Modern Criticism and Theory

A READER

Modern Criticism and Theory

A READER

Edited by David Lodge

Longman

London and New York

Longman Group UK Limited
Longman House, Burnt Mill, Harlow,
Essex CM20 2JE, England
and Associated Companies throughout the world.

*Published in the United States of America
by Longman Inc., New York*

First published 1988
Eighth impression 1993

British Library Cataloguing in Publication Data
Modern criticism and theory: a reader.
 1. Criticism
 I. Lodge, David
 801'.95   PN81

ISBN 0-582-01598-7 CSD
ISBN 0-582-49460-5 PPR

Library of Congress Cataloging in Publication Data
Modern criticism and theory.

 A companion volume to: 20th century literary
criticism
 Includes bibliographies and index.
 1. Criticism—History—20th century. I. Lodge,
David, 1935–
PN94.M57   1988   801'.95'0904   87–3068
ISBN 0-582-01598-7
ISBN 0-582-49460-5 (pbk.)

Set in Linotron 202 10/11^1/$_2$ pt Erhardt

Produced by Longman Singapore Publishers (Pte) Ltd.
Printed in Singapore.

Contents

A = Contents arranged historically

B = Contents arranged thematically

Contents

B. CONTENTS ARRANGED THEMATICALLY

[Items marked with an asterisk appear in more than one category]

I Formalist, structuralist and post-structuralist poetics, linguistics and narratology

Contents

II Deconstruction

III Psychoanalysis

IV Politics, ideology, cultural history

V *Feminism*

VI *Hermeneutics, reception theory, reader-response*

VII *Cognitive literary scholarship*

Foreword

This book is a companion volume, and in some sense a sequel, to my *20th Century Literary Criticism: A Reader*, which was published by Longman in 1972. As such books go, *20th Century Literary Criticism* has been very successful. It has sold some 35,000 copies to date, and is used as a textbook in universities and colleges all around the world. Fifteen years later, however, it seems, not surprisingly, a little dated, and in need of supplementation. The most recent essay included in it (Frank Kermode's 'Objects, Jokes and Art') was first published in 1966. An enormous amount of important criticism and literary theory has been published since then, and entire new schools or movements have arisen (for example, deconstruction, reader-response criticism, feminist criticism). Moreover, much of this work has built upon or reacted against an intellectual tradition that goes back well before 1966, but was barely reflected in *20th Century Literary Criticism*—the tradition, loosely speaking, of 'structuralism'.

What is structuralism—or perhaps one should ask, what *was* structuralism? In the opinion of many qualified judges, structuralism is a thing of the past—was already in terminal decline by the time the English-speaking world became aware of its existence in the late 1960s. We live in the age of post-structuralism—but to understand *that* we must know what came before. Structuralism is, or was, a movement in what Continental Europeans call 'the human sciences', which sought to explain and understand cultural phenomena (from poems to menus, from primitive myths to modern advertisements) as manifestations of underlying systems of signification, of which the exemplary model is verbal language itself, especially as elucidated by the Swiss linguist Ferdinand de Saussure. One can trace a line from Saussure to the Russian Formalists, from the Russian Formalists (via Roman Jakobson) to the Prague Linguistic Circle, and from there to the structuralist anthropology of Claude Lévi-Strauss and the eruption of *la nouvelle critique* in Paris in the 1960s. This tradition was very inadequately represented in *20th Century Literary Criticism* (represented, in fact, by two short pieces by Lévi-Strauss and Roland Barthes, respectively) for the simple reason that it had only just begun to impinge on my consciousness at the time when I was compiling that Reader. In this respect I do not think that I lagged conspicuously behind my peer group in the British academic world. *20th Century Literary Criticism* was intended primarily for readers in Britain and America, and was heavily biassed towards Anglo–American criticism, as I admitted in the Foreword. That bias, however, seemed increasingly obvious as Anglo–American criticism itself became increasingly oriented to European criticism and theory.

'Theory' has more than one meaning in this context. Structuralism has generated in literary critics a much greater interest in, and anxiety about, the theory of their own subject (what is sometimes called, after Aristotle, poetics) than was formerly the case, at least in Britain and America. But the recent theorization of literary studies has borrowed its terms and concepts very largely from other disciplines—linguistics, psychoanalysis, philosophy, marxism. In the process, literary criticism has been drawn into the vortex of a powerful new field of study in which all these disciplines are merged and interfused, and which goes under the general name of 'theory'. The aim of this collective enterprise would appear to be nothing less than a totalizing account of human consciousness and human culture (or else a tireless demonstration of the impossibility of such a project). A good deal of what goes on in university departments of language and literature nowadays, and is written in journals ostensibly dedicated to literary criticism, is contributing to Theory in this wide sense. The title and the contents of this Reader recognize the importance of theory in contemporary criticism, and its ambiguous status—both part of and larger than literary studies. Every item has an explicit theoretical dimension. What I wrote in the Foreword to *20th Century Literary Criticism*—'in our era, criticism is not merely a library of secondary aids to the understanding and appreciation of literary texts, but also a rapidly increasing body of knowledge in its own right'—has been emphatically confirmed in the last fifteen years by the explosion of theory.

This development, predictably, has created strains and stresses within the institutional structures that contain and maintain the academic study of literature. In the Foreword to *20th Century Literary Criticism* I felt obliged to rebut the view that students should be discouraged from reading criticism because, by supplying them with ready-made interpretations and judgments, it was likely to blunt their capacity for independent response to primary texts. The complaint more commonly heard today is that modern criticism's obsession with theory undermines the study of literature in a more fundamental way, by questioning its very foundations, such as the idea of the author as origin of a text's meaning, the possibility of objective interpretation, the validity of empirical historical scholarship and the authority of the literary canon.

By no means all of modern critical theory is hostile to these traditional humanist principles, but much of it certainly is, and it is easy to understand the anxiety that provokes this complaint. A premature and dogmatically enforced exposure to post-structuralist theory can be confusing and disabling to the student. I am sure, however, that the answer is not to try and ignore or suppress the existence of theory. We have eaten the apple of knowledge and must live with the consequences. Literary criticism can no longer be taught and practised as if its methods, aims and institutional forms were innocent of theoretical assumptions and ideological implications. What is essential, however, is that the new theoretical self-consciousness should be earned, not borrowed, that it should be based on a study of the seminal texts that gave rise to it. These are, for the most part, difficult texts, and coming to grips with them, seeking to understand them, is an educative process in itself, whether or not one accepts their conclusions.

There are numerous guides to structuralism and post-structuralism now available, and introductions to the work of individual critics and theorists. These publications are often extremely useful, but they are no substitute for the texts upon which they comment, though paradoxically they are often cheaper and easier to obtain. There are also several critical anthologies which represent particular types of criticism, such as deconstruction, or reader-response criticism. *Modern Criticism and Theory* aims to provide within the covers of a single book a selection of important and representative work from all the major theoretical schools or tendencies in contemporary criticism, and to provide materials for tracing their historical evolution.

I have confined my selection to authors who have an established reputation, usually based on a substantial body of work, and who are firmly associated with particular theories or methods of criticism. Even with that limitation, the anthology could easily have been twice as long with no loss of quality. To keep it to a manageable length I excluded writers already represented in *20th Century Literary Criticism*. I made two exceptions to this rule: Roland Barthes, perhaps the most brilliant and original of all the critics in the structuralist–post-structuralist tradition, whose work was quite inadequately represented in the earlier Reader; and M. H. Abrams, whose 'The Deconstructive Angel' I found, as an editor, an irresistible short account and critique of Derridean deconstruction. As in *20th Century Literary Criticism*, I have tried to select items that naturally invite comparison in pairs or larger groups, and Abrams's essay is very much a case in point. As far as possible (there are very few exceptions) I have preferred complete, self-contained essays to extracts from longer works.

The format of this Reader is essentially the same as that of the earlier one. The items are arranged, generally speaking, in chronological order of first publication (in the case of translated texts I have used my discretion in choosing between the date of original publication and the date of the translation; and where two items are included by the same author the chronological sequence is inevitably disturbed). This order is presented in the first list of Contents (A), and should enable a reader to follow the historical development of modern criticism and theory, especially the transition from structuralism to post-structuralism. A second list of Contents (B) categorises items thematically, according to the school or approach which they exemplify. Each author's work is preceded by a brief note giving basic biographical and bibliographical information, and placing him or her in the general context of modern criticism and theory. After each headnote there are, where appropriate, suggestions for comparison with other items in the Reader ('Cross Reference') and for further reading about the writer's work ('Commentary'). Finally, by means of the index, the Reader can be used as a reference guide to modern criticism and theory.

Author's notes, and the notes of editors and translators of the original texts, are keyed by numbers and gathered at the end of each item. Explanatory notes by the present editor are keyed by letters of the alphabet, and printed at the foot of the page. In writing these notes I have borne in mind that this book, like its predecessor, is likely to be used by students from many different cultures and educational backgrounds, and that what may be self-evident to an English reader could be puzzling or obscure to a reader in another country or continent. When practicable, translations of foreign words and phrases into English are interpolated in the main texts inside square brackets. Foreign words inside square brackets are interpolations by the translators of non-English texts.

20th Century Literary Criticism was based on an undergraduate course called 'Comparative Critical Approaches' which I taught for many years at Birmingham University. The materials for this Reader have, to a large extent, been gathered and sifted in connection with a weekly postgraduate seminar on post-Renaissance literature and modern critical theory for which I have been responsible for an even longer period at Birmingham. I would like to thank the many postgraduate students and occasional visitors who attended this seminar over the years for their contributions to my own education, and to thank the colleagues who regularly shared the strain of grappling with difficult and demanding texts—especially Deirdre Burton and Tom Davis. I also gratefully acknowledge the research assistance of Adrian Stokes and the help of Jackie Evans in compiling the index. Finally I should like to thank the colleagues in the Arts Faculty at the University of Birmingham—especially Anthony Bryer, Michael Butler, Ceri Crossley and Bob Smith—who generously assisted me in identifying quotations and allusions, and translating foreign words.

Birmingham, January 1987

Acknowledgements

We are grateful to the following for permission to reproduce copyright material:

Associated Book Publishers Ltd for 'Textual Analysis: Poe's "Valdemar"' by Robert Young from *Untying the Text*, pubd Routledge & Kegan Paul plc; Associated Book Publishers Ltd/Cornell University Press for 'What is an Author?' by Michel Foucault, trans. from the French by Josue V. Harari in *Textual Strategies: Perspectives in Post-Structuralist Criticism*, ed. Josue V. Harari, copyright © 1977 by Cornell University Press, pubd in the UK by Methuen & Co.; Associated Book Publishers Ltd/Pantheon Books, a Division of Random House Inc., for 'Crisis [in orientalism]' by Edward Said from *Orientalism*, pubd Routledge & Kegan Paul plc/Pantheon Books, pp. 92–100; Associated Book Publishers Ltd/University of Chicago Press/George Borchardt Inc. for Editions du Seuil for 'Structure, Sign and Play in the Discourse of the Human Sciences' by Jacques Derrida from *Writing and Difference*, trans. Bass 1978, pp. 278–93, & notes p. 339, pubd Routledge & Kegan Paul plc/University of Chicago Press; the Author, Catherine Belsey, for her article 'Literature, History, Politics', *Literature and History* Vol. 9 (Spring 1983) pp. 17–27, pubd Thames Polytechnic; Basil Blackwell Ltd/Columbia University Press for 'The Ethics of Linguistics' by Julia Kristeva from *Desire in Language*, ed. Leon S. Roudiez, trans. Thomas Gora, Alice Jardine & Leon S. Roudiez, and for 'Structuralism and Literary Criticism' by Gérard Genette from *Figures of Literary Discourse*, trans. Alan Sheridan, copyright © 1982 Columbia University Press; Basil Blackwell Ltd/Cornell University Press for 'The Typology of Detective Fiction' by Tzvetan Todorov from *The Poetics of Prose*, trans. from the French by Richard Howard, originally pubd in French under the title *La Poetique de la prose*, copyright © 1971 by Editions du Seuil, © 1977 by Cornell University; Columbia University Press for 'The Interpreter's Freud' by Geoffrey Hartman from *Easy Pieces*, 1985; Gerald Duckworth & Co. Ltd/Open Court Publishing Co. for 'The Object of Study' and 'Nature of the Linguistic Sign' by Ferdinand de Saussure from *Course in General Linguistics*, trans. Roy Harris, © 1983; Editions du Seuil for 'The Death of the Author' by Roland Barthes from *Image-Music-Text*, ed. & trans. Stephen Heath, pubd Fontana 1979; The Harvester Press Ltd/Wheatsheaf Books Ltd/University of Massachusetts Press for 'Sorties' by Hélène Cixous from *New French Feminisms*, ed. Elaine Marks & Isabelle de Courtivron (Amherst: University of Massachusetts Press 1980), copyright © 1980 by The University of Massachusetts Press; The Jakobson Trust for 'Two Aspects of Language and Two Types of Linguistic Disturbances' by Roman Jakobson from *Selected Writings II* (The Hague: Mouton 1971) pp. 254–59, © The Jakobson Trust; Johns Hopkins University Press for 'The Reading Process: A Phenomenological Approach' by Wolfgang Iser from *New Literary History* Vol. 3 (Winter 1972) pp. 279–99; Manchester University Press for 'Language, Linguistics and the Study of Literature' by Colin MacCabe from *Theoretical Essays*, pp. 113–30; MIT Press Inc./The Jakobson Trust for 'Linguistics and Poetics' by Roman Jakobson, originally 'Closing Statement: Linguistics and Poetics', from *Style in Language*, MIT Press, Cambridge, Massachusetts 1960; the Editor, *New German Critique*, and the Author for 'The Politics of Theory: Ideological Positions in the Postmodernism Debate' by Fredric Jameson, *New German Critique* No 33 (Fall 1984), pubd by Dept. German at the University of Wisconsin-Milwaukie; Oxford University Press Inc. for 'Poetic Origins and Final Phases' by Harold Bloom from *A Map of Misreading*, copyright © 1979 by Oxford University Press Inc.; Martin Secker & Warburg Ltd/Gruppo Editoriale Fabbri for 'Casablanca: Cultural Movies and Intertextual Collage' by Umberto Eco from *Faith in Fakes*; The University of Chicago Press & the Authors for 'The Deconstructive Angel' by M. H. Abrams, *Critical Inquiry* Vol. 3 (1977) pp. 425–32, 'Interpreting the *Variorum*' by Stanley E. Fish, *Critical Inquiry* Vol. 2, No 3, pp. 465–86, 'The Critic as Host' by J. H. Miller, *Critical Inquiry* Vol. 31 (1977) pp. 439–47, 'Feminist Criticism in the Wilderness' by Prof. Elaine Showalter, *Critical Inquiry* Vol. 8 (Winter 1981) pp. 179–205 and 'Faulty Perspectives' by E. D. Hirsch Jr. from *The Aims of Interpretation*, 1976, pp. 36–49; University of Nebraska Press for 'Art as Technique' by Victor Shklovsky from *Russian*

Formalist Criticism: Four Essays, pp. 5–24, trans. & ed. by Lee T. Lemon & Marion J. Reis, copyright © 1965 by University of Nebraska Press; University of Texas Press for 'From the Prehistory of Novelistic Discourse' by M. M. Bakhtin from *The Dialogic Imagination: Four Essays*, ed. Michael Holquist, trans. Caryl Emerson & Michael Holquist, pp. 41–83, copyright 1981 University of Texas Press; Verso Ltd for part of 'Capitalism, Modernism and Postmodernism' by Terry Eagleton from *Against the Grain*, Verso 1986, originally pubd in *New Left Review* 152 (July/Aug 1985); Virago Press Ltd/the Author's Agents for 'Femininity, Narrative and Psychoanalysis' by Juliet Mitchell from *Women: The Longest Revolution*, © Juliet Mitchell 1984; Yale French Studies for 'The Insistence of the Letter in the Unconscious' by Jacques Lacan, *YFS* 36–7, 1966, 'The Resistance to Theory' by Paul de Man, *YFS 63*, 1982.

We have, unfortunately, been unable to trace the Foucault family as original copyright holders of Michel Foucault's 'What is an Author?', and we would appreciate any information which would enable us to do so.

1 Ferdinand de Saussure

Ferdinand de Saussure (1857–1913) was a Swiss linguist who studied in Germany and France before taking up a university chair in his native city of Geneva, which he occupied for the rest of his life. Saussure is widely regarded as the father of modern linguistics. He is included in this reader because his theory of language and how it should be studied played a seminal part in the development of 'structuralism' as a method in the human sciences, and thus significantly affected the course of literary studies in this century. The theory was never published by Saussure himself in a complete and authoritative form. The *Course in General Linguistics* (first published in Paris in 1915) which goes under his name was compiled by colleagues after his death, based on lecture notes taken down by Saussure's students in his lifetime. Its most recent translator and editor, Roy Harris, has described it as 'without doubt one of the most far-reaching works concerning the study of human cultural activities to have been published at any time since the Renaissance.'

Before Saussure, the study of language, or philology as it was usually called, had been essentially historical, tracing change and development in phonology and semantics within and between languages or groups of languages. Saussure argued that a scientific linguistics could never be based on such a 'diachronic' study but only by approaching language as a 'synchronic' *system*, i.e., a system of which all the elements and rules are in theory simultaneously available to the user of the language. Saussure's discussion of 'the object of study' in linguistics, reprinted below, depends crucially on a distinction between *langage, langue* and *parole*, translated here as 'language' (i.e., the universal human phenomenon of language), 'a language' (i.e., a particular language system, for example English) and 'speech' (i.e., language in use, specific speech acts).

Language is made up of words, and another seminal contribution of Saussure's was his analysis of the word as a verbal sign having two sides, an acoustic image or sound pattern and a concept. The former he called *signifiant*, translated by Harris as 'signal', and the other *signifié*, translated as 'significance'. (The more usual translations are 'signifier' and 'signified'.) Saussure's crucial point was that the connection between the two is arbitrary—that is to say, a convention accepted by all users of a given language, not the result of some existential link between word and thing. It is the arbitrariness of the verbal sign that necessitates a systematic structure for language.

Some implications for literary studies which may be glimpsed in the brief extracts from the *Course* reprinted below (from Roy Harris's translation of 1983),

1

are : (1) the idea that literary texts could be seen as manifestations of a literary system (such as narrative) the underlying rules of which might be understood, thus making literary criticism a more 'scientific' discipline; (2) scepticism about historical explanations of literary phenomena, especially research into the 'origins' of meaning; (3) a corresponding emphasis on the collective or social construction of meaning in the production and reception of literary texts; (4) a critique of naive theories of literary 'realism'. Many of the essays included in this book are directly or indirectly indebted to Saussure's theory of language.

CROSS REFERENCES: 3. Jakobson
                     5. Lacan
                     6. Derrida
                     7. Bakhtin
                    27. MacCabe
COMMENTARY: Jonathan Culler, *Saussure* (1976)

The object of study

1. On defining a language

What is it that linguistics sets out to analyse? What is that actual object of study in its entirety? The question is a particularly difficult one. We shall see why later. First, let us simply try to grasp the nature of the difficulty.

Other sciences are provided with objects of study given in advance, which are then examined from different points of view. Nothing like that is the case in linguistics. Suppose someone pronounces the French word *nu* ('naked'). At first sight, one might think this would be an example of an independently given linguistic object. But more careful consideration reveals a series of three or four quite different things, depending on the viewpoint adopted. There is a sound, there is the expression of an idea, there is a derivative of Latin *nūdum*, and so on. The object is not given in advance of the viewpoint: far from it. Rather, one might say that it is the viewpoint adopted which creates the object. Furthermore, there is nothing to tell us in advance whether one of these ways of looking at it is prior to or superior to any of the others.

Whichever viewpoint is adopted, moreover, linguistic phenomena always present two complementary facets, each depending on the other. For example:

(1) The ear perceives articulated syllables as auditory impressions. But the sounds in question would not exist without the vocal organs. There would be no *n*, for instance, without these two complementary aspects to it. So one cannot equate the language simply with what the ear hears. One cannot divorce what is heard from oral articulation. Nor, on the other hand, can one specify the

relevant movements of the vocal organs without reference to the corresponding auditory impression.

(2) But even if we ignored this phonetic duality, would language then be reducible to phonetic facts? No. Speech sounds are only the instrument of thought, and have no independent existence. Here another complementarity emerges, and one of great importance. A sound, itself a complex auditory–articulatory unit, in turn combines with an idea to form another complex unit, both physiologically and psychologically. Nor is this all.

(3) Language has an individual aspect and a social aspect. One is not conceivable without the other. Furthermore:

(4) Language at any given time involves an established system and an evolution. At any given time, it is an institution in the present and a product of the past. At first sight, it looks very easy to distinguish between the system and its history, between what it is and what it was. In reality, the connexion between the two is so close that it is hard to separate them. Would matters be simplified if one considered the ontogenesis of linguistic phenomena, beginning with a study of children's language, for example? No. It is quite illusory to believe that where language is concerned the problem of origins is any different from the problem of permanent conditions. There is no way out of the circle.

So however we approach the question, no one object of linguistic study emerges of its own accord. Whichever way we turn, the same dilemma confronts us. Either we tackle each problem on one front only, and risk failing to take into account the dualities mentioned above: or else we seem committed to trying to study language in several ways simultaneously, in which case the object of study becomes a muddle of disparate, unconnected things. By proceeding thus one opens the door to various sciences—psychology, anthropology, prescriptive grammar, philology, and so on—which are to be distinguished from linguistics. These sciences could lay claim to language as falling in their domain: but their methods are not the ones that are needed.

One solution only, in our view, resolves all these difficulties. *The linguist must take the study of linguistic structure as his primary concern, and relate all other manifestations of language to it.* Indeed, amid so many dualities, linguistic structure seems to be the one thing that is independently definable and provides something our minds can satisfactorily grasp.

What, then, is linguistic structure? It is not, in our opinion, simply the same thing as language. Linguistic structure is only one part of language, even though it is an essential part. The structure of a language is a social product of our language faculty. At the same time, it is also a body of necessary conventions adopted by society to enable members of society to use their language faculty. Language in its entirety has many different and disparate aspects. It lies astride the boundaries separating various domains. It is at the same time physical, physiological and psychological. It belongs both to the individual and to society. No classification of human phenomena provides any single place for it, because language as such has no discernible unity.

A language as a structured system, on the contrary, is both a self-contained whole and a principle of classification. As soon as we give linguistic structure pride of place among the facts of language, we introduce a natural order into an aggregate which lends itself to no other classification.

It might be objected to this principle of classification that our use of language depends on a faculty endowed by nature: whereas language systems are acquired and conventional, and so ought to be subordinated to—instead of being given priority over—our natural ability.

To this objection one might reply as follows.

First, it has not been established that the function of language, as manifested in speech, is entirely natural: that is to say, it is not clear that our vocal apparatus is made for speaking as our legs for walking. Linguists are by no means in agreement on this issue. Whitney, for instance, who regards languages as social institutions on exactly the same footing as all other social institutions, holds it to be a matter of chance or mere convenience that it is our vocal apparatus we use for linguistic purposes. Man, in his view, might well have chosen to use gestures, thus substituting visual images for sound patterns. Whitney's is doubtless too extreme a position. For languages are not in all respects similar to other social institutions. Moreover, Whitney goes too far when he says that the selection of the vocal apparatus for language was accidental. For it was in some measure imposed upon us by Nature. But the American linguist is right about the essential point: the language we use is a convention, and it makes no difference what exactly the nature of the agreed sign is. The question of the vocal apparatus is thus a secondary one as far as the problem of language is concerned.

This idea gains support from the notion of *language articulation*. In Latin, the word *articulus* means 'member, part, subdivision in a sequence of things'. As regards language, articulation may refer to the division of the chain of speech into syllables, or to the division of the chain of meanings into meaningful units. It is in this sense that one speaks in German of *gegliederte Sprache* [articulate speech]. On the basis of this second interpretation, one may say that it is not spoken language which is natural to man, but the faculty of constructing a language, i.e. a system of distinct signs corresponding to distinct ideas.

Broca discovered that the faculty of speech is localised in the third frontal convolution of the left hemisphere of the brain. This fact has been seized upon to justify regarding language as a natural endowment. But the same localisation is known to hold for *everything* connected with language, including writing. Thus what seems to be indicated, when we take into consideration also the evidence from various forms of aphasia due to lesions in the centres of localisation is: (1) that the various disorders which affect spoken language are interconnected in many ways with disorders affecting written language, and (2) that in all cases of aphasia or agraphia what is affected is not so much the ability to utter or inscribe this or that, but the ability to produce in any given mode signs corresponding to normal language. All this leads us to believe that, over and above the functioning of the various organs, there exists a more general faculty governing signs, which may be regarded as the linguistic faculty *par excellence*. So by a different route we are once again led to the same conclusion.

Finally, in support of giving linguistic structure pride of place in our study of language, there is this argument: that, whether natural or not, the faculty of articulating words is put to use only by means of the linguistic instrument created and provided by society. Therefore it is no absurdity to say that it is linguistic structure which gives language what unity it has.

2. *Linguistic structure: its place among the facts of language*

In order to identify what role linguistic structure plays within the totality of language, we must consider the individual act of speech and trace what takes place in the speech circuit. This act requires at least two individuals: without this minimum the circuit would not be complete. Suppose, then, we have two people, *A* and *B*, talking to each other:

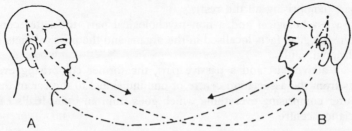

The starting point of the circuit is in the brain of one individual, for instance *A*, where facts of consciousness which we shall call concepts are associated with representations of linguistic signs or sound patterns by means of which they may be expressed. Let us suppose that a given concept triggers in the brain a corresponding sound pattern. This is an entirely *psychological* phenomenon, followed in turn by a *physiological* process: the brain transmits to the organs of phonation an impulse corresponding to the pattern. Then sound waves are sent from *A*'s mouth to *B*'s ear: a purely *physical* process. Next, the circuit continues in *B* in the opposite order: from ear to brain, the physiological transmission of the sound pattern; in the brain, the psychological association of this pattern with the corresponding concept. If *B* speaks in turn, this new act will pursue—from his brain to *A*'s—exactly the same course as the first, passing through the same successive phases, which we may represent as follows:

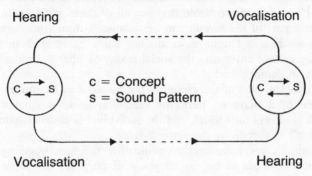

5

This analysis makes no claim to be complete. One could go on to distinguish the auditory sensation itself, the identification of that sensation with the latent sound pattern, the patterns of muscular movement associated with phonation, and so on. We have included only those elements considered essential; but our schematisation enables us straight away to separate the parts which are physical (sound waves) from those which are physiological (phonation and hearing) and those which are psychological (the sound patterns of words and the concepts). It is particularly important to note that the sound patterns of the words are not to be confused with actual sounds. The word patterns are psychological, just as the concepts associated with them are.

The circuit as here represented may be further divided:

(a) into an external part (sound vibrations passing from mouth to ear) and an internal part (comprising all the rest);

(b) into a psychological and a non-psychological part, the latter comprising both the physiological facts localised in the organs and the physical facts external to the individual; and

(c) into an active part and a passive part, the former comprising everything which goes from the association centre of one individual to the ear of the other, and the latter comprising everything which goes from an individual's ear to his own association centre.

Finally, in the psychological part localised in the brain, one may call everything which is active 'executive' ($c \rightarrow s$), and everything which is passive 'receptive' ($s \rightarrow c$).

In addition, one must allow for a faculty of association and co-ordination which comes into operation as soon as one goes beyond individual signs in isolation. It is this faculty which plays the major role in the organisation of the language as a system.

But in order to understand this role, one must leave the individual act, which is merely language in embryo, and proceed to consider the social phenomenon.

All the individuals linguistically linked in this manner will establish among themselves a kind of mean; all of them will reproduce—doubtless not exactly, but approximately—the same signs linked to the same concepts.

What is the origin of this social crystallisation? Which of the parts of the circuit is involved? For it is very probable that not all of them are equally relevant.

The physical part of the circuit can be dismissed from consideration straight away. When we hear a language we do not know being spoken, we hear the sounds but we cannot enter into the social reality of what is happening, because of our failure to comprehend.

The psychological part of the circuit is not involved in its entirety either. The executive side of it plays no part, for execution is never carried out by the collectivity: it is always individual, and the individual is always master of it. This is what we shall designate by the term *speech*.

The individual's receptive and co-ordinating faculties build up a stock of imprints which turn out to be for all practical purposes the same as the next

6

person's. How must we envisage this social product, so that the language itself can be seen to be clearly distinct from the rest? If we could collect the totality of word patterns stored in all those individuals, we should have the social bond which constitutes their language. It is a fund accumulated by the members of the community through the practice of speech, a grammatical system existing potentially in every brain, or more exactly in the brains of a group of individuals; for the language is never complete in any single individual, but exists perfectly only in the collectivity.

By distinguishing between the language itself and speech, we distinguish at the same time: (1) what is social from what is individual, and (2) what is essential from what is ancillary and more or less accidental.

The language itself is not a function of the speaker. It is the product passively registered by the individual. It never requires premeditation, and reflexion enters into it only for the activity of classifying to be discussed below.

Speech, on the contrary, is an individual act of the will and the intelligence, in which one must distinguish: (1) the combinations through which the speaker uses the code provided by the language in order to express his own thought, and (2) the psycho-physical mechanism which enables him to externalise these combinations.

It should be noted that we have defined things, not words. Consequently the distinctions established are not affected by the fact that certain ambiguous terms have no exact equivalents in other languages. Thus in German the word *Sprache* covers individual languages as well as language in general, while *Rede* answers more or less to 'speech', but also has the special sense of 'discourse'. In Latin the word *sermo* covers language in general and also speech, while *lingua* is the word for 'a language'; and so on. No word corresponds precisely to any one of the notions we have tried to specify above. That is why all definitions based on words are vain. It is an error of method to proceed from words in order to give definitions of things.

To summarise, then, a language as a structured system may be characterised as follows:

1. Amid the disparate mass of facts involved in language, it stands out as a well defined entity. It can be localised in that particular section of the speech circuit where sound patterns are associated with concepts. It is the social part of language, external to the individual, who by himself is powerless either to create it or to modify it. It exists only in virtue of a kind of contract agreed between the members of a community. On the other hand, the individual needs an apprenticeship in order to acquaint himself with its workings: as a child, he assimilates it only gradually. It is quite separate from speech: a man who loses the ability to speak none the less retains his grasp of the language system, provided he understands the vocal signs he hears.

2. A language system, as distinct from speech, is an object that may be studied independently. Dead languages are no longer spoken, but we can perfectly well acquaint ourselves with their linguistic structure. A science which studies linguistic structure is not only able to dispense with other elements of language,

but is possible only if those other elements are kept separate.

3. While language in general is heterogeneous, a language system is homogeneous in nature. It is a system of signs in which the one essential is the union of sense and sound pattern, both parts of the sign being psychological.

4. Linguistic structure is no less real than speech, and no less amenable to study. Linguistic signs, although essentially psychological, are not abstractions. The associations, ratified by collective agreement, which go to make up the language are realities localised in the brain. Moreover, linguistic signs are, so to speak, tangible: writing can fix them in conventional images, whereas it would be impossible to photograph acts of speech in all their details. The utterance of a word, however small, involves an infinite number of muscular movements extremely difficult to examine and to represent. In linguistic structure, on the contrary, there is only the sound pattern, and this can be represented by one constant visual image. For if one leaves out of account that multitude of movements required to actualise it in speech, each sound pattern, as we shall see, is only the sum of a limited number of elements or speech sounds, and these can in turn be represented by a corresponding number of symbols in writing. Our ability to identify elements of linguistic structure in this way is what makes it possible for dictionaries and grammars to give us a faithful representation of a language. A language is a repository of sound patterns and writing is their tangible form.

3. Languages and their place in human affairs. Semiology

The above characteristics lead us to realise another, which is more important. A language, defined in this way from among the totality of facts of language, has a particular place in the realm of human affairs, whereas language does not.

A language, as we have just seen, is a social institution. But it is in various respects distinct from political, juridical and other institutions. Its special nature emerges when we bring into consideration a different order of facts.

A language is a system of signs expressing ideas, and hence comparable to writing, the deaf-and-dumb alphabet, symbolic rites, forms of politeness, military signals, and so on. It is simply the most important of such systems.

It is therefore possible to conceive of a science *which studies the role of signs as part of social life*. It would form part of social psychology, and hence of general psychology. We shall call it *semiology*[1] (from the Greek *sēmeion*, 'sign'). It would investigate the nature of signs and the laws governing them. Since it does not yet exist, one cannot say for certain that it will exist. But it has a right to exist, a place ready for it in advance. Linguistics is only one branch of this general science. The laws which semiology will discover will be laws applicable in linguistics, and linguistics will thus be assigned to a clearly defined place in the field of human knowledge.

It is for the psychologist to determine the exact place of semiology[2] The linguist's task is to define what makes languages a special type of system within the totality of semiological facts. The question will be taken up later on: here we shall make just one point, which is that if we have now for the first time succeeded in assigning linguistics its place among the sciences, that is because we have grouped it with semiology.

Why is it that semiology is not yet recognised as an autonomous science with its own object of study, like other sciences? The fact is that here we go round in a circle. On the one hand, nothing is more appropriate than the study of languages to bring out the nature of the semiological problem. But to formulate the problem suitably, it would be necessary to study what a language is in itself: whereas hitherto a language has usually been considered as a function of something else, from other points of view.

In the first place, there is the superficial view taken by the general public, which sees a language merely as a nomenclature. This is a view which stifles any inquiry into the true nature of linguistic structure.

Then there is the viewpoint of the psychologist, who studies the mechanism of the sign in the individual. This is the most straightforward approach, but it takes us no further than individual execution. It does not even take us as far as the linguistic sign itself, which is social by nature.

Even when due recognition is given to the fact that the sign must be studied as a social phenomenon, attention is restricted to those features of languages which they share with institutions mainly established by voluntary decision. In this way, the investigation is diverted from its goal. It neglects those characteristics which belong only to semiological systems in general, and to languages in particular. For the sign always to some extent eludes control by the will, whether of the individual or of society: that is its essential nature, even though it may be by no means obvious at first sight.

So this characteristic emerges clearly only in languages, but its manifestations appear in features to which least attention is paid. All of which contributes to a failure to appreciate either the necessity or the particular utility of a science of semiology. As far as we are concerned, on the other hand, the linguistic problem is first and foremost semiological. All our proposals derive their rationale from this basic fact. If one wishes to discover the true nature of language systems, one must first consider what they have in common with all other systems of the same kind. Linguistic factors which at first seem central (for example, the workings of the vocal apparatus) must be relegated to a place of secondary importance if it is found that they merely differentiate languages from other such systems. In this way, light will be thrown not only upon the linguistic problem. By considering rites, customs, etc., as signs, it will be possible, we believe, to see them in a new perspective. The need will be felt to consider them as semiological phenomena and to explain them in terms of the laws of semiology.

NOTES

1. Not to be confused with *semantics*, which studies changes of meaning. Saussure gave no detailed exposition of semantics. (Editorial note)
2. Cf. A. Naville, *Classification des sciences*, 2nd ed., p. 104. (Editorial note)

Nature of the linguistic sign

1. Sign, signification, signal

For some people a language, reduced to its essentials, is a nomenclature: a list of terms corresponding to a list of things. For example, Latin would be represented as:

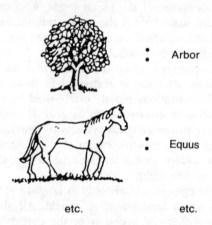

Arbor

Equus

etc.   etc.

This conception is open to a number of objections. It assumes that ideas already exist independently of words. It does not clarify whether the name is a vocal or a psychological entity, for *ARBOR* might stand for either. Furthermore, it leads one to assume that the link between a name and a thing is something quite unproblematic, which is far from being the case. None the less, this naive view contains one element of truth, which is that linguistic units are dual in nature, comprising two elements.

As has already been noted in connexion with the speech circuit, the two elements involved in the linguistic sign are both psychological and are connected in the brain by an associative link.[1] This is a point of major importance.

A linguistic sign is not a link between a thing and a name, but between a concept and a sound pattern.[2] The sound pattern is not actually a sound; for a sound is something physical. A sound pattern is the hearer's psychological impression of a sound, as given to him by the evidence of his senses. This sound pattern may be called a 'material' element only in that it is the representation of our sensory impressions. The sound pattern may thus be distinguished from the other element associated with it in a linguistic sign. This other element is generally of a more abstract kind: the concept.

The psychological nature of our sound patterns becomes clear when we consider our own linguistic activity. Without moving either lips or tongue, we can talk to ourselves or recite silently a piece of verse. We grasp the words of a language as sound patterns. That is why it is best to avoid referring to them as composed of 'speech sounds'. Such a term, implying the activity of the vocal apparatus, is appropriate to the spoken word, to the actualisation of the sound pattern in discourse. Speaking of the *sounds* and *syllables* of a word need not give rise to any misunderstanding,[3] provided one always bears in mind that this refers to the sound pattern.

The linguistic sign is, then, a two-sided psychological entity, which may be represented by the diagram below.

These two elements are intimately linked and each triggers the other. Whether we are seeking the meaning of the Latin word *arbor* or the word by which Latin designates the concept 'tree', it is clear that only the connexions institutionalised

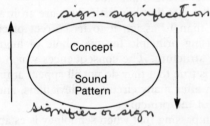

in the language appear to us as relevant. Any other connexions there may be we set on one side.

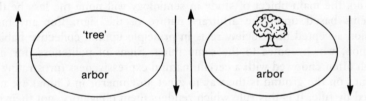

This definition raises an important question of terminology. In our terminology a *sign* is the combination of a concept and a sound pattern. But in current usage the term *sign* generally refers to the sound pattern alone, e.g. the word form *arbor*. It is forgotten that if *arbor* is called a sign, it is only because it carries with it the concept 'tree', so that the sensory part of the term implies reference to the whole.

The ambiguity would be removed if the three notions in question were designated by terms which are related but contrast. We propose to keep the term *sign* to designate the whole, but to replace *concept* and *sound pattern* respectively by *signification* and *signal*. The latter terms have the advantage of indicating the distinction which separates each from the other and both from the whole of which they are part. We retain the term *sign*, because current usage suggests no alternative by which it might be replaced.

11

The linguistic sign thus defined has two fundamental characteristics. In specifying them, we shall lay down the principles governing all studies in this domain.

2. First principle: the sign is arbitrary

The link between signal and signification is arbitrary. Since we are treating a sign as the combination in which a signal is associated with a signification, we can express this more simply as: *the linguistic sign is arbitrary*.

There is no internal connexion, for example, between the idea 'sister' and the French sequence of sounds *s-ö-r* which acts as its signal. The same idea might as well be represented by any other sequence of sounds. This is demonstrated by differences between languages, and even by the existence of different languages. The signification 'ox' has as its signal *b-ö-f* on one side of the frontier,[4] but *o-k-s* (*Ochs*) on the other side.

No one disputes the fact that linguistic signs are arbitrary. But it is often easier to discover a truth than to assign it to its correct place. The principle stated above is the organising principle for the whole of linguistics, considered as a science of language structure. The consequences which flow from this principle are innumerable. It is true that they do not all appear at first sight equally evident. One discovers them after many circuitous deviations, and so realises the fundamental importance of the principle.

It may be noted in passing that when semiology is established one of the questions that must be asked is whether modes of expression which rely upon signs that are entirely natural (mime, for example) fall within the province of semiology. If they do, the main object of study in semiology will none the less be the class of systems based upon the arbitrary nature of the sign. For any means of expression accepted in a society rests in principle upon a collective habit, or on convention, which comes to the same thing. Signs of politeness, for instance, although often endowed with a certain natural expressiveness (prostrating oneself nine times on the ground is the way to greet an emperor in China) are none the less fixed by rule. It is this rule which renders them obligatory, not their intrinsic value. We may therefore say that signs which are entirely arbitrary convey better than others the ideal semiological process. That is why the most complex and the most widespread of all systems of expression, which is the one we find in human languages, is also the most characteristic of all. In this sense, linguistics serves as a model for the whole of semiology, even though languages represent only one type of semiological system.

The word *symbol* is sometimes used to designate the linguistic sign, or more exactly that part of the linguistic sign which we are calling the signal. This use of the word *symbol* is awkward, for reasons connected with our first principle. For it is characteristic of symbols that they are never entirely arbitrary. They are not empty configurations. They show at least a vestige of natural connexion between the signal and its signification. For instance, our symbol of justice, the scales, could hardly be replaced by a chariot.

The word *arbitrary* also calls for comment. It must not be taken to imply that a signal depends on the free choice of the speaker. (We shall see later than the individual has no power to alter a sign in any respect once it has become established in a linguistic community.) The term implies simply that the signal is *unmotivated*: that is to say arbitrary in relation to its signification, with which it has no natural connexion in reality.

In conclusion, two objections may be mentioned which might be brought against the principle that linguistic signs are arbitrary.

1. *Onomatopoeic* words might be held to show that a choice of signal is not always arbitrary. But such words are never organic elements of a linguistic system. Moreover, they are far fewer than is generally believed. French words like *fouet* ('whip') or *glas* ('knell'), may strike the ear as having a certain suggestive sonority. But to see that this is in no way intrinsic to the words themselves, it suffices to look at their Latin origins. *Fouet* comes from Latin *fāgus* ('beech tree') and *glas* from Latin *classicum* ('trumpet call'). The suggestive quality of the modern pronunciation of these words is a fortuitous result of phonetic evolution.

As for genuine onomatopoeia (e.g. French *glou-glou* ('gurgle'), *tictac* 'ticking (of a clock)'), not only is it rare but its use is already to a certain extent arbitrary. For onomatopoeia is only the approximate imitation, already partly conventionalised, of certain sounds. This is evident if we compare a French dog's *ouaoua* and a German dog's *wauwau*. In any case, once introduced into the language, onomatopoeic words are subjected to the same phonetic and morphological evolution as other words. The French word *pigeon* ('pigeon') comes from Vulgar Latin *pipiō*, itself of onomatopoeic origin, which clearly proves that onomatopoeic words themselves may lose their original character and take on that of the linguistic sign in general, which is unmotivated.

2. Similar considerations apply to *exclamations*. These are not unlike onomatopoeic words, and they do not undermine the validity of our thesis. People are tempted to regard exclamations as spontaneous expressions called forth, as it were, by nature. But in most cases it is difficult to accept that there is a necessary link between the exclamatory signal and its signification. Again, it suffices to compare two languages in this respect to see how much exclamations vary. For example, the French exclamation *aie!* corresponds to the German *au!* Moreover, it is known that many exclamations were originally meaningful words (e.g. *diable!* 'devil', *mordieu*! 'God's death').

In short, onomatopoeic and exclamatory words are rather marginal phenomena, and their symbolic origin is to some extent disputable.

3. Second principle: linear character of the signal

The linguistic signal, being auditory in nature, has a temporal aspect, and hence certain temporal characteristics: (a) *it occupies a certain temporal space*, and (b) *this space is measured in just one dimension:* it is a line.

This principle is obvious, but it seems never to be stated, doubtless because it is considered too elementary. However, it is a fundamental principle and its consequences are incalculable. Its importance equals that of the first law. The whole mechanism of linguistic structure depends upon it. Unlike visual signals (e.g. ships' flags) which can exploit more than one dimension simultaneously, auditory signals have available to them only the linearity of time. The elements of such signals are presented one after another: they form a chain. This feature appears immediately when they are represented in writing, and a spatial line of graphic signs is substituted for a succession of sounds in time.

In certain cases, this may not be easy to appreciate. For example, if I stress a certain syllable, it may seem that I am presenting a number of significant features simultaneously. But that is an illusion. The syllable and its accentuation constitute a single act of phonation. There is no duality within this act, although there are various contrasts with what precedes and follows.

NOTES

1. This associative link is to be distinguished from the associative relations which link one sign with another. (Translator's note)
2. Saussure's term 'sound pattern' may appear too narrow. For in addition to the representation of what a word sounds like, the speaker must also have a representation of how it is articulated, the muscular pattern of the act of phonation. But for Saussure a language is essentially something acquired by the individual from the outside world. Saussure's 'sound pattern' is above all the natural representation of the word form as an abstract linguistic item, independently of any actualization in speech. Hence the articulatory aspect of the word may be taken for granted, or relegated to a position of secondary importance in relation to its sound pattern. (Editorial note)
3. None the less, as various passages in the *Cours* bear witness, it would have been in the interests of clarity to introduce a terminological distinction and keep to it. (Translator's note)
4. The frontier between France and Germany. (Translator's note)

2 Victor Shklovsky

Victor Shklovsky (b. 1893) was a leading figure in the school of literary and linguistic theory known as Russian formalism, which flourished in the immediately pre- and post-revolutionary period in Russia. Two groups of scholars and students were involved—the Moscow Linguistic Circle, whose most famous member was Roman Jakobson (see below, pp. 31–61) and the *Opayaz* group based in St Petersburg, which was more interested in literary criticism, and whose leader was Shklovsky. Both groups were committed to the study and support of experimental, avant-garde literature and art. Shklovsky's 'Art as Technique', first published in 1917, was described by Boris Eikhenbaum, another member of the *Opoyaz* group, as 'a kind of manifesto of the Formal Method'.

Shklovsky's essay begins with a polemic against the Symbolist school of poets and critics, especially their chief theoretical spokesman Potebnya. Russian symbolism was evidently not identical to the French symbolist movement of the late nineteenth century, which had such a profound effect on English and American modernist writing, though they clearly had a common origin in Romantic poetics. In any case, it is not necessary to be familiar with Russian symbolism in order to appreciate the more formal, less idealist character of Shklovsky's approach to the question of what makes poetry poetic.

In a significant aside, Shklovsky praises another writer, Jakubinsky, for producing 'one of the first examples of scientific criticism'. This dream (or mirage), of making the study of literature an exact science, inspired the tradition that ran from the Russian formalists, via the Prague School of the 1930s, to the exponents of 'structuralism' in Western Europe in the 1960s and 70s. It had its equivalent in England and America in the efforts of the New Critics, from I. A. Richards to W. K. Wimsatt, to make literary criticism a more precise and objective discipline. There is an obvious parallel between Shklovsky's distinction between poetic and prose language and I. A. Richards' distinction between emotive and referential language (see I. A. Richards, 'The Two Uses of Language', Section 9 in *20th Century Literary Criticism*).

Shklovsky's crucially important concept of defamiliarization (*ostranenie*, 'making strange') is, however, essentially structuralist in that it treats literary technique, as Saussure had treated language, as a 'system of differences'. What startles us into a new way of seeing is a new way of saying, and we can only appreciate the novelty of *that* against what is habitual and expected in any given context.

The focus of Russian formalists upon the medium rather than the message of literary artefacts brought it into conflict with the official ideology of post-Revolutionary Russia, and under Stalin it was suppressed. Most of its exponents were silenced, or forced into exile. Shklovsky, however, by a judicious revision of his views, managed amazingly to survive as a practising scholar and critic into the 1980s. 'Art as Technique' is reprinted here from *Russian Formalist Criticism* (1965) translated by Lee T. Lemon and Marion J. Reis.

CROSS REFERENCES: 1. Saussure
                    3. Jakobson
    COMMENTARY: Boris M. Eichenbaum, 'The Theory of the Formal Method', in L. Matejka and K. Pomorska (eds), *Readings in Russian Poetics* (1978).
                  Victor Erlich, *Russian Formalism: history-doctrine* (1955)

Art as technique

'Art is thinking in images.' This maxim, which even high school students parrot, is nevertheless the starting point for the erudite philologist who is beginning to put together some kind of systematic literary theory. The idea, originated in part by Potebnya, has spread. 'Without imagery there is no art, and in particular no poetry,' Potebnya writes.[1] And elsewhere, 'Poetry, as well as prose, is first and foremost a special way of thinking and knowing.'[2]

Poetry is a special way of thinking; it is, precisely, a way of thinking in images, a way which permits what is generally called 'economy of mental effort,' a way which makes for 'a sensation of the relative ease of the process.' Aesthetic feeling is the reaction to this economy. This is how the academician Ovsyaniko-Kulikovsky,[3] who undoubtedly read the works of Potebnya attentively, almost certainly understood and faithfully summarized the ideas of his teacher. Potebnya and his numerous disciples consider poetry a special kind of thinking—thinking by means of images; they feel that the purpose of imagery is to help channel various objects and activities into groups and to clarify the unknown by means of the known. Or, as Potebnya wrote:

> The relationship of the image to what is being clarified is that: (a) the image is the fixed predicate of that which undergoes change—the unchanging means of attracting what is perceived as changeable. . . . (b) the image is far clearer and simpler than what it clarifies.[4]

In other words:

> Since the purpose of imagery is to remind us, by approximation, of those meanings for which the image stands, and since, apart from this, imagery is unnecessary for thought, we must be more familiar with the image than with what it clarifies.[5]

It would be instructive to try to apply this principle to Tyutchev's comparison of summer lightning to deaf and dumb demons or to Gogol's comparison of the sky to the garment of God.[6]

'Without imagery there is no art'—'Art is thinking in images.' These maxims have led to far-fetched interpretations of individual works of art. Attempts have been made to evaluate even music, architecture, and lyric poetry as imagistic thought. After a quarter of a century of such attempts Ovsyaniko-Kulikovsky finally had to assign lyric poetry, architecture, and music to a special category of imageless art and to define them as lyric arts appealing directly to the emotions. And thus he admitted an enormous area of art which is not a mode of thought. A part of this area, lyric poetry (narrowly considered), is quite like the visual arts; it is also verbal. But, much more important, visual art passes quite imperceptibly into nonvisual art; yet our perceptions of both are similar.

Nevertheless, the definition 'Art is thinking in images,' which means (I omit the usual middle terms of the argument) that art is the making of symbols, has survived the downfall of the theory which supported it. It survives chiefly in the wake of Symbolism, especially among the theorists of the Symbolist movement.

Many still believe, then, that thinking in images—thinking in specific scenes of 'roads and landscape' and 'furrows and boundaries'[7]—is the chief characteristic of poetry. Consequently, they should have expected the history of 'imagistic art,' as they call it, to consist of a history of changes in imagery. But we find that images change little; from century to century, from nation to nation, from poet to poet, they flow on without changing. Images belong to no one: they are 'the Lord's.' The more you understand an age, the more convinced you become that the images a given poet used and which you thought his own were taken almost unchanged from another poet. The works of poets are classified or grouped according to the new techniques that poets discover and share, and according to their arrangement and development of the resources of language; poets are much more concerned with arranging images than with creating them. Images are given to poets; the ability to remember them is far more important than the ability to create them.

Imagistic thought does not, in any case, include all the aspects of art nor even all the aspects of verbal art. A change in imagery is not essential to the development of poetry. We know that frequently an expression is thought to be poetic, to be created for aesthetic pleasure, although actually it was created without such intent—e.g., Annensky's opinion that the Slavic languages are especially poetic and Andrey Bely's ecstasy over the technique of placing adjectives after nouns, a technique used by eighteenth-century Russian poets. Bely joyfully accepts the technique as something artistic, or more exactly, as intended, if we consider intention as art. Actually, this reversal of the usual adjective–noun order is a peculiarity of the language (which had been influenced by Church Slavonic). Thus a work may be (1) intended as prosaic and accepted as poetic, or (2) intended as poetic and accepted as prosaic. This suggests that the artistry attributed to a given work results from the way we perceive it. By 'works of art,' in the narrow sense, we mean works created by special techniques designed to make the works as obviously artistic as possible.

Potebnya's conclusion, which can be formulated 'poetry equals imagery,' gave rise to the whole theory that 'imagery equals symbolism,' that the image may serve as the invariable predicate of various subjects. (This conclusion, because it expressed ideas similar to the theories of the Symbolists, intrigued some of their leading representatives—Andrey Bely, Merezhkovsky and his 'eternal companions' and, in fact, formed the basis of the theory of Symbolism.) The conclusion stems partly from the fact that Potebnya did not distinguish between the language of poetry and the language of prose. Consequently, he ignored the fact that there are two aspects of imagery: imagery as a practical means of thinking, as a means of placing objects within categories; and imagery as poetic, as a means of reinforcing an impression. I shall clarify with an example. I want to attract the attention of a young child who is eating bread and butter and getting the butter on her fingers. I call, 'Hey, butterfingers!' This is a figure of speech, a clearly prosaic trope. Now a different example. The child is playing with my glasses and drops them. I call, 'Hey, butterfingers!'[8] This figure of speech is a poetic trope. (In the first example, 'butterfingers' is metonymic; in the second, metaphoric—but this is not what I want to stress.)[a]

Poetic imagery is a means of creating the strongest possible impression. As a method it is, depending upon its purpose, neither more nor less effective than other poetic techniques; it is neither more nor less effective than ordinary or negative parallelism, comparison, repetition, balanced structure, hyperbole, the commonly accepted rhetorical figures, and all those methods which emphasize the emotional effect of an expression (including words or even articulated sounds).[9] But poetic imagery only externally resembles either the stock imagery of fables and ballads or thinking in images—e.g., the example in Ovsyaniko-Kulikovsky's *Language and Art* in which a little girl calls a ball a little watermelon. Poetic imagery is but one of the devices of poetic language. Prose imagery is a means of abstraction: a little watermelon instead of a lampshade, or a little watermelon instead of a head, is only the abstraction of one of the object's characteristics, that of roundness. It is no different from saying that the head and the melon are both round. This is what is meant, but it has nothing to do with poetry.

The law of the economy of creative effort is also generally accepted. [Herbert] Spencer[b] wrote:

> On seeking for some clue to the law underlying these current maxims, we may see shadowed forth in many of them, the importance of economizing the reader's or the hearer's attention. To so present ideas that they may be apprehended with the least possible mental effort, is the desideratum towards which most of the rules above quoted point. . . . Hence, carrying out the metaphor that language is the vehicle of thought, there seems reason to think that in all cases the friction and inertia of the vehicle deduct from its efficiency; and that in composition, the chief, if

[a] See Roman Jakobson, 'The Metaphoric and Metonymic Poles', below pp. 57–61.
[b] British philosopher (1820–1903).

18

not the sole thing to be done, is to reduce this friction and inertia to the smallest possible amount.[10]

And R[ichard] Avenarius:

If a soul possess inexhaustible strength, then, of course, it would be indifferent to how much might be spent from this inexhaustible source; only the necessarily expended time would be important. But since its forces are limited, one is led to expect that the soul hastens to carry out the apperceptive process as expediently as possible—that is, with comparatively the least expenditure of energy, and, hence, with comparatively the best result.

Petrazhitsky, with only one reference to the general law of mental effort, rejects [William] James's theory of the physical basis of emotion, a theory which contradicts his own. Even Alexander Veselovsky acknowledged the principle of the economy of creative effort, a theory especially appealing in the study of rhythm, and agreed with Spencer: 'A satisfactory style is precisely that style which delivers the greatest amount of thought in the fewest words.' And Andrey Bely, despite the fact that in his better pages he gave numerous examples of 'roughened' rhythm[11] and (particularly in the examples from Baratynsky) showed the difficulties inherent in poetic epithets, also thought it necessary to speak of the law of the economy of creative effort in his book[12]—a heroic effort to create a theory of art based on unverified facts from antiquated sources, on his vast knowledge of the techniques of poetic creativity, and on Krayevich's high school physics text.

These ideas about the economy of energy, as well as about the law and aim of creativity, are perhaps true in their application to 'practical' language; they were, however, extended to poetic language. Hence they do not distinguish properly between the laws of practical language and the laws of poetic language. The fact that Japanese poetry has sounds not found in conversational Japanese was hardly the first factual indication of the differences between poetic and everyday language. Leo Jakubinsky has observed that the law of the dissimilation of liquid sounds does not apply to poetic language.[13] This suggested to him that poetic language tolerated the admission of hard-to-pronounce conglomerations of similar sounds. In his article, one of the first examples of scientific criticism, he indicates inductively the contrast (I shall say more about this point later) between the laws of poetic language and the laws of practical language.[14]

We must, then, speak about the laws of expenditure and economy in poetic language not on the basis of an analogy with prose, but on the basis of the laws of poetic language.

If we start to examine the general laws of perception, we see that as perception becomes habitual, it becomes automatic. Thus, for example, all of our habits retreat into the area of the unconsciously automatic; if one remembers the sensations of holding a pen or of speaking in a foreign language for the first time and compares that with his feeling at performing the action for the ten thousandth time, he will agree with us. Such habituation explains the principles by which, in ordinary speech, we leave phrases unfinished and words half expressed. In this process, ideally realized in algebra, things are replaced by symbols. Complete words are not expressed in rapid speech; their initial sounds are barely perceived. Alexander Pogodin offers the example of a boy considering the sentence 'The Swiss mountains are beautiful' in the form of a series of letters: *T, S, m, a, b*.[15]

This characteristic of thought not only suggests the method of algebra, but even prompts the choice of symbols (letters, especially initial letters). By this 'algebraic' method of thought we apprehend objects only as shapes with imprecise extensions; we do not see them in their entirety but rather recognize them by their main characteristics. We see the object as though it were enveloped in a sack. We know what it is by its configuration, but we see only its silhouette. The object, perceived thus in the manner of prose perception, fades and does not leave even a first impression; ultimately even the essence of what it was is forgotten. Such perception explains why we fail to hear the prose word in its entirety (see Leo Jakubinsky's article[16]) and, hence, why (along with other slips of the tongue) we fail to pronounce it. The process of 'algebrization,' the over-automatization of an object, permits the greatest economy of perceptive effort. Either objects are assigned only one proper feature—a number, for example— or else they function as though by formula and do not even appear in cognition:

> I was cleaning a room and, meandering about, approached the divan and couldn't remember whether or not I had dusted it. Since these movements are habitual and unconscious, I could not remember and felt that it was impossible to remember—so that if I had dusted it and forgot—that is, had acted unconsciously, then it was the same as if I had not. If some conscious person had been watching, then the fact could be established. If, however, no one was looking, or looking on unconsciously, if the whole complex lives of many people go on unconsciously, then such lives are as if they had never been.[17]

And so life is reckoned as nothing. Habitualization devours works, clothes, furniture, one's wife, and the fear of war. 'If the whole complex lives of many people go on unconsciously, then such lives are as if they had never been.' And art exists that one may recover the sensation of life; it exists to make one feel things, to make the stone *stony*. The purpose of art is to impart the sensation of things as they are perceived and not as they are known. The technique of art is to make objects 'unfamiliar,' to make forms difficult, to increase the difficulty and length of perception because the process of perception is an aesthetic end in itself and must be prolonged. *Art is a way of experiencing the artfulness of an object; the object is not important.*[c]

The range of poetic (artistic) work extends from the sensory to the cognitive, from poetry to prose, from the concrete to the abstract: from Cervantes' Don

[c] The translation of this crucial and often quoted sentence by Lemon and Reis has been criticized by Robert Scholes, who offers his own version: 'In art, it is our experience of the process of construction that counts, not the finished product.' *Structuralism in Literature* (1974) p. 84.

20

Quixote—scholastic and poor nobleman, half consciously bearing his humiliation in the court of the duke—to the broad but empty Don Quixote of Turgenev; from Charlemagne to the name 'king' [in Russian 'Charles' and 'king' obviously derive from the same root, *korol*]. The meaning of a work broadens to the extent that artfulness and artistry diminish; thus a fable symbolizes more than a poem, and a proverb more than a fable. Consequently, the least self-contradictory part of Potebnya's theory is his treatment of the fable, which, from his point of view, he investigated thoroughly. But since his theory did not provide for 'expressive' works of art, he could not finish his book. As we know, *Notes on the Theory of Literature* was published in 1905, thirteen years after Potebnya's death. Potebnya himself completed only the section on the fable.[18]

After we see an object several times, we begin to recognize it. The object is in front of us and we know about it, but we do not see it[19]—hence we cannot say anything significant about it. Art removes objects from the automatism of perception in several ways. Here I want to illustrate a way used repeatedly by Leo Tolstoy, that writer who, for Merezhkovsky at least, seems to present things as if he himself saw them, saw them in their entirety, and did not alter them.

Tolstoy makes the familiar seem strange by not naming the familiar object. He describes an object as if he were seeing it for the first time, an event as if it were happening for the first time. In describing something he avoids the accepted names of its parts and instead names corresponding parts of other objects. For example, in 'Shame' Tolstoy 'defamiliarizes' the idea of flogging in this way: 'to strip people who have broken the law, to hurl them to the floor, and to rap on their bottoms with switches,' and, after a few lines, 'to lash about on the naked buttocks.' Then he remarks:

> Just why precisely this stupid, savage means of causing pain and not any other—why not prick the shoulders or any part of the body with needles, squeeze the hands or the feet in a vise, or anything like that?

I apologize for this harsh example, but it is typical of Tolstoy's way of pricking the conscience. The familiar act of flogging is made unfamiliar both by the description and by the proposal to change its form without changing its nature. Tolstoy uses this technique of 'defamiliarization' constantly. The narrator of 'Kholstomer,' for example, is a horse, and it is the horse's point of view (rather than a person's) that makes the content of the story seem unfamiliar. Here is how the horse regards the institution of private property:

> I understood well what they said about whipping and Christianity. But then I was absolutely in the dark. What's the meaning of 'his own,' 'his colt'? From these phrases I saw that people thought there was some sort of connection between me and the stable. At the time I simply could not understand the connection. Only much later, when they separated me from the other horses, did I begin to understand. But even then I simply could not see what it meant when they called me 'man's property.' The words 'my horse' referred to me, a living horse, and seemed as strange to me as the words 'my land,' 'my air,' 'my water.'

21

But the words made a strong impression on me. I thought about them constantly, and only after the most diverse experiences with people did I understand, finally, what they meant. They meant this: In life people are guided by words, not by deeds. It's not so much that they love the possibility of doing or not doing something as it is the possibility of speaking with words, agreed on among themselves, about various topics. Such are the words 'my' and 'mine,' which they apply to different things, creatures, objects, and even to land, people, and horses. They agree that only one may say 'mine' about this, that, or the other thing. And the one who says 'mine' about the greatest number of things is, according to the game which they've agreed to among themselves, the one they consider the most happy. I don't know the point of all this, but it's true. For a long time I tried to explain it to myself in terms of some kind of real gain, but I had to reject that explanation because it was wrong.

Many of those, for instance, who called me their own never rode on me—although others did. And so with those who fed me. Then again, the coachman, the veterinarians, and the outsiders in general treated me kindly, yet those who called me their own did not. In due time, having widened the scope of my observations, I satisfied myself that the notion 'my,' not only in relation to us horses, has no other basis than a narrow human instinct which is called a sense of or right to private property. A man says 'this house is mine' and never lives in it; he only worries about its construction and upkeep. A merchant says 'my shop,' 'my dry goods shop,' for instance, and does not even wear clothes made from the better cloth he keeps in his own shop.

There are people who call a tract of land their own, but they never set eyes on it and never take a stroll on it. There are people who call others their own, yet never see them. And the whole relationship between them is that the so-called 'owners' treat the others unjustly.

There are people who call women their own, or their 'wives', but their women live with other men. And people strive not for the good in life, but for goods they can call their own.

I am now convinced that this is the essential difference between people and ourselves. And therefore, not even considering the other ways in which we are superior, but considering just this one virtue, we can bravely claim to stand higher than men on the ladder of living creatures. The actions of men, at least those with whom I have had dealings, are guided by *words*—ours, by deeds.

The horse is killed before the end of the story, but the manner of the narrative, its technique, does not change:

Much later they put Serpukhovsky's body, which had experienced the world, which had eaten and drunk, into the ground. They could profitably send neither his hide, nor his flesh, nor his bones anywhere.

But since his dead body, which had gone about in the world for twenty

years, was a great burden to everyone, its burial was only a superfluous
embarrassment for the people. For a long time no one had needed him;
for a long time he had been a burden on all. But nevertheless, the dead
who buried the dead found it necessary to dress this bloated body, which
immediately began to rot, in a good uniform and good boots; to lay it in a
good new coffin with new tassels at the four corners, then to place this
new coffin in another of lead and ship it to Moscow; there to exhume
ancient bones and at just that spot, to hide this putrefying body,
swarming with maggots, in its new uniform and clean boots, and to cover
it over completely with dirt.

Thus we see that at the end of the story Tolstoy continues to use the technique
even though the motivation for it [the reason for its use] is gone.

In *War and Peace* Tolstoy uses the same technique in describing whole battles
as if battles were something new. These descriptions are too long to quote; it
would be necessary to extract a considerable part of the four-volume novel. But
Tolstoy uses the same method in describing the drawing room and the theater:

The middle of the stage consisted of flat boards; by the sides stood
painted pictures representing trees, and at the back a linen cloth was
stretched down to the floor boards. Maidens in red bodices and white
skirts sat on the middle of the stage. One, very fat, in a white silk dress,
sat apart on a narrow bench to which a green pasteboard box was glued
from behind. They were all singing something. When they had finished,
the maiden in white approached the prompter's box. A man in silk with
tight-fitting pants on his fat legs approached her with a plume and began
to sing and spread his arms in dismay. The man in the tight pants
finished his song alone; then the girl sang. After that both remained silent
as the music resounded; and the man, obviously waiting to begin singing
his part with her again, began to run his fingers over the hand of the girl
in the white dress. They finished their song together, and everyone in
the theater began to clap and shout. But the men and women on stage,
who represented lovers, started to bow, smiling and raising their hands.

In the second act there were pictures representing monuments and
openings in the linen cloth representing the moonlight, and they raised
lamp shades on a frame. As the musicians started to play the bass horn
and counter-bass, a large number of people in black mantles poured onto
the stage from right and left. The people, with something like daggers in
their hands, started to wave their arms. Then still more people came
running out and began to drag away the maiden who had been wearing a
white dress but who now wore one of sky blue. They did not drag her
off immediately, but sang with her for a long time before dragging her
away. Three times they struck on something metallic behind the side
scenes, and everyone got down on his knees and began to chant a prayer.
Several times all of this activity was interrupted by enthusiastic shouts
from the spectators.

The third act is described:

> But suddenly a storm blew up. Chromatic scales and chords of
> diminished sevenths were heard in the orchestra. Everyone ran about and
> again they dragged one of the bystanders behind the scenes as the
> curtain fell.

In the fourth act, 'There was some sort of devil who sang, waving his hands,
until the boards were moved out from under him and he dropped down.[20]
In *Resurrection* Tolstoy describes the city and the court in the same way; he
uses a similar technique in 'Kreutzer Sonata' when he describes marriage—'Why,
if people have an affinity of souls, must they sleep together?' But he did not
defamiliarize only those things he sneered at:

> Pierre stood up from his new comrades and made his way between the
> campfires to the other side of the road where, it seemed, the captive
> soldiers were held. He wanted to talk with them. The French sentry
> stopped him on the road and ordered him to return. Pierre did so, but
> not to the campfire, not to his comrades, but to an abandoned,
> unharnessed carriage. On the ground, near the wheel of the carriage, he
> sat cross-legged in the Turkish fashion, and lowered his head. He sat
> motionless for a long time, thinking. More than an hour passed. No one
> disturbed him. Suddenly he burst out laughing with his robust, good
> natured laugh—so loudly that the men near him looked around, surprised
> at his conspicuously strange laughter.
> 'Ha, ha, ha,' laughed Pierre. And he began to talk to himself. 'The
> soldier didn't allow me to pass. They caught me, barred me. Me—me—
> my immortal soul. Ha, ha, ha,' he laughed with tears starting in his eyes.
> Pierre glanced at the sky, into the depths of the departing, playing
> stars. 'And all this is mine, all this is in me, and all this is I,' thought
> Pierre. 'And all this they caught and put in a planked enclosure.' He
> smiled and went off to his comrades to lie down to sleep.[21]

Anyone who knows Tolstoy can find several hundred such passages in his
work. His method of seeing things out of their normal context is also apparent
in his last works. Tolstoy described the dogmas and rituals he attacked as if they
were unfamiliar, substituting everyday meanings for the customarily religious
meanings of the words common in church ritual. Many persons were painfully
wounded; they considered it blasphemy to present as strange and monstrous what
they accepted as sacred. Their reaction was due chiefly to the technique through
which Tolstoy perceived and reported his environment. And after turning to what
he had long avoided, Tolstoy found that his perceptions had unsettled his faith.

The technique of defamiliarization is not Tolstoy's alone. I cited Tolstoy
because his work is generally known.
Now, having explained the nature of this technique, let us try to determine
the approximate limits of its application. I personally feel that defamiliarization
is found almost everywhere form is found. In other words, the difference between

Potebnya's point of view and ours is this: An image is not a permanent referent for those mutable complexities of life which are revealed through it; its purpose is not to make us perceive meaning, but to create a special perception of the object—*it creates a 'vision' of the object instead of serving as a means for knowing it.*

The purpose of imagery in erotic art can be studied even more accurately; an erotic object is usually presented as if it were seen for the first time. Gogol, in 'Christmas Eve,' provides the following example:

> Here he approached her more closely, coughed, smiled at her, touched her plump, bare arm with his fingers, and expressed himself in a way that showed both his cunning and his conceit.
>
> 'And what is this you have, magnificent Solokha?' and having said this, he jumped back a little.
>
> 'What? An arm, Osip Nikiforovich!' she answered.
>
> 'Hmmm, an arm! *He, he, he!*' said the secretary cordially, satisfied with his beginning. He wandered about the room.
>
> 'And what is this you have, dearest Solokha?' he said in the same way, having approached her again and grasped her lightly by the neck, and in the very same way he jumped back.
>
> 'As if you don't see, Osip Nikiforovich!' answered Solokha, 'a neck, and on my neck a necklace.'
>
> 'Hmm! On the neck a necklace! *He, he, he!*' and the secretary again wandered about the room, rubbing his hands.
>
> 'And what is this you have, incomparable Solokha?' . . . It is not known to what the secretary would stretch his long fingers now.

And Knut Hamsun has the following in 'Hunger': 'Two white prodigies appeared from beneath her blouse.'

Erotic subjects may also be presented figuratively with the obvious purpose of leading us away from their 'recognition.' Hence sexual organs are referred to in terms of lock and key[22] or quilting tools[23] or bow and arrow, or rings and marlinspikes, as in the legend of Stavyor, in which a married man does not recognize his wife, who is disguised as a warrior. She proposes a riddle:

> 'Remember, Stavyor, do you recall
> How we little ones walked to and fro in the street?
> You and I together sometimes played with a marlinspike—
> You had a silver marlinspike,
> But I had a gilded ring?
> I found myself at it just now and then,
> But you fell in with it ever and always.'
> Says Stavyor, son of Godinovich,
> 'What! I didn't play with you at marlinspikes!'
> Then Vasilisa Mikulichna: 'So he says.
> Do you remember, Stavyor, do you recall,
> Now must you know, you and I together learned to
> > read and write;

> Mine was an ink-well of silver,
> And yours a pen of gold?
> But I just moistened it a little now and then,
> And I just moistened it ever and always.'[24]

In a different version of the legend we find a key to the riddle:

> Here the formidable envoy Vasilyushka
> Raised her skirts to the very navel,
> And then the young Stavyor, son of Godinovich,
> Recognized her gilded ring . . .[25]

But defamiliarization is not only a technique of the erotic riddle—a technique of euphemism—it is also the basis and point of all riddles. Every riddle pretends to show its subject either by words which specify or describe it but which, during the telling, do not seem applicable (the type: 'black and white and 'red'—read—all over)' or by means of odd but imitative sounds ("Twas brillig, and the slithy toves/Did gyre and gimble in the wabe"[a]).[26]

Even erotic images not intended as riddles are defamiliarized ('boobies,' 'tarts,' 'piece,' etc.). In popular imagery there is generally something equivalent to 'trampling the grass' and 'breaking the guelder-rose.' The technique of defamiliarization is absolutely clear in the widespread image—a motif of erotic affectation—in which a bear and other wild beasts (or a devil, with a different reason for nonrecognition) do not recognize a man.[27]

The lack of recognition in the following tale is quite typical:

> A peasant was plowing a field with a piebald mare. A bear approached him and asked, 'Uncle, what's made this mare piebald for you?'
> 'I did the piebalding myself.'
> 'But how?'
> 'Let me, and I'll do the same for you.'
> The bear agreed. The peasant tied his feet together with a rope, took the ploughshare from the two-wheeled plough, heated it on the fire, and applied it to his flanks. He made the bear piebald by scorching his fur down to the hide with the hot ploughshare. The man untied the bear, which went off and lay down under a tree.
> A magpie flew at the peasant to pick at the meat on his shirt. He caught her and broke one of her legs. The magpie flew off to perch in the same tree under which the bear was lying. Then, after the magpie, a horsefly landed on the mare, sat down, and began to bite. The peasant caught the fly, took a stick, shoved it up its rear, and let it go. The fly went to the tree where the bear and the magpie were. There all three sat.
> The peasant's wife came to bring his dinner to the field. The man and his wife finished their dinner in the fresh air, and he began to wrestle with her on the ground.

[a] The quotation is from the poem 'Jaberwocky' in Lewis Carroll's *Through the Looking-Glass, and what Alice found there* (1872).

The bear saw this and said to the magpie and the fly, 'Holy priests!
The peasant wants to piebald someone again.'
The magpie said, 'No, he wants to break someone's legs.'
The fly said, 'No, he wants to shove a stick up someone's rump.'[28]

The similarity of technique here and in Tolstoy's 'Kholstomer,' is, I think, obvious.

Quite often in literature the sexual act itself is defamiliarized; for example, the *Decameron* refers to 'scraping out a barrel,' 'catching nightingales,' 'gay wool-beating work,' (the last is not developed in the plot). Defamiliarization is often used in describing the sexual organs.

A whole series of plots is based on such a lack of recognition; for example, in Afanasyev's *Intimate Tales* the entire story of 'The Shy Mistress' is based on the fact that an object is not called by its proper name—or, in other words, on a game of nonrecognition. So too in Onchukov's 'Spotted Petticoats,' tale no. 525, and also in 'The Bear and the Hare' from *Intimate Tales*, in which the bear and the hare make a 'wound.'

Such constructions as 'the pestle and the mortar,' or 'Old Nick and the infernal regions' (*Decameron*), are also examples of the technique of defamiliarization. And in my article on plot construction I write about defamiliarization in psychological parallelism. Here, then I repeat that the perception of disharmony in a harmonious context is important in parallelism. The purpose of parallelism, like the general purpose of imagery, is to transfer the usual perception of an object into the sphere of a new perception—that is, to make a unique semantic modification.

In studying poetic speech in its phonetic and lexical structure as well as in its characteristic distribution of words and in the characteristic thought structures compounded from the words, we find everywhere the artistic trademark—that is, we find material obviously created to remove the automatism of perception; the author's purpose is to create the vision which results from that deautomatized perception. A work is created 'artistically' so that its perception is impeded and the greatest possible effect is produced through the slowness of the perception. As a result of this lingering, the object is perceived not in its extension in space, but, so to speak, in its continuity. Thus 'poetic language' gives satisfaction. According to Aristotle, poetic language must appear strange and wonderful; and, in fact, it is often actually foreign: the Sumerian used by the Assyrians, the Latin of Europe during the Middle Ages, the Arabisms of the Persians, the Old Bulgarian of Russian literature, or the elevated, almost literary language of folk songs. The common archaisms of poetic language, the intricacy of the sweet new style [*dolce stil nuovo*],[29] the obscure style of the language of Arnaut Daniel with the 'roughened' [*harte*] forms *which make pronunciation difficult*—these are used in much the same way. Leo Jakubinsky has demonstrated the principle of phonetic 'roughening' of poetic language in the particular case of the repetition of identical sounds. The language of poetry is, then, a difficult, roughened, impeded language. In a few special instances the language of poetry approximates the language of prose, but this does not violate the principle of 'roughened' form.

> Her sister was called Tatyana.
> For the first time we shall
> Wilfully brighten the delicate
> Pages of a novel with such a name.

wrote Pushkin. The usual poetic language for Pushkin's contemporaries was the elegant style of Derzhavin; but Pushkin's style, because it seemed trivial then, was unexpectedly difficult for them. We should remember the consternation of Pushkin's contemporaries over the vulgarity of his expressions. He used the popular language as a special device for prolonging attention, just as his contemporaries generally used Russian words in their usually French speech (see Tolstoy's examples in *War and Peace*).

Just now a still more characteristic phenomenon is under way. Russian literary language, which was originally foreign to Russia, has so permeated the language of the people that it has blended with their conversation. On the other hand, literature has now begun to show a tendency towards the use of dialects (Remizov, Klyuyev, Essenin, and others,[30] so unequal in talent and so alike in language, are intentionally provincial) and of barbarisms (which gave rise to the Severyanin group[31]). And currently Maxim Gorky is changing his diction from the old literary language to the new literary colloquialism of Leskov.[32] Ordinary speech and literary language have thereby changed places (see the work of Vyacheslav Ivanov and many others). And finally, a strong tendency, led by Khlebnikov, to create a new and properly poetic language has emerged. In the light of these developments we can define poetry as *attenuated, tortuous* speech. Poetic speech is *formed speech*. Prose is ordinary speech—economical, easy, proper, the goddess of prose [*dea prosae*] is a goddess of the accurate, facile type, of the 'direct' expression of a child. I shall discuss roughened form and retardation as the general *law* of art at greater length in an article on plot construction.[33]

Nevertheless, the position of those who urge the idea of the economy of artistic energy as something which exists in and even distinguishes poetic language seems, at first glance, tenable for the problem of rhythm. Spencer's description of rhythm would seem to be absolutely incontestable:

> Just as the body in receiving a series of varying concussions, must keep the muscles ready to meet the most violent of them, as not knowing when such may come: so, the mind in receiving unarranged articulations, must keep its perspectives active enough to recognize the least easily caught sounds. And as, if the concussions recur in definite order, the body may husband its forces by adjusting the resistance needful for each concussion; so, if the syllables be rhythmically arranged, the mind may economize its energies by anticipating the attention required for each syllable.[34]

This apparently conclusive observation suffers from the common fallacy, the confusion of the laws of poetic and prosaic language. In *The Philosophy of Style* Spencer failed utterly to distinguish between them. But rhythm may have two functions. The rhythm of prose, or of a work song like 'Dubinushka,' permits the members of the work crew to do their necessary 'groaning together' and also eases the work by making it automatic. And, in fact, it is easier to march with music than without it, and to march during an animated conversation is even easier, for the walking is done unconsciously. Thus the rhythm of prose is an important automatizing element; the rhythm of poetry is not. There is 'order' in art, yet not a single column of a Greek temple stands exactly in its proper order; poetic rhythm is similarly disordered rhythm. Attempts to systematize the irregularities have been made, and such attempts are part of the current problem in the theory of rhythm. It is obvious that the systematization will not work, for in reality the problem is not one of complicating the rhythm but of disordering the rhythm—a disordering which cannot be predicted. Should the disordering of rhythm become a convention, it would be ineffective as a device for the roughening of language. But I will not discuss rhythm in more detail since I intend to write a book about it.[35]

NOTES

1. Alexander Potebnya, *Iz zapisok po teorii slovesnosti* [*Notes on the Theory of Language*] (Kharkov, 1905), p. 38.
2. *Ibid.*, p. 97.
3. Dmitry Ovsyaniko-Kulikovsky (1835–1920), a leading Russian scholar, was an early contributor to Marxist periodicals and a literary conservative, antagonistic towards the deliberately meaningless poems of the Futurists. *Ed. note.*
4. Potebnya, *Iz zapisok po teorii slovesnosti*, p. 314.
5. *Ibid.*, p. 291.
6. Fyodor Tyutchev (1803–1873), a poet, and Nicholas Gogol (1809–1852), a master of prose fiction and satire, are mentioned here because their bold use of imagery cannot be accounted for by Potebnya's theory. Shklovsky is arguing that writers frequently gain their effects by comparing the commonplace to the exceptional rather than vice versa. *Ed. note.*
7. This is an allusion to Vyacheslav Ivanov's *Borozdy i mezhi* [*Furrows and Boundaries*] (Moscow, 1916), a major statement of Symbolist theory. *Ed. note.*
8. The Russian text involves a play on the word for 'hat,' colloquial for 'clod,' 'duffer,' etc. *Ed. note.*
9. Shklovsky is here doing two things of major theoretical importance: (1) he argues that different techniques serve a single function, and that (2) no single technique is all-important. The second permits the Formalists to be concerned with any and all literary devices; the first permits them to discuss the devices from a single consistent theoretical position. *Ed. note.*
10. Herbert Spencer, *The Philosophy of Style* [(Humboldt Library, Vol. XXXIV; New York, 1882), pp. 2–3. Shklovsky's quoted reference, in Russian, preserves the idea of the original but shortens it].
11. The Russian *zatrudyonny* means 'made difficult.' The suggestion is that poems with 'easy' or smooth rhythms slip by unnoticed; poems that are difficult or 'roughened' force the reader to attend to them. *Ed. note.*
12. *Simvolizm*, probably. *Ed. note.*
13. Leo Jakubinsky, 'O zvukakh poeticheskovo yazyka' ['On the Sounds of Poetic Language'], *Sborniki*, I (1916), p. 38.
14. Leo Jakubinsky, 'Skopleniye odinakovykh plavnykh v prakticheskom i poeticheskom yazykakh' ['The Accumulation of Identical Liquids in Practical and Poetic Language'], *Sborniki*, II (1917), pp. 13–21.

29

15. Alexander Pogodin, *Yazyk, kak tvorchestvo* [*Language as Art*] (Kharkov, 1913), p. 42. [The original sentence was in French, '*Les montagnes de la Suisse sont belles*,' with the appropriate initials.]
16. Jakubinsky, *Sborniki*, I (1916).
17. Leo Tolstoy's *Diary*, entry dated February 29, 1897. [The date is transcribed incorrectly; it should read March 1, 1897.]
18. Alexander Potebnya, *Iz lektsy po teorii slovesnosti* [*Lectures on the Theory of Language*] (Kharkov, 1914).
19. Victor Shklovsky, *Voskresheniye slova* [*The Resurrection of the Word*] (Petersburg, 1914).
20. The Tolstoy and Gogol translations are ours. The passage occurs in Vol. II, Part 8, Chap. 9 of the edition of *War and Peace* published in Boston by the Dana Estes Co. in 1904–1912. *Ed. note.*
21. Leo Tolstoy, *War and Peace*, IV, Part 13. Chap. 14. *Ed. note.*
22. [Dimitry] Savodnikov, *Zagadki russkovo naroda* [*Riddles of the Russian People*] (St. Petersburg, 1901), Nos. 102–107.
23. *Ibid.*, Nos. 588–591.
24. A. E. Gruzinsky, ed., *Pesni, sobrannye P* [*avel*] *N. Rybnikovym* [*Songs Collected by P. N. Rybnikov*] (Moscow, 1909–1910), No. 30.
25. *Ibid.*, No. 171.
26. We have supplied familiar English examples in place of Shklovsky's wordplay. Shklovsky is saying that we create words with no referents or with ambiguous referents in order to force attention to the objects represented by the similar-sounding words. By making the reader go through the extra step of interpreting the nonsense word, the writer prevents an automatic response. A toad is a toad, but 'tove' forces one to pause and think about the beast. *Ed. note.*
27. E. R. Romanov, 'Besstrashny barin,' *Velikorusskiye skazki* (Zapiski Imperskovo Russkovo Geograficheskovo Obschestva, XLII, No. 52). Belorussky sbornik, 'Spravyadlivy soldat' ['The Intrepid Gentleman,' *Great Russian Tales* (Notes of the Imperial Russian Geographical Society, XLII, No. 52). White Russian Anthology, 'The Upright Soldier' (1886–1912)].
28. D[mitry] S. Zelenin, *Velikorusskiye skazki Permskoy gubernii* [*Great Russian Tales of the Permian Province* (St. Petersburg, 1913)], No. 70.
29. Dante, *Purgatorio*, 24:56. Dante refers to the new lyric style of his contemporaries. *Ed. note.*
30. Alexy Remizov (1877–1957) is best known as a novelist and satirist; Nicholas Klyuyev (1885–1937) and Sergey Essenin (1895–1925), were 'peasant poets.' All three were noted for their faithful reproduction of Russian dialects and colloquial language. *Ed. note.*
31. A group noted for its opulent and sensuous verse style. *Ed. note.*
32. Nicholas Leskov (1831–1895), novelist and short story writer, helped popularize the *skaz*, or yarn, and hence, because of the part dialect peculiarities play in the *skaz*, also altered Russian literary language. *Ed. note.*
33. Shklovsky is probably referring to his *Razvyortyvaniye syuzheta* [*Plot Development*] (Petrograd, 1921). *Ed. note.*
34. Spencer, [p. 169. Again the Russian text is shortened from Spencer's original].
35. We have been unable to discover the book Shklovsky promised. *Ed. note.*

3 Roman Jakobson

Roman Jakobson (1896–1982) was one of the most powerful minds in twentieth-century intellectual history, though general recognition of this fact came rather late in his long life. He was born in Russia and was a founder-member of the Moscow Linguistic Circle which played a major part in the development of Russian formalism (see headnote to Victor Shklovsky, p. 15, above). At this time, Jakobson was an enthusiastic supporter of the Russian futurist poets, and he never lost this commitment to modernist experiment and innovation. In 1920, he moved to Czechoslovakia and helped to found the Prague Linguistic Circle, which was the source of some of the important foundation work in structuralist linguistics and poetics. The Nazi invasion of Czechoslovakia in 1939 forced Jakobson to move on again, and in 1941 he arrived in the United States, where he lived until his death, teaching at Columbia, Harvard and MIT.

Most of Jakobson's published work consists of highly technical articles on matters of grammar and phonology, expecially in Slavonic languages. But he was able to apply his immense learning and speculative intelligence to theoretical questions of universal interest and importance, and to incisive linguistic analysis of classic literary texts in English and French. The French anthropologist Claude Lévi-Strauss, whose work gave such a powerful impetus to structuralism in the 1960s (see 'Incest and Myth', section 40 in *20th Century Literary Criticism*), acknowledged his indebtedness to the linguistic theory of Roman Jakobson, and the two men collaborated on an analysis of Baudelaire's poem 'Les Chats', published in the journal *L'Homme* in 1962, which acquired considerable fame, or notoriety, as a set piece of structuralist criticism (especially after Michael Riffaterre's critique of it in *Yale French Studies* in 1966).

Two ideas in Jakobson's contribution to modern literary theory deserve special mention. One was his identification of the rhetorical figures, metaphor and metonymy, as models for two fundamental ways of organizing discourse that can be traced in every kind of cultural production. (See 'The Metaphoric and Metonymic Poles', reprinted below, pp. 57–61, an extract from 'Two Aspects of Language and Two Types of Aphasic Disturbances' in Jakobson and Morris Halle, *Fundamentals of Language* [1956].) The other was his attempt to understand 'literariness'—to define in linguistic terms what makes a verbal message a work of art. This was a preoccupation of the Russian formalists from the inception of the movement, but in 'Linguistics and Poetics', reprinted below, we find a lucid exposition of Jakobson's mature thought on the subject, enlivened and illuminated by a staggering range of illustration. This paper was first delivered as a 'Closing

Statement' to a conference on 'Style in Language' held at Indiana University in 1958, and is reprinted here from the proceedings of that conference, edited by Thomas Sebeok, and published under the title *Style in Language* in 1960. It had an incalculable effect in bringing to the attention of Anglo-American critics the richness of the structuralist tradition of poetics and textual analysis that originated in Eastern and Central Europe.

CROSS REFERENCES: 1. Saussure
                      2. Shklovsky
                      4. Genette
                      12. Kristeva
                      27. MacCabe

COMMENTARY: Krystyna Pomorska and Stephen Rudy (eds), *Roman Jakobson: Verbal Art, Verbal Sign, Verbal Time* (1985)
David Lodge, *The Modes of Modern Writing: metaphor, metonymy and the typology of modern literature* (1977)
Michael Riffaterre, 'Describing Poetic Structures: two approaches to Baudelaire's 'Les Chats',' *Yale French Studies* 36–7 (1966) pp. 200–42

Linguistics and poetics

I have been asked for summary remarks about poetics in its relation to linguistics. Poetics deals primarily with the question, *What makes a verbal message a work of art?* Because the main subject of poetics is the *differentia specifica* [specific differences] of verbal art in relation to other arts and in relation to other kinds of verbal behavior, poetics is entitled to the leading place in literary studies.

Poetics deals with problems of verbal structure, just as the analysis of painting is concerned with pictorial structure. Since linguistics is the global science of verbal structure, poetics may be regarded as an integral part of linguistics.

Arguments against such a claim must be thoroughly discussed. It is evident that many devices studied by poetics are not confined to verbal art. We can refer to the possibility of transposing *Wuthering Heights* into a motion picture, medieval legends into frescoes and miniatures, or *L'aprés-midi d'un faune*[a] into music, ballet, and graphic art. However ludicrous may appear the idea of the *Iliad* and *Odyssey* in comics, certain structural features of their plot are preserved despite the disappearance of their verbal shape. The question whether Blake's illustrations to the *Divina Commedia* are or are not adequate is a proof that different

---

[a] *The Afternoon of a Faun*, poem by Stéphane Mallarmé (1842–98) which inspired, among other works, Debussy's tone poem of the same title.

arts are comparable. The problems of baroque or any other historical style transgress the frame of a single art. When handling the surrealistic metaphor, we could hardly pass by Max Ernst's pictures or Luis Buñuel's films, *The Andalusian Dog* and *The Golden Age*. In short, many poetic features belong not only to the science of language but to the whole theory of signs, that is, to general semiotics. This statement, however, is valid not only for verbal art but also for all varieties of language since language shares many properties with some other systems of signs or even with all of them (pansemiotic features).

Likewise a second objection contains nothing that would be specific for literature: the question of relations between the word and the world concerns not only verbal art but actually all kinds of discourse. Linguistics is likely to explore all possible problems of relation between discourse and the 'universe of discourse': what of this universe is verbalized by a given discourse and how is it verbalized. The truth values, however, as far as they are—to say with the logicians—'extralinguistic entities,' obviously exceed the bounds of poetics and of linguistics in general.

Sometimes we hear that poetics, in contradistinction to linguistics, is concerned with evaluation. This separation of the two fields from each other is based on a current but erroneous interpretation of the contrast between the structure of poetry and other types of verbal structure: the latter are said to be opposed by their 'casual,' designless nature to the 'noncasual,' purposeful character of poetic language. In the point of fact, any verbal behavior is goal-directed, but the aims are different and the conformity of the means used to the effect aimed at is a problem that evermore preoccupies inquirers into the diverse kinds of verbal communication. There is a close correspondence, much closer than critics believe, between the question of linguistic phenomena expanding in space and time and the spatial and temporal spread of literary models. Even such discontinuous expansion as the resurrection of neglected or forgotten poets—for instance, the posthumous discovery and subsequent canonization of Gerard Manley Hopkins (d. 1889), the tardy fame of Lautréamont (d. 1870) among surrealist poets, and the salient influence of the hitherto ignored Cyprian Norwid (d. 1883) on Polish modern poetry—find a parallel in the history of standard languages which are prone to revive outdated models, sometimes long forgotten, as was the case in literary Czech which toward the beginning of the nineteenth century leaned to sixteenth-century models.

Unfortunately the terminological confusion of 'literary studies' with 'criticism' tempts the student of literature to replace the description of the intrinsic values of a literary work by a subjective, censorious verdict. The label 'literary critic' applied to an investigator of literature is as erroneous as 'grammatical (or lexical) critic' would be applied to a linguist. Syntactic and morphologic research cannot be supplanted by a normative grammar, and likewise no manifesto, foisting a critic's own tastes and opinions on creative literature, may act as substitute for an objective scholarly analysis of verbal art. This statement is not to be mistaken for the quietist principle of *laissez faire*; any verbal culture involves programmatic, planning, normative endeavors. Yet why is a clear-cut discrimination made between pure and applied linguistics or between phonetics and orthoëpy[b] but not between literary studies and criticism?

Literary studies, with poetics as their focal portion, consist like linguistics of two sets of problems: synchrony and diachrony. The synchronic description envisages not only the literary production of any given stage but also that part of the literary tradition which for the stage in question has remained vital or has been revived. Thus, for instance, Shakespeare on the one hand and Donne, Marvell, Keats, and Emily Dickinson on the other are experienced by the present English poetic world, whereas the works of James Thomson and Longfellow, for the time being, do not belong to viable artistic values. The selection of classics and their reinterpretation by a novel trend is a substantial problem of synchronic literary studies. Synchronic poetics, like synchronic linguistics, is not to be confused with statics; any stage discriminates between more conservative and more innovatory forms. Any contemporary stage is experienced in its temporal dynamics, and, on the other hand, the historical approach both in poetics and in linguistics is concerned not only with changes but also with continuous, enduring, static factors. A thoroughly comprehensive historical poetics or history of language is a superstructure to be built on a series of successive synchronic descriptions.

Insistence on keeping poetics apart from linguistics is warranted only when the field of linguistics appears to be illicitly restricted, for example, when the sentence is viewed by some linguists as the highest analyzable construction or when the scope of linguistics is confined to grammar alone or uniquely to non-semantic questions of external form or to the inventory of denotative devices with no reference to free variations. Voegelin has clearly pointed out the two most important and related problems which face structural linguistics, namely, a re-vision of 'the monolithic hypothesis of language' and a concern with 'the inter-dependence of diverse structures within one language'. No doubt, for any speech community, for any speaker, there exists a unity of language, but this over-all code represents a system of interconnected subcodes; each language encompasses several concurrent patterns which are each characterized by a different function.

Obviously we must agree with Sapir that, on the whole, 'ideation reigns supreme in language . . .' (40), but this supremacy does not authorize linguistics to disregard the 'secondary factors.' The emotive elements of speech which, as Joos is prone to believe, cannot be described 'with a finite number of absolute categories,' are classified by him 'as non-linguistic elements of the real world.' Hence, 'for us they remain vague, protean, fluctuating phenomena,' he concludes, 'which we refuse to tolerate in our science' (19). Joos is indeed a brilliant expert in reduction experiments, and his emphatic requirement for an 'expulsion' of the emotive elements 'from linguistic science' is a radical experiment in reduction—*reductio ad absurdum*.

Language must be investigated in all the variety of its functions. Before discussing the poetic function we must define its place among the other functions of language. An outline of these functions demands a concise survey of the

[b] That part of grammar which deals with pronunciation.

constitutive factors in any speech event, in any act of verbal communication. The ADDRESSER sends a MESSAGE to the ADDRESSEE. To be operative the message requires a CONTEXT referred to ('referent' in another, somewhat ambiguous, nomenclature), seizable by the addressee, and either verbal or capable of being verbalized; a CODE fully, or at least partially, common to the addresser and addressee (or in other words, to the encoder and decoder of the message); and, finally, a CONTACT, a physical channel and psychological connection between the addresser and the addressee, enabling both of them to enter and stay in communication. All these factors inalienably involved in verbal communication may be schematized as follows:

CONTEXT

ADDRESSER   MESSAGE   ADDRESSEE

CONTACT

CODE

Each of these six factors determines a different function of language. Although we distinguish six basic aspects of language, we could, however, hardly find verbal messages that would fulfill only one function. The diversity lies not in a monopoly of some one of these several functions but in a different hierarchical order of functions. The verbal structure of a message depends primarily on the predominant function. But even though a set (*Einstellung*) toward the referent, an orientation toward the CONTEXT—briefly the so-called REFERENTIAL, 'denotative,' 'cognitive' function—is the leading task of numerous messages, the accessory participation of the other functions in such messages must be taken into account by the observant linguist.

The so-called EMOTIVE or 'expressive' function, focused on the ADDRESSER, aims a direct expression of the speaker's attitude toward what he is speaking about. It tends to produce an impression of a certain emotion whether true or feigned; therefore, the term 'emotive,' launched and advocated by Marty (30) has proved to be preferable to 'emotional.' The purely emotive stratum in language is presented by the interjections. They differ from the means of referential language both by their sound pattern (peculiar sound sequences or even sounds elsewhere unusual) and by their syntactic role (they are not components but equivalents of sentences). '*Tut! Tut!* said McGinty': the complete utterance of Conan Doyle's character consists of two suction clicks. The emotive function, laid bare in the interjections, flavors to some extent all our utterances, on their phonic, grammatical, and lexical level. If we analyze language from the standpoint of the information it carries, we cannot restrict the notion of information to the cognitive aspect of language. A man, using expressive features to indicate his angry or ironic attitude, conveys ostensible information, and evidently this verbal behaviour cannot be likened to such nonsemiotic, nutritive activities as 'eating grapefruit' (despite Chatman's bold simile). The difference between [big] and the emphatic prolongation of the vowel [bi:g] is a conventional, coded linguistic feature like the difference between the short and long vowel in such Czech pairs as [vi] 'you' and [vi:] 'knows,' but in the latter pair the differential information is phonemic and in the former emotive. As long as we are interested in phonemic invariants, the English /i/ and /i:/ appear to be mere variants of one and the same phoneme, but if we are concerned with emotive units, the relation between the invariant and variants is reversed: length and shortness are invariants implemented by variable phonemes. Saporta's surmise that emotive difference is a nonlinguistic feature, 'attributable to the delivery of the message and not to the message,' arbitrarily reduces the informational capacity of messages.

A former actor of Stanislavskij's Moscow Theater told me how at his audition he was asked by the famous director to make forty different messages from the phrase *Segodnja večerom* 'This evening,' by diversifying its expressive tint. He made a list of some forty emotional situations, then emitted the given phrase in accordance with each of these situations, which his audience had to recognize only from the changes in the sound shape of the same two words. For our research work in the description and analysis of contemporary Standard Russian (under the auspices of the Rockfeller Foundation) this actor was asked to repeat Stanislavskij's test. He wrote down some fifty situations framing the same elliptic sentence and made of it fifty corresponding messages for a tape record. Most of the messages were correctly and circumstantially decoded by Moscovite listeners. May I add that all such emotive cues easily undergo linguistic analysis.

Orientation toward the ADDRESSEE, the CONATIVE function, finds its purest grammatical expression in the vocative and imperative, which syntactically, morphologically, and often even phonemically deviate from other nominal and verbal categories. The imperative sentences cardinally differ from declarative sentences: the latter are and the former are not liable to a truth test. When in O'Neill's play *The Fountain*, Nano, '(in a fierce tone of command),' says 'Drink!'—the imperative cannot be challenged by the question 'is it true or not?' which may be, however, perfectly well asked after such sentences as 'one drank,' 'one will drink,' 'one would drink.' In contradistinction to the imperative sentences, the declarative sentences are convertible into interrogative sentences: 'did one drink?' 'will one drink?' 'would one drink?'

The traditional model of language as elucidated particularly by Bühler (4) was confined to these three functions—emotive, conative, and referential—and the three apexes of this model—the first person of the addresser, the second person of the addressee, and the 'third person,' properly—someone or something spoken of. Certain additional verbal functions can be easily inferred from this triadic model. Thus the magic, incantatory function is chiefly some kind of conversion of an absent or inanimate 'third person' into an addressee of a conative message. 'May this sty dry up, *tfu, tfu, tfu, tfu*' (Lithuanian spell: 28, p. 69). 'Water, queen river, daybreak! Send grief beyond the blue sea, to the sea-bottom, like a grey stone never to rise from the sea-bottom, may grief never come to burden the light heart of God's servant, may grief be removed and sink away.' (North Russian incantation: 39, p. 217 f.). 'Sun, stand thou still upon Gibeon; and thou, Moon, in the valley of Aj-a-lon. And the sun stood still, and the moon stayed . . .' (Josh. 10.12). We observe, however, three further constitutive factors of verbal communication and three corresponding functions of language.

There are messages primarily serving to establish, to prolong, or to discontinue communication, to check whether the channel works ('Hello, do you hear me?'), to attract the attention of the interlocutor or to confirm his continued attention ('Are you listening?' or in Shakespearean diction, 'Lend me your ears!'—and on the other end of the wire 'Um-hum!'). This set for CONTACT, or in Malinowski's terms PHATIC function (26), may be displayed by a profuse exchange of ritualized formulas, by entire dialogues with the mere purport of prolonging communication. Dorothy Parker[c] caught eloquent examples: '"Well!" the young man said. "Well!" she said. "Well, here we are," he said. "Here we are," she said, "Aren't we?" "I should say we were," he said, "Eeyop! Here we are." "Well!' she said. "Well!" he said, "well."' The endeavor to start and sustain communication is typical of talking birds; thus the phatic function of language is the only one they share with human beings. It is also the first verbal function acquired by infants; they are prone to communicate before being able to send or receive informative communication.

A distinction has been made in modern logic between two levels of language, 'object language' speaking of objects and 'metalanguage' speaking of language. But metalanguage is not only a necessary scientific tool utilized by logicians and linguists; it plays also an important role in our everyday language. Like Molière's Jourdain who used prose without knowing it, we practice metalanguage without realizing the metalingual character of our operations. Whenever the addresser and/or the addressee need to check up whether they use the same code, speech is focused on the CODE: it performs a METALINGUAL (i.e., glossing) function. 'I don't follow you—what do you mean?' asks the addressee, or in Shakespearean diction, 'What is't thou say'st?' And the addresser in anticipation of such recapturing questions inquires: Do you know what I mean?' Imagine such an exasperating dialogue: 'The sophomore was plucked.' 'But what is *plucked?* '*Plucked* means the same as *flunked.*' 'And *flunked?*' '*To be flunked* is *to fail in an exam.*' 'And what is *sophomore?*' persists the interrogator innocent of school vocabulary. '*A sophomore* is (or means) a *second-year student.*' All these equational sentences convey information merely about the lexical code of English; their function is strictly metalingual. Any process of language learning, in particular child acquisition of the mother tongue, makes wide use of such metalingual operations; and aphasia may often be defined as a loss of ability for metalingual operations.

We have brought up all the six factors involved in verbal communication except the message itself. The set (*Einstellung*) toward the MESSAGE as such, focus on the message for its own sake, is the POETIC function of language. This function cannot be productively studied out of touch with the general problems of language, and, on the other hand, the scrutiny of language requires a thorough consideration of its poetic function. Any attempt to reduce the sphere of poetic function to poetry or to confine poetry to poetic function would be a delusive oversimplification. Poetic function is not the sole function of verbal art but only its dominant, determining function, whereas in all other verbal activities it acts as a subsidiary, accessory constituent. This function, by promoting the palpability

[c] American humourist (1893–1967), and one of *The New Yorker's* most celebrated contributors.

of signs, deepens the fundamental dichotomy of signs and objects. Hence, when dealing with poetic function, linguistics cannot limit itself to the field of poetry.

'Why do you always say *Joan and Margery*, yet never *Margery and Joan*? Do you prefer Joan to her twin sister?' 'Not at all, it just sounds smoother.' In a sequence of two coordinate names, as far as no rank problems interfere, the precedence of the shorter name suits the speaker, unaccountably for him, as a well-ordered shape of the message.

A girl used to talk about 'the horrible Harry.' 'Why horrible?' 'Because I hate him.' 'But why not *dreadful, terrible, frightful, disgusting?*' 'I don't know why, but *horrible* fits him better.' Without realizing it, she clung to the poetic device of paronomasia[d].

The political slogan 'I like Ike'[e]/ay layk ayk/, succinctly structured, consists of three monosyllables and counts three diphthongs /ay/, each of them symmetrically followed by one consonantal phoneme, /..1..k..k/. The make-up of the three words presents a variation: no consonantal phonemes in the first word, two around the diphthong in the second, and one final consonant in the third. A similar dominant nucleus /ay/ was noticed by Hymes in some of the sonnets of Keats. Both cola of the trisyllabic formula 'I like /Ike' rhyme with each other, and the second of the two rhyming words is fully included in the first one (echo rhyme), /layk/—/ayk/, a paronomastic image of a feeling which totally envelops its object. Both cola alliterate with each other, and the first of the two alliterating words is included in the second: /ay/—/ayk/, a paronomastic image of the loving subject enveloped by the beloved object. The secondary, poetic function of this electional catch phrase reinforces its impressiveness and efficacy.

As we said, the linguistic study of the poetic function must overstep the limits of poetry, and, on the other hand, the linguistic scrutiny of poetry cannot limit itself to the poetic function. The particularities of diverse poetic genres imply a differently ranked participation of the other verbal functions along with the dominant poetic function. Epic poetry, focused on the third person, strongly involves the referential function of language; the lyric, oriented toward the first person, is intimately linked with the emotive function; poetry of the second person is imbued with the conative function and is either supplicatory or exhortative, depending on whether the first person is subordinated to the second one or the second to the first.

Now that our cursory description of the six basic functions of verbal communication is more or less complete, we may complement our scheme of the fundamental factors by a corresponding scheme of the functions:

REFERENTIAL

EMOTIVE   POETIC   CONATIVE
PHATIC

METALINGUAL

[d] The term in traditional rhetoric for playing on words with similar sounds.

[e] 'Ike' was a familiar name for General Dwight David Eisenhower, President of the United States 1956–61. 'I Like Ike' was a political campaign slogan.

What is the empirical linguistic criterion of the poetic function? In particular, what is the indispensable feature inherent in any piece of poetry? To answer this question we must recall the two basic modes of arrangement used in verbal behavior, *selection* and *combination*. If 'child' is the topic of the message, the speaker selects one among the extant, more or less similar, nouns like child, kid, youngster, tot, all of them equivalent in a certain respect, and then, to comment on this topic, he may select one of the semantically cognate verbs—sleeps, dozes, nods, naps. Both chosen words combine in the speech chain. The selection is produced on the base of equivalence, similarity and dissimilarity, synonymity and antonymity, while the combination, the build up of the sequence, is based on contiguity. *The poetic function projects the principle of equivalence from the axis of selection into the axis of combination.* Equivalence is promoted to the constitutive device of the sequence. In poetry one syllable is equalized with any other syllable of the same sequence; word stress is assumed to equal word stress, as unstress equals unstress; prosodic long is matched with long, and short with short; word boundary equals word boundary, no boundary equals no boundary; syntactic pause equals syntactic pause, no pause equals no pause. Syllables are converted into units of measure, and so are morae or stresses.

It may be objected that metalanguage also makes a sequential use of equivalent units when combining synonymic expressions into an equational sentence: $A = A$ ('*Mare* is *the female of the horse*'). Poetry and metalanguage, however, are in diametrical opposition to each other: in metalanguage the sequence is used to build an equation, whereas in poetry the equation is used to build a sequence.

In poetry, and to a certain extent in latent manifestations of poetic function, sequences delimited by word boundaries become commensurable whether they are sensed as isochronic [having the same duration] or graded. 'Joan and Margery' showed us the poetic principle of syllable gradation, the same principle which in the closes of Serbian folk epics has been raised to a compulsory law (cf. 29). Without its two dactylic words the combination '*innocent bystander*' would hardly have become a hackneyed phrase. The symmetry of three disyllabic verbs with an identical initial consonant and identical final vowel added splendor to the laconic victory message of Caesar: '*Veni, vidi, vici.*' ['I came, I saw, I conquered.']

Measure of sequences is a device which, outside of poetic function, finds no application in language. Only in poetry with its regular reiteration of equivalent units is the time of the speech flow experienced, as it is—to cite another semiotic pattern—with musical time. Gerard Manley Hopkins, an outstanding searcher in the science of poetic language, defined verse as 'speech wholly or partially repeating the same figure of sound' (12). Hopkins' subsequent question, 'but is all verse poetry?' can be definitely answered as soon as poetic function ceases to be arbitrarily confined to the domain of poetry. Mnemonic lines cited by Hopkins (like 'Thirty days hath September'), modern advertising jingles, and versified medieval laws, mentioned by Lotz, or finally Sanscrit scientific treaties in verse which in Indic tradition are strictly distinguished from true poetry (*kāvya*)—all these metrical texts make use of poetic function without, however, assigning to this function the coercing, determining role it carries in poetry. Thus verse actually exceeds the limits of poetry, but at the same time verse always implies poetic function. And apparently no human culture ignores versemaking, whereas there are many cultural patterns without 'applied' verse; and even in such cultures which possess both pure and applied verses, the latter appear to be a secondary, unquestionably derived phenomenon. The adaptation of poetic means for some heterogeneous purpose does not conceal their primary essence, just as elements of emotive language, when utilized in poetry, still maintain their emotive tinge. A filibusterer may recite *Hiawatha* because it is long, yet poetical- ness still remains the primary intent of this text itself. Self-evidently, the exist- ence of versified, musical, and pictorial commercials does not separate the questions of verse or of musical and pictorial form from the study of poetry, music, and fine arts.

To sum up, the analysis of verse is entirely within the competence of poetics, and the latter may be defined as that part of linguistics which treats the poetic function in its relationship to the other functions of language. Poetics in the wider sense of the word deals with the poetic function not only in poetry, where this function is superimposed upon the other functions of language, but also outside of poetry, when some other function is superimposed upon the poetic function.

The reiterative 'figure of sound,' which Hopkins saw to be the constitutive principle of verse, can be further specified. Such a figure always utilizes at least one (or more than one) binary contrast of a relatively high and relatively low prominence effected by the different sections of the phonemic sequence.

Within a syllable the more prominent, nuclear, syllabic part, constituting the peak of the syllable, is opposed to the less prominent, marginal, nonsyllabic phonemes. Any syllable contains a syllabic phoneme, and the interval between two successive syllabics is in some languages always and in others overwhelmingly carried out by marginal, nonsyllabic phonemes. In the so-called syllabic versifi- cation the number of syllabics in a metrically delimited chain (time series) is a constant, whereas the presence of a nonsyllabic phoneme or cluster between every two syllabics of a metrical chain is a constant only in languages with an indispensable occurrence of nonsyllabics between syllabics and, furthermore, in those verse systems where hiatus is prohibited. Another manifestation of a tend- ency toward a uniform syllabic model is the avoidance of closed syllables at the end of the line, observable, for instance, in Serbian epic songs. The Italian syllabic verse shows a tendency to treat a sequence of vowels unseparated by consonantal phonemes as one single metrical syllable (cf. 21, secs. VIII–IX).

In some patterns of versification the syllable is the only constant unit of verse measure, and a grammatical limit is the only constant line of demarcation between measured sequences, whereas in other patterns syllables in turn are dichotomized into more and less prominent, and/or two levels of grammatical limits are distinguished in their metrical function, word boundaries and syntactic pauses.

Except the varieties of the so-called 'vers libre' that are based on conjugate intonations and pauses only, any meter uses the syllable as a unit of measure at least in certain sections of the verse. Thus in the purely accentual verse ('sprung rhythm' in Hopkins' vocabulary), the number of syllables in the upbeat (called 'slack' by Hopkins) may vary, but the downbeat (ictus) constantly contains one single syllable.

In any accentual verse the contrast between higher and lower prominence is achieved by syllables under stress versus unstressed syllables. Most accentual patterns operate primarily with the contrast of syllables with and without word stress, but some varieties of accentual verse deal with syntactic, phrasal stresses, those which Wimsatt and Beardsley cite as 'the major stresses of the major words' and which are opposed as prominent to syllables without such major, syntactic stress.

In the quantitative ('chronemic') verse, long and short syllables are mutually opposed as more and less prominent. This contrast is usually carried out by syllable nuclei, phonemically long and short. But in metrical patterns like Ancient Greek and Arabic, which equalize length 'by position' with length 'by nature,' the minimal syllables consisting of a consonantal phoneme and one mora vowel are opposed to syllables with a surplus (a second mora or a closing consonant) as simpler and less prominent syllables opposed to those that are more complex and prominent.

The question still remains open whether, besides the accentual and the chronemic verse, there exists a 'tonemic' type of versification in languages where differences of syllabic intonations are used to distinguish word meanings (15). In classical Chinese poetry (3), syllables with modulations (in Chinese *tsê*, 'deflected tones') are opposed to the nonmodulated syllables (*p'ing*, 'level tones'), but apparently a chronemic principle underlies this opposition, as was suspected by Polivanov (34) and keenly interpreted by Wang Li (46); in the Chinese metrical tradition the level tones prove to be opposed to the deflected tones as long tonal peaks of syllables to short ones, so that verse is based on the opposition of length and shortness.

Joseph Greenberg brought to my attention another variety of tonemic versification—the verse of Efik riddles based on the level feature. In the sample cited by Simmons (42, p. 228), the query and the response form two octosyllables with an alike distribution of *h*(igh)- and *l*(ow)-tone syllabics; in each hemistich, moreover, the last three of the four syllables present an identical tonemic pattern: *lhhl/hhhl//lhhl/hhhl//*. Whereas Chinese versification appears as a peculiar variety of the quantitative verse, the verse of the Efic riddles is linked with the usual accentual verse by an opposition of two degrees of prominence (strength or height) of the vocal tone. Thus a metrical system of versification can be based only on the opposition of syllabic peaks and slopes (syllabic verse), on the relative level of the peaks (accentual verse), and on the relative length of the syllabic peaks or entire syllables (quantitative verse).

In textbooks of literature we sometimes encounter a superstitious contraposition of syllabism as a mere mechanical count of syllables to the lively pulsation of accentual verse. If we examine, however, the binary meters of the strictly syllabic and at the same time, accentual versification, we observe two homogeneous successions of wavelike peaks and valleys. Of these two undulatory curves, the syllabic one carries nuclear phonemes in the crest and usually marginal phonemes in the bottom. As a rule the accentual curve superposed upon the syllabic curve alternates stressed and unstressed syllables in the crests and bottoms respectively.

For comparison with the English meters which we have lengthily discussed, I bring to your attention the similar Russian binary verse forms which for the last fifty years have verily undergone an exhaustive investigation (see particularly 44). The structure of the verse can be very thoroughly described and interpreted in terms of enchained probabilities. Besides the compulsory word boundary between the lines, which is an invariant throughout all Russian meters, in the classic pattern of Russian syllabic accentual verse ('syllabo-tonic' in native nomenclature) we observe the following constants: (1) the number of syllables in the line from its beginning to the last downbeat is stable; (2) this very last downbeat always carries a word stress; (3) a stressed syllable cannot fall on the upbeat if a downbeat is fulfilled by an unstressed syllable of the same word unit (so that a word stress can coincide with an upbeat only as far as it belongs to a monosyllabic word unit).

Along with these characteristics compulsory for any line composed in a given meter, there are features that show a high probability of occurrence without being constantly present. Besides signals certain to occur ('probability one'), signals likely to occur ('probabilities less than one') enter into the notion of meter. Using Cherry's description of human communication (5), we could say that the reader of poetry obviously 'may be unable to attach numerical frequencies' to the constituents of the meter, but as far as he conceives the verse shape, he unwittingly gets an inkling of their 'rank order.'

In the Russian binary meters all odd syllables counting back from the last downbeat—briefly, all the upbeats—are usually fulfilled by unstressed syllables, except some very low percentage of stressed monosyllables. All even syllables, again counting back from the last downbeat, show a sizable preference for syllables under word stress, but the probabilities of their occurrence are unequally distributed among the successive downbeats of the line. The higher the relative frequency of word stresses in a given downbeat, the lower the ratio shown by the preceding downbeat. Since the last downbeat is constantly stressed, the next to last gives the lowest percentage of word stresses; in the preceding downbeat their amount is again higher, without attaining the maximum, displayed by the final downbeat; one downbeat further toward the beginning of the line, the amount of the stresses sinks once more, without reaching the minimum of the next-to-last downbeat; and so on. Thus the distribution of word stresses among the downbeats within the line, the split into strong and weak downbeats, creates a *regressive undulatory curve* superposed upon the wavy alternation of downbeats and upbeats. Incidentally, there is a captivating question of the relationship between the strong downbeats and phrasal stresses.

The Russian binary meters reveal a stratified arrangement of three undulatory curves: (I) alternation of syllabic nuclei and margins; (II) division of syllabic nuclei into alternating downbeats and upbeats; and (III) alternation of strong and weak downbeats. For example, Russian masculine iambic tetrameter of the nineteenth and present centuries may be represented by Figure 1, and a similar triadic pattern appears in the corresponding English forms.

Three of five downbeats are deprived of word stress in Shelley's iambic line 'Laugh with an inextinguishable laughter.' Seven of sixteen downbeats are stress-less in the following quatrain from Pasternak's recent iambic tetrameter *Zemlja* ('Earth'):

> I úlica za panibráta
> S okónnicej podslepovátoj,
> I béloj noči i zakátu
> Ne razminút'sja u reki.

Since the overwhelming majority of downbeats concur with word stresses, the listener or reader of Russian verses is prepared with a high degree of probability to meet a word stress in any even syllable of iambic lines, but at the very beginning of Pasternak's quatrain the fourth and, one foot further, the sixth syllable, both in the first and in the following line, present him with a *frustrated expectation*.

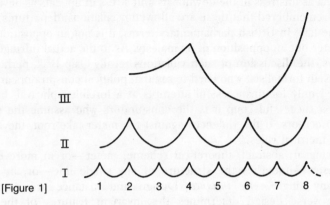

[Figure 1]   1   2   3   4   5   6   7   8

The degree of such a 'frustration' is higher when the stress is lacking in a strong downbeat and becomes particularly outstanding when two successive downbeats are carrying unstressed syllables. The stresslessness of two adjacent downbeats is the less probable and the most striking when it embraces a whole hemistich as in a later line of the same poem: 'Čtoby za gorodskjóu grán' ju' [stəbyzəgərackóju grán'ju]. The expectation depends on the treatment of a given downbeat in the poem and more generally in the whole extant metrical tradition. In the last downbeat but one, unstress may, however, outweigh the stress. Thus in this poem only 17 of 41 lines have a word stress on their sixth syllable. Yet in such a case the inertia of the stressed even syllables alternating with the unstressed odd syllables prompts some expectancy of stress also for the sixth syllable of the iambic tetrameter.

Quite naturally it was Edgar Allan Poe, the poet and theoretician of defeated anticipation, who metrically and psychologically appraised the human sense of gratification for the unexpected arising from expectedness, both of them unthinkable without the opposite, 'as evil cannot exist without good' (33). Here we could easily apply Robert Frost's formula from 'The Figure A Poem Makes': 'The figure is the same as for love' (8).

The so-called shifts of word stress in polysyllabic words from the downbeat to the upbeat ('reversed feet'), which are unknown to the standard forms of

Russian verse, appear quite usually in English poetry after a metrical and/or syntactic pause. A noticeable example is the rhythmical variation of the same adjective in Milton's 'Infinite wrath and infinite despair.' In the line 'Nearer, my God, to Thee, nearer to Thee,'[f] the stressed syllable of one and the same word occurs twice in the upbeat, first at the beginning of the line and a second time at the beginning of a phrase. This licence, discussed by Jespersen (18) and current in many languages, is entirely explainable by the particular import of the relation between an upbeat and the immediately preceding downbeat. Where such an immediate precedence is impeded by an inserted pause, the upbeat becomes a kind of *syllaba anceps* [double or undecided syllable].

Besides the rules which underlie the compulsory features of verse, the rules governing its optional traits also pertain to meter. We are inclined to designate such phenomena as unstress in the downbeats and stress in upbeats as deviations, but it must be remembered that these are allowed oscillations, departures within the limits of the law. In British parliamentary terms, it is not an opposition to its majesty the meter but an opposition of its majesty. As to the actual infringements of metrical laws, the discussion of such violations recalls Osip Brik, perhaps the keenest of Russian formalists, who used to say that political conspirators are tried and condemned only for unsuccessful attempts at a forcible upheaval, because in the case of a successful coup it is the conspirators who assume the role of judges and prosecutors. If the violences against the meter take root, they themselves become metrical rules.

Far from being an abstract, theoretical scheme, meter—or in more explicit terms, *verse design*—underlies the structure of any single line—or, in logical terminology, any single *verse instance*. Design and instance are correlative concepts. The verse design determines the invariant features of the verse instances and sets up the limits of variations. A Serbian peasant reciter of epic poetry memorizes, performs, and, to a high extent, improvises thousands, sometimes tens of thousands of lines, and their meter is alive in his mind. Unable to abstract its rules, he nonetheless notices and repudiates even the slightest infringement of these rules. Any line of Serbian epics contains precisely ten syllables and is followed by a syntactic pause. There is furthermore a compulsory word boundary before the fifth syllable and a compulsory absence of word boundary before the fourth and tenth syllable. The verse has, moreover, significant quantitative and accentual characteristics (16, 17).

This Serbian epic break, along with many similar examples presented by comparative metrics, is a persuasive warning against the erroneous identification of a break with a syntactic pause. The obligatory word boundary must not be combined with pause and is not even meant to be perceptible by the ear. The analysis of Serbian epic songs phonographically recorded proves that there are no compulsory audible clues to the break, and yet any attempt to abolish the word boundary before the fifth syllable by a mere insignificant change in word order is immediately condemned by the narrator. The grammatical fact that the fourth and fifth syllables pertain to two different word units is sufficient for the

[f] Words of a hymn written by Sarah Flower Adams (1805–48).

appraisal of the break. Thus verse design goes far beyond the questions of sheer sound shape; it is a much wider linguistic phenomenon, and it yields to no isolating phonetic treatment.

I say 'linguistic phenomenon' even though Chatman states that 'the meter exists as a system outside the language.' Yes, meter appears also in other arts dealing with time sequence. There are many linguistic problems—for instance, syntax— which likewise overstep the limit of language and are common to different semiotic systems. We may speak even about the grammar of traffic signals. There exists a signal code, where a yellow light when combined with green warns that free passage is close to being stopped and when combined with red announces the approaching cessation of the stoppage; such a yellow signal offers a close analogue to the verbal completive aspect. Poetic meter, however, has so many intrinsically linguistic particularities that it is most convenient to describe it from a purely linguistic point of view.

Let us add that no linguistic property of the verse design should be disregarded. Thus, for example, it would be an unfortunate mistake to deny the constitutive value of intonation in English meters. Not even speaking about its fundamental role in the meters of such a master of English free verse as Whitman, it is impossible to ignore the metrical significance of pausal intonation ('final juncture'), whether 'cadence' or 'anticadence' (20), in poems like [Alexander Pope's] 'The Rape of The Lock' with its intentional avoidance of enjambments. Yet even a vehement accumulation of enjambments never hides their digressive, variational status; they always set off the normal coincidence of syntactic pause and pausal intonation with the metrical limit. Whatever is the reciter's way of reading, the intonational constraint of the poem remains valid. The intonational contour inherent to a poem, to a poet, to a poetic school is one of the most notable topics brought to discussion by the Russian formalists (6, 49).

The verse design is embodied in verse instances. Usually the free variation of these instances is denoted by the somewhat equivocal label 'rhythm.' A variation of *verse instances* within a given poem must be strictly distinguished from the variable *delivery instances*. The intention 'to describe the verse line as it is actually performed' is of lesser use for the synchronic and historical analysis of poetry than it is for the study of its recitation in the present and the past. Meanwhile the truth is simple and clear: 'There are many performances of the same poem—differing among themselves in many ways. A performance is an event, but the poem itself, if there *is* any poem, must be some kind of enduring object.' This sage memento of Wimsatt and Beardsley belongs indeed to the essentials of modern metrics.

In Shakespeare's verses the second, stressed syllable of the word 'absurd' usually falls on the downbeat, but once in the third act of *Hamlet* it falls on the upbeat: 'No, let the candied tongue lick absurd pomp.' The reciter may scan the word 'absurd' in this line with an initial stress on the first syllable or observe the final word stress in accordance with the standard accentuation. He may also subordinate the word stress of the adjective in favor of the strong syntactic stress of the following head word, as suggested by Hill: 'Nó, lèt thě cândied tóngue lick ăbsùrd pómp' (11), as in Hopkins' conception of English antispasts—'regrét néver' (12). There is finally a possibility of emphatic modifications either through a 'fluctuating accentuation' (*schwebende Betonung*) embracing both syllables or through an exclamational reinforcement of the first syllable [àb-súrd]. But whatever solution the reciter chooses, the shift of the word stress from the downbeat to the upbeat with no antecedent pause is still arresting, and the moment of frustrated expectation stays viable. Wherever the reciter puts the accent, the discrepancy between the English word stress on the second syllable of 'absurd' and the downbeat attached to the first syllable persists as a constitutive feature of the verse instance. The tension between the ictus [metrical stress] and the usual word stress is inherent in this line independently of its different implementations by various actors and readers. As Gerard Manley Hopkins observes, in the preface to his poems, 'two rhythms are in some manner running at once' (13). His description of such a contrapuntal run can be reinterpreted. The superinducing of an equivalence principle upon the word sequence or, in other terms, the *mounting* of the metrical form upon the usual speech form, necessarily gives the experience of a double, ambiguous shape to anyone who is familiar with the given language and with verse. Both the convergences and the divergences between the two forms, both the warranted and the frustrated expectations, supply this experience.

How the given verse-instance is implemented in the given delivery instance depends on the *delivery design* of the reciter; he may cling to a scanning style or tend toward prose-like prosody or freely oscillate between these two poles. We must be on guard against simplistic binarism which reduces two couples into one single opposition either by suppressing the cardinal distinction between verse design and verse instance (as well as between delivery design and delivery instance) or by an erroneous identification of delivery instance and delivery design with the verse instance and verse design.

> 'But tell me, child, your choice; what shall I buy
> You?'—'Father, what you buy me I like best.'

These two lines from 'The Handsome Heart' by Hopkins contain a heavy enjambment which puts a verse boundary before the concluding monosyllable of a phrase, of a sentence, of an utterance. The recitation of these pentameters may be strictly metrical with a manifest pause between 'buy' and 'you' and a suppressed pause after the pronoun. Or, on the contrary, there may be displayed a prose-oriented manner without any separation of the words 'buy you' and with a marked pausal intonation at the end of the question. None of these ways of recitation may, however, hide the intentional discrepancy between the metrical and syntactic division. The verse shape of a poem remains completely independent of its variable delivery, whereby I do not intend to nullify the alluring question of *Autorenleser* [author-reader] and *Selbstleser* [self-reader] launched by Sievers (41).

No doubt, verse is primarily a recurrent 'figure of sound.' Primarily, always, but never uniquely. Any attempts to confine such poetic conventions as meter, alliteration, or rhyme to the sound level are speculative reasonings without any empirical justification. The projection of the equational principle into the sequence has a much deeper and wider significance. Valéry's view of poetry as 'hesitation between the sound and the sense' (cf. 45) is much more realistic and scientific than any bias of phonetic isolationism.

Although rhyme by definition is based on a regular recurrence of equivalent phonemes or phonemic groups, it would be an unsound oversimplification to treat rhyme merely from the standpoint of sound. Rhyme necessarily involves the semantic relationship between rhyming units ('rhyme-fellows' in Hopkins' nomenclature). In the scrutiny of a rhyme we are faced with the question of whether or not it is a homoeoteleuton, which confronts similar derivational and/or inflexional suffixes (congratulations-decorations), or whether the rhyming words belong to the same or to different grammatical categories. Thus, for example, Hopkins' fourfold rhyme is an agreement of two nouns—'kind' and 'mind'—both contrasting with the adjective 'blind' and with the verb 'find.' Is there a semantic propinquity, a sort of simile between rhyming lexical units, as in dove-love, light-bright, place-space, name-fame? Do the rhyming members carry the same syntactic function? The difference between the morphological class and the syntactic application may be pointed out in rhyme. Thus in Poe's lines, 'While I nodded, nearly *napping*, suddenly there came a *tapping*, As of someone gently *rapping*,' the three rhyming words, morphologically alike, are all three syntactically different. Are totally or partly homonymic rhymes prohibited, tolerated, or favored? Such full homonyms as son-sun, I-eye, eve-eave, and on the other hand, echo rhymes like December-ember, infinite-night, swarm-warm, smiles-miles? What about compound rhymes (such as Hopkins' enjoyment-toy meant' or 'began some-ransom'), where a word unit accords with a word group?

A poet or poetic school may be oriented toward or against grammatical rhyme; rhymes must be either grammatical or antigrammatical; an agrammatical rhyme, indifferent to the relation between sound and grammatical structure, would, like any agrammatism, belong to verbal pathology. If a poet tends to avoid grammatical rhymes, for him, as Hopkins said, 'There are two elements in the beauty rhyme has to the mind, the likeness or sameness of sound and the unlikeness or difference of meaning' (13). Whatever the relation between sound and meaning in different rhyme techniques, both spheres are necessarily involved. After Wimsatt's illuminating observations about the meaningfulness of rhyme (48) and the shrewd modern studies of Slavic rhyme patterns, a student in poetics can hardly maintain that rhymes signify merely in a very vague way.

Rhyme is only a particular, condensed case of a much more general, we may even say the fundamental, problem of poetry, namely *parallelism*. Here again Hopkins, in his student papers of 1865, displayed a prodigious insight into the structure of poetry:

The artificial part of poetry, perhaps we shall be right to say all artifice, reduces itself to the principle of parallelism. The structure of poetry is that of continuous parallelism, ranging from the technical so-called Parallelisms of Hebrew poetry and the antiphons of Church music up to the intricacy of Greek or Italian or English verse. But parallelism is of two kinds necessarily—where the opposition is clearly marked, and where it is transitional rather or chromatic. Only the first kind, that of marked parallelism, is concerned with the structure of verse—in rhythm, the recurrence of a certain sequence of syllables, in metre, the recurrence of a certain sequence of rhythm, in alliteration, in assonance and in rhyme. Now the force of this recurrence is to beget a recurrence or parallelism answering to it in the words or thought and, speaking roughly and rather for the tendency than the invariable result, the more marked parallelism in structure whether of elaboration or of emphasis begets more marked parallelism in the words and sense. . . . To the marked or abrupt kind of parallelism belong metaphor, simile, parable, and so on, where the effect is sought in likeness of things, and antithesis, contrast, and so on, where it is sought in unlikeness (12).

Briefly, equivalence in sound, projected into the sequence as its constitutive principle, inevitably involves semantic equivalence, and on any linguistic level any constituent of such a sequence prompts one of the two correlative experiences which Hopkins neatly defines as 'comparison for likeness' sake' and 'comparison for unlikeness' sake.'

Folklore offers the most clear-cut and stereotyped forms of poetry, particularly suitable for structural scrutiny (as Sebeok illustrated with Cheremis samples). Those oral traditions that use grammatical parallelism to connect consecutive lines, for example, Finno-Ugric patterns of verse (see 2, 43) and to a high degree also Russian folk poetry, can be fruitfully analyzed on all linguistic levels—phonological, morphological, syntactic, and lexical: we learn what elements are conceived as equivalent and how likeness on certain levels is tempered with conspicuous difference on other ones. Such forms enable us to verify Ransom's wise suggestion that 'the meter-and-meaning process is the organic act of poetry, and involves all its important characters' (37). These clear-cut traditional structures may dispel Wimsatt's doubts about the possibility of writing a grammar of the meter's interaction with the sense, as well as a grammar of the arrangement of metaphors. As soon as parallelism is promoted to canon, the interaction between meter and meaning and the arrangement of tropes cease to be 'the free and individual and unpredictable parts of the poetry.'

Let us translate a few typical lines from Russian wedding songs about the apparition of the bridegroom:

> A brave fellow was going to the porch,
> Vasilij was walking to the manor.

The translation is literal; the verbs, however, take the final position in both Russian clauses (Dobroj mólodec k sénickam privoráčival, // Vasilij k téremu prixážival). The lines wholly correspond to each other syntactically and morphologically. Both predicative verbs have the same prefixes and suffixes and the same vocalic alternant in the stem; they are alike in aspect, tense, number, and gender; and, moreover, they are synonymic. Both subjects, the common noun and the proper name, refer to the same person and form an appositional group. The two modifiers of place are expressed by identical prepositional constructions, and the first one stands to the second in synecdochic relation.

These verses may occur preceded by another line of similar grammatical (syntactic and morphologic) make-up: 'Not a bright falcon was flying beyond the hills' or 'Not a fierce horse was coming at gallop to the court.' The 'bright falcon' and the 'fierce horse' of these variants are put in metaphorical relation with 'brave fellow.' This is traditional Slavic negative parallelism—the refutation of the metaphorical state in favor of the factual state. The negation *ne* may, however, be omitted: 'Jasjón sokol zá gory zaljótyval' (A bright falcon was flying beyond the hills) or 'Retiv kon' kó dvoru priskákival' (A fierce horse was coming at a gallop to the court). In the first of the two examples the *metaphorical* relation is maintained: a brave fellow appeared at the porch, like a bright falcon from behind the hills. In the other instance, however, the semantic connection becomes ambiguous. A comparison between the appearing bridegroom and the galloping horse suggests itself, but at the same time the halt of the horse at the court actually anticipates the approach of the hero to the house. Thus before introducing the rider and the manor of his fiancée, the song evokes the contiguous, *metonymical* images of the horse and of the courtyard: possession instead of possessor, and outdoors instead of inside. The exposition of the groom may be broken up into two consecutive moments even without substituting the horse for the horseman: 'A brave fellow was coming at a gallop to the court, // Vasilij was walking to the porch.' Thus the 'fierce horse,' emerging in the preceding line at a similar metrical and syntactic place as the 'brave fellow,' figures simultaneously as a likeness to and as a representative possession of this fellow, properly speaking—*pars pro toto* [part for the whole] for the horseman. The horse image is on a border line between metonymy and synecdoche. From these suggestive connotations of the 'fierce horse' there ensues a metaphorical synecdoche: in the wedding songs and other varieties of Russian erotic lore, the masculine *retiv kon* becomes a latent or even patent phallic symbol.

As early as the 1880's, Potebnja, a remarkable inquirer into Slavic poetics, pointed out that in folk poetry a symbol appears to be materialized (*oveščestvlen*), converted into an accessory of the ambiance. 'Still a symbol, it is put, however, in a connection with the action. Thus a simile is presented under the shape of a temporal sequence' (35). In Potebnja's examples from Slavic folklore, the willow, under which a girl passes, serves at the same time as her image; the tree and the girl are both copresent in the same verbal simulacrum of the willow. Quite similarly the horse of the love songs remains a virility symbol not only when the maid is asked by the lad to feed his steed but even when being saddled or put into the stable or attached to a tree.

In poetry not only the phonological sequence but in the same way any sequence of semantic units strives to build an equation. Similarity superimposed on contiguity imparts to poetry its throughgoing symbolic, multiplex, polysemantic essence which is beautifully suggested by Goethe's 'Alles Vergängliche ist nur ein Gleichnis' (Anything transient is but a likeness). Said more technically, anything sequent is a simile. In poetry where similarity is superinduced upon contiguity, any metonymy is slightly metaphorical and any metaphor has a metonymical tint.

Ambiguity is an intrinsic, inalienable character of any self-focused message, briefly a corollary feature of poetry. Let us repeat with Empson: 'The machinations of ambiguity are among the very roots of poetry' (7). Not only the message itself but also its addresser and addressee become ambiguous. Besides the author and the reader, there is the 'I' of the lyrical hero or of the fictitious storyteller and the 'you' or 'thou' of the alleged addressee of dramatic monologues, supplications, and epistles. For instance the poem 'Wrestling Jacob' is addressed by its title hero to the Saviour and simultaneously acts as a subjective message of the poet Charles Wesley to his readers. Virtually any poetic message is a quasiquoted discourse with all those peculiar, intricate problems which 'speech within speech' offers to the linguist.

The supremacy of poetic function over referential function does not obliterate the reference but makes it ambiguous. The double-sensed message finds correspondence in a split addresser, in a split addressee, and besides in a split reference, as it is cogently exposed in the preambles to fairy tales of various peoples, for instance, in the usual exordium of the Majorca storytellers: 'Aixo era y no era' (It was and it was not) (9). The repetitiveness effected by imparting the equivalence principle to the sequence makes reiterable not only the constituent sequences of the poetic message but the whole message as well. This capacity for reiteration whether immediate or delayed; this reification of a poetic message and its constituents, this conversion of a message into an enduring thing, indeed all this represents an inherent and effective property of poetry.

In a sequence, where similarity is superimposed on contiguity, two similar phonemic sequences near to each other are prone to assume a paronomastic function. Words similar in sound are drawn together in meaning. It is true that the first line of the final stanza in Poe's 'Raven' makes wide use of repetitive alliterations, as noted by Valéry (45), but 'the overwhelming effect' of this line and of the whole stanza is due primarily to the sway of poetic etymology.

> And the Raven, never flitting, still is sitting, *still* is sitting
> On the pallid bust of Pallas just above my chamber door;
> And his eyes have all the seeming of a demon's that is dreaming,
> And the lamp-light o'er him streaming throws his shadow on the floor;
> And my soul from out that shadow that lies floating on the floor
> Shall be lifted—nevermore.

The perch of the raven, 'the pallid bust of Pallas,' is merged through the 'sonorous' paronomasia /páeləd/—/páeləs/ into one organic whole (similar to Shelley's molded line 'Sculptured on alabaster obelisk' /sk.lp/—/l.b.st/—/b.l.sk/). Both confronted words were blended earlier in another epithet of the same bust—*placid* /pláesld/—a poetic portmanteau, and the bond between the sitter and the seat was in turn fastened by a paronomasia: '*b*ird or *b*east upon the . . . *b*ust.' The bird 'is sitting // On the pallid bust of Pallas just above my chamber door,' and the raven on his perch, despite the lover's imperative 'take thy form from off my door,' is nailed to the place by the words ʒʌst əbʌv/, both of them blended in /bʌst/.

The never-ending stay of the grim guest is expressed by a chain of ingenious paronomasias, partly inversive, as we would expect from such a deliberate experimenter in anticipatory, regressive *modus operandi*, [method of working], such a master in 'writing backwards' as Edgar Allan Poe. In the introductory line of this concluding stanza, 'raven,' contiguous to the bleak refrain word 'never,' appears once more as an embodied mirror image of this 'never:' /n.v.r./—/r.v.n./. Salient paronomasias interconnect both emblems of the everlasting despair, first 'the Raven, never flitting,' at the beginning of the very last stanza, and second, in its very last lines the 'shadow that lies floating on the floor' and 'shall be lifted—nevermore': /nɛvər flitiŋ/—/flótiŋ/ . . . /flór/ . . . /liftəd nɛvər/. The alliterations which struck Valéry build a paronomastic string: /sti . . . /—/sit . . . /—/sti . . . /—/sit . . ./. The invariance of the group is particularly stressed by the variation in its order. The two luminous effects in the chiaroscuro—the 'fiery eyes' of the black fowl and the lamplight throwing 'his shadow on the floor'—are evoked to add to the gloom of the whole picture and are again bound by the 'vivid effect' of paronomasias: /ɔlðə simiŋ/ . . . /dimənz/ . . . /ɪz drimiŋ/—/ɔrim strimiŋ/. 'That shadow that lies /láyz/' pairs with the Raven's 'eyes' /áyz/ in an impressively misplaced echo rhyme.

In poetry, any conspicuous similarity in sound is evaluated in respect to similarity and/or dissimilarity in meaning. But Pope's alliterative precept to poets—'the sound must seem an Echo of the sense'—has a wider application. In referential language the connection between *signans* [signifier] and *signatum* [signified] is overwhelmingly based on their codified contiguity, which is often confusingly labelled 'arbitrariness of the verbal sign.'[g] The relevance of the sound-meaning nexus is a simple corollary of the superposition of similarity upon contiguity. Sound symbolism is an undeniably objective relation founded on a phenomenal connection between different sensory modes, in particular between the visual and auditory experience. If the results of research in this area have sometimes been vague or controversial, it is primarily due to an insufficient care for the methods of psychological and/or linguistic inquiry. Particularly from the linguistic point of view the picture has often been distorted by lack of attention to the phonological aspect of speech sounds or by inevitably vain operations with complex phonemic units instead of with their ultimate components. But when, on testing, for example, such phonemic oppositions as grave versus acute we ask whether /i/ or /u/ is darker, some of the subjects may respond that this question makes no sense to them, but hardly one will state that /i/ is the darkest of the two.

Poetry is not the only area where sound symbolism makes itself felt, but it is a province where the internal nexus between sound and meaning changes from latent into patent and manifests itself most palpably and intensely, as it has been noted in Hymes's stimulating paper. The super-average accumulation of a certain class of phonemes or a contrastive assemblage of two opposite classes in the sound texture of a line, of a stanza, of a poem acts like an 'undercurrent of meaning,' to use Poe's picturesque expression. In two polar words phonemic relationship may be in agreement with semantic opposition, as in Russian /d,en,/ 'day' and /noč/ 'night' with the acute vowel and sharped consonants in the diurnal name and the corresponding grave vowel in the nocturnal name. A reinforcement of this contrast by surrounding the first word with acute and sharped

---

[g] An allusion to the linguistic theory of Ferdinand de Saussure (see above pp. 12–13)

phonemes, in contradistinction to a grave phonemic neighborhood of the second word, makes the sound into a thorough echo of the sense. But in the French *jour* 'day' and *nuit* 'night' the distribution of grave and acute vowels is inverted, so that Mallarmé's *Divagations* accuse his mother tongue of a deceiving perversity for assigning to day a dark timbre and to night a light one (27). Whorf states that when in its sound shape 'a word has an acoustic similarity to its own meaning, we can notice it . . . But, when the opposite occurs, nobody notices it.' Poetic language, however, and particularly French poetry in the collision between sound and meaning detected by Mallarmé, either seeks a phonological alternation of such a discrepancy and drowns the 'converse' distribution of vocalic features by surrounding *nuit* with grave and *jour* with acute phonemes, or it resorts to a semantic shift and its imagery of day and night replaces the imagery of light and dark by other synesthetic correlates of the phonemic opposition grave/acute and, for instance, puts the heavy, warm day in contrast to the airy, cool night; because 'human subjects seem to associate the experiences of bright, sharp, hard, high, light (in weight), quick, high-pitched, narrow, and so on in a long series, with each other; and conversely the experiences of dark, warm, yielding, soft, blunt, low, heavy, slow, low-pitched, wide, etc., in another long series' (47, p. 267f).

However effective is the emphasis on repetition in poetry, the sound texture is still far from being confined to numerical contrivances, and a phoneme that appears only once, but in a key word, in a pertinent position, against a contrastive background, may acquire a striking significance. As painters used to say, 'Un kilo de vert n'est pas plus vert qu'un demi kilo' [a kilo of green is no greener than half a kilo].

Any analysis of poetic sound texture must consistently take into account the phonological structure of the given language and, beside the over-all code, also the hierarchy of phonological distinctions in the given poetic convention. Thus the approximate rhymes used by Slavic peoples in oral and in some stages of written tradition admit unlike consonants in the rhyming members (e.g. Czech *boty, boky, stopy, kosy, sochy*) but, as Nitch noticed, no mutual correspondence between voiced and voiceless consonants is allowed (31), so that the quoted Czech words cannot rhyme with *body, doby, kozy, rohy*. In the songs of some American Indian peoples such as Pima-Papago and Tepecano, according to Herzog's observations—only partly communicated in print (10)—the phonemic distinction between voiced and voiceless plosives and between them and nasals is replaced by a free variation, whereas the distinction between labials, dentals, velars, and palatals is rigorously maintained. Thus in the poetry of these languages consonants lose two of the four distinctive features, voiced/voiceless and nasal/oral, and preserve the other two, grave/acute and compact/diffuse. The selection and hierarchic stratification of valid categories is a factor of primary importance for poetics both on the phonological and on the grammatical level.

Old Indic and Medieval Latin literary theory keenly distinguished two poles of verbal art, labelled in Sanskrit *Pāñcali* and *Vaidarbhí* and correspondingly in Latin *ornatus difficilis* [difficult ornament] and *ornatus facilis* [easy ornament] (see 1), the latter style evidently being much more difficult to analyze linguistically because in such literary forms verbal devices are unostentatious and language seems a nearly transparent garment. But one must say with Charles Sanders Peirce: 'This clothing never can be completely stripped off, it is only changed for something more diaphanous' (32, p. 171). 'Verseless composition,' as Hopkins calls the prosaic variety of verbal art—where parallelisms are not so strictly marked and strictly regular as 'continuous parallelism' and where there is no dominant figure of sound—present more entangled problems for poetics, as does any transitional linguistic area. In this case the transition is between strictly poetic and strictly referential language. But Propp's pioneering monograph on the structure of the fairy tale (36) shows us how a consistently syntactic approach may be of paramount help even in classifying the traditional plots and in tracing the puzzling laws that underlie their composition and selection. The new studies of Lévi-Strauss (22, 23, also, 24) display a much deeper but essentially similar approach to the same constructional problem.

It is no mere chance that metonymic structures are less explored than the field of metaphor. May I repeat my old observation that the study of poetic tropes has been directed mainly toward metaphor, and the so-called realistic literature, intimately tied with the metonymic principle, still defies interpretation, although the same linguistic methodology, which poetics uses when analyzing the metaphorical style of romantic poetry, is entirely applicable to the metonymical texture of realistic prose (14)[h].

Textbooks believe in the occurrence of poems devoid of imagery, but actually scarcity in lexical tropes is counterbalanced by gorgeous grammatical tropes and figures. The poetic resources concealed in the morphological and syntactic structure of language, briefly the poetry of grammar, and its literary product, the grammar of poetry, have been seldom known to critics and mostly disregarded by linguists but skillfully mastered by creative writers.

The main dramatic force of Antony's exordium to the funeral oration for Caesar is achieved by Shakespeare's playing on grammatical categories and constructions. Mark Antony lampoons Brutus's speech by changing the alleged reasons for Caesar's assassination into plain linguistic fictions. Brutus's accusation of Caesar, 'as he was ambitious, I slew him,' undergoes successive transformations. First Antony reduces it to a mere quotation which puts the responsibility for the statement on the speaker quoted: 'The noble Brutus // Hath told you . . . .' When repeated, this reference to Brutus is put into opposition to Antony's own assertions by an adversative 'but' and further degraded by a concessive 'yet.' The reference to the alleger's honor ceases to justify the allegation, when repeated with a substitution of the merely copulative 'and' instead of the previous causal 'for,' and when finally put into question through the malicious insertion of a modal 'sure':

> The noble Brutus
> Hath told you Caesar was ambitious;
>
> For Brutus is an honourable man,

[h] See pp. 60–61 below.

> But Brutus says he was ambitious,
> And Brutus is an honourable man.

> Yet Brutus says he was ambitious,
> And Brutus is an honourable man.

> Yet Brutus says he was ambitious,
> And, sure, he is an honourable man.

The following polyptoton—'I speak ... Brutus spoke ... I am to speak'—presents the repeated allegation as mere reported speech instead of reported facts. The effect lies, modal logic would say, in the oblique context of the arguments adduced which makes them into unprovable belief sentences:

> I speak not to disprove what Brutus spoke,
> But here I am to speak what I do know.

The most effective device of Antony's irony is the *modus obliquus* [indirect method] of Brutus's abstracts changed into a *modus rectus* [direct method] to disclose that these reified attributes are nothing but linguistic fictions. To Brutus's saying 'he was ambitious,' Antony first replies by transferring the adjective from the agent to the action ('Did this in Caesar seem ambitious?'), then by eliciting the abstract noun 'ambition' and converting it into a subject of a concrete passive construction 'Ambition should be made of sterner stuff' and subsequently to a predicate noun of an interrogative sentence, 'Was this ambition?'—Brutus's appeal 'hear me for my cause' is answered by the same noun *in recto*, the hypostatized subject of an interrogative, active construction: 'What cause withholds you ...?' While Brutus calls 'awake your senses, that you may the better judge,' the abstract substantive derived from 'judge' becomes an apostrophized agent in Antony's report: 'O judgement, thou art fled to brutish beasts ...' Incidentally, this apostrophe with its murderous paronomasia Brutus-brutish is reminiscent of Caesar's parting exclamation 'Et tu, Brute!' Properties and activities are exhibited *in recto*, whereas their carriers appear either *in obliquo* ('withholds you,' 'to brutish beasts,' 'back to me') or as subjects of negative actions ('men have lost,' 'I must pause'):

> You all did love him once, not without cause;
> What cause withholds you then to mourn for him?
> O judgment, thou art fled to brutish beasts,
> And men have lost their reason!

The last two lines of Antony's exordium display the ostensible independence of these grammatical metonymies. The stereotyped 'I mourn for so-and-so' and the figurative but still stereotyped 'so-and-so is in the coffin and my heart is with him' or 'goes out to him' give place in Antony's speech to a daringly realized metonymy; the trope becomes a part of poetic reality:

> My heart is in the coffin there with Caesar,
> And I must pause till it come back to me.

In poetry the internal form of a name, that is, the semantic load of its constituents, regains its pertinence. The 'Cocktails' may resume their obliterated kinship with plumage. Their colors are vivified in Mac Hammond's lines 'The ghost of a Bronx pink lady // With orange blossoms afloat in her hair,' and the etymological metaphor attains its realization: 'O, Bloody Mary, // The cocktails have crowed not the cocks!' ('At an Old Fashion Bar in Manhattan'). Wallace Stevens' poem 'An Ordinary Evening in New Haven' revives the head word of the city name first through a discreet allusion to heaven and then through a direct pun-like confrontation similar to Hopkins' 'Heaven-Haven.'

> The dry eucalyptus *seeks god in the rainy cloud.*
> Professor Eucalyptus of New Haven *seeks him in New Haven* . . .

> The instinct *for heaven* had its counterpart:
> The instinct for earth, *for New Haven*, for his room . . .

The adjective 'New' of the city name is laid bare through the concatenation of opposites:

> The oldest-newest day is the newest alone.
> The oldest-newest night does not creak by . . .

When in 1919 the Moscow Linguistic Circle discussed how to define and delimit the range of *epitheta ornantia* [decorative epithets] the poet Majakovskij rebuked us by saying that for him any adjective while in poetry was thereby a poetic epithet, even 'great' in the *Great Bear* or 'big' and 'little' in such names of Moscow streets as *Bol'shaja Presnja* and *Malaja Presnja*. In other words, poeticalness is not a supplementation of discourse with rhetorical adornment but a total re-evaluation of the discourse and of all its components whatsoever.

A missionary blamed his African flock for walking undressed. 'And what about yourself?' they pointed to his visage, 'are not you, too, somewhere naked?' 'Well, but that is my face.' 'Yet in us,' retorted the natives, 'everywhere it is face.' So in poetry any verbal element is converted into a figure of poetic speech.

My attempt to vindicate the right and duty of linguistics to direct the investigation of verbal art in all its compass and extent can come to a conclusion with the same burden which summarized my report to the 1953 conference here at Indiana University: 'Linguista sum; linguistici nihil a me alienum puto'[i] (25). If the poet Ransom is right (and he is right) that 'poetry is a kind of language' (38) the linguist whose field is any kind of language may and must include poetry in his study. The present conference has clearly shown that the time when both linguists and literary historians eluded questions of poetic structure is now safely behind us. Indeed, as Hollander stated, 'there seems to be no reason for trying to separate the literary from the overall linguistic.' If there are some critics who still doubt the competence of linguistics to embrace the field of poetics, I privately believe that the poetic incompetence of some bigoted linguists has been mistaken for an inadequacy of the linguistic science itself. All of us here, however, definitely realize that a linguist deaf to the poetic function of language and a literary scholar indifferent to linguistic problems and unconversant with linguistic methods are equally flagrant anachronisms.

---

[i] 'I am a linguist; I consider nothing linguistic alien to me.' An adaptation of a famous quotation from the Roman playwright Terence: 'I am human and I consider nothing human alien to me.'

NOTES

1. Arbusow, L., *Colores rhetorici*, Göttingen, 1948.
2. Austerlitz, R., *Ob-Ugric Metrics; Folklore Fellows Communications*, 174 (1958).
3. Bishop, J. L., 'Prosodic Elements in T'ang Poetry,' *Indiana University Conference on Oriental-Western Literary Relations*, Chapel Hill, 1955.
4. Bühler, K., 'Die Axiomatik der Sprachwissenschaft,' *Kant-Studien*, 38, pp. 19–90 (Berlin, 1933).
5. Cherry, C., *On Human Communication*, New York, 1957.
6. Ejxenbaum, B., *Melodika stixa*, Leningrad, 1922.
7. Empson, W., *Seven Types of Ambiguity*, New York, third edition, 1955.
8. Frost, R., *Collected Poems*, New York, 1939.
9. Giese, W., 'Sind Märchen Lügen?' *Cahiers S. Puscariu*, 1, pp. 137ff. (1952).
10. Herzog, G., 'Some Linguistic Aspects of American Indian Poetry,' *Word*, 2, p. 82 (1946).
11. Hill, A. A., Review in *Language*, 29, pp. 549–61 (1953).
12. Hopkins, G. M., *The Journals and Papers*, H. House, ed., London, 1959.
13. ——, *Poems*, W. H. Gardner, ed., New York and London, third edition, 1948.
14. Jakobson, R., 'The Metaphoric and Metonymic Poles,' in *Fundamentals of Language*, pp. 76–82, 's-Gravenhage and New York, 1956.
15. ——, *O čéšskom stixe preimušćestvenno v sopostavlenii s russkim* (= Sborniki po teorii poètičeskogo jazyka, 5), Berlin and Moscow, 1923.
16. ——, 'Studies in Comparative Slavic Metrics,' *Oxford Slavonic Papers*, 3, pp. 21–66 (1952).
17. ——, 'Über den Versbau der serbokroatischen Volksepen,' *Archives néerlandaises de phonétique expérimentale*, pp. 7–9, 44–53 (1933).
18. Jespersen, O., 'Cause psychologique de quelques phénomènes de métrique germanique,' *Psychologie du langage*, Paris, 1933.
19. Joos, M., 'Description of language design,' *Journal of the Acoustical Society of America*, 22, pp. 701–08 (1950).
20. Karcevskij, S., 'Sur la phonologie de la phrase,' *Travaux du cercle linguistique de Prague*, 4, pp. 188–223 (1931).
21. Levi, A., 'Della versificazione italiana,' *Archivum Romanicum*, 14, pp. 449–526 (1930).
22. Lévi-Strauss, C., 'Analyse morphologique des contes russes,' *International Journal of Slavic Linguistics and Poetics*, 3 (1960).
23. ——, *La geste d' Asdival*, Ecole Pratique des Hautes Etudes, Paris, 1958.
24. ——, 'The Structural Study of Myth,' in T. A. Sebeok, ed., *Myth: a Symposium*, pp. 50–66, Philadelphia, 1955.
25. ——, R. Jakobson, C. F. Voegelin, and T. A. Sebeok, *Results of the Conference of Anthropologists and Linguists*, Baltimore, 1953.
26. Malinowski, B., 'The Problem of Meaning in Primitive Languages,' in C. K. Ogden and I. A. Richards, *The Meaning of Meaning*, pp. 296–336, New York and London, ninth edition, 1953.
27. Mallarmé, S., *Divagations*, Paris, 1899.
28. Mansikka, V. T., *Litauische Zaubersprüche, Folklore Fellows Communications*, 87 (1929).
29. Maretić, T., 'Metrika narodnih naših pjesama,' *Rad Yugoslavenske Akademije*, 168, 170 (Zagreb, 1907).
30. Marty, A., *Untersuschungen zur Grundlegung der allgemeinen Grammatik und Sprachphilosophie*, Vol. 1., Halle, 1908.
31. Nitsch, K., 'Z historii polskich rymow,' *Wybor pism polonisty-cznych*, 1, pp. 33–77 (Wroclaw, 1954).
32. Peirce, C. S., *Collected Papers*, Vol. 1, Cambridge, Mass. 1931.
33. Poe, E. A., 'Marginalia,' *The Works*, Vol. 3, New York, 1857.
34. Polivanov, E. D., 'O metričeskom xaraktere kitajskogo stixosloženija,' *Doklady Rossijskoj Akademii Nauk*, serija V, 156–58 (1924).
35. Potebnja, A., *Ob' jasnenija malorusskix i srodnyx narodnyx pesen*, Warsaw, 1 (1883); 2 (1887).
36. Propp, V., *Morphology of the Folktale*, Bloomington, 1958.
37. Ransom, J. C., *The New Criticism*, Norfolk, Conn., 1941.
38. ——, *The World's Body*, New York, 1938.
39. Rybnikov, P. N., *Pesni*, Vol. 3, Moscow, 1910.

40. Sapir, E., *Language*, New York, 1921.
41. Sievers, E., *Ziele und Wege der Schallanalyse*, Heidelberg, 1924.
42. Simmons, D. C., 'Specimens of Efik folklore,' *Folk-Lore*, 66, pp. 417–24 (1955).
43. Steinitz, W., *Der Parallelismus in der finnisch-karelischen Volksdichtung, Folklore Fellows Communications*, 115 (1934).
44. Taranovski, K., *Ruski dvodelni ritmovi*, Belgrade, 1955.
45. Valéry, P., *The Art of Poetry*, Bollingen series 45, New York, 1958.
46. Wang Li, *Han-yü shih-lü hsüeh* (= Versification in Chinese), Shanghai, 1958.
47. Whorf, B. L., *Language, Thought, and Reality*, J. B. Carroll, ed., New York, 1956.
48. Wimsatt, W. K., Jr., *The Verbal Icon*, Lexington, 1954.
49. Zirmunskij, V., *Voprosy teorii literatury*, Leningrad, 1928.

The metaphoric and metonymic poles[a]

The varieties of aphasia are numerous and diverse, but all of them lie between the two polar types just described. Every form of aphasic disturbance consists in some impairment, more or less severe, either of the faculty for selection and substitution or for combination and contexture. The former affliction involves a deterioration of metalinguistic operations, while the latter damages the capacity for maintaining the hierarchy of linguistic units. The relation of similarity is suppressed in the former, the relation of contiguity in the latter type of aphasia. Metaphor is alien to the similarity disorder, and metonymy to the contiguity disorder.

The development of a discourse may take place along two different semantic lines: one topic may lead to another either through their similarity or through

---

[a] Jakobson's seminal discussion of metaphor and metonymy comes at the end of a highly technical discussion of aphasia (i.e., language disorder). He begins by formulating one of the basic principles of Saussurian linguistics, that language, like all systems of signs, has a twofold character, involving two distinct operations, selection and combination. To produce a sentence like 'ships crossed the sea' (the example is not Jakobson's), I *select* the words I need from the appropriate sets or paradigms of the English language and *combine* them according to the rules of that language. If I substitute 'ploughed' for 'crossed', I create a *metaphor* based on a *similarity* between things otherwise different—the movement of a ship through water and the movement of a plough through the earth. If I substitute 'keels' for 'ships', I have used the figure of *synecdoche* (part for whole or whole for part). If I substitute 'deep' for 'sea' I have used the figure of metonymy (an attribute or cause or effect of a thing signifies the thing). According to Jakobson, synecdoche is a subspecies of metonymy: both depend on *contiguity* in space/time (the keel is part of the ship, depth is a property of the sea), and thus correspond to the *combination* axis of language. Metaphor, in contrast, corresponds to the *selection* axis of language, and depends on similarity between things not normally contiguous. Aphasics tend to be more affected in one or other of the selection and combination functions. Those who suffer from 'selection deficiency' or 'similarity disorder' are heavily dependent on context or contiguity to speak, and make 'metonymic' mistakes, substituting 'fork' for 'knife', 'table' for 'lamp', etc. Conversely, patients suffering from 'contexture deficiency' or 'contiguity disorder' are unable to combine words into a grammatical sentence, and make 'metaphorical' mistakes—'spyglass' for 'microscope', or 'fire' for 'gaslight'.

their contiguity. The metaphoric way would be the most appropriate term for the first case and the metonymic way for the second, since they find their most condensed expression in metaphor and metonymy respectively. In aphasia one or the other of these two processes is restricted or totally blocked—an effect which makes the study of aphasia particularly illuminating for the linguist. In normal verbal behavior both processes are continually operative, but careful observation will reveal that under the influence of a cultural pattern, personality, and verbal style, preference is given to one of the two processes over the other.

In a well-known psychological test, children are confronted with some noun and told to utter the first verbal response that comes into their heads. In this experiment two opposite linguistic predilections are invariably exhibited: the response is intended either as a substitute for, or as a complement to the stimulus. In the latter case the stimulus and the response together form a proper syntactic construction, most usually a sentence. These two types of reaction have been labeled substitutive and predicative.

To the stimulus *hut* one response was *burnt out*; another, *is a poor little house*. Both reactions are predicative; but the first creates a purely narrative context, while in the second there is a double connection with the subject *hut*: on the one hand, a positional (namely, syntactic) contiguity, and on the other a semantic similarity.

The same stimulus produced the following substitutive reactions: the tautology *hut*; the synonyms *cabin* and *hovel*; the antonym *palace*, and the metaphors *den* and *burrow*. The capacity of two words to replace one another is an instance of positional similarity, and, in addition, all these responses are linked to the stimulus by semantic similarity (or contrast). Metonymical responses to the same stimulus, such as *thatch*, *litter*, or *poverty*, combine and contrast the positional similarity with semantic contiguity.

In manipulating these two kinds of connection (similarity and contiguity) in both their aspects (positional and semantic)—selecting, combining, and ranking them—an individual exhibits his personal style, his verbal predilections and preferences.

In verbal art the interaction of these two elements is especially pronounced. Rich material for the study of this relationship is to be found in verse patterns which require a compulsory parallelism between adjacent lines, for example in Biblical poetry or in the Finnic and, to some extent, the Russian oral traditions. This provides an objective criterion of what in the given speech community acts as a correspondence. Since on any verbal level—morphemic, lexical, syntactic, and phraseological—either of these two relations (similarity and contiguity) can appear—and each in either of two aspects, an impressive range of possible configurations is created. Either of the two gravitational poles may prevail. In Russian lyrical songs, for example, metaphoric constructions predominate, while in the heroic epics the metonymic way is preponderant.

In poetry there are various motives which determine the choice between these alternants. The primacy of the metaphoric process in the literary schools of romanticism and symbolism has been repeatedly acknowledged, but it is still insufficiently realized that it is the predominance of metonymy which underlies and actually predetermines the so-called 'realistic' trend, which belongs to an intermediary stage between the decline of romanticism and the rise of symbolism and is opposed to both. Following the path of contiguous relationships, the realist author metonymically digresses from the plot to the atmosphere and from the characters to the setting in space and time. He is fond of synecdochic details. In the scene of Anna Karenina's suicide Tolstoj's artistic attention is focused on the heroine's handbag; and in *War and Peace* the synecdoches 'hair on the upper lip' and 'bare shoulders' are used by the same writer to stand for the female characters to whom these features belong.

The alternative predominance of one or the other of these two processes is by no means confined to verbal art. The same oscillation occurs in sign systems other than language.[1] A salient example from the history of painting is the manifestly metonymical orientation of cubism, where the object is transformed into a set of synecdoches; the surrealist painters responded with a patently metaphorical attitude. Ever since the productions of D. W. Griffith, the art of the cinema, with its highly developed capacity for changing the angle, perspective, and focus of 'shots', has broken with the tradition of the theater and ranged an unprecedented variety of synecdochic 'close-ups' and metonymic 'set-ups' in general. In such motion pictures as those of Charlie Chaplin and Eisenstein,[2] these devices in turn were overlayed by a novel, metaphoric 'montage' with its 'lap dissolves'—the filmic similes.[3]

The bipolar structure of language (or other semiotic systems) and, in aphasia, the fixation on one of these poles to the exclusion of the other require systematic comparative study. The retention of either of these alternatives in the two types of aphasia must be confronted with the predominance of the same pole in certain styles, personal habits, current fashions, etc. A careful analysis and comparison of these phenomena with the whole syndrome of the corresponding type of aphasia is an imperative task for joint research by experts in psychopathology, psychology, linguistics, poetics, and semiotics, the general science of signs. The dichotomy discussed here appears to be of primal significance and consequence for all verbal behavior and for human behavior in general.[4]

To indicate the possibilities of the projected comparative research, we choose an example from a Russian folktale which employs parallelism as a comic device: 'Thomas is a bachelor; Jeremiah is unmarried' (*Fomá xólost; Erjóma neženát*). Here the predicates in the two parallel clauses are associated by similarity: they are in fact synonymous. The subjects of both clauses are masculine proper names and hence morphologically similar, while on the other hand they denote two contiguous heroes of the same tale, created to perform identical actions and thus to justify the use of synonymous pairs of predicates. A somewhat modified version of the same construction occurs in a familiar wedding song in which each of the wedding guests is addressed in turn by his first name and patronymic: 'Gleb is a bachelor; Ivanovič is unmarried.' While both predicates here are again synonyms, the relationship between the two objects is changed: both are proper names denoting the same man and are normally used contiguously as a mode of polite address.

In the quotation from the folktale, the two parallel clauses refer to two separate facts, the marital status of Thomas and the similar status of Jeremiah. In the verse from the wedding song, however, the two clauses are synonymous: they redundantly reiterate the celibacy of the same hero, splitting him into two verbal hypostases.

The Russian novelist Gleb Ivanovič Uspenskij (1840–1902) in the last years of his life suffered from a mental illness involving a speech disorder. His first name and patronymic, Gleb Ivanovic, traditionally combined in polite intercourse, for him split into two distinct names designating two separate beings: Gleb was endowed with all his virtues, while Ivanovič, the same relating a son to his father, became the incarnation of all Uspenskij's vices. The linguistic aspect of this split personality is the patient's inability to use two symbols for the same thing, and it is thus a similarity disorder. Since the similarity disorder is bound up with the metonymical bent, an examination of the literary manner Uspenskij had employed as a young writer takes on particular interest. And the study of Anatolij Kamegulov, who analyzed Uspenskij's style, bears out our theoretical expectations. He shows that Uspenskij had a particular penchant for metonymy, and especially for synecdoche, and that he carried it so far that 'the reader is crushed by the multiplicity of detail unloaded on him in a limited verbal space, and is physically unable to grasp the whole, so that the portrait is often lost.'[5]

To be sure, the metonymical style in Uspenkij is obviously prompted by the prevailing literary canon of his time, late nineteenth-century 'realism'; but the personal stamp of Gleb Ivanovič made his pen particularly suitable for this artistic trend in its extreme manifestations and finally left its mark upon the verbal aspect of his mental illness.

A competition between both devices, metonymic and metaphoric, is manifest in any symbolic process, be it intrapersonal or social. Thus in an inquiry into the structure of dreams, the decisive question is whether the symbols and the temporal sequences used are based on contiguity (Freud's metonymic 'displacement' and synecdochic 'condensation') or on similarity (Freud's 'identification and symbolism').[6] The principles underlying magic rites have been resolved by Frazer into two types: charms based on the law of similarity and those founded on association by contiguity. The first of these two great branches of sympathetic magic has been called 'homoeopathic' or 'imitative', and the second, 'contagious magic'.[7] This bipartition is indeed illuminating. Nonetheless, for the most part, the question of the two poles is still neglected, despite its wide scope and importance for the study of any symbolic behavior, especially verbal, and of its impairments. What is the main reason for this neglect?

Similarity in meaning connects the symbols of a metalanguage with the symbols of the language referred to. Similarity connects a metaphorical term with the term for which it is substituted. Consequently, when constructing a metalanguage to interpret tropes, the researcher possesses more homogeneous means to handle metaphor, whereas metonymy, based on a different principle, easily defies interpretation. Therefore nothing comparable to the rich literature on metaphor[8] can be cited for the theory of metonymy. For the same reason, it is generally realized that romanticism is closely linked with metaphor, whereas the equally intimate ties of realism with metonymy usually remain unnoticed. Not only the tool of the observer but also the object of observation is responsible for the preponderance of metaphor over metonymy in scholarship. Since poetry is focused upon the sign, and pragmatical prose primarily upon the referent, tropes and figures, were studied mainly as poetic devices. The principle of similarity underlies poetry; the metrical parallelism of lines, or the phonic equivalence of rhyming words prompts the question of semantic similarity and contrast; there exist, for instance, grammatical and anti-grammatical but never agrammatical rhymes. Prose, on the contrary, is forwarded essentially by contiguity. Thus, for poetry, metaphor, and for prose, metonymy is the line of least resistance and, consequently, the study of poetical tropes is directed chiefly toward metaphor. The actual bipolarity has been artificially replaced in these studies by an amputated, unipolar scheme which, strikingly enough coincides with one of the two aphasic patterns, namely with the contiguity disorder.

NOTES

1. I ventured a few sketchy remarks on the metonymical turn in verbal art (*'Prosa* realizm u mystectvi', *Vaplite*, Kharkov, 1927, No. 2; 'Randbemerkungen zur *Prosa* des Dichters Pasternak', *Slavische Rundschau*, VII, 1935), in painting ('Futurizm Iskusstvo, Moscow, Aug. 2, 1919), and in motion pictures ('Úpadek filmu' *Listy pro uměni a kritiku*, I, Prague, 1933), but the crucial problem of the two polar processes awaits a detailed investigation.
2. Cf. his striking essay 'Dickens, Griffith, and We': S. Eisenstein, *Izbrannye star* (Moscow, 1950), p. 153 ff.
3. Cf. B. Balazs, *Theory of the Film* (London, 1952).
4. For the psychological and sociological aspects of this dichotomy, see Bateson's views on 'progressional' and 'selective integration' and Parsons' on the 'conjunction disjunction dichotomy' in child development: J. Ruesch and G. Bateson, *Communication, the Social Matrix of Psychiatry* (New York, 1951), pp. 183 ff.; T. Parsons and R. F. Bales, *Family, Socialization and Interaction Process* (Glencoe, 1955), pp. 119
5. A. Kamegulov, *Stil' Gleba Uspenskogo* (Leningrad, 1930), pp.65, 145. One of such disintegrated portraits cited in the monograph: 'From underneath an ancient straw cap, with a black spot on its visor, peeked two braids resembling the tusks of a wild boar, a chin, grown fat and pendulous, had spread definitively over the greasy collar of the calico dicky and lay in a thick layer on the coarse collar of the canvas coat, firmly buttoned at the neck. From underneath this coat to the eyes of the observer protruded massive hands with a ring which had eaten into the fat finger, a cane with a copper top, a significant bulge of the stomach, and the presence of very broad pants, almost of muslin quality, in the wide bottoms of which hid the toes of the boots.'
6. S. Freud, *Die Traumdeutung*, 9th ed. (Vienna, 1950).
7. J. G. Frazer, *The Golden Bough: A Study in Magic and Religion*, Part I, 3rd ed. (Vienna, 1950), chapter III.
8. C. F. P. Stutterheim, *Het begrip metaphoor* (Amsterdam, 1941).

4 Gérard Genette

Gérard Genette (b. 1930) teaches at the *Ecole des Hautes Etudes* in Paris. He is the author of several distinguished works of literary theory, including three collections of essays austerely entitled *Figures I* (1966), *Figures II* (1969) and *Figures III* (1972). The last of these consists mainly of a treatise on narrative method (illustrated with particular reference to Marcel Proust's *A la recherche du temps perdu*) which was translated into English under the title *Narrative Discourse* (1980). This is arguably the most refined and comprehensive working out of the Russian formalist distinction between *fabula* (the story as it would have been enacted in reality) and *sjuzet* (the presentation of that story in a discourse) that has so far been accomplished, and it has had considerable influence on criticism of the novel in Britain and America as well as in Europe. (For a lucid account of this work, which does not lend itself to representation in extracts, see Shlomith Rimmon-Kenan under 'Commentary', below.)

Genette's starting point as a theorist is invariably the poetics of Plato and Aristotle, and the classical tradition of rhetoric. He was quick to appreciate the possibility of reviving and extending this approach to literature by means of structuralist methodology. 'Literary Criticism and Structuralism', first published in 1964, is a remarkably balanced, perceptive and, considering its date, prescient consideration of this topic. Genette gives due credit to the pioneering work of the Russian Formalists: 'Literature had long enough been regarded as a message without a code for it to become necessary to regard it for a time as a code without a message.' But in the phrase 'for a time' Genette perhaps hints at the fate which would overcome structuralism. He shows how Jakobson revised the more extreme doctrines of the Formalists to take into account the semantic dimension of literature, but in his observation that structuralism's privileging of structure is an ideological stance, 'the prejudice of which is to value structures at the expense of substances, and which may therefore overestimate their explanatory value', he anticipated many poststructuralist critiques of structuralism. At the time of writing, however, Genette was concerned to emphasize the ways in which structuralism could usefully extend and complement the hermeneutic or interpretative activity of literary criticism: the study of genres and the conventions which govern their production and reception; of popular literature and culture; of canon formation and the evolution of literary forms.

'Structuralism and Literary Criticism' is reprinted here from Gérard Genette, *Figures of Literary Discourse*, trans. Alan Sheridan (1982).

COMMENTARY: Shlomith Rimmon-Kenan, 'A Comprehensive Theory of
Narrative: Genette's *Figures III* and the structuralist study
of fiction,' *Poetics and Theory of Literature* 1 (1976) pp. 33–62
Marie-Rose Logan, '*Ut Figura Poiesis*: the work of Gérard
Genette,' introduction to Gérard Genette, *Figures of Literary
Discourse* (1982)

Structuralism and literary criticism

In a now classic chapter of *La Pensée sauvage*, Claude Lévi-Strauss defines mythical thought as 'a kind of intellectual *bricolage*.' The nature of *bricolage* is to make
use of materials and tools that, unlike those of the engineer, for example, were
not intended for the task in hand. The rule of *bricolage* is 'always to make do
with whatever is available' and to use in a new structure the remains of previous
constructions or destructions, thus making the specific manufacture of materials
and tools unnecessary, though at the cost of a double operation of analysis (the
extraction of various elements from various already-constituted wholes) and of
synthesis (the forming of these heterogeneous elements into a new whole in which
none of the re-used elements will necessarily be used as originally intended).[1]
It should be remembered that this typically 'structuralist' operation, which makes
up for a lack of production by means of an extreme ingenuity in the distribution
of remnants, was discovered by an ethnologist attempting to account for the way
myths are invented by so-called 'primitive' civilizations. But there is another
intellectual activity, peculiar to more 'developed' cultures, to which this analysis
might be applied almost word for word: I mean criticism, more particularly literary
criticism, which distinguishes itself formally from other kinds of criticism by the
fact that it uses the same materials—writing—as the works with which it is
concerned; art criticism or musical criticism are obviously not expressed in sound
or in color, but literary criticism speaks the same language as its object: it is a
metalanguage, 'discourse upon a discourse.'[2] It can therefore be a metaliterature,
that is to say, 'a literature of which literature itself is the imposed object.'[3]

If in fact one isolates the two most obvious functions of the critical activity—
the 'critical' function in the literal sense of the term, which consists of judging
and appreciating recent works with a view to helping the public make up its mind
(a function linked to the institution of journalism), and the 'scientific' function
(linked, generally speaking, to the institution of the university), which consists

of a positive study, solely with a view to knowledge, of the conditions of existence of literary works (the materiality of the text, sources, psychological or historical origins, etc.)—there is obviously a third, which is strictly literary. A book of criticism like Sainte-Beuve's *Port-Royal* or Maurice Blanchot's *L'Espace littéraire* is among other things a book, and its author is in his own way and at least to a certain extent what Roland Barthes calls an *écrivain* (a writer, in contradistinction to the mere *écrivant*, or someone who happens to write), that is to say, the author of a message which to some extent tends to be absorbed into spectacle. This 'frustration' of meaning, which is frozen and constituted in an object of esthetic consumption is no doubt the movement (or rather the *halt*) that constitutes all literature. The literary object only exists through it; on the other hand, it is dependent upon it alone and, depending on the circumstances, any text may or may not be literature, according to whether it is received (either) as spectacle or (else) as message: literary history is made up of these comings-and-goings, these fluctuations. That is, there is no literary object strictly speaking, but only a *literary function*, which can invest or abandon any object of writing in turn. Its partial, unstable, ambiguous literariness is not therefore a property of criticism: what distinguishes criticism from the other literary 'genres' is its *secondary* character, and it is here that Lévi-Strauss' remarks on *bricolage* may find a somewhat unexpected application.

The instrumental universe of the *bricoleur*, says Lévi-Strauss, is a 'closed' universe. Its repertoire, however extended, 'remains limited.' This limitation distinguishes the *bricoleur* from the engineer, who (in principle) can at any time obtain the tool specially adapted to a particular technical need. The engineer 'questions the universe, while the *bricoleur* addresses himself to a collection of oddments left over from human endeavors, that is, only a subset of the culture.'[4] One has only to replace in the last sentence the words 'engineer' and *bricoleur* by 'novelist' (for example) and 'critic' respectively to define the literary status of criticism. The materials of the critical task are indeed those 'oddments left over from human endeavors,' which is what works of literature are once they have been reduced to themes, motifs, key-words, obsessive metaphors, quotations, index cards, and references. The initial work is a structure, like those primary wholes that the *bricoleur* dismantles in order to extract parts which may prove useful; the critic too breaks down a structure into its elements—one element per card—and the *bricoleur's* motto, 'that might always come in handy,' is the very postulate that inspires the critic when he is making up his card-index, literally or figuratively, of course. His next task is to build up a new structure while 'arranging these oddments.' '*Critical* thought,' one might say, paraphrasing Lévi-Strauss, 'builds structured sets by means of a structured set, namely, *the work*. But it is not at the structural level that it makes use of it: it builds ideological castles out of the debris of what was once a *literary* discourse.'

The distinction between the critic and the writer lies not only in the secondary and limited character of the critical material (literature) as opposed to the unlimited and primary character of the poetic or fictional material (the universe); this as it were quantitative inferiority, which derives from the fact that the critic always comes after the writer and has at his disposal only materials imposed by the previous choice of the writer, is perhaps aggravated, perhaps compensated by another difference: '*The writer* works by means of concepts and *the critic* by means of signs. Within the opposition between nature and culture, there is only an imperceptible discrepancy between the sets employed by each. One way indeed in which signs can be opposed to concepts is that whereas concepts seem to be wholly transparent with respect to reality, signs allow and even require the interposing and incorporation of a certain amount of human culture into reality.' If the writer questions the universe, the critic questions literature, that is to say, the universe of signs. But what was a sign for the writer (the work) becomes meaning for the critic (since it is the object of the critical discourse), and in another way what was meaning for the writer (his view of the world) becomes a sign for the critic, as the theme and symbol of a certain literary nature. This, again, is what Lévi-Strauss says of mythical thought, which, as Franz Boas remarked, constantly creates new worlds, but by reversing means and ends: 'signifieds change into signifiers, and vice versa.' This constant interchange, this perpetual inversion of signs and meaning is a good description of the dual function of the critic's work, which is to produce meaning with the work of others, but also to produce his own work out of this meaning. If such a thing as 'critical poetry' exists, therefore, it is in the sense in which Lévi-Strauss speaks of a 'poetry of *bricolage*': just as the *bricoleur* 'speaks through things,' the critic speaks—in the full sense, that is to say, speaks up—through books, and we will paraphrase Lévi-Strauss once more by saying that 'without ever completing his project he always puts something of himself into it.'

In this sense, therefore, one can regard literary criticism as a 'structuralist activity'; but it is not—as is quite clear—merely an implicit, unreflective structuralism. The question posed by the present orientation of such human sciences as linguistics or anthropology is whether criticism is being called upon to organize its structuralist vocation explicitly in a structural method. My aim here is simply to elucidate the meaning and scope of this question, suggesting the principal ways in which structuralism could reach the object of criticism, and offer itself to criticism as a fruitful method.

Literature being primarily a work of language, and structuralism, for its part, being preeminently a linguistic method, the most probable encounter should obviously take place on the terrain of linguistic material: sounds, forms, words, and sentences constitute the common object of the linguist and the philologist to such an extent that it was possible, in the early enthusiasm of the Russian Formalist movement, to define literature as a mere dialect, and to envisage its study as an annex of general dialectology.[5] Indeed, Russian Formalism, which is rightly regarded as one of the matrices of structural linguistics, was at first nothing more than a meeting of critics and linguists on the terrain of 'poetic language.' This assimilation of literature to a dialect raises objections that are too obvious for it to be taken literally. If literature *were* a dialect, it would be a translinguistic dialect effecting on all languages a number of transformations, different in their procedures but similar in their function, rather as the various forms of slang are parasitical in various ways on the various languages, but are similar in their parasitical function: nothing of the kind can be proposed in the case of dialects. In particular, the difference between 'literary language' and ordinary language resides not so much in the means as in the ends; apart from a few inflections, the writer uses the same language as other users, but he uses it neither in the same way nor with the same intention—identical material, displaced function: this status is exactly the reverse of that of a dialect. But, like other 'excesses' committed by Formalism, this particular one had cathartic value: by temporarily ignoring content, the provisional reduction of literature's 'literary being'[6] to its linguistic being made it possible to revise certain traditional 'verities' concerning the 'truth' of literary discourse, and to study more closely the system of its conventions. Literature had long enough been regarded as a message without a code for it to become necessary to regard it for a time as a code without a message.

Structuralist method as such is constituted at the very moment when one rediscovers the message in the code, uncovered by an analysis of the immanent structures and not imposed from the outside by ideological prejudices. This moment was not to be long in coming,[7] for the existence of the sign, at every level, rests on the connection of form and meaning. Thus Roman Jakobson, in his study of Czech verse of 1923, discovered a relationship between the prosodic value of a phonic feature and its signifying value, each language tending to give the greatest prosodic importance to the system of oppositions most relevant on the semantic plane: stress or 'dynamic accent' in Russian, length in Greek, pitch or 'musical accent' in Serbo-Croatian.[8] This passage from the phonetic to the phonemic, that is to say, from the pure sound substance, dear to early Formalist thinking, to the organization of this substance in a signifying system (or at least one capable of signification) is of interest not only to the study of metrics, since it was rightly seen as an anticipation of the phonological method.[9] It represents rather well what the contribution of structuralism might be to the study of literary morphology as a whole: poetics, stylistics, composition. Between pure Formalism, which reduces literary 'forms' to a sound material that is ultimately formless, because nonsignifying,[10] and traditional realism, which accords to each form an autonomous, substantial 'expressive value,' structural analysis must make it possible to uncover the connection that exists between a system of forms and a system of meanings, by replacing the search for term-by-term analogies with one for overall homologies.

A simplistic example might serve to clarify the matter: one of the traditional unsolved problems of the theory of expressivity is the question of the 'color' of vowels, which was put into the forefront by Rimbaud's sonnet.[a] The advocates of phonic expressivity, such as Otto Jespersen or Maurice Grammont, tried to attribute to each phoneme its own suggestive value, which, it was thought, governed the makeup of certain words in all languages. Others exposed the weakness of these hypotheses,[11] and, as far as the color of vowels was concerned,

---

[a] The French Symbolist poet Arthur Rimbaud (1854–91) wrote a sonnet on the colour of vowel sounds: 'A black, E white, I red, U green, O blue.'

the comparative tables drawn up by Etiemble[12] show quite clearly that the advo-cates of 'colored sounds' agree on none of their attributions.[13] Their adversaries naturally concluded from this that 'colored sounds' were a myth—and as a fact of *nature*, they may well be nothing more. But the disparity of the individual tables does not destroy the authenticity of each of them, and structuralism can suggest an explanation here that takes account both of the arbitrariness of each vowel-color and of the very widespread sense of a vocalic chromaticism: it is true that no vowel evokes, naturally and in isolation, a particular color; but it is also true that the distribution of colors in the spectrum (which indeed is itself, as Gelb and Goldstein have shown, as much a fact of language as of vision) can find its correspondence in the distribution of vowels in a given language. Hence the idea of a table of concordance, variable in its details but constant in its function: there is a spectrum of vowels as there is a spectrum of colors; the two systems evoke and attract one another, and the overall homology creates the illusion of a term-by-term analogy, which each realizes in its own way by an act of symbolic motiv-ation comparable to the one analyzed by Lévi-Strauss in the case of totemism. Each individual motivation, objectively arbitrary but subjectively based, can be regarded, then, as the index of a particular psychic configuration. The structural hypothesis, in this case, gives back to the stylistics of the subject what it takes from the stylistics of the object.

So structuralism is under no obligation to confine itself to 'surface' analyses, quite the reverse: here as elsewhere, the horizon of its approach is the analysis of significations. 'No doubt verse is primarily a recurrent "figure of sound." Primarily, always, but never uniquely . . . . Valéry's view of poetry as "hesitation between the sound and the sense" is much more realistic and scientific than any bias of phonetic isolationism.'[14] The importance attached by Jakobson, since his 1935 article on Pasternak, to the concepts of metaphor and metonymy, borrowed from the rhetoric of tropes, is characteristic of this orientation, especially if one remembers that one of the war-horses of early Formalism was a contempt for images, and the devaluation of tropes as marks of poetic language. Speaking of a poem by Pushkin, Jakobson himself was still insisting, in 1936, on the possibility of poetry without imagery.[15] In 1958 he took up this question with a very marked shift of emphasis: 'Textbooks believe in the occurrence of poems devoid of imagery, but actually scarcity in lexical tropes is counterbalanced by gorgeous grammatical tropes and figures.'[16] Tropes, as we know, are figures of signifi-cation, and in adopting metaphor and metonymy as poles of his typology of language and literature, Jakobson not only pays homage to ancient rhetoric: he places the categories of meaning at the heart of the structural method.

The structural study of 'poetic language' and of the forms of literary expression in general cannot, in fact, reject the analysis of the relations between code and message. Jakobson's analysis, 'Linguistics and Poetics,' in which he refers at the same time to the technicians of communication and to poets like Hopkins and Valéry or to critics like John Crowe Ransom and William Empson, shows this quite explicitly: 'Ambiguity is an intrinsic, inalienable character of any self-focused message, briefly a corollary feature of poetry. Let us repeat with Empson: "The machinations of ambiguity are among the very roots of poetry."'[17] The ambition of structuralism is not confined to counting feet and to observing the repetitions of phonemes: it must also attack semantic phenomena which, as Mallarmé showed us, constitute the essence of poetic language, and more generally the problems of literary semiology. In this respect one of the newest and most fruitful directions that are now opening up for literary research ought to be the structural study of the 'large unities' of discourse, beyond the frame-work—which linguistics in the strict sense cannot cross—of the sentence. The Formalist Vladimir Propp was no doubt the first to deal (in regard to a series of Russian folktales) with texts of a particular scope,[18] made up of a large number of sentences, like statements capable in turn, and on an equal footing with the traditional units of linguistics, of an analysis that could distinguish in them, by a play of superimpositions, variable elements and constant functions, and to rediscover in them the bi-axial system, familiar to Saussurean linguistics, of syntagmatic relations (real connections of functions in the continuity of a text) and paradigmatic relations (virtual relations between similar or opposed functions, from one text to another, in the whole of the corpus considered). One would thus study systems from a much higher level of generality, such as narrative,[19] description, and the other major forms of literary expression. There would then be a linguistics of discourse that was a *translinguistics*, since the facts of language would be handled by it in great bulk, and often at one remove—to put it simply, a rhetoric, perhaps that 'new rhetoric' which Francis Ponge once called for, and which we still lack.

The structural character of language at every level is sufficiently accepted by all today for the structuralist 'approach' to literary expression to be adopted as it were without question. As soon as one abandons the level of linguistics (or that 'bridge thrown between linguistics and literary history,' as Leo Spitzer called studies of form and style) and approaches the domain traditionally reserved for criticism, that of 'content,' the legitimacy of the structural point of view raises very serious questions of principle. *A priori*, of course, structuralism as a method is based on the study of structures wherever they occur; but to begin with, struc-tures are not directly encountered objects—far from it; they are systems of latent relations, conceived rather than perceived, which analysis constructs as it uncovers them, and which it runs the risk of inventing while believing that it is discovering them. Furthermore, structuralism is not only a method; it is also what Ernst Cassirer calls a 'general tendency of thought,' or as others would say (more crudely) an ideology, the prejudice of which is precisely to value structures at the expense of substances, and which may therefore overestimate their explana-tory value. Indeed, the question is not so much to know whether there is or is not a system of relations in a particular object of research, since such systems are everywhere, but to determine the relative importance of this system in relation to other elements of understanding: this importance measures the degree of validity of the structural method; but how are we to measure this importance, in turn, without recourse to this method? A circular argument.

Apparently, structuralism ought to be on its own ground whenever criticism abandons the search for the conditions of existence or the external determinations—psychological, social, or other—of the literary work, in order to concentrate its attention on that work itself, regarded no longer as an effect, but as an absolute being. In this sense, structuralism is bound up with the general movement away from positivism, 'historicizing history' and the 'biographical illusion,' a movement represented in various ways by the critical writings of a Proust, an Eliot, a Valéry, Russian Formalism, French 'thematic criticism' or Anglo-American 'New Criticism.'[20] In a way, the notion of structural analysis can be regarded as a simple equivalent of what Americans call 'close reading' and which would be called in Europe, following Spitzer, the 'immanent study' of works. It is precisely in this sense that Spitzer, retracing in 1960 the evolution that had led him from the psychologism of his first studies of style to a criticism free of any reference to the *Erlebnis* [experience], 'subordinating stylistic analysis to an explanation of the particular works as *poetic organisms in themselves*, without recourse to the psychology of the author,'[21] called this new attitude 'structuralist.' Any analysis that confines itself to a work without considering its sources or motives would, therefore, be implicitly structuralist, and the structural method ought to intervene in order to give to this immanent study a sort of rationality of understanding that would replace the rationality of explanation abandoned with the search for causes. A somewhat spatial determinism of structure would thus take over, but in a quite modern spirit, from the temporal determinism of genesis, each unity being defined in terms of relations, instead of filiation.[22] 'Thematic analysis, then, would tend spontaneously to culminate and to be tested in a structural synthesis in which the different themes are grouped in *networks*, in order to extract their full meaning from their place and function in the system of the work. This is the aim clearly expressed by Jean-Pierre Richard in his *Univers imaginaire de Mallarmé*, or by Jean Rousset when he writes: 'There is a graspable form only when there emerges a harmony or a relation, a line of force, an obsessive figure, a texture of presences or echoes, a network of convergences; I will call "structures" those formal constants, those links that betray a mental world and which each artist reinvents according to his own needs.'[23]

Structuralism, then, would appear to be a refuge for all immanent criticism against the danger of fragmentation that threatens thematic analysis: the means of reconstituting the unity of a work, its principle of coherence, what Spitzer called its spiritual *etymon*. In fact, the question is no doubt more complex, for immanent criticism can adopt two very different and even antithetical attitudes to a work, depending on whether it regards this work as an object or as a subject. The opposition between these two attitudes is brought out with great clarity by Georges Poulet in a text in which he declares himself to be an advocate of the second:

Like everybody else, I believe that the end of criticism is to arrive at an intimate knowledge of the reality criticized. Now it seems to me that such intimacy is possible only insofar as critical thought *becomes* the thought criticized, insofar as it succeeds in re-feeling, re-thinking, re-imagining that thought from the inside. Nothing could be less objective than such a movement of the mind. Contrary to common belief, criticism must avoid attending to any *object* whatever (whether it be the person of the author, considered as someone else, or his work, considered as a thing); for what must be obtained is a *subject*, that is to say a spiritual activity that can only be understood if one puts oneself in its place and revives within us its role as subject.[24]

This intersubjective criticism, which is admirably illustrated in Poulet's own work,[b] is related to the type of understanding that Paul Ricoeur, following Dilthey and others (including Spitzer), calls *hermeneutics*.[25] The meaning of a work is not conceived through a series of intellectual operations; it is relived, 'taken up again' as a message that is both old and forever renewed. Conversely, it is clear that structural criticism is emerging from the objectivism condemned by Poulet, for structures are *experienced* neither by the creative consciousness, nor by the critical consciousness. They are at the heart of the work, no doubt, but as its latent armature, as a principle of objective intelligibility, accessible only, through analysis and substitutions, to a sort of geometrical mind that is not consciousness. Structural criticism is untainted by any of the transcendent reductions of psychoanalysis, for example, or Marxist explanation, but it exerts, in its own way, a sort of internal reduction, traversing the substance of the work in order to reach its bone-structure: certainly not a superficial examination, but a sort of radioscopic penetration, and all the more external in that it is more penetrating.

There emerges, then, a limit rather comparable to the one Ricoeur fixed on structural mythology: wherever the hermeneutic resumption of meaning is possible and desirable, in the intuitive convergence of two consciousness, structural analysis would (partially at least) be illegitimate and irrelevant. One might then imagine a sort of division of the literary field into two domains, that of 'living' literature, that is to say, capable of being experienced by the critical consciousness, and which would have to be reserved for hermeneutic criticism, just as Ricoeur claims for hermeneutics the domain of the Judaic and Hellenic traditions, with their inexhaustible and forever indefinitely present *surplus of meaning*; and that of a literature which is not exactly 'dead' but in some sense distant and difficult to decipher: its lost meaning would be perceptible only to the operations of the structural intelligence, like that of 'totemic' cultures, the exclusive domain of the ethnologists. There is nothing absurd in principle about such a division of labor and it should be noted at the outset that it corresponds to the limitations of prudence that structuralism imposes on itself, tackling primarily those areas that best lend themselves, and with the least 'remainder,' to the application of its method;[26] it should also be recognized that such a division would leave an immense and almost virgin field for structuralist research. Indeed, the sort of literature that has 'lost' its meaning is much greater than the other, and not always

[b] Georges Poulet was a leading figure of the so-called Geneva School of phenomenological criticism which enjoyed considerable prestige, especially in the United States, in the late 1950s and early 1960s. See J. Hillis Miller, 'The Geneva School' in John K. Simon (ed.), *Modern French Criticism* (1972).

of less interest. There is as it were a whole ethnographic domain of literature, the exploration of which would be of great interest to structuralism: literatures distant in time and place, children's and popular literature, including such recent forms as the melodrama or serialized fiction, which criticism has always ignored, not only out of academic prejudice, but also because no intersubjective participation could animate it or guide it in its research, and which a structural criticism could treat like anthropological material and study in great bulk and in terms of their recurrent functions, following the lines laid down by such folklore specialists as Propp and Skaftymov. These works, like those of Lévi-Strauss on primitive mythologies, already show how fruitful the structural method applied to texts of this kind can be, and how much it can reveal of the hitherto unknown foundations of the canonical 'literatures.' Fantomas or Bluebeard may not speak to us as intimately as Swann or Hamlet; they might have as much to teach us. And certain officially consecrated works, which have in fact become largely alien to us, like those of Corneille, might speak better in that language of distance and strangeness than in that of the false proximity that we insist on imposing on them, often to no avail.

Here perhaps structuralism would begin to reconquer part of the terrain ceded to hermeneutics: for the true division between these two 'methods' lies not in the object, but in the critical position. To Ricoeur, who suggested to him the division described above, alleging that 'one part of civilization, precisely the part which did not produce our own culture, lends itself to the structural method better than any other,' Lévi-Strauss replied by asking: 'Are we dealing with an intrinsic difference between two kinds of thought and civilization, or simply with the relative position of the observer, who cannot adopt the same perspectives vis-à-vis his own civilization as would seem normal to him vis-à-vis a different civilization?'[27] The inappropriateness that Ricoeur finds in the possible application of structuralism to the Judeo-Christian mythologies, a Melanesian philosopher would no doubt find in the structural analysis of his own mythical tradition, which he *interiorizes* just as a Christian interiorizes the biblical message; but conversely this Melanesian might find a structural analysis of the Bible quite appropriate. What Merleau-Ponty wrote of ethnology as a discipline can be applied to structuralism as a method: 'It is not a specialty defined by a particular object, 'primitive societies.' It is a way of thinking, the way which imposes itself when the object is different, and requires us to transform ourselves. We also become the ethnologists of our own society if we set ourselves at a distance from it.'[28]

Thus the relation that binds structuralism and hermeneutics together might not be one of mechanical separation and exclusion, but of complementarity: on the subject of the same work, hermeneutic criticism might speak the language of the resumption of meaning and of internal recreation, and structural criticism that of distant speech and intelligible reconstruction. They would thus bring out complementary significations, and their dialogue would be all the more fruitful, on condition that one could never speak these two languages at once.[29] In any case, literary criticism has no reason to refuse to listen to the new significations that structuralism can obtain from the works that are apparently closest and most familiar by 'distancing' their speech;[30] for one of the most profound lessons of modern anthropology is that the distant is also close to us, by virtue of its very distance.

Moreover, the effort of psychological understanding initiated by nineteenth-century criticism and continued in our own time by the various kinds of thematic criticism has perhaps concerned itself too exclusively with the psychology of the authors, and not sufficiently with that of the public, or the reader. We know for example that one of the dangers of thematic analysis lies in the difficulty it often has in distinguishing between what is properly of concern to the irreducible singularity of an individual creator and what more generally belongs to the taste, sensibility, or ideology of a period, or more generally still to the permanent conventions and traditions of a genre or literary form. The heart of this difficulty lies in a sense in the encounter between the original, 'deep' thematics of the creative individual and of what ancient rhetoric called *topics*, that is to say, the treasury of subjects and forms that constitute the common wealth of tradition and culture. Personal thematics represents only a choice made between the possibilities offered by the collective topics. It is evidence—to speak in a very schematic way—that the contribution of the *topos* is greater in the so-called 'inferior,' or as one ought rather to say *fundamental*, genres, such as the folktale or the adventure novel, and the role of the creative personality is sufficiently weakened in such works for critical investigation to turn spontaneously, when dealing with them, to the tastes, requirements, and needs that constitute what is commonly called the *expectations* of the public. But we should also be aware of what the 'great works'—and even the most original of them—owe to these common dispositions. How can we appreciate, for example, the particular quality of the Stendhalian novel without considering in its historical and transhistorical generality the common thematics of the fictional imagination?[31] Spitzer recounts how the belated—and it would seem somewhat ingenuous—discovery that he made of the importance of the traditional *topos* in classical literature was one of the events that helped to 'discourage' him from psychoanalytic stylistics.[32] But the passage from what one might call the psychologism of the author to an absolute anti-psychologism may not be as inevitable as it seems, for, conventional as it may be, the *topos* is not psychologically more arbitrary than the personal theme: it simply belongs to another, collective psychology, for which contemporary anthropology has done something to prepare us and the literary implications of which deserve to be explored systematically. The fault of modern criticism is perhaps not so much its psychologism as its over-individualistic conception of psychology.

Classical criticism—from Aristotle to La Harpe—was in a sense much more attentive to these anthropological aspects of literature; it knew how to measure, narrowly but precisely, the requirements of what it called *verisimilitude*, that is to say, the idea that the public has of the true or possible. The distinctions between the genres, the notions of epic, tragic, heroic, comic, fictional, corresponded to certain broad categories of mental attitudes that predispose the reader's imagination in one way or another and make him want or expect particular types of situations and actions, of psychological, moral, and esthetic values. It cannot be said that the study of these broad diatheses that divide up and inform the literary sensibility of mankind (and which Gilbert Durand has rightly called *the anthropological structures of the imaginary*) has been taken sufficiently seriously by literary criticism and theory. Gaston Bachelard gave us a typology of the 'material' imagination: no doubt there also exists, for example, an imagination of behavior, situations, human relationships, a *dramatic* imagination, in the broad sense of the term, which strongly animates the production and consumption of theatrical and fictional work. The topics of this imagination, the structural laws of its functioning are obviously, and fundamentally, of importance to literary criticism: they will no doubt constitute one of the tasks of that vast axiomatics of literature that Valéry believed to be such an urgent necessity. The highest efficacity of literature rests on a subtle play between expectation and surprise 'against which all the expectation in the world cannot prevail,'[33] between the 'verisimilitude' expected and desired by the public and the unpredictability of creation. But does not the very unpredictability, the infinite shock of the great works, resound with all its force in the secret depths of verisimilitude? 'The great poet,' says Borges[c], 'is not so much an inventor as a discoverer.'

Valéry dreamed of a history of Literature understood 'not so much as a history of authors and of the accidents of their careers, or that of their works, than as a History of the mind, insofar as it produces or consumes literature, and this history might even be written without the name of a single writer being mentioned.' We know what echoes this idea has found in such authors as Borges or Maurice Blanchot, and Albert Thibaudet had already been pleased, by means of constant comparisons and transferences, to set up a Republic of Letters in which distinctions of person tended to be blurred. This unified view of the literary field is a very profound utopia, and one that is not unreasonably attractive, since literature is not only a collection of autonomous works, which may 'influence' one another by a series of fortuitous and isolated encounters; it is a coherent whole, a homogeneous space, within which works touch and penetrate one another; it is also, in turn, a part linked to other parts in the wider space of 'culture,' in which its own value is a function of the whole. Thus it doubly belongs to a study of structure, internal and external.

We know that the acquisition of language by a child proceeds not by a simple extension of vocabulary, but by a series of internal divisions, without modification of the overall acquisition: at each stage, the few words at its disposal are for the child the whole of language and it uses them to designate everything, with increasing precision, but without gaps. Similarly, for a man who has read only one book, this book is for him the whole of 'literature,' in the primary sense of the term; when he has read two, these two books will share his entire literary field, with no gap between them, and so on; it is precisely because it has no gaps to fill that a culture may *enrich itself*: it becomes deeper and more diversified, because it does not have to extend itself.

In a way, the 'literature' of mankind as a whole (that is to say, the way in which written works are organized in men's minds) can be regarded as being constituted

[c] Jorge Luis Borges, modern Argentinian writer whose ingenious, paradoxical stories and essays have fascinated and stimulated critics and creative writers alike.

in accordance with a similar process—bearing in mind the crude simplification that is involved here: literary 'production' is a *parole*, in the Saussurian sense, a series of partially autonomous and unpredictable individual acts; but the 'consumption' of this literature by society is a *langue*, that is to say, a whole the parts of which, whatever their number and nature, tend to be ordered into a coherent system. Raymond Queneau makes the amusing remark that all literature is either an *Iliad* or an *Odyssey*. This dichotomy has not always been a metaphor, and one often finds in Plato the echo of a 'literature' that was almost reduced to these two poems, and which was not regarded as incomplete for that reason. Ion[d] knew and wished to know nothing other than Homer. 'That seems to be enough for me,' he says, for Homer speaks sufficiently well of all things, and the competence of the bard would be encyclopedic, if poetry really proceeded from knowledge (it is this point, and not the universality of the work, that Plato challenges). Since then, literature has tended to subdivide rather than to extend, and for centuries the Homeric *oeuvre* has continued to be seen as the embryo and source of all literature. This myth is not devoid of truth, and the bookburner of Alexandria[e] was not entirely wrong, from his point of view, to place the Koran alone in the scale against a whole library: whether it contains one book, two books, or several thousand, a library is a civilization that is always complete, because in men's minds it always forms a whole and a system.

Classical rhetoric was acutely aware of this system, which is formalized into the theory of genres. There was epic, tragedy, comedy, and so on—and all these genres shared without remainder the totality of the literary field. What was lacking in this theory was the temporal dimension, the idea that a system could evolve. Boileau himself witnessed the death of the epic and the birth of the novel without being able to integrate these modifications into his *Ars poetica*. The nineteenth century discovered history, but it forgot the coherence of the whole; the individual history of works, and of authors, effaced the table of the genres. Ferdinand Brunetière alone attempted a synthesis, but we know that this marriage of Boileau and Darwin was not a very happy one: the evolution of genres according to Brunetière is a matter of pure organicism, each genre being born, developing, and dying like a solitary species, without concern for its neighbor.

The structuralist idea, in this matter, is to follow literature in its overall evolution, while making synchronic cuts at various stages and comparing the tables one with another. Literary evolution then appears in all its richness, which derives from the fact that the system survives while constantly altering. Here, again, the Russian Formalists showed the way by paying special attention to the phenomena of structural dynamics, and by isolating the notion of *change of function*. Noting the presence or absence, in isolation, of a literary form or theme at a particular point in diachronic evolution is meaningless until the synchronic study has shown the function of this element in the system. An element can remain while changing function, or on the contrary disappear while leaving its

---

[d] Character in Plato's dialogue, *Ion*. He is a rhapsode, or reciter of epic poetry.
[e] Alexandria was the site of the greatest library of the ancient world. It was destroyed by fire in AD 651.

function to another. 'In this way the mechanism of literary evolution,' says Boris Tomachevski, tracing the development of Formalist work on this point,

> became gradually more precise: it was presented not as a succession of forms, each replacing the other, but as a continual variation of the aesthetic function of literary methods. Each work finds itself oriented in relation to the literary milieu, and each element in relation to the whole work. An element that has a particular value in a certain period will completely change its function in another period. The grotesque forms, which were regarded in the period of Classicism as resources for the comic, became, in the Romantic period, one of the sources of tragedy. It is in this continual change of function that the true life of the elements of the literary work are to be found.[34]

In particular Viktor Shklovsky and Jurij Tynianov made a study, in relation to Russian literature, of those functional variations by which, for example, the same form can be transformed from a minor rank to that of a 'canonical form,' and which maintain a perpetual transference between popular literature and official literature, between academicism and the avant-garde, between poetry and prose, etc. Inheritance, Shklovsky was fond of saying, usually passes from the uncle to the nephew, and evolution canonizes the junior branch. Thus Pushkin imported into great poetry the effects of eighteenth-century album verse, Nekrassov borrowed from journalism and vaudeville, Blok from gypsy songs, Dostoevsky from the detective novel.[35]

In this sense literary history becomes the history of a system: it is the evolution of the functions that is significant, not that of the elements, and knowledge of the synchronic relations necessarily precedes that of the processes. But on the other hand, as Jakobson has remarked, the literary table of a period describes not only a present of creation, but also a present of culture, and therefore a certain image of the past, 'not only the literary production of any given period, but also that part of the literary tradition which for the stage in question has remained vital or has been revived ... The selection of a new tendency from among the classics and their reinterpretation by a novel trend is a substantial problem for synchronic literary studies,'[36] and consequently for the structural history of literature, which is simply the placing in diachronic perspective of these successive synchronic tables: in the table of French classicism, Homer and Vergil have a place, Dante and Shakespeare do not. In our present literary landscape, the discovery (or invention) of the Baroque is more important than the Romantic inheritance, and our Shakespeare is not Voltaire's Shakespeare or Hugo's: he is a contemporary of Brecht and Claudel, as Cervantes is a contemporary of Kafka. A period is manifested as much by what it reads as by what it writes, and these two aspects of its 'literature' act upon one another. As Borges puts it: 'If it were given to me to read any page written today—this one for example—as one will read it in the year 2000, I would know the literature of the year 2000.'[37]

To this history of the *internal divisions* of the literary field, with its already very rich program (one has only to think what a universal history of the opposition between prose and poetry would be like: a fundamental, elementary, constant,

75

immutable opposition in its function, constantly renewed in its means), one should add that of the much wider division between literature and everything that is not literature; this would be, not literary history, but the history of the relations between literature and social life as a whole: the history of the *literary function*. The Russian Formalists insisted on the *differential* character of the literary fact. Literariness is also a function of non-literariness, and no stable definition can be given of it: one is left simply with the awareness of limit. Everyone knows that the birth of the cinema altered the status of literature: by depriving it of certain of its functions, but also by giving it some of its own means. And this transformation is obviously no more than a beginning. How will literature survive the development of other media of communication? Already we no longer believe, as it was believed from Aristotle to La Harpe, that art is an imitation of nature, and where the classics sought above all a fine resemblance, we seek on the contrary a radical originality and an absolute creation. The day when the Book ceases to be the principal vehicle of knowledge, will not literature have changed its meaning once again? Perhaps we are quite simply living through the last days of the Book. This continuing adventure ought to make us more attentive to certain episodes in the past: we cannot go on speaking of literature as if its existence were self-evident, as if its relation to the world and to men had never varied. We do not have, for example, a history of reading. Such a history would be an intellectual, social, and even physical history: if St. Augustine is to be believed,[38] his master Ambrose was the first man in Antiquity to read with his eyes, without speaking the text aloud. True history is made up of these great silent moments. And the value of the method may lie in its ability to find, beneath each silence, a question.

NOTES

1. Claude Lévi-Strauss, *La Pensée sauvage* (Paris; Plon, 1962), p. 26; *The Savage Mind* (Chicago: University of Chicago Press, 1966), p. 17.
2. Roland Barthes, *Essais critiques* (Paris: Seuil, 1964), p. 255; *Critical Essays*, Richard Howard, tr. (Evanston, Ill.: Northwestern University Press, 1972), p. 258.
3. Paul Valéry, 'Albert Thibaudet,' *Nouvelle revue française* (July 1936), p. 6.
4. Lévi-Strauss, *Pensée sauvage*, p. 29; *S. M.*, p. 19.
5. Boris Tomachevski, 'La nouvelle école d'histoire littéraire en Russie,' *Revue des Études slaves* (1928), p. 231.
6. 'The object of literary study is not literature as a whole, but its literariness (*literaturnost*), that is to say, that which makes a work literary.' This sentence written by Jakobson in 1921 was one of the watchwords of Russian Formalism.
7. 'In mythology, as in linguistics, formal analysis immediately raises the question of meaning.' Claude Lévi-Strauss, *Anthropologie structurale* (Paris: Plon, 1958), p. 266; *Structural Anthropology*, Claire Jacobson and Brooke Grundiest Schoepf, trs. (New York: Basic Books, 1963), p. 241.
8. Cf. Victor Erlich, *Russian Formalism* (2d. rev. ed.; The Hague: Mouton, 1969), p. 219.
9. N. S. Trubetzkoy, *The Principles of Phonology* (1939), C. A. M. Baltaxe, tr. (Berkeley: University of California Press, 1969), pp. 3–4.
10. Cf. in particular the criticism by Eichenbaum, Jakobson, and Tynianov of Sievers's methods of acoustic metrics, which tried to study the sounds of a poem as if it had been written in a totally unknown language. Erlich, *Russian Formalism*, p. 218.

11. A synthesis of these criticisms is to be found in Paul Delbouille, *Poéste et sonorités*. (Paris: Les Belles Lettres, 1961).
12. René Etiemble, *Le Mythe de Rimbaud* (Paris: Gallimard, 1952), 2: 81–104.
13. 'All colors have been attributed at least once to each of the vowels.' Delbouille, *Poésie*, p. 248.
14. Roman Jakobson, 'Closing Statement: Linguistics and Poetics,' in T. A. Sebeok, ed., *Style in Language* (Cambridge, Mass: M.I.T. Press, 1960), p. 367.
15. Erlich, *Russian Formalism*, p. 175.
16. Jakobson, 'Closing Statement,' p. 375.
17. Jakobson, 'Closing Statement,' pp. 370–71.
18. Vladimir Propp, *The Morphology of the Folktale* (1928), L. Scott, tr. (Bloomington: Indiana University Press, 1958; 2d. rev. ed., Louis A. Wagner, ed.; Austin: Univeristy Press, 1968).
19. Claude Bremond, 'Le message narratif,' *Communications*, 4 (1964).
20. One can however find a purely methodological state of structuralism, as it were, in authors who do not claim allegiance to this 'philosophy.' This applies to Georges Dumézil, who puts at the service of a typically historical investigation the analysis of the *functions* that unite the elements of Indo-European mythology, these functions being regarded as more significant than the elements themselves. It also applies to Charles Mauron, whose psychocriticism interprets not isolated themes, but networks, the terms of which may vary without alteration to their structure. The study of systems does not necessarily *exclude* that of genesis or filiations: the minimum program of structuralism is that such a study should precede it and *govern* it.
21. Leo Spitzer, 'Les études de style et les différents pays,' *Langue et Littérature* (Paris: Les Belles Lettres, 1961).
22. 'Structural linguistics, like quantum mechanics, gains in morphic determinism what it loses in temporal determinism.' Roman Jakobson, Report presented to the VIIIth International Congress of Linguists, Oslo, 1957, published in *Proceedings of the VIIIth International Congress of Linguists* (Oslo, 1958).
23. Jean Rousset, *Forme et signification* (Paris: J. Corti, 1964), p. xii.
24. Georges Poulet, 'Response de,' *Les Lettres nouvelles* (June 1959), pp. 10–13.
25. Paul Ricoeur, 'Structure et herméneutique,' *Esprit* (November 1963); 'Structuralism and Hermeneutics,' Kathleen McLaughlin, tr., in Ricoeur, *The Conflict of Interpretations*, Don Ihde, ed. (Evanston, Ill: North-western University Press, 1974).
26. Cf. Claude Lévi-Strauss, *Esprit* (November 1963), p. 632; 'A Confrontation,' *New Left Review* (July–August 1970) 62:61. [This is Lévi-Strauss' paraphrase of Ricoeur's remark—M.-R. L.]
27. Lévi-Strauss, *Esprit*, p. 633; 'A Confrontation' p. 61.
28. Maurice Merleau-Ponty, *Signes* (Paris: Gallimard, 1960), p. 50; *Signs*, R. C. McCleary, tr. (Evanston, Ill: Northwestern University Press, 1964), p. 120.
29. Lévi-Strauss suggests a relation of the same kind between history and ethnology: 'Structures appear only to an observation practised from the outside. Conversely, this observation can never grasp the processes, which are not analytic objects, but only the particular way in which a temporality is experienced by a subject .... A historian can sometimes work as an ethnologist, and an ethnologist as a historian, but the methods themselves are complementary, in the sense the physicists give to this term; that is to say, one cannot, at one and the same time, rigorously define a stage A and a stage B (which is possible only from the outside and in structural terms), and reexperience empirically the passage from one to the other (which would be the only intelligible way of understanding it). Even the sciences of man have their relations of uncertainty.' 'Les limites de la notion de structure en ethnologie,' *Sens et usage du mot structure*, R. Bastide, ed. (The Hague: Mouton, 1962), pp. 44–45.
30. A new signification is not necessarily a new *meaning*: it is a new connection between form and meaning. If literature is an art of significations, it is renewed, and with it criticism, by modifying this connection, either through the meaning or through the form. It thus happens that modern criticism is rediscovering in 'themes' or 'styles' what classical criticism had already found in 'ideas' or 'feelings.' An old meaning comes back to us linked to a new form, and this 'shift' displaces a whole work.
31. It is in this light that I introduce the very fine book by Gilbert Durand, *Le Décor mythique de la Chartreuse de Parme* (Paris: J. Corti, 1961).

32. Spitzer, 'Les études de style,' p.27.
33. Paul Valéry, *Oeuvres*, Pléiade (Paris: Gallimard, 1960), II: 560; 'Odds and Ends' in Valery, *Analects*, Stuart Gilbert, tr. (Princeton: Princeton University Press, 1970), p.113.
34. Tomachevski, 'La nouvelle école,' pp. 238–39.
35. On the Formalist views of literary history, cf. Boris Eichenbaum, 'The Theory of the Formal Method,' and Jurij Tynianov, 'On Literary Evolution' in *Readings in Russian Poetics*, Ladislav Matejka and Krystyna Pomorska, eds. (Cambridge, Mass: M.I.T. Press, 1970). See also Erlich, *Formalism*, pp. 254–55 and Nina Gourfinkel, 'Les nouvelles méthodes d'histoire littéraire en Russie,' *Le Monde slave*, (February 1929).
36. Jakobson, 'Closing statement,' p. 352.
37. Jorge Luis Borges, *Other Inquisitions*, Ruth L. C. Simms, tr. (New York: Simon & Schuster, 1965).
38. St. Augustine, *Confessions*, Book VI. Quoted by Borges, *Other Inquisitions*, pp. 117–18.

5 Jacques Lacan

Jacques Lacan (1901–81) studied medicine in Paris and entered the Freudian psychoanalytical movement in 1936. His radical critique of orthodox psychoanalytical theory and practice led to his expulsion in 1959 from the International Psychoanalytical Association and the setting up of his own Ecole Freudienne in Paris in 1964. The publication of a collection of his papers and seminars, *Ecrits*, in Paris in 1964 made him one of the most fashionable figures on the French intellectual scene, and one of the most influential in the international dissemination of structuralist and post-structuralist ideas about language, literature and the nature of the human subject. The last years of his life were marred by increasingly eccentric behaviour and rancorous quarrels with many of his own disciples.

'The Insistence of the Letter in the Unconscious' was originally delivered as a lecture at the Sorbonne in 1957, and published in an annual volume edited by Lacan called *La Psychoanalyse*. The present translation by Jan Miel first appeared in *Yale French Studies* in 1966. With Lacan's seminar on Poe's story, 'The Purloined Letter' (*Yale French Studies*, 48 (1972) pp. 39–72) it is probably the work of Lacan's best known to English-speaking readers. Lacan was a notoriously, wilfully difficult writer, and the present editor certainly does not claim fully to understand everything in this essay. The algebraic formulae for metaphor and metonymy, for instance, seem designed to mystify and intimidate rather than to shed light. However, the main drift of Lacan's discourse is clear.

Psychoanalysis aims to understand and, if appropriate, 'cure' the disturbances caused by the pressure of the unconscious upon conscious existence as manifested by neurotic symptoms, dreams, etc. Orthodox Freudian doctrine views the unconscious as chaotic, primordial, instinctual, pre-verbal. Lacan's most celebrated dictum, 'the unconscious is structured like a language', implies that psychoanalysis as a discipline must borrow the methods and concepts of modern linguistics; but he also aims at a critique of modern linguistics from his psychoanalytical vantage point. Thus at the outset of his essay Lacan questions Saussure's assumption that there is nothing problematic about the bond between the signified and the signifier in the verbal sign, by pointing out that the two signifiers, 'Ladies' and 'Gentlemen' may refer to the same signified (a WC), or be interpreted in a certain context as apparently contradictory place names. In short, language, the signifying chain, has a life of its own which cannot be securely anchored to a world of things. 'There is a perpetual sliding of the signified under the signifier.' 'No meaning is sustained by anything other than reference to another meaning.' Such dicta were to have major repercussions on the theory and practice of interpretation.

Lacan's other principal borrowing from modern linguistics was Jakobson's distinction between metaphor and metonymy (see 'The Metaphoric and Metonymic Poles', pp. 57–61 above), which Lacan identified with Freud's categories of condensation and displacement, respectively. Here he seems to offer a revised version of his linguistic model without acknowledging the fact (see note *i*, p. 92 below). His equation of neurotic symptoms with metaphor and of desire with metonymy is, however, quite compatible with Jakobson's scheme.

The points that emerge with most force from this dazzling, wayward, teasing discourse are: (1) that there is no getting outside language, and that language is innately figurative, not transparently referential; (2) that the human subject is constituted precisely by the entry into language, and that the Christian–humanist idea of an autonomous individual self or soul that transcends the limits of language is a fallacy and an illusion. Both ideas (which are fundamental to the Deconstruction school of criticism) can be traced back to Nietzsche, whose cryptic, idiosyncratic expository style also seems to have been a model for Lacan.

COMMENTARY: Malcolm Bowie, 'Jacques Lacan', in John Sturrock (ed.), *Structuralism and Since* (1979)
              Sherry Turkle, *Psychoanalytical Politics: Freud's French Revolution* (1979)
              Elizabeth Wright, *Psychoanalytic Criticism: theory in practice* (1984)

The insistence of the letter in the unconscious

Of Children in Swaddling Clothes
O cities of the sea, I behold in you your citizens, women as well as men tightly bound with stout bonds around their arms and legs by folk who will have no understanding of our speech; and you will only be able to give vent to your griefs and sense of loss of liberty by making tearful complaints, and sighs, and lamentations one to another; for those who bind you will not have understanding of your speech nor will you understand them.

—Leonardo da Vinci

If the nature of this contribution has been set by the theme of this volume of *La Psychanalyse*, I yet owe to what will be found in it to insert it at a point somewhere between the written and spoken word—it will be halfway between the two.

A written piece is in fact distinguished by a prevalence of the 'text' in the sense which that factor of speech will be seen to take on in this essay, a factor which makes possible the kind of tightening up that I like in order to leave the reader no other way out than the way in, which I prefer to be difficult. In that sense, then, this will not be a written work.

The priority I accord to the nourishing of my seminars each time with something new has until now prevented my drawing on such a text, with one exception, not outstanding in the context of the series, and I refer to it at all only for the general level of its argument.

For the urgency which I now take as a pretext for leaving aside such an aim only masks the difficulty that, in trying to maintain this discourse on the level at which I ought in these writings to present my teaching, I might push it too far from the spoken word which, with its own measures, differs from writing and is essential to the instructive effect I am seeking.

That is why I have taken the expedient offered me by the invitation to lecture to the philosophy group of the union of humanities students[1] to produce an adaptation suitable to my talk; its necessary generality having to accommodate itself to the exceptional character of the audience, but its sole object encountering the collusion of their common preparation, a literary one, to which my title pays homage.

How should we forget in effect that until the end of his life Freud constantly maintained that such a preparation was the first requisite in the formation of analysts, and that he designated the eternal *universitas litterarum* [universe of letters] as the ideal place for its institution?[2]

And thus my recourse to the movement of this speech, feverishly restored, by showing whom I meant it for, marks even more clearly those for whom it is not meant. I mean that it is not meant for those who for any reason, psychoanalytic or other, allow their discipline to parade under a false identity; a fault of habit, but its effect on the mind is such that the true identity may appear as simply one alibi among others, a sort of refined reduplication whose implications will not be missed by the most acute.

So one observes the curious phenomenon of a whole new tack concerning language and symbolization in the *International Journal of Psychoanalysis*, buttressed by many sticky fingers in the pages of Sapir and Jespersen[a]—amateurish exercise so far, but it is even more the tone which is lacking. A certain seriousness is cause for amusement from the standpoint of veracity.

And how could a psychoanalyst of today not realize that his realm of truth is in fact the word, when his whole experience must find in the word alone its instrument, its framework, its material, and even the static of its uncertainties.

[a] Edward Sapir (1881–1939) and Jens Otto Jespersen (1860–1943) were among the most important modern linguists.

I The Meaning of the Letter

As our title suggests, beyond what we call 'the word,' what the psychoanalytic experience discovers in the unconscious is the whole structure of language. Thus from the outset we have altered informed minds to the extent to which the notion that the unconscious is merely the seat of the instincts will have to be rethought.

But this 'letter,' how are we to take it here? How indeed but literally.

By 'letter' we designate that material support which concrete speech borrows from language.

This simple definition assumes that language not be confused with the diverse psychic and somatic functions which serve it in the individual speaker.

For the primary reason that language and its structure exist prior to the moment at which each individual at a certain point in his mental development makes his entry into it.

Let us note, then, that aphasia, although caused by purely anatomical lesions in the cerebral apparatus which supplies the mental center for these linguistic functions, produces language deficiencies which divide naturally between the two poles of the signifying effect of what we call here 'the letter' in the creation of meaning.[3] A point which will be clarified later.

The speaking subject, if he seems to be thus a slave of language, is all the more so of a discourse in the universal moment of which he finds himself at birth, even if only by dint of his proper name.

Reference to the 'experience of the community' as the substance of this discourse settles nothing. For this experience has as its essential dimension the tradition which the discourse itself founds. This tradition, long before the drama of history gets written into it, creates the elementary structures of culture. And these structures reveal an ordering of possible exchanges which, even unconscious, is inconceivable outside the permutations authorized by language.

With the result that the ethnographic duality of nature and culture is giving way to a ternary conception of the human condition: nature, society, and culture, the last term of which could well be equated to language, or that which essentially distinguishes human society from natural societies.

But we shall not make of this distinction either a point or a point of departure, leaving to its own obscurity the question of the original relation between work and the signifier. We shall be content, for our little jab at the general function of *praxis* in the genesis of history, to point out that the very society which wished to restore, along with the privileges of the producer, the causal hierarchy of the relations between production and the ideological superstructure to their full political rights, has none the less failed to give birth to an esperanto in which the relations of language to socialist realities would have rendered any literary formalism radically impossible.[4]

As for us, we shall have faith only in those assumptions which have already proven their value by virtue of the fact that language through them has attained the status of an object of scientific investigation.

For it is by dint of this fact that linguistics[5] is seen to occupy the key position in this domain, and the reclassification of sciences and regrouping of them around

82

it points up, as is the rule, a revolution in knowledge; only the necessities of communication made us call this volume and this grouping the 'human sciences' given the confusion that this term can be made to hide.

To pinpoint the emergence of linguistic science we may say that, as in the case of all sciences in the modern sense, it is contained in the constitutive moment of a formula which is its foundation. This formula is the following:

$$\frac{S}{s}$$

which is read as: the signifier over the signified, 'over' corresponding to the line separating the two levels.

This sign should be attributed to Ferdinand de Saussure although it is not found in exactly this form in any of the numerous schemas which none the less express it in the printed version of his lectures of the years 1906–07, 1908–09, and 1910–11, which the piety of a group of his disciples caused to be published under the title, *Cours de linguistique générale*, a work of prime importance for the transmission of a teaching worthy of the name, that is, that one can come to terms with only in its own terms.

That is why it is legitimate for us to give him credit for the formulation S/s by which, in spite of the differences among schools, the beginning of modern linguistics can be recognized.

The thematics of this science is henceforth suspended, in effect, at the primordial placement of the signifier and the signified as being distinct orders separated initially by a barrier resisting signification. And that is what was to make possible an exact study of the relations proper to the signifier, and of the breadth of their function in the birth of the signified.

For this primordial distinction goes way beyond the debates on the arbitrariness of the sign which have been elaborated since the earliest reflections of the ancients, and even beyond the impasse which, through the same period, has been encountered in every discussion of the bi-univocal correspondence between the word and the thing, even in the mere act of naming. All this, of course, is quite contrary to the appearances suggested by the importance often imputed to the role of the index finger pointing to an object in the learning process of the infant subject learning his mother tongue, or the use in foreign language teaching of methods sometimes called 'concrete.'

One cannot and need not go further along this line of thought than to demonstrate that no meaning is sustained by anything other than reference to another meaning;[6] in its extreme form this is tantamount to the proposition that there is no language in existence for which there is any question of its inability to cover the whole field of the signified, it being an effect of its existence as a language that it necessarily answer all needs. Should we try to grasp in the realm of language the constitution of the object, how can we help but notice that the object is to be found only at the level of concept, a very different thing from a simple nominative, and that the thing, to take it at its word reduces to two divergent factors: the cause in which it has taken shelter in the French word *chose*, and the nothing (*rien*) to which it has abandoned its Latin dress (*rem*).

83

These considerations, however stimulating they may seem to philosophers, turn us aside from the area in which language questions us on its very nature. And one will fail even to keep the question in view as long as one has not got rid of the illusion that the signifier answers to the function of representing the signified, or better, that the signifier has to answer for its existence in the name of any signification whatever.

For even reduced to this latter formulation, the heresy is the same, the heresy that leads logical positivism[b] in search of the 'meaning of meaning' as its object is called in the language its disciples like to wallow in. Whence we can observe that even a text charged with meaning reduces itself, through this sort of analysis, to meaningless bagatelles, all that survives being mathematical formulas which are, of course, meaningless.[7]

To return to our formula S/s: if we could infer nothing from it beyond the notion of the parallelism of its upper and lower terms, each one taken in its globality, it would remain only the enigmatic sign of a total mystery. Which of course is not the case.

In order to grasp its function I shall begin by reproducing the classical, yet faulty illustration by which its usage is normally presented. It is:

Tree

and one can see already how it seems to favor the sort of erroneous interpretation just mentioned.

I replaced this in my lecture with another, which has no greater claim to correctness than that it has been transplanted into that incongruous dimension which the psychoanalyst has not yet altogether renounced because of his quite justified feeling that his conformism takes its value entirely from it. Here is the other diagram:

Ladies   **Gentlemen**

where we see that, without greatly extending the scope of the signifier concerned in the experiment, that is, by doubling a noun through the mere juxtaposition

---

[b] Logical positivism was a school of philosophy that originated in Vienna in the 1920s. It had affinities with the tradition of British empiricist philosophy and found a sympathetic reception in England, especially through the advocacy of A. J. Ayer. Lacan seems to be using the term to refer primarily to British philosophy (see his note 7).

of two terms whose complementary meanings ought apparently to reinforce each other, a surprise is produced by an unexpected precipitation of meaning: the image of twin doors symbolizing, through the solitary confinement offered Western Man for the satisfaction of his natural needs away from home, the imperative that he seems to share with the great majority of primitive communities which submits his public life to the laws of urinary segregation.

It is not only with the idea of silencing the nominalist debate[c] with a low blow that I use this example, but rather to show how in fact the signifier intrudes into the signified, namely in a form which, not being immaterial, raises the very question of its place in reality. For the blinking gaze of a near-sighted person would be quite justified in doubting whether this was indeed the signifier as he peered closely at the little enamel signs which bore it, a signifier of which the signified received its final honors from the double and solemn procession from the upper nave.

But no contrived example can equal the sharpness of the encounter with a lived truth. And so I am happy to have invented the above since it awoke in the person whose word I most trust this memory of childhood which having thus happily come to my knowledge could well be inserted here.

A train arrives at a station. A little boy and a little girl, brother and sister, are seated in a compartment face to face next to the window through which the buildings along the station platform can be seen passing as the train pulls to a stop. 'Look,' says the brother, 'we're at Ladies!' 'Idiot,' replies his sister, 'can't you see we're at Gentlemen.'

Besides the fact that the rails in this story offer a material counterpart to the line in the Saussurian formula (and in a form designed to suggest that its resistance may be other than dialectical), we should add that only someone who didn't have his eyes in front of the holes (it's the appropriate image here) could possibly confuse the place of the signifier and the signified in this story, or not see from what shining center the signifier goes forth to reflect its light into the shadow of incomplete meanings. For this signifier will now carry a purely animal Dissension, meant for the usual oblivion of natural mists, to the unbridled power of ideological Warfare, relentless for families, a torment to the Gods. Ladies and Gentlemen will be henceforth for these children two countries towards which each of their souls will strive on divergent wings, and between which a cessation of hostilities will be the more impossible since they are in truth the same country and neither can compromise on its own superiority without detracting from the glory of the other.

But enough. It begins to sound like the history of France. Which it is more human, as it ought to be, to evoke here than that of England, destined to tumble from the Large to the Small End of Dean Swift's egg[d].

---

[c] The philosophical debate about whether the abstract universals which enable us to group discrete phenomena into categories are real or arbitrary.

[d] In the Lilliput section of *Gulliver's Travels*, Swift satirised doctrinal disagreement between Catholics and Protestants by representing it as a dispute about at which end a boiled egg should be opened.

It remains to be conceived what steps, what corridor, the S of the signifier, visible here in the plurals in which it focuses its welcome beyond the window, must take in order to rest its elbows on the ventilators through which, like warm and cold air, scorn and indignation come hissing out below.

One thing is certain: if the formula S/s with its line is appropriate, access from one to the other cannot in any case have a meaning. For the formula, insofar as it is itself only pure function of the signifier, can reveal only the structure of a signifier in the transfer.

Now the structure of the signifier is, as it is commonly said of language itself, that it be articulated.

This means that no matter where one starts from in order to describe the zones of reciprocal infringement and the areas of expanding inclusiveness of its units, these units are submitted to the double condition of reducing to ultimate distinctive features and of combining according to the laws of a closed order.

These units, one of the decisive discoveries of linguistics, are *phonemes*; but we must not expect to find any *phonetic* constancy in the modulatory variability to which this term applies, but rather the synchronic system of distinguishing connections necessary for the discernment of sounds in a given language. Through this, one sees that an essential element of the word itself was predestined to slide down into the mobile characters which—in a scurry of lower-case Didots or Garamonds—render validly present what we call the 'letter,' namely the essentially localized structure of the signifier.

With the second property of the signifier, that of combining according to the laws of a closed order, is affirmed the necessity of the topological substratum of which the term I ordinarily use, namely, the signifying chain, gives an approximate idea: rings of a necklace that is a ring in another necklace made of rings.

Such are the conditions of structure which define grammar as the order of constitutive infringements of the signifier up to the level of the unit immediately superior to the sentence, and lexicology as the order of constitutive inclusions of the signifier to the level of the verbal locution.

In examining the limits by which these two exercises in the understanding of linguistic usage are determined, it is easy to see that only the correlations between signifier and signifier supply the standard for all research into meaning, as is indicated in fact by the very notion of 'usage' of a taxeme or semanteme which in fact refers to the context just above that of the units concerned.

But it is not because the undertakings of grammar and lexicology are exhausted within certain limits that we must think that beyond those limits meaning reigns supreme. That would be an error.

For the signifier, by its very nature, always anticipates on meaning by unfolding its dimension before it. As is seen at the level of the sentence when it is interrupted before the significant term: 'I shall never . . .,' 'All the same it is . . .,' 'And yet there may be . . .' Such sentences are not without meaning, a meaning all the more oppressive in that it is content to make us wait for it.[8]

But the phenomenon is no different which by the mere recoil of a 'but' brings to the light, comely as the Shulamite, honest as the dew, the negress adorned for the wedding and the poor woman ready for the auction-block.[9]

From which we can say that it is in the chain of the signifier that the meaning 'insists' but that none of its elements 'consists' in the meaning of which it is at the moment capable.

We are forced, then, to accept the notion of an incessant sliding of the signified under the signifier—which F. de Saussure illustrates with an image resembling the wavy lines of the upper and lower Waters in miniatures from manuscripts of Genesis; a double flow in which the guidelines of fine streaks of rain, vertical dotted lines supposedly confining segments of correspondence, seem too slight.

All our experience runs counter to this linearity, which made me speak once, in one of my seminars on psychosis, of something more like spaced upholstery buttons as a schema for taking into account the dominance of the letter in the dramatic transformation which the dialogue can bring about in a subject.[10]

The linearity which F. de Saussure holds to be constitutive of the chain of discourse, in conformity with its emission by a single voice and with its horizontal position in our writing—if this linearity is necessary in fact, it is not sufficient. It applies to the chain of discourse only in the direction in which it is oriented in time, being taken as a signifying factor in all languages in which 'Peter hits Paul' reverses its time when the terms are inverted.

But one has only to listen to poetry, which perhaps Saussure was not in the habit of doing, to hear a true polyphony emerge, to know in fact that all discourse aligns itself along the several staves of a score.

There is in effect no signifying chain which does not have attached to the punctuation of each of its units a whole articulation of relevant context suspended 'vertically' from that point.

Let us take our word 'tree' again, this time not as an isolated noun, but at the point of one of these punctuations, and see how it crosses the line of the Saussurian formula.

For even broken down into the double spectre of its vowels and consonants, it can still call up with the robur and the plane tree the meanings it takes on, in the context of our flora, of strength and majesty. Drawing on all the symbolic contexts suggested in the Hebrew of the Bible, it erects on a barren hill the shadow of the cross. Then reduces to the capital Y, the sign of dichotomy which, except for the illustration used by heraldry, would owe nothing to the tree however genealogical we may think it. Circulatory tree, tree of life of the cerebellum, tree of Saturn, tree of Diana, crystals formed in a tree struck by lightning, is it your figure which traces our destiny for us in the tortoise-shell cracked by the fire, or your lightning which causes that slow shift in the axis of being to surge up from an unnamable night into the 'Εν παντα [one in all] of language':

> No! says the Tree, it says No! in the shower of sparks
> Of its superb head

lines which require the harmonics of the tree just as much as their continuation:

> Which the storm treats as universally
> As it does a blade of grass.[11]

For this modern verse is ordered according to the same law of the parallelism of the signifier which creates the harmony governing the primitive Slavic epic or the most refined Chinese poetry.

As is seen in the fact that the tree and the blade of grass are chosen from the same mode of the existent in order for the signs of contradiction—saying 'No!' and 'treat as'—to affect them, and also so as to bring about, through the categorical contrast of the particularity of 'superb' with the 'universally' which reduces it, in the condensation of the 'head' and the 'storm,' the indiscernible shower of sparks of the eternal instant.

But this whole signifier can only operate, someone may object, if it is present in the subject. It is this objection that I answer by supposing that it has passed over to the level of the signified.

For what is important is not that the subject know anything whatsoever. (If LADIES and GENTLEMEN were written in a language unknown to the little boy and girl, their quarrel would simply be the more exclusively a quarrel over words, but none the less ready to take on meaning.)

One thing this structure of the signifying chain makes evident is the possibility I have, precisely insofar as I have this language in common with other subjects, that is insofar as it exists as a language, to use it in order to say something quite other than what it says. This function of the word is more worth pointing out than that of 'disguising the thought' (more often than not indefinable) of the subject; it is no less than the function of indicating the place of the subject in the search for the truth.

I have only to plant my tree in a locution: climb the tree, indeed illuminate it by playing on it the light of a descriptive context; plant it firm so as not to let myself be trapped in some sort of *communiqué*, however official, and if I know the truth, let it be heard, in spite of all the between-the-lines censures, by the only signifier I know how to create with my acrobatics among the branches of the tree, tantalizing to the point of burlesque, or sensible only to the experienced eye, according to whether I wish to be heard by the mob or the few.

The properly signifying function thus described in language has a name. We learned this name in some grammar of our childhood, on the last page, where the shade to Quintilian[e], relegated to a phantom chapter of 'ultimate considerations on style,' seemed in a hurry to get his word in as though threatened with the hook.

It is among the figures of style, or tropes, that we find the word: the name is *metonymy*.

We shall recall only the example given there: thirty sails. For the anxiety we felt over the fact that the word 'boat' lurking in the background was only part of the craft employed in this example did less to veil these illustrious sails than did the definition they were supposed to illustrate.

---

[e] Roman rhetorician, author of *Institutiones Oratoriae*, in which all the figures of speech are defined and classified.

The part taken for the whole,[f] we said to ourselves, and if we take it seriously, we are left with very little idea of the importance of this fleet, which 'thirty sails' is precisely supposed to give us: for each boat to have just one sail is in fact the least likely possibility.

By which we see that the connection between boat and sail is nowhere but in the signifier, and that it is in the word-to-word connection that metonymy is based.[12]

We shall designate as metonymy, then, the one slope of the effective field of the signifier in the constitution of meaning.

Let us name the other: it is *metaphor*. Let us find again an illustration; Quillet's dictionary seemed an appropriate place to find a sample which would not seem to be chosen for my own purposes, and for an appropriate dressing I didn't have to go any further than the well known line of Victor Hugo:

His sheaves were not miserly nor spiteful[13]

under which aspect I presented metaphor to my seminar on psychosis.

Let us admit that modern poetry and especially the surrealist school have taken us quite far in this domain by showing that any conjunction of two signifiers would be equally sufficient to constitute a metaphor, except for the additional requirement of the greatest possible disparity of the images signified, needed for the production of the poetic spark, or in other words for there to be metaphoric creation.

It is true this radical position is based on the experiment known as automatic writing which would not have been tried if its pioneers had not been reassured by the Freudian discovery. But it remains a position branded with confusion because the doctrine behind it is false.

The creative spark of the metaphor does not spring from the conjunction of two images, that is of two signifiers equally actualized. It springs from two signifiers one of which has taken the place of the other in the signifying chain, the hidden signifier then remaining present through its (metonymic) relation to the rest of the chain.

One word for another: that is the formula for the metaphor and if you are a poet you will produce for your own delight a continuous stream, a dazzling tissue of metaphors. If the result is the sort of intoxication of the dialogue that Jean Tardieu[g] wrote under this title, that is only because he was giving us a demonstration of the radical superfluousness of all meaning to a perfectly convincing representation of a bourgeois comedy.

It is manifest that in the line of Hugo cited above, not the slightest spark of light springs from the proposition that his sheaves were neither miserly nor spiteful, for the reason that there is no question of the sheaves having either

---

[f] Strictly speaking, 'the part taken for the whole' is the figure of synecdoche, but Roman Jakobson, on whom Lacan is drawing in this passage, treats synecdoche as a sub-category of metonymy. (See p. 57, n. *a*, above.)

[g] Jean Tardieu (b. 1903) is an experimental French poet and dramatist.

the merit or demerit of these attributes, since the attributes, as the sheaves, belong to Booz who exercises the former in disposing of the latter and without informing the latter of his sentiments in the case.

If, however, his sheaves do refer us to Booz, and this is indeed the case, it is because they have replaced him in the signifying chain at the very spot where he was to be exalted by the sweeping away of greed and spite. But now Booz himself has been swept away by the sheaves, and hurled into the outer darkness where greed and spite harbor him in the hollow of their negation.

But once *his* sheaves have thus usurped his place, Booz can no longer return there; the slender thread of the little word *his* which binds him to it is only one more obstacle to his return in that it links him to the notion of possession which retains him in the very zone of greed and spite. So *his* generosity, affirmed in the passage, is yet reduced to less than nothing by the munificence of the sheaves which, coming from nature, know not our caution or our casting out, and even in their accumulation remain prodigal by our standards.

But if in this profusion, the giver has disappeared along with his gift, it is only in order to rise again in what surrounds this figure by which he was annihilated. For it is the figure of the burgeoning of fecundity, and this it is which announces the surprise which the poem sings, namely the promise which the old man will receive in a sacred context of his accession to paternity.

So, it is between the signifier in the form of the proper name of a man, and the signifier which metaphorically abolishes him that the poetic spark is produced, and it is in this case all the more effective in realizing the meaning of paternity in that it reproduces the mythic event in terms of which Freud reconstructed the progress, in the individual unconscious, of the mystery of the father.

Modern metaphor has the same structure. So this ejaculation:

Love is a pebble laughing in the sunlight,

recreates love in a dimension that seems to me most tenable in the face of its imminent lapse into the mirage of narcissistic altruism.

We see, then, that metaphor occurs at the precise point at which sense comes out of non-sense, that is, at that frontier which, as Freud discovered, when crossed the other way produces what we generally call 'wit' (*Witz*); it is at this frontier that we can glimpse the fact that man tempts his very destiny when he derides the signifier.

But to draw back from that place, what do we find in metonymy other than the power to bypass the obstacles of social censure? This form which lends itself to the truth under oppression, doesn't it show the very servitude inherent in its presentation?

One may read with profit a book by Leo Strauss, of the land which traditionally offers asylum to those who chose freedom, in which the author gives his reflections on the relation between the art of writing and persecution.[14] By pushing to its limits the sort of connaturality which links that art to that condition, he lets us glimpse a certain something which in this matter imposes its form, in the effect of the truth on desire.

But haven't we felt for some time now that, having followed the path of the letter in search of the truth we call Freudian, we are getting very warm indeed, that it is burning all about us?

Of course, as it is said, the letter killeth while the spirit giveth life. We can't help but agree, having had to pay homage elsewhere to a noble victim of the error of seeking the spirit in the letter; but we should like to know, also, how the spirit could live without the letter. Even so, the claims of the spirit would remain unassailable if the letter had not in fact shown us that it can produce all the effects of truth in man without involving the spirit at all.

It is none other than Freud who had this revelation, and he called his discovery the Unconscious.

II *The Letter in the Unconscious*

One out of every three pages in the complete works of Freud is devoted to philological references, one out of every two pages to logical inferences, and everywhere the apprehension of experience is dialectical, with the proportion of linguistic analysis increasing just insofar as the unconscious is directly concerned.

Thus in *The Interpretation of Dreams* every page deals with what we are calling the letter of the discourse, in its texture, its usage, its immanence in the matter in question. For it is with this work that the work of Freud begins to open the royal road to the unconscious. And Freud gave us notice of this; his confidence at the time of launching this book in the early days of this century[15] only confirms what he continued to proclaim to the end: that his whole message was at stake in this, the whole of his discovery.

The first sentence of the opening chapter announces what for the sake of the exposition could not be postponed: that the dream is a rebus.[h] And Freud goes on to stipulate what I have said from the start, that it must be understood literally. This derives from the persistence in the dream of that same literal (or phonematic) structure through which the signifier in ordinary discourse is articulated and analyzed. So the unnatural images of the boat on the roof, or the man with a comma for a head which are specifically mentioned by Freud, are examples of dream-images which have importance only as signifiers, that is, insofar as they allow us to spell out the 'proverb' presented by the rebus of the dream. The structure of language which enables us to read dreams is the very principle of the 'meaning of dreams,' the *Traumdeutung*.

Freud shows us in every possible way that the image's value as signifier has nothing whatever to do with what it signifies, giving as an example Egyptian hieroglyphics in which it would be sheer buffoonery to pretend that in a given text the frequency of a vulture which is an *aleph*, or of a chick which is a *vau*, and which indicate a form of the verb 'to be' or a plural, prove that the text has anything at all to do with these ornithological specimens. Freud finds in this script certain uses of the signifier which are lost in ours, such as the use of determinatives, where a categorical figure is added to the literal figuration of a

[h] A rebus is a puzzle in which pictures represent words or syllables.

verbal term; but this is only to show us that even in this script, the so-called 'ideogram' is a letter.

But the current confusion on this last term was not needed for there to prevail in the minds of psychoanalysts lacking linguistic training the prejudice in favor of a symbolism by natural analogy, that is of the image as fitted to the instinct. And to such an extent that, outside of the French school which has been alerted, one must draw the line between reading coffee grounds and reading hieroglyphics, by recalling to its own principles a technique which nothing could possibly justify except the very aim and content of the unconscious.

It must be said that this truth is admitted only with difficulty and that the bad mental habits denounced above enjoy such favor that today's psychoanalyst can be expected to say that he decodes before he will come around to taking the necessary tour with Freud (turn at the statue of Champollion, says the guide) which will make him understand that he deciphers; the distinction is that a cryptogram takes on its full dimension only when it is in a lost language.

Taking the tour is nothing other than continuing in the *Traumdeutung*.

Entstellung, translated as distortion, is what Freud shows to be the general precondition for the functioning of dreams, and it is what we described above, following Saussure, as the sliding of the signified under the signifier which is always active in speech (its action, let us note, is unconscious).

But what we called the two slopes of the incidence of the signifier on the signified are also found here.

The *Verdichtung*, or condensation, is the structure of the superimposition of signifiers which is the field of metaphor, and its very name, condensing in itself the word *Dichtung*, shows how the process is connatural with the mechanism of poetry to the point that it actually envelops its properly traditional function.[i]

In the case of *Verschiebung*, displacement, the German term is closer to the idea of that veering off of meaning that we see in metonymy, and which from its first appearance in Freud is described as the main method by which the unconscious gets around censorship.

What distinguishes these two mechanisms which play such a privileged role in the dream-work (*Traumarbeit*), from their homologous functions in speech?

---

[i] Here, whether consciously or not, Lacan departs from Roman Jakobson's application of the metaphor/metonymy distinction to Freudian dream analysis. According to Jakobson, *both* condensation *and* displacement correspond to metonymy. (See above, p. 60).

Condensation is the process by which one element in a dream may represent more than one dream-thought and refer to more than one event, anxiety, etc., in the dreamer's waking life. The examples Freud gives in the chapter, 'The Work of Condensation' in *The Interpretation of Dreams* seem to support Jakobson's classification: the multiple sources of a given dream-image usually turn out to be contiguous in the dreamer's life. Displacement refers to the way a dream is often differently centred from the preoccupations which give rise to it, a trivial event in reality being of prime importance in the dream. Freud links this phenomenon very closely to condensation, and uses the same examples to illustrate it.

According to Jakobson, the metaphors of dream are what Freud calls 'symbolism', e.g. the representation of male and female genitalia by objects of similar properties—long and pointed, round and hollow.

Nothing except a condition imposed on the signifying material by the dream, called *Rücksicht auf Darstellbarkeit*, translated as Considerations of Representability. But this condition constitutes a limitation operating *within* the system of notation; it is a long way from dissolving the system into a figurative semiology on a level with certain phenomena of natural expression. This fact could perhaps shed light on the problems involved in certain modes of pictography which, simply because they have been abandoned by writing systems as imperfect, are not therefore to be considered as mere evolutionary stages. Let us say, then, that the dream is like the parlor-game in which one is put on the spot to cause a group of spectators to guess some known utterance or variant of it by means solely of a silent performance. That the dream uses words makes no difference since for the unconscious they are but one among several elements of the performance. It is exactly the fact that both the game and the dream run up against a lack of taxematic material for the representation of such logical articulations as causality, contradiction, hypothesis, etc., that proves they are both writing systems rather than pantomime. The subtle processes which dreams are seen to use to represent these logical articulations, in a much less artificial way than the game brings to bear, are the object of a special study in Freud in which we see once more confirmed that dream-work follows the laws of the signifier.

The rest of the dream-elaboration is designated as secondary by Freud, the nature of which indicates its value: they are fantasies or day-dreams (*Tagtraum*) to use the term Freud prefers in order to emphasize their function of wish-fulfillment (*Wunscherfüllung*). Given the fact that these fantasies can remain unconscious, their distinctive trait is in this case their meaning. Now concerning these fantasies, Freud tells us that their place in dreams is either to be taken up and used as signifying elements in the message of the dream-thought (*Traumgedanke*), or else to be used in the secondary elaboration just mentioned, that is in a function not to be distinguished from our waking thought (*von unserem wachen Denken nicht zu unterschieden*). No better idea of this function can be got than by comparing it to splotches of color which when applied here and there to a stencil would create for our view in a topical painting the pictures, rather grim in themselves, of the rebus or hieroglyph.

Excuse me if I seem to have to spell out the text of Freud; I do it not only to show how much is to be gained by not cutting or abridging it, but also in order to situate the development of psychoanalysis according to its first guide-lines, which were fundamental and never revoked.

Yet from the beginning there was a general failure to recognize the formative role of the signifier in the status which Freud from the first assigned to the unconscious and in the most precise formal manner. And for a double reason, of which the least obvious, naturally, is that this formalization was not sufficient in itself to bring about a recognition of the insistence of the signifier because the time of the appearance of the *Traumdeutung* was well ahead of the formalizations of linguistics for which one could no doubt show that it paved the way by the sheer weight of its truth.

And the second reason, which is after all only the underside of the first, is that if psychoanalysts were fascinated exclusively by the meanings revealed in the unconscious, that is because the secret attraction of these meanings arises from the dialectic which seems to inhere in them.

I showed in my seminars that it is the necessity of counteracting the continuously accelerating effects of this bias which alone explains the apparent sudden changes, or rather changes of tack, which Freud, through his primary concern to preserve for posterity both his discovery and the fundamental revisions it effected in our other knowledge, felt it necessary to apply to his doctrine.

For, I repeat: in the situation in which he found himself, having nothing which corresponded to the object of his discovery which was the same level of scientific development—in this situation, at least he never failed to maintain this object on the level of its proper ontological dignity.

The rest was the work of the gods and took such a course that analysis today takes as its basis those imaginary forms which I have just shown to be written on the margin of the text they mutilate—and analysis tries to accommodate its goal according to them, in the interpretation of dreams confusing them with the visionary liberation of the hieroglyphic apiary, and seeking generally the control of the exhaustion of the analysis in a sort of scanning process[16] of these forms whenever they appear, with the idea that, just as they are a sign of the exhaustion of regressions, they are also signs of the remodeling of the 'object-relation' which characterizes the subject.

The technique which is based on such positions can be fertile in its diverse results, and under the aegis of therapy, difficult to criticize. But an internal criticism must none the less arise from the flagrant disparity between the mode of operation by which the technique is justified—namely the analytic rule, all the instruments of which, from 'free association' on up, depend on the conception of the unconscious of their inventor—and on the other hand the general ignorance which reigns regarding this conception of the unconscious. The most peremptory champions of this technique think themselves freed of any need to reconcile the two by the simplest pirouette: the analytic rule (they say) must be all the more religiously observed since it is only the result of a lucky accident. In other words, Freud never knew what he was doing.

A return to Freud's text shows on the contrary the absolute coherence between his technique and his discovery, and at the same time this coherence allows us to put all his procedures in their proper place.

That is why the rectification of psychoanalysis must inevitably involve a return to the truth of that discovery which, taken in its original moment, is impossible to mistake.

For in the analysis of dreams, Freud intends only to give us the laws of the unconscious in the most general extension. One of the reasons why dreams were most propitious for this demonstration is exactly, Freud tells us, that they reveal the same laws whether in the normal person or in the neurotic.

But in the one case as in the other, the efficacy of the unconscious does not cease in the waking state. The psychoanalytic experience is nothing other than the demonstration that the unconscious leaves none of our actions outside its scope. The presence of the unconscious in the psychological order, in other words in the relation-functions of the individual, should, however, be more precisely defined: it is not coextensive with that order, for we know that if unconscious motivation is manifest in conscious psychic effects, as well as in unconscious ones, conversely it is only elementary to recall to mind that a large number of psychic effects which are quite legitimately designated as unconscious, in the sense of excluding the characteristic of consciousness, never the less are without any relation whatever to the unconscious in the Freudian sense. So it is only by an abuse of the term that unconscious in that sense is confused with psychic, and that one may thus designate as psychic what is in fact an effect of the unconscious, as on the somatic for instance.

It is a matter, therefore, of defining the locus of this unconscious. I say that it is the very locus defined by the formula S/s. What we have been able to unfold concerning the incidence of the signifier on the signified suggests its transformation into.

$$f(S)\,\frac{1}{s}$$

We have shown the effects not only of the elements of the horizontal signifying chain, but also of its vertical dependencies, divided into two fundamental structures called metonymy and metaphor. We can symbolize them by, first:

$$f(S\ldots S')\ S \sim S\ (-)s$$

that is, the metonymic structure, indicating that it is the connection between signifier and signifier which alone permits the elision in which the signifier inserts the lack of being into the object relation, using the reverberating character of meaning to invest it with the desire aimed at the very lack it supports. The sign— placed between ( ) represents here the retention of the line—which in the original formula marked the irreducibility in which, in the relations between signifier and signified, the resistance of meaning is constituted.[17]

Secondly,

$$f\left(\frac{S'}{S}\right)\ S \sim S\ (+)s$$

the metaphoric structures, indicates that it is in the substitution of signifier for signifier that an effect of signification is produced which is creative or poetic, in other words which is the advent of the signification in question.[18] The sign + between ( ) represents here the leap over the line—and the constitutive value of the leap for the emergence of meaning.

This leap is an expression of the condition of passage of the signifier into the signified which I pointed out above, although provisionally confusing it with the place of the subject. It is the function of the subject, thus introduced, which we must now turn to as it is the crucial point of our problem.

Je pense, donc je suis (cogito ergo sum)[j] is not merely the formula in which is

---

[j] 'I think, therefore I am'—the famous axiom of the French rationalist philosopher, Descartes (1596–1650).

constituted, along with the historical apogee of reflection on the conditions of knowledge, the link between the transparence of the transcendental subject and his existential affirmation.

Perhaps I am only object and mechanism (and so nothing more than phenomenon), but assuredly insofar as I think so, I am—absolutely. No doubt philosophers have made important corrections on this formulation, notably that in that which thinks (*cogitans*), I can never pose myself as anything but object (*cogitatum*). None the less it remains true that by way of this extreme purification of the transcendental subject, my existential link to its project seems irrefutable, at least in its present form, and that:

$$\text{`cogito ergo sum' ubi cogito, ibi sum,}^{k}$$

overcomes this objection.

Of course this confines me to being there in my being only insofar as I think that I am in my thought; just how far I actually think this concerns only myself and if I say it, interests no one.[19]

To elude this problem on the pretext of its philosophical pretensions is simply to show our inhibition. For the notion of subject is indispensable even to the operation of a science such as strategy (in the modern sense) whose calculations exclude all subjectivism.

It is also to deny oneself access to what we may call the Freudian universe—in the way that we speak of the Copernican universe. It was in fact the so-called Copernican revolution to which Freud himself compared his discovery, emphasizing that it was once again a question of the place man assigns to himself at the center of a universe.

The place that I occupy as the subject of a signifier: is it, in relation to the place I occupy as subject of the signified, concentric or ex-centric?—that is the question.

It is not a question of knowing whether I speak of myself in a way that conforms to what I am, but rather of knowing whether I am the same as that of which I speak. And it is not at all inappropriate to use the word 'thought' here. For Freud uses the term to designate the elements involved in the unconscious, that is the signifying mechanisms which we now recognize as being there.

It is none the less true that the philosophical *cogito* is at the center of that mirage which renders modern man so sure of being himself even in his uncertainties about himself, or rather in the mistrust he has learned to erect against the traps of self-love.

Likewise, if I charge nostalgia with being in the service of metonymy and refuse to seek meaning beyond tautology; if in the name of 'war is war' and 'a penny's a penny' I determine to be only what I am, yet how even here can I eliminate the obvious fact that in that very act I am?

And it is no less true if I take myself to the other, metaphorical pole in my quest for meaning, and if I dedicate myself to becoming what I am, to coming into being, I cannot doubt that even if I lose myself in the process, in that process, I am.

---

k 'I think, therefore I am' where I think, there I am.

Now it is on these very points where evidence will be subverted by the empirical, that the trick of the Freudian conversion lies.

This meaningful game between metonymy and metaphor up to and including the active edge which splits my desire between a refusal of meaning or a lack of being and links my fate to the question of my destiny, this game, in all its inexorable subtlety, is played until the match is called, there where I am not because I cannot locate myself there.

That is, what is needed is more than these words with which I disconcerted my audience: I think where I am not, therefore I am where I think not. Words which render sensible to an ear properly attuned with what weasling ambiguity the ring of meaning flees from our grasp along the verbal thread.

What one ought to say is: I am not, wherever I am the plaything of my thought; I think of what I am wherever I don't think I am thinking.

This two-faced mystery is linked to the fact that the truth can be evoked only in that dimension of alibi in which all 'realism' in creative works takes its virtue from metonymy; it is likewise linked to this other fact that we accede to meaning only through the double twist of metaphor when we have the unique key: the S and the s of the Saussurian formula are not on the same level, and man only deludes himself when he believes his true place is at their axis, which is nowhere.

Was nowhere, that is, until Freud discovered it; for if what Freud discovered isn't that, it isn't anything.

The content of the unconscious with all its disappointing ambiguities gives us no reality in the subject more consistent than the immediate; its force comes from the truth and in the dimension of being: *Kern unseres Wesen* [the nucleus of our being] are Freud's own terms.

The double-triggered mechanism of metaphor is in fact the very mechanism by which the symptom, in the analytic sense, is determined. Between the enigmatic signifier of a sexual trauma and its substitute term in a present signifying chain there passes the spark which fixes in a symptom the meaning inaccessible to the conscious subject in which is its resolution—a symptom which is in effect a metaphor in which flesh or function are taken as signifying elements.

And the enigmas which desire seems to pose for a 'natural philosophy'—its frenzy mocking the abyss of the infinite, the secret collusion by which it obscures the pleasure of knowing and of joyful domination, these amount to nothing more than that derangement of the instincts that comes from being caught on the rails—eternally stretching forth towards the desire for something else—of metonymy. Wherefore its 'perverse' fixation at the very suspension-point of the signifying chain where the memory-screen freezes and the fascinating image of the fetish petrifies.

There is no other way to conceive the indestructibility of unconscious desire, when there is no natural need which, when prevented from satisfying itself, isn't dissipated even if it means the destruction of the organism itself. It is in a memory, comparable to what they call by that name in our modern thinking-machines (which are in turn based on an electronic realization of the signifying compound), it is in this sort of memory that is found that chain which insists on reproducing itself in the process of transference, and which is the chain of dead desire.

It is the truth of what this desire was in its history which the patient cries out through his symptom, as Christ said that the stones themselves would have cried out if the children of Israel had not lent them their voice.

And that is why only psychoanalysis allows us to differentiate within memory the function of recall. Rooted in the signifier, it resolves the Platonic puzzles of reminiscence through the ascendancy of the historic in man.

One has only to read the 'Three Essays on Sexuality' to observe, in spite of the pseudo-biological glosses with which it is decked out for popular consumption, that Freud there derives any accession to the object from the dialectic of the return.

Starting from Hölderlin's νοστος [return] Freud will arrive less than twenty years later at Kierkegaard's repetition; that is, through submitting his thought solely to the humble but inflexible consequences of the talking cure, he was unable ever to escape the living servitudes which led him from the regal principle of the Logos to re-thinking the mortal Empedoclean antinomies.[1]

And how else are we to conceive the recourse of a man of science to a *Deus ex machina*[m] than on that other stage of which he speaks as the dream place, a *Deus ex machina* only less derisory for the fact that it is revealed to the spectator that the machine directs the director? How else can we imagine that a scientist of the nineteenth century, unless we realize that he had to bow before the force of evidence that over-whelmed his prejudices, put more stock in his *Totem and Taboo* than in all his other works, with its obscene and ferocious figure of the primordial father, not to be exhausted in the expiation of Oedipus' blindness, and before which the ethnologists of today bow as before the growth of an authentic myth?

So that imperious proliferation of particular symbolic creations, such as what are called the sexual theories of the child, which supply the motivation down to the smallest detail of neurotic compulsions, these reply to the same necessities as do myths.

Likewise, to speak of the precise point we are treating in my seminars on Freud, little Hans,[n] left in the lurch at the age of five by his symbolic environment, and suddenly forced to face the enigma of his sex and his existence, under the direction of Freud and of his father, Freud's disciple, developed in a mythic form, around the signifying crystal of his phobia, all the permutations possible on a limited number of signifiers.

The operation shows that even on the individual level the solution of the impossible is brought within man's reach by the exhaustion of all possible forms

[1] Friedrich Holderlin (1770–1843) was a German poet and enthusiastic Hellenist. The theme of 'return' runs through all his work. The Danish philosopher Soren Kierkegaard (1813–55) published his book on Repetition in 1843. Psychoanalysis was dubbed 'the talking cure' by one of its earliest patients. Empedocles was a pre-Socratic Greek philosopher.

[m] Originally the representation of a god in classical drama, who was lowered on to the stage by machinery to resolve the plot. Metaphorically applied to any arbitrary or artificial resolution of a problem.

[n] Subject of one of Freud's most celebrated case histories.

of the impossibilities encountered in solution by recourse to the signifying equation. It is a striking demonstration for the clarifying of this labyrinth of observation which so far has only been used as a source of demolished fragments. We should be struck also with the fact that the coextensivity of the unfolding of the symptom and of its curative resolution shows the true nature of neurosis: whether phobic, hysterical or obsessive, a neurosis is a question which being poses for the subject 'from the place where it was before the subject came into the world' (Freud's phrase which he used in explaining the Oedipal complex to little Hans).

The 'being' referred to is that which appears in a lightning moment in the void of the verb 'to be' and I said that it poses its question for the subject. What does that mean? It does not pose it *before* the subject, since the subject cannot come to the place where it is posed, but it poses it *in place* of the subject, that is, in that place it poses the question *with* the subject, as one poses a problem *with* a pen, or as man in antiquity thought *with* his soul.

It is only in this way that Freud fits the ego into his doctrine. Freud defined the ego by the resistances which are proper to it. They are of an imaginary nature much in the same sense as those adaptational activities which the ethology of animal behavior shows us in courting-pomp or combat. Freud showed their reduction in man to a narcissistic relation, which I elaborated in my essay on the mirror-stage.[o] And he grouped within it the synthesis of the perceptive functions in which the sensori-motor selections are integrated which determine for man what he calls reality.

But this resistance, essential for the solidifying of the inertias of the imaginary order which obstruct the message of the unconscious, is only secondary in relation to the specific resistances of the journey in the signifying order of the truth.

That is the reason why an exhaustion of the mechanisms of defence, which Fenichel the practitioner shows us so well in his studies of technique (while his whole reduction on the theoretical level of neuroses and psychoses to genetic anomalies in libidinal development is pure platitude), manifests itself, without Fenichel's accounting for it or realizing it himself, as simply the underside or reverse aspect of the mechanisms of the unconscious. Periphrasis, hyperbaton, ellipsis, suspension, anticipation, retraction, denial, digression, irony, these are the figures of style (Quintilian's *figurae sententiarum*); as catachresis, litotes, antonomasia, hypotyposis are the tropes, whose terms impose themselves as the most proper for the labelling of these mechanisms. Can one really see these as mere figures of speech when it is the figures themselves which are the active principle of the rhetoric of the discourse which the patient in fact utters?

By the obstinacy with which today's psychoanalysts reduce to a sort of emotional police station the reality of the resistance of which the patient's discourse is only a cover, they have sunk beneath one of the fundamental truths which Freud rediscovered through psychoanalysis. One is never happy making way for a new truth, for it always means making our way into it: the truth demands

---

[o] The stage in childhood, usually between six and eighteen months, when the individual, recognizing his own reflection in a mirror, is first able to conceive of him/herself as an autonomous being.

that we bestir ourselves. We cannot even manage to get used to the idea most of the time. We get used to reality. But the truth we repress.

Now it is quite specially necessary to the scientist and the magician, and even the quack, that he be the only one to *know*. The idea that deep in the simplest (and even sick) souls there is something ready to blossom—perish the thought! but if someone seems to know as much as the savants about what we ought to make of it . . . come to our aid, categories of primitive, prelogical, archaic, or even magical thought, so easy to impute to others! It is not right that these nibblers keep us breathless with enigmas which turn out to be only malicious.

To interpret the unconscious as Freud did, one would have to be as he was, an encyclopedia of the arts and muses, as well as an assiduous reader of the *Fliegendle Blätter*.[20] And the task is made no easier by the fact that we are at the mercy of a thread woven with allusions, quotations, puns, and equivocations. And is that our profession; to be antidotes to trifles?

Yet that is what we must resign ourselves to. The unconscious is neither primordial nor instinctual; what it knows about the elementary is no more than the elements of the signifier.

The three books that one might call canonical with regard to the unconscious—the *Traumdeutung*, the *Psychopathology of Everyday Life*, and *Wit in its Relation to the Unconscious*—are but a web of examples whose development is furnished by the formulas of connection and substitution (though carried to the tenth degree by their particular complexity—the rundown of them is sometimes given by Freud outside the text); these are the formulas we give to the signifier in its *transference*-function. For in the *Traumdeutung* it is in the sense of such a function that the term *Ubertragung*, or transference, is introduced, which only later will give its name to the mainspring of the intersubjective link between analyst and analysed.

Such diagrams (of the various transfers of the signifier) are not only constitutive of each of the symptoms in a neurosis, but they alone make possible the understanding of the thematic of its course and resolution. The great observations of analyses which Freud gave amply demonstrate this.

To fall back on data that are more limited but more apt to furnish us with the final seal to bind up our proposition, let me cite the article on fetishism of 1927,[21] and the case Freud reports there of a patient who, to achieve sexual satisfaction, needed something shining on the nose (*Glanz auf der Nase*); analysis showed that his early, English-speaking years had seen the displacement of the burning curiosity which he felt for the phallus of his mother, that is for that eminent failure-to-be the privileged signification of which Freud revealed to us, into a *glance at the nose* in the forgotten language of his childhood, rather than a *shine on the nose*.

That a thought makes itself heard in the abyss, that is an abyss open before all thought—and that is what provoked from the outset resistance to psychoanalysis. And not, as is commonly said, the emphasis on man's sexuality. This latter is after all the dominant object in the literature of the ages. And in fact the more recent evolution of psychoanalysis has succeeded by a bit of comical legerdemain in turning it into a quite moral affair, the cradle and trysting-place of attraction and oblativity. The Platonic setting of the soul, blessed and illuminated, rises straight to paradise.

The intolerable scandal in the time before Freudian sexuality was sanctified was that it was so 'intellectual.' It was precisely in that that it showed itself to be the worthy ally of the terrorists plotting to ruin society.

At a time when psychoanalysts are busy remodeling psychoanalysis into a right-thinking movement whose crowning expression is the sociological poem of the autonomous ego, and by this I mean what will identify, for those who understand me, bad psychoanalysts, this is the term they use to deprecate all technical or theoretical research which carries forward the Freudian experience along its authentic lines: *intellectualization* is the word—execrable to all those who, living in fear of being tried and found wanting by the wine of truth, spit on the bread of men, although their slaver can no longer have any effect other than that of leavening.

III Being, the Letter and the Other

Is what thinks in my place then another I? Does Freud's discovery represent the confirmation on the psychological level of Manicheism?[22]

In fact there is no confusion on this point: what Freud's researches led us to is not a few more or less curious cases of split personality. Even at the heroic epoch we were talking about, when, like the animals in fairy stories, sexuality talked, the demonic atmosphere that such an orientation might have given rise to never materialized.[23]

The end which Freud's discovery proposes for man was defined by him at the apex of his thought in these moving terms: *Wo es war, soll Ich werden*. I must come to the place where that (id) was.

The goal is one of reintegration and harmony, I could even say of reconciliation (*Versöhnung*).

But if we ignore the self's radical ex-centricity to itself with which man is confronted, in other words, the truth discovered by Freud, we shall falsify both the order and methods of psychoanalytic mediation; we shall make of it nothing more than the compromise operation which it has effectively become, namely just what the letter as well as the spirit of Freud's work most repudiates. For since he constantly invoked the notion of compromise as the main support of all the miseries which analysis is meant to help, we can say that any recourse to compromise, explicit or implicit, will necessarily disorient psychoanalytic action and plunge it into darkness.

Neither does it suffice, moreover, to associate oneself with the moralistic tartufferies[p] of our times or to be forever spouting something about the 'total personality' in order to have said anything articulate about the possibility of mediation.

[p] An allusion to the hypocritical antihero of Moliere's play *Tartuffe* (1664)

The radical heteronomy which Freud's discovery shows gaping within man can never again be covered over without whatever is used to hide it being fundamentally dishonest.

Then who is this other to whom I am more attached than to myself, since, at the heart of my assent to my own identity it is still he who wags me?

Its presence can only be understood at a second degree of otherness which puts it in the position of mediating between me and the double of myself, as it were my neighbour.

If I have said elsewhere that the unconscious is the discourse of the Other (with a capital O), I meant by that to indicate the beyond in which the recognition of desire is bound up with the desire of recognition.

In other words this other is the Other which my lie invokes as a gage of the truth in which it thrives.

By which we can also see that the dimension of truth emerges only with the appearance of language.

Prior to this point, we can recognize in psychological relations which can be easily isolated in the observation of animal behavior the existence of subjects, not on account of any projective mirage, the phantoms of which a certain type of psychologist delights in hacking to pieces, but simply on account of the manifest presence of intersubjectivity. In the animal hidden in his lookout, in the well-laid trap of certain others, in the feint by which an apparent straggler leads a bird of prey away from a fugitive band, we see something more emerge than in the fascinating display of mating or combat ritual. Yet there is nothing even there which transcends the function of decoy in the service of a need, nor which affirms a presence in that Beyond where we think we can question the designs of Nature.

For there even to be a question (and we know that it is one Freud himself posed in *Beyond the Pleasure Principle*), there must be language.

For I can decoy my adversary by means of a movement contrary to my actual plan of battle, and this movement will have its deceiving effect only insofar as I produce it in reality and for my adversary.

But in the propositions with which I open peace negotiations with him, what my negotiations propose to him is situated in third place which is neither my words nor my interlocutor.

This place is none other than the area of signifying convention, of the sort revealed in the comedy of the sad plaint of the Jew to his crony: 'Why do you tell me you are going to Cracow so I'll believe you are going to Lvov, when you are really going to Cracow?'

Of course the troop-movement I just spoke of could be understood in the conventional context of game-strategy where it is in function of a rule that I deceive my adversary, but in that case my success is evaluated within the connotation of betrayal, that is, in relation to the Other who is the guarantee of Good Faith.

Here the problems are of an order the basic heteronomy of which is completely misunderstood if it is reduced to an 'awareness of the other' by whatever name we call it. For the 'existence of the other' having once upon a time reached the ears of the Midas of psychoanalysis through the partition which separates him from the Privy Council of phenomenology, the news is now bruited through the reeds: 'Midas, King Midas is the other of his patient. He himself has said it.'*q*

What sort of breakthrough is that? The other, what other?

The young André Gide,*r* defying the landlady to whom his mother had confided him to treat him as a responsible being, opening with a key (false only in that it opened all locks of the same make) the lock which this lady took to be a worthy signifier of her educational intentions, and doing it with ostentation in her sight—what 'other' was he aiming at? She who was supposed to intervene and to whom he would then say: 'Do you think my obedience can be secured with a ridiculous lock?' But by remaining out of sight and holding her peace until that evening in order, after primly greeting his return, to lecture him like a child, she showed him not just another with the face of anger, but another André Gide who is no longer sure, either then or later in thinking back on it, of just what he really meant to do—whose own truth has been changed by the doubt thrown on his good faith.

Perhaps it would be worth our while pausing a moment over this dominion of confusion which is none other than that in which the whole human opera-buffa plays itself out, in order to understand the ways in which analysis can proceed not just to restore an order but to found the conditions for the possibility of its restoration.

Kern unseres Wesen, the nucleus of our being, but it is not so much that Freud commands us to seek it as so many others before him have with the empty adage 'Know thyself'—as to reconsider the ways which lead to it, and which he shows us.

Or rather that which he proposes for us to attain is not that which can be the object of knowledge, but that (doesn't he tell us as much?) which creates our being and about which he teaches us that we bear witness to it as much and more in our whims, our aberrations, our phobias and fetishes, as in our vaguely civilized personalities.

Folly, you are no longer the object of the ambiguous praise with which the sage decorated the impregnable burrow of his terror; and if after all he finds himself tolerably at home there, it is only because the supreme agent forever at work digging its galleries and labyrinths is none other than reason, the very Logos which he serves.

So how do you imagine that a scholar with so little talent for the '*engagements*' which solicited him in his age (as they do in all ages), that a scholar such as Erasmus held such an eminent place in the revolution of a Reformation in which man has much of a stake in each man as in all men?

The answer is that the slightest alteration in the relation between man and the signifier, in this case in the procedures of exegesis, changes the whole course

---

q Midas was a king in classical mythology whom Apollo punished by giving him ass's ears. Midas' barber, unable to keep the secret, whispered it into a hole in the ground, then filled it up. The reeds that grew upon the spot, however, whispered the secret when the wind blew.

r André Gide (1869–1951), French novelist, critic, playwright and diarist.

of history by modifying the lines which anchor his being.

It is in precisely this way that Freudianism, however misunderstood it has been, and confused the consequences, to anyone capable of perceiving the changes we have lived through in our own lives, is seen to have founded an intangible but radical revolution. No need to collect witnesses to the fact:[24] everything involving not just the human sciences, but the destiny of man, politics, metaphysics, literature, art, advertising, propaganda, and through these even the economy, everything has been affected.

Is all this anything more than the unharmonized effect of an immense truth in which Freud traced for us a clear path? What must be said, however, is that any technique which bases its claim on the mere psychological categorization of its object is not following this path, and this is the case of psychoanalysis today except insofar as we return to the Freudian discovery.

Likewise the vulgarity of the concepts by which it recommends itself to us, the embroidery of Freudery which is no longer anything but decoration, as well as the bad repute in which it seems to prosper, all bear witness to its fundamental denial of its founder.

Freud, by his discovery, brought within the circle of science the boundary between being and the object which seemed before to mark its outer limit.

That this is the symptom and the prelude of a reexamination of the situation of man in the existent such as has been assumed up to the present by all our postulates of knowledge—don't be content, I beg of you, to write this off as another case of Heideggerianism[s], even prefixed by a neo- which adds nothing to the trashcan style in which currently, by the use of his ready-made mental jetsam, one excuses oneself from any real thought.

When I speak of Heidegger, or rather when I translate him, I at least make the effort to leave the word he proffers us its sovereign significance.

If I speak of being and the letter, if I distinguish the other and the Other, it is only because Freud shows me that they are the terms to which must be referred the effects of resistance and transfer against which, in the twenty years I have engaged in what we all call after him the impossible practice of psychoanalysis, I have done unequal battle. And it is also because I must help others not to lose their way there.

It is to prevent the field of which they are the inheritors from becoming barren, and for that reason to make it understood that if the symptom is a metaphor, it is not a metaphor to say so, no more than to say that man's desire is a metonymy. For the symptom *is* a metaphor whether one likes it or not, as desire *is* a metonymy for all that men mock the idea.

Finally, if I am to rouse you to indignation that, after so many centuries of religious hypocrisy and philosophical bravado, nothing valid has yet been articulated on what links metaphor to the question of being and metonymy to its lack, there must be an object there to answer to that indignation both as its provocator and its victim; it is humanistic man and the credit, affirmed beyond reparation, which he has drawn on his intentions.

[s] Martin Heidegger (1889–1976), German existentialist philosopher.

NOTES

1. The lecture took place on 9th May 1957 in the Descartes Amphi-theatre of the Sorbonne.
2. *Die Frage der Laienanalyse, G. W., XIV*, pp. 281–283.
3. This aspect of aphasia, very suggestive in the direction of an overthrow of the concept of 'psychological function,' which only obscures every aspect of the question, appears in its proper luminosity in the purely linguistic analysis of the two major forms of aphasia worked out by one of the leaders of modern linguistics, Roman Jakobson. See the most available of his works, the *Fundamentals of Language*, with Morris Halle (Mouton and Co., 'S-Gravenhage), part II, Chs. 1 to 4.
4. We may recall that the discussion of the necessity for a new language in the communist society did in fact take place, and Stalin, much to the relief of those depending on his philosophy, cut off the discussion with the decision: language is not a superstructure.
5. By 'linguistics' we understand the study of existing languages in their structure and in the laws revealed therein; this leaves out any theory of abstract codes sometimes included under the heading of communication theory, as well as the theory, originating in the physical sciences, called information theory, or any semiology more or less hypothetically generalized.
6. Cf. the *De Magistro* of Saint Augustine, especially the chapter 'De significatione locutionis' which I analysed in my seminar of 23rd June 1954.
7. So, Mr. I. A. Richards, author of a work precisely in accord with such an objective, has in another work shown us its application. He took for his purposes a page from Mong-tse (Mencius to the Jesuits) and called the piece, *Mencius on the Mind*. The guarantees of the purity of the experiment are nothing to the luxury of the approaches. And our expert on the traditional Canon which contains the text is found right on the spot in Peking where our demonstration-model mangle has been transported regardless of cost.

    But we shall be no less transported, if less expensively, to see a bronze which gives out bell-tones at the slightest contact with true thought, transformed into a rag to wipe the blackboard of the most dismaying British psychologism. And not without eventually being identified with the meninx of the author himself—all that remains of him or his object after having exhausted the meaning of the latter and the good sense of the former.
8. To which verbal hallucination, when it takes this form, opens a communicating door with the Freudian structure of psychosis—a door until now unnoticed.
9. The allusions are to the 'I am black, but comely . . .' of the *Song of Solomon* and to the nineteenth-century cliché of the 'poor but honest' woman. (Trans.)
10. We spoke in our seminar of 6th June 1956, of the first scene of *Athalie*, incited by an allusion—tossed off by a high-brow critic in the *New Statesman and Nation*—to the 'high whoredom' of Racine's heroines, to renounce reference to the savage dramas of Shakespeare, which have become compulsional in analytic milieux where they play the role of status-symbol for the Philistines.
11.

    > Non! dit l'Arbre, il dit: Non! dans l'étincellement
    >   De sa tête superbe
    > Que la tempête traite universellement
    >   Comme elle fait une herbe.

    Lines from Valery's 'Au Platane' in *Les Charmes*. (Trans.)

12. We give homage here to the works of Roman Jakobson—to which we owe much of this formulation; works to which a psychoanalyst can constantly refer in order to structure his own experience, and which render superfluous the 'personal communications' of which we could boast as much as the next fellow.

    Let us thank also, in this context, the author [R. M Loewenstein] of 'Some remarks on the role of speech in psycho-analytic technique' (I.J.P., Nov.–Dec., 1956, XXXVII, 6, p. 467) for taking the trouble to point out that his remarks are 'based on' work dating from 1952. This is no doubt the explanation for the fact that he has learned nothing from work done since then, yet which he is not ignorant of, as he cites me as their editor (sic).
13. 'Sa gerbe n'était pas avare ni haineuse,' a line from 'Booz endormi.' (Trans.)

14. Leo Strauss, *Persecution and the Art of Writing*, The Free Press, Glencoe, Ill.
15. See the correspondence, namely letters 107 and 109.
16. That is the process by which the results of a piece of research are assured through a mechanical exploration of the entire extent of the field of its object.
17. The sign ~ here represents congruence.
18. (S' i.e. prime) designating here the term productive of the signifying effect (or significance); one can see that the term is latent in metonymy, patent in metaphor.
19. It is quite otherwise if by posing a question such as 'Why philosophers?' I become more candid than nature, for then I am asking the question which philosophers have been asking themselves for all time and also the one in which they are in fact the most interested.
20. A German comic newspaper of the late nineteenth and early twentieth centuries. (Trans.)
21. *Fetischismus*, G. W., XIV, p. 311.
22. One of my Colleagues went so far in this direction as to wonder if the Id of the last phase wasn't in fact the 'bad Ego.'
23. Note, none the less, the tone with which one spoke in that period of the 'elfin pranks' of the unconscious; a work of Silberer's is called, *Der Zufall und die Koboldstreiche des Unbewussten*—completely anachronistic in the context of our present soul-managers.
24. To pick the most recent in date, François Mauriac, in the *Figaro Littéraire* of May 25, excuses himself for not 'narrating his life.' If no one these days can undertake to do that with the old enthusiasm, the reason is that, 'a half century since, Freud, whatever we think of him' has already passed that way. And after being briefly tempted by the old saw that this is only the 'history of our body,' Mauriac returns to the truth that his sensitivity as a writer makes him face: to write the history of oneself is to write the confession of the deepest part of our neighbors' souls as well.

6 Jacques Derrida

Jacques Derrida (b. 1930) is a French philosopher, who teaches philosophy at the Ecole Normale Supérieure in Paris. He has, however, arguably had more influence on literary studies than on philosophy, especially in the universities of America, where a school of 'deconstructive' criticism, drawing much of its inspiration from Derrida, has been a major force in the 1970s and 80s, and where he himself is a frequent visitor.

'Structure, Sign and Play in the Human Sciences' in fact belongs to a historic moment in the traffic of ideas between Europe and America. It was originally a paper contributed to a conference entitled 'The Languages of Criticism and the Sciences of Man', held at Johns Hopkins University, Baltimore, in 1966, at which the American academic world experienced at first hand the challenge of the new ideas and methodologies in the humanities generated by European structuralism. (Present on this occasion, as well as Derrida, were Lucien Goldmann, Tzvetan Todorov, Roland Barthes and Jacques Lacan.)

'Structure, Sign and Play' marks the moment at which 'post-structuralism' as a movement begins, opposing itself to classical structuralism as well as to traditional humanism and empiricism: the moment, as Derrida himself puts it, when 'the structurality of structure had to begin to be thought'. Classical structuralism, based on Saussure's linguistics, held out the hope of achieving a 'scientific' account of culture by identifying the *system* that underlies the infinite manifestations of any form of cultural production. The structural anthropology of Claude Lévi-Strauss tried to do this for myth. (See Lévi-Strauss, 'Incest and Myth', section 40 in *20th Century Literary Criticism*.) But, says Derrida, all such analyses imply that they are based on some secure ground, a 'centre' or 'transcendental signified', that is outside the system under investigation and guarantees its intelligibility. There is, however, no such secure ground, according to Derrida—it is a philosophical fiction. He sees Lévi-Strauss as making this disconcerting discovery in the course of his researches, and then retreating from a full recognition of its implications. Lévi-Strauss renounces the hope of a totalizing scientific explanation of cultural phenomena, but on equivocal grounds—sometimes because it is impossible (new data will always require modification of the systematic model) and sometimes because it is useless (discourse is a field not of finite meanings but of infinite play).

Derrida himself had no qualms about embracing 'a world of signs without fault, without truth and without origin, which is offered to our active interpretation', and fathered a new school of criticism based on this *donnée*: deconstruction.

Taking its cue from Derrida's assertion in 'Structure, Sign and Play' that 'language bears within itself the necessity of its own critique', deconstructive criticism aims to show that any text inevitably undermines its own claim to have a determinate meaning, and licences the reader to produce his own meanings out of it by an activity of semantic 'freeplay'.

'Structure, Sign and Play in the Discourse of the Human Sciences' is reprinted here from Jacques Derrida, *Writing and Difference*, trans. Alan Bass (1978). Other books by Derrida which have been influential in literary studies and have been translated into English include *Of Grammatology* (1976) and *Dissemination* (1982).

CROSS-REFERENCES: 4. Genette
5. Lacan
9. Barthes
15. Abrams
16. Miller

COMMENTARY: Jonathan Culler, 'Derrida', in John Sturrock, *Structuralism and Since* (1979) and *On Deconstruction: theory and criticism after structuralism* (1983)
Christopher Norris, *Deconstruction: theory and practice* (1982)

Structure, sign and play in the discourse of the human sciences

We need to interpret interpretations more than to interpret things.
(Montaigne)

Perhaps something has occurred in the history of the concept of structure that could be called an 'event,' if this loaded word did not entail a meaning which it is precisely the function of structural—or structuralist—thought to reduce or to suspect. Let us speak of an 'event,' nevertheless, and let us use quotation marks to serve as a precaution. What would this event be then? Its exterior form would be that of a *rupture* and a redoubling.

It would be easy enough to show that the concept of structure and even the word 'structure' itself are as old as the *epistēmē* [a]—that is to say, as old as Western science and Western philosophy—and that their roots thrust deep into the soil of ordinary language, into whose deepest recesses the *epistēmē* plunges in order

[a] A term coined by Michel Foucault (see below, pp. 196–210) to refer to 'the total set of relations that unite, at a given period, the discursive practices that give rise to epistemological figures, sciences, and possibly formalized systems of knowledge'.

to gather them up and to make them part of itself in a metaphorical displacement. Nevertheless, up to the event which I wish to mark out and define, structure— or rather the structurality of structure—although it has always been at work, has always been neutralized or reduced, and this by a process of giving it a center or of referring it to a point of presence, a fixed origin. The function of this center was not only to orient, balance, and organize the structure—one cannot in fact conceive of an unorganized structure—but above all to make sure that the organizing principle of the structure would limit what we might call the *play* of the structure. By orienting and organizing the coherence of the system, the center of a structure permits the play of its elements inside the total form. And even today the notion of a structure lacking any center represents the unthinkable itself.

Nevertheless, the center also closes off the play which it opens up and makes possible. As center, it is the point at which the substitution of contents, elements, or terms is no longer possible. At the center, the permutation of the transform-ation of elements (which may of course be structures enclosed within a structure) is forbidden. At least this permutation has always remained *interdicted* (and I am using this word deliberately). Thus it has always been thought that the center, which is by definition unique, constituted that very thing within a structure which while governing the structure, escapes structurality. This is why classical thought concerning structure could say that the center is, paradoxically, *within* the struc-ture and *outside it*. The center is at the center of the totality, and yet, since the center does not belong to the totality (is not part of the totality), the totality *has its center elsewhere*. The center is not the center. The concept of centered struc-ture—although it represents coherence itself, the condition of the *epistēmē* as philosophy or science—is contradictorily coherent. And as always, coherence in contradiction expresses the force of a desire.[1] The concept of centered structure is in fact the concept of a play based on a fundamental ground, a play constituted on the basis of a fundamental immobility and a reassuring certitude, which itself is beyond the reach of play. And on the basis of this certitude anxiety can be mastered, for anxiety is invariably the result of a certain mode of being implicated in the game, of being caught by the game, of being as it were at stake in the game from the outset. And again on the basis of what we call the center (and which, because it can be either inside or outside, can also indifferently be called the origin or end, *archē* or *telos*), repetitions, substitutions, transformations, and permutations are always *taken* from a history of meaning [*sens*]—that is, in a word, a history—whose origin may always be reawakened or whose end may always be anticipated in the form of presence. This is why one perhaps could say that the movement of any archaeology, like that of any eschatology, is an accomplice of this reduction of the structurality of structure and always attempts to conceive of structure on the basis of a full presence which is beyond play.

If this is so, the entire history of the concept of structure, before the rupture of which we are speaking, must be thought of as a series of substitutions of center for center, as a linked chain of determinations of the center. Successively, and in a regulated fashion, the center receives different forms or names. The history of metaphysics, like the history of the West, is the history of these metaphors and metonymies. Its matrix—if you will pardon me for demonstrating so little and for being so elliptical in order to come more quickly to my principal theme—is the determination of Being as *presence* in all senses of this word. It could be shown that all the names related to fundamentals, to principles, or to the center have always designated an invariable presence—*eidos, archē, telos, energeia, ousia* (essence, existence, substance, subject) *alētheia*, transcendentality, consciousness, God, man, and so forth.

The event I called a rupture, the disruption I alluded to at the beginning of this paper, presumably would have come about when the structurality of structure had to begin to be thought, that is to say, repeated, and this is why I said that this disruption was repetition in every sense of the word. Henceforth, it became necessary to think both the law which somehow governed the desire for a center in the constitution of structure, and the process of signification which orders the displacements and substitutions for this law of central presence—but a central presence which has never been itself, has always already been exiled from itself into its own substitute. The substitute does not substitute itself for anything which has somehow existed before it. Henceforth, it was necessary to begin thinking that there was no center, that the center could not be thought in the form of a present-being, that the center had no natural site, that it was not a fixed locus but a function, a sort of nonlocus in which an infinite number of sign-substitutions came into play. This was the moment when language invaded the universal problematic, the moment when, in the absence of a center or origin, everything became discourse—provided we can agree on this word—that is to say, a system in which the central signified, the original or transcendental signified, is never absolutely present outside a system of differences. The absence of the transcendental signified extends the domain and the play of signification infinitely.

Where and how does this decentering, this thinking the structurality of structure, occur? It would be somewhat naive to refer to an event, a doctrine, or an author in order to designate this occurrence. It is no doubt part of the totality of an era, our own, but still it has always already begun to proclaim itself and begun to *work*. Nevertheless, if we wished to choose several 'names,' as indications only, and to recall those authors in whose discourse this occurrence has kept most closely to its most radical formulation, we doubtless would have to cite the Nietzchean critique of metaphysics, the critique of the concepts of Being and truth, for which were substituted the concepts of play, interpretation, and sign (sign without present truth); the Freudian critique of self-presence, that is, the critique of consciousness, of the subject, of self-identity and of self-proximity or self-possession; and, more radically, the Heideggerean destruction of metaphysics, of onto-theology, of the determination of Being as presence.[b] But all these destructive discourses and all their analogues are trapped in a kind of circle. This circle is unique. It describes the form of the relation between the history of metaphysics and the destruction of the history of metaphysics. There is no sense in doing without the concepts of metaphysics in order to shake

[b] See p. 104 n.s, above.

metaphysics. We have no language—no syntax and no lexicon—which is foreign to this history; we can pronounce not a single destructive proposition which has not already had to slip into the form, the logic, and the implicit postulations of precisely what it seeks to contest. To take one example from many: the metaphysics of presence is shaken with the help of the concept of *sign*. But, as I suggested a moment ago, as soon as one seeks to demonstrate in this way that there is no transcendental or privileged signified and that the domain or play of signification henceforth has no limit, one must reject even the concept and word 'sign' itself—which is precisely what cannot be done. For the signification 'sign' has always been understood and determined, in its meaning, as sign-of, a signifier referring to a signified, a signifier different from its signified. If one erases the radical difference between signifier and signified, it is the word 'signifier' itself which must be abandoned as a metaphysical concept. When Lévi-Strauss says in the preface to *The Raw and the Cooked* that he has 'sought to transcend the opposition between the sensible and the intelligible by operating from the outset at the level of signs,'[2] the necessity, force, and legitimacy of his act cannot make us forget that the concept of the sign cannot in itself surpass this opposition between the sensible[c] and the intelligible. The concept of the sign, in each of its aspects, has been determined by this opposition throughout the totality of its history. It has lived only on this opposition and its system. But we cannot do without the concept of the sign, for we cannot give up this metaphysical complicity without also giving up the critique we are directing against this complicity, or without the risk of erasing difference in the self-identity of a signified reducing its signifier into itself or, amounting to the same thing, simply expelling its signifier outside itself. For there are two heterogenous ways of erasing the difference between the signifier and the signified: one, the classic way, consists in reducing or deriving the signifier, that is to say, ultimately in *submitting* the sign to thought; the other, the one we are using here against the first one, consists in putting into question the system in which the preceding reduction functioned: first and foremost, the opposition between the sensible and the intelligible. For the *paradox* is that the metaphysical reduction of the sign needed the opposition it was reducing. The opposition is systematic with the reduction. And what we are saying here about the sign can be extended to all the concepts and all the sentences of metaphysics, in particular to the discourse on 'structure.' But there are several ways of being caught in this circle. They are all more or less naive, more or less empirical, more or less systematic, more or less close to the formulation—that is, to the formalization—of this circle. It is these differences which explain the multiplicity of destructive discourses and the disagreement between those who elaborate them. Nietzsche, Freud, and Heidegger, for example, worked within the inherited concepts of metaphysics. Since these concepts are not elements or atoms, and since they are taken from a syntax and a system, every particular borrowing brings along with it the whole of metaphysics. This is what allows these destroyers to destroy each other reciprocally—for example, Heidegger regarding Nietzsche, with as much lucidity and

[c] 'Sensible' meaning 'perceptible through the senses'.

111

rigor as bad faith and misconstruction, as the last metaphysician, the last 'Platonist.' One could do the same for Heidegger himself, for Freud, or for a number of others. And today no exercise is more widespread.

What is the relevance of this formal schema when we turn to what are called the 'human sciences'? One of them perhaps occupies a privileged place—ethnology. In fact one can assume that ethnology could have been born as a science only at the moment when a decentering had come about: at the moment when European culture—and, in consequence, the history of metaphysics and of its concepts—had been *dislocated*, driven from its locus, and forced to stop considering itself as the culture of reference. This moment is not first and foremost a moment of philosophical or scientific discourse. It is also a moment which is political, economic, technical, and so forth. One can say with total security that there is nothing fortuitous about the fact that the critique of ethnocentrism—the very condition for ethnology—should be systematically and historically contemporaneous with the destruction of the history of metaphysics. Both belong to one and the same era. Now, ethnology—like any science—comes about within the element of discourse. And it is primarily a European science employing traditional concepts, however much it may struggle against them. Consequently, whether he wants to or not—and this does not depend on a decision on his part—the ethnologist accepts into his discourse the premises of ethnocentrism at the very moment when he denounces them. This necessity is irreducible; it is not a historical contingency. We ought to consider all its implications very carefully. But if no one can escape this necessity, and if no one is therefore responsible for giving in to it, however little he may do so, this does not mean that all the ways of giving in to it are of equal pertinence. The quality and fecundity of a discourse are perhaps measured by the critical rigor with which this relation to the history of metaphysics and to inherited concepts is thought. Here it is a question both of a critical relation to the language of the social sciences and a critical responsibility of the discourse itself. It is a question of explicitly and systematically posing the problem of the status of a discourse which borrows from a heritage the resources necessary for the deconstruction of that heritage itself. A problem of *economy* and *strategy*.

If we consider, as an example, the texts of Claude Lévi-Strauss, it is not only because of the privilege accorded to ethnology among the social sciences, nor even because the thought of Lévi-Strauss weighs heavily on the contemporary theoretical situation. It is above all because a certain choice has been declared in the work of Lévi-Strauss and because a certain doctrine has been elaborated there, and precisely, in a *more or less explicit manner*, as concerns both this critique of language and this critical language in the social sciences.

In order to follow this movement in the text of Lévi-Strauss, let us choose as one guiding thread among others the opposition between nature and culture. Despite all its rejuvenations and disguises, this opposition is congenital to philosophy. It is even older than Plato. It is at least as old as the Sophists[d]. Since the statement of the opposition *physis/nomos, physis/technē*, it has been relayed to

[d] Philosophers and teachers active in Greece in the fifth century BC.

us by means of a whole historical chain which opposes 'nature' to law, to education, to art, to technics—but also to liberty, to the arbitrary, to history, to society, to the mind, and so on. Now, from the outset of his researches, and from his first book (*The Elementary Structures of Kinship*) on, Lévi-Strauss simultaneously has experienced the necessity of utilizing this opposition and the impossibility of accepting it. In the *Elementary Structures*, he begins from this axiom or definition: that which is *universal* and spontaneous, and not dependent on any particular culture or on any determinate norm, belongs to nature. Inversely, that which depends upon a system of *norms* regulating society and therefore is capable of *varying* from one social structure to another, belongs to culture. These two definitions are of the traditional type. But in the very first pages of the *Elementary Structures* Lévi-Strauss, who has begun by giving credence to these concepts, encounters what he calls a *scandal*, that is to say, something which no longer tolerates the nature/culture opposition he has accepted, something which *simultaneously* seems to require the predicates of nature and of culture. This scandal is the *incest prohibition*. The incest prohibition is universal; in this sense one could call it natural. But it is also a prohibition, a system of norms and interdicts; in this sense one could call it cultural:

> Let us suppose then that everything universal in man relates to the
> natural order, and is characterized by spontaneity, and that everything
> subject to a norm is cultural and is both relative and particular. We are
> then confronted with a fact, or rather, a group of facts, which, in the
> light of previous definitions, are not far removed from a scandal: we refer
> to that complex group of beliefs, customs, conditions and institutions
> described succinctly as the prohibition of incest, which presents, without
> the slightest ambiguity, and inseparably combines, the two characteristics
> in which we recognize the conflicting features of two mutually exclusive
> orders. It constitutes a rule, but a rule which, alone among all the social
> rules, possesses at the same time a universal character.[3]

Obviously there is no scandal except within a system of concepts which accredits the difference between nature and culture. By commencing his work with the *factum* of the incest prohibition, Lévi-Strauss thus places himself at the point at which this difference, which has always been assumed to be self-evident, finds itself erased or questioned. For from the moment when the incest prohibition can no longer be conceived within the nature/culture opposition, it can no longer be said to be a scandalous fact, a nucleus of opacity within a network of transparent significations. The incest prohibition is no longer a scandal one meets with or comes up against in the domain of traditional concepts; it is something which escapes these concepts and certainly precedes them—probably as the condition of their possibility. It could perhaps be said that the whole of philosophical conceptualization, which is systematic with the nature/culture opposition, is designed to leave in the domain of the unthinkable the very thing that makes this conceptualization possible: the origin of the prohibition of incest.

This example, too cursorily examined, is only one among many others, but nevertheless it already shows that language bears within itself the necessity of its own critique. Now this critique may be undertaken along two paths, in two 'manners.' Once the limit of the nature/culture opposition makes itself felt, one might want to question systematically and rigorously the history of these concepts. This is a first action. Such a systematic and historic questioning would be neither a philological nor a philosophical action in the classic sense of these words. To concern oneself with the founding concepts of the entire history of philosophy, to deconstitute them, is not to undertake the work of the philologist or of the classic historian of philosophy. Despite appearances, it is probably the most daring way of making the beginnings of a step outside of philosophy. The step 'outside philosophy' is much more difficult to conceive than is generally imagined by those who think they made it long ago with cavalier ease, and who in general are swallowed up in metaphysics in the entire body of discourse which they claim to have disengaged from it.

The other choice (which I believe corresponds more closely to Lévi-Strauss's manner), in order to avoid the possibly sterilizing effects of the first one, consists in conserving all these old concepts within the domain of empirical discovery while here and there denouncing their limits, treating them as tools which can still be used. No longer is any truth value attributed to them: there is a readiness to abandon them, if necessary, should other instruments appear more useful. In the meantime, their relative efficacy is exploited, and they are employed to destroy the old machinery to which they belong and of which they themselves are pieces. This is how the language of the social sciences criticizes *itself*. Lévi-Strauss thinks that in this way he can separate *method* from *truth*, the instruments of the method and the objective significations envisaged by it. One could almost say that this is the primary affirmation of Lévi-Strauss; in any event, the first words of the *Elementary Structures* are: 'Above all, it is beginning to emerge that this distinction between nature and society ('nature' and 'culture' seem preferable to us today), while of no acceptable historical significance, does contain a logic, fully justifying its use by modern sociology as a methodological tool.'[4]

Lévi-Strauss will always remain faithful to this double intention: to preserve as an instrument something whose truth value he criticizes.

On the one hand, he will continue, in effect, to contest the value of the nature/culture opposition. More than thirteen years after the *Elementary Structures*, *The Savage Mind* faithfully echoes the text I have just quoted: 'The opposition between nature and culture to which I attached much importance at one time . . . now seems to be of primarily methodological importance.' And this methodological value is not affected by its 'ontological' nonvalue (as might be said, if this notion were not suspect here): 'However, it would not be enough to re-absorb particular humanities into a general one. This first enterprise opens the way for others which . . . are incumbent on the exact natural sciences: the reintegration of culture in nature and finally of life within the whole of its physico-chemical conditions.'[5]

On the other hand, still in *The Savage Mind*, he presents as what he calls *bricolage* what might be called the discourse of this method. The *bricoleur*, says Lévi-Strauss, is someone who uses 'the means at hand,' that is, the instruments he finds at his disposition around him, those which are already there, which had not been especially conceived with an eye to the operation for which they are to be used and to which one tries by trial and error to adapt them, not hesitating to change them whenever it appears necessary, or to try several of them at once, even if their form and their origin are heterogenous—and so forth. There is therefore a critique of language in the form of *bricolage*, and it has even been said that *bricolage* is critical language itself. I am thinking in particular of the article of G. Genette, 'Structuralisme et critique littéraire,'[e] published in homage to Lévi-Strauss in a special issue of *L'Arc* (no. 26, 1965), where it is stated that the analysis of *bricolage* could 'be applied almost word for word' to criticism, and especially to 'literary criticism.'

If one calls *bricolage* the necessity of borrowing one's concepts from the text of a heritage which is more or less coherent or ruined, it must be said that every discourse is *bricoleur*. The engineer, whom Lévi-Strauss opposes to the *bricoleur*, should be the one to construct the totality of his language, syntax, and lexicon. In this sense the engineer is a myth. A subject who supposedly would be the absolute origin of his own discourse and supposedly would construct it 'out of nothing,' 'out of whole cloth,' would be the creator of the verb, the verb itself. The notion of the engineer who supposedly breaks with all forms of *bricolage* is therefore a theological idea; and since Lévi-Strauss tells us elsewhere that *bricolage* is mythopoetic, the odds are that the engineer is a myth produced by the *bricoleur*. As soon as we cease to believe in such an engineer and in a discourse which breaks with the received historical discourse, and as soon as we admit that every finite discourse is bound by a certain *bricolage* and that the engineer and the scientist are also species of *bricoleurs*, then the very idea of *bricolage* is menaced and the difference in which it took on its meaning breaks down.

This brings us to the second thread which might guide us in what is being contrived here.

Lévi-Strauss describes *bricolage* not only as an intellectual activity but also as a mythopoetical activity. One reads in *The Savage Mind* 'Like *bricolage* on the technical plane, mythical reflection can reach brilliant unforeseen results on the intellectual plane. Conversely, attention has often been drawn to the mytho-poetical nature of *bricolage*.'[6]

But Lévi-Strauss's remarkable endeavor does not simply consist in proposing, notably in his most recent investigations, a structural science of myths and of mythological activity. His endeavor also appears—I would say almost from the outset—to have the status which he accords to his own discourse on myths, to what he calls his 'mythologicals.' It is here that his discourse on the myth reflects on itself and criticizes itself. And this moment, this critical period, is evidently of concern to all the languages which share the field of the human sciences. What does Lévi-Strauss say of his 'mythologicals'? It is here that we rediscover the mythopoetical virtue of *bricolage*. In effect, what appears most fascinating in this critical search for a new status of discourse is the stated abandonment of all reference to a *center*, to a *subject*, to a privileged *reference*, to an origin, or to an

---

[e] See Gérard Genette, 'Structuralism and Literary Criticism', pp. 62–78 above.

absolute *archia* [beginning]. The theme of this decentering could be followed throughout the 'Overture' to his last book, *The Raw and the Cooked*. I shall simply remark on a few key points.

1. From the very start, Lévi-Strauss recognizes that the Bororo myth which he employs in the book as the 'reference myth' does not merit this name and this treatment. The name is specious and the use of the myth improper. This myth deserves no more than any other its referential privilege: 'In fact, the Bororo myth, which I shall refer to from now on as the key myth, is, as I shall try to show, simply a transformation, to a greater or lesser extent, of other myths originating either in the same society or in neighboring or remote societies. I could, therefore, have legitimately taken as my starting point any one representative myth of the group. From this point of view, the key myth is interesting not because it is typical, but rather because of its irregular position within the group.'[7]

2. There is no unity or absolute source of the myth. The focus or the source of the myth are always shadows and virtualities which are elusive, unactualizable, and nonexistent in the first place. Everything begins with structure, configuration, or relationship. The discourse on the acentric structure that myth itself is, cannot itself have an absolute subject or an absolute center. It must avoid the violence that consists in centering a language which describes an acentric structure if it is not to shortchange the form and movement of myth. Therefore it is necessary to forego scientific or philosophical discourse, to renounce the *epistémē* which absolutely requires, which is the absolute requirement that we go back to the source, to the center, to the founding basis, to the principle, and so on. In opposition to *epistemic* discourse, structural discourse on myths—*mythological* discourse—must itself be *mythomorphic*. It must have the form of that of which it speaks. This is what Lévi-Strauss says in *The Raw and the Cooked*, from which I would now like to quote a long and remarkable passage:

> The study of myths raises a methodological problem, in that it cannot be carried out according to the Cartesian principle of breaking down the difficulty into as many parts as may be necessary for finding the solution. There is no real end to methodological analysis, no hidden unity to be grasped once the breaking-down process has been completed. Themes can be split up *ad infinitum*. Just when you think you have disentangled and separated them, you realize that they are knitting together again in response to the operation of unexpected affinities. Consequently the unity of the myth is never more than tendential and projective and cannot reflect a state or a particular moment of the myth. It is a phenomenon of the imagination, resulting from the attempt at interpretation; and its function is to endow the myth with synthetic form and to prevent its disintegration into a confusion of opposites. The science of myths might therefore be termed 'anaclastic,' if we take this old term in the broader etymological sense which includes the study of both reflected rays and broken rays. But unlike philosophical reflection, which aims to go back to its own source, the reflections we are dealing with here concern rays whose only source is hypothetical. . . . And in seeking to imitate the

spontaneous movement of mythological thought, this essay, which is also both too brief and too long, has had to conform to the requirements of that thought and to respect its rhythm. It follows that this book on myths is itself a kind of myth.[8]

This statement is repeated a little farther on: 'As the myths themselves are based on secondary codes (the primary codes being those that provide the substance of language), the present work is put forward as a tentative draft of a tertiary code, which is intended to ensure the reciprocal translatability of several myths. This is why it would not be wrong to consider this book itself as a myth: it is, as it were, the myth of mythology.'[9] The absence of a center is here the absence of a subject and the absence of an author: 'Thus the myth and the musical work are like conductors of an orchestra, whose audience becomes the silent performers. If it is now asked where the real center of the work is to be found, the answer is that this is impossible to determine. Music and mythology bring man face to face with potential objects of which only the shadows are actualized. . . . Myths are anonymous.'[10] The musical model chosen by Lévi-Strauss for the composition of his book is apparently justified by this absence of any real fixed center of the mythical or mythological discourse.

Thus it is at this point that ethnographic *bricolage* deliberately assumes its mythopoetic function. But by the same token, this function makes the philosophical or epistemological requirement of a center appear as mythological, that is to say, as a historical illusion.

Nevertheless, even if one yields to the necessity of what Lévi-Strauss has done, one cannot ignore its risks. If the mythological is mythomorphic, are all discourses on myths equivalent? Shall we have to abandon any epistemological requirement which permits us to distinguish between several qualities of discourse on the myth? A classic, but inevitable question. It cannot be answered—and I believe that Lévi-Strauss does not answer it—for as long as the problem of the relations between the philosopheme or the theorem, on the one hand, and the mytheme or the mythopoem, on the other, has not been posed explicitly, which is no small problem. For lack of explicitly posing this problem, we condemn ourselves to transforming the alleged trangression of philosophy into an unnoticed fault within the philosophical realm. Empiricism would be the genus of which these faults would always be the species. Transphilosophical concepts would be transformed into philosophical naivetés. Many examples could be given to demonstrate this risk: the concepts of sign, history, truth, and so forth. What I want to emphasize is simply that the passage beyond philosophy does not consist in turning the page of philosophy (which usually amounts to philosophizing badly), but in continuing to read philosophers *in a certain way*. The risk I am speaking of is always assumed by Lévi-Strauss, and it is the very price of this endeavor. I have said that empiricism is the matrix of all faults menacing a discourse which continues, as with Lévi-Strauss in particular, to consider itself scientific. If we wanted to pose the problem of empiricism and *bricolage* in depth, we would probably end up very quickly with a number of absolutely contradictory propositions concerning the status of discourse in structural ethnology. On the one hand, structuralism justifiably claims to be the critique of empiricism. But at the same time there is not a single book or study by Lévi-Strauss which is not proposed as an empirical essay which can always be completed or invalidated by new information. The structural schemata are always proposed as hypotheses resulting from a finite quantity of information and which are subjected to the proof of experience. Numerous texts could be used to demonstrate this double postulation. Let us turn once again to the 'Overture' of *The Raw and the Cooked*, where it seems clear that if this postulation is double, it is because it is a question here of a language on language:

> If critics reproach me with not having carried out an exhaustive inventory of South American myths before analyzing them, they are making a grave mistake about the nature and function of these documents. The total body of myth belonging to a given community is comparable to its speech. Unless the population dies out physically or morally, this totality is never complete. You might as well criticize a linguist for compiling the grammar of a language without having complete records of the words pronounced since the language came into being, and without knowing what will be said in it during the future part of its existence. Experience proves, that a linguist can work out the grammar of a given language from a remarkably small number of sentences. . . . And even a partial grammar or an outline grammar is a precious acquisition when we are dealing with unknown languages. Syntax does not become evident only after a (theoretically limitless) series of events has been recorded and examined, because it is itself the body of rules governing their production. What I have tried to give is an outline of the syntax of South American mythology. Should fresh data come to hand, they will be used to check or modify the formulation of certain grammatical laws, so that some are abandoned and replaced by new ones. But in no instance would I feel constrained to accept the arbitrary demand for a total mythological pattern, since, as has been shown, such a requirement has no meaning.[11]

Totalization, therefore, is sometimes defined as *useless*, and sometimes as *impossible*. This is no doubt due to the fact that there are two ways of conceiving the limit of totalization. And I assert once more that these two determinations coexist implicitly in Lévi-Strauss's discourse. Totalization can be judged impossible in the classical style: one then refers to the empirical endeavor of either a subject or a finite richness which it can never master. There is too much, more than one can say. But nontotalization can also be determined in another way: no longer from the standpoint of a concept of finitude as relegation to the empirical, but from the standpoint of the concept of *play*. If totalization no longer has any meaning, it is not because the infiniteness of a field cannot be covered by a finite glance or a finite discourse, but because the nature of the field—that is, language and a finite language—excludes totalization. This field is in effect that of *play*, that is to say, a field of infinite substitutions only because it is finite, that is to say, because instead of being too large, there is something missing from it: a center which arrests and grounds the play of substitutions. One could say—rigorously using that word whose scandalous signification is always obliterated in French—that this movement of play, permitted by the lack or absence of a center or origin, is the movement of *supplementarity*. One cannot determine the center and exhaust totalization because the sign which replaces the center, which supplements it, taking the center's place in its absence—this sign is added, occurs as a surplus, as a *supplement*.[12] The movement of signification adds something, which results in the fact that there is always more, but this addition is a floating one because it comes to perform a vicarious function, to supplement a lack on the part of the signified. Although Lévi-Strauss in his use of the word 'supplementary' never emphasizes, as I do here, the two directions of meaning which are so strangely compounded within it, it is not by chance that he uses this word twice in his 'Introduction to the Work of Marcel Mauss,' at one point where he is speaking of the 'overabundance of signifier, in relation to the signifieds to which this overabundance can refer':

> In his endeavor to understand the world, man therefore always has at his disposal a surplus of signification (which he shares out amongst things according to the laws of symbolic thought—which is the task of ethnologists and linguists to study). This distribution of a *supplementary* allowance [*ration supplémentaire*]—if it is permissible to put it that way—is absolutely necessary in order that on the whole the available signifier and the signified it aims at may remain in the relationship of complementarity which is the very condition of the use of symbolic thought.[13]

(It could no doubt be demonstrated that this *ration supplémentaire* of signification is the origin of the *ratio* itself.) The word reappears a little further on, after Lévi-Strauss has mentioned 'this floating signifier, which is the servitude of all finite thought':

> In other words—and taking as our guide Mauss's precept that all social phenomena can be assimilated to language—we see in *mana, Wakau, oranda* and other notions of the same type, the conscious expression of a semantic function, whose role it is to permit symbolic thought to operate in spite of the contradiction which is proper to it. In this way are explained the apparently insoluble antinomies attached to this notion. . . . At one and the same time force and action, quality and state, noun and verb; abstract and concrete, omnipresent and localized—*mana* is in effect all these things. But is it not precisely because it is none of these things that *mana* is a simple form, or more exactly, a symbol in the pure state, and therefore capable of becoming charged with any sort of symbolic content whatever? In the system of symbols constituted by all cosmologies, *mana* would simply be a zero symbolic value, that is to say, a sign marking the necessity of a symbolic content *supplementary* [my italics] to that with which the signified is already loaded, but which can take on any value required, provided only that this value still remains part of the available reserve and is not, as phonologists put it, a group-term.

Lévi-Strauss adds the note:

'Linguists have already been led to formulate hypotheses of this type. For example: "A zero phoneme is opposed to all the other phonemes in French in that it entails no differential characters and no constant phonetic value. On the contrary, the proper function of the zero phoneme is to be opposed to phoneme absence." (R. Jakobson and J. Lutz, 'Notes on the French Phonemic Pattern,' *Word* 5, no. 2 [August 1949]:155). Similarly, if we schematize the conception I am proposing here, it could almost be said that the function of notions like *mana* is to be opposed to the absence of signification, without entailing by itself any particular signification.'[14]

The *overabundance* of the signifier, its *supplementary* character, is thus the result of a finitude, that is to say, the result of a lack which must be *supplemented*.

It can now be understood why the concept of play is important in Lévi-Strauss. His references to all sorts of games, notably to roulette, are very frequent, especially in his *Conversations*,[15] in *Race and History*,[16] and in *The Savage Mind*. Further, the reference to play is always caught up in tension.

Tension with history, first of all. This is a classical problem, objections to which are now well worn. I shall simply indicate what seems to me the formality of the problem: by reducing history, Lévi-Strauss has treated as it deserves a concept which has always been in complicity with a teleological and eschatological metaphysics, in other words, paradoxically, in complicity with that philosophy of presence to which it was believed history could be opposed. The thematic of historicity, although it seems to be a somewhat late arrival in philosophy, has always been required by the determination of Being as presence. With or without etymology, and despite the classic antagonism which opposes these significations throughout all of classical thought, it could be shown that the concept of *epistēmē* has always called forth that of *historia*, if history is always the unity of a becoming, as the tradition of truth or the development of science or knowledge oriented toward the appropriation of truth in presence and self-presence, toward knowledge in consciousness-of-self. History has always been conceived as the movement of a resumption of history, as a detour between two presences. But if it is legitimate to suspect this concept of history, there is a risk, if it is reduced without an explicit statement of the problem I am indicating here, of falling back into an ahistoricism of a classical type, that is to say, into a determined moment of the history of metaphysics. Such is the algebraic formality of the problem as I see it. More concretely, in the work of Lévi-Strauss it must be recognized that the respect for structurality, for the internal originality of the structure, compels a neutralization of time and history. For example, the appearance of a new structure, of an original system, always comes about—and this is the very condition of its structural specificity—by a rupture with its past, its origin, and its cause. Therefore one can describe what is peculiar to the structural organization only by not taking into account, in the very moment of this description, its past conditions: by omitting to posit the problem of the transition from one structure to another, by putting history between brackets. In this 'structuralist' moment, the concepts of chance and discontinuity are indispensable. And Lévi-Strauss does in fact often appeal to them, for example, as concerns that structure of structures, language, of which he says in the 'Introduction to the Work of Marcel Mauss' that it 'could only have been born in one fell swoop':

> Whatever may have been the moment and the circumstances of its appearance on the scale of animal life, language could only have been born in one fell swoop. Things could not have set about acquiring signification progressively. Following a transformation the study of which is not the concern of the social sciences, but rather of biology and psychology, a transition came about from a stage where nothing had a meaning to another where everything possessed it.[17]

This standpoint does not prevent Lévi-Strauss from recognizing the slowness, the process of maturing, the continuous toil of factual transformations, history (for example, *Race and History*). But, in accordance with a gesture which was also Rousseau's and Husserl's, he must 'set aside all the facts' at the moment when he wishes to recapture the specificity of a structure. Like Rousseau, he must always conceive of the origin of a new structure on the model of catastrophe—an overturning of nature in nature, a natural interruption of the natural sequence, a setting aside *of* nature.

Besides the tension between play and history, there is also the tension between play and presence. Play is the disruption of presence. The presence of an element is always a signifying and substitutive reference inscribed in a system of differences and the movement of a chain. Play is always play of absence and presence, but if it is to be thought radically, play must be conceived of before the alternative of presence and absence. Being must be conceived as presence or absence on the basis of the possibility of play and not the other way around. If Lévi-Strauss, better than any other, has brought to light the play of repetition and the repetition of play, one no less perceives in his work a sort of ethic of presence, an ethic of nostalgia for origins, an ethic of archaic and natural innocence, of a purity of presence and self-presence in speech—an ethic, nostalgia, and even remorse, which he often presents as the motivation of the ethnological project when he moves toward the archaic societies which are exemplary societies in his eyes. These texts are well known.[18]

Turned towards the lost or impossible presence of the absent origin, this structuralist thematic of broken immediacy is therefore the saddened, *negative*, nostalgic, guilty, Rousseauistic side of the thinking of play whose other side would be the Nietzschean *affirmation*, that is the joyous affirmation of the play of the world and of the innocence of becoming, the affirmation of a world of signs without fault, without truth, and without origin which is offered to an active interpretation. *This affirmation then determines the noncenter otherwise than as loss of the center.* And it plays without security. For there is a *sure* play: that which is limited to the *substitution* of *given* and *existing, present*, pieces. In absolute chance, affirmation also surrenders itself to *genetic* indetermination, to the *seminal* adventure of the trace.

There are thus two interpretations of interpretation, of structure, of sign, of play. The one seeks to decipher, dreams of deciphering a truth or an origin which escapes play and the order of the sign, and which lives the necessity of interpretation as an exile. The other, which is no longer turned toward the origin, affirms play and tries to pass beyond man and humanism, the name of man being the name of that being who, throughout the history of metaphysics or of ontotheology—in other words, throughout his entire history—has dreamed of full presence, the reassuring foundation, the origin and the end of play. The second interpretation of interpretation, to which Nietzsche pointed the way, does not seek in ethnography, as Lévi-Strauss does, the 'inspiration of a new humanism' (again citing the 'Introduction to the Work of Marcel Mauss').

There are more than enough indications today to suggest we might perceive that these two interpretations of interpretation—which are absolutely irreconcilable even if we live them simultaneously and reconcile them in an obscure economy—together share the field which we call, in such a problematic fashion, the social sciences.

For my part, although these two interpretations must acknowledge and accentuate their difference and define their irreducibility, I do not believe that today there is any question of *choosing*—in the first place because here we are in a region (let us say, provisionally, a region of historicity) where the category of choice seems particularly trivial; and in the second, because we must first try to conceive of the common ground, and the *différance* of this irreducible difference. Here there is a kind of question, let us still call it historical, whose *conception, formation, gestation,* and *labor* we are only catching a glimpse of today. I employ these words, I admit, with a glance toward the operations of childbearing—but also with a glance toward those who, in a society from which I do not exclude myself, turn their eyes away when faced by the as yet unnamable which is proclaiming itself and which can do so, as is necessary whenever a birth is in the offing, only under the species of the nonspecies, in the formless, mute, infant, and terrifying form of monstrosity.

NOTES

1. The reference, in a restricted sense, is to the Freudian theory of neurotic symptoms and of dream interpretation in which a given symbol is understood contradictorily as both the desire to fulfill an impulse and the desire to suppress the impulse. In a general sense the reference is to Derrida's thesis that logic and coherence themselves can only be understood contradictorily, since they presuppose the suppression of *différance*, 'writing' in the sense of the general economy. Cf. 'La pharmacie de Platon,' in *La dissemination*, pp. 125–26, where Derrida uses the Freudian model of dream interpretation in order to clarify the contractions embedded in philosophical coherence. [Translator's Note]
2. *The Raw and the Cooked*, trans. John and Doreen Wightman (New York: Harper and Row, 1969), p. 14. [Translation somewhat modified.]
3. *The Elementary Structures of Kinship*, trans. James Bell, John von Sturmer, and Rodney Needham (Boston: Beacon Press, 1969), p. 8.
4. Ibid., p. 3.
5. *The Savage Mind* (London: George Weidenfeld and Nicolson; Chicago: The University of Chicago Press, 1966), p. 247.
6. Ibid., p. 17.

f Derrida's term punningly unites the senses of 'to differ' and 'to defer'.

7. *The Raw and the Cooked*, p. 2.
8. Ibid., pp. 5–6.
9. Ibid., p. 12.
10. Ibid., pp. 17–18.
11. Ibid., pp. 7–8.
12. This double sense of supplement—to supply something which is missing, or to supply something additional—is at the center of Derrida's deconstruction of traditional linguistics in *De la grammatologie*. In 'The Violence of the Letter: From Lévi-Strauss to Rousseau' Derrida expands the analysis of Lévi-Strauss begun in this essay in order further to clarify the ways in which the contradictions of traditional logic 'program' the most modern conceptual apparatuses of linguistics and the social sciences. [Translator's Note]
13. 'Introduction à l'oeuvre de Marcel Mauss,' in Marcel Mauss, *Sociologie et anthropologie* (Paris: P.U.F., 1950), p. xlix.
14. Ibid., pp. xlix–l.
15. George Charbonnier, *Entretiens avec Claude Lévi-Strauss* (Paris: Plon, 1961).
16. *Race and History* (Paris: Unesco Publications, 1958).
17. 'Introduction à l'oeuvre de Marcel Mauss,' p. xlvi.
18. The reference is to *Tristes tropiques*, trans. John Russell (London: Hutchinson and Co., 1961). [Translator's Note]

7 Mikhail Bakhtin

The life and work of Mikhail Bakhtin (1895–1975), and the reception of his work both before and after his death, constitute one of the most remarkable stories in modern intellectual history. Bakhtin was Russian and studied classics at St Petersburg University. As a student and teacher in the 1920s, he began to define his linguistic and literary theories against the dominant school of Russian formalism (see headnote to Victor Shklovsky, pp. 15–16 above). *The Formal Method in Literary Scholarship*, published in 1928 under the name of Bakhtin's associate P. N. Medvedev, but thought to have been written wholly or largely by Bakhtin, was a critique of formalism based on an assertion of the essentially *social* nature of language. This view of language was explored further in *Marxism and The Philosophy of Language* (1929) published by another member of the Bakhtin Circle, V. Volosinov, and also thought to have been written in part by Bakhtin himself.

In 1929, Bakhtin published, under his own name, *Problems of Dostoevsky's Art*, arguing that Dostoevsky inaugurated a new 'polyphonic' type of fiction in which a variety of discourses expressing different ideological positions are set in play without being ultimately placed and judged by a totalizing authorial discourse. Later Bakhtin came to think that this was not a unique discovery of Dostoevsky's, but an inherent characteristic of the novel as a literary form—one that he traced back to its origins in the 'parodying-travestying' genres of classical and medieval culture—the satyr play, the Menippean satire and the popular culture of carnival. These ideas were expounded in a revised and expanded edition of the Dostoevsky book, *Problems in Dostoevsky's Poetics* (1963) and a monumental study of Rabelais and the carnivalesque, *Rabelais and His World* (1966). In the intervening decades, dominated by Stalin, Bahktin was harassed and persecuted by the state, exiled from Moscow and Leningrad, and prevented from publishing his work under his own name. In the more liberal Russian political climate of the 1960s, Mikhail Bakhtin enjoyed a measure of rehabilitation, and his work began to be published and translated to an ever-increasing chorus of admiration and excitement. He is, as his biographer and editor Michael Holquist has said, 'gradually emerging as one of the leading thinkers of the twentieth century'.

Bakhtin's perception that language in use is essentially 'dialogic', every speech act springing from previous utterances and being structured in expectation of a future response, has implications that spread far beyond the field of literary studies. For the latter his major contribution has been twofold: establishing the novel and comedy at the centre instead of at the margins of poetics; and offering an attractive theoretical alternative to traditional humanist, orthodox marxist, and deconstructionist approaches.

'From the Prehistory of Novelistic Discourse' conveys some sense of two of Bakhtin's key ideas. The first is that a given utterance may be, not just the representation of something in the world, but also a representation of another speech act about that thing (*Problems of Dostoevsky's Poetics* contains an elaborate typology of such 'doubly-oriented discourse'.) The second is that prose fiction does greater justice to this aspect of language and human behaviour than the 'canonical' genres of epic, lyric and tragedy privileged by orthodox poetics—a capacity that it derives from the parodic-travestying genres of classical and medieval literature. This tradition is valued by Bakhtin because it offers permanent resistance to the tyranny of totalitarian 'monologic' ideologies, one of which he experienced at first hand.

'From the Prehistory of Novelistic Discourse' was probably written in 1940, but first published in Russia in 1967. It is reprinted here from *The Dialogic Imagination: four essays* (1981), translated by Caryl Emerson and Michael Holquist. Holquist's very full explanatory footnotes have been retained, marked [Tr.].

CROSS-REFERENCES: 1. Saussure
2. Shklovsky
COMMENTARY: Katerina Clark and Michael Holquist, *Mikhail Bakhtin* (1984)
Tzvetan Todorov, *Mikhail Bakhtin: the dialogical principle* (1984)

From the prehistory of novelistic discourse

I

The stylistic study of the novel began only very recently. Classicism of the seventeenth and eighteenth centuries did not recognize the novel as an independent poetic genre and classified it with the mixed rhetorical genres. The first theoreticians of the novel—Abbé Huet (*Essay [Traité] sur l'origine des romans*, 1670), Wieland (in his celebrated preface to *Agathon*, 1766–1767), Blankenburg (*Versuch über den Roman*, 1774, published anonymously) and the Romantics (Friedrich Schlegel, Novalis) barely touched upon questions of style.[1] In the second half of the nineteenth century there was an intensification of interest in the theory of the novel, as it had become the leading European genre[2]—but scholarship was concentrated almost exclusively on questions of composition and thematics.[3] Questions of stylistics were touched upon only in passing and then in a manner that was completely unsystematic.

Beginning with the 1920s, this situation changed rather abruptly: there appeared a large number of works dealing with the stylistics of individual novelists and of individual novels. These works are often rich in valuable observations.[4] But the distinctive features of novelistic discourse, the stylistic *specificum* of the novel as a genre, remained as before unexplored. Moreover, the problem of this *specificum* itself, its full significance, has to this day not yet been posed. Five different stylistic approaches to novelistic discourse may be observed: (1) the author's portions alone in the novel are analyzed, that is, only direct words of the author more or less correctly isolated—an analysis constructed in terms of the usual, direct poetic methods of representation and expression (metaphors, comparisons, lexical register, etc.); (2) instead of a stylistic analysis of the novel as an artistic whole, there is a neutral linguistic description of the novelist's language;[5] (3) in a given novelist's language, elements characteristic of his particular literary tendency are isolated (be it Romanticism, Naturalism, Impressionism, etc.);[6] (4) what is sought in the language of the novel is examined as an expression of the individual personality, that is, language is analyzed as the individual style of the given novelist;[7] (5) the novel is viewed as a rhetorical genre, and its devices are analyzed from the point of view of their effectiveness as rhetoric.[8]

All these types of stylistic analysis to a greater or lesser degree are remote from those peculiarities that define the novel as a genre, and they are also remote from the specific conditions under which the word lives in the novel. They all take a novelist's language and style not as the language and style of a *novel* but merely as the expression of a specific individual artistic personality, or as the style of a particular literary school or finally as a phenomenon common to poetic language in general. The individual artistic personality of the author, the literary school, the general characteristics of poetic language or of the literary language of a particular era all serve to conceal from us the genre itself, with the specific demands it makes upon language and the specific possibilities it opens up for it. As a result, in the majority of these works on the novel, relatively minor stylistic variations—whether individual or characteristic of a particular school—have the effect of completely covering up the major stylistic lines determined by the development of the novel as a unique genre. And all the while discourse in the novel has been living a life that is distinctly its own, a life that is impossible to understand from the point of view of stylistic categories formed on the basis of poetic genres in the narrow sense of that term.

The differences between the novel (and certain forms close to it) and all other genres—*poetic* genres in the narrow sense—are so fundamental, so categorical, that all attempts to impose on the novel the concepts and norms of *poetic* imagery are doomed to fail. Although the novel does contain poetic imagery in the narrow sense (primarily in the author's direct discourse), it is of secondary importance for the novel. What is more, this direct imagery often acquires in the novel quite special functions that are not direct. Here, for example, is how Pushkin characterizes Lensky's poetry [*Evgenij Onegin*, 2. 10, 1–4]:

> He sang love, he was obedient to love,
> And his song was as clear
> As the thoughts of a simple maid,
> As an infant's dream, as the moon. . . .*[a]*

(a development of the final comparison follows).

The poetic images (specifically the metaphoric comparisons) representing Lensky's 'song' do not here have any direct poetic significance at all. They cannot be understood as the direct poetic images of Pushkin himself (although formally, of course, the characterization is that of the author). Here Lensky's 'song' is characterizing itself, in its own language, in its own poetic manner. Pushkin's direct characterization of Lensky's 'song'—which we find as well in the novel—sounds completely different [6. 23, 1]:

> Thus he wrote gloomily and *languidly*. . . .

In the four lines cited by us above it is Lensky's song itself, his voice, his poetic style that sounds, but it is permeated with the parodic and ironic accents of the author; that is the reason why it need not be distinguished from authorial speech by compositional or grammatical means. What we have before us is in fact an *image* of Lensky's song, but not an image in the narrow sense; it is rather a *novelistic* image: the image of another's [*čužoj*] language, in the given instance the image of another's poetic style (sentimental and romantic). The poetic metaphors in these lines ('as an infant's dream,' 'as the moon' and others) in no way function here as the *primary means of representation* (as they would function in a direct, 'serious' song written by Lensky himself); rather they themselves have here become the object of representation, or more precisely of a representation that is parodied and stylized. This novelistic image of another's style (with the direct metaphors that it incorporates) must be taken in *intonational quotation marks* within the system of direct authorial speech (postulated by us here), that is, taken as if the image were parodic and ironic. Were we to discard intonational question marks and take the use of metaphors here as the direct means by which the author represents himself, we would in so doing destroy the novelistic image [*obraz*] of another's style, that is, destroy precisely that image that Pushkin, as novelist, constructs here. Lensky's represented poetic speech is very distant from the direct word of the author himself as we have postulated it: Lensky's language functions merely as an *object* of representation (almost as a material thing); the author himself is almost completely outside Lensky's language (it is only his parodic and ironic accents that penetrate this 'language of another').

Another example from *Onegin* [1. 46, 1–7]:

---

[a] These lines and the following citations from *Eugene Onegin* are taken from Walter Arndt's translation (New York: Dutton, 1963), slightly modified in places to correspond with Bakhtin's remarks about particular words used. [Tr.] (Pushkin's *Eugene Onegin*, first published in Russia in 1831, is 'a novel in verse'. The fact that it is written in verse does not, however, make it a poem rather than a novel in Bakhtin's terms.)

> He who has lived and thought can never
> Look on mankind without disdain;
> He who has felt is haunted ever
> By days that will not come again;
> No more for him enchantment's semblance,
> On him the serpent of remembrance
> Feeds, and remorse corrodes his heart.

One might think that we had before us a direct poetic maxim of the author himself. But these ensuing lines:

> All this is likely to impart
> An added charm to conversation

(spoken by the posited author to Onegin) already give an objective coloration to this maxim. Although it is part of authorial speech, it is structured in a realm where Onegin's voice and Onegin's style hold sway. We once again have an example of the novelistic image of another's style. But it is structured somewhat differently. All the images in this excerpt become in turn the object of representation: they are represented as Onegin's style, Onegin's world view. In this respect they are similar to the images in Lensky's song. But unlike Lensky's song these images, being the object of representation, at the same time represent themselves, or more precisely they express the thought of the author, since the author agrees with this maxim to a certain extent, while nevertheless seeing the limitations and insufficiency of the Onegin–Byronic world view and style. Thus the author (that is, the direct authorial word we are postulating) is considerably closer to Onegin's 'language' than to the 'language' of Lensky: he is no longer merely outside it but in it as well; he not only represents this 'language' but to a considerable extent he himself speaks in this 'language.' The hero is located in a zone of potential conversation with the author, in a zone of *dialogical contact*. The author sees the limitations and insufficiency of the Oneginesque language and world view that was still fashionable in his (the author's) time; he sees its absurd, atomized and artificial face ('A Muscovite in the cloak of a Childe Harold,' 'A lexicon full of fashionable words,' 'Is he not really a parody?'); at the same time however the author can express some of his most basic ideas and observations only with the help of this 'language,' despite the fact that as a system it is a historical dead end. The image of another's language and outlook on the world [*čužoe jazyk- mirovozzrenie*], simultaneously represented *and* representing, is extremely typical of the novel; the greatest novelistic images (for example, the figure of Don Quixote) belong precisely to this type. These descriptive and expressive means that are direct and poetic (in the narrow sense) retain their direct significance when they are incorporated into such a figure, but at the same time they are 'qualified' and 'externalized,' shown as something historically relative, delimited and incomplete—in the novel they, so to speak, criticize themselves.

They both illuminate the world and are themselves illuminated. Just as all there is to know about a man is not exhausted by his situation in life, so all there is to know about the world is not exhausted by a particular discourse about it; every available style is restricted, there are protocols that must be observed.

The author represents Onegin's 'language' (a period-bound language associated with a particular world view) as an image that speaks, and that is therefore preconditioned [*ogovorennij govorjaščij*]. Therefore, the author is far from neutral in his relationship to this image: to a certain extent he even polemicizes with this language, argues with it, agrees with it (although with conditions), interrogates it, eavesdrops on it, but also ridicules it, parodically exaggerates it and so forth— in other words, the author is in a dialogical relationship with Onegin's language; the author is actually *conversing* with Onegin, and such a conversation is the fundamental constitutive element of all novelistic style as well as of the controlling image of Onegin's language. The author represents this language, carries on a conversation with it, and the conversation penetrates into the interior of this language-image and dialogizes it from within. And all essentially novelistic images share this quality: they are internally dialogized images—of the languages, styles, world views of another (all of which are inseparable from their concrete linguistic and stylistic embodiment). The reigning theories of poetic imagery are completely powerless to analyze these complex internally dialogized images of whole languages.

Analyzing *Onegin*, it is possible to establish without much trouble that in addition to the images of Onegin's language and Lensky's language there exists yet another complex language-image, a highly profound one, associated with Tatiana. At the heart of this image is a distinctive internally dialogized combination of the language of a 'provincial miss'—dreamy, sentimental, Richardsonian[b]—with the folk language of fairy tales and stories from everyday life told to her by her nurse, together with peasant songs, fortune telling and so forth. What is limited, almost comical, old-fashioned in Tatiana's language is combined with the boundless, serious and direct truth of the language of the folk. The author not only represents this language but is also in fact speaking in it. Considerable sections of the novel are presented in Tatiana's voice-zone (this zone, as is the case with zones of all other characters, is not set off from authorial speech in any formally compositional or syntactical way; it is a zone demarcated purely in terms of style).

In addition to the character-zones, which take up a considerable portion of authorial speech in the novel, we also find in *Onegin* individual parodic stylizations of the language associated with various literary schools and genres of the time (such as a parody on the neoclassical epic formulaic opening, parodic epitaphs, etc.). And the author's lyrical digressions themselves are by no means free of parodically stylized or parodically polemicizing elements, which to a certain degree enter into the zones of the characters as well. Thus, from a stylistic point of view, the lyrical digressions in the novel are categorically distinct from the direct lyrics of Pushkin. The former are not lyrics, they are the novelistic

[b] The allusion is to the eighteenth-century English novelist Samuel Richardson, author of the epistolary novels, *Pamela* (1740) and *Clarissa* (1747–8).

image of lyrics (and of the poet as lyricist). As a result, under careful analysis almost the entire novel breaks down into images of languages that are connected to one another and with the author via their own characteristic dialogical relationships. These languages are, in the main, the period-bound, generic and common everyday varieties of the epoch's literary language, a language that is in itself ever evolving and in process of renewal. All these languages, with all the direct expressive means at their disposal, themselves become the object of representation, are presented as images of whole languages, characteristically typical images, highly limited and sometimes almost comical. But at the same time these represented languages themselves do the work of representing to a significant degree. The author participates in the novel (he is omnipresent in it) with *almost no direct language of his own*. The language of the novel is a *system* of languages that mutually and ideologically interanimate each other. It is impossible to describe and analyze it as a single unitary language.

We pause on one more example. Here are four excerpts from different sections of *Onegin*:

(1) Thus a young [*Molodoj*] good-for-nothing muses .... [1. 2, 1]
(2) ... Our youthful [*mladoj*] singer
   Has gone to his untimely end! ... [6. 31, 10–11]
(3) I sing of a young [*mladoj*] friend, his checkered
   Career in fortune's cruel coil. [7. 55, 6–7]
(4) What if your pistol-shot has shattered
   The temple of a dear young [*molodoj*] boy.... [6. 34, 1–2]

We see here in two instances the Church Slavonic form *mladoj* and in two instances the Russian metathesized form *molodoj*. Could it be said that both forms belong to a single authorial language and to a single authorial style, one or the other of them being chosen, say, 'for the meter'? Any assertion of the sort would be, of course, barbaric. Certainly it *is* the author speaking in all four instances. But analysis shows us that these forms belong to different stylistic systems of the novel.

The words '*mladoj pevec*' [youthful singer] (the second excerpt) lie in Lensky's zone, are presented in his style, that is, in the somewhat archaicized style of Sentimental Romanticism. The words '*pet*' [to sing] in the sense of *pisat' stixi* [to write verses] and '*pevec*' [singer] and '*poet*' [poet] are used by Pushkin in Lensky's zone or in other zones that are parodied and objectified (in his own language Pushkin himself says of Lensky: 'Thus he wrote. . . .'). The scene of the duel and the 'lament' for Lensky ('My friends, you mourn the poet . . . .' [6. 36, 1], etc.) are in large part constructed in Lensky's zone, in his poetic style, but the realistic and soberminded authorial voice is forever breaking in; the orchestration in this section of the novel is rather complex and highly interesting.

The words 'I sing of a young friend' (third excerpt) involve a parodic travesty on the formulaic opening of the neoclassical epic. The stylistically crude link-up of the archaic, high word *mladoj* with the low word *prijatel'* [acquaintance, friend] is justified by the requirements of parody and travesty.

The words *molodoj povesa* [young good-for-nothing] and *molodoj prijate'* [young friend] are located on the plane of direct authorial language, consistent with the spirit of the familiar, conversational style characteristic of the literary language of the era.

Different linguistic and stylistic forms may be said to belong to different systems of languages in the novel. If we were to abolish all the intonational quotation marks, all the divisions into voices and styles, all the various gaps between the represented 'languages' and direct authorial discourse, then we would get a conglomeration of *heterogeneous* linguistic and stylistic forms lacking any real sense of style. It is impossible to lay out the languages of the novel on a single plane, to stretch them out along a single line. It is a system of intersecting planes. In *Onegin*, there is scarcely a word that appears as Pushkin's direct word, in the unconditional sense that would for instance be true of his lyrics or romantic poems. Therefore, there is no unitary language or style in the novel. But at the same time there does exist a center of language (a verbal-ideological center) for the novel. The author (as creator of the novelistic whole) cannot be found at any one of the novel's language levels: he is to be found at the center of organization where all levels intersect. The different levels are to varying degrees distant from this authorial center.

Belinsky called Pushkin's novel 'an encyclopedia of Russian life.' But this is no inert encyclopedia that merely catalogues the things of everyday life. Here Russian life speaks in all its voices, in all the languages and styles of the era. Literary language is not represented in the novel as a unitary, completely finished-off and indisputable language—it is represented precisely as a living mix of varied and opposing voices [*raznorečivost'*], developing and renewing itself. The language of the author strives to overcome the superficial 'literariness' of moribund, outmoded styles and fashionable period-bound languages; it strives to renew itself by drawing on the fundamental elements of folk language (which does not mean, however, exploiting the crudely obvious, vulgar contradictions between folk and other languages).

Pushkin's novel is a self-critique of the literary language of the era, a product of this language's various strata (generic, everyday, 'currently fashionable') mutually illuminating one another. But this interillumination is not of course accomplished at the level of linguistic abstraction: images of language are inseparable from images of various world views and from the living beings who are their agents—people who think, talk, and act in a setting that is social and historically concrete. From a stylistic point of view we are faced with a complex system of languages of the era being appropriated into one unitary dialogical movement, while at the same time separate 'languages' within this system are located at different distances from the unifying artistic and ideological center of the novel.

The stylistic structure of *Evgenij Onegin* is typical of all authentic novels. To a greater or lesser extent, every novel is a dialogized system made up of the images of 'languages,' styles and consciousnesses that are concrete and inseparable from language. Language in the novel not only represents, but itself serves as the object of representation. Novelistic discourse is always criticizing itself.

In this consists the categorical distinction between the novel and all straightforward genres—the epic poem, the lyric and the drama (strictly conceived). All directly descriptive and expressive means at the disposal of these genres, as well as the genres themselves, become upon entering the novel an object of representation within it. Under conditions of the novel every direct word—epic, lyric, strictly dramatic—is to a greater or lesser degree made into an object, the word itself becomes a bounded [*ograničennij*] image, one that quite often appears ridiculous in this framed condition.

The basic tasks for a stylistics in the novel are, therefore: the study of specific images of languages and styles; the organization of these images; their typology (for they are extremely diverse); the combination of images of languages within the novelistic whole; the transfers and switchings of languages and voices; their dialogical interrelationships.

The stylistics of direct genres, of the direct poetic word, offer us almost no help in resolving these problems.

We speak of a special novelistic discourse because it is only in the novel that discourse can reveal all its specific potential and achieve its true depth. But the novel is a comparatively recent genre. Indirect discourse, however, the representation of another's word, another's language in intonational quotation marks, was known in the most ancient times; we encounter it in the earliest stages of verbal culture. What is more, long before the appearance of the novel we find a rich world of diverse forms that transmit, mimic and represent from various vantage points another's word, another's speech and language, including also the languages of the direct genres. These diverse forms prepared the ground for the novel long before its actual appearance. Novelistic discourse has a lengthy prehistory, going back centuries, even thousands of years. It was formed and matured in the genres of familiar speech found in conversational folk language (genres that are as yet little studied) and also in certain folkloric and low literary genres. During its germination and early development, the novelistic word reflected a primordial struggle between tribes, peoples, cultures and languages—it is still full of echoes of this ancient struggle. In essence this discourse always developed on the boundary line between cultures and languages. The prehistory of novelistic discourse is of great interest and not without its own special drama.

In the prehistory of novelistic discourse one may observe many extremely heterogeneous factors at work. From our point of view, however, two of these factors prove to be of decisive importance: one of these is *laughter*, the other *polyglossia* [*mnogojazycie*]. The most ancient forms for representing language were organized by laughter—these were originally nothing more than the ridiculing of another's language and another's direct discourse. Polyglossia and the *inter-animation of languages* associated with it elevated these forms to a new artistic and ideological level, which made possible the genre of the novel.

These two factors in the prehistory of novelistic discourse are the subject of the present article.

II

One of the most ancient and widespread forms for representing the direct word of another is *parody*. What is distinctive about parody as a form?

Take, for example, the parodic *sonnets* with which *Don Quixote* begins. Although they are impeccably structured as sonnets, we could never possibly assign them to the sonnet genre. In *Don Quixote* they appear as part of a novel— but even the isolated parodic sonnet (outside the novel) could not be classified generically as a sonnet. In a parodied sonnet, the sonnet form is not a genre at all; that is, it is not the form of a whole but is rather *the object of representation*: the sonnet here is the *hero of the parody*. In a parody on the sonnet, we must first of all recognize a sonnet, recognize its form, its specific style, its manner of seeing, its manner of selecting from and evaluating the world—the world view of the sonnet, as it were. A parody may represent and ridicule these distinctive features of the sonnet well or badly, profoundly or superficially. But in any case, what results is not a sonnet, but rather the *image of a sonnet*.

For the same reasons one could not under any circumstances assign to the genre of 'epic poem' the parodic epic 'War between the Mice and the Frogs.'[c] This is an *image of the Homeric style*. It is precisely style that is the true hero of the work. We would have to say the same of Scarron's *Virgil travesti*.[d] One could likewise not include the fifteenth-century *sermons joyeux*[e] in the genre of the sermon, or parodic 'Pater nosters' or 'Ave Marias' in the genre of the prayer and so forth.

All these parodies on genres and generic styles ('languages') enter the great and diverse world of verbal forms that ridicule the straightforward, serious word in all its generic guises. This world is very rich, considerably richer than we are accustomed to believe. The nature and methods available for ridiculing something are highly varied, and not exhausted by parodying and travestying in a strict sense. These methods for making fun of the straightforward word have as yet received little scholarly attention. Our general conceptions of parody and travesty in literature were formed as a scholarly discipline solely by studying very late forms of literary parody, forms of the type represented by Scarron's *Énéide travestie*, or Platen's 'Verhängnisvolle Gabel,'[f] that is, the impoverished, super-ficial and historically least significant forms. These impoverished and limited conceptions of the nature of the parodying and travestying word were then retroactively applied to the supremely rich and varied world of parody and trav-esty in previous ages.

[c] The *Batrachomyomachia*, a still extant parody of Homer thought to have been written about 500 B.C., but with many later interpolations. It is now usually ascribed to Pigres of Halicarnassus (brother-in-law of Mausoleus, whose tomb was one of the seven wonders of the ancient world). The *Margites* (cf. note *aa*) has also been ascribed to Pigres. [Tr.]

[d] This work, comprising seven books (1638–1653), was considered the masterpiece of Paul Scarron (1610–1660) in his day. Scarron is now best remembered for his picaresque novel, *Le Roman comique* (2 vol., 1651–1657, unfinished, 3rd vol. by other hands, 1659). [Tr.]

[e] These were mock sermons originally given in the churches of medieval France as part of the *Fête des fous*; later they were expelled from the church and became a secular genre in their own right, satires in verse form, often directed against women. The humor consisted in pious passages inter-mingled with ribaldry. [Tr.]

[f] 'Die verhängnissvolle Gabel' (1826), a parody of Romantic 'fate tragedies' by August, Graf von Platen-Hallermünde (1796–1835), who was concerned to re-establish classical norms in the face of what he saw as the excesses of the *Stürmer und Dränger* (see his Venetian sonnets [1825]). [Tr.]

The importance of parodic-travestying forms in world literature is enormous. Several examples follow that bear witness to their wealth and special significance.

Let us first take up the ancient period. The 'literature of erudition' of late antiquity—Aulus Gellius[g], Plutarch[h] (in his *Moralia*), Macrobius[i] and, in particular, Athenaeus[j]—provide sufficiently rich data for judging the scope and special character of the parodying and travestying literature of ancient times. The commentaries, citations, references and allusions made by these 'erudites' add substantially to the fragmented and random material on the ancient world's literature of laughter that has survived.

The works of such literary scholars as Dietrich,[k] Reich,[l] Cornford[m] and others have prepared us for more correct assessment of the role and significance of parodic-travestying forms in the verbal culture of ancient times.

It is our conviction that there never was a single strictly straightforward genre, no single type of direct discourse—artistic, rhetorical, philosophical, religious, ordinary everyday—that did not have its own parodying and travestying double, its own comic-ironic *contre-partie*. What is more, these parodic doubles and laughing reflections of the direct word were, in some cases, just as sanctioned by tradition and just as canonized as their elevated models.

I will deal only very briefly with the problem of the so-called 'fourth drama,' that is, the satyr play.[n] In most instances this drama, which follows upon the tragic trilogy, developed the same narrative and mythological motifs as had the trilogy that preceded it. It was, therefore, a peculiar type of parodic-travestying *contre-partie* to the myth that had just received a tragic treatment on the stage; it showed the myth in a different aspect.

---

[g] Aulus Gellius (c. 130–c. 180 A.D.), author of the *Noctes Atticae* in twenty books, a collection of small chapters dealing with a great variety of topics: literary criticism, the law, grammar, history, etc. His Latin is remarkable for its mixture of classical purity and affected archaism. [Tr.]

[h] The *Moralia* of Plutarch (translated in fourteen volumes by F. C. Babbitt et al. [1927–1959] are essays and dialogues on a wide variety of literary, historical and ethical topics, with long sections of quotations from the ancient dramatists. [Tr.]

[i] Ambrosius Theodosius Macrobius (a figure variously identified with several Macrobii), author of the *Saturnalia*, a symposium presented in the form of a dialogue in seven books, drawing heavily on Aulus Gellius (cf. note g). [Tr.]

[j] Athenaeus (fl. 200 A.D.), author of *Deipnosophistai* (*Doctors at Dinner*, or as it is sometimes translated, *Experts on Dining*). This is a work of fifteen books filled with all kinds of miscellaneous information on medicine, literature, the law, etc., intermingled with anecdotes and quotations from a large number of other authors, many of whose works are otherwise lost or unknown. [Tr.]

[k] A. Dietrich, author of *Pulcinella: Pompeyanische Wandbilder und Romische Satyrspiele* (Leipzig, 1897), a book that played a major role in shaping some of Bakhtin's early ideas about the role of fools in history. [Tr.]

[l] Hermann Reich, author of *Der Mimus* (Berlin, 1903), a theoretical attempt to reconstruct the reasons for the mime's importance in ancient Greece. [Tr.]

[m] F. M. Cornford (1874–1943), from whose many works Bakhtin here has in mind *The Origin of Greek Comedy* (London, 1914). [Tr.]

[n] In ancient Greece, the tragic dramas were normally written and performed in groups of three (e.g., Sophocles' *Oedipus Rex*, *Oedipus at Colonus* and *Antigone*). The satyr play was a ribald comedy with a chorus of satyrs, performed immediately after the tragic trilogy.

These parodic-travestying counter-presentations of lofty national myths were just as sanctioned and canonical as their straightforward tragic manifestations. All the tragedians—Phrynicous,[o] Sophocles, Euripides—were writers of satyr plays as well, and Aeschylus, the most serious and pious of them all, an initiate into the highest Eleusinian Mysteries, was considered by the Greeks to be the greatest master of the satyr play. From fragments of Aeschylus' satyr play *The Bone-Gatherers'*[p] we see that this drama gave a parodic, travestying picture of the events and heroes of the Trojan War, and particularly the episode involving Odysseus' quarrel with Achilles and Diomedes, where a stinking chamber pot is thrown at Odysseus' head.

It should be added that the figure of 'comic Odysseus,' a parodic travesty of his high epic and tragic image, was one of the most popular figures of satyr plays, of ancient Doric farce and pre-Aristophanic comedy, as well as of a whole series of minor comic epics, parodic speeches and disputes in which the comedy of ancient times was so rich (especially in southern Italy and Sicily). Characteristic here is that special role that the motif of madness played in the figure of the 'comic Odysseus': Odysseus, as is well known, donned a clown's fool's cap (*pileus*) and harnessed his horse and ox to a plow, pretending to be mad in order to avoid participation in the war. It was the motif of madness that switched the figure of Odysseus from the high and straightforward plane to the comic plane of parody and travesty.[9]

But the most popular figure of the satyr play and other forms of the parodic travestying word was the figure of the 'comic Hercules.' Hercules, the powerful and simple servant to the cowardly, weak and false king Euristheus; Hercules, who had conquered death in battle and had descended into the nether world; Hercules the monstrous glutton, the playboy, the drunk and scrapper, but especially Hercules the madman—such were the motifs that lent a comic aspect to his image. In this comic aspect, heroism and strength are retained, but they are combined with laughter and with images from the material life of the body.

The figure of the comic Hercules was extremely popular, not only in Greece but also in Rome, and later in Byzantium (where it became one of the central figures in the marionette theater). Until quite recently this figure lived on in the Turkish game of 'shadow puppets.' The comic Hercules is one of the most profound folk images for a cheerful and simple heroism, and had an enormous influence on all of world literature.

When taken together with such figures as the 'comic Odysseus' and the 'comic Hercules,' the 'fourth drama,' which was an *indispensable* conclusion to the tragic trilogy, indicates that the literary consciousness of the Greeks did not view the parodic-travestying reworkings of national myth as any particular profanation or blasphemy. It is characteristic that the Greeks were not at all embarrassed to

---

[o] Phrynicous, one of the originators of Greek tragedy. He was first to introduce the feminine mask, and was greatly admired by Aristophanes. His first victory was in 511 B.C. Some of his titles are *Pleuroniae, Aegyptii, Alcestis, Acteon*; he wrote several other plays as well. [Tr.]

[p] The *Ostologoi* may have been part of a tetralogy with *Penelope*, deriving its title from the hungry beggars in the palace at Ithaca who collected bones hurled at them by the suitors. [Tr.]

attribute the authorship of the parodic work 'War between the Mice and the Frogs' to Homer himself. Homer is also credited with a comic work (a long poem) about the fool *Margit*. For any and every straightforward genre, any and every direct discourse—epic, tragic, lyric, philosophical—may and indeed must itself become the object of representation, the object of a parodic travestying 'mimicry.' It is as if such mimicry rips the word away from its object, disunifies the two, shows that a given straightforward generic word—epic or tragic—is one-sided, bounded, incapable of exhausting the object; the process of parodying forces us to experience those sides of the object that are not otherwise included in a given genre or a given style. Parodic-travestying literature introduces the permanent corrective of laughter, of a critique on the one-sided seriousness of the lofty direct word, the corrective of reality that is always richer, more fundamental and most importantly *too contradictory and heteroglot* to be fitted into a high and straightforward genre. The high genres are monotonic, while the 'fourth drama' and genres akin to it retain the ancient binary tone of the word. Ancient parody was free of any nihilistic denial. It was not, after all, the heroes who were parodied, nor the Trojan War and its participants; what was parodied was only its epic heroization; not Hercules and his exploits but their tragic heroization. The genre itself, the style, the language are all put in cheerfully irreverent quotation marks, and they are perceived against a backdrop of a contradictory reality that cannot be confined within their narrow frames. The direct and serious word was revealed, in all its limitations and insufficiency, only after it had become the laughing image of that word—but it was by no means discredited in the process. Thus it did not bother the Greeks to think that Homer himself wrote a parody of Homeric style.

Evidence from Roman literature casts additional light on the problem of the 'fourth drama.' In Rome its functions were filled by the Atellan literary farces. When, beginning with the period of Sulla, the Atellan farces were reworked for literature and, fixed in texts, they were staged after the tragedy, during the exordium.[q] Thus the Atellan farces[r] of Pomponius[s] and Novius[t] were performed after the tragedies of Accius.[u] The strictest correspondence was observed between the Atellan farces and the tragedies. The insistence upon a single source for both the serious and the comic material was more strict and sustained in Rome than had been the case in Greece. At a later date, the Atellan farces

---

[q] The exordium was, in Greek drama, the end or catastrophe of a play, but is used here by Bakhtin as it applied in Roman plays, where the word means a comic interlude or farce following something more serious. Its function is comparable with the satyr play in Athenian tetralogies. (Not to be confused with *exodos*, the portion near the end of Greek plays where the chorus leaves the stage.) [Tr.]

[r] First-century B.C. farces that emphasized crude physiological details and bawdy jokes. [Tr.]

[s] Lucius Pomponius of Bononia (fl. 100–85 B.C.), author of at least seventy Atellan farces. [Tr.]

[t] Novius (fl. 95–80 B.C.), younger contemporary of Pomponius, and author of forty-three farces. [Tr.]

[u] Lucius Accius (170–90 B.C.), historian of literature, but cited here by Bakhtin because he was generally regarded as the last real tragedian of Rome. [Tr.]

that had been performed during the tragedic exodium were replaced by mimes: apparently they also travestied the material of the preceding tragedy.

The attempt to accompany every tragic (or serious) treatment of material with a parallel comic (parodic-travestying) treatment also found its reflection in the graphic arts of the Romans. In the so-called 'consular diptychs,' comic scenes in grotesque masks were usually depicted on the left, while on the right were found tragic scenes. An analogous counterposing of scenes can also be observed in the mural paintings in Pompeii. Dieterich, who made use of the Pompeiian paintings to unlock the secret of ancient comic forms, describes, for example, two frescoes arranged facing each other: on the one we see Andromeda being rescued by Perseus, on the opposite wall is a picture of a naked woman bathing in a pond with a serpent wrapped around her; peasants are trying to come to her aid with sticks and stones.[10] This is an obvious parodic travesty of the first mythological scene. The plot of the myth is relocated in a specifically prosaic reality; Perseus himself is replaced by peasants with rude weapons (compare the knightly world of Don Quixote translated into Sancho's language).

From a whole series of sources, and particularly from the fourteenth book of Athenaeus, we know of the existence of an enormous world of highly hetero-geneous parodic-travestying forms; we know, for instance, of the performances of phallophors[v] and deikelists[w] [mimers] who on the one hand travestied national and local myths and on the other mimicked the characteristically typical 'languages' and speech mannerisms of foreign doctors, procurers, *hetaerae* [concubines], peasants, slaves and so forth. The parodic travestying literature of southern Italy was especially rich and varied. Comic parodic plays and riddles flourished there, as did parodies of the speeches of scholars and judges, and forms of parodic and agonic dialogues, one of whose variants became a structural component of Greek comedy. Here the word lived an utterly different life from that which it lived in the high, straightforward genres of Greece.

It is worth remembering that the most primitive mime, that is, a wandering actor of the most banal sort, always had to possess, as a professional minimum, two skills: the ability to imitate the voices of birds and animals, and the ability to mimic the speech, facial expressions and gesticulation of a slave, a peasant, a procurer, a scholastic pedant and a foreigner. To this very day this is still the stock-in-trade for the farcical actor-impersonators at annual fairs.

The culture of laughter was no less rich and diverse in the Roman world than it had been in the Greek. Especially characteristic for Rome was the stubborn vitality of ritualistic ridicule. Everyone is familiar with the soldiers' sanctioned ritualistic ridicule of the commander returning in triumph, or the ritualistic laughter at Roman funerals and the license granted the laughter. of the mime;

---

[v] Phallophors, 'phallus bearers,' the figures who carried carved *phalloi* in religious processions and whose role was to joke and cavort obscenely. [Tr.]

[w] Deikelists, from the Greek *deikeliktas*, simply 'one who represents,' but according to Athenaeus (cf. note *j*), in book 14 of the *Deipnosophistai*, they were actors who specialized in burlesque parts. [Tr.]

there is no need to expand further on the Saturnalia.[x] What is important for us here is not the ritual roots of this laughter, but rather the literature it produced, and the role played by Roman laughter in the ultimate destinies of discourse. Laughter proved to be just as profoundly productive and deathless a creation of Rome as Roman law. This laughter broke through the grim atmosphere of seriousness of the Middle Ages to fertilize the great creations of Renaissance literature; up to this day it continues to resonate in many aspects of European literature.

The literary and artistic consciousness of the Romans could not imagine a serious form without its comic equivalent. The serious, straightforward form was perceived as only a fragment, only half of a whole; the fullness of the whole was achieved only upon adding the comic *contre-partie* of this form. Everything serious had to have, and indeed did have, its comic double. As in the Saturnalia the clown was the double of the ruler and the slave the double of the master, so such comic doubles were created in all forms of culture and literature. For this reason Roman literature, and especially the low literature of the folk, created an immense number of parodic-travestying forms: they provided the matter for mimes, satires, epigrams, table talk, rhetorical genres, letters, various types of low comic folk art. It was oral tradition preeminently that transmitted many of these forms to the Middle Ages, transmitting as well the very style and logic of Roman parody, a logic that was bold and consistent. It was Rome that taught European culture how to laugh and ridicule. But of the rich heritage of laughter that was part of the written tradition of Rome only a miniscule quantity has survived: those upon whom the transmission of this heritage depended were agelasts[y] who elected the serious word and rejected its comic reflections as a profanation (as happened, for example, with the numerous parodies on Virgil).

Thus we see that alongside the great and significant models of straightforward genres and direct discourses, discourses with no conditions attached, there was created in ancient times a rich world of the most varied forms and variations of parodic-travestying, indirect, conditional discourse. Of course our term 'parodic-travestying discourse' far from expresses the full richness of types, variants and nuances of the laughing word. But the question arises: what unifies all these diverse forms of laughter, and what relationship do they bear to the novel?

Some forms of parodic-travestying literature issue directly from the form of the genres being parodied—parodic poems, tragedies (Lucian's *Tragopodagra*[z] 'Gout-Tragedy', for example), parodic judicial speeches and so forth. This is a parody and travesty in the narrow sense of the word. In other cases we find special forms of parody constituted as genres—satyr-drama, improvised comedy, satire, plotless dialogue [*bessjužetnyi dialog*] and others. As we have said above, parodied genres

---

[x] A Roman festival in honour of the god Saturn, which lasted for seven days in late December. It was characterized by merrymaking and the suspension of normal laws and constraints on licentious behaviour.

[y] Agelasts, from the Greek 'without-laughter,' is an example of Bakhtin's often rarified vocabulary. The word implies grim ideologues. [Tr.]

[z] Cf. note *bb*.

do not belong to the genres that they parody; that is, a parodic poem is not a poem at all. But the particular genres of the parodic-travestying word of the sort we have enumerated here are unstable, compositionally still unshaped, lacking a firm or definite generic skeleton. It can be said, then, that in ancient times the parodic-travestying word was (generically speaking) homeless. All these diverse parodic-travestying forms constituted, as it were, a special extra-generic or inter-generic world. But this world was unified, first of all, by a common purpose: to provide the corrective of laughter and criticism to all existing straightforward genres, languages, styles, voices; to force men to experience beneath these categories a different and contradictory reality that is otherwise not captured in them. Such laughter paved the way for the impiety of the novelistic form. In the second place, all these forms are unified by virtue of their shared subject: language itself, which everywhere serves as a means of direct expression, becomes in this new context the image of language, the image of the direct word. Consequently this extra-generic or inter-generic world is internally unified and even appears as its own kind of totality. Each separate element in it—parodic dialogue, scenes from everyday life, bucolic humor, etc.—is presented as if it were a fragment of some kind of unified whole. I imagine this whole to be something like an immense novel, multi-generic, multi-styled, mercilessly critical, soberly mocking, reflecting in all its fullness the heteroglossia and multiple voices to a given culture, people and epoch. In this huge novel—in this mirror of constantly evolving heteroglossia—any direct word and especially that of the dominant discourse is reflected as something more or less bounded, typical and characteristic of a particular era, aging, dying, ripe for change and renewal. And in actual fact, out of this huge complex of parodically reflected words and voices the ground was being prepared in ancient times for the rise of the novel, a genre formed of many styles and many images. But the novel could not *at that time* gather unto itself and make use of all the material that language images had made available. I have in mind here the 'Greek romance,' and Apuleius and Petronius. The ancient world was apparently not capable of going further than these.

These parodic-travestying forms prepared the ground for the novel in one very important, in fact decisive, respect. They liberated the object from the power of language in which it had become entangled as if in a net; they destroyed the homogenizing power of myth over language; they freed consciousness from the power of the direct word, destroyed the thick walls that had imprisoned consciousness within its own discourse, within its own language. A distance arose between language and reality that was to prove an indispensable condition for authentically realistic forms of discourse.

Linguistic consciousness—parodying the direct word, direct style, exploring its limits, its absurd sides, the face specific to an era—constituted itself *outside* this direct word and outside all its graphic and expressive means of representation. A new mode developed for working creatively with language: the creating artist began to look at language from the outside, with another's eyes, from the point of view of a potentially different language and style. It is, after all, precisely in the light of another potential language or style that a given straightforward style is parodied, travestied, ridiculed. The creating consciousness stands, as it were, on the boundary line between languages and styles. This is, for the creating consciousness, a highly peculiar position to find itself in with regard to language. The aedile or rhapsode experienced himself in his own language, in his own discourse, in an utterly different way from the creator of 'War between the Mice and the Frogs,' or the creators of *Margites.*[aa]

One who creates a direct word—whether epic, tragic or lyric—deals only with the subject whose praises he sings, or represents, or expresses, and he does so in his own language that is perceived as the sole and fully adequate tool for realizing the word's direct, objectivized meaning. This meaning and the objects and themes that compose it are inseparable from the straightforward language of the person who creates it: the objects and themes are born and grow to maturity in this language, and in the national myth and national tradition that permeate this language. The position and tendency of the parodic-travestying consciousness is, however, completely different: it, too, is oriented toward the object—but toward another's word as well, a parodied word *about* the object that in the process becomes *itself* an image. Thus is created that distance between language and reality we mentioned earlier. Language is transformed from the absolute dogma it had been within the narrow framework of a sealed-off and impermeable monoglossia into a working hypothesis for comprehending and expressing reality.

But such a full and complete transformation can occur only under certain conditions, namely, under the condition of thoroughgoing *polyglossia*. Only polyglossia fully frees consciousness from the tyranny of its own language and its own myth of language. Parodic-travestying forms flourish under these conditions, and only in this milieu are they capable of being elevated to completely new ideological heights.

Roman literary consciousness was bilingual. The purely national Latin genres, conceived under monoglotic conditions, fell into decay and did not achieve the level of literary expression. From start to finish, the creative literary consciousness of the Romans functioned against the background of the Greek language and Greek forms. From its very first steps, the Latin literary word viewed itself in the light of the Greek word, *through the eyes* of the Greek word; it was from the very beginning a word 'with a sideways glance,' a stylized word enclosing itself, as it were, in its own piously stylized quotation marks.

Latin literary language in all its generic diversity was created in the light of Greek literary language. Its national distinctiveness and the specific verbal thought process inherent in it were realized in creative literary consciousness in a way that would have been absolutely impossible under conditions of monoglossia. After all, it is possible to objectivize one's own particular language, its internal form, the peculiarities of its world view, its specific linguistic habitus, only in the light of another language belonging to someone else, which is almost as much 'one's own' as one's native language.

In his book on Plato, Wilamowitz-Moellendorff writes: 'Only knowledge of a language that possesses another mode of conceiving the world can lead to the appropriate knowledge of one's own language. . . .'[11] I do not continue the

---

[aa] An early satirical epic, traditionally ascribed to Homer, but to Pigres as well (cf. note *c*). [Tr.]

quotation, for it primarily concerns the problem of understanding one's own language in purely cognitive linguistic terms, an understanding that is realized only in the light of a different language, one not one's own; but this situation is no less pervasive where the literary imagination is conceiving language in actual artistic practice. Moreover, in the process of literary creation, languages inter-animate each other and objectify precisely that side of one's own (and of the other's) language *that pertains to its world view*, its inner form, the axiologically accentuated system inherent in it. For the creating literary consciousness, existing in a field illuminated by another's language, it is not the phonetic system of its own language that stands out, nor is it the distinctive features of its own morphology nor its own abstract lexicon—what stands out is precisely that which makes language concrete and which makes its world view ultimately untranslatable, that is, precisely the *style of the language as a totality*.

For a creative, literary bilingual consciousness (and such was the consciousness of the literary Roman) language taken as a whole, that is, able to comprehend the language *I* call *my* own [*svoj-rodnoj*] as well as the language that someone else calls *his* own [*svoj-čužoj*]—was a concrete *style*, but not an abstract linguistic system. It was extremely characteristic for the literary Roman to perceive all of language, from top to bottom, as style—a conception of language that is somewhat cold and 'exteriorizing.' Speaking as well as writing, the Roman *stylized*, and not without a certain cold sense of alienation from his own language. For this reason the objective and expressive *directness* of the Latin literary word was always somewhat conventionalized (as indeed is every sort of stylization). An element of stylizing is inherent in all the major straightforward genres of Roman literature; it is even present in such a great Roman creation as the *Aeneid*.

But we have to do here not only with the cultural *bi*lingualism of literary Rome. Roman literature at the outset was characterized by *tri*lingualism. 'Three souls' lived in the breast of Ennius. But three souls—three language-cultures—lived in the breast of all the initiators of Roman literary discourse, all the translator-stylizers who had come to Rome from lower Italy, where the boundaries of three languages and cultures intersected with one another—Greek, Oscan and Roman. Lower Italy was the home of a specific kind of hybrid culture and hybrid literary forms. The rise of Roman literature is connected in a fundamental way with this trilingual cultural home; this literature was born in the interanimation of three languages—one that was indigenously its own, and two that were other but that were *experienced* as indigenous.

From the point of view of polyglossia, Rome was merely the concluding phase of Hellenism, a phase whose final gesture was to carry over into the barbarian world of Europe a radical polyglossia, and thus make possible the creation of a new type of medieval polyglossia.

For all the barbarian peoples who came in contact with it, Hellenism provided a powerful and illuminating model of other-languagedness. This model played a fateful role in national, straightforward forms of artistic discourse. It overwhelmed almost all of the tender shoots of national epic and lyric, born in an environment muffled by a dense monoglossia, it turned the direct word of barbarian peoples—their epic and lyric word—into a discourse that was somewhat conventional, somewhat stylized. And this greatly facilitated the development of all forms of parodic-travestying discourse. On Hellenistic and Helleno-Roman soil there became possible a maximal distance between the speaker (the creating artist) and his language, as well as a maximal distance between language itself and the world of themes and objects. Only under such conditions could Roman laughter have developed so powerfully.

A complex polyglossia was, as we have seen, characteristic of Hellenism. But the Orient, which was itself always a place of many languages and many cultures, crisscrossed with the intersecting boundary lines of ancient cultures and languages, was anything but a naive monoglotic world, passive in its relationship to Greek culture. The Orient was itself bearer of an ancient and complex polyglossia. Scattered throughout the entire Hellenistic world were centers, cities, settlements where several cultures and languages directly cohabited, interweaving with one another in distinctive patterns. Such, for instance, was Samosata, Lucian's*bb* native city, which has played such an immense role in the history of the European novel. The original inhabitants of Samosata were Syrians who spoke Aramaic. The entire literary and educated upper classes of the urban population spoke and wrote in Greek. The official language of the administration and chancellery was Latin, all the administrators were Romans, and there was a Roman legion stationed in the city. A great thoroughfare passed through Samosata (strategically very important) along which flowed the languages of Mesopotamia, Persia and even India. Lucian's cultural and linguistic consciousness was born and shaped at this point of intersection of cultures and languages. The cultural and linguistic environment of the African Apuleius and of the writers of Greek novels—who were for the most part Hellenized barbarians—is analogous to Lucian's.

In his book on the history of the Greek novel,[12] Erwin Rohde analyzes the dissolution of the Greek national myth on Hellenistic soil, and the concomitant decline and diminution of the epic and drama forms—forms that can be sustained only on the basis of a unitary national myth that perceives itself as a totality. Rohde does not have much to say on the role of polyglossia. For him, the Greek novel was solely a product of the decay of the major straightforward genres. In part this is true: everything new is born out of the death of something old. But Rohde was no dialectician. It was precisely what was new in all this that he failed to see.*cc* He did define, more or less correctly, the significance of a unitary and totalizing national myth for the creation of the major forms of Greek epic, lyric and drama. But the disintegration of this national myth, which was so fatal for

---

bb Lucian (c. 120–180 A.D.), greatest of all the second-century Sophists, is one of Bakhtin's favorites. Lucian is the author of some 130 works, most of them dialogues that hold up to ridicule the pretensions of his age, such as the *Lexiphanes*, an attack on the stilted Atticists who larded their works with polysyllabic, obsolete words. [Tr.]

cc Compare Mandelstam's insight: 'Just as there are two geometries, Euclid's and Lobachevsky's, there may be two histories of literature, written in different keys: one that speaks only of acquisitions, another only of losses, and both would be speaking of one and the same thing' ('About the Nature of the Word,' in *Osip Mandelstam: Selected Essays*, tr. Sidney Monas, [Austin, Tx., 1977], p. 67). [Tr.]

the straightforward monoglotic genres of Hellenism, proved productive for the birth and development of a new prosaic, novelistic discourse. The role of polyglossia in this slow death of the myth and the birth of novelistic matter-of-factness is extremely great. Where languages and cultures interanimated each other, language became something entirely different, its very nature changed: in place of a single, unitary sealed-off Ptolemaic world of language, there appeared the open Galilean world of many languages, mutually animating each other.

Unfortunately the Greek novel only weakly embodied this new discourse that resulted from polyglot consciousness. In essence this novel-type resolved only the problem of plot, and even that only partially. What was created was a new and large multi-genred genre, one which included in itself various types of dialogues, lyrical songs, letters, speeches, descriptions of countries and cities, short stories and so forth. It was an encyclopedia of genres. But this multi-generic novel was almost exclusively cast in a single style. Discourse was partially conventionalized, stylized. The stylizing attitude toward language, characteristic of all forms of polyglossia, found its paradigmatic expression in such novels. But semiparodic, travestying and ironic forms were present in them as well; there were probably many more such forms than literary scholars admit. The boundaries between semi-stylized and semiparodic discourse were very unstable: after all, one need only emphasize ever so slightly the conventionality in stylized discourse for it to take on a light overtone of parody or irony, a sense that words have 'conditions attached to them': it is not, strictly speaking, *I* who speak; I, perhaps, would speak quite differently. But images of languages that are capable of reflecting in a polyglot manner speakers of the era are almost entirely absent in the Greek novel. In this respect certain varieties of Hellenistic and Roman satire are incomparably more 'novelistic' than the Greek novel.

At this point it becomes necessary to broaden the concept of polyglossia somewhat. We have been speaking so far of the interanimation of major national languages (Greek, Latin), each of which was in itself already *fully formed* and *unitary*, languages that had already passed through a lengthy phase of comparatively stable and peaceful monoglossia. But we saw that the Greeks, even in their classical period, had at their disposal a very rich world of parodic-travestying forms. It is hardly likely that such a wealth of images of language would arise under conditions of a deaf, sealed-off monoglossia.

It must not be forgotten that monoglossia is always in essence relative. After all, one's own language is never a single language: in it there are always survivals of the past and a potential for other-languagedness that is more or less sharply perceived by the working literary and language consciousness.

Contemporary scholarship has accumulated a mass of facts that testify to the intense struggle that goes on between languages and within languages, a struggle that preceded the relatively stable condition of Greek as we know it. A significant number of Greek roots belong to the language of the people who had settled the territory before the Greeks. In the Greek literary language we encounter behind each separate genre the consolidation of a particular dialect. Behind these gross facts a complex trial-at-arms is concealed, a struggle between languages and dialects, between hybridizations, purifications, shifts and renovations, the long and twisted path of struggle for the unity of a literary language and for the unity of its system of genres. This was followed by a lengthy period of relative stabilization. But the memory of these past linguistic disturbances was retained, not only as congealed traces in language but also in literary and stylistic figuration—and preeminently in the parodying and travestying verbal forms.

In the historical period of ancient Greek life—a period that was, linguistically speaking, stable and monoglotic—all plots, all subject and thematic material, the entire basic stock of images, expressions and intonations, arose from within the very heart of the native language. Everything that entered from outside (and that was a great deal) was assimilated in a powerful and confident environment of closed-off monoglossia, one that viewed the polyglossia of the barbarian world with contempt. Out of the heart of this confident and uncontested monoglossia were born the major straightforward genres of the ancient Greeks—their epic, lyric and tragedy. These genres express the centralizing tendencies in language. But alongside these genres, especially among the folk, there flourished parodic and travestying forms that kept alive the memory of the ancient linguistic struggle and that were continually nourished by the ongoing process of linguistic stratification and differentiation.

Closely connected with the problem of polyglossia and inseparable from it is the problem of heteroglossia *within* a language, that is, the problem of internal differentiation, the stratification characteristic of any national language. This problem is of primary importance for understanding the style and historical destinies of the modern European novel, that is, the novel since the seventeenth century. This latecomer reflects, in its stylistic structure, the struggle between two tendencies in the languages of European peoples: one a centralizing (unifying) tendency, the other a decentralizing tendency (that is, one that stratifies languages). The novel senses itself on the border between the completed, dominant literary language and the extraliterary languages that know heteroglossia; the novel either serves to further the centralizing tendencies of a new literary language in the process of taking shape (with its grammatical, stylistic and ideological norms), or—on the contrary—the novel fights for the renovation of an antiquated literary language, in the interests of those strata of the national language that have remained (to a greater or lesser degree) outside the centralizing and unifying influence of the artistic and ideological norm established by the dominant literary language. The literary-artistic consciousness of the modern novel, sensing itself on the border between two languages, one literary, the other extraliterary, each of which now knows heteroglossia, also senses itself on the border of time: it is extraordinarily sensitive to time in language, it senses time's shifts, the aging and renewing of language, the past and the future—and all in language.

Of course all these processes of shift and renewal of the national language that are reflected *by* the novel do not bear an abstract linguistic character *in* the novel: they are inseparable from social and ideological struggle, from processes of evolution and of the renewal of society and the folk.

The speech diversity within language thus has primary importance for the novel. But this speech diversity achieves its full creative consciousness only under conditions of an active polyglossia. Two myths perish simultaneously: the myth of a language that presumes to be the only language, and the myth of a language that presumes to be completely unified. Therefore even the modern European novel, reflecting intra-language heteroglossia as well as processes of aging and renewal of the literary language and its generic types, was prepared for by the polyglossia of the Middle Ages—which was experienced by all European peoples—and by that intense interanimation of languages that took place during the Renaissance, during that shifting away from an ideological language (Latin) and the move of European peoples toward the critical monoglossia characteristic of modern times.

III

The laughing, parodic-travestying literature of the Middle Ages was extremely rich. In the wealth and variety of its parodic forms, the Middle Ages was akin to Rome. It must in fact be said that in a whole series of ways the medieval literature of laughter appears to be the direct heir to Rome, and the Saturnalian tradition in particular continued to live in altered form throughout the Middle Ages. The Rome of the Saturnalia, crowned with a fool's cap—'pileata Roma' (Martial)[dd]—successfully retained its force and its fascination, even during the very darkest days of the Middle Ages. But the original products of laughter among the European peoples, which grew out of local folklore, were also important.

One of the more interesting stylistic problems during the Hellenistic period was the problem of quotation. The forms of direct, half-hidden and completely hidden quoting were endlessly varied, as were the forms for framing quotations by a context, forms of intonational quotation marks, varying degrees of alienation or assimilation of another's quoted word. And here the problem frequently arises: is the author quoting with reverence or on the contrary with irony, with a smirk? Double entendre as regards the other's word was often deliberate.

The relationship to another's word was equally complex and ambiguous in the Middle Ages. The role of the other's word was enormous at that time: there were quotations that were openly and reverently emphasized as such, or that were half-hidden, completely hidden, half-conscious, unconscious, correct, intentionally distorted, unintentionally distorted, deliberately reinterpreted and so forth. The boundary lines between someone else's speech and one's own speech were flexible, ambiguous, often deliberately distorted and confused. Certain types of texts were constructed like mosaics out of the texts of others. The so-called *cento*[ee]

[dd] Martial (Marcus Valerius Martialis), famous for his epigrams, many of which contain vivid, almost novelistic details of everyday life in Rome (i.e., sausage vendors, wounded slaves, etc.). [Tr.]

[ee] *Cento* (Latin, 'patchwork'), a poetic compilation made up of passages selected from the work of great poets of the past. A recent example of what a *cento* might be is provided by Andrew Field's collection of writings by modern Russian critics: *The Complection of Russian Literature: A Cento* (London, 1971). [Tr.]

(a specific genre) was, for instance, composed exclusively out of others' verse-lines and hemistichs. One of the best authorities on medieval parody, Paul Lehmann, states outright that the history of medieval literature and its Latin literature in particular 'is the history of the appropriation, re-working and imitation of someone else's property' ['eine Geschichte der Aufnahme, Verarbeitung und Nachahmung fremden Gutes']¹³—or as we would say, of another's language, another's style, another's word.

The primary instance of appropriating another's discourse and language was the use made of the authoritative and sanctified word of the Bible, the Gospel, the Apostles, the fathers and doctors of the church. This word continually infiltrates the context of medieval literature and the speech of educated men (clerics). But how does this infiltration occur, how does the receiving context relate to it, in what sort of intonational quotation marks is it enclosed? Here a whole spectrum of possible relationships toward this word comes to light, beginning at one pole with the pious and inert quotation that is isolated and set off like an icon, and ending at the other pole with the most ambiguous, disrespectful, parodic-travestying use of a quotation. The transitions between various nuances on this spectrum are to such an extent flexible, vacillating and ambiguous that it is often difficult to decide whether we are confronting a reverent use of a sacred word or a more familiar, even parodic playing with it; if the latter, then it is often difficult to determine the degree of license permitted in that play.

At the very dawning of the Middle Ages there appeared a whole series of remarkable parodic works. Among them is the well-known *Cena Cypriani* or *Cyprian Feasts*,ᶠᶠ a fascinating gothic symposium. But how was it constituted? The entire Bible, the entire Gospel was as it were cut up into little scraps, and these scraps were then arranged in such a way that a picture emerged of a grand feast at which all the personages of sacred history from Adam and Eve to Christ and his Apostles eat, drink and make merry. In this work a correspondence of all details to Sacred Writ is strictly and precisely observed, but at the same time the entire Sacred Writ is transformed into carnival, or more correctly into Saturnalia. This is 'pileata Biblia.'

But what purpose motivates the author of this work? What was his attitude toward Holy Writ? Scholars answer this question in various ways. All are agreed, of course, that some sort of play with the sacred word figures in here, but the degree of license enjoyed by this play and its larger sense are evaluated in

---

ᶠᶠ The *Cena* seem to have been composed to be recited at table, following the advice given by Bishop Zeno of Verona (in his tract *ad neophytos post baptisma*) that instruction be provided in this pleasant way. The work is a narrative concerning the marriage feast of King Johel at Cana of Galilee. All kinds of persons from both the Old and the New Testament are invited. The work was popular enough to be set to verse during the Carolingian Revival by John the Deacon, a contemporary of Charles the Bad. The verse redaction was intended to amuse Pope John VIII, to whom it is dedicated. F. J. E. Raby, the great expert on medieval Latin, says somewhat sententiously of this version that, 'while puerile in itself, it might serve the purpose of instruction, if it did not rather move those who heard it recited to unseemly laughter' (*A History of Secular Latin Poetry in the Middle Ages*, 2 vols. [Oxford, 1934], vol. 1, p. 220). [Tr.]

different ways. There are those scholars who insist that the purpose of such play is innocent, that is, purely mnemonic: to teach through play. In order to help those believers (who had not long before been pagans) better remember the figures and events of Sacred Writ, the author of the *Feasts* wove out of them the mnemonic pattern of a banquet. Other scholars see the *Feasts* as straightforward blasphemous parody.

We mention these scholarly opinions only as an example. They testify to the complexity and ambiguity of the medieval treatment of the sacred word as another's word. *Cyprian Feasts* is not, of course, a mnemonic device. It is parody, and more precisely a parodic travesty. But one must not transfer contemporary concepts of parodic discourse onto medieval parody (as one also must not do with ancient parody). In modern times the functions of parody are narrow and unproductive. Parody has grown sickly, its place in modern literature is insignificant. We live, write and speak today in a world of free and democratized language; the complex and multi-leveled hierarchy of discourses, forms, images, styles that used to permeate the entire system of official language and linguistic consciousness was swept away by the linguistic revolutions of the Renaissance. European *literary* languages—French, German, English—came into being while this hierarchy was in the process of being destroyed, and while the laughing, travestying genres of the late Middle Ages and Renaissance—novellas, Mardi Gras, *soties*, farces and finally novels—were in the process of shaping these languages. The language of French literary prose was created by Calvin and Rabelais—but Calvin's language, the language of the middle classes ('of shopkeepers and tradesmen') was an intentional and conscious lowering of, almost a travesty on, the sacred language of the Bible. The middle strata of national languages, while being transformed into the language of the higher ideological spheres and into the language of Sacred Writ, were perceived as a denigrating travesty of these higher spheres. For this reason these new languages provided only very modest space for parody: these languages hardly knew, and now do not know at all, sacred words, since they themselves were to a significant extent born out of a parody of the sacred word.

However, in the Middle Ages the role of parody was extremely important: it paved the way for a new literary and linguistic consciousness, as well as for the great Renaissance novel.

Cyprian Feasts is an ancient and excellent example of medieval 'parodia sacra,' that is, sacred parody—or to be more accurate, parody on sacred texts and rituals. Its roots go deep into ancient ritualistic parody, ritual degrading and the ridiculing of higher powers. But these roots are distant; the ancient ritualistic element in them has been re-interpreted; parody now fulfills the new and highly important functions of which we spoke above.

We must first of all take into account the recognized and legalized freedom then enjoyed by parody. The Middle Ages, with varying degrees of qualification, respected the freedom of the fool's cap and allotted a rather broad license to laughter and the laughing word. This freedom was bounded primarily by feast days and school festivals. Medieval laughter is holiday laughter. The parodic-travestying 'Holiday of Fools'[gg] and 'Holiday of the Ass' are well known, and were even celebrated in the churches themselves by the lower clergy. Highly characteristic of this tendency is *risus paschalis*, or paschal laughter. During the paschal days laughter was traditionally permitted in church. The preacher permitted himself risqué jokes and gay-hearted anecdotes from the church pulpit in order to encourage laughter in the congregation—this was conceived as a cheerful rebirth after days of melancholy and fasting. No less productive was 'Christmas laughter' (*risus natalis*); as distinct from *risus paschalis* it expressed itself not in stories but in songs. Serious church hymns were sung to the tunes of street ditties and were thus given a new twist. In addition a huge store of special Christmas carols existed in which reverent nativity themes were interwoven with folk motifs on the cheerful death of the old and the birth of the new. Parodic-travestying ridicule of the old often became dominant in these songs, especially in France, where the 'Noël,' or Christmas carol, became one of the most popular generic sources for the revolutionary street song (we recall Pushkin's 'Noël,' with its parodic-travestying use of the nativity theme). To holiday laughter, almost everything was permitted.

Equally broad were the rights and liberties enjoyed by the school festivals, which played a large role in the cultural and literary life of the Middle Ages. Works created for these festivals were predominantly parodies and travesties. The medieval monastic pupil (and in later times the university student) ridiculed with a clear conscience during the festival everything that had been the subject of reverent studies during the course of the year—everything from Sacred Writ to his school grammar. The Middle Ages produced a whole series of variants on the parodic-travestying Latin grammar. Case inflection, verbal forms and all grammatical categories in general were reinterpreted either in an indecent, erotic context, in a context of eating and drunkenness or in a context ridiculing church and monastic principles of hierarchy and subordination. Heading this unique grammatical tradition is the seventh-century work of Virgilius Maro Grammaticus.[hh] This is an extraordinarily learned work, stuffed with an incredible quantity of references, quotations from all possible authorities of the ancient world including some that had never existed; in a number of cases even the quotations themselves are parodic. Interwoven with serious and rather subtle grammatical analysis is a sharp parodic exaggeration of this very subtlety, and of the scru-

---

[gg] Reference here is to the *festa stultorum*, a form of *ludus* in which everything is reversed, even clothing: trousers were worn on the head, for instance, an operation that symbolically reflects in some measure the jongleurs, who are depicted in miniatures head-downward. [Tr.]

[hh] Virgilius Maro the Grammarian lived in Toulouse in the seventh century and wrote a number of remarkable meditations on the secrets of Latin grammar (*Opera*, ed. J. Heumer [Teubner], 1886). Bakhtin has two of these in mind, apparently, the *Epist. de verbo* and *Epist. de pron.* Helen Waddell (*The Wandering Scholars* [New York, 1927]) says of this dark age that 'the grammarians of Toulouse argue over the vocative of *ego* amid the crash of empires' (p. 8), but she singles Virgilius Maro the Grammarian out as a bright (?) spot: 'It was low tide on the continent of Europe, except for one deep pool at Toulouse, where the grammarian Virgilius Maro agitated strangely on the secret tongues of Latin, and told his story of the two scholars who argued for fifteen days and nights without sleeping or eating on the frequentative of the verb *to be*, till it almost came to knives, rather like the monsters one expects to find stranded in an ebb' (p. 28). [Tr.]

pulousness of scholarly analyses; there is a description, for example, of a scholarly discussion lasting two weeks on the question of the vocative case of *ego*, that is, the vocative case of 'I.' Taken as a whole, Virgilius Grammaticus' work is a magnificent and subtle parody of the formalistic-grammatical thinking of late antiquity. It is grammatical Saturnalia, *grammatica pileata*.

Characteristically, many medieval scholars apparently took this grammatical treatise completely seriously. And even contemporary scholars are far from unanimous in their evaluation of the character and degree of the parodic impulse in it. This is additional evidence, were it needed, for just how flexible the boundaries were between the straightforward and the parodically refracted word in medieval literature.

Holiday and school-festival laughter was fully legalized laughter. In those days it was permitted to turn the direct sacred word into a parodic-travestying mask; it could be born again, as it were, out of the grave of authoritative and reverential seriousness. Under these conditions, the fact that *Cyprian Feasts* could enjoy enormous popularity even in strict church circles becomes understandable. In the ninth century the severe abbot of Fulda, Raban Maur,[ii] put the work into verse: the *Feasts* were read at the banquet tables of kings, and were performed during the paschal festivals by pupils of monastic schools.

The great parodic literature of the Middle Ages was created in an atmosphere of holidays and festivals. There was no genre, no text, no prayer, no saying that did not receive its parodic equivalent. Parodic liturgies have come down to us— liturgies of drunks[jj] and gamblers, liturgies about money. Numerous evangelical readings have also survived, readings that began with the traditional 'ab illo tempore,' that is, 'in former times . . .' and that often included highly indiscreet stories. A great number of parodic prayers and hymns are intact as well. In his dissertation, 'Parodies des thèmes pieux dans la poésie française du moyen age' [Helsinki, 1914], the Finnish scholar Eero Ilvoonen published the texts of six parodies on the 'Pater noster' two on the 'Credo' and one on the 'Ave Maria,' but he gives only the macaronic Latin-French texts. One cannot begin to conceive of the huge number of parodic Latin and macaronic prayers and hymns in medieval manuscript codices. In his *Parodia Sacra*, F. Novati surveys but a small part of this literature.[14] The stylistic devices employed in this parodying, travestying, reinterpreting and re-accentuating are extremely diverse. These devices have so far been very little studied, and such studies as there are have lacked the necessary stylistic depth.

Alongside the specific 'parodia sacra' we find a diverse parodying and travestying of the sacred word in other comic genres and in literary works of the Middle Ages—for example, in the comic beast epics.

[ii] Magnentius Raban Maur (780–856) was the greatest ecclesiastic of his age, generally regarded as the first in the still unbroken line of German theologians. His reputation for severity is caught in Raby's description: 'Strict, and not too sympathetic by nature; he ruled the Abbey well, caring little for politics and testing all things by a high standard of duty' (*A History of Christian Latin Poetry* [Oxford, 1927], p. 179). [Tr.]

[jj] Liturgies for drunks constitute a whole medieval genre, the *missa potatorum*. [Tr.]

The sacred, authoritative, direct word in another's language—that was the hero of this entire grand parodic literature, primarily Latin, but in part macaronic. This word, its style and the way it means, became an object of representation; both word and style were transformed into a bounded and ridiculous image. The Latin 'parodia sacra' is projected against the background of the vulgar national language. The accentuating system of this vulgar language penetrates to the very heart of the Latin text. In essence Latin parody is, therefore, a bilingual phenomenon: although there is only one language, this language is structured and perceived in the light of another language, and in some instances not only the accents but also the syntactical forms of the vulgar language are clearly sensed in the Latin parody. Latin parody is an intentional bilingual hybrid. We now come upon the problem of the *intentional hybrid*.

Every type of parody or travesty, every word 'with conditions attached,' with irony, enclosed in intonational quotation marks, every type of indirect word is in a broad sense an intentional hybrid—but a hybrid compounded of two orders: one linguistic (a single language) and one stylistic. In actual fact, in parodic discourse two styles, two 'languages' (both intra-lingual) come together and to a certain extent are crossed with each other: the language being parodied (for example, the language of the heroic poem) and the language that parodies (low prosaic language, familiar conversational language, the language of the realistic genres, 'normal' language, 'healthy' literary language as the author of the parody conceived it). This second parodying language, against whose background the parody is constructed and perceived, does not—if it is a strict parody—enter as such into the parody itself, but is invisibly present in it.

It is the nature of every parody to transpose the values of the parodied style, to highlight certain elements while leaving others in the shade: parody is always biased in some direction, and this bias is dictated by the distinctive features of the parodying language, its accentual system, its structure—we feel its presence in the parody and we can recognize that presence, just as we at other times recognize clearly the accentual system, syntactic construction, tempi and rhythm or a specific vulgar language within purely Latin parody (that is, we recognize a Frenchman or a German as the author of the parody). Theoretically it is possible to sense and recognize in any parody that 'normal' language, that 'normal' style, in light of which the given parody was created. But in practice it is far from easy and not always possible.

Thus it is that in parody two languages are crossed with each other, as well as two styles, two linguistic points of view, and in the final analysis two speaking subjects. It is true that only one of these languages (the one that is parodied) is present in its own right; the other is present invisibly, as an actualizing background for creating and perceiving. Parody is an intentional hybrid, but usually it is an intra-linguistic one, one that nourishes itself on the stratification of the literary language into generic languages and languages of various specific tendencies.

Every type of intentional stylistic hybrid is more or less dialogized. This means that the languages that are crossed in it relate to each other as do rejoinders in a dialogue; there is an argument between languages, an argument between styles of language. But it is not a dialogue in the narrative sense, nor in the abstract sense; rather it is a dialogue between points of view, each with its own concrete language that cannot be translated into the other.

Thus every parody is an intentional dialogized hybrid. Within it, languages and styles actively and mutually illuminate one another.

Every word used 'with conditions attached,' every word enclosed in intonational quotation marks, is likewise an intentional hybrid—if only because the speaker insulates himself from this word as if from another 'language,' as if from a style, when it sounds to him (for example) too vulgar, or on the contrary too refined, or too pompous, or if it bespeaks a specific tendency, a specific linguistic manner and so forth.

But let us return to the Latin 'parodia sacra.' It is an intentional dialogized hybrid, but a hybrid of different languages. It is a dialogue between languages, although one of them (the vulgar) is present only as an actively dialogizing backdrop. What we have is a never-ending folkloric dialogue: the dispute between a dismal sacred word and a cheerful folk word, a dispute that resembles the well-known medieval dialogues between Solomon and the cheerful rogue Marcolph—except that Marcolph argued with Solomon in Latin, and here the arguments are carried on in various languages.[kk] Another's sacred word, uttered in a foreign language, is degraded by the accents of vulgar folk languages, re-evaluated and reinterpreted against the backdrop of these languages, and congeals to the point where it becomes a ridiculous image, the comic carnival mask of a narrow and joyless pedant, an unctious hypocritical old bigot, a stingy and dried-up miser. This manuscript tradition of 'parodia sacra,' prodigious in scope and almost a thousand years long, is a remarkable and as yet poorly read document testifying to an intense struggle and interanimation among languages, a struggle that occurred everywhere in Western Europe. This was a language drama played out as if it were a gay farce. It was linguistic Saturnalia—*lingua sacra pileata*.

The sacred Latin word was a foreign body that invaded the organism of the European languages. And throughout the Middle Ages, national languages, as organisms, repulsed this body. It was not, however, the repelling of a *thing*, but rather of a conceptualizing discourse that had made a home for itself in all the higher reaches of national ideological thought processes. The repulsion of this foreign-born sacred word was a dialogized operation, and was accomplished under cover of holiday and festival merrymaking; it was precisely the old ruler, the old year, the winter, the fast that was driven out. Such was the 'parodia sacra.'

But the remainder of medieval Latin literature was also in its essence a great and complex dialogized hybrid. It is no wonder that Paul Lehmann defines it as the appropriation, reworking and imitation of someone else's property, that is,

---

[kk] Reference here is to the *Dialogus Salomonis et Marcolphus*, available in the edition of W. Benary (Heidelberg, 1914). See also Piero Camporesi, *La Maschera di Bertoldo* (Turin, 1976). A re-edition, with a re-publication of the first printed vernacular version (Venice, 1502) is contained in an appendix to Giulio Cesare Croce, *La Sottilissime astuzie di Bertoldo: Le piacevoli ridicoloso simplicita di Bertoldino* (Turin, 1978). [Tr.]

of someone else's word. This reciprocal orientation of each word to the other occurs across the entire spectrum of tones—from reverent acceptance to parodic ridicule—so that it is often very difficult to establish precisely where reverence ends and ridicule begins. It is exactly like the modern novel, where one often does not know where the direct authorial word ends and where a parodic or stylized playing with the characters' language begins. Only here, in the Latin literature of the Middle Ages, the complex and contradictory process of accepting and then resisting the other's word, the process of reverently heeding it while at the same time ridiculing it, was accomplished on a grand scale throughout all the Western European world, and left an irradicable mark on the literary and linguistic consciousness of its peoples.

In addition to Latin parody there also existed, as we have already mentioned, macaronic parody.*ll* This is an already fully developed, intentionally dialogized bilingual (and sometimes trilingual) hybrid. In the bilingual literature of the Middle Ages we also find all possible types of relationships to the other's word— from reverence to merciless ridicule. In France, for example, the so-called 'épitres farcies' were widespread. Here, a verse of Sacred Writ (part of the Apostolic Epistles read during the mass) is accompanied by lines of octo-syllabic verse in French that piously translate and paraphrase the Latin text. The French language functioned in such a pious and commentating way in a whole series of macaronic prayers. Here, for example, is an excerpt from a macaronic 'Pater noster' of the thirteenth century (the beginning of the final stanza):

> Sed libera nos, mais delivre nous, Sire,
> a malo, de tout mal et de cruel martire.

In this hybrid the French portion piously and affirmatively translates and completes the Latin portion.

But here is the beginning of a 'Pater noster' of the fourteenth century describing the disasters of war:

> Pater noster, tu n'ies pas foulz
> Quar tu t'ies mis en grand repos
> Qui es montés haut in celis.[15]

Here the French portion*mm* sharply ridicules the sacred Latin word. It interrupts the opening words of the prayer and gives a picture of life in heaven as something peaceful and marvelous compared to our earthly woes. The style of the French portion does not correspond to the high style of the prayer, as it does in the first example; high style is in fact deliberately vulgarized. This is a crude earthly rejoinder to the other-wordly pomposity of the prayer.

There are an extraordinarily large number of macaronic texts of varying degrees of piety and parody. The macaronic verse from *Carmina burana* is universally known. We might also recall the macaronic language of liturgical dramas. There, national languages often serve as a comic rejoinder, lowering the

---

ll Macaronic verse combines Latin with a vernacular language.

mm 'Our Father, who ascended to high heaven, Thou art not stupid, for there Thou art in great peace.'

lofty Latin portions of the drama.

The macaronic literature of the Middle Ages is likewise an extremely important and interesting document in the struggle and interanimation among languages.

There is no need to expand upon the great parodic-travestying literature of the Middle Ages that exists in national folk languages. This literature constituted a fully articulated superstructure of laughter, erected over all serious straight-forward genres. Here, as in Rome, the tendency was toward a laughing double for every serious form. We recall the role of medieval clowns, those professional creators of the 'second level,' who with the doubling effect of their laughter insured the wholeness of the seriolaughing word. We recall all the different kinds of comic intermedia and entr'actes that played a role in the 'fourth drama' of Greece and in the cheerful exodium of Rome. A clear example of just this doubling effect of laughter can be found at the second level, the level of the fool, in the tragedies and comedies of Shakespeare. Echoes of this comic parallelism can still be heard today—for example, in the rather common doubling by a circus clown of the serious and dangerous numbers of a program, or in the half-joking role of our masters of ceremonies.

All the parodic-travestying forms of the Middle Ages, and of the ancient world as well, modeled themselves on folk and holiday merrymaking, which throughout the Middle Ages bore the character of carnival and still retained in itself ineradicable traces of Saturnalia.

At the waning of the Middle Ages and during the Renaissance the parodic-travestying word broke through all remaining boundaries. It broke through into all strict and closed straightforward genres; it reverberated loudly in the epics of the *Spielmänner* and *cantastorie*;[nn] it penetrated the lofty chivalric romance. Devilry almost completely overwhelmed the mystery rites, of which devilry was originally only a part. Such major and extremely important genres as the *sotie*[oo] made their appearance. And there arrived on the scene, at last, the great Renaissance novel—the novels of Rabelais and Cervantes. It is precisely in these two works that the novelistic word, prepared for by all the forms analyzed above as well as by a more ancient heritage, revealed its full potential and began to play such a titanic role in the formulation of a new literary and linguistic consciousness.

In the Renaissance, this interanimation of languages that was working to destroy bilingualism reached its highest point. It became, in addition, extraordinarily more complex. In the second volume of his classic work, Ferdinand Bruno,[pp] the historian of the French language, poses the question: why was the

[nn] *Cantastorie* were the medieval singers of the Carolingian epic in Tuscany. Although the battle between Christians and Moors is still the subject, the dignified Charlemagne is less important in the rhymes of the *cantastorie* than erotic love stories and improbable adventures. They are an important source for the *Orlando Furioso*. [Tr.]

[oo] *Sotie*, a type of French comic play of the fifteenth and sixteenth centuries, differing from the farce essentially because of its political and social satire. Twenty of these are still extant, the best known of which is Pierre Gringoire's *La Sottie du Prince des Sots* (1512), directed against Pope Julius II. See E. Picot, *La Sottie en France* (Paris, 1878). [Tr.]

[pp] Ferdinand Bruno, author of the magisterial *Histoire de la langue française des origines à 1900* (Paris, 1924–). [Tr.]

task of transition to a national language accomplished precisely during the Renaissance, that period whose tendencies were otherwise overwhelmingly toward the classical? And the answer he provides is absolutely correct: the very attempt of the Renaissance to establish the Latin language in all its classical purity inevitably transformed it into a dead language. It was impossible to sustain the classic Ciceronian purity of Latin while using it in the course of everyday life and in the world of objects of the sixteenth century, that is, while using it to express concepts and objects from the contemporary scene. The re-establishment of a classically pure Latin restricted its area of application to essentially the sphere of stylization alone. It was as if the language were being measured against a new world. And the language could not be stretched to fit. At the same time classical Latin illuminated the face of medieval Latin. This face, as it turned out, was hideous; but this face could only be seen in the light of classical Latin. And thus there came about that remarkable image of a language—*The Letters of Obscure People.*[qq]

This satire is a complex intentional linguistic hybrid. The language of obscure people is parodied; that is, it coalesces into a stereotype, it is exaggerated, reduced to a type—when measured against the standard of the proper and correct Latin of the humanists. At the same time, beneath the Latin language of these obscure people their native German tongue shines distinctly through: they take the syntactical constructions of the German language and fill them with Latin words, and they even translate specific German expressions literally into Latin; their intonation is coarse, Germanic. From the point of view of the obscure people this hybrid is not intentional; they write in the only way they can. But this Latin–German hybrid is intentionally exaggerated and highlighted by the parodying intention of the authors of the satire. One must note, however, that this linguistic satire has something of the air of the study about it, a somewhat abstract and grammatical character.

The poetry of the macaronics was also complex linguistic satire, but it was not a parody on kitchen Latin; it was a travesty that aimed at lowering the Latin used by the Ciceronian purists with their lofty and strict lexical norms. The macaronics worked with correct Latin constructions (as distinct from the obscure people), but into these constructions they introduced an abundance of words from their native vulgar tongue (Italian), having given them an external Latin formulation. The Italian language and the style of the low genres—the facetious tales and so forth—functioned as an actualizing backdrop against which macaronic poetry could be perceived, with the themes of body and material emphasized and thereby degraded. The language of the Ciceronians featured a high style; it was, in essence, a style rather than a language. It was this style that the macaronics parodied.

[qq] *Letters of Obscure People*, or *Epistolae obscurorum virorum* (1515), a collection of satirical letters making fun of the obscurantist enemies of the great humanist Johann Reuchlin (1455–1522) by two of his younger—and more irreverent—supporters, Crotus Rubianus and Ulrich von Hutten. The letters were ordered burnt by Pope Adrian. See David Friedrich Strauss, *Ulrich von Hutten*, tr. G. Sturge (London, 1874), pp. 120–140. [Tr.]

In the linguistic satires of the Renaissance (*The Letters of Obscure People*, the poetry of the macaronics) three languages thus animate one another: medieval Latin, the purified and rigorous Latin of the humanists and the national vulgar tongue. At the same time two worlds are animating each other: a medieval one and a new folk-humanist one. We also hear the same old folkloric quarrel of old with new; we hear the same old folkloric disgracing and ridiculing of the old— old authority, old truth, the old word.

The Letters of Obscure People, the poetry of the macaronics and a series of other analogous phenomena indicate to what extent this process of interanimation of languages, the measuring of them against their current reality and their epoch, was a conscious process. They indicate further to what extent forms of language, and forms of world view, were inseparable from each other. And they indicate, finally, to what extent the old and new worlds were characterized precisely by their own peculiar languages, by the image of language that attached to each. Languages quarreled with each other, but this quarrel—like any quarrel among great and significant cultural and historical forces—could not pass on to a further phase by means of abstract and rational dialogue, nor by a purely dramatic dialogue, but only by means of complexly dialogized hybrids. The great novels of the Renaissance were such hybrids, although stylistically they were monoglot.

In the process of this linguistic change, the dialects within national languages were also set into new motion. Their period of dark and deaf co-existence came to an end. Their unique qualities began to be sensed in a new way, in the light of the evolving and centralizing norm of a national language. Ridiculing dialecto-logical peculiarities, making fun of the linguistic and speech manners of groups living in different districts and cities throughout the nation, is something that belongs to every people's most ancient store of language images. But during the Renaissance this mutual ridiculing of different groups among the folk took on a new and fundamental significance—occurring as it did in the light of a more general interanimation of languages, and when a general, national norm for the country's language was being created. The parodying images of dialects began to receive more profound artistic formulation, and began to penetrate major literature.

Thus in the commedia dell'arte, Italian dialects were knit together with the specific types and masks of the comedy. In this respect one might even call the commedia dell'arte a comedy of dialects. It was an intentional dialectological hybrid.

Thus did the interanimation of languages occur in the very epoch that saw the creation of the European novel. Laughter and polyglossia had paved the way for the novelistic discourse of modern times.

In our essay we have touched upon only two factors that were at work in the prehistory of novelistic discourse. There remains before us the very important task of studying speech genres—primarily the familiar strata of folk language that played such an enormous role in the formulation of novelistic discourse and that, in altered form, entered into the composition of the novel as a genre. But this already takes us beyond the boundaries of our present study. Here, at the conclusion, we wish only to emphasize that the novelistic word arose and developed not as the result of a narrowly literary struggle among tendencies, styles, abstract world views—but rather in a complex and centuries-long struggle of cultures and languages. It is connected with the major shifts and crises in the fates of various European languages, and of the speech life of peoples. The prehistory of the novelistic word is not to be contained within the narrow perimeters of a history confined to mere literary styles.

NOTES

1. The Romantics maintained that the novel was a mixed genre (a mixture of verse and prose) incorporating into its composition various genres (in particular the lyrical)—but the Romantics did not draw any stylistic conclusions from this. Cf., for example, Friedrich Schlegel's *Brief über den Roman.*
2. In Germany, in a series of works by Spielhagen (which began to appear in 1864) and especially with R. Riemanns' work, *Goethes Romantechnik* (1902); in France, beginning in the main with Brunetière and Lanson.
3. Literary scholars studying the technique of framing ('Ramenerzählung') in literary prose and the role of the storyteller in the epic (Käte Friedemann, *Die Rolle des Erzählers in der Epik* [Leipzig, 1910]) came close to dealing with this fundamental problem of the plurality of styles and levels characteristic of the novel as a genre, but this problem remained unresolved on the stylistic plane.
4. Of special value is the work by H. Hatzfeld, *Don-Quijote als Wortkunstwerk* (Leipzig-Berlin, 1927).
5. Such, for example, is L. Sainéan's book, *La Langue de Rabelais* (Paris, vol. 1, 1922; vol. 2, 1923).
6. Such, for example, is G. Loesch's book, *Die impressionistische Syntax der Goncourts* (Nuremberg, 1919).
7. Of such a type are the works by the Vosslerians devoted to style: we should mention as especially worthwhile the works of Leo Spitzer on the stylistics of Charles-Louis Philippe, Charles Péguy and Marcel Proust, brought together in his book *Stilstudien* (vol. 2, *Stilsprachen*, 1928).
8. V. V. Vinogradov's book *On Artistic Prose* [O xudožestvennoj proze] (Moscow-Leningrad, 1930) assumes this position.
9. Cf. J. Schmidt, *Ulixes comicus.*
10. Cf. A. Dieterich, *Pulcinella: Pompeyanische Wandbilder und römische Satyrspiele* (Leipzig, 1897), p. 131.
11. U. Wilamowitz-Moellendorff, *Platon*, vol. 1 (Berlin, 1920), p. 290.
12. Cf. Erwin Rohde, *Der griechische Roman und seine Vorläufer* (n.p., 1896).
13. Cf. Paul Lehmann, *Die Parodie im Mittelalter* (Munich, 1922), p. 10.
14. F. Novati, *Parodia sacra nelle letterature moderne* (see: 'Novatis Studi critici e letterari,' Turin, 1889).
15. Cf. Eero Ilvoonen, *Parodies des thèmes pieux dans la poésie française du moyen âge* (Helsinki, 1914).

8 Tzvetan Todorov

Tzvetan Todorov (b. 1939) was born in Sofia, Bulgaria, and is an authority on Slavic literature as well as being a distinguished literary theorist. He settled in Paris, and took a leading part in the emergence of structuralism as a force in literary studies in France in the 1960s, firstly by translating and disseminating the work of the Russian Formalists from which structuralism derived much of its methodology, and secondly by his own original contributions, especially in the field of narratology. He taught, like Roland Barthes, at the Ecole Pratique des Hautes Etudes, and now works at the Centre Nationale de la Recherche Scientifique, in Paris. He is a frequent academic visitor to the United States. His publications include *Grammaire du Decameron* (1969), *Introduction à la littérature fantastique* (1970) translated as *The Fantastic: a Structural Approach to a Literary Genre* (1975), *La Poetique de la Prose* (1971), translated as *The Poetics of Prose* (1977), and *Mikhail Bakhtin: le principe dialogique* (1981), translated as *Mikhail Bakhtin: the dialogical principle* (1984).

'The Typology of Detective Fiction', first published in 1966, is reprinted from *The Poetics of Prose*, probably Todorov's most generally accessible work of criticism, translated by Richard Howard. It exemplifies the characteristic structuralist pursuit of explanatory models with which masses of literary data may be classified and explained. It is also typical of Todorov's cool, lucid and economical expository style—qualities not frequently encountered in structuralist criticism.

CROSS-REFERENCES: 4. Genette
                           9. Barthes
                          28. Eco
COMMENTARY: Jonathan Culler, 'Foreword' to Tzvetan Todorov, *The Poetics of Prose* (1977)
                          Terence Hawkes, *Structuralism and Semiotics* (1977) pp. 95–106.

The typology of detective fiction

> Detective fiction cannot be subdivided into kinds.
> It merely offers historically different forms.
> —Boileau and Narcejac, *Le Roman policier*, 1964

If I use this observation as the epigraph to an article dealing precisely with 'kinds' of 'detective fiction,' it is not to emphasize my disagreement with the authors in question, but because their attitude is very widespread; hence it is the first thing we must confront. Detective fiction has nothing to do with this question: for nearly two centuries, there has been a powerful reaction in literary studies against the very notion of genre. We write either about literature in general or about a single work, and it is a tacit convention that to classify several works in a genre is to devalue them. There is a good historical explanation for this attitude: literary reflection of the classical period, which concerned genres more than works, also manifested a penalizing tendency—a work was judged poor if it did not sufficiently obey the rules of its genre. Hence such criticism sought not only to describe genres but also to prescribe them; the grid of genre preceded literary creation instead of following it.

The reaction was radical: the romantics and their present-day descendants have refused not only to conform to the rules of the genres (which was indeed their privilege) but also to recognize the very existence of such a notion. Hence the theory of genres has remained singularly undeveloped until very recently. Yet now there is a tendency to seek an intermediary between the too-general notion of literature and those individual objects which are works. The delay doubtless comes from the fact that typology is implied by the description of these individual works; yet this task of description is still far from having received satisfactory solutions. So long as we cannot describe the structure of works, we must be content to compare certain measurable elements, such as meter. Despite the immediate interest in an investigation of genres (as Albert Thibaudet remarked, such an investigation concerns the problem of universals), we cannot undertake it without first elaborating structural description: only the criticism of the classical period could permit itself to deduce genres from abstract logical schemas.

An additional difficulty besets the study of genres, one which has to do with the specific character of every esthetic norm. The major work creates, in a sense, a new genre and at the same time transgresses the previously valid rules of the genre. The genre of *The Charterhouse of Parma*, that is, the norm to which this novel refers, is not the French novel of the early nineteenth century; it is the genre 'Stendhalian novel' which is created by precisely this work and a few others. One might say that every great book establishes the existence of two genres, the reality of two norms: that of the genre it transgresses, which dominated the preceding literature, and that of the genre it creates.

Yet there is a happy realm where this dialectical contradiction between the work and its genre does not exist: that of popular literature. As a rule, the literary masterpiece does not enter any genre save perhaps its own; but the masterpiece of popular literature is precisely the book which best fits its genre. Detective fiction has its norms; to 'develop' them is also to disappoint them: to 'improve upon' detective fiction is to write 'literature,' not detective fiction. The whodunit par excellence is not the one which transgresses the rules of the genre, but the one which conforms to them: *No Orchids for Miss Blandish*[a] is an incarnation of its genre, not a transcendence. If we had properly described the genres of popular literature, there would no longer be an occasion to speak of its master-pieces. They are one and the same thing; the best novel will be the one about which there is nothing to say. This is a generally unnoticed phenomenon, whose consequences affect every esthetic category. We are today in the presence of a discrepancy between two essential manifestations; no longer is there one single esthetic norm in our society, but two; the same measurements do not apply to 'high' art and 'popular' art.

The articulation of genres within detective fiction therefore promises to be relatively easy. But we must begin with the description of 'kinds,' which also means with their delimitation. We shall take as our point of departure the classic detective fiction which reached its peak between the two world wars and is often called the whodunit. Several attempts have already been made to specify the rules of this genre (we shall return below to S. S. Van Dine's twenty rules); but the best general characterization I know is the one Butor gives in his own novel *Passing Time* (*L'Emploi du temps*). George Burton, the author of many murder mysteries, explains to the narrator that 'all detective fiction is based on two murders of which the first, committed by the murderer, is merely the occasion for the second, in which he is the victim of the pure and unpunishable murderer, the detective,' and that 'the narrative . . . superimposes two temporal series: the days of the investigation which begin with the crime, and the days of the drama which lead up to it.'

At the base of the whodunit we find a duality, and it is this duality which will guide our description. This novel contains not one but two stories: the story of the crime and the story of the investigation. In their purest form, these two stories have no point in common. Here are the first lines of a 'pure' whodunit:

a small green index-card on which is typed:
    Odel, Margaret.
184 W. Seventy-first Street. Murder: Strangled about
11 P.M. Apartment robbed. Jewels stolen. Body found by
Amy Gibson, maid. [S. S. Van Dine, *The 'Canary' Murder Case*]

The first story, that of the crime, ends before the second begins. But what happens in the second? Not much. The characters of this second story, the story

---

[a] Thriller by James Hadley Chase, first published in 1939. It is the subject of a famous essay by George Orwell, 'Raffles and Miss Blandish', (*Collected Essays, Journalism and Letters*, Vol 3).

of the investigation, do not act, they learn. Nothing can happen to them: a rule of the genre postulates the detective's immunity. We cannot imagine Hercule Poirot or Philo Vance[b] threatened by some danger, attacked, wounded, even killed. The hundred and fifty pages which separate the discovery of the crime from the revelation of the killer are devoted to a slow apprenticeship: we examine clue after clue, lead after lead. The whodunit thus tends toward a purely geometric architecture: Agatha Christie's *Murder on the Orient Express*, for example, offers twelve suspects; the book consists of twelve chapters, and again twelve interrogations, a prologue, and an epilogue (that is, the discovery of the crime and the discovery of the killer).

This second story, the story of the investigation, thereby enjoys a particular status. It is no accident that it is often told by a friend of the detective, who explicitly acknowledges that he is writing a book; the second story consists, in fact, in explaining how this very book came to be written. The first story ignores the book completely, that is, it never confesses its literary nature (no author of detective fiction can permit himself to indicate directly the imaginary character of the story, as it happens in 'literature'). On the other hand, the second story is not only supposed to take the reality of the book into account, but it is precisely the story of that very book.

We might further characterize these two stories by saying that the first—the story of the crime—tells 'what really happened,' whereas the second—the story of the investigation—explains 'how the reader (or the narrator) has come to know about it.' But these definitions concern not only the two stories in detective fiction, but also two aspects of every literary work which the Russian Formalists isolated forty years ago. They distinguished, in fact, the *fable* (story) from the *subject* (plot)[c] of a narrative: the story is what has happened in life, the plot is the way the author presents it to us. The first notion corresponds to the reality evoked, to events similar to those which take place in our lives; the second, to the book itself, to the narrative, to the literary devices the author employs. In the story, there is no inversion in time, actions follow their natural order; in the plot, the author can present results before their causes, the end before the beginning. These two notions do not characterize two parts of the story or two different works, but two aspects of one and the same work; they are two points of view about the same thing. How does it happen then that detective fiction manages to make both of them present, to put them side by side?

To explain this paradox, we must first recall the special status of the two stories. The first, that of the crime, is in fact the story of an absence: its most accurate characteristic is that it cannot be immediately present in the book. In other words, the narrator cannot transmit directly the conversations of the

[b] Hercule Poirot is the detective in many of Agatha Christie's novels, and Philo Vance is the detective in many of S. S. van Dine's novels.

[c] This translation of the Russian formalists' terms, *fabula* and *sjuzet*, is not entirely satisfactory, since 'story' and 'plot' are used loosely and sometimes interchangeably in much criticism of prose fiction. 'Discourse' is perhaps a more satisfactory rendering of *sjuzet*. For a useful account of the interpretation and modification of this crucial distinction in modern narratology, see the essay by Shlomith Rimmon-Kenan listed under 'Commentary' on Gérard Genette, p. 63 above.

characters who are implicated, nor describe their actions: to do so, he must necessarily employ the intermediary of another (or the same) character who will report, in the second story, the words heard or the actions observed. The status of the second story is, as we have seen, just as excessive; it is a story which has no importance in itself, which serves only as a mediator between the reader and the story of the crime. Theoreticians of detective fiction have always agreed that style, in this type of literature, must be perfectly transparent, imperceptible; the only requirement it obeys is to be simple, clear, direct. It has even been attempted—significantly—to suppress this second story altogether. One publisher put out real dossiers, consisting of police reports, interrogations, photographs, fingerprints, even locks of hair; these 'authentic' documents were to lead the reader to the discovery of the criminal (in case of failure, a sealed envelope, pasted on the last page, gave the answer to the puzzle: for example, the judge's verdict).

We are concerned then in the whodunit with two stories of which one is absent but real, the other present but insignificant. This presence and this absence explain the existence of the two in the continuity of the narrative. The first involves so many conventions and literary devices (which are in fact the 'plot' aspects of the narrative) that the author cannot leave them unexplained. These devices are, we may note, of essentially two types, temporal inversions and individual 'points of view': the tenor of each piece of information is determined by the person who transmits it, no observation exists without an observer; the author cannot, by definition, be omniscient as he was in the classical novel. The second story then appears as a place where all these devices are justified and 'naturalized': to give them a 'natural' quality, the author must explain that he is writing a book! And to keep this second story from becoming opaque, from casting a useless shadow on the first, the style is to be kept neutral and plain, to the point where it is rendered imperceptible.

Now let us examine another genre within detective fiction, the genre created in the United States just before and particularly after World War II, and which is published in France under the rubric '*série noire*' (the thriller); this kind of detective fiction fuses the two stories or in other words, suppresses the first and vitalizes the second. We are no longer told about a crime anterior to the moment of the narrative; the narrative coincides with the action. No thriller is presented in the form of memoirs: there is no point reached where the narrator comprehends all past events, we do not even know if he will reach the end of the story alive. Prospection takes the place of retrospection.

There is no story to be guessed; and there is no mystery, in the sense that it was present in the whodunit. But the reader's interest is not thereby diminished; we realize here that two entirely different forms of interest exist. The first can be called *curiosity*; it proceeds from effect to cause: starting from a certain effect (a corpse and certain clues) we must find its cause (the culprit and his motive). The second form is *suspense*, and here the movement is from cause to effect: we are first shown the causes, the initial *données* (gangsters preparing a heist), and our interest is sustained by the expectation of what will happen, that is, certain effects (corpses, crimes, fights). This type of interest was inconceivable in the whodunit, for its chief characters (the detective and his friend the narrator) were, by definition, immunized: nothing could happen to them. The situation is reversed in the thriller: everything is possible, and the detective risks his health, if not his life.

I have presented the opposition between the whodunit and the thriller as an opposition between two stories and a single one; but this is a logical, not a historical classification. The thriller did not need to perform this specific transformation in order to appear on the scene. Unfortunately for logic, genres are not constituted in conformity with structural descriptions; a new genre is created around an element which was not obligatory in the old one: the two encode different elements. For this reason the poetics of classicism was wasting its time seeking a logical classification of genres. The contemporary thriller has been constituted not around a method of presentation but around the milieu represented, around specific characters and behavior; in other words, its constitutive character is in its themes. This is how it was described, in 1945, by Marcel Duhamel, its promoter in France: in it we find 'violence—in all its forms, and especially the most shameful—beatings, killings. . . . Immorality is as much at home here as noble feelings. . . . There is also love—preferably vile—violent passion, implacable hatred.' Indeed it is around these few constants that the thriller is constituted: violence, generally sordid crime, the amorality of the characters. Necessarily, too, the 'second story,' the one taking place in the present, occupies a central place. But the suppression of the first story is not an obligatory feature: the early authors of the thriller, Dashiell Hammett and Raymond Chandler, preserve the element of mystery; the important thing is that it now has a secondary function, subordinate and no longer central as in the whodunit.

This restriction in the milieu described also distinguishes the thriller from the adventure story, though this limit is not very distinct. We can see that the properties listed up to now—danger, pursuit, combat—are also to be found in an adventure story; yet the thriller keeps its autonomy. We must distinguish several reasons for this: the relative effacement of the adventure story and its replacement by the spy novel; then the thriller's tendency toward the marvelous and the exotic, which brings it closer on the one hand to the travel narrative, and on the other to contemporary science fiction; last, a tendency to description which remains entirely alien to the detective novel. The difference in the milieu and behavior described must be added to these other distinctions, and precisely this difference has permitted the thriller to be constituted as a genre.

One particularly dogmatic author of detective fiction, S. S. Van Dine, laid down, in 1928, twenty rules to which any self-respecting author of detective fiction must conform. These rules have been frequently reproduced since then (see for instance the book, already quoted from, by Boileau and Narcejac) and frequently contested. Since we are not concerned with prescribing procedures for the writer but with describing the genres of detective fiction, we may profitably consider these rules a moment. In their original form, they are quite prolix and may be readily summarized by the eight following points:

1. The novel must have at most one detective and one criminal, and at least one victim (a corpse).

2. The culprit must not be a professional criminal, must not be the detective, must kill for personal reasons.

3. Love has no place in detective fiction.

4. The culprit must have a certain importance:
   (a) in life: not be a butler or a chambermaid.
   (b) in the book: must be one of the main characters.

5. Everything must be explained rationally; the fantastic is not admitted.

6. There is no place for descriptions nor for psychological analyses.

7. With regard to information about the story, the following homology must be observed: 'author : reader = criminal : detective.'

8. Banal situations and solutions must be avoided (Van Dine lists ten).

If we compare this list with the description of the thriller, we will discover an interesting phenomenon. A portion of Van Dine's rules apparently refers to all detective fiction, another portion to the whodunit. This distribution coincides, curiously, with the field of application of the rules: those which concern the themes, the life represented (the 'first story'), are limited to the whodunit (rules 1–4a); those which refer to discourse, to the book (to the 'second story'), are equally valid for the thriller (rules 4b–7; rule 8 is of a much broader generality). Indeed in the thriller there is often more than one detective (Chester Himes's *For Love of Imabelle*) and more than one criminal (James Hadley Chase's *The Fast Buck*). The criminal is almost obliged to be a professional and does not kill for personal reasons ('the hired killer'); further, he is often a policeman. Love—'preferably vile'—also has its place here. On the other hand, fantastic explanations, descriptions, and psychological analyses remain banished; the criminal must still be one of the main characters. As for rule 7, it has lost its pertinence with the disappearance of the double story. This proves that the development has chiefly affected the thematic part, and not the structure of the discourse itself (Van Dine does not note the necessity of mystery and consequently of the double story, doubtless considering this self-evident).

Certain apparently insignificant features can be codified in either type of detective fiction: a genre unites particularities located on different levels of generality. Hence the thriller, to which any accent on literary devices is alien, does not reserve its surprises for the last lines of the chapter; whereas the whodunit, which legalizes the literary convention by making it explicit in its 'second story,' will often terminate the chapter by a particular revelation ('You are the murderer,' Poirot says to the narrator of *The Murder of Roger Ackroyd*). Further, certain stylistic features in the thriller belong to it specifically. Descriptions are made without rhetoric, coldly, even if dreadful things are being described; one might say 'cynically' ('Joe was bleeding like a pig. Incredible that an old man could bleed so much,' Horace McCoy, *Kiss Tomorrow Goodbye*). The comparisons suggest a certain brutality (description of hands: 'I felt that if ever his hands got around my throat, they would make the blood gush out of my ears,' Chase, *You Never Know with Women*). It is enough to read such a passage to be sure one has a thriller in hand.

It is not surprising that between two such different forms there has developed a third, which combines their properties: the suspense novel. It keeps the mystery of the whodunit and also the two stories, that of the past and that of the present; but it refuses to reduce the second to a simple detection of the truth. As in the thriller, it is this second story which here occupies the central place. The reader is interested not only by what has happened but also by what will happen next; he wonders as much about the future as about the past. The two types of interest are thus united here—there is the curiosity to learn how past events are to be explained; and there is also the suspense: what will happen to the main characters? These characters enjoyed an immunity, it will be recalled, in the whodunit; here they constantly risk their lives. Mystery has a function different from the one it had in the whodunit: it is actually a point of departure, the main interest deriving from the second story, the one taking place in the present.

Historically, this form of detective fiction appeared at two moments: it served as transition between the whodunit and the thriller and it existed at the same time as the latter. To these two periods correspond two subtypes of the suspense novel. The first, which might be called 'the story of the vulnerable detective' is mainly illustrated by the novels of Hammett and Chandler. Its chief feature is that the detective loses his immunity, gets beaten up, badly hurt, constantly risks his life, in short, he is integrated into the universe of the other characters, instead of being an independent observer as the reader is (we recall Van Dine's detective-as-reader analogy). These novels are habitually classified as thrillers because of the milieu they describe, but we see that their composition brings them closer to suspense novels.

The second type of suspense novel has in fact sought to get rid of the conventional milieu of professional crime and to return to the personal crime of the whodunit, though conforming to the new structure. From it has resulted a novel we might call 'the story of the suspect-as-detective.' In this case, a crime is committed in the first pages and all the evidence in the hands of the police points to a certain person (who is the main character). In order to prove his innocence, this person must himself find the real culprit, even if he risks his life in doing so. We might say that, in this case, this character is at the same time the detective, the culprit (in the eyes of the police), and the victim (potential victim of the real murderers). Many novels by William Irish, Patrick Quentin, and Charles Williams are constructed on this model.

It is quite difficult to say whether the forms we have just described correspond to the stages of an evolution or else can exist simultaneously. The fact that we can encounter several types by the same author, such as Arthur Conan Doyle or Maurice Leblanc, preceding the great flowering of detective fiction, would make us tend to the second solution, particularly since these three forms coexist today. But it is remarkable that the evolution of detective fiction in its broad outlines has followed precisely the succession of these forms. We might say that at a certain point detective fiction experiences as an unjustified burden the constraints of this or that genre and gets rid of them in order to constitute a new code. The rule of the genre is perceived as a constraint once it becomes pure form and is no longer justified by the structure of the whole. Hence in novels by Hammett and Chandler, mystery had become a pure pretext, and the thriller which succeeded the whodunit got rid of it, in order to elaborate a new form of interest, suspense, and to concentrate on the description of a milieu. The suspense novel, which appeared after the great years of the thriller, experienced this milieu as a useless attribute, and retained only the suspense itself. But it has been necessary at the same time to reinforce the plot and to re-establish the former mystery. Novels which have tried to do without both mystery and the milieu proper to the thriller—for example, Francis Iles's *Premeditations* and Patricia Highsmith's *The Talented Mr Ripley*—are too few to be considered a separate genre.

Here we reach a final question: what is to be done with the novels which do not fit our classification? It is no accident, it seems to me, that the reader habitually considers novels such as those I have just mentioned marginal to the genre, an intermediary form between detective fiction and the novel itself. Yet if this form (or some other) becomes the germ of a new genre of detective fiction, this will not in itself constitute an argument against the classification proposed; as I have already said, the new genre is not necessarily constituted by the negation of the main feature of the old, but from a different complex of properties, not by necessity logically harmonious with the first form.

9 Roland Barthes

Roland Barthes (1915–80) was the most brilliant and influential of the generation of literary critics who came to prominence in France in the 1960s. After a slow start to his academic career (due mainly to illness), Barthes became a teacher at the Ecole Pratique des Hautes Etudes in Paris, and at the time of his death was Professor of Literary Semiology (a title of his own choice) at the prestigious Collège de France. His first book, *Writing Degree Zero* (1953; English translation 1972) was a polemical essay on the history of French literary style, in which the influence of Jean-Paul Sartre is perceptible. *Mythologies* (1957; translated 1973), perhaps Barthes' most accessible work, wittily analysed various manifestations of popular and high culture at the expense of bourgeois 'common sense'. A controversy with a traditionalist Sorbonne professor, Raymond Picard, in the mid-1960s, made Barthes famous, or notorious, as the leading iconoclast of '*la nouvelle critique*'. This movement, a rather loose alliance of critics opposed to traditional academic criticism and literary history, drew some of its inspiration from the experiments of the *nouveau roman* (see Alain Robbe-Grillet, 'A Future for the Novel', section 34 in *20th Century Literary Criticism*), and in the late 60s and early 70s was associated with radical left-wing politics (especially in the journal *Tel Quel*—see headnote on Julia Kristeva, below p. 229); but methodologically it depended heavily on structuralist semiotics in the tradition of Saussure and Jakobson.

Barthes himself produced an austere treatise on *The Elements of Semiology* in 1964 (translated 1967) and an influential essay entitled 'Introduction to the Structural Analysis of Narrative' in 1966 (included in *Image-Music-Text* (1977), essays by Barthes selected and translated by Stephen Heath). At this period he seems to have shared the structuralist ambition to found a 'science' of literary criticism. Later, perhaps partly under the influence of Derrida and Lacan, his interest shifted from the general rules and constraints of narrative to the production of meaning in the process of reading. In a famous essay written in 1968, reprinted below, Barthes proclaimed that 'the birth of the reader must be at the cost of the death of the Author'—an assertion that struck at the very heart of traditional literary studies, and that has remained one of the most controversial tenets of post-structuralism.

Barthes' most important work of literary criticism was probably *S/Z* (1970; translated 1974), an exhaustive commentary on a Balzac short story, 'Sarrasine', interleaved with bold theoretical speculation. The method of analysis, which is confessedly improvised and provisional and claims none of the rigour of structuralist narratology, is exemplified on a smaller scale by 'Textual Analysis of a Tale by Poe' (1973), reprinted below. By breaking down the text into small units of sense, or 'lexias', Barthes aims to show how they carry many different meanings simultaneously on different levels or in different codes. In *S/Z*, this demonstration is linked to a distinction between the '*lisible*' or 'readerly' classic text, which makes its readers passive consumers, and the '*scriptible*' or 'writerly' modern text, which invites its readers to an active participation in the production of meanings that are infinite and inexhaustible. Paradoxically, the effect of Barthes' brilliant interpretation of 'Sarrasine' is to impress one with the plurality rather than the limitation of meanings in the so-called classic realist text.

In the last decade of his life, Barthes moved further and further away from the concerns and methods of literary criticism and produced a series of highly idiosyncratic texts which consciously challenge the conventional distinctions between critic and creator, fiction and non-fiction, literature and non-literature: *The Pleasure of the Text* (1975), *Roland Barthes by Roland Barthes* (1977) [first published in France 1975], and *A Lover's Discourse*: Fragments (1978) [1977]. He was a writer who disconcerted his disciples as well as his opponents by continually rejecting one kind of discourse in favour of another, and to this extent lived the assertion in 'The Death of the Author', that 'the modern scriptor is born simultaneously with the text ... and every text is eternally written *here and now*'.

'The Death of the Author' is reprinted here from *Image-Music-Text*, and 'Textual Analysis of Poe's "Valdemar"', translated by Geoff Bennington, from *Untying The Text: a post-structuralist reader* (1981), ed. Robert Young, whose contributions to the numbered notes are in square brackets.

CROSS-REFERENCES: 8. Todorov
10. Foucault
COMMENTARY: Jonathan Culler, *Barthes* (1983)
Annette Lavers, *Roland Barthes: structuralism and after* (1982)
Philip Thody, *Roland Barthes: a conservative estimate* (revised edn 1984)

The death of the author

In his story *Sarrasine* Balzac, describing a castrato disguised as a woman, writes the following sentence: '*This was woman herself, with her sudden fears, her irrational whims, her instinctive worries, her impetuous boldness, her fussings, and her delicious sensibility.*' Who is speaking thus? Is it the hero of the story bent on remaining ignorant of the castrato hidden beneath the woman? Is it Balzac the individual, furnished by his personal experience with a philosophy of Woman? Is it Balzac the author professing 'literary' ideas on femininity? Is it universal wisdom? Romantic psychology? We shall never know, for the good reason that writing is the destruction of every voice, of every point of origin. Writing is that neutral, composite, oblique space where our subject slips away, the negative where all identity is lost, starting with the very identity of the body writing.

No doubt it has always been that way. As soon as a fact is *narrated* no longer with a view to acting directly on reality but intransitively, that is to say, finally outside of any function other than that of the very practice of the symbol itself, this disconnection occurs, the voice loses its origin, the author enters into his own death, writing begins. The sense of this phenomenon, however, has varied; in ethnographic societies the responsibility for a narrative is never assumed by a person but by a mediator, shaman or relator whose 'performance'—the mastery of the narrative code—may possibly be admired but never his 'genius'. The author is a modern figure, a product of our society insofar as, emerging from the Middle Ages with English empiricism, French rationalism and the personal faith of the Reformation, it discovered the prestige of the individual, of, as it is more nobly put, the 'human person'. It is thus logical that in literature it should be this positivism, the epitome and culmination of capitalist ideology, which has attached the greatest importance to the 'person' of the author. The *author* still reigns in histories of literature, biographies of writers, interviews, magazines, as in the very consciousness of men of letters anxious to unite their person and their work through diaries and memoirs. The image of literature to be found in ordinary culture is tyrannically centred on the author, his person, his life, his tastes, his passions, while criticism still consists for the most part in saying that Baudelaire's work is the failure of Baudelaire the man, Van Gogh's his madness, Tchaikovsky's his vice. The *explanation* of a work is always sought in the man or woman who produced it, as if it were always in the end, through the more or less transparent allegory of the fiction, the voice of a single person, the *author* 'confiding' in us.

Though the sway of the Author remains powerful (the new criticism[a] has often done no more than consolidate it), it goes without saying that certain writers have long since attempted to loosen it. In France, Mallarmé[b] was doubtless the first to see and to foresee in its full extent the necessity to substitute language itself for the person who until then had been supposed to be its owner. For him, for us too, it is language which speaks, not the author; to write is, through a prerequisite impersonality (not at all to be confused with the castrating objectivity of the realist novelist), to reach that point where only language acts, 'performs', and not 'me'. Mallarmé's entire poetics consists in suppressing the author in the interests of writing (which is, as will be seen, to restore the place of the reader).

[a] Barthes refers not to the Anglo–American 'New Criticism' of the 1930s, 40s and 50s, but to the French *nouvelle critique* of the 1960s.

[b] Stéphane Mallarmé (1871–1945), French symbolist poet.

Valéry[c], encumbered by a psychology of the Ego, considerably diluted Mallarmé's theory but, his taste for classicism leading him to turn to the lessons of rhetoric, he never stopped calling into question and deriding the Author; he stressed the linguistic and, as it were, 'hazardous' nature of his activity, and throughout his prose works he militated in favour of the essentially verbal condition of literature, in the face of which all recourse to the writer's interiority seemed to him pure superstition. Proust himself, despite the apparently psychological character of what are called his *analyses*, was visibly concerned with the task of inexorably blurring, by an extreme subtilization, the relation between the writer and his characters; by making of the narrator not he who has seen and felt nor even he who is writing, but he who *is going to write* (the young man in the novel—but, in fact, how old is he and who is he?—wants to write but cannot; the novel ends when writing at last becomes possible), Proust gave modern writing its epic. By a radical reversal, instead of putting his life into his novel, as is so often maintained, he made of his very life a work for which his own book was the model; so that it is clear to us that Charlus does not imitate Montesquiou but that Montesquiou—in his anecdotal, historical reality—is no more than a secondary fragment, derived from Charlus.[d] Lastly, to go no further than this prehistory of modernity, Surrealism, though unable to accord language a supreme place (language being system and the aim of the movement being, romantically, a direct subversion of codes—itself moreover illusory: a code cannot be destroyed, only 'played off'), contributed to the desacrilization of the image of the Author by ceaselessly recommending the abrupt disappointment of expectations of meaning (the famous surrealist 'jolt'), by entrusting the hand with the task of writing as quickly as possible what the head itself is unaware of (automatic writing), by accepting the principle and the experience of several people writing together. Leaving aside literature itself (such distinctions really becoming invalid), linguistics has recently provided the destruction of the Author with a valuable analytical tool by showing that the whole of the enunciation is an empty process, functioning perfectly without there being any need for it to be filled with the person of the interlocutors. Linguistically, the author is never more than the instance writing, just as *I* is nothing other than the instance saying *I*: language knows a 'subject', not a 'person', and this subject, empty outside of the very enunciation which defines it, suffices to make language 'hold together', suffices, that is to say, to exhaust it.

The removal of the Author (one could talk here with Brecht of a veritable 'distancing', the Author diminishing like a figurine at the far end of the literary stage) is not merely an historical fact or an act of writing; it utterly transforms the modern text (or—which is the same thing—the text is henceforth made and read in such a way that at all its levels the author is absent). The temporality is different. The Author, when believed in, is always conceived of as the past of

[c] Paul Valéry (1871–1945), French poet and critic. See section 20 of *20th Century Literary Criticism*.

[d] The Baron de Charlus is a character in Marcel Proust's *A la recherche du temps perdu* (1913–27) thought to be modelled on Proust's friend, Count Robert de Montesquiou.

his own book: book and author stand automatically on a single line divided into a *before* and an *after*. The Author is thought to *nourish* the book, which is to say that he exists before it, thinks, suffers, lives for it, is in the same relation of ante-cedence to his work as a father to his child. In complete contrast, the modern scriptor is born simultaneously with the text, is in no way equipped with a being preceding or exceeding the writing, is not the subject with the book as predi-cate; there is no other time than that of the enunciation and every text is eternally written *here and now*. The fact is (or, it follows) that *writing* can no longer designate an operation of recording, notation, representation, 'depiction' (as the Classics would say); rather, it designates exactly what linguists, referring to Oxford philosophy, call a performative, a rare verbal form (exclusively given in the first person and in the present tense) in which the enunciation has no other content (contains no other proposition) than the act by which it is uttered—something like the *I declare* of kings or the *I sing* of very ancient poets. Having buried the Author, the modern scriptor can thus no longer believe, as according to the pathetic view of his predecessors, that this hand is too slow for his thought or passion and that consequently, making a law of necessity, he must emphasize this delay and indefinitely 'polish' his form. For him, on the contrary, the hand, cut off from any voice, borne by a pure gesture of inscription (and not of expression), traces a field without origin—or which, at least, has no other origin than language itself, language which ceaselessly calls into question all origins.

We know now that a text is not a line of words releasing a single 'theological' meaning (the 'message' of the Author-God) but a multi-dimensional space in which a variety of writings, none of them original, blend and clash. The text is a tissue of quotations drawn from the innumerable centres of culture. Similar to Bouvard and Pécuchet,[e] those eternal copyists, at once sublime and comic and whose profound ridiculousness indicates precisely the truth of writing, the writer can only imitate a gesture that is always anterior, never original. His only power is to mix writings, to counter the ones with the others, in such a way as never to rest on any one of them. Did he wish to *express himself*, he ought at least to know that the inner 'thing' he thinks to 'translate' is itself only a ready-formed dictionary, its words only explainable through other words, and so on indefi-nitely; something experienced in exemplary fashion by the young Thomas de Quincey,[f] he who was so good at Greek that in order to translate absolutely modern ideas and images into that dead language, he had, so Baudelaire tells us (in *Paradis Artificiels*), 'created for himself an unfailing dictionary, vastly more extensive and complex than those resulting from the ordinary patience of purely literary themes'. Succeeding the Author, the scriptor no longer bears within him passions, humours, feelings, impressions, but rather this immense dictionary from which he draws a writing that can know no halt: life never does more than imitate

---

[e] The names of the principal characters in Gustave Flaubert's novel *Bouvard and Pécuchet*, a study in bourgeois stupidity posthumously published in 1881.

[f] Thomas de Quincey (1785–1859), English essayist, author of *Confessions of an English Opium Eater*.

the book, and the book itself is only a tissue of signs, an imitation that is lost, infinitely deferred.

Once the Author is removed, the claim to decipher a text becomes quite futile. To give a text an Author is to impose a limit on that text, to furnish it with a final signified, to close the writing. Such a conception suits criticism very well, the latter then allotting itself the important task of discovering the Author (or its hypostases: society, history, psyché, liberty) beneath the work: when the Author has been found, the text is 'explained'—victory to the critic. Hence there is no surprise in the fact that, historically, the reign of the Author has also been that of the Critic, nor again in the fact that criticism (be it new) is today under-mined along with the Author. In the multiplicity of writing, everything is to be *disentangled*, nothing *deciphered*; the structure can be followed, 'run' (like the thread of a stocking) at every point and at every level, but there is nothing beneath: the space of writing is to be ranged over, not pierced; writing ceaselessly posits meaning ceaselessly to evaporate it, carrying out a systematic exemption of meaning. In precisely this way literature (it would be better from now on to say *writing*), by refusing to assign a 'secret', an ultimate meaning, to the text (and to the world as text), liberates what may be called an anti-theological activity, an activity that is truly revolutionary since to refuse to fix meaning is, in the end, to refuse God and his hypostases—reason, science, law.

Let us come back to the Balzac sentence. No one, no 'person', says it: its source, its voice, is not the true place of the writing, which is reading. Another—very precise—example will help to make this clear: recent research (J.-P. Vernant[1]) has demonstrated the constitutively ambiguous nature of Greek tragedy, its texts being woven from words with double meanings that each character understands unilaterally (this perpetual misunderstanding is exactly the 'tragic'); there is, however, someone who understands each word in its duplicity and who, in addition, hears the very deafness of the characters speaking in front of him—this someone being precisely the reader (or here, the listener). Thus is revealed the total existence of writing: a text is made of multiple writings, drawn from many cultures and entering into mutual relations of dialogue, parody, contestation, but there is one place where this multiplicity is focused and that place is the reader, not, as was hitherto said, the author. The reader is the space on which all the quotations that make up a writing are inscribed without any of them being lost; a text's unity lies not in its origin but in its destination. Yet this destination cannot any longer be personal: the reader is without history, biography, psychology; he is simply that *someone* who holds together in a single field all the traces by which the written text is constituted. Which is why it is derisory to condemn the new writing in the name of a humanism hypocritically turned champion of the reader's rights. Classic criticism has never paid any attention to the reader; for it, the writer is the only person in literature. We are now beginning to let ourselves be fooled no longer by the arrogant antiphrastical[g]

[g] Antiphrasis is the rhetorical figure which uses a word in an opposite sense to its usual meaning.

171

recriminations of good society in favour of the very thing it sets aside, ignores, smothers, or destroys; we know that to give writing its future, it is necessary to overthrow the myth: the birth of the reader must be at the cost of the death of the Author.

NOTE

1. Cf. Jean-Pierre Vernant (with Pierre Vidal-Naquet), *Mythe et tragédie en Grèce ancienne*, Paris 1972, esp. pp. 19–40, 99–131. [Tr.]

Textual analysis: Poe's 'Valdemar'

The structural analysis of narrative is at present in the course of full elaboration. All research in this area has a common scientific origin: semiology or the science of signification; but already (and this is a good thing) divergences within that research are appearing, according to the critical stance each piece of work takes with respect to the scientific status of semiology, or in other words, with respect to its own discourse. These divergences (which are constructive) can be brought together under two broad tendencies: in the first, faced with all the narratives in the world, the analysis seeks to establish a narrative model—which is evidently formal—, a structure or grammar of narrative, on the basis of which (once this model, structure or grammar has been discovered) each particular narrative will be analysed in terms of divergences. In the second tendency, the narrative is immediately subsumed (at least when it lends itself to being subsumed) under the notion of 'text', space, process of meanings at work, in short, 'signifiance' (we shall come back to this word at the end), which is observed not as a finished, closed product, but as a production in progress, 'plugged in' to other texts, other codes (this is the intertextual), and thereby articulated with society and history in ways which are not determinist but citational. We have then to distinguish in a certain way structural analysis and textual analysis, without here wishing to declare them enemies: structural analysis, strictly speaking, is applied above all to oral narrative (to myth); textual analysis, which is what we shall be attempting to practise in the following pages, is applied exclusively to written narrative.[1]

Textual analysis does not try to describe the structure of a work; it is not a matter of recording a structure, but rather of producing a mobile structuration of the text (a structuration which is displaced from reader to reader throughout history), of staying in the signifying volume of the work, in its 'signifiance'. Textual analysis does not try to find out what it is that determines the text (gathers it together as the end-term of a causal sequence), but rather how the text explodes and disperses. We are then going to take a narrative text, and we're going to read it, as slowly as is necessary, stopping as often as we have to (being at ease is an essential dimension of our work), and try to locate and classify without rigour, not all the meanings of the text (which would be impossible because the text is open to infinity: no reader, no subject, no science can arrest the text) but the forms and codes according to which meanings are possible. We are going to locate the avenues of meaning. Our aim is not to find the meaning, nor even a meaning of the text, and our work is not akin to literary criticism of. the hermeneutic type (which tries to interpret the text in terms of the truth believed to be hidden therein), as are Marxist or psychoanalytical criticism. Our aim is to manage to conceive, to imagine, to live the plurality of the text, the opening of its 'signifiance'. It is clear then that what is at stake in our work is not limited to the university treatment of the text (even if that treatment were openly methodological), nor even to literature in general; rather it touches on a theory, a practice, a choice, which are caught up in the struggle of men and signs.

In order to carry out the textual analysis of a narrative, we shall follow a certain number of operating procedures (let us call them elementary rules of manipulation rather than methodological principles, which would be too ambitious a word and above all an ideologically questionable one, in so far as 'method' too often postulates a positivistic result). We shall reduce these procedures to four briefly laid out measures, preferring to let the theory run along in the analysis of the text itself. For the moment we shall say just what is necessary to begin as quickly as possible the analysis of the story we have chosen.

1 We shall cut up the text I am proposing for study into contiguous, and in general very short, segments (a sentence, part of a sentence, at most a group of three or four sentences); we shall number these fragments starting from 1 (in about ten pages of text there are 150 segments). These segments are units of reading, and this is why I have proposed to call them 'lexias'.[2] A lexia is obviously a textual signifier; but as our job here is not to observe signifiers (our work is not stylistic) but meanings, the cutting-up does not need to be theoretically founded (as we are in discourse, and not in 'langue',[a] we must not expect there to be an easily-perceived homology between signifier and signified; we do not know how one corresponds to the other, and consequently we must be prepared to cut up the signifier without being guided by the underlying cutting-up of the signified). All in all the fragmenting of the narrative text into lexias is purely empirical, dictated by the concern of convenience: the lexia is an arbitrary product, it is simply a segment within which the distribution of meanings is observed; it is what surgeons would call an operating field: the useful lexia is one where only one, two or three meanings take place (superposed in the volume of the piece of text).

2 For each lexia, we shall observe the meanings to which that lexia gives rise. By meaning, it is clear that we do not mean the meanings of the words or groups of words which dictionary and grammar, in short a knowledge of the French language, would be sufficient to account for. We mean the connotations of the lexia, the secondary meanings. These connotation-meanings can be associations

---

[a] 'Discourse' here corresponds to *parole* in Saussure's distinction between *langue* and *parole* (see above, pp. 1–9).

(for example, the physical description of a character, spread out over several sentences, may have only one connoted signified, the 'nervousness' of that character, even though the word does not figure at the level of denotation); they can also be relations, resulting from a linking of two points in the text, which are sometimes far apart, (an action begun here can be completed, finished, much further on). Our lexias will be, if I can put it like this, the finest possible sieves, thanks to which we shall 'cream off' meanings, connotations.

3 Our analysis will be progressive: we shall cover the length of the text step by step, at least in theory, since for reasons of space we can only give two fragments of analysis here. This means that we shan't be aiming to pick out the large (rhetorical) blocks of the text; we shan't construct a plan of the text and we shan't be seeking its thematics; in short, we shan't be carrying out an explication of the text, unless we give the word 'explication' its etymological sense, in so far as we shall be unfolding the text, the foliation of the text. Our analysis will retain the procedure of reading; only this reading will be, in some measure, filmed in slow-motion. This method of proceeding is theoretically important: it means that we are not aiming to reconstitute the structure of the text, but to follow its structuration, and that we consider the structuration of reading to be more important than that of composition (a rhetorical, classical notion).

4 Finally, we shan't get unduly worried if in our account we 'forget' some meanings. Forgetting meanings is in some sense part of reading: the important thing is to show departures of meaning, not arrivals (and is meaning basically anything other than a departure?). What founds the text is not an internal, closed, accountable structure, but the outlet of the text on to other texts, other signs; what makes the text is the intertextual. We are beginning to glimpse (through other sciences) the fact that research must little by little get used to the conjunction of two ideas which for a long time were thought incompatible: the idea of structure and the idea of combinational infinity; the conciliation of these two postulations is forced upon us now because language, which we are getting to know better, is at once infinite and structured.

I think that these remarks are sufficient for us to begin the analysis of the text (we must always give in to the impatience of the text, and never forget that whatever the imperatives of study, the pleasure of the text is our law). The text which has been chosen is a short narrative by Edgar Poe, in Baudelaire's translation: —The Facts in the Case of M. Valdemar—.[3] My choice—at least consciously, for in fact it might be my unconscious which made the choice—was dictated by two didactic considerations: I needed a very short text so as to be able to master entirely the signifying surface (the succession of lexias), and one which was symbolically very dense, so that the text analysed would touch us continuously, beyond all particularism: who could avoid being touched by a text whose declared 'subject' is death?

To be frank, I ought to add this: in analysing the 'signifiance' of a text, we shall abstain voluntarily from dealing with certain problems; we shall not speak of the author, Edgar Poe, nor of the literary history of which he is a part; we shall not take into account the fact that the analysis will be carried out on a translation: we shall take the text as it is, as we read it, without bothering about whether in a university it would belong to students of English rather than students of French or philosophers. This does not necessarily mean that these problems will not pass into our analysis; on the contrary, they will pass, in the proper sense of the term: the analysis is a crossing of the text; these problems can be located in terms of cultural quotations, of departures of codes, not of determinations.

A final word, which is perhaps one of conjuration, exorcism: the text we are going to analyse is neither lyrical nor political, it speaks neither of love nor society, it speaks of death. This means that we shall have to lift a particular censorship: that attached to the sinister. We shall do this, persuaded that any censorship stands for all others: speaking of death outside all religion lifts at once the religious interdict and the rationalist one.

Analysis of lexias 1–17

(1) —The Facts in the Case of M. Valdemar—

(2) Of course I shall not pretend to consider it any matter for wonder, that the extraordinary case of M. Valdemar has excited discussion. It would have been a miracle had it not—especially under the circumstances. (3) Through the desire of all parties concerned, to keep the affair from the public, at least for the present, or until we had further opportunities for investigation— through our endeavours to effect this—(4) a garbled or exaggerated account made its way into society, and became the source of many unpleasant mis-representations, and, very naturally, of a great deal of disbelief.

(5) It is now rendered necessary that I give the *facts*—as far as I comprehend them myself.

(6) They are, succinctly, these:

(7) My attention, for the last three years, had been repeatedly drawn to the subject of Mesmerism; (8) and, about nine months ago, it occurred to me, quite suddenly, that in a series of experiments made hitherto, (9) there had been a very remarkable and most unaccountable omission: (10)—no person had as yet been mesmerised 'in articulo mortis'. (11) It remained to be seen, (12) first, whether, in such condition, there existed in the patient any susceptibility to the magnetic influence; (13) secondly, whether if any existed, it was impaired or increased by the condition; (14) thirdly, to what extent, or for how long a period, the encroachments of Death might be arrested by the process. (15) There were other points to be ascertained, (16) but these most excited my curiosity (17)—the last in especial, from the immensely important character of its consequences.

(1) —The Facts in the Case of M. Valdemar—[—La Vérité sur le cas de M. Valdemar—]

The function of the title has not been well studied, at least from a structural point of view. What can be said straight away is that for commercial reasons, society, needing to assimilate the text to a product, a commodity, has need of markers: the function of the title is to mark the beginning of the text, that is, to constitute the text as a commodity. Every title thus has several simultaneous meanings, including at least these two: (i) what it says linked to the contingency of what follows it; (ii) the announcement itself that a piece of literature (which means, in fact, a commodity) is going to follow; in other words, the title always has a double function; enunciating and deictic.

(a) Announcing a truth involves the stipulation of an enigma. The posing of the enigma is a result (at the level of the signifiers): of the word 'truth' [in the French title]; of the word 'case' (that which is exceptional, therefore marked, therefore signifying, and consequently of which the meaning must be found); of the definite article 'the' [in the French title] (there is only one truth, all the work of the text will, then, be needed to pass through this narrow gate); of the cataphorical[b] form implied by the title: what follows will realise what is announced, the resolution of the enigma is already announced; we should note that the English says:—The Facts in the Case ...—: the signified which Poe is aiming at is of an empirical order, that aimed at by the French translator (Baudelaire) is hermeneutic: the truth refers then to the exact facts, but also perhaps to their meaning. However this may be, we shall code this first sense of the lexia: 'enigma, position' (the enigma is the general name of a code, the position is only one term of it).

(b) The truth could be spoken without being announced, without there being a reference to the word itself. If one speaks of what one is going to say, if language is thus doubled into two layers of which the first in some sense caps the second, then what one is doing is resorting to the use of a metalanguage. There is then here the presence of the metalinguistic code.

(c) This metalinguistic announcement has an aperitive function: it is a question of whetting the reader's appetite (a procedure which is akin to 'suspense'). The narrative is a commodity the proposal of which is preceded by a 'patter'. This 'patter', this 'appetiser' is a term of the narrative code (rhetoric of narration).

(d) A proper name should always be carefully questioned, for the proper name is, if I can put it like this, the prince of signifiers; its connotations are rich, social and symbolic. In the name Valdemar, the following two connotations at least can be read: (i) presence of a socio-ethnic code: is the name German? Slavic? In any case, not Anglo-Saxon; this little enigma here implicitly formulated, will be resolved at number 19 (Valdemar is Polish); (ii) 'Valdemar' is 'the valley of the sea'; the oceanic abyss; the depths of the sea is a theme dear to Poe: the gulf refers to what is twice outside nature, under the waters and under the earth.

---

[b] There is no English equivalent to this word, by which Barthes seems to mean, 'answering or reflecting back on itself'.

176

From the point of view of the analysis there are, then, the traces of two codes: a socio-ethnic code and a (or the) symbolic code (we shall return to these codes a little later).

(e) Saying 'M(onsieur) Valdemar' is not the same thing as saying 'Valdemar'. In a lot of stories Poe uses simple christian names (Ligeia, Eleonora, Morella). The presence of the 'Monsieur' brings with it an effect of social reality, of the historically real: the hero is socialised, he forms part of a definite society, in which he is supplied with a civil title. We must therefore note: social code.

> (2) 'Of course I shall not pretend to consider it any matter for wonder, that the extraordinary case of M. Valdemar has excited discussion. It would have been a miracle had it not—especially under the circumstances.'

(a) This sentence (and those immediately following) have as their obvious function that of exciting the reader's expectation, and that is why they are apparently meaningless: what one wants is the solution of the enigma posed in the title (the 'truth'), but even the exposition of this enigma is held back. So we must code: delay in posing the enigma.

(b) Same connotation as in (1c): it's a matter of whetting the reader's appetite (narrative code).

(c) The word 'extraordinary' is ambiguous: it refers to that which departs from the norm but not necessarily from nature (if the case remains 'medical'), but it can also refer to what is supernatural, what has moved into transgression (this is the 'fantastic' element of the stories—'extraordinary', precisely [The French title of Poe's Collected Stories is 'Histoires extraordinaires']—that Poe tells). The ambiguity of the word is here meaningful: the story will be a horrible one (outside the limits of nature) which is yet covered by the scientific alibi (here connoted by the 'discussion', which is a scientist's word). This bonding is in fact cultural: the mixture of the strange and the scientific had its high-point in the part of the nineteenth century to which Poe, broadly speaking, belongs: there was great enthusiasm for observing the supernatural scientifically (magnetism, spiritism, telepathy, etc.); the supernatural adopts a scientific, rationalist alibi; the cry from the heart of that positivist age runs thus: if only one could believe scientifically in immortality! This cultural code, which for simplicity's sake we shall here call the scientific code, will be of great importance throughout the narrative.

> (3) 'Through the desire of all parties concerned, to keep the affair from the public, at least for the present, or until we had further opportunities for investigation—through our endeavours to effect this—'

(a) Same scientific code, picked up by the word 'investigation' (which is also a detective story word: the fortune of the detective novel in the second half of the

177

nineteenth century—starting from Poe, precisely—is well known: what is important here, ideologically and structurally, is the conjunction of the code of the detective enigma and the code of science—scientific discourse—which proves that structural analysis can collaborate perfectly well with ideological analysis).

(b) The motives of the secret are not given; they can proceed from two different codes, present together in reading (to read is also silently to imagine what is not said): (i) the scientific-deontological[c] code: the doctors and Poe, out of loyalty and prudence, do not want to make public a phenomenon which has not been cleared up scientifically; (ii) the symbolic code: there is a taboo on living death: one keeps silent because it is horrible. We ought to say straight away (even though we shall come back and insist on this later) that these two codes are undecidable (we can't choose one against the other), and that it is this very undecidability which makes for a good narrative.

(c) From the point of view of narrative actions (this is the first one we have met), a sequence is here begun: 'to keep hidden' in effect implies, logically or pseudo-logically, consequent operations (for example: to unveil). We have then here to posit the first term of an actional sequence: to keep hidden, the rest of which we shall come across later.

> (4) 'a garbled or exaggerated account made its way into society, and became the source of many unpleasant misrepresentations, and, very naturally, of a great deal of disbelief'

(a) The request for truth, that is, the enigma, has already been placed twice (by the word 'truth' [in the French title] and by the expression 'extraordinary case'). The enigma is here posed a third time (to pose an enigma, in structural terms, means to utter: there is an enigma), by the invocation of the error to which it gave rise: the error, posed here, justifies retroactively, anaphorically[d], the [French] title (—La Vérité sur . . .—). The redundancy operated on the position of the enigma (the fact that there is an enigma is repeated in several ways) has an aperitive value: it is a matter of exciting the reader, of procuring clients for the narrative.

(b) In the actional sequence 'to hide', a second term appears: this is the effect of the secret: distortion, mistaken opinion, accusation of mystification.

> (5) 'It is now rendered necessary that I give the *facts*—as far as I comprehend them myself'

[c] 'Deontology' is the branch of ethics dealing with moral duty and obligation.
[d] Anaphora is the use of repetition for rhetorical effect.

(a) The emphasis placed on 'the facts' supposes the intrication of two codes, between which—as in (3b), it is impossible to decide: (i) the law, the deontology of science, makes the scientist, the observer, a slave to the fact; the opposition of fact and rumour is an old mythical theme; when it is invoked in a fiction (and invoked emphatically), the fact has as its structural function (for the real effect of this artifice fools no one) that of authenticating the story, not that of making the reader believe that it really happened, but that of presenting the discourse of the real, and not that of the fable. The fact is then caught up in a paradigm in which it is opposed to mystification (Poe admitted in a private letter that the story of M. Valdemar was a pure mystification: *it is a mere hoax*).[4] The code which structures the reference to the fact is then the scientific code which we have already met. (ii) However, any more or less pompous recourse to the fact can also be considered to be the symptom of the subject's being mixed up with the symbolic; protesting aggressively in favour of the fact alone, protesting the triumph of the referent, involves suspecting signification, mutilating the real of its symbolic supplement;[e] it is an act of censorship against the signifier which displaces the fact; it involves refusing the other scene, that of the unconscious. By pushing away the symbolical supplement, even if to our eyes this is done by a narrative trick, the narrator takes on an imaginary role, that of the scientist: the signified of the lexia is then the asymbolism of the subject of the enunciation; 'I' presents itself as asymbolic; the negation of the symbolic is clearly part of the symbolic code itself.[5]

(b) The actional sequence 'to hide' develops: the third term posits the necessity of rectifying the distortion located in (4b); this rectification stands for: wanting to unveil (that which was hidden). This narrative sequence 'to hide' clearly constitutes a stimulation for the narrative; in a sense, it justifies it, and by that very fact points to its value (its 'standing-for' ['valant-pour']), makes a commodity of it: I am telling the story, says the narrator, in exchange for a demand for counter-error, for truth (we are in a civilisation where truth is a value, that is, a commodity). It is always very interesting to try to pick out the 'valant-pour' of a narrative: in exchange for what is the story told? In the 'Arabian Nights', each story stands for a day's survival. Here we are warned that the story of M. Valdemar stands for the truth (first presented as a counter-distortion).

(c) The 'I' appears [in French] for the first time—it was already present in the 'we' in 'our endeavours' (3). The enunciation in fact includes three I's, or in other words, three imaginary roles (to say 'I' is to enter the imaginary): (i) a narrating 'I', an artist, whose motive is the search for effect; to this 'I' there corresponds a 'You', that of the literary reader, who is reading 'a fantastic story by the great writer Edgar Poe'; (ii) an I-witness, who has the power to bear witness to a scientific experiment; the corresponding 'You' is that of a panel of scientists, that of serious opinion, that of the scientific reader: (iii) an I-actor,

---

[e] Cf. Derrida, pp. 119–20 above.

experimenter, the one who will magnetise Valdemar; the 'You' is in this case Valdemar himself; in these two last instances, the motive for the imaginary role is the 'truth'. We have here the three terms of a code which we shall call, perhaps provisionally, the code of communication. Between these three roles, there is no doubt another language, that of the unconscious, which is spoken neither in science, nor in literature; but that language, which is literally the language of the interdict, does not say 'I': our grammar, with its three persons, is never directly that of the unconscious.

(6) 'They are, succinctly, these:'

(a) Announcing what is to follow involves metalanguage (and the rhetorical code); it is the boundary marking the beginning of a story in the story.

(b) 'Succinctly' carries three mixed and undecidable connotations: (i) 'Don't be afraid, this won't take too long': this, in the narrative code, is the phatic mode (located by Jakobson)ᶠ, the function of which is to hold the attention, maintain contact; (ii) 'It will be short because I'll be sticking strictly to the facts'; this is the scientific code, allowing the announcement of the scientist's 'spareness', the superiority of the instance of the fact over the instance of discourse; (iii) to pride oneself on talking briefly is in a certain sense an assertion against speech, a limitation of the supplement of discourse, that is, the symbolic; this is to speak the code of the asymbolic.

(7) 'My attention, for the last three years, had been repeatedly drawn to the subject of Mesmerism;'

(a) The chronological code must be observed in all narratives; here in this code ('last three years'), two values are mixed; the first is in some sense naive; one of the temporal elements of the experiment to come is noted: the time of its preparation; the second does not have a diegetical, operative function (this is made clear by the test of commutation; if the narrator had said seven years instead of three, it would have had no effect on the story); it is therefore a matter of a pure reality-effect: the number connotes emphatically the truth of the fact: what is precise is reputed to be real (this illusion, moreover, since it does exist, is well known; a delirium of figures). Let us note that linguistically the word 'last' is a 'shifter': it refers to the situation of the speaker in time; it thus reinforces the *presence of* the following account.[6]

(b) A long actional sequence begins here, or at the very least a sequence well-furnished with terms; its object is the starting-off of an experiment (we are under the alibi of experimental science); structurally, this setting-off is not the experiment itself, but an experimental programme. This sequence in fact stands for the formulation of the enigma, which has already been posed several times ('there

ᶠ See above, p. 37.

is an enigma'), but which has not yet been formulated. So as not to weigh down the report of the analysis, we shall code the 'programme' separately, it being understood that by procuration the whole sequence stands for a term of the enigma-code. In this 'programme' sequence, we have here the first term: the posing of the scientific field of the experiment, magnetism.

(c) The reference to magnetism is extracted from a cultural code which is very insistent in this part of the nineteenth century. Following Mesmer (in English, 'magnetism' can be called 'mesmerism') and the Marquis Armand de Puységur, who had discovered that magnetism could provoke somnambulism, magnetisers and magnetist societies had multiplied in France (around 1820); in 1829, it appears that it had been possible, under hypnosis, to carry out the painless ablation of a tumour; in 1845, the year of our story, Braid of Manchester codified hypnosis by provoking nervous fatigue through the contemplation of a shining object; in 1850, in the Mesmeric Hospital of Calcutta, painless births were achieved. We know that subsequently Charcot classified hypnotic states and circumscribed hypnosis under hysteria (1882), but that since then hysteria has disappeared from hospitals as a clinical entity (from the moment it was no longer observed). The year 1845 marks the peak of scientific illusion: people believed in a psychological reality of hypnosis (although Poe, pointing out Valdemar's 'nervousness', may allow the inference of the subject's hysterical predisposition).

(d) Thematically, magnetism connotes (at least at that time) an idea of fluid: something passes from one subject to another; there is an exchange [un entrédit] (an interdict) between the narrator and Valdemar: this is the code of communication.

(8) 'and, about nine months ago, it occured to me, quite suddenly, that in a series of experiments made hitherto,'

(a) The chronological code ('nine months') calls for the same remarks as those made in (7a).

(b) Here is the second term of the 'programme' sequence: in (7b) a domain was chosen, that of magnetism; now it is cut up; a particular problem will be isolated.

(9) 'there had been a very remarkable and most unaccountable omission:'

(a) The enunciation of the structure of the 'programme' continues: here is the third term: the experiment which has not yet been tried—and which, therefore, for any scientist concerned with research, is to be tried.

(b) This experimental lack is not a simple oversight, or at least this oversight is heavily significant; it is quite simply the oversight of death: there has been a taboo (which will be lifted, in the deepest horror); the connotation belongs to the symbolic code.

181

(10) '—no person had as yet been mesmerised "in articulo mortis".'

(a) Fourth term of the 'programme' sequence: the content of the omission (there is clearly a reduction of the link between the assertion of the omission and its definition, in the rhetorical code: to announce/to specify).

(b) The use of Latin (in articulo mortis), a juridical and medical language, produces an effect of scientificity (scientific code), but also, through the inter-mediary of euphemism (saying in a little-known language something one does not dare say in everyday language), designates a taboo (symbolic code). It seems clear that what is taboo in death, what is essentially taboo, is the passage, the threshold, the dying; life and death are relatively well-classified states, and more-over they enter into a paradigmatic opposition, they are taken in hand by meaning, which is always reassuring; but the transition between the two states, or more exactly, as will be the case here, their mutual encroachment, outplays meaning and engenders horror: there is the transgression of an antithesis, of a classification.

(11) 'It remained to be seen'

The detail of the 'programme' is announced (rhetorical code and action sequence 'programme').

(12) 'first, whether, in such conditions, there existed in the patient any susceptibility to the magnetic influence;'

(a) In the 'programme' sequence, this is the first coining of the announcement made in (11): this is the first problem to elucidate.

(b) This Problem I itself entitles an organised sequence (or a sub-sequence of the 'programme'): here we have the first term: the formulation of the problem; its object is the very being of magnetic communication: does it exist, yes or no? (there will be an affirmative reply to this in (78): the long textual distance separating the question and the answer is specific to narrative structure, which authorises and even demands the careful construction of sequences, each of which is a thread which weaves in with its neighbours).

(13) 'secondly, whether if any existed, it was impaired or increased by the condition;'

(a) In the 'programme' sequence, the second problem here takes its place (it will be noted that Problem II is linked to Problem I by a logic of implication: 'if yes . . . then'; if not, then the whole story would fall down; the alternative, according to the instance of discourse, is thus faked).

(b) Second sub-sequence of 'programme': this is Problem II: the first problem concerned the being of the phenomenon; the second concerns its measurement (all this is very 'scientific'); the reply to the question will be given in (82); receptivity is increased: 'In such experiments with this patient I had never perfectly succeeded before ... but to my astonishment, ...'.

(14) 'thirdly, to what extent, or for how long a period, the encroachments of Death might be arrested by the process.'

(a) This is Problem III posed by the 'programme'.

(b) This Problem III is formulated, like the others—this formulation will be taken up again emphatically in (17); the formulation implies two sub-questions: (i) to what extent does hypnosis allow life to encroach on death? The reply is given in (110): *up to and including language*; (ii) for how long? There will be no direct reply to this question: the encroachment of life on death (the survival of the hypnotized dead man) will end after seven months, but only through the arbitrary intervention of the experimenter. We can then suppose: infinitely, or at the very least indefinitely within the limits of observation.

(15) 'There were other points to be ascertained,'

The 'programme' mentioned other problems which could be posed with respect to the planned experiment, in a global form. The phrase is equivalent to 'etcetera'. Valéry said that in nature there was no etcetera; we can add: nor in the unconscious. In fact the etcetera only belongs to the discourse of pretence; on the one hand it pretends to play the scientific game of the vast experimental programme; it is an operator of the pseudo-real: on the other hand, by glossing over and avoiding the other problems, it reinforces the meaning of the questions already posed: the powerfully symbolic has been announced, and the rest, under the instance of discourse, is only play acting.

(16) 'but these most excited my curiosity,'

Here, in the 'programme', it's a matter of a global reminder of the three problems (the 'reminder', or the 'résumé', like the 'announcement', are terms in the rhetorical code).

(17) '—this last in especial, from the immensely important character of its consequences.'

(a) An emphasis (a term in the rhetorical code) is placed on Problem III.

(b) Two more undecidable codes: (i) scientifically, what is at stake is the pushing back of a biological given, death; (ii) symbolically, this is the transgression of meaning, which opposes life and death.

Actional analysis of lexias 18–102

Among all the connotations that we have met with or at least located in the opening of Poe's story, we have been able to define some as progressive terms in sequences of narrative actions; we shall come back at the end to the different codes which analysis has brought to light, including, precisely, the actional code. Putting off this theoretical clarification, we can isolate these sequences of actions so as to account with less trouble (and yet maintaining a structural import in our purpose) for the rest of the story. It will be understood that in effect it is impossible to analyse minutely (and even less exhaustively: textual analysis is never, and never wants to be, exhaustive) the whole of Poe's story: it would take too long; but we do intend to undertake the textual analysis of some lexias again at the culminating point of the work (lexias 103–110). In order to join the fragment we have analysed and the one we are going to analyse, at the level of intelligibility, it will suffice to indicate the principal actional sequences which begin and develop (but do not necessarily end) between lexia 18 and lexia 102. Unfortunately, through lack of space, we cannot give the text which separates our two fragments, nor the numeration of the intermediate lexias; we shall give only the actional sequences (and moreover without even being able to bring out the detail of them by term), to the detriment of the other codes, which are more numerous and certainly more interesting. This is essentially because the actional sequences constitute by definition the anecdotic framework of the story (I shall make a slight exception for the chronological code, indicating by an initial and a final notation, the point of the narrative at which the beginning of each sequence is situated).

I Programme: the sequence has begun and been broadly developed in the fragment analysed. The problems posed by the planned experiment are known. The sequence continues and closes with the choice of the subject (the patient) necessary for the experiment: it will be M. Valdemar (the posing of the programme takes place nine months before the moment of narration).

II Magnetisation (or rather, if this heavy neologism is permitted: magnetisability). Before choosing M. Valdemar as subject of the experiment, P. tested his magnetic receptiveness; it exists, but the results are nonetheless disappointing: M. V's obedience involves some resistances. The sequence enumerates the terms of this test, which is anterior to the decision on the experiment and whose chronological position is not specified.

III Medical death: actional sequences are most often distended, and intertwined with other sequences. In informing us of M. V's bad state of health and the fatal outcome predicted by the doctors, the narrative begins a very long sequence which runs throughout the story, to finish only in the last lexia (150), with the liquefaction of M. V's body. The episodes of this sequence are numerous, split up, but still scientifically logical: ill-health, diagnosis, death-sentence, deterioration, agony, mortification (physiological signs of death)—it is at this point in the sequence that our second textual analysis is situated—, disintegration, liquefaction.

IV Contract: P. makes the proposal to M. Valdemar of hypnotising him when he reaches the threshold of death (since he knows he is to die) and M. V. accepts; there is a contract between the subject and the experimenter: conditions, proposition, acceptance, conventions, decision to proceed, official registration in the presence of doctors (this last point constitutes a sub-sequence).

V Catalepsy (7 months before the moment of narration, a Saturday at 7.55): as the last moments of M. V have come and the experimenter has been notified by the patient himself, P. begins the hypnosis 'in articulo mortis', in conformity with the programme and the contract. This sequence can be headed 'catalepsy'; among other terms, it involves: magnetic passes, resistances from the subject, signs of a cataleptic state, observation by the experimenter, verification by the doctor (the actions of this sequence take up 3 hours: it is 10.55).

VI Interrogation I (Sunday, 3 o'clock in the morning): P. four times interrogates M. Valdemar under hypnosis; it is pertinent to identify each interrogative sequence by the reply made by the hypnotised M. Valdemar. The replay to this first interrogation is: 'I am asleep' (canonically, the interrogative sequences involve the announcement of the question, the question, delay or resistance of the reply, and the reply).

VII Interrogation II: this interrogation follows shortly after the first. This time M. Valdemar replies: 'I am dying.'

VIII Interrogation III: the experimenter interrogates the dying, hypnotised M. Valdemar again ('do you still sleep?'); he replies by linking the two replies already made: 'still asleep—dying'.

IX Interrogation IV: P. attempts to interrogate M. V a fourth time; he repeats his question (M. V will reply beginning with lexia 105, see below).

At this point we reach the moment in the narrative at which we are going to take up the textual analysis again, lexia by lexia. Between Interrogation III and the beginning of the analysis to follow, an important term of the sequence 'medical death' intervenes: this is the mortification of M. Valdemar (101–102). Under hypnosis, M. Valdemar is henceforth dead, medically speaking. We know that recently, with the transplantation of organs, the diagnosis of death has been called into question: today the evidence of electro-encephalography is required. In order to certify M. V's death, Poe gathers (in 101 and 102) all the clinical signs which in his day certified scientifically the death of a patient: open rolled-back eyes, corpse-like skin, extinction of hectic spots, fall and relaxation of the lower jaw, blackened tongue, a general hideousness which makes those present shrink back from the bed (here again the weave of the codes should be noted: all the medical signs are also elements of horror; or rather, horror is always given under the alibi of science: the scientific code and the symbolic code are actualised at the same time, undecidably).

With M. Valdemar medically dead, the narrative ought to finish: the death of the hero (except in cases of religious resurrection) ends the story. The re-launching of the anecdote (beginning with lexia 103) appears then at once as a narrative necessity (to allow the text to continue) and a logical scandal. This scandal is that of the supplement: for there to be a supplement of narrative, there will have to be a supplement of life: once again, the narrative stands for life.

Textual analysis of lexias 103–110

(103) 'I feel that I have reached a point of this narrative at which every reader will be startled into positive disbelief. It is my business, however, simply to proceed.'

(a) We know that announcing a discourse to come is a term in the rhetorical code (and the metalinguistic code); we also know the 'aperitive' value of this connotation.

(b) It being one's business to speak the facts, without worrying about the unpleasantness, forms part of the code of scientific deontology. [At this point the French text has 'mon devoir est de continuer.']

(c) The promise of an unbelievable 'real' forms part of the field of the narrative considered as a commodity; it raises the 'price' of the narrative; here, then, in the general code of communication, we have a sub-code, that of exchange, of which every narrative is a term, cf. (5b).

(104) 'There was no longer the faintest sign of vitality in M. Valdemar; and concluding him to be dead, we were consigning him to the charge of the nurses,'

In the long sequence of 'medical death', which we have pointed out, the mortification was noted in (101): here it is confirmed; in (101), M. Valdemar's state of death was described (through a framework of indices); here it is asserted by means of a metalanguage.

(105) 'when a strong vibratory motion was observable in the tongue. This continued for perhaps a minute. At the expiration of this period,'

(a) The chronological code ('one minute') supports two effects: an effect of reality-precision, cf. (7a), and a dramatic effect: the laborious welling-up of the voice, the delivery of the cry recalls the combat of life and death: life is trying to break free of the bogging-down of death, it is struggling (or rather it is here rather death which is unable to break free of life: we should not forget that M. V is dead: it is not life, but death, that he has to hold back).

(b) Shortly before the point we have reached, P. has interrogated M. V (for the fourth time); and before M. V replies, he is clinically dead. Yet the sequence Interrogation IV is not closed (this is where the supplement we have mentioned intervenes): the movement of the tongue indicates that M. V is going to speak. We must, then, construct the sequence as follows: question (100)/(medical death)/attempt to reply (and the sequence will continue).

(c) There is quite clearly a symbolism of the tongue. The tongue is speech (cutting off the tongue is a mutilation of language, as can be seen in the symbolic ceremony of punishment of blasphemers); further, there is something visceral about the tongue (something internal), and at the same time, something phallic. This general symbolism is here reinforced by the fact that the tongue which moves is (paradigmatically) opposed to the black, swollen tongue of medical death (101). It is, then, visceral life, the life of the depths, which is assimilated to speech, and speech itself is fetishized in the form of a phallic organ which begins to vibrate, in a sort of pre-orgasm: the one-minute vibration is the desire to come ['le désir de la jouissance'] and the desire for speech: it is the movement of desire to get somewhere.

(106) 'there issued from the distended and motionless jaws a voice,'

(a) Little by little the sequence Interrogation IV continues, with great detail in the global term 'reply'. Certainly, the delayed reply is well known in the grammar of narrative; but it has in general a psychological value; here, the delay (and the detail it brings with it) is purely physiological: it is the welling-up of the voice, filmed and recorded in slow-motion.

(b) The voice comes from the tongue (105), the jaws are only the gateway; it does not come from the teeth: the voice in preparation is not dental, external, civilised (a marked dentalism is the sign of 'distinction' in pronunciation), but internal, visceral, muscular. Culture valorises what is sharp, bony, distinct, clear (the teeth); the voice of death, on the other hand, comes from what is viscous, from the internal muscular magma, from the depths. Structurally, we have here a term in the symbolic code.

(107) '—such as it would be madness in me to attempt describing. There are, indeed, two or three epithets which might be considered as applicable to it in part; I might say, for example, that the sound was harsh, and broken and hollow; but the hideous whole is indescribable, for the simple reason that no similar sounds have ever jarred upon the ear of humanity.'

(a) The metalinguistic code is present here, through a discourse on the difficulty of holding a discourse; hence the use of frankly metalinguistic terms: epithets, describing, indescribable.

(b) The symbolism of the voice unfolds: it has two characteristics: the internal ('hollow'), and the discontinuous ('harsh', 'broken'): this prepares a logical contradiction (a guarantee of the supernatural): the contrast between the 'broken-up' and the 'glutinous' (108), whilst the internal gives credit to a feeling of distance (108).

(108) 'There were two particulars, nevertheless, which I thought then, and still think, might be stated as characteristic of the intonation—as well adapted to convey some idea of its unearthly peculiarity. In the first place, the voice

seemed to reach our ears—at least mine—from a vast distance, or from some deep cavern within the earth. In the second place, it impressed me (I fear, indeed, that it will be impossible to make myself comprehended) as gelatinous or glutinous matters impress the sense of touch.

I have spoken both of "sound" of "voice". I mean to say that the sound was one of distinct—of even wonderfully, thrillingly distinct—syllabification.'

(a) Here there are several terms of the metalinguistic (rhetorical) code: the announcement ('characteristic'), the résumé ('I have spoken') and the oratorical precaution ('I fear that it will be impossible to make myself comprehended').

(b) The symbolic field of the voice spreads, through the taking-up of the 'in part' expressions of lexia (107): (i) the far-off (absolute distance): the voice is distant because/so that the distance between death and life is/should be total (the 'because' implies a motive belonging to the real, to what is 'behind' the paper; the 'so that' to the demand of the discourse which wants to continue, survive as discourse; by noting 'because/so that' we accept that the two instances, that of the real and that of discourse are twisted together, and we bear witness to the structural duplicity of all writing). The distance (between life and death) is affirmed the better to be denied: it permits the transgression, the 'encroach-ment', the description of which is the very object of the story; (ii) 'under the earth'; the thematics of voice are in general double, contradictory: sometimes the voice is a light, bird-like thing that flies off with life, and sometimes a heavy, cavernous thing, which comes up from below: it is voice tied down, anchored like a stone: this is an old mythical theme: the chthonic voice, the voice from beyond the grave (as is the case here); (iii) discontinuity founds language; there is there-fore a supernatural effect in hearing a gelatinous, glutinous, viscous language; the notation has a double value: on the one hand it emphasizes the strangeness of this language which is contrary to the very structure of language; and on the other hand it adds up the malaises and dysphorias: the broken-up and the clinging, sticking (cf. the suppuration of the eyelids when the dead man is brought round from hypnosis, that is, when he is about to enter real death, (133)); (iv) the distinct syllabification constitutes the imminent speech of the dead man as a full, complete, adult language, as an essence of language, and not as a mumbled, approximate, stammered language, a lesser language, troubled by non-language; hence the fright, the terror: there is a glaring contradiction between death and language; the contrary of life is not death (which is a stereotype), but language: it is undecidable whether Valdemar is alive or dead; what is certain, is that he speaks, without one's being able to refer his speech to life or death.

(c) Let us note here an artifice which belongs to the chronological code: 'I thought then and I still think': there is here a co-presence of three temporalities: the time of the story, the diegesis ('I thought then'), the time of writing ('I think it at the time at which I'm writing'), and the time of reading (carried along by the present tense of writing, we think it ourselves at the moment of reading). The whole produces a reality-effect.

(109) 'M. Valdemar *spoke*—obviously in reply to the question I had propounded to him a few minutes before. I had asked him, it will be remembered, if he still slept.'

(a) Interrogation IV is here in progress: the question is here recalled (cf. 100), the reply is announced.

(b) The words of the hypnotised dead man are the very reply to Problem III, posed in (14): to what extent can hypnosis stop death? Here the question is answered: up to and including language.

(110) 'He now said:—"Yes;—no;—I *have been* sleeping—and now—now— I am dead."'

From the structural point of view, this lexia is simple: it is the term 'reply' ('I am dead') to Interrogation IV. However, outside the diegetical structure (i.e. the presence of the lexia in an actional sequence) the connotation of the words ('I am dead') is of inexhaustible richness. Certainly there exist numerous mythical narratives in which death speaks; but only to say: 'I am alive'. There is here a true hapax[g] of narrative grammar, a staging of words impossible as such: I am dead. Let us attempt to unfold some of these connotations:
(i) We have already extracted the theme of encroachment (of life on death); encroachment is a paradigmatic disorder, a disorder of meaning; in the life/death paradigm, the bar is normally read as 'against' (versus); it would suffice to read it as 'on' for encroachment to take place and the paradigm to be destroyed. That's what happens here; one of the spaces bites unwarrantedly into the other. The interesting thing here is that the encroachment occurs at the level of language. The idea that, once dead, the dead man can continue to act is banal; it is what is said in the proverb 'the dead man seizes the living'; it is what is said in the great myths of remorse or of posthumous vengeance; it is what is said comically in Forneret's sally: 'Death teaches incorrigible people to live'.[7] But here the action of the dead man is a purely linguistic action; and, to crown all, this language serves no purpose, it does not appear with a view to acting on the living, it says nothing but itself, it designates itself tautologically. Before saying 'I am dead', the voice says simply 'I am speaking'; a little like a grammatical example which refers to nothing but language; the uselessness of what is proffered is part of the scandal: it is a matter of affirming an essence which is not in its place (the displaced is the very form of the symbolic).
(ii) Another scandal of the enunciation is the turning of the metaphorical into the literal. It is in effect banal to utter the sentence 'I am dead!': it is what is said by the woman who has been shopping all afternoon at Printemps, and who has gone to her hairdresser's, etc.[8] The turning of the metaphorical into the literal, precisely for this metaphor, is impossible: the enunciation 'I am dead', is

---

[g] *Hapax legomenon* is the Greek term for a word coined for a particular occasion.

literally foreclosed (whereas 'I sleep' remained literally possible in the field of hypnotic sleep). It is, then, if you like, scandal of language which is in question.

(iii) There is also a scandal at the level of 'language' (and no longer at the level of discourse). In the ideal sum of all the possible utterances of language, the link of the first person (I) and the attribute 'dead' is precisely the one which is radically impossible: it is this empty point, this blind spot of language which the story comes, very exactly, to occupy. What is said is no other than this impossibility: the sentence is not descriptive, it is not constative, it delivers no message other than its own enunciation. In a sense we can say that we have here a performative, but such, certainly, that neither Austin nor Benveniste had foreseen it in their analyses (let us recall that the performative is the mode of utterance according to which the utterance refers only to its enunciation: 'I declare war'; performatives are always, by force, in the first person, otherwise they would slip towards the constative: 'he declares war'); here, the unwarranted sentence performs an impossibility.[9]

(iv) From a strictly semantic point of view, the sentence 'I am dead' asserts two contrary elements at once (life, death): it is an enantioseme, but is, once again, unique: the signifier expresses a signified (death) which is contradictory with its enunciation. And yet, we have to go further still: it is not simply a matter of a simple negation, in the psychoanalytical sense, 'I am dead' meaning in that case 'I am not dead', but rather an affirmation–negation: 'I am dead and not dead'; this is the paroxysm of transgression, the invention of an unheard-of category: the 'true–false', the 'yes–no', the 'death–life' is thought of as a whole which is indivisible, uncombinable, non-dialectic, for the antithesis implies no third term; it is not a two-faced entity, but a term which is one and new.

(v) A further psychoanalytical reflection is possible on the 'I am dead'. We have said that the sentence accomplished a scandalous return to the literal. That means that death, as primordially repressed, irrupts directly into language; this return is radically traumatic, as the image of explosion later shows (147: 'ejaculations of "dead! dead!" absolutely bursting from the tongue and not from the lips of the sufferer'): the utterance 'I am dead' is a taboo exploded. Now, if the symbolic is the field of neurosis, the return of the literal, which implies the foreclosure of the symbol, opens up the space of psychosis: at this point of the story, all symbolism ends, and with it all neurosis, and it is psychosis which enters the text, through the spectacular foreclosure of the signifier: what is extraordinary in Poe is indeed madness.

Other commentaries are possible, notably that of Jacques Derrida.[10] I have limited myself to those that can be drawn from structural analysis, trying to show that the unheard-of sentence 'I am dead' is in no way the unbelievable utterance, but much more radically the impossible enunciation.

Before moving on to methodological conclusions, I shall recall, at a purely anecdotal level, the end of the story: Valdemar remains dead under hypnosis for seven months; with the agreement of the doctors, P. then decides to wake him; the passes succeed and a little colour returns to Valdemar's cheeks; but while P. attempts to activate the patient by intensifying the passes, the cries of 'Dead! dead' explode on his tongue, and all at once his whole body escapes, crumbles, rots under the experimenter's hands, leaving nothing but a 'nearly liquid mass of loathsome—of detestable putridity'.

Methodological conclusions

The remarks which will serve as a conclusion to these fragments of analysis will not necessarily be theoretical; theory is not abstract, speculative: the analysis itself, although it was carried out on a contingent text, was already theoretical, in the sense that it observed (that was its aim) a language in the process of formation. That is to say—or to recall—that we have not carried out an explication of the text: we have simply tried to grasp the narrative as it was in the process of self-construction (which implies at once structure and movement, system and infinity). Our structuration does not go beyond that spontaneously accomplished by reading. In concluding, then, it is not a question of delivering the 'structure' of Poe's story, and even less that of all narratives, but simply of returning more freely, and with less attachment to the progressive unfolding of the text, to the principal codes which we have located.

The word 'code' itself should not be taken here in the rigorous, scientific, sense of the term. The codes are simply associative fields, a supra-textual organization of notations which impose a certain idea of structure; the instance of the code is, for us, essentially cultural: the codes are certain types of 'déjà-lu' [already read], of 'déjà-fait' [already done]: the code is the form of this 'déjà', constitutive of all the writing in the world.

Although all the codes are in fact cultural, there is yet one, among those we have met with, which we shall privilege by calling it the *cultural code*: it is the code of knowledge, or rather of human knowledges, of public opinions, of culture as it is transmitted by the book, by education, and in a more general and diffuse form, by the whole of sociality. We met several of these cultural codes (or several sub-codes of the general cultural code): the scientific code, which (in our story) is supported at once by the principles of experimentation and by the principles of medical deontology; the rhetorical code, which gathers up all the social rules of what is said: coded forms of narrative, coded forms of discourse (the announcement, the résumé, etc.); metalinguistic enunciation (discourse talking about itself) forms part of this code; the chronological code: 'dating', which seems natural and objective to us today, is in fact a highly cultural practice—which is to be expected since it implies a certain ideology of time ('historical' time is not the same as 'mythical' time); the set of chronological reference-points thus constitute a strong cultural code (a historical way of cutting up time for purposes of dramatisation, of scientific appearance, of reality-effect); the socio-historical code allows the mobilisation in the enunciation, of all the inbred knowledge that we have about our time, our society, our country (the fact of saying 'M. Valdemar' and not 'Valdemar', it will be remembered, finds its place here). We must not be worried by the fact that we can constitute extremely banal notations into code: it is on the contrary their banality, their apparent insignificance that predisposes them to codification, given our definition of code: a corpus of rules that are so worn we take them to be marks of nature; but if the narrative departed from them, it would very rapidly become unreadable.

The code of communication could also be called the code of destination. Communication should be understood in a restricted sense; it does not cover the whole of the signification which is in a text and still less its 'signifiance'; it simply designates every relationship in the text which is stated as an address (this is the case of the 'phatic' code, charged with the accentuation of the relationship between narrator and reader), or as an exchange (the narrative is exchanged for truth, for life). In short, communication should here be understood in an economic sense (communication, circulation of goods).

The symbolic field (here 'field' is less inflexible than 'code') is, to be sure, enormous; the more so in that here we are taking the word 'symbol' in the most general possible sense, without being bothered by any of its usual connotations; the sense to which we are referring is close to that of psychoanalysis: the symbol is broadly that feature of language which displaces the body and allows a 'glimpse' of a scene other than that of the enunciation, such as we think we read it; the symbolic framework in Poe's story is evidently the transgression of the taboo of death, the disorder of classification, that Baudelaire has translated (very well) by the 'empiètement' ('encroachment') of life on death (and not, banally, of death on life); the subtletly of the story comes in part from the fact that the enunciation seems to come from an asymbolic narrator, who has taken on the role of the objective scientist, attached to the fact alone, a stranger to the symbol (which does not fail to come back in force in the story).

What we have called the code of actions supports the anecdotal framework of the narrative; the actions, or the enunciations which denote them, are organized in sequences; the sequence has an approximate identity (its contour cannot be determined rigorously, nor unchallengeably); it is justified in two ways: first because one is led spontaneously to give it a generic name (for example a certain number of notations, ill-health, deterioration, agony, the mortification of the body, its liquefaction, group naturally under a stereotyped idea, that of 'medical death'); and, second, because the terms of the actional sequence are interlinked (from one to the next, since they follow one another throughout the narrative) by an apparent logic; we mean by that that the logic which institutes the actional sequence is very impure from a scientific point of view; it is only an apparent logic which comes not from the laws of formal reasoning, but from our habits of reasoning and observing: it is an endoxal, cultural logic (it seems 'logical' to us that a severe diagnosis should follow the observation of a poor state of health); and what is more this logic becomes confused with chronology: what comes 'after' seems to us to be 'caused by'. Although in narrative they are never pure, temporality and causality seem to us to found a sort of naturality, intelligibility, readability for the anecdote: for example, they allow us to resume it (what the ancients called the argument, a word which is at once logical and narrative).

One last code has traversed our story from its beginning: that of the enigma. We have not had the chance to see it at work, because we have only analysed a very small part of Poe's story. The code of the enigma gathers those terms through the stringing-together of which (like a narrative sentence) an enigma is posed, and which, after some 'delays', make up the piquancy of the narrative, the solution unveiled. The terms of the enigmatic (or hermeneutic) code are well differentiated: for example, we have to distinguish the positing of the enigma (every notation whose meaning is 'there is an enigma') from the formulation of the enigma (the question is exposed in its contingency); in our story, the enigma is posed in the [French] title itself (the 'truth' is announced, but we don't yet know about what question), formulated from the start (the scientific account of the problems linked to the planned experiment), and even, from the very start, delayed: obviously it is in the interests of every narrative to delay the solution of the enigma it poses, since that solution will toll its death-knell as a narrative: we have seen that the narrator uses a whole paragraph to delay the account of the case, under cover of scientific precautions. As for the solution of the enigma, it is not here of a mathematical order; it is in sum the whole narrative which replies to the question posed at the beginning, the question of the truth (this truth can however be condensed into two points: the proffering of 'I am dead', and the sudden liquefaction of the dead man when he awakes from hypnosis); the truth here is not the object of a revelation, but of a revulsion.

These are the codes which traverse the fragments we have analysed. We deliberately don't structure them further, nor do we try to distribute the terms within each code according to a logical or semiological schema; this is because for us the codes are only departures of 'déjà-lu', beginnings of intertextuality: the frayed nature of the codes does not contradict structure (as, it is thought, life, imagination, intuition, disorder, contradict system and rationality), but on the contrary (this is the fundamental affirmation of textual analysis) is an integral part of structuration. It is this 'fraying' of the text which distinguishes structure—the object of structural analysis, strictly speaking—from structuration—the object of the textual analysis we have attempted to practise here.

The textile metaphor we have just used is not fortuitous. Textual analysis indeed requires us to represent the text as a tissue (this is moreover the etymological sense), as a skein of different voices and multiple codes which are at once interwoven and unfinished. A narrative is not a tabular space, a flat structure, it is a volume, a stereophony (Eisenstein placed great insistence on the counterpoint of his directions, thus initiating an identity of film and text): there is a field of listening for written narrative; the mode of presence of meaning (except perhaps for actional sequences) is not development, but 'explosion' [éclat]: call for contact, communication, the position of contracts, exchange, flashes [éclats] of references, glimmerings of knowledge, heavier, more penetrating blows, coming from the 'other scene', that of the symbolic, a discontinuity of actions which are attached to the same sequence but in a loose, ceaselessly interrupted way.

All this 'volume' is pulled forward (towards the end of the narrative), thus provoking the impatience of reading, under the effect of two structural dispositions: (a) distortion: the terms of a sequence or a code are separated, threaded with heterogeneous elements: a sequence seems to have been abandoned (for example, the degradation of Valdemar's health), but it is taken up again further on, sometimes much later; an expectation is created; we can now even define the sequence: it is the floating micro-structure which constructs not a logical object, but an expectation and its resolution; (b) irreversibility: despite the floating character of structuration, in the classical, readable narrative (such as Poe's story), there are two codes which maintain a directional order; the actional code (based on a logico-temporal order) and the code of the enigma (the question is capped by its solution); and in this way an irreversibility of narrative is created. It is clearly on this point that modern subversion will operate: the avant-garde (to keep a convenient word) attempts to make the text thoroughly reversible, to expel the logico-temporal residue, to attack empiricism (the logic of behaviour, the actional code) and truth (the code of the enigma).

We must not, however, exaggerate the distance separating the modern text from the classical narrative. We have seen, in Poe's story, that one sentence very often refers to two codes simultaneously, without one's being able to choose which is the 'true' one (for example, the scientific code and the symbolic code): what is specific to the text, once it attains the quality of a text, is to constrain us to the undecidability of the codes. In the name of what could we decide? In the author's name? But the narrative gives us only an enunciator, a performer caught up in his own production. In the name of such and such a criticism? All are challengeable, carried off by history (which is not to say that they are useless: each one participates, but only as one voice, in the text's volume). Undecidability is not a weakness, but a structural condition of narration: there is no unequivocal determination of the enunciation: in an utterance, several codes and several voices are there, without priority. Writing is precisely this loss of origin, this loss of 'motives' to the profit of a volume of indeterminations or over-determinations: this volume is, precisely, 'signifiance'. Writing [écriture] comes along very precisely at the point where speech stops, that is from the moment one can no longer locate who is speaking and one simply notes that speaking has started.

NOTES

1. I have attempted the textual analysis of a whole narrative (which could not be the case here for reasons of space) in my book *S/Z*, Seuil, 1970, [trans. Richard Miller, London, Cape, 1975.]
2. For a tighter analysis of the notion of the lexia, and moreover of the operating procedures to follow, I am obliged to refer to *S/Z* [pp. 13ff].
3. *Histoires extraordinaires*, trans. Charles Baudelaire, Paris, N.R.F.; Livre de poche, 1969, pp. 329–345 [*The Collected Works*, 3 vols. ed T. O. Mabbott, Cambridge, Harvard University Press, 1978, III, 1233–43. Translator's note: The fact that Barthes is working on the translation of a text originally in English evidently causes some extra problems of translation. Naturally I have used Poe's text; the quality of Baudelaire's translation is such that most of Barthes's comments apply equally to the original. The notable exception to this is the title, and Barthes in fact explicitly comments on this, continuing, however, to use the word 'vérité' in the French title in support of his analysis. I have specified by notes in square brackets wherever this might lead to confusion.]
4. [Cf Shoshana Felman's discussion of James's comparable statement that *The Turn of the Screw* is a 'trap', in 'Turning the Screw of Interpretation', *Yale French Studies*, 55/6, 1977, pp. 101ff.]
5. [According to Barthes, it was the inability to read the plurality of texts ('asymbolism') that was precisely the failure of his critical adversary Raymond Picard. See *Critique et vérité*, Paris, Seuil, 1966, pp. 35–42.]

6. [In Jakobson's definition ('Shifters, Verbal Categories, and the Russian Verb', in *Selected Writings*, 5 vols, The Hague, Mouton, 1962–, II, pp. 130–2) 'shifters' are the units in language which create the difference between the 'message' per se and the 'meaning' of a communication. Specifically, they refer to those units which refer to the mode of utterance or context, such as 'I', 'you', 'him', etc. But, typically, Barthes elsewhere modifies this to see 'shifting' as characteristic of all writing; see 'The Shifter as Utopia', in *Roland Barthes by Roland Barthes*, trans. Richard Howard, London, Macmillan, 1977, pp. 165–6.]

7. [Xavier Forneret (1809–84), poet. His 'Vapeurs, ni vers ni prose' passed unnoticed when it was published in 1838, but was reissued in 1952 by Andreé Breton, who situated him in the tradition of Lautréamont and the Surrealists.]

8. [In French this metaphorical usage corresponds to the English expression 'I'm dead tired.']

9. [See J. L. Austin, *Philosophical Papers*, ed J. O. Urmson and G. J. Warnock, Oxford, Oxford University Press, 1961; *How To Do Things With Words*, ed J. O. Urmson and Marina Sbisa, Oxford, Oxford University Press, 1962; John R. Searle, *Speech Acts: An Essay in the Philosophy of Language*, Cambridge, Cambridge University Press, 1969. Cf. Stanley E. Fish, 'How To Do Things With Austin and Searle: Speech Act Theory and Literary Criticism' in *Modern Language Notes*, 91, 1976, pp. 983–1025; and Jacques Derrida, 'Signature Event Context', in *Glyph* 1, 1977, pp. 172–97; John R. Searle, 'Reiterating the Differences: a Reply to Derrida', ibid. pp. 198–208; and Derrida's reply, Limited inc., in *Glyph* 2, 1977, pp. 162–254. Cf. also, Paul de Man, 'Action and Identity in Nietzsche', *Yale French Studies*, 52, 1975, pp. 16–30.]

10. Jacques Derrida, *La Voix et le phénomène*, Paris, P.U.F., 1967, pp. 60–1, ['Speech and Phenomena', trans. David B. Allison, Evanston, Northwestern University Press, 1973, pp. 54–5.]

10 Michel Foucault

Michel Foucault (1926–84) was, at the time of his death, Professor of the History of Systems of Thought at the Collège de France in Paris, a title that succeeds (or fails) as much as any other single phrase in the effort to encapsulate his unique, inter-disciplinary field of research. He has been variously described as philosopher, social scientist, and historian of ideas. He was certainly one of the most powerful and influential figures in a remarkable galaxy of intellectual stars who shone in Paris in the 1960s and 70s.

Foucault was often at pains to deny that he was a 'structuralist', but he may legitimately be described as a post-structuralist. Structuralism ignored or distrusted the superficial appearances or commonsense view of cultural phenomena in its efforts to grasp the conditions of their possibility. Foucault did the same, but where the structuralists, like Lévi-Strauss, or the early Barthes, used language and linguistics as their methodological model or tool, Foucault used the history of social and political institutions and discourses. As one of his commentators (Paul Robinow) has said, 'Foucault is highly suspicious of claims to universal truths. He doesn't refute them; instead his consistent response is to historicize grand abstractions.' His example has had a powerful effect upon the writing of literary history in Britain and America.

The essay 'What is an Author' is typical of this historicizing approach. Foucault shows that the idea of the author, which we tend to take for granted, as a timeless, irreducible category, is, rather, a 'function' of discourse which has changed in the course of history. For example, whereas before the Renaissance the attribution of a text to an author was more important in science than in litera-ture, the reverse is true in the era of humanism and capitalism.

In the early part of the essay, Foucault acknowledges the effort of some radical modern criticism (he may be thinking of Barthes' essay 'The Death of the Author', see above pp. 167–72) to abolish the idea of the author as origin and owner of his work, but suggests that this is easier said than done. The essay ends with a vision of a culture in which literature would circulate 'anonymously'; but whether this vision (which has something in common with the conclusion to Derrida's essay 'Structure, Sign and Play'—see pp. 121–22, above) offers an attractive prospect is open to argument. Though Foucault's focus on the histor-ical and institutional contexts of discourse has inspired many critics on the intel-lectual left, his Nietzschean insistence on the struggle for power as the ultimate determinant of all human action is not encouraging to progressive political philosophies.

Foucault's many publications include *Madness and Civilization* (1965) [first published in France, 1961], *The Order of Things* (1970) [1966], *The Archaeology of Knowledge* (1972) [1969], *Discipline and Punish* (1977) [1975], and a multivolumed history of sexuality left unfinished at his death. 'What Is an Author?' was first published in France in 1969, and the English translation by Joseph V. Harari, reprinted below, was first published in 1979.

CROSS REFERENCES: 9. Barthes
                       18. Said
                       24. Belsey
COMMENTARY: Alan Sheridan, *Michel Foucault: the Will to Truth* (1980)
                 Hayden White, 'Michel Foucault' in John Sturrock (ed.), *Structuralism and Since* (1979)

What is an author?

The coming into being of the notion of 'author' constitutes the privileged moment of *individualization* in the history of ideas, knowledge, literature, philosophy, and the sciences. Even today, when we reconstruct the history of a concept, literary genre, or school of philosophy, such categories seem relatively weak, secondary, and superimposed scansions in comparison with the solid and fundamental unit of the author and the work.

I shall not offer here a sociohistorical analysis of the author's persona. Certainly it would be worth examining how the author became individualized in a culture like ours, what status he has been given, at what moment studies of authenticity and attribution began, in what kind of system of valorization the author was involved, at what point we began to recount the lives of authors rather than of heroes, and how this fundamental category of 'the-man-and-his-work criticism' began. For the moment, however, I want to deal solely with the relationship between text and author and with the manner in which the text points to this 'figure' that, at least in appearance, is outside it and antecedes it.

Beckett nicely formulates the theme with which I would like to begin: '"What does it matter who is speaking", someone said, "what does it matter who is speaking."' In this indifference appears one of the fundamental ethical principles of contemporary writing [*écriture*]. I say 'ethical' because this indifference is not really a trait characterizing the manner in which one speaks and writes, but rather a kind of immanent rule, taken up over and over again, never fully applied, not designating writing as something completed, but dominating it as a practice. Since it is too familiar to require a lengthy analysis, this immanent rule can be adequately illustrated here by tracing two of its major themes.

First of all, we can say that today's writing has freed itself from the dimension of expression. Referring only to itself, but without being restricted to the confines of its interiority, writing is identified with its own unfolded exteriority. This means that it is an interplay of signs arranged less according to its signified content than according to the very nature of the signifier. Writing unfolds like a game [*jeu*] that invariably goes beyond its own rules and transgresses its limits. In writing, the point is not to manifest or exalt the act of writing, nor is it to pin a subject within language; it is rather a question of creating a space into which the writing subject constantly disappears.

The second theme, writing's relationship with death, is even more familiar. This link subverts an old tradition exemplified by the Greek epic, which was intended to perpetuate the immortality of the hero: if he was willing to die young, it was so that his life, consecrated and magnified by death, might pass into immortality; the narrative then redeemed this accepted death. In another way, the motivation, as well as the theme and the pretext of Arabian narratives—such as *The Thousand and One Nights*—was also the eluding of death: one spoke, telling stories into the early morning, in order to forestall death, to postpone the day of reckoning that would silence the narrator. Scheherazade's narrative is an effort, renewed each night, to keep death outside the circle of life.

Our culture has metamorphosed this idea of narrative, or writing, as something designed to ward off death. Writing has become linked to sacrifice, even to the sacrifice of life: it is now a voluntary effacement which does not need to be represented in books, since it is brought about in the writer's very existence. The work, which once had the duty of providing immortality, now possesses the right to kill, to be its author's murderer, as in the cases of Flaubert, Proust, and Kafka. That is not all, however: this relationship between writing and death is also manifested in the effacement of the writing subject's individual characteristics. Using all the contrivances that he sets up between himself and what he writes, the writing subject cancels out the signs of his particular individuality. As a result, the mark of the writer is reduced to nothing more than the singularity of his absence; he must assume the role of the dead man in the game of writing.

None of this is recent; criticism and philosophy took note of the disappearance—or death—of the author some time ago. But the consequences of their discovery of it have not been sufficiently examined, nor has its import been accurately measured. A certain number of notions that are intended to replace the privileged position of the author actually seem to preserve that privilege and suppress the real meaning of his disappearance. I shall examine two of these notions, both of great importance today.

The first is the idea of the work. It is a very familiar thesis that the task of criticism is not to bring out the work's relationships with the author, nor to reconstruct through the text a thought or experience, but rather, to analyze the work through its structure, its architecture, its intrinsic form, and the play of its internal relationships. At this point, however, a problem arises: 'What is a work? What is this curious unity which we designate as a work? Of what elements is it composed? Is it not what an author has written?' Difficulties appear immediately. If an individual were not an author, could we say that what he wrote, said, left behind in his papers, or what has been collected of his remarks, could be called a 'work'? When Sade was not considered an author, what was the status of his papers? Were they simply rolls of paper onto which he ceaselessly uncoiled his fantasies during his imprisonment?

Even when an individual has been accepted as an author, we must still ask whether everything that he wrote, said, or left behind is part of his work. The problem is both theoretical and technical. When undertaking the publication of Nietzsche's works, for example, where should one stop? Surely everything must be published, but what is 'everything'? Everything that Nietzsche himself published, certainly. And what about the rough drafts for his works? Obviously. The plans for his aphorisms? Yes. The deleted passages and the notes at the bottom of the page? Yes. What if, within a workbook filled with aphorisms, one finds a reference, the notation of a meeting or of an address, or a laundry list: is it a work, or not? Why not? And so on, ad infinitum. How can one define a work amid the millions of traces left by someone after his death? A theory of the work does not exist, and the empirical task of those who naively undertake the editing of works often suffers in the absence of such a theory.

We could go even further: does *The Thousand and One Nights* constitute a work? What about Clement of Alexandria's *Miscellanies* or Diogenes Laertius' *Lives?*[a] A multitude of questions arises with regard to this notion of the work. Consequently, it is not enough to declare that we should do without the writer (the author) and study the work in itself. The word 'work' and the unity that it designates are probably as problematic as the status of the author's individuality.

Another notion which has hindered us from taking full measure of the author's disappearance, blurring and concealing the moment of this effacement and subtly preserving the author's existence, is the notion of writing [*écriture*]. When rigorously applied, this notion should allow us not only to circumvent references to the author, but also to situate his recent absence. The notion of writing, as currently employed, is concerned with neither the act of writing nor the indication—be it symptom or sign—of a meaning which someone might have wanted to express. We try, with great effort, to imagine the general condition of each text, the condition of both the space in which it is dispersed and the time in which it unfolds.

In current usage, however, the notion of writing seems to transpose the empirical characteristics of the author into a transcendental anonymity. We are content to efface the more visible marks of the author's empiricity by playing off, one against the other, two ways of characterizing writing, namely, the critical and the religious approaches. Giving writing a primal status seems to be a way of retranslating, in transcendental terms, both the theological affirmation of its sacred character and the critical affirmation of its creative character. To admit that writing is, because of the very history that it made possible, subject to the test of oblivion and repression, seems to represent, in transcendental terms, the religious principle of the hidden meaning (which requires interpretation) and the

[a] Clement of Alexandria was a Christian theologian of the second century whose *Stromata* or *Miscellanies* was a commentary on the history of philosophy. Diogenes Laertius was a native of Cicilia who probably lived at about the same time. His *Lives of the Philosophers* ran to ten volumes.

critical principle of implicit significations, silent determinations, and obscured contents (which gives rise to commentary). To imagine writing as absence seems to be a simple repetition, in transcendental terms, of both the religious principle of inalterable and yet never fulfilled tradition, and the aesthetic principle of the work's survival, its perpetuation beyond the author's death, and its enigmatic *excess* in relation to him.

This usage of the notion of writing runs the risk of maintaining the author's privileges under the protection of writing's a priori status: it keeps alive, in the grey light of neutralization, the interplay of those representations that formed a particular image of the author. The author's disappearance, which, since Mallarmé, has been a constantly recurring event, is subject to a series of transcendental barriers. There seems to be an important dividing line between those who believe that they can still locate today's discontinuities [*ruptures*] in the historico-transcendental tradition of the nineteenth century, and those who try to free themselves once and for all from that tradition.

It is not enough, however, to repeat the empty affirmation that the author has disappeared. For the same reason, it is not enough to keep repeating (after Nietzsche) that God and man have died a common death. Instead, we must locate the space left empty by the author's disappearance, follow the distribution of gaps and breaches, and watch for the openings that this disappearance uncovers.

First, we need to clarify briefly the problems arising from the use of the author's name. What is an author's name? How does it function? Far from offering a solution, I shall only indicate some of the difficulties that it presents.

The author's name is a proper name, and therefore it raises the problems common to all proper names. (Here I refer to Searle's analyses, among others.[b]) Obviously, one cannot turn a proper name into a pure and simple reference. It has other than indicative functions: more than an indication, a gesture, a finger pointed at someone, it is the equivalent of a description. When one says 'Aristotle,' one employs a word that is the equivalent of one or a series of, definite descriptions, such as 'the author of the *Analytics*,' 'the founder of ontology,' and so forth. One cannot stop there, however, because a proper name does not have just one signification. When we discover that Rimbaud did not write *La Chasse spirituelle*[c] [*The Spiritual Pursuit*], we cannot pretend that the meaning of this proper name, or that of the author, has been altered. The proper name and the author's name are situated between the two poles of description and designation: they must have a certain link with what they name, but one that is neither entirely in the mode of designation nor in that of description; it must be a *specific* link. However—and it is here that the particular difficulties of the author's name arise—the links between the proper name and the individual named and between the author's name and what it names are not isomorphic and do not function in

---

[b] See John Searle, *Speech Acts: an Essay in the Philosophy of Language* (1969).

[c] A supposedly lost poem by the French Symbolist poet Arthur Rimbaud (1854–91) which was published in the French newspaper *Combat* on 19 May 1949. It was eventually revealed to be a pastiche written by Akakia-Viala and Nicolas Bataille.

the same way. There are several differences.

If, for example, Pierre Dupont does not have blue eyes, or was not born in Paris, or is not a doctor, the name Pierre Dupont will still always refer to the same person; such things do not modify the link of designation. The problems raised by the author's name are much more complex, however. If I discover that Shakespeare was not born in the house that we visit today, this is a modification which, obviously, will not alter the functioning of the author's name. But if we proved that Shakespeare did not write those sonnets which pass for his, that would constitute a significant change and affect the manner in which the author's name functions. If we proved that Shakespeare wrote Bacon's *Organon* by showing that the same author wrote both the works of Bacon and those of Shakespeare, that would be a third type of change which would entirely modify the functioning of the author's name. The author's name is not, therefore, just a proper name like the rest.

Many other facts point out the paradoxical singularity of the author's name. To say that Pierre Dupont does not exist is not at all the same as saying that Homer or Hermes Trismegistus[d] did not exist. In the first case, it means that no one has the name Pierre Dupont; in the second, it means that several people were mixed together under one name, or that the true author had none of the traits traditionally ascribed to the personae of Homer or Hermes. To say that X's real name is actually Jacques Durand instead of Pierre Dupont is not the same as saying that Stendhal's name was Henri Beyle. One could also question the meaning and functioning of propositions like 'Bourbaki is so-and-so, so-and-so, etc.' and 'Victor Eremita, Climacus, Anticlimacus, Frater Taciturnus, Constantine Constantius, all of these are Kierkegaard.'

These differences may result from the fact that an author's name is not simply an element in a discourse (capable of being either subject or object, of being replaced by a pronoun, and the like); it performs a certain role with regard to narrative discourse, assuring a classificatory function. Such a name permits one to group together a certain number of texts, define them, differentiate them from and contrast them to others. In addition, it establishes a relationship among the texts. Hermes Trismegistus did not exist, nor did Hippocrates[e]—in the sense that Balzac existed—but the fact that several texts have been placed under the same name indicates that there has been established among them a relationship of homogeneity, filiation, authentification of some texts by the use of others, reciprocal explication, or concomitant utilization. The author's name serves to characterize a certain mode of being of discourse: the fact that the discourse has an author's name, that one can say 'this was written by so-and-so' or 'so-and-so is its author,' shows that this discourse is not ordinary everyday speech that merely comes and goes, not something that is immediately consumable. On the contrary, it is a speech that must be received in a certain mode and that, in a given culture, must receive a certain status.

[d] Reputed author of ancient books of occult wisdom.

[e] Greek physician of the 5th century BC. He is honoured as the father of medicine, but the details of his life and work are obscure.

It would seem that the author's name, unlike other proper names, does not pass from the interior of a discourse to the real and exterior individual who produced it; instead, the name seems always to be present, marking off the edges of the text, revealing, or at least characterizing, its mode of being. The author's name manifests the appearance of a certain discursive set and indicates the status of this discourse within a society and a culture. It has no legal status, nor is it located in the fiction of the work; rather, it is located in the break that founds a certain discursive construct and its very particular mode of being. As a result, we could say that in a civilization like our own there are a certain number of discourses that are endowed with the 'author-function,' while others are deprived of it. A private letter may well have a signer—it does not have an author; a contract may well have a guarantor—it does not have an author. An anonymous text posted on a wall probably has a writer—but not an author. The author-function is therefore characteristic of the mode of existence, circulation, and functioning of certain discourses within a society.

Let us analyze this 'author-function' as we have just described it. In our culture, how does one characterize discourse containing the author-function? In what way is this discourse different from other discourses? If we limit our remarks to the author of a book or a text, we can isolate four different characteristics.

First of all, discourses are objects of appropriation. The form of ownership from which they spring is of a rather particular type, one that has been codified for many years. We should note that, historically, this type of ownership has always been subsequent to what one might call penal appropriation. Texts, books, and discourses really began to have authors (other than mythical, 'sacralized' and 'sacralizing' figures) to the extent that authors became subject to punishment, that is, to the extent that discourses could be transgressive. In our culture (and doubtless in many others), discourse was not originally a product, a thing, a kind of goods; it was essentially an act—an act placed in the bipolar field of the sacred and the profane, the licit and the illicit, the religious and the blasphemous. Historically, it was a gesture fraught with risks before becoming goods caught up in a circuit of ownership.

Once a system of ownership for texts came into being, once strict rules concerning author's rights, author–publisher relations, rights of reproduction, and related matters were enacted—at the end of the eighteenth and the beginning of the nineteenth century—the possibility of transgression attached to the act of writing took on, more and more, the form of an imperative peculiar to literature. It is as if the author, beginning with the moment at which he was placed in the system of property that characterizes our society, compensated for the status that he thus acquired by rediscovering the old bipolar field of discourse, systematically practicing transgression and thereby restoring danger to a writing which was now guaranteed the benefits of ownership.

The author-function does not affect all discourses in a universal and constant way, however. This is its second characteristic. In our civilization, it has not always been the same types of texts which have required attribution to an author. There was a time when the texts that we today call 'literary' (narratives, stories, epics, tragedies, comedies) were accepted, put into circulation, and valorized without any question about the identity of their author; their anonymity caused no difficulties since their ancientness, whether real or imagined, was regarded as a sufficient guarantee of their status. On the other hand, those texts that we now would call scientific—those dealing with cosmology and the heavens, medicine and illnesses, natural sciences and geography—were accepted in the Middle Ages, and accepted as 'true,' only when marked with the name of their author. 'Hippocrates said,' 'Pliny recounts,'[f] were not really formulas of an argument based on authority; they were the markers inserted in discourses that were supposed to be received as statements of demonstrated truth.

A reversal occurred in the seventeenth or eighteenth century. Scientific discourses began to be received for themselves, in the anonymity of an established or always redemonstrable truth; their membership in a systematic ensemble, and not the reference to the individual who produced them, stood as their guarantee. The author-function faded away, and the inventor's name served only to christen a theorem, proposition, particular effect, property, body, group of elements, or pathological syndrome. By the same token, literary discourses came to be accepted only when endowed with the author-function. We now ask of each poetic or fictional text: from where does it come, who wrote it, when, under what circumstances, or beginning with what design? The meaning ascribed to it and the status or value accorded it depend upon the manner in which we answer these questions. And if a text should be discovered in a state of anonymity—whether as a consequence of an accident or the author's explicit wish—the game becomes one of rediscovering the author. Since literary anonymity is not tolerable, we can accept it only in the guise of an enigma. As a result, the author-function today plays an important role in our view of literary works. (These are obviously generalizations that would have to be refined insofar as recent critical practice is concerned.)

The third characteristic of this author-function is that it does not develop spontaneously as the attribution of a discourse to an individual. It is, rather, the result of a complex operation which constructs a certain rational being that we call 'author.' Critics doubtless try to give this intelligible being a realistic status, by discerning, in the individual, a 'deep' motive, a 'creative' power, or a 'design,' the milieu in which writing originates. Nevertheless, these aspects of an individual which we designate as making him an author are only a projection, in more or less psychologizing terms, of the operations that we force texts to undergo, the connections that we make, the traits that we establish as pertinent, the continuities that we recognize, or the exclusions that we practice. All these operations vary according to periods and types of discourse. We do not construct a 'philosophical author' as we do a 'poet,' just as, in the eighteenth century, one did not construct a novelist as we do today. Still, we can find through the ages certain constants in the rules of author-construction.

[f] Caius Plinius Secundus, Roman naturalist of the first century AD, author of the encyclopaedic *Natural History.*

It seems, for example, that the manner in which literary criticism once defined the author—or rather constructed the figure of the author beginning with existing texts and discourses—is directly derived from the manner in which Christian tradition authenticated (or rejected) the texts at its disposal. In order to 'rediscover' an author in a work, modern criticism uses methods similar to those that Christian exegesis employed when trying to prove the value of a text by its author's saintliness. In *De viris illustribus* [*Concerning Illustrious Men*], Saint Jerome explains that homonymy is not sufficient to identify legitimately authors of more than one work: different individuals could have had the same name, or one man could have, illegitimately, borrowed another's patronymic. The name as an individual trademark is not enough when one works within a textual tradition.

How then can one attribute several discourses to one and the same author? How can one use the author-function to determine if one is dealing with one or several individuals? Saint Jerome proposes four criteria: (1) if among several books attributed to an author one is inferior to the others, it must be withdrawn from the list of the author's works (the author is therefore defined as a constant level of value); (2) the same should be done if certain texts contradict the doctrine expounded in the author's other works (the author is thus defined as a field of conceptual or theoretical coherence): (3) one must also exclude works that are written in a different style, containing words and expressions not ordinarily found in the writer's production (the author is here conceived as a stylistic unity); (4) finally, passages quoting statements that were made, or mentioning events that occurred after the author's death must be regarded as interpolated texts (the author is here seen as a historical figure at the crossroads of a certain number of events).

Modern literary criticism, even when—as is now customary—it is not concerned with questions of authentication, still defines the author the same way: the author provides the basis for explaining not only the presence of certain events in a work, but also their transformations, distortions, and diverse modifications (through his biography, the determination of his individual perspective, the analysis of his social position, and the revelation of his basic design). The author is also the principle of a certain unity of writing—all differences, having to be resolved, at least in part, by the principles of evolution, maturation, or influence. The author also serves to neutralize the contradictions that may emerge in a series of texts: there must be—at a certain level of his thought or desire, of his consciousness or unconscious—a point where contradictions are resolved, where incompatible elements are at last tied together or organized around a fundamental or originating contradiction. Finally, the author is a particular source of expression that, in more or less completed forms, is manifested equally well, and with similar validity, in works, sketches, letters, fragments, and so on. Clearly, Saint Jerome's four criteria of authenticity (criteria which seem totally insufficient for today's exegetes) do define the four modalities according to which modern criticism brings the author-function into play.

But the author-function is not a pure and simple reconstruction made second-hand from a text given as passive material. The text always contains a certain number of signs referring to the author. These signs, well known to grammarians, are personal pronouns, adverbs of time and place, and verb conjugation. Such elements do not play the same role in discourses provided with the author-function as in those lacking it. In the latter, such 'shifters' refer to the real speaker and to the spatio-temporal coordinates of his discourse (although certain modifications can occur, as in the operation of relating discourses in the first person). In the former, however, their role is more complex and variable. Everyone knows that, in a novel narrated in the first person, neither the first person pronoun, nor the present indicative refer exactly either to the writer or to the moment in which he writes, but rather to an alter ego whose distance from the author varies, often changing in the course of the work. It would be just as wrong to equate the author with the real writer as to equate him with the fictitious speaker; the author-function is carried out and operates in the scission itself, in this division and this distance.

One might object that this is a characteristic peculiar to novelistic or poetic discourse, a 'game' in which only 'quasi-discourses' participate. In fact, however, all discourses endowed with the author-function do possess this plurality of self. The self that speaks in the preface to a treatise on mathematics—and that indicates the circumstances of the treatise's composition—is identical neither in its position nor in its functioning to the self that speaks in the course of a demonstration, and that appears in the form of 'I conclude' or 'I suppose.' In the first case, the 'I' refers to an individual without an equivalent who, in a determined place and time, completed a certain task; in the second, the 'I' indicates an instance and a level of demonstration which any individual could perform provided that he accept the same system of symbols, play of axioms, and set of previous demonstrations. We could also, in the same treatise, locate a third self, one that speaks to tell the work's meaning, the obstacles encountered, the results obtained, and the remaining problems; this self is situated in the field of already existing or yet-to-appear mathematical discourses. The author-function is not assumed by the first of these selves at the expense of the other two, which would then be nothing more than a fictitious splitting in two of the first one. On the contrary, in these discourses the author-function operates so as to effect the dispersion of these three simultaneous selves.

No doubt analysis could discover still more characteristic traits of the author-function. I will limit myself to these four, however, because they seem both the most visible and the most important. They can be summarized as follows: (1) the author-function is linked to the juridical and institutional system that encompasses, determines, and articulates the universe of discourses; (2) it does not affect all discourses in the same way at all times and in all types of civilization; (3) it is not defined by the spontaneous attribution of a discourse to its producer, but rather by a series of specific and complex operations; (4) it does not refer purely and simply to a real individual, since it can give rise simultaneously to several selves, to several subjects—positions that can be occupied by different classes of individuals.

Up to this point I have unjustifiably limited my subject. Certainly the author-function in painting, music, and other arts should have been discussed, but even supposing that we remain within the world of discourse, as I want to do, I seem to have given the term 'author' much too narrow a meaning. I have discussed the author only in the limited sense of a person to whom the production of a text, a book, or a work can be legitimately attributed. It is easy to see that in the sphere of discourse one can be the author of much more than a book—one can be the author of a theory, tradition, or discipline in which other books and authors will in their turn find a place. These authors are in a position which we shall call 'transdiscursive.' This is a recurring phenomenon—certainly as old as our civilization. Homer, Aristotle, and the Church Fathers, as well as the first mathematicians and the originators of the Hippocratic tradition, all played this role.

Furthermore, in the course of the nineteenth century, there appeared in Europe another, more uncommon, kind of author, whom one should confuse with neither the 'great' literary authors, nor the authors of religious texts, nor the founders of science. In a somewhat arbitrary way we shall call those who belong in this last group 'founders of discursivity.' They are unique in that they are not just the authors of their own works. They have produced something else: the possibilities and the rules for the formation of other texts. In this sense, they are very different, for example, from a novelist, who is, in fact, nothing more than the author of his own text. Freud is not just the author of *The Interpretation of Dreams* or *Jokes and their Relation to the Unconscious*; Marx is not just the author of the *Communist Manifesto* or *Capital*: they both have established an endless possibility of discourse.

Obviously, it is easy to object. One might say that it is not true that the author of a novel is only the author of his own text; in a sense, he also, provided that he acquires some 'importance,' governs and commands more than that. To take a very simple example, one could say that Ann Radcliffe not only wrote *The Castles of Athlin and Dunbayne* and several other novels, but also made possible the appearance of the Gothic horror novel at the beginning of the nineteenth century; in that respect, her author-function exceeds her own work. But I think there is an answer to this objection. These founders of discursivity (I use Marx and Freud as examples, because I believe them to be both the first and the most important cases) make possible something altogether different from what a novelist makes possible. Ann Radcliffe's texts opened the way for a certain number of resemblances and analogies which have their model or principle in her work. The latter contains characteristic signs, figures, relationships, and structures which could be reused by others. In other words, to say that Ann Radcliffe founded the Gothic horror novel means that in the nineteenth-century Gothic novel one will find, as in Ann Radcliffe's works, the theme of the heroine caught in the trap of her own innocence, the hidden castle, the character of the black cursed hero devoted to making the world expiate the evil done to him, and all the rest of it.

On the other hand, when I speak of Marx or Freud as founders of discursivity, I mean that they made possible not only a certain number of analogies, but also (and equally important) a certain number of differences. They have created a possibility for something other than their discourse, yet something belonging to what they founded. To say that Freud founded psychoanalysis does not (simply) mean that we find the concept of the libido or the technique of dream analysis in the works of Karl Abraham or Melanie Klein; it means that Freud made possible a certain number of divergences—with respect to his own texts, concepts, and hypotheses—that all arise from the psychoanalytical discourse itself.

This would seem to present a new difficulty, however: is the above not true, after all, of any founder of a science, or of any author who has introduced some important transformation into a science? After all, Galileo made possible not only those discourses that repeated the laws that he had formulated, but also statements very different from what he himself had said. If Cuvier is the founder of biology or Saussure the founder of linguistics, it is not because they were imitated, nor because people have since taken up again the concept of organism or sign; it is because Cuvier made possible, to a certain extent, a theory of evolution diametrically opposed to his own fixism; it is because Saussure made possible a generative grammar radically different from his structural analyses. Superficially, then, the initiation of discursive practices appears similar to the founding of any scientific endeavor.

Still, there is a difference, and a notable one. In the case of a science, the act that founds it is on an equal footing with its future transformations; this act becomes in some respects part of the set of modifications that it makes possible. Of course, this belonging can take several forms. In the future development of a science, the founding act may appear as little more than a particular instance of a more general phenomenon which unveils itself in the process. It can also turn out to be marred by intuition and empirical bias; one must then reformulate it, making it the object of a certain number of supplementary theoretical operations which establish it more rigorously, etc. Finally, it can seem to be a hasty generalization which must be limited, and whose restricted domain of validity must be retraced. In other words, the founding act of a science can always be reintroduced within the machinery of those transformations that derive from it.

In contrast, the initiation of a discursive practice is heterogeneous to its subsequent transformations. To expand a type of discursivity, such as psychoanalysis as founded by Freud, is not to give it a formal generality that it would not have permitted at the outset, but rather to open it up to a certain number of possible applications. To limit psychoanalysis as a type of discursivity is, in reality, to try to isolate in the founding act an eventually restricted number of propositions or statements to which, alone, one grants a founding value, and in relation to which certain concepts or theories accepted by Freud might be considered as derived, secondary, and accessory. In addition, one does not declare certain propositions in the work of these founders to be false: instead, when trying to seize the act of founding, one sets aside those statements that are not pertinent, either because they are deemed inessential, or because they are considered 'prehistoric' and derived from another type of discursivity. In other words, unlike the founding of a science, the initiation of a discursive practice does not participate in its later transformations.

As a result, one defines a proposition's theoretical validity in relation to the work of the founders—while, in the case of Galileo and Newton, it is in relation to what physics or cosmology *is* (in its intrinsic structure and 'normativity') that one affirms the validity of any proposition that those men may have put forth. To phrase it very schematically: the work of initiators of discursivity is not situated in the space that science defines; rather, it is the science or the discursivity which refers back to their work as primary coordinates.

In this way we can understand the inevitable necessity, within these fields of discursivity, for a 'return to the origin.' This return, which is part of the discursive field itself, never stops modifying it. The return is not a historical supplement which would be added to the discursivity, or merely an ornament; on the contrary, it constitutes an effective and necessary task of transforming the discursive practice itself. Re-examination of Galileo's text may well change our knowledge of the history of mechanics, but it will never be able to change mechanics itself. On the other hand, re-examining Freud's texts, modifies psychoanalysis itself just as a re-examination of Marx's would modify Marxism.

What I have just outlined regarding the initiation of discursive practices is, of course, very schematic; this is true, in particular, of the opposition that I have tried to draw between discursive initiation and scientific founding. It is not always easy to distinguish between the two; moreover, nothing proves that they are two mutually exclusive procedures. I have attempted the distinction for only one reason: to show that the author-function, which is complex enough when one tries to situate it at the level of a book or a series of texts that carry a given signature, involves still more determining factors when one tries to analyze it in larger units, such as groups of works or entire disciplines.

To conclude, I would like to review the reasons why I attach a certain importance to what I have said.

First, there are theoretical reasons. On the one hand, an analysis in the direction that I have outlined might provide for an approach to a typology of discourse. It seems to me, at least at first glance, that such a typology cannot be constructed solely from the grammatical features, formal structures, and objects of discourse: more likely there exist properties or relationships peculiar to discourse (not reducible to the rules of grammar and logic), and one must use these to distinguish the major categories of discourse. The relationship (or nonrelationship) with an author, and the different forms this relationship takes, constitute—in a quite visible manner—one of these discursive properties.

On the other hand, I believe that one could find here an introduction to the historical analysis of discourse. Perhaps it is time to study discourses not only in terms of their expressive value or formal transformations, but according to their modes of existence. The modes of circulation, valorization, attribution, and appropriation of discourses vary with each culture and are modified within each. The manner in which they are articulated according to social relationships can be more readily understood, I believe, in the activity of the author-function and in its modifications, than in the themes or concepts that discourses set in motion.

It would seem that one could also, beginning with analyses of this type, re-examine the privileges of the subject. I realize that in undertaking the internal and architectonic analysis of a work (be it a literary text, philosophical system, or scientific work), in setting aside biographical and psychological references, one has already called back into question the absolute character and founding role of the subject. Still, perhaps one must return to this question, not in order to re-establish the theme of an originating subject, but to grasp the subject's points of insertion, modes of functioning, and system of dependencies. Doing so means overturning the traditional problem, no longer raising the questions 'How can a free subject penetrate the substance of things and give it meaning? How can it activate the rules of a language from within and thus give rise to the designs which are properly its own?' Instead, these questions will be raised: 'How, under what conditions and in what forms can something like a subject appear in the order of discourse? What place can it occupy in each type of discourse, what functions can it assume, and by obeying what rules?' In short, it is a matter of depriving the subject (or its substitute) of its role as originator, and of analyzing the subject as a variable and complex function of discourse.

Second, there are reasons dealing with the 'ideological' status of the author. The question then becomes: How can one reduce the great peril, the great danger with which fiction threatens our world? The answer is: One can reduce it with the author. The author allows a limitation of the cancerous and dangerous proliferation of significations within a world where one is thrifty not only with one's resources and riches, but also with one's discourses and their significations. The author is the principle of thrift in the proliferation of meaning. As a result, we must entirely reverse the traditional idea of the author. We are accustomed, as we have seen earlier, to saying that the author is the genial creator of a work in which he deposits, with infinite wealth and generosity, an inexhaustible world of significations. We are used to thinking that the author is so different from all other men, and so transcendent with regard to all languages that, as soon as he speaks, meaning begins to proliferate, to proliferate indefinitely.

The truth is quite the contrary: the author is not an indefinite source of significations which fill a work; the author does not precede the works, he is a certain functional principle by which, in our culture, one limits, excludes, and chooses; in short, by which one impedes the free circulation, the free manipulation, the free composition, decomposition, and recomposition of fiction. In fact, if we are accustomed to presenting the author as a genius, as a perpetual surging of invention, it is because, in reality, we make him function in exactly the opposite fashion. One can say that the author is an ideological product, since we represent him as the opposite of his historically real function. (When a historically given function is represented in a figure that inverts it, one has an ideological production.) The author is therefore the ideological figure by which one marks the manner in which we fear the proliferation of meaning.

In saying this, I seem to call for a form of culture in which fiction would not be limited by the figure of the author. It would be pure romanticism, however, to imagine a culture in which the fictive would operate in an absolutely free state, in which fiction would be put at the disposal of everyone and would develop without passing through something like a necessary or constraining figure. Although, since the eighteenth century, the author has played the role of the regulator of the fictive, a role quite characteristic of our era of industrial and bourgeois society, of individualism and private property, still, given the historical modifications that are taking place, it does not seem necessary that the author-function remain constant in form, complexity, and even in existence. I think that, as our society changes, at the very moment when it is in the process of changing, the author-function will disappear, and in such a manner that fiction and its polysemic texts will once again function according to another mode, but still with a system of constraint—one which will no longer be the author, but which will have to be determined or, perhaps, experienced.

All discourses, whatever their status, form, value, and whatever the treatment to which they will be subjected, would then develop in the anonymity of a murmur. We would no longer hear the questions that have been rehashed for so long: 'Who really spoke? Is it really he and not someone else? With what authenticity or originality? And what part of his deepest self did he express in his discourse?' Instead, there would be other questions, like these: 'What are the modes of existence of this discourse? Where has it been used, how can it circulate, and who can appropriate it for himself? What are the places in it where there is room for possible subjects? Who can assume these various subject-functions?' And behind all these questions, we would hear hardly anything but the stirring of an indifference: 'What difference does it make who is speaking?'

11 Wolfgang Iser

Wolfgang Iser (b. 1926) is Professor of English and Comparative Literature at the University of Constance, West Germany, and has taught at many other universities in Europe and America. He and his colleague at Constance, Hans Robert Jauss, are the best-known exponents of a distinctively German school of modern criticism known as 'reception-theory' (*Rezeption-aesthetik*). This developed in Germany concurrently with, but more or less independently of, a shift in French and Anglo–American criticism from a structuralist focus on the literary text as a realization of underlying systems to a post-structuralist view of the text as a site for the production and proliferation of meaning. *Rezeption-aesthetik* shares with deconstruction a scepticism about the reified, objective text presupposed by formalist criticism, but its account of reading is less subversive of the values of traditional humanist scholarship. It owes much to the philosophical tradition of phenomenology that began with Husserl, especially the aesthetics of the Polish scholar Roman Ingarden and the hermeneutics of the German philosopher Hans-Georg Gadamer—a tradition which stresses the centrality of consciousness in all investigations of meaning.

Iser's work has affinities with the so-called Geneva school of phenomenological criticism, whose doyen, Georges Poulet, he discusses at the end of the essay reprinted here. Iser is less 'mystical', more 'scientific' than the Geneva critics in his account of literary meaning as a convergence of text and reader, but like them, and like Gadamer and Ingarden, he privileges the experience of reading literary texts as a uniquely valuable consciousness-raising activity: 'reading literature gives us the chance to formulate the unformulated'. One of the most useful ideas in Iser's impressively coherent theory is his discussion of indeterminacy—the way in which 'gaps' or 'blanks' in literary texts stimulate the reader to construct meanings which would not otherwise come into existence. 'The Reading Process: a phenomenological approach' is reprinted here from *New Literary History* 3 (1972). For a fuller exposition of Iser's theory see *The Act of Reading: a theory of aesthetic response* (1978) [first published in German 1976]; and for Jauss's theory see 'Literary History as a Challenge to Literary Theory', *New Literary History* 5 (1974).

CROSS-REFERENCES: 2. Shklovsky
19. Fish
COMMENTARY: Robert C. Holub, *Reception Theory: a critical introduction* (1984)

The reading process: a phenomenological approach

I

The phenomenological theory of art lays full stress on the idea that, in considering a literary work, one must take into account not only the actual text but also, and in equal measure, the actions involved in responding to that text. Thus Roman Ingarden confronts the structure of the literary text with the ways in which it can be *konkretisiert* (realized).[1] The text as such offers different 'schematised views'[2] through which the subject matter of the work can come to light, but the actual bringing to light is an action of *Konkretisation*. If this is so, then the literary work has two poles, which we might call the artistic, and the aesthetic: the artistic refers to the text created by the author, and the aesthetic to the realization accomplished by the reader. From this polarity it follows that the literary work cannot be completely identical with the text, or with the realization of the text, but in fact must lie halfway between the two. The work is more than the text, for the text only takes on life when it is realized, and furthermore the realization is by no means independent of the individual disposition of the reader—though this in turn is acted upon by the different patterns of the text. The convergence of text and reader brings the literary work into existence, and this convergence can never be precisely pinpointed, but must always remain virtual, as it is not to be identified either with the reality of the text or with the individual disposition of the reader.

It is the virtuality of the work that gives rise to its dynamic nature, and this in turn is the precondition for the effects that the work calls forth. As the reader uses the various perspectives offered him by the text in order to relate the patterns and the 'schematised views' to one another, he sets the work in motion, and this very process results ultimately in the awakening of responses within himself. Thus, reading causes the literary work to unfold its inherently dynamic character. That this is no new discovery is apparent from references made even in the early days of the novel. Laurence Sterne remarks in *Tristram Shandy*: '. . . no author, who understands the just boundaries of decorum and good-breeding, would presume to think all: The truest respect which you can pay to the reader's understanding, is to halve this matter amicably, and leave him something to imagine, in his turn, as well as yourself. For my own part, I am eternally paying him compliments of this kind, and do all that lies in my power to keep his imagination as busy as my own.'[3] Sterne's conception of a literary text is that it is something like an arena in which reader and author participate in a game of the imagination. If the reader were given the whole story, and there were nothing left for him to do, then his imagination would never enter the field, the result would be the boredom which inevitably arises when everything is laid out cut and dried before us. A literary text must therefore be conceived in such a way that it will engage the reader's imagination in the task of working things out for himself, for reading is only a pleasure when it is active and creative. In this process of creativity, the text may either not go far enough, or may go too far, so we may say that boredom and overstrain form the boundaries beyond which the reader will leave the field of play.

The extent to which the 'unwritten' part of a text stimulates the reader's creative participation is brought out by an observation of Virginia Woolf's in her study of *Jane Austen*: 'Jane Austen is thus a mistress of much deeper emotion than appears upon the surface. She stimulates us to supply what is not there. What she offers is, apparently, a trifle, yet is composed of something that expands in the reader's mind and endows with the most enduring form of life scenes which are outwardly trivial. Always the stress is laid upon character . . . . The turns and twists of the dialogue keep us on the tenterhooks of suspense. Our attention is half upon the present moment, half upon the future. . . . Here, indeed, in this unfinished and in the main inferior story, are all the elements of Jane Austen's greatness.'[4] The unwritten aspects of apparently trivial scenes, and the unspoken dialogue within the 'turns and twists,' not only draw the reader into the action, but also lead him to shade in the many outlines suggested by the given situations, so that these take on a reality of their own. But as the reader's imagination animates these 'outlines,' they in turn will influence the effect of the written part of the text. Thus begins a whole dynamic process: the written text imposes certain limits on its unwritten implications in order to prevent these from becoming too blurred and hazy, but at the same time these implications, worked out by the reader's imagination, set the given situation against a background which endows it with far greater significance than it might have seemed to possess on its own. In this way, trivial scenes suddenly take on the shape of an 'enduring form of life.' What constitutes this form is never named, let alone explained, in the text, although in fact it is the end product of the interaction between text and reader.

II

The question now arises as to how far such a process can be adequately described. For this purpose a phenomenological analysis recommends itself, especially since the somewhat sparse observations hitherto made of the psychology of reading tend mainly to be psychoanalytical, and so are restricted to the illustration of predetermined ideas concerning the unconscious. We shall, however, take a closer look later at some worthwhile psychological observations.

As a starting point for a phenomenological analysis we might examine the way in which sequent sentences act upon one another. This is of especial importance in literary texts in view of the fact that they do not correspond to any objective reality outside themselves. The world presented by literary texts is constructed out of what Ingarden has called *intentionale Satzkorrelate* (intentional sentence correlatives):

> Sentences link up in different ways to form more complex units of
> meaning that reveal a very varied structure giving rise to such entities as
> a short story, a novel, a dialogue, a drama, a scientific theory. . . . In the
> final analysis, there arises a particular world, with component parts
> determined in this way or that, and with all the variations that may occur
> within these parts—all this as a purely intentional correlative of a
> complex of sentences. If this complex finally forms a literary work, I call
> the whole sum of sequent intentional sentence correlatives the 'world
> presented' in the work.[5]

This world, however, does not pass before the reader's eyes like a film. The sentences are 'component parts' insofar as they make statements, claims, or observations, or convey information, and so establish various perspectives in the text. But they remain only 'component parts'—they are not the sum total of the text itself. For the intentional correlatives disclose subtle connections which individually are less concrete than the statements, claims, and observations, even though these only take on their real meaningfulness through the interaction of their correlatives.

How is one to conceive the connection between the correlatives? It marks those points at which the reader is able to 'climb aboard' the text. He has to accept certain given perspectives, but in doing so he inevitably causes them to interact. When Ingarden speaks of intentional sentence correlatives in literature, the statements made, or information conveyed in the sentence are already in a certain sense qualified: the sentence does not consist solely of a statement—which after all, would be absurd, as one can only make statements about things that exist—but aims at something beyond what it actually says. This is true of all sentences in literary works, and it is through the interaction of these sentences that their common aim is fulfilled. This is what gives them their own special quality in literary texts. In their capacity as statements, observations, purveyors of information, etc., they are always indications of something that is to come, the structure of which is foreshadowed by their specific content.

They set in motion a process out of which emerges the actual content of the text itself. In describing man's inner consciousness of time, Husserl once remarked: 'Every originally constructive process is inspired by pre-intentions, which construct and collect the seed of what is to come, as such, and bring it to fruition.'[6] For this bringing to fruition, the literary text needs the reader's imagination, which gives shape to the interaction of correlatives foreshadowed in structure by the sequence of the sentences. Husserl's observation draws our attention to a point that plays a not insignificant part in the process of reading. The individual sentences not only work together to shade in what is to come; they also form an expectation in this regard. Husserl calls this expectation 'pre-intentions.' As this structure is characteristic of *all* sentence correlatives, the interaction of these correlatives will not be a fulfilment of the expectation so much as a continual modification of it.

For this reason, expectations are scarcely ever fulfilled in truly literary texts. If they were, then such texts would be confined to the individualization of a given expectation, and one would inevitably ask what such an intention was supposed to achieve. Strangely enough, we feel that any confirmative effect—such as we implicitly demand of expository texts, as we refer to the objects they are meant to present—is a defect in a literary text. For the more a text individualizes or confirms an expectation it has initially aroused, the more aware we become of its didactic purpose, so that at best we can only accept or reject the thesis forced upon us. More often than not, the very clarity of such texts will make us want to free ourselves from their clutches. But generally the sentence correlatives of literary texts do not develop in this rigid way, for the expectations they evoke tend to encroach on one another in such a manner that they are continually modified as one reads. One might simplify by saying that each intentional sentence correlative opens up a particular horizon, which is modified, if not completely changed, by succeeding sentences. While these expectations arouse interest in what is to come, the subsequent modification of them will also have a retrospective effect on what has already been read. This may now take on a different significance from that which it had at the moment of reading.

Whatever we have read sinks into our memory and is foreshortened. It may later be evoked again and set against a different background with the result that the reader is enabled to develop hitherto unforeseeable connections. The memory evoked, however, can never reassume its original shape, for this would mean that memory and perception were identical, which is manifestly not so. The new background brings to light new aspects of what we had committed to memory; conversely these, in turn, shed their light on the new background, thus arousing more complex anticipations. Thus, the reader, in establishing these interrelations between past, present and future, actually causes the text to reveal its potential multiplicity of connections. These connections are the product of the reader's mind working on the raw material of the text, though they are not the text itself—for this consists just of sentences, statements, information, etc.

This is why the reader often feels involved in events which, at the time of reading, seem real to him, even though in fact they are very far from his own reality. The fact that completely different readers can be differently affected by the 'reality' of a particular text is ample evidence of the degree to which literary texts transform reading into a creative process that is far above mere perception of what is written. The literary text activates our own faculties, enabling us to recreate the world it presents. The product of this creative activity is what we might call the virtual dimension of the text, which endows it with its reality. This virtual dimension is not the text itself, nor is it the imagination of the reader: it is the coming together of text and imagination.

As we have seen, the activity of reading can be characterized as a sort of kaleidoscope of perspectives, preintentions, recollections. Every sentence contains a preview of the next and forms a kind of viewfinder for what is to come; and this in turn changes the 'preview' and so becomes a 'viewfinder' for what has been read. This whole process represents the fulfilment of the potential, unexpressed reality of the text, but it is to be seen only as a framework for a great variety of means by which the virtual dimension may be brought into being. The process of anticipation and retrospection itself does not by any means develop in a smooth flow. Ingarden has already drawn attention to this fact, and ascribes a quite remarkable significance to it:

> Once we are immersed in the flow of *Satzdenken* (sentence-thought); we are ready, after completing the thought of one sentence, to think out the 'continuation,' also in the form of a sentence—and that is, in the form of a sentence that connects up with the sentence we have just thought through. In this way the process of reading goes effortlessly forward. But if by chance the following sentence has no tangible connection whatever with the sentence we have just thought through, there then comes a blockage in the stream of thought. This hiatus is linked with a more or less active surprise, or with indignation. This blockage must be overcome if the reading is to flow once more.[7]

The hiatus that blocks the flow of sentences is, in Ingarden's eyes, the product of chance, and is to be regarded as a flaw; this is typical of his adherence to the classical idea of art. If one regards the sentence sequence as a continual flow, this implies that the anticipation aroused by one sentence will generally be realized by the next, and the frustration of one's expectations will arouse feelings of exasperation. And yet literary texts are full of unexpected twists and turns, and frustration of expectations. Even in the simplest story there is bound to be some kind of blockage, if only for the fact that no tale can ever be told in its entirety. Indeed, it is only through inevitable omissions that a story will gain its dynamism. Thus whenever the flow is interrupted and we are led off in unexpected directions, the opportunity is given to us to bring into play our own faculty for establishing connections—for filling in the gaps left by the text itself.[8]

These gaps have a different effect on the process of anticipation and retrospection, and thus on the 'gestalt' of the virtual dimension, for they may be filled in different ways. For this reason, one text is potentially capable of several different realizations, and no reading can ever exhaust the full potential, for each individual reader will fill in the gaps in his own way, thereby excluding the various other possibilities; as he reads, he will make his own decision as to how the gap is to be filled. In this very act the dynamics of reading are revealed. By making his decision he implicitly acknowledges the inexhaustibility of the text; at the same time it is this very inexhaustibility that forces him to make his decision. With 'traditional' texts this process was more or less unconscious, but modern texts frequently exploit it quite deliberately. They are often so fragmentary that one's attention is almost exclusively occupied with the search for connections between the fragments; the object of this is not to complicate the 'spectrum' of connections, so much as to make us aware of the nature of our own capacity for providing links. In such cases, the text refers back directly to our own preconceptions—which are revealed by the act of interpretation that is a basic element of the reading process. With all literary texts, then, we may say that the reading process is selective, and the potential text is infinitely richer than any of its individual realizations. This is borne out by the fact that a second reading of a piece of literature often produces a different impression from the first. The reasons for this may lie in the reader's own change of circumstances; still, the text must be such as to allow this variation. On a second reading familiar occurrences now tend to appear in a new light and seem to be at times corrected, at times enriched.

In every text there is a potential time-sequence which the reader must inevitably realize, as it is impossible to absorb even a short text in a single moment. Thus the reading process always involves viewing the text through a perspective that is continually on the move, linking up the different phases, and so constructing what we have called the virtual dimension. This dimension, of course, varies all the time we are reading. However, when we have finished the text, and read it again, clearly our extra knowledge will result in a different time-sequence; we shall tend to establish connections by referring to our awareness of what is to come, and so certain aspects of the text will assume a significance we did not attach to them on a first reading, while others will recede into the background. It is a common enough experience for a person to say that on a second reading he noticed things he had missed when he read the book for the first time, but this is scarcely surprising in view of the fact that the second time he is looking at the text through a different perspective. The time-sequence that he realized on his first reading cannot possibly be repeated on a second reading and this unrepeatability is bound to result in modifications of his reading experience. This is not to say that the second reading is 'truer' than the first—they are, quite simply, different: the reader establishes the virtual dimension of the text by realizing a new time-sequence. Thus even on repeated viewings a text allows and, indeed, induces innovative reading.

In whatever way, and under whatever circumstances, the reader may link the different phases of the text together, it will always be the process of anticipation and retrospection that leads to the formation of the virtual dimension, which in turn transforms the text into an experience for the reader. The way in which this experience comes about through a process of continual modification is closely akin to the way in which we gather experience in life. And thus the 'reality' of the reading experience can illuminate basic patterns of real experience:

> We have the experience of a world, not understood as a system of
> relations which wholly determine each event, but as an open totality the
> synthesis of which is inexhaustible. . . . From the moment that
> experience—that is, the opening on to our de facto world—is recognized
> as the beginning of knowledge, there is no longer any way of
> distinguishing a level of a priori truths and one of factual ones, what the
> world must necessarily be and what it actually is.[9]

The manner in which the reader experiences the text will reflect his own disposition, and in this respect the literary text acts as a kind of mirror; but at the same time, the reality which this process helps to create is one that will be *different* from his own (since, normally, we tend to be bored by texts that present us with things we already know perfectly well ourselves). Thus we have the apparently paradoxical situation in which the reader is forced to reveal aspects of himself in order to experience a reality which is different from his own. The impact this reality makes on him will depend largely on the extent to which he himself actively provides the unwritten part of the text, and yet in supplying all the missing links, he must think in terms of experiences different from his own; indeed, it is only by leaving behind the familiar world of his own experience that the reader can truly participate in the adventure the literary text offers him.

III

We have seen that, during the process of reading, there is an active interweaving of anticipation and retrospection, which on a second reading may turn into a kind of advance retrospection. The impressions that arise as a result of this process will vary from individual to individual but only within the limits imposed by the written as opposed to the unwritten text. In the same way, two people gazing at the night sky may both be looking at the same collection of stars, but one will see the image of a plough, and the other will make out a dipper. The 'stars' in a literary text are fixed; the lines that join them are variable. The author of the text may, of course, exert plenty of influence on the reader's imagination—he has the whole panoply of narrative techniques at his disposal—but no author worth his salt will ever attempt to set the *whole* picture before his reader's eyes. If he does, he will very quickly lose his reader, for it is only by activating the reader's imagination that the author can hope to involve him and so realize the intentions of his text.

Gilbert Ryle, in his analysis of imagination, asks: 'How can a person fancy that he sees something, without realizing that he is not seeing it?' He answers as follows:

> Seeing Helvellyn (the name of a mountain) in one's mind's eye does not entail, what seeing Helvellyn and seeing snapshots of Helvellyn entail, the having of visual sensations. It does involve the thought of having a view of Helvellyn and it is therefore a more sophisticated operation than that of having a view of Helvellyn. It is one utilization among others of the knowledge of how Helvellyn should look, or, in one sense of the verb, it is thinking how it should look. The expectations which are fulfilled in the recognition at sight of Helvellyn are not indeed fulfilled in picturing it, but the picturing of it is something like a rehearsal of getting them fulfilled. So far from picturing involving the having of faint sensations, or wraiths of sensations, it involves missing just what one would be due to get, if one were seeing the mountain.[10]

If one sees the mountain, then of course one can no longer imagine it, and so the act of picturing the mountain presupposes its absence. Similarly, with a literary text we can only picture things which are not there; the written part of the text gives us the knowledge, but it is the unwritten part that gives us the opportunity to picture things; indeed without the elements of indeterminacy, the gaps in the text, we should not be able to use our imagination.[11]

218

The truth of this observation is borne out by the experience many people have on seeing, for instance, the film of a novel. While reading *Tom Jones*, they may never have had a clear conception of what the hero actually looks like, but on seeing the film, some may say, 'That's not how I imagined him.' The point here is that the reader of *Tom Jones* is able to visualize the hero virtually for himself, and so his imagination senses the vast number of possibilites; the moment these possibilites are narrowed down to one complete and immutable picture, the imagination is put out of action, and we feel we have somehow been cheated. This may perhaps be an oversimplification of the process, but it does illustrate plainly the vital richness of potential that arises out of the fact that the hero in the novel must be pictured and cannot be seen. With the novel the reader must use his imagination to synthesize the information given him, and so his perception is simultaneously richer and more private; with the film he is confined merely to physical perception, and so whatever he remembers of the world he had pictured is brutally cancelled out.

IV

The 'picturing' that is done by our imagination is only one of the activities through which we form the 'gestalt' of a literary text. We have already discussed the process of anticipation and retrospection, and to this we must add the process of grouping together all the different aspects of a text to form the consistency that the reader will always be in search of. While expectations may be continually modified, and images continually expanded, the reader will still strive, even if unconsciously, to fit everything together in a consistent pattern. 'In the reading of images, as in the hearing of speech, it is always hard to distinguish what is given to us from what we supplement in the process of projection which is triggered off by recognition ... it is the guess of the beholder that tests the medley of forms and colours for coherent meaning, crystallizing it into shape when a consistent interpretation has been found.'[12] By grouping together the written parts of the text, we enable them to interact, we observe the direction in which they are leading us, and we project onto them the consistency which we, as readers, require. This 'gestalt' must inevitably be colored by our own characteristic selection process. For it is not given by the text itself; it arises from the meeting between the written text and the individual mind of the reader with its own particular history of experience, its own consciousness, its own outlook. The 'gestalt' is not the true meaning of the text; at best it is a configurative meaning; '... comprehension is an individual act of seeing-things-together, and only that.'[13] With a literary text such comprehension is inseparable from the reader's expectations, and where we have expectations, there too we have one of the most potent weapons in the writer's armory—illusion.

Whenever 'consistent reading suggests itself ... illusion takes over.'[14] Illusion, says Northrop Frye, is 'fixed or definable, and reality is at best understood as its negation.'[15] The 'gestalt' of a text normally takes on (or, rather, is given) this fixed or definable outline, as this is essential to our own understanding, but on the other hand, if reading were to consist of nothing but an uninterrupted building up of illusions, it would be a suspect, if not downright dangerous, process: instead of bringing us into contact with reality, it would wean us away from realities. Of course, there is an element of 'escapism' in all literature, resulting from this very creation of illusion, but there are some texts which offer nothing but a harmonious world, purified of all contradiction and deliberately excluding anything that might disturb the illusion once established, and these are the texts that we generally do not like to classify as literary. Women's magazines and the brasher forms of detective story might be cited as examples.

However, even if an overdose of illusion may lead to triviality, this does not mean that the process of illusion-building should ideally be dispensed with alto-gether. On the contrary, even in texts that appear to resist the formation of illusion, thus drawing our attention to the cause of this resistance, we still need the abiding illusion that the resistance itself is the consistent pattern underlying the text. This is especially true of modern texts, in which it is the very precision of the written details which increases the proportion of indeterminacy; one detail appears to contradict another, and so simultaneously stimulates and frustrates our desire to 'picture,' thus continually causing our imposed 'gestalt' of the text to disintegrate. Without the formation of illusions, the unfamiliar world of the text would remain unfamiliar; through the illusions, the experience offered by the text becomes accessible to us, for it is only the illusion, on its different levels of consistency, that makes the experience 'readable.' If we cannot find (or impose) this consistency, sooner or later we will put the text down. The process is virtually hermeneutic. The text provokes certain expectations which in turn we project onto the text in such a way that we reduce the polysemantic possibilities to a single interpretation in keeping with the expectations aroused, thus extracting an individual, configurative meaning. The polysemantic nature of the text and the illusion-making of the reader are opposed factors. If the illusion were complete, the polysemantic nature would vanish; if the polysemantic nature were all-powerful, the illusion would be totally destroyed. Both extremes are conceiv-able, but in the individual literary text we always find some form of balance between the two conflicting tendencies. The formation of illusions, therefore, can never be total, but it is this very incompleteness that in fact gives it its productive value.

With regard to the experience of reading, Walter Pater once observed: 'For to the grave reader words too are grave; and the ornamental word, the figure, the accessory form or colour or reference, is rarely content to die to thought precisely at the right moment, but will inevitably linger awhile, stirring a long "brainwave" behind it of perhaps quite alien associations.'[16] Even while the reader is seeking a consistent pattern in the text, he is also uncovering other impulses which cannot be immediately integrated or will even resist final integration. Thus the semantic possibilities of the text will always remain far richer than any configurative meaning formed while reading. But this impression is, of course, only to be gained through reading the text. Thus the configurative meaning can be nothing but a *pars pro toto* [part for the whole] fulfilment of the text, and yet this fulfilment gives rise to the very richness which it seeks to restrict, and indeed in some modern texts, our awareness of this richness takes precedence over any configurative meaning.

This fact has several consequences which, for the purpose of analysis, may be dealt with separately, though in the reading process they will all be working together. As we have seen, a consistent, configurative meaning is essential for the apprehension of an unfamiliar experience, which through the process of illusion-building we can incorporate in our own imaginative world. At the same time, this consistency conflicts with the many other possibilities of fulfillment it seeks to exclude, with the result that the configurative meaning is always accompanied by 'alien associations' that do not fit in with the illusions formed. The first consequence, then, is the fact that in forming our illusions, we also produce at the same time a latent disturbance of these illusions. Strangely enough, this also applies to texts in which our expectations are actually fulfilled—though one would have thought that the fulfilment of expectations would help to complete the illusion. 'Illusion wears off once the expectation is stepped up; we take it for granted and want more.'[17]

The experiments in 'gestalt' psychology referred to by Gombrich in *Art and Illusion* make one thing clear: '. . . though we may be intellectually aware of the fact that any given experience must be an illusion, we cannot, strictly speaking, watch ourselves having an illusion.'[18] Now, if illusion were not a transitory state, this would mean that we could be, as it were, permanently caught up in it. And if reading were exclusively a matter of producing illusion—necessary though this is for the understanding of an unfamiliar experience—we should run the risk of falling victim to a gross deception. But it is precisely during our reading that the transitory nature of the illusion is revealed to the full.

As the formation of illusions is constantly accompanied by 'alien associations' which cannot be made consistent with the illusions, the reader constantly has to lift the restrictions he places on the 'meaning' of the text. Since it is he who builds the illusions, he oscillates between involvement in and observation of those illusions; he opens himself to the unfamiliar world without being imprisoned in it. Through this process the reader moves into the presence of the fictional world and so experiences the realities of the text as they happen.

In the oscillation between consistency and 'alien associations,' between involvement in and observation of the illusion, the reader is bound to conduct his own balancng operation, and it is this that forms the aesthetic experience offered by the literary text. However, if the reader were to achieve a balance, obviously he would then no longer be engaged in the process of establishing and disrupting consistency. And since it is this very process that gives rise to the balancing operation, we may say that the inherent non-achievement of balance is a prerequisite for the very dynamism of the operation. In seeking the balance we inevitably have to start out with certain expectations, the shattering of which is integral to the aesthetic experience.

Furthermore, to say merely that 'our expectations are satisfied' is to be guilty of another serious ambiguity. At first sight such a statement seems to deny the obvious fact that much of our enjoyment is derived from

221

surprises, from betrayals of our expectations. The solution of this paradox is to find some ground for a distinction between 'surprise' and 'frustration.' Roughly, the distinction can be made in terms of the effects which the two kinds of experiences have upon us. Frustration blocks or checks activity. It necessitates new orientation for our activity, if we are to escape the *cul de sac*. Consequently, we abandon the frustrating object and return to blind impulsive activity. On the other hand, surprise merely causes a temporary cessation of the exploratory phase of the experience, and a recourse to intense contemplation and scrutiny. In the latter phase the surprising elements are seen in their connection with what has gone before, with the whole drift of the experience, and the enjoyment of these values is then extremely intense. Finally, it appears that there must always be some degree of novelty or surprise in all these values if there is a progressive specification of the direction of the total act . . . and any aesthetic experience tends to exhibit a continuous interplay between 'deductive' and 'inductive' operation.[19]

It is this interplay between 'deduction' and 'induction' that gives rise to the configurative meaning of the text, and not the individual expectations, surprises, or frustrations arising from the different perspectives. Since this interplay obviously does not take place in the text itself, but can only come into being through the process of reading, we may conclude that this process formulates something that is unformulated in the text, and yet represents its 'intention.' Thus, by reading, we uncover the unformulated part of the text, and this very indeterminacy is the force that drives us to work out a configurative meaning while at the same time giving us the necessary degree of freedom to do so.

As we work out a consistent pattern in the text, we will find our 'interpretation' threatened, as it were, by the presence of other possibilities of 'interpretation,' and so there arise new areas of indeterminacy (though we may only be dimly aware of them, if at all, as we are continually making 'decisions' which will exclude them). In the course of a novel, for instance, we sometimes find that characters, events, and backgrounds seem to change their significance; what really happens is that the other 'possibilities' begin to emerge more strongly, so that we become more directly aware of them. Indeed, it is this very shifting of perspectives that makes us feel a novel is that much more 'true-to-life.' Since it is we ourselves who establish the levels of interpretation and switch from one to another as we conduct our balancing operation, we ourselves impart to the text the dynamic lifelikeness which, in turn, enables us to absorb an unfamiliar experience into our personal world.

As we read, we oscillate to a greater or lesser degree between the building and the breaking of illusions. In a process of trial and error, we organize and reorganize the various data offered us by the text. These are the given factors, the fixed point on which we base our 'interpretation,' trying to fit them together in the way we think the author meant them to be fitted. 'For to perceive, a beholder must create his own experience. And his creation must include relations comparable to those which the original producer underwent. They are not the same in any literal sense. But with the perceiver, as with the artist, there must be an ordering of the elements of the whole that is in form, although not in details, the same as the process of organization the creator of the work consciously experienced. Without an act of recreation the object is not perceived as a work of art.'[20]

The act of recreation is not a smooth or continuous process, but one which, in its essence, relies on *interruptions* of the flow to render it efficacious. We look forward, we look back, we decide, we change our decisions, we form expectations, we are shocked by their nonfulfilment, we question, we muse, we accept, we reject; this is the dynamic process of recreation. This process is steered by two main structural components within the text: first, a repertoire of familiar literary patterns and recurrent literary themes, together with allusions to familiar social and historical contexts; second, techniques or strategies used to set the familiar against the unfamiliar. Elements of the repertoire are continually backgrounded or foregrounded with a resultant strategic overmagnification, trivialization, or even annihilation of the allusion. This defamiliarization of what the reader thought he recognized is bound to create a tension that will intensify his expectations as well as his distrust of those expectations. Similarly, we may be confronted by narrative techniques that establish links between things we find difficult to connect, so that we are forced to reconsider data we at first held to be perfectly straightforward. One need only mention the very simple trick, so often employed by novelists, whereby the author himself takes part in the narrative, thus establishing perspectives which would not have arisen out of the mere narration of the events described. Wayne Booth once called this the technique of the 'unreliable narrator,'[21] to show the extent to which a literary device can counter expectations arising out of the literary text. The figure of the narrator may act in permanent opposition to the impressions we might otherwise form. The question then arises as to whether this strategy, opposing the formation of illusions, may be integrated into a consistent pattern, lying, as it were, a level deeper than our original impressions. We may find that our narrator, by opposing us, in fact turns us against him and thereby strengthens the illusion he appears to be out to destroy; alternatively, we may be so much in doubt that we begin to question all the processes that lead us to make interpretative decisions. Whatever the cause may be, we will find ourselves subjected to this same interplay of illusion-forming and illusion-breaking that makes reading essentially a recreative process.

We might take, as a simple illustration of this complex process, the incident in Joyce's *Ulysses* in which Bloom's cigar alludes to Ulysses's spear. The context (Bloom's cigar) summons up a particular element of the repertoire (Ulysses's spear); the narrative technique relates them to one another as if they were identical. How are we to 'organize' these divergent elements, which, through the very fact that they are put together, separate one element so clearly from the other? What are the prospects here for a consistent pattern? We might say that it is ironic—at least that is how many renowned Joyce readers have understood it.[22] In this case, irony would be the form of organization that integrates the material. But if this is so, what is the object of the irony? Ulysses's spear, or Bloom's cigar?

The uncertainty surrounding this simple question already puts a strain on the consistency we have established, and indeed begins to puncture it, especially when other problems make themselves felt as regards the remarkable conjunction of spear and cigar. Various alternatives come to mind, but the variety alone is sufficient to leave one with the impression that the consistent pattern has been shattered. And even if, after all, one can still believe that irony holds the key to the mystery, this irony must be of a very strange nature; for the formulated text does not merely mean the opposite of what has been formulated. It may even mean something that cannot be formulated at all. The moment we try to impose a consistent pattern on the text, discrepancies are bound to arise. These are, as it were, the reverse side of the interpretative coin, an involuntary product of the process that creates discrepancies by trying to avoid them. And it is their very presence that draws us into the text, compelling us to conduct a creative examination not only of the text, but also of ourselves.

This entanglement of the reader is, of course, vital to any kind of text, but in the literary text we have the strange situation that the reader cannot know what his participation actually entails. We know that we share in certain experiences, but we do not know what happens to us in the course of this process. This is why, when we have been particularly impressed by a book, we feel the need to talk about it; we do not want to get away from it by talking about it— we simply want to understand more clearly what it is that we have been entangled in. We have undergone an experience, and now we want to know consciously *what* we have experienced. Perhaps this is the prime usefulness of literary criticism—it helps to make conscious those aspects of the text which would otherwise remain concealed in the subconscious; it satisfies (or helps to satisfy) our desire to talk about what we have read.

The efficacy of a literary text is brought about by the apparent evocation and subsequent negation of the familiar. What at first seemed to be an affirmation of our assumptions leads to our own rejection of them, thus tending to prepare us for a re-orientation. And it is only when we have outstripped our preconceptions and left the shelter of the familiar that we are in a position to gather new experiences. As the literary text involves the reader in the formation of illusion and the simultaneous formation of the means whereby the illusion is punctured, reading reflects the process by which we gain experience. Once the reader is entangled, his own preconceptions are continually overtaken, so that the text becomes his 'present' whilst his own ideas fade into the 'past;' as soon as this happens he is open to the immediate experience of the text, which was impossible so long as his preconceptions were his 'present.'

V

In our analysis of the reading process so far, we have observed three important aspects that form the basis of the relationship between reader and text: the process of anticipation and retrospection, the consequent unfolding of the text as a living event, and the resultant impression of lifelikeness.

Any 'living event' must, to a greater or lesser degree, remain open. In reading, this obliges the reader to seek continually for consistency, because only then can he close up situations and comprehend the unfamiliar. But consistency-building is itself a living process, in which one is constantly forced to make selective decisions—and these decisions in their turn give a reality to the possibilities which they exclude, insofar as they may take effect as a latent disturbance of the consistency established. This is what causes the reader to be entangled in the text 'gestalt' that he himself has produced.

Through this entanglement the reader is bound to open himself up to the workings of the text, and so leave behind his own preconceptions. This gives him the chance to have an experience in the way George Bernard Shaw once described it: 'You have learnt something. That always feels at first as if you had lost something.'[23] Reading reflects the structure of experience to the extent that we must suspend the ideas and attitudes that shape our own personality before we can experience the unfamiliar world of the literary text. But during this process, something happens to us.

This 'something' needs to be looked at in detail, especially as the incorporation of the unfamiliar into our own range of experience has been to a certain extent obscured by an idea very common in literary discussion: namely, that the process of absorbing the unfamiliar is labelled as the *identification* of the reader with what he reads. Often the term 'identification' is used as if it were an explanation, whereas in actual fact it is nothing more than a description. What is normally meant by 'identification' is the establishment of affinities between oneself and someone outside oneself—a familiar ground on which we are able to experience the unfamiliar. The author's aim, though, is to convey the experience and, above all, an attitude towards that experience. Consequently, 'identification' is not an end in itself, but a stratagem by means of which the author stimulates attitudes in the reader.

This of course is not to deny that there does arise a form of participation as one reads; one is certainly drawn into the text in such a way that one has the feeling that there is no distance between oneself and the events described. This involvement is well summed up by the reaction of a critic to reading Charlotte Brontë's *Jane Eyre*: 'We took up *Jane Eyre* one winter's evening, somewhat piqued at the extravagant commendations we had heard, and sternly resolved to be as critical as Croker. But as we read on we forgot both commendations and criticism, identified ourselves with Jane in all her troubles, and finally married Mr. Rochester about four in the morning.'[24] The question is how and why did the critic identify himself with Jane?

In order to understand this 'experience,' it is well worth considering Georges Poulet's observations on the reading process. He says that books only take on their full existence in the reader.[25] It is true that they consist of ideas thought out by someone else, but in reading the reader becomes the subject that does the thinking. Thus there disappears the subject-object division that otherwise is a prerequisite for all knowledge and all observation, and the removal of this division puts reading in an apparently unique position as regards the possible absorption of new experiences. This may well be the reason why relations with the world of the literary text have so often been misinterpreted as identification. From the idea that in reading we must think the thoughts of someone else, Poulet draws the following conclusion: 'Whatever I think is a part of *my* mental world. And yet here I am thinking a thought which manifestly belongs to another mental world, which is being thought in me just as though I did not exist. Already the notion is inconceivable and seems even more so if I reflect that, since every thought must have a subject to think it, this *thought* which is alien to me and yet in me, must also have in me a *subject* which is alien to me. . . . Whenever I read, I mentally pronounce an I, and yet the I which I pronounce is not myself.'[26]

But for Poulet this idea is only part of the story. The strange subject that thinks the strange thought in the reader indicates the potential presence of the author, whose ideas can be 'internalized' by the reader: 'Such is the characteristic condition of every work which I summon back into existence by placing consciousness at its disposal. I give it not only existence, but awareness of existence.'[27] This would mean that consciousness forms the point at which author and reader converge, and at the same time it would result in the cessation of the temporary self-alienation that occurs to the reader when his consciousness brings to life the ideas formulated by the author. This process gives rise to a form of communication which, however, according to Poulet, is dependent on two conditions: the life-story of the author must be shut out of the work, and the individual disposition of the reader must be shut out of the act of reading. Only then can the thoughts of the author take place subjectively in the reader, who thinks what he is not. It follows that the work itself must be thought of as a consciousness, because only in this way is there an adequate basis for the author-reader relationship—a relationship that can only come about through the negation of the author's own life-story and the reader's own disposition. This conclusion is actually drawn by Poulet when he describes the work as the self-presentation or materialization of consciousness: 'And so I ought not to hesitate to recognize that so long as it is animated by this vital inbreathing inspired by the act of reading, a work of literature becomes (at the expense of the reader whose own life it suspends) a sort of human being, that it is a mind conscious of itself and constituting itself in me as the subject of its own objects.'[28] Even though it is difficult to follow such a substantialist conception of the consciousness that constitutes itself in the literary work, there are, nevertheless, certain points in Poulet's argument that are worth holding on to. But they should be developed along somewhat different lines.

If reading removes the subject-object division that constitutes all perception, it follows that the reader will be 'occupied' by the thoughts of the author, and these in their turn will cause the drawing of new 'boundaries.' Text and reader no longer confront each other as object and subject, but instead the 'division' takes place within the reader himself. In thinking the thoughts of another, his own individuality temporarily recedes into the background since it is supplanted by these alien thoughts, which now become the theme on which his attention is focussed. As we read, there occurs an artificial division of our personality because we take as a theme for ourselves something that we are not. Consequently when reading we operate on different levels. For although we may be thinking the thoughts of someone else, what we are will not disappear completely—it will merely remain a more or less powerful virtual force. Thus, in reading there are these two levels—the alien 'me' and the real, virtual 'me'—which are never completely cut off from each other. Indeed, we can only make someone else's thoughts into an absorbing theme for ourselves, provided the virtual background of our own personality can adapt to it. Every text we read draws a different boundary within our personality, so that the virtual background (the real 'me') will take on a different form, according the theme of the text concerned. This is inevitable, if only for the fact that the relationship between alien theme and virtual background is what makes it possible for the unfamiliar to be understood.

In this context there is a revealing remark made by D. W. Harding, arguing against the idea of identification with what is read: 'What is sometimes called wish-fulfilment in novels and plays can . . . more plausibly be described as wish-formulation or the definition of desires. The cultural levels at which it works may vary widely; the process is the same. . . . It seems nearer the truth . . . to say that fictions contribute to defining the reader's or spectator's values, and perhaps stimulating his desires, rather than to suppose that they gratify desire by some mechanism of vicarious experience.'[29] In the act of reading, having to think something that we have not yet experienced does not mean only being in a position to conceive or even understand it; it also means that such acts of conception are possible and successful to the degree that they lead to something being formulated in us. For someone else's thoughts can only take a form in our consciousness if, in the process, our unformulated faculty for deciphering those thoughts is brought into play—a faculty which, in the act of deciphering, also formulates itself. Now since this formulation is carried out on terms set by someone else, whose thoughts are the theme of our reading, it follows that the formulation of our faculty for deciphering cannot be along our own lines of orientation.

Herein lies the dialectical structure of reading. The need to decipher gives us the chance to formulate our own deciphering capacity—i.e., we bring to the fore an element of our being of which we are not directly conscious. The production of the meaning of literary texts—which we discussed in connection with forming the 'gestalt' of the test—does not merely entail the discovery of the unformulated, which can then be taken over by the active imagination of the reader; it also entails the possibility that we may formulate ourselves and so discover what had previously seemed to elude our consciousness. These are the ways in which reading literature gives us the chance to formulate the unformulated.

NOTES

1. Cf. Roman Ingarden, *Vom Erkennen des literarischen Kunstwerks* (Tübingen, 1968), pp. 49 ff.
2. For a detailed discussion of this term see Roman Ingarden, *Das literarische Kunstwerk* (Tübingen, 1960), pp. 270 ff.
3. Laurence Sterne, *Tristram Shandy* (London, 1956), II, chap. 11, 79.
4. Virginia Woolf, *The Common Reader*, First Series (London, 1957), p. 174.

5. Ingarden, *Vom Erkennen des literarischen Kunstwerks*, p. 29.
6. Edmund Husserl, *Zur Phänomenologie des inneren Zeitbewusstseins, Gesammelte Werke* 10 (Haag, 1966), 52.
7. Ingarden, *Vom Erkennen des literarischen Kunstwerks*, p. 32.
8. For a more detailed discussion of the function of 'gaps' in literary texts see Wolfgang Iser, 'Indeterminacy and the Reader's Response in Prose Fiction,' *Aspects of Narrative*, English Institute Essays, ed. by J. Hillis Miller (New York, 1971), pp. 1–45.
9. M. Merleau-Ponty, *Phenomenology of Perception*, trans. Colin Smith (New York, 1962), pp. 219, 221.
10. Gilbert Ryle, *The Concept of Mind* (Harmondsworth, 1968), p. 255.
11. Cf. Iser, pp. II ff., 42 ff.
12. E. H. Gombrich, *Art and Illusion* (London, 1962), p. 204.
13. Louis O. Mink, 'History and Fiction as Modes of Comprehension,' *New Literary History*, I (1970), 553.
14. Gombrich, p. 278.
15. Northrop Frye, *Anatomy of Criticism* (New York, 1967), pp. 169 f.
16. Walter Pater, *Appreciations* (London, 1920), p. 18.
17. Gombrich, p. 54.
18. *Ibid.*, p. 5.
19. B. Ritchie, 'The Formal Structure of the Aesthetic Object,' *The Problems of Aesthetics*, ed. by Eliseo Vivas and Murray Krieger (New York, 1965), pp. 230.
20. John Dewey, *Art as Experience* (New York, 1958), p. 54.
21. Cf. Wayne C. Booth, *The Rhetoric of Fiction* (Chicago, 1963), pp. 211 ff., 339 ff.
22. Richard Ellmann, 'Ulysses. The Divine Nobody,' *Twelve Original Essays on Great English Novels*, ed. by Charles Shapiro (Detroit 1960), p. 247, classified this particular allusion as 'mock-heroic.'
23. G. B. Shaw, *Major Barbara* (London, 1964), p. 316.
24. William George Clark, *Fraser's*, December, 1849, 692, quoted by Kathleen Tillotson, *Novels of the Eighteen-Forties* (Oxford, 1961), pp. 19 f.
25. Cf. Georges Poulet, 'Phenomenology of Reading,' *New Literary History*, 1 (1969), 54.
26. *Ibid.*, 56.
27. *Ibid.*, 59.
28. *Ibid.*, p. 59.
29. D. W. Harding, 'Psychological Processes in the Reading of Fiction,' *Aesthetics in the Modern World*, ed by Harold Osborne (London, 1968), pp. 313 ff.

12 Julia Kristeva

Julia Kristeva (b. 1941), like Tzvetan Todorov (see above pp. 157–65), was born in Bulgaria and has made her intellectual career in France, writing in French and teaching at the University of Paris. She is one of the most brilliant and versatile of the French intellectual figures of the last two decades. Roland Barthes said of her (it could have been equally well said of himself) that 'Julia Kristeva always destroys the latest preconception, the one we thought we could be comforted by, the one of which we could be proud.'

Beginning as a linguist and semiotician, she became a key figure in the group associated with the journal *Tel Quel*, which in the late 1960s and early 70s promoted a heady (and, as it proved, unstable) mixture of literary semiotics and Maoist politics. The ideas of Barthes, Lacan, and Derrida were all grist to her mill, but her Slavic background made her also a shrewd and illuminating commentator on Jakobson and Bakhtin. In the mid-1970s, Julia Kristeva began to write on topics related to women and feminism, and her work became increasingly oriented to psychoanalysis, which she now practices. To the dismay of many of her early admirers, she has in recent years repudiated the leftism of her *Tel Quel* period and espoused some very right-wing views. In her intellectual brilliance, epigrammatic poise, conceptual eclecticism, sometimes wilful obscurity, and determination to stay ahead of the game, she typifies everything that is, to outsiders, most impressive and most irritating in contemporary French intellectual life.

'The Ethics of Linguistics' questions the attempt of that discipline to give a totally scientific and systematic account of language, by invoking, and in part borrowing, the mysterious eloquence of poetic discourse. In calling for an anti-authoritarian linguistics of the speaking subject, the essay perhaps reflects Kristeva's familiarity with Bakhtin, though she conceives 'the subject' very much in terms of a post-structuralist reading of Marx, Freud and Nietzsche. 'The Ethics of Linguistics' was first published in 1974, and is reprinted here from *Desire in Language: a semiotic approach to literature and art* (1980), edited by Leon S. Roudiez and translated by Thomas Gora, Alice Jardine, and Leon S. Roudiez.

CROSS-REFERENCES: 1. Saussure
2. Shklovsky
3. Jakobson
27. MacCabe

COMMENTARY: Toril Moi, 'Marginality and Subversion: Julia Kristeva', in Moi's *Sexual/Textual Politics* (1985)
Allon White, '"*L'éclatement du sujet*": the theoretical work of Julia Kristeva.' University of Birmingham Centre for Contemporary Cultural Studies Occasional Paper, no. 49 (1977)

The ethics of linguistics

Should a linguist, today, ever happen to pause and query the ethics of his own discourse, he might well respond by doing something else, e.g., engaging in political activity; or else, he might accommodate ethics to the ingenuousness of his good conscience—seeking socio-historical motives for the categories and relations involved in his model. One could thus account for the Janus-like behavior of a prominent modern grammarian; in his linguistic theories he sets forth a logical, normative basis for the speaking subject, while in politics he claims to be an anarchist. Then there are scholars, quite numerous but not so well known, who squeeze into modern linguistic theory a few additional considerations on the role of ideology; or who go no further than to lift their examples out of leftist newspapers when illustrating linguistic propositions.

Now, since the end of the nineteenth century, there have been intellectual, political, and, generally speaking, social ventures that have signaled the outbreak of something quite new within Western society and discourse, which is subsumed in the names of Marx, Nietzsche, and Freud, and their primary goal has been to reformulate an ethics. Ethics used to be a coercive, customary manner of ensuring the cohesiveness of a particular group through the repetition of a code—a more or less accepted apologue. Now, however, the issue of ethics crops up wherever a code (mores, social contract) must be shattered in order to give way to the free play of negativity, need, desire, pleasure, and jouissance [ecstasy], before being put together again, although temporarily and with full knowledge of what is involved. Fascism and Stalinism stand for the barriers that the new adjustment between a law and its transgression comes against.

Meanwhile, linguistics is still bathed in the aura of *systematics* that prevailed at the time of its inception. It is discovering the rules governing the coherence of our fundamental social code: language, either system of signs or strategy for the transformation of logical sequences. The ethical foundations for this belong to the past: in their work, contemporary linguists think like seventeenth century men, while structuralist logic can be made to work only with primitive societies or their surviving elements. As wardens of repression and rationalizers of the social contract in its most solid substratum (discourse), linguists carry the Stoic tradition to its conclusion. The epistemology underlying linguistics and the ensuing cognitive processes (structuralism, for example), even though constituting a bulwark against irrational destruction and sociologizing dogmatism, seem helplessly anachronistic when faced with the contemporary mutations of subject and society. Even though 'formalism' might have been right, contrary to Zhdanov, neither can think the rhythm of Mayakovsky through to his suicide or Khlebnikov's glossolalias to his disintegration—with the young Soviet state as backdrop.[a]

For, as soon as linguistics was established as a science (through Saussure, for all intents and purposes) its field of study was thus hemmed in [*suturé*]; the problem of *truth* in linguistic discourse became dissociated from any notion of the *speaking subject*. Determining *truth* was reduced to a seeking out of the object-utterance's internal coherence, which was predetermined by the coherence of the particular metalinguistic theory within which the search was conducted. Any attempt at reinserting the 'speaking subject,' whether under the guise of a Cartesian subject or any other subject of enunciation more or less akin to the transcendental ego (as linguists make use of it), resolves nothing as long as that subject is not posited as the place, not only of structure and its regulated transformation, but especially, of its loss, its outlay.

It follows that formulating the problem of linguistic ethics means, above all, compelling linguistics to change its object of study. The speech practice that should be its object is one in which signified structure (sign, syntax, signification) is defined within boundaries that can be shifted by the advent of a semiotic rhythm that no system of linguistic communication has yet been able to assimilate. It would deflect linguistics toward a consideration of language as articulation of a heterogeneous process, with the speaking subject leaving its imprint on the dialectic between the articulation and its process. In short, this would establish *poetic language* as the object of linguistics' attention in its pursuit of truth in language. This does not necessarily mean, as is often said today, that poetic language is subject to *more* constraints than 'ordinary language.' It does mean that we must analyze those elements of the complex operation that I should call poetic language (in which the dialectics of the subject is inscribed) that are screened out by ordinary language, i.e., *social constraint*. I shall then be talking about something other than language—a practice *for which any particular language is the margin*. The term 'poetry' has meaning only insofar as it makes this kind of studies acceptable to various educational and cultural institutions. But the stakes it entails are totally different; what is implied is that language, and thus sociability, are defined by boundaries admitting of upheaval, dissolution, and transformation. Situating our discourse near such boundaries might enable us to endow it with a current ethical impact. In short, the ethics of a linguistic discourse may be gauged in proportion to the poetry that it presupposes.

[a] Andrey Aleksandrovich Zhdanov (1896–1948) was a Russian Communist politician who played a leading part in the suppression of artistic freedom in Soviet Russia under Stalin. Vladimir Mayakovsky (1893–1930) was a leading Russian futurist poet who identified enthusiastically with the Revolution in its early stages, but was criticized for 'individualism' when Stalin came to power. His suicide was probably motivated by personal as well as political factors. Viktor Khlebnikov (1885–1921) was one of the founders of Russian futurism, and another enthusiastic, if unorthodox, early supporter of the Revolution.

A most eminent modern linguist believed that, in the last hundred years, there had been only two significant linguists in France: Mallarmé and Artaud.[b] As to Heidegger, he retains currency, *in spite of everything*, because of his attentiveness to language and 'poetic language' as an opening up of beings; as an openness that is checked but nonetheless occurs; as a struggle between world and earth; artistic creations are all conceived in the image of poetic language where the 'Being' of 'beings' is fulfilled and on which, as a consequence, 'History' is grounded. If modern art, which is post-Hegelian, sounds a rhythm in language capable of stymieing any subjugated work or logic, this discredits only that closure in Heidegger's reflections that systematizes Being, beings and their historial veracity. But such discredit does not jeopardize poetry's logical stake, inasmuch as poetry is a practice of the speaking subject, consequently implying a dialectic between limits, both signified and signifying, and the setting of a pre- and trans-logical rhythm solely within this limit. Similarly, modern art's odyssey nevertheless remains the field where the possibility of History and dialectic struggle can be played out (before these become a particular history and a concrete struggle), since this artistic practice is the laboratory of a minimal signifying structure, its maximum dissolution, and the eternal return of both.

One might submit that Freud's discovery of the unconscious provided the necessary conditions for such a reading of poetic language. This would be true for the history of *thought*, but not for the history of *poetic practice*. Freud himself considered writers as his predecessors. Avant-garde movements of the twentieth century, more or less unaware of Freud's discovery, propounded a practice, and sometimes even a knowledge of language and its subject, that kept pace with, when they did not precede, Freudian breakthroughs. Thus, it was entirely possible to remain alert to this avant-garde laboratory, to perceive its experiments in a way that could be qualified only as a 'love' relationship—and therefore, while bypassing Freud, to perceive the high stakes of any language as *always-already* poetic. Such, I believe, was the path taken by Roman Jakobson. It should not be surprising, then, that it is his discourse and his conception of linguistics, and those of no other linguist, that could contribute to the theory of the unconscious—allowing us to see it being made and unmade—*poiein* [ποιεῖν]—like the language of any subject.

There is no denying Jakobson's contributions toward establishing phonology and structural linguistics in general, toward Slavic studies and research into language acquisition, and toward epistemology and the history of linguistic discourse in its relationship to contemporary or past philosophy and society. But beyond these contributions lies *foremost* the heed given by Jakobson to poetic language; this constitutes the uniqueness of his research, providing its ethical dimension, while at the same time maintaining the openness of present-day linguistic discourse, pointing out, for example, those blockings that cause it to have problems with semantics. Consequently, by virtue of its equally historical and poetic concern, Jakobson's linguistics appears to bracket the technical nature of some contemporary tendencies (such as generative grammar), and to leap from

---

[b] Antonin Artaud (1896–1948) was a French actor, stage producer and theorist of drama, who advocated a violent and ritualistic form of drama known as 'theatre of cruelty'.

the beginning of our century, when linguistics was not yet hemmed in, to the contemporary period when it must open up in order to have something to say about the speaking subject. Precursor and predecessor, Jakobson nevertheless also accepted the task of providing a concrete and rigorous description, thereby maintaining science's limitative requirements; in this way, he defined the origin and the end of the linguistic episteme, which in recent years has taken upon itself to oversee all thinking although in fact it is merely a symptom of the drama experienced by the Western subject as it attempts to master and structure not only the logos but also its pre- and trans-logical breakouts. *Irony*, alone, piercing through the linguist's metalanguage, is the timid witness to this drama. There is, however, an *other*, modestly filed away among the 'objects' of research, as if to safeguard the sovereignty of the scholarwarden, standing watch over the structures of communication and sociality; there is an *other* besides the irony of the learned man; there is the poem, in the sense that it is *rhythm, death*, and *future*. The linguist projects himself into it, identifies with it, and in the end, extracts a few concepts necessary for building a new model of language. But he also and foremost comes away suspecting that the signifying process is not limited to the language system, but that there are also speech, discourse, and, within them, a causality other than linguistic: a heterogeneous, destructive causality.

It is quite an experience to listen to Harvard University's recording of Roman Jakobson's 1967 lecture, 'Russian Poetry of my Generation'—he gave a reading of Mayakovsky and Khlebnikov, imitating their voices, with the lively, rhythmic accents, thrust out throat and fully militant tone of the first; and the softly whispered words, sustained swishing and whistling sounds, vocalizations of the disintegrating voyage toward the mother constituted by the 'trans-mental' ('zaum') language of the second. To understand the real conditions needed for producing scientific models, one should listen to the story of their youth, of the aesthetic and always political battles of Russian society on the eve of the Revolution and during the first years of victory, of the friendships and sensitivities that coalesced into lives and life projects. From all this, one may perceive what initiates a science, what it stops, what deceptively ciphers its models. No longer will it be possible to read any treatise on phonology without deciphering within every phoneme the statement, 'Here lies a poet.' The linguistics professor doesn't know this, and that is another problem, allowing him blithely to put forward his models, never to invent any new notion of language, and to preserve the sterility of theory.

I shall not, then, summarize the linguistic models, much less the tools of poetic analysis, proposed by Jakobson. I shall only review a few themes or mythemes inherent in his listening to futurist poetry, insofar as they are hidden recesses— silent causality and ethics—of the linguistic process.

The Struggle between Poet and Sun

Two tendencies seem to dominate Mayakovsky's poetic craft: *rhythmic* rapture and the simultaneous affirmation of the '*ego*.'

Rhythm: 'I walk along, waving my arms and mumbling almost wordlessly, now shortening my steps so as not to interrupt my mumbling, now mumbling more rapidly in time with my steps. So the rhythm is trimmed and takes shape—and rhythm is the basis of any poetic work, resounding through the whole thing. Gradually individual words begin to ease themselves free of this dull roar. . . . When the fundamentals are already there, one has a sudden sensation that the rhythm is strained: there's some little syllable or sound missing. You begin to shape all the words anew, and the work drives you to distraction. It's like having a tooth crowned. A hundred times (or so it seems) the dentist tries a crown on the tooth, and it's the wrong size; but at last, after a hundred attempts, he presses one down, and it fits. The analogy is all the more apposite in my case, because when at last the crown fits, I (quite literally) have tears in my eyes, from pain and relief. Where this basic dull roar of a rhythm comes from is a mystery. In my case, it's all kinds of repetitions in my mind of noises, rocking motions or in fact, of any phenomenon with which I can associate a sound. The sound of the sea, endlessly repeated, can provide my rhythm, or a servant who slams the door every morning, recurring and intertwining with itself, trailing through my consciousness; or even the rotation of the earth, which in my case, as in a shop full of visual aids, gives way to, and inextricably connects with, the whistle of a high wind.'[1]

On the one hand, then, we have this rhythm; this repetitive sonority; this thrusting tooth pushing upwards before being capped with the crown of language; this struggle between word and force gushing with the pain and relief of a desperate delirium; the repetition of this growth, of this gushing forth around the crown-word, like the earth completing its revolution around the sun.

On the other hand, we have the 'ego' situated within the space of language, crown, system: no longer rhythm, but sign, word, structure, contract, constraint; an 'ego' declaring itself poetry's sole interest (cf. the poem 'I Am Alone'), and comparing itself to Napoleon ('Napoleon and I': 'Today, I am Napoleon / I am the chief of armies and more. / Compare / him and me!'). Trotsky called this erection of the poetic 'I' a 'Mayakomorphism,' which he opposed to anthropomorphism (one can think of other word associations on the basis of *mayak* = 'beacon').

Once the rhythm has been centered in the fixed position of an all powerful 'ego', the poetic 'I' thrusts at the sun—a paternal image that is coveted but also feared, murderous, and sentenced to die, a legislative seat which must be usurped. Thus: 'one more minute / and you will meet / the monarch of the skies / if I want, I'll kill him for you, the sun!' ('Napoleon and I'); 'Sun! / My father! / Won't you melt and stop torturing me! / My blood spilled by you runs along the road' ('A Few Words about Myself').

I could give many references, evoke Lautréamont, Bataille, Cyrano, or Schreber;[c] the struggle between poet and sun, which Jakobson brought out, runs

---

[c] Comte de Lautréamont was the pseudonym of Isidore Ducasse (1846–70), writer of prose poems which are seen as precursors of surrealism. Georges Bataille (1897–1962) was the author of erotic texts, such as *The History of an Eye*, which have enjoyed something of a posthumous vogue among Parisian literary intellectuals. Cyrano de Bergerac (1619–55) was a French writer of plays and philosophical fictions. Daniel Schreber was a German judge whose autobiography, *Memorabilia of a Nerve Patient*, originally published in 1903, was the subject of a famous analysis by Sigmund Freud.

through such texts. We should understand it as a summary leading from the poet's condition to poetic formulation. Sun: agency of language since it is the 'crown' of rhythmic thrust, limiting structure, paternal law abrading rhythm, destroying it to a large degree, but also bringing it to light, out of its earthy revolutions, to enunciate itself. Inasmuch as the 'I' is poetic, inasmuch as it wants to enunciate rhythm, to socialize it, to channel it into linguistic structure if only to break the structure, this 'I' is bound to the sun. It is a part of this agency because it must master rhythm, it is threatened by it because solar mastery cuts off rhythm. Thus, there is no choice but to struggle eternally against the sun; the 'I' is successively the sun and its opponent, language and its rhythm, never one without the other, and poetic formulation will continue as long as the struggle does. The essential point to note is that there would be no struggle but for the sun's agency. Without it, rhythm incapable of formulation, would flow forth, growling, and in the end would dig itself in. Only by vying with the agency of limiting and structuring language does rhythm become a contestant—formulating and transforming.

Khlebnikov evokes another aspect of this solar contest; a mother, coming to the aid of her children in their fight against the sun. 'The otter's children' are squared off against three suns, one white, one purple, the other dark green. In 'The God of the Virgins,' the protagonist is 'the daughter of the sun prince.' The poem 'Ka' calls forth the 'hairy-armed sun of Egypt.' All of Khlebnikov's pagan mythology is underlain with a contest against the sun supported by a feminine figure, all-powerful mother or forbidden virgin, gathering into one representation and thus substantifying all that which, with Mayakovsky, hammered in sonorous thrusts within and against the system of language—that is, rhythm.

Here, pagan mythology is probably nothing more than rhythm become substantive: this *other* of the linguistic and/or social contract, this ultimate and primordial leash holding the body close to the mother before it can become a social speaking subject. In any case, what in Khlebnikov Tynanov called 'infantilism' or 'the poet's pagan attitude regarding words'[2] is essentially manifest in the *glossolalias* unique to Khlebnikov. He invented words by onomatopoeia, with a great deal of alliteration, demanding of him an acute awareness of the articulatory base and instinctual charge of that articulation. This entire strategy broke up the lexicon of the Russian language, drawing it closer to childhood soliloquy. But above all, it threaded through metaphor and metonymy a network of meaning supplementary to the normative signifying line, a network of phonemes or phonic groups charged with instinctual drives and meaning, constituting what for the author was a *numerical* code, a *ciphering*, underlying the verbal signs: for example, 'Veter-penie / kogo i o chem? / neterpenie—mecha stat' mjachom' (Wind-song / of whom and for what? / Impatience of the sword to become a bullet). Jakobson notes the phonic displacement *mech-mjach* (sword-bullet) dominating several lines of Khlebnikov's poetry, where one notices also a tendency toward infantile regression and/or toward lessening of tension on the level of pronunciation as well as on the more general level of sexualized semantic areas.) The vocalization of language thus becomes a way of deflecting the censorship that, for rhythm, is constituted by the structuring agency. Having become 'trans-mental' Khlebnikov's instinctual, ciphered language projects itself as prophetic and seeks for homologues within this tradition: for example, 'Through Zarathustra's golden mouth let us swear / Persia shall become a Soviet country, thus has the prophet spoken'.[3]

Rhythm and Death

'But how do we speak about the poetry of Mayakovsky, now that what prevails is not rhythm but the poet's death . . .?' asks Jakobson in 'The Generation That Wasted Its Poets.'[4] We tend to read this article as if it were exclusively an indictment of a society founded on the murder of its poets. This is probably true; when the article first appeared in 1931, even psychoanalysts were not all convinced that 'society was now based on complicity in the common crime,' as Freud had written in *Totem and Taboo*.[5] On the basis of his work on Mayakovsky, Jakobson suggested that the crime was more concretely the murder of poetic language. By 'society,' he probably meant more than just Russian or Soviet society; there are frequent and more general allusions to the 'stability of the unchanging present,' to 'life, hardened along narrow and rigid models,' and to 'daily existence.' Consequently we have this Platonistic acknowledgement on the eve of Stalinism and fascism: a (any) society may be stabilized only if it excludes poetic language.

On the other hand, but simultaneously, poetic language alone carries on the struggle against such a death, and so harries, exorcises, and invokes it. Jakobson is fascinated by murder and suicide as themes with poets of his generation as well as of all time. The question is unavoidable: if we are not on the side of those whom society wastes in order to reproduce itself, where are we?

Murder, death, and unchanging society represent precisely the inability to hear and understand the signifier as such—as ciphering, as rhythm, as a presence that precedes the signification of object or emotion. The poet is put to death because he wants to turn rhythm into a dominant element; because he wants to make language perceive what it doesn't want to say, provide it with its matter independently of the sign, and free it from denotation. For it is this *eminently parodic* gesture that changes the system.

> The word is experienced as word and not as a simple substitute for a named object nor as the explosion of emotion [. . .] beside the immediate consciousness of the identity existing between the object and its sign (A is A), the immediate consciousness of the absence of this identity (A is not A) is necessary; this antinomy is inevitable, for, without contradiction, there is no interplay of concepts, no interplay of signs, the relationship between the concept and the sign becomes automatic, the progress of events comes to a halt, and all consciousness of reality dies [. . .] Poetry protects us from this automatization from the rust that threatens our formulation of love, hate, revolt and reconciliation, faith and negation.[6]

Today, the analyst boasts of his ability to hear 'pure signifiers.' Can he hear them in what is known as 'private life'? There is good reason to believe that these 'wasted poets' are alone in meeting the challenge. Whoever understands them cannot 'practice linguistics' without passing through whole geographic and discursive continents as an impertinent traveller, a 'faun in the house' [*faune au logis* = *phonologie*—Tr.].

The Futurists' Future

According to Jakobson, Mayakovsky was interested in resurrection. It is easy, at that, to see that his poems, like those of Khlebnikov and other futurists, take up the theme of Messianic resurrection, a privileged one in Russian Medieval poetry. Such a theme is a very obvious and direct descendant of the contest against the sun myth that I mentioned earlier. The son assumes from his sun-father the task of completing the 'self' and 'rhythm' dialectic within the poem. But the irruption of semiotic rhythm within the signifying system of language will never be a Hegelian *Aufhebung*[d], that is, it will not truly be experienced in the present. The rigid, imperious, immediate present kills, puts aside, and fritters away the poem. Thus, the irruption within the order of language of the anteriority of language evokes a later time, that is, a forever. The poem's time frame is some 'future anterior' that will never take place, never come about as such, but only as an upheaval of present place and meaning. Now, by thus suspending the present moment, by straddling rhythmic, meaningless, anterior memory with meaning intended for later or forever, poetic language structures itself as the very nucleus of a monumental historicity. Futurism succeeded in making this poetic law explicit solely because it extended further than anyone else the signifier's autonomy, restored its instinctual value, and aimed at a 'trans-mental language.' Consequently attuned to a scene preceding the logical systematicity of communication, Futurism managed to do so without withdrawing from its own historical period; instead, it paid strong attention to the explosion of the October Revolution. It heard and understood the Revolution only because its present was dependent on a future. Mayakovsky's and Khlebnikov's pro-Soviet proposals and leaps into mythology came from a nonexistent place in the future. Anteriority and future join together to open that historical axis in relation to which concrete history will always be wrong: murderous, limiting, subject to regional imperatives (economic, tactical, political, familial...). Although, confronted with such regional necessities, poetic language's future anterior is an impossible, 'aristocratic' and 'elitist' demand, it is nonetheless the only signifying strategy allowing the speaking animal to shift the limits of its enclosure. In 'As for the Self,' Khlebnikov writes:

Short pieces are important when they serve as a break into the future,
like a shooting star, leaving behind a trail of fire. They should move
rapidly enough so that they pierce the present. While we wait, we cannot

[d] In Hegel's philosophy, thesis generates antithesis, and the opposites are taken up into a synthesis which Hegel terms the *Aufhebung*, usually translated as 'sublation'.

yet define the reason for this speech. But we know the piece is good when, in its role as a piece of the future it sets the present ablaze. [. . .] the homeland of creation is the future. The wind of the gods of the word blows from that direction.[7]

Poetic discourse measures rhythm against the meaning of language structure and is thus always eluded by meaning in the present while continually postponing it to an impossible time-to-come. Consequently, it is assuredly the most appropriate *historical* discourse, if and only if we attribute to this word its new resonance; it is neither flight in the face of a supposed metaphysics of the notion of 'history,' nor mechanistic enclosure of this notion within a project oblivious to the violence of the social contract and evolution's being, above all, a refinement of the various forms of dissipating the tension we have been calling 'poetic language.'

It should come as no surprise that a movement such as the October Revolution, striving to remain antifeudal and antibourgeois, should call forth the same mythemes that dominated feudalism and were suppressed by the bourgeoisie, in order to exploit solely their dynamics producing exchange value. Beyond these mythemes, however, futurism stressed equally its participation in the anamnesis of a culture as well as a basic feature of Western discourse. 'You have to bring the poem to the highest pitch of expressiveness' (Mayakovsky, 'How are Verses Made'). At that point the code becomes receptive to the rhythmic body and it forms, in opposition to present meaning, another meaning, but a future, impossible meaning. The important element of this 'future anterior' of language is 'the word perceived as word,' a phenomenon in turn induced by the contest between rhythm and sign system.

Mayakovsky's suicide, Khlebnikov's disintegration, and Artaud's incarceration prove that this contest can be prevented. Does this mean there is no future (no history) for this discourse, which found its own 'anteriority' within the 'poetic' experience of the twentieth century? Linguistic ethics, as it can be understood through Jakobson's practice, consists in following the resurgence of an 'I' coming back to rebuild an ephemeral structure in which the constituting struggle of language and society would be spelled out.

Can contemporary linguistics hear this conception of language of which Jakobson's work is the major token?

The currently dominant course, generative grammar, surely rests on many of Jakobson's approaches, notably phonological, in the study of the linguistic system. Nonetheless, it is hard to see how notions of elision, metaphor, metonymy, and parallelism (cf. his study on biblical and Chinese verse) could fit into the generative apparatus, including generative semantics, except perhaps under the rubric of 'additional rules,' necessitating a cutoff point in the specific generation of a language. But the dramatic notion of language as a risky practice, allowing the speaking animal to sense the rhythm of the body as well as the upheavals of history, seems tied to a notion of signifying process that contemporary theories do not confront. Jakobson's linguistic ethics therefore unmistakably demands first a *historical epistemology of linguistics* (one wonders which Eastern or Western theories linked with what ideological corpus of Antiquity, the Middle Ages, or the Renaissance were able to formulate the problematic of language as a place of structure as well as of its bodily, subjective, and social outlay). Secondly, it demands a *semiology*, understood as moving beyond simple linguistic studies toward a typology of signifying systems composed of semiotic materials and varied social functions. Such an affirmation of Saussurian semiological exigencies in a period dominated by generative grammar is far from archaistic; rather, it is integrated into a tradition where linguistics is inseparable from concepts of subject and society. As it epitomizes the experiences of language and linguistics of our entire European century, it allows us to foresee what the discourse on the signifying process might be in times to come.

NOTES

1. Vladimir Mayakovsky, *How Are Verses Made?* G. M. Hyde, trans. (London: J. Cape, 1970), pp. 36–37. The other Mayakovsky quotations are from *Electric Iron*, Jack Hirschman and Victor Erlich, trans (Berkeley: Maya, 1971), p. 46.
2. From the preface of Velimir Khlebnikov, *Sobranie Sochninenij* (Moscow, 1927–1933).
3. Velimir Khlebnikov, *Oeuvres*, L. Schnitzer, trans. (Paris: Oswald, 1967).
4. In Tzvetan Todorov, ed., *Questions de poétique*, (Paris: Seuil, 1973). First appeared as 'O pokolenii rastrativshem svoikh poetov' in *Smeri Vladimira Majakovskoga* (Berlin, 1931), pp. 7–45. This essay will appear in English translation in a future volume of Jakobson's *Selected Writings*, published by Mouton in The Hague.
5. *Totem and Taboo* in *The Standard Edition of the Complete Works of Sigmund Freud* (London: Hogarth & The Institute of Psycho-Analysis, 1953), 13:146.
6. 'Qu'est-ce que la poésie,' in *Questions de poétique*, pp. 124–25.
7. Khlebnikov, *Oeuvres*.

13 Harold Bloom

Harold Bloom (b. 1930) is Du Van Professor of the Humanities at Yale University, where he has been closely associated with Paul de Man, Geoffrey Hartman and J. Hillis Miller, a group whose great influence on contemporary American criticism has earned them the soubriquet (at once respectful and resentful) 'the hermeneutic Mafia'. In fact, Bloom's intellectual relationship with his Yale colleagues is complicated and not easy to define. Though he collaborated with them, and with Jacques Derrida, to produce the symposium *Deconstruction and Criticism* (1979), he has frequently and explicitly dissociated himself from deconstructionist principles and methods. His own critical approach is in part derived from Freud, but it is not Lacan's Freud, or indeed anyone else's. Bloom is very much his own man, one of the most idiosyncratic critics writing today.

Harold Bloom has always been primarily interested in the tradition of English and American poetry, of which he has a remarkable knowledge, especially Romantic and post-Romantic poetry. In four books produced in rapid succession, *The Anxiety of Influence* (1973), *A Map of Misreading* (1975), *Kabbalah and Criticism* (1975) and *Poetry and Repression* (1976), he undertook a bold theorization of this interest. Major, or, as Bloom calls them, 'strong' poets are obliged to define the originality of their work against the achievement of their poetic predecessors or father-figures (the model of Freud's Oedipus complex is quite explicitly invoked). Nineteenth- and twentieth-century poets suffer from a particularly acute 'anxiety of influence' or sense of 'belatedness'. Overcoming this disablement entails a creative 'misreading' or 'misprision' of the precursor by the 'ephebe' or aspirant poet, a licence Bloom extends to 'strong' critics, such as himself. (It is this blurring of the usual hierarchical distinction between creative and critical writing that constitutes Bloom's common ground with the deconstructionists.) This theory of poetic revisionism is elaborated in a complex and esoteric terminology drawn from classical rhetoric and the Jewish mystical tradition of the Kaballah, and produces readings of English and American poetry that oscillate between the brilliant and the bizarre. Harold Bloom is also the author of a visionary novel, *The Flight To Lucifer: a Gnostic Fantasy* (1979).

'Poetic Origins and Final Phases' is the first chapter of *A Map of Misreading*, probably the most accessible of his theoretical tetralogy.

COMMENTARY: Leon Wieseltier, 'Summoning up the Kabballah,' *New York Review of Books*, 19 February 1976, pp. 27–31.

Poetic origins and final phases

Strong poets are infrequent; our own century, in my judgment, shows only Hardy and Stevens writing in English. Great poets—even Yeats and Lawrence, even Frost—may fail of continuous strength, and major innovators—even Pound and Williams—may never touch strength at all. Browning, Whitman, Dickinson are strong, as are the High Romantics, and Milton may be taken as the apotheosis of strength. Poetic strength comes only from a triumphant wrestling with the greatest of the dead, and from an even more triumphant solipsism. Enormous gifts, the endowment of a Coleridge, or of a lesser but still considerable talent like Eliot, do not avail where strength is evaded, or never attained. Poetic strength, in this sense, rises only from a particular kind of catastrophe—as ordinary consciousness must regard the terrible incarnation that can lead to a poet like the very old Hardy or the very old Stevens. This chapter will move from the primal catastrophe of poetic incarnation on to a description of the relation of poetic strength to poetic influence, and then to the final phases of Hardy and Stevens.

I rely in this discussion upon the theory of poetry, Vichian[a] and Emersonian in origin, that I have expounded recently in *The Anxiety of Influence*. The theory, deliberately an attempt at de-idealizing, has encountered considerable resistance during my presentation of it in a number of lectures at various universities, but whether the theory is correct or not may be irrelevant to its usefulness for practical criticism, which I think can be demonstrated. I take the resistance shown to the theory by many poets, in particular, to be likely evidence for its validity, for poets rightly idealize their activity; and all poets, weak and strong, agree in denying any share in the anxiety of influence. More than ever, contemporary poets insist that they are telling the truth in their work, and more than ever they tell continuous lies, particularly about their relations to one another, and most consistently about their relations to their precursors. One of the functions of criticism, as I understand it, is to make a good poet's work even more difficult for him to perform, since only the overcoming of genuine difficulties can result in poems wholly adequate to an age consciously as late as our own. All that a critic, as critic, can give poets is the deadly encouragement that never ceases to remind them of how heavy their inheritance is.

Catastrophe, as Freud and Ferenczi[b] viewed it, seems to me the central element in poetic incarnation, in the fearsome process by which a person is re-born as

---

[a] The reference is to Gianbattista Vico (1668–1744), Italian philosopher of history.
[b] S. Ferenczi, early psychoanalyst, associated with Freud.

241

a poet. Perhaps I should say catastrophe as Empedocles viewed it, for the dualistic vision of Empedocles is the necessary start of any valid theory of poetic
origins; but then Empedocles was Freud's acknowledged ultimate precursor, even
as Schopenhauer[c] was a closer and rather less acknowledged precursor. The
dialectic of cosmic love and hate governs poetic incarnation: 'At one time they
are all brought together into one order by Love; at another, they are carried each
in different directions by repulsion of Strife.' Initial love for the precursor's
poetry is transformed rapidly enough into revisionary strife, without which indi-
viduation is not possible. Strife, Empedocles held, caused the initial catastrophe,
separating out the elements and bringing the Promethean fire of consciousness
into being. Poetry is identical neither with a particular mode of consciousness
nor with a particular instinct, yet its birth in an individual is analogous to the
Empedoclean catastrophe of consciousness and the Freudian catastrophe of
instinctual genesis. Empedocles and Freud alike are theorists of *influence*, of the
giving that famishes the taker. We move from ocean to land by a drying-up of
the oceanic sense, and we learn sublimation through our preconscious memories
of a glacial catastrophe. It follows that our most valued activities are regressive.
The great Ferenczi, more fecund than Freud or Empedocles at envisioning
catastrophes, almost as fecund as Blake, rather frighteningly saw all sexual love
as regression, a drive back to ocean. Poetry, perhaps unlike sexual intercourse,
most certainly is regressive, as Peacock so charmingly saw.[d] I turn therefore to
some surmises upon the catastrophe of poetic incarnation. How are true poets
born? Or better, as the Age of Sensibility liked to ask, what makes possible the
incarnation of the Poetical Character?

   Desiccation combined with an unusually strong oceanic sense is the highly
dualistic yet not at all paradoxical answer. Here we can cite the most truly poetic
of all true, strong poets, P. B. Shelley, whom it is no longer quite so fashionable
to malign, a welcome change from the days of my youth. I will summarize the
dedicatory stanzas to *The Revolt of Islam*, stanzas as much one of Whitman's
starting-points as one of Yeats's, and stanzas highly relevant to those similarly
Shelley-obsessed poets, Hardy, who owed Shelley so many of his ecstatic breakthroughs, and Stevens, who owed Shelley his fiction of the leaves, and of the
wind, and of most other movements of the spirit. There is no fuller vision of
poetic incarnation in the language, not in Collins, Coleridge, Blake, Keats, not
even in *Out of the Cradle Endlessly Rocking*, for Shelley was at once a major skeptical intellect and a unique master of the heart's impulses, and he turned both
these forces to the study of poetic origins, seeking there the daemonic ground
of his own incurable and involuntary dualism. Stevens, however one loves him,
hardly compares well with Shelley on this frightening ground, for he lacked both
Shelley's intellectual penetration and Shelley's astonishing *speed* of perception,
a speed crucial in the dark realms of origins.

   At a particular hour, Shelley says, his spirit's sleep was burst, when he found
himself weeping, he knew not why, as he walked forth upon the glittering grass,

[c] Arthur Schopenhauer (1788–1860), German philosopher, author of *The World as Will and Idea*.
[d] An allusion to Thomas Love Peacock's ironic essay, *The Four Ages of Poetry* (1820).

on a May dawn. But this hour, though it turned quickly from tears to a sense of power, of a sublime hope, was followed rapidly by 'A sense of loneliness, a thirst with which I pined.' To repair this desiccation, the young poet set forth upon erotic quests, all of which failed him, until he encountered his true epi-psyche, Mary Wollstonecraft Godwin, whereupon the spirit of solitude left him. He tries to end in the sense of 'a serener hour,' yet this hope seems vain, for 'I am worn away,/And Death and Love are yet contending for Their prey.' The Dedication's climax anticipates the close of *Adonais* some four turbulent years later, for the last vision of Shelley and Mary shows them:

> Like lamps into the world's tempestuous night,—
> Two tranquil stars, while clouds are passing by
> Which wrap them from the foundering seaman's sight,
> That burn from year to year with unextinguished light.

Poetic incarnation results from poetic influence, here the influence of Wordsworth, particularly of his Great Ode, *Intimations of Immortality*. No poet, I amend that to no strong poet, can choose his precursor, any more than any person can choose his father. The *Intimations* Ode chose Shelley, as Shelley's *To a Skylark* chose Hardy, the way starlight flows where it flows, gratuitously. Whether we can be found by what is not already somehow ourselves has been doubted from Heraclitus through Emerson to Freud, but the daemon is not our destiny until we yield to his finding us out. Poetic influence, in its first phase, is not to be distinguished from love, though it will shade soon enough into revisionary strife. '*Protection against* stimuli is an almost more important function for the living organism than *reception* of stimuli' is a fine reminder in [Freud's] *Beyond the Pleasure Principle*, a book whose true subject is influence. Poets tend to think of themselves as stars because their deepest desire is to be an influence, rather than to be influenced, but even in the strongest, whose desire is accomplished, the anxiety of having been formed by influence still persists.

Shelley understood that the *Intimations* Ode, and *its* precursor, *Lycidas*, took divination as their true subject, for the goal of divination is to attain a power that frees one from all influence, but particularly from the influence of an expected death, or necessity for dying. Divination, in this sense, is both a rage and a program, offering desperate intimations of immortality through a proleptic magic that would evade every danger, including nature itself. Take the darkest of Freudian formulae, that 'the aim of all life is death,' reliant on the belief that 'inanimate things existed before living ones.' Oppose to it the inherent belief of all strong poets, that the animate always had priority, and that death is only a failure in imagination. Say then that in the process of poetic incarnation the ephebe or new poet, through love, experiences an influx of an antithetical power, antithetical both to the entropy that is nature's and to the unacceptable sublimity of Ananke, goddess who turns the spindle of the Freudian instinctual drive back to the inanimate. All poetic odes of incarnation are therefore Immortality odes, and all of them rely upon a curious divinity that the ephebe has imparted successfully, not to himself, but to the precursor. In making the precursor a god, the ephebe already has begun a movement away from him, a primary revision that imputes error to the father, a sudden inclination or swerve away from obligation; for even in the context of incarnation, of becoming a poet, obligation shines clear as a little death, premonitory of the greater fall down to the inanimate.

Poets tend to incarnate by the side of ocean, at least in vision, if inland far they be. Or if some blocking agent excludes any glimpse of that immortal sea, various surrogates readily enough are found. Poets whose sexual natures manifest unusual complexity—Byron, Beddoes, Darley, Whitman, Swinburne, Hart Crane, among so many others—rarely get very far away from the ocean of incarnation. Poets of more primary sexuality avoid this overt obsession, generally following the Wordsworthian pattern, in which a haunting noise of waters echoes every imaginative crisis. Here we need to brood on the full context of poetic incarnation, remembering that every strong poet in Western tradition is a kind of Jonah or renegade prophet[c].

Jonah, the aggrieved one, whose name means 'dove,' descends into the ship, and every such ship 'was like to be broken.' When he descends from ship into the sea, 'the sea ceased from its raging.' 'I leaped headlong into the Sea,' Keats said, to learn there 'the Soundings, the quicksands, and the rocks.' The Sea:

> . . . with its mighty swell
> Gluts twice ten thousand caverns, till the spell
> Of Hecate leaves them their old shadowy sound.

Jonah, in flight from open vision, was swallowed up and closed in darkness. When the sirocco blew upon the rescued prophet, he wished again for darkness, and the author of his book, giving God the last word, never tells us whether Jonah returned to his vocation. Call Jonah the model of the poet who fails of strength, and who wishes to return to the Waters of Night, the Swamp of Tears, where he began, before the catastrophe of vocation. It is only later, awash in the Word, that the poet questing for strength can sing, with Thoreau:

> Now chiefly is my natal hour,
> And only now my prime of life;
> Of manhood's strength it is the flower,
> 'Tis peace's end, and war's beginning strife.

This does not sound, in its first hush, like a strife's beginning, as here in Whitman:

> The yellow half-moon enlarged, sagging down, drooping, the face of the
>   sea almost touching,
> The boy ecstatic, with his bare feet the waves, with his hair the
>   atmosphere dallying,
> The love in the heart long pent, now loose, at last tumultuously
>   bursting. . . .

[c] The Book of Jonah in the Old Testament tells how Jonah, trying 'to flee from the presence of the Lord', was shipwrecked and swallowed by a whale.

The dallying hair is the young Apollo's, and every ephebe is a new Phoebus, looking to name what cannot be named, finding it again as mysteriously as Ammons does here, in a long-dead hunchback playmate of remote childhood:

> So I said I am Ezra
> and the wind whipped my throat
> gaming for the sounds of my voice
>   I listened to the wind
> go over my head and up into the night
> Turning to the sea I said
>   I am Ezra
> but there were no echoes from the waves. . . .

Poetic origins: the Incarnation of the Poetic Character, if an inland matter, takes place near caverns and rivulets, replete with mingled measures and soft murmurs, promises of an improved infancy when one hears the sea again. Just when the promises were betrayed, the Strong Poet himself will never know, for his strength (as poet) is never to suffer such knowing. No Strong Poet can deign to be a good reader of his own works. The Strong Poet is strong by virtue of and in proportion to his *thrownness*; having been thrown farther, his consciousness of such primal outrage is greater. This consciousness informs his more intense awareness of the precursors, for he knows how far our being can be thrown, out and down, as lesser poets cannot know.

Ocean, the matter of Night, the original Lilith or 'feast that famished,' mothers what is antithetical to her, the makers who fear (rightly) to accept her and never cease to move towards her. If not to have conceived oneself is a burden, so for the strong poet there is also the more hidden burden: not to have brought oneself forth, not to be a god breaking one's own vessels, but to be awash in the Word not quite one's own. And so many greatly surrender, as Swinburne did:

> A land that is thirstier than ruin;
>   A sea that is hungrier than death;
> Heaped hills that a tree never grew in;
>   Wide sands where the wave draws breath;
> All solace is here for the spirit
>   That ever forever may be
> For the soul of thy son to inherit,
>   My mother, my sea.

Even the strongest, who surrender only at the end, brood too deep upon this beauty, as Shelley brooded: 'The sea was so translucent that you could see the caverns clothed with the glaucous sea-moss and the leaves and branches of those delicate weeds that pave the bottom of the water.' Their epigoni drown too soon, as Beddoes drowned:

> Come follow us, and smile as we;
>   We sail to the rock in the ancient waves,
> Where the snow falls by thousands into the sea,
>   And the drowned and the shipwrecked have happy graves.

The sea of poetry, of poems already written, is no redemption for the Strong Poet. Only a poet already slain under the shadow of the Covering Cherub's wings can deceive himself this profoundly, with Auden:

> Restored! Returned! The lost are borne
> On seas of shipwreck home at last:
> See! In the fire of praising burns
>   The dry dumb past, and we
> The life-day long shall part no more.

To know that we are object as well as subject of the quest is not poetic knowledge, but rather the knowledge of defeat, a knowledge fit for the pragmaticists of communication, not for that handful who hope to fathom (if not to master) the wealth of ocean, the ancestry of voice. Who could set forth on the poet's long journey, upon the path of laboring Heracles, if he knew that at last he must wrestle with the dead? Wrestling Jacob could triumph, because his Adversary was the Everliving, but even the strongest poets must grapple with phantoms. The strength of these phantoms—which is their beauty—increases as the struggling poet's distance from them lengthens in time. Homer, a greater poet in the Enlightenment than he was even among the Hellenes, is greater yet now in our Post-Enlightenment. The splendors of the firmament of time blaze with a greater fury even as time seems to droop in its decay.

How (even with all hindsight) can we know the true ephebe, the potentially strong poet, from the mass of ocean's nurslings around him? By hearing in his first voices what is most central in the precursors' voices, rendered with a directness, clarity, even a sweetness that they do not often give to us. For the revisionary ratios that will be employed as means-of-defense by the maturing poet do not manifest themselves in the ephebe. They appear only when he quests for fire, when he seeks to burn through every context that the precursors created or themselves accepted. What we see in the ephebe is the incarnation of the poetical character, the second birth into supposed imagination that fails to displace the first birth into nature, but fails only because desire fails when confronted by so antithetical a quest, fiercer than the human can bear to undergo.

Why invoke a process that merely begins poets, as prelude to a consideration of the last phases of Hardy and Stevens? Because poets, as poets, and particularly the strongest poets, return to origins at the end, or whenever they sense the imminence of the end. Critics may be wary of origins, or consign them disdainfully to those carrion-eaters of scholarship, the source hunters, but the poet-in-a-poet is desperately obsessed with poetic origins, generally despite himself, as the person-in-a-person at last becomes obsessed with personal origins. Emerson, most undervalued (in our time) of American moral psychologists, is acutely aware of the mind's catastrophic growth into full self-awareness:

> It is very unhappy, but too late to be helped, the discovery we have
> made that we exist. That discovery is called the Fall of Man. Ever
> afterwards we suspect our instruments. We have learned that we do not

see directly, but mediately, and that we have no means of correcting these colored and distorting lenses which we are, or of computing the amount of their errors. . . .

When the strong poet learns that he does not see directly, but mediately through the precursor (frequently a composite figure), he is less able than Emerson to accept a helplessness at correcting the eye of the self, or at computing the angle of vision that is also an angle of fall, a blindness of error. Nothing is less generous than the poetic self when it wrestles for its own survival. Here the Emersonian formula of Compensation is demonstrated: 'Nothing is got for nothing.' If we have been ravished by a poem, it will cost us our own poem. If the poetic self in us loves another, it loves itself in the other; but if it is loved, and accepts love, then it loves itself less, because it knows itself less worthy of self-love. Poets-as-poets are not lovable and critics have been slow to know this, which is why criticism has not yet turned to its rightful function: the study of the problematics of loss.

Let me reduce my argument to the hopelessly simplistic; poems, I am saying, are neither about 'subjects' nor about 'themselves.' They are necessarily about *other poems*; a poem is a response to a poem, as a poet is a response to a poet, or a person to his parent. Trying to write a poem takes the poet back to the origins of what a poem *first was for him*, and so takes the poet back beyond the pleasure principle to the decisive initial encounter and response that began him. We do not think of W. C. Williams as a Keatsian poet, yet he *began and ended as one*, and his late celebration of his Greeny Flower is another response to Keats's odes. *Only a poet challenges a poet as poet*, and so only a poet makes a poet. To the poet-in-a-poet, a poem is always *the other man*, the precursor, and so a poem is always a person, always the father of one's Second Birth. To live, the poet must *misinterpret* the father, by the crucial act of misprision, which is the re-writing of the father.

But who, what is the poetic father? The voice of the other, of the *daimon*, is always speaking in one; the voice that cannot die because already it has survived death—*the dead poet lives in one*. In the last phase of strong poets, they attempt to join the undying *by living in the dead poets* who are already alive in them. This late Return of the Dead recalls us, as readers, to a recognition of the original motive for the catastrophe of poetic incarnation. Vico, who identified the origins of poetry with the impulse towards divination (to foretell, but also to become a god by foretelling), implicitly understood (as did Emerson, and Wordsworth) that a poem is written to escape dying. Literally, poems are refusals of mortality. Every poem therefore has two makers: the precursor, and the ephebe's rejected mortality.

A poet, I argue in consequence, is not so much a man speaking to men as a man rebelling against being spoken to by a dead man (the precursor) outrageously more alive than himself. A poet dare not regard himself as being *late*, yet cannot accept a substitute for the first vision he reflectively judges to have been the precursor's also. Perhaps this is why the poet-in-a-poet *cannot marry*, whatever the person-in-a-poet chooses to have done.

Poetic influence, in the sense I give to it, has almost nothing to do with the verbal resemblances between one poet and another. Hardy, on the surface, scarcely resembles Shelley, his prime precursor, but then Browning, who resembles Shelley even less, was yet more fully Shelley's ephebe than even Hardy was. The same observation can be made of Swinburne and of Yeats in relation to Shelley. What Blake called the Spiritual Form, at once the aboriginal poetical self and the True Subject, is what the ephebe is so dangerously obliged to the precursor for ever possessing. Poets need not *look* like their fathers, and the anxiety of influence more frequently than not is quite distinct from the anxiety of style. Since poetic influence is necessarily misprision, a taking or doing amiss of one's burden, it is to be expected that such a process of malformation and misinterpretation will, at the very least, produce deviations in style between strong poets. Let us remember always Emerson's insistence as to what it is that makes a poem:

> For it is not meters, but a meter-making argument that makes a poem,—a thought so passionate and alive that like the spirit of a plant or an animal it has an architecture of its own, and adorns nature with a new thing. The thought and the form are equal in the order of time, but in the order of genesis the thought is prior to the form. The poet has a new thought; he has a whole new experience to unfold; he will tell us how it was with him, and all men will be the richer in his fortune. For the experience of each new age requires a new confession, and the world seems always waiting for its poet. . . .

Emerson would not acknowledge that meter-making arguments themselves were subject to the tyrannies of inheritance, but that they are so subject is the saddest truth I know about poets and poetry. In Hardy's best poems, the central meter-making argument is what might be called a skeptical lament for the hopeless incongruity of ends and means in all human acts. Love and the means of love cannot be brought together, and the truest name for the human condition is simply that it is loss:

> And brightest things that are theirs. . . .
> Ah, no; the years, the years;
> Down their carved names the raindrop plows.

These are the closing lines of *During Wind and Rain*, as good a poem as our century has given us. The poem, like so many others, is a grandchild of the *Ode to the West Wind*, as much as Stevens' *The Course of a Particular* or any number of major lyrics by Yeats. A carrion-eater, Old Style, would challenge my observations, and to such a challenge I could offer, in its own terms, only the first appearance of the refrain:

> Ah, no; the years O!
> How the sick leaves reel down in throngs!

But such terms can be ignored. Poetic influence, between strong poets, works in the depths, as all love antithetically works. At the center of Hardy's verse, whether in the early *Wessex Poems* or the late *Winter Words*, is this vision:

> And much I grieved to think how power and will
> In opposition rule our mortal day,
>
> And why God made irreconcilable
> Good and the means of good; and for despair
> I have disdained mine eyes' desire to fill
>
> With the spent vision of the times that were
> And scarce have ceased to be—

Shelley's *The Triumph of Life* can give us also the heroic motto for the major characters in Hardy's novels: 'For in the battle Life and they did wage, / She remained conqueror.' The motto would serve as well for the superb volume *Winter Words in Various Moods and Metres*, published on October 2 in 1928, the year that Hardy died on January 11. Hardy had hoped to publish the book on June 2, 1928, which would have been his eighty-eighth birthday. Though a few poems in the book go back as far as the 1860's, most were written after the appearance of Hardy's volume of lyrics, *Human Shows*, in 1925. A few books of twentieth-century verse in English compare with *Winter Words* in greatness, but very few. Though the collection is diverse, and has no central design, its emergent theme is a counterpoise to the burden of poetic incarnation, and might be called the Return of the Dead, who haunt Hardy as he faces towards death.

In his early poem (1887), *Shelley's Skylark*, Hardy, writing rather in the style of his fellow Shelleyan, Browning, speaks of his ancestor's 'ecstatic heights in thought and rhyme.' Recent critics who admire Shelley are not particularly fond of *To a Skylark*, and it is rather too ecstatic for most varieties of modern sensibility, but we can surmise why it so moved Hardy:

> We look before and after,
>   And pine for what is not:
> Our sincerest laughter
> With some pain is fraught;
> Our sweetest songs are those that tell of saddest thought.
>
> Yet if we could scorn
>   Hate, and pride, and fear;
> If we were things born
>   Not to shed a tear,
> I know not how thy joy we ever should come near.

The thought here, as elsewhere in Shelley, is not so simple as it may seem. Our divided consciousness, keeping us from being able to unperplex joy from pain, and ruining the presentness of the moment, at least brings us an aesthetic gain. But even if we lacked our range of negative affections, even if grief were not our birthright, the pure joy of the lark's song would still surpass us. We may think of Shelleyan ladies like Marty South, and even more Sue Bridehead, who seems to have emerged from the *Epipsychidion*. Or perhaps we may remember

Angel Clare, as a kind of parody of Shelley himself.[f] Hardy's Shelley is very close to the most central of Shelleys, the visionary skeptic, whose head and whose heart could never be reconciled, for they both told truths, but contrary truths. In *Prometheus Unbound*, we are told that in our life the shadow cast by love is always ruin, which is the head's report, but the heart in Shelley goes on saying that if there is to be coherence at all, it must come through Eros.

Winter Words, as befits a man going into his later eighties, is more in ruin's shadow than in love's realm. The last poem, written in 1927, is called *He Resolves To Say No More*, and follows directly on *We Are Getting to The End* which may be the bleakest sonnet in the language. Both poems explicitly reject any vision of hope, and are set against the Shelleyan rational meliorism of *Prometheus Unbound*. 'We are getting to the end of visioning/The impossible within this universe,' Hardy flatly insists, and he recalls Shelley's vision of rolling time backward, only to dismiss it as the doctrine of Shelley's Ahasuerus: '(Magians who drive the midnight quill/With brain aglow/Can see it so)'. Behind this rejection is the mystery of misprision, of deep poetic influence in its final phase, which I have called *Apophrades* or the Return of the Dead. Hovering everywhere in *Winter Words*, though far less explicitly than it hovers in *The Dynasts*, is Shelley's *Hellas*. The peculiar strength and achievement of *Winter Words* is not that we are compelled to remember Shelley when we read in it, but rather that it makes us read much of Shelley as though Hardy were Shelley's ancestor, the dark father whom the revolutionary idealist failed to cast out.

Nearly every poem in *Winter Words* has a poignance unusual even in Hardy, but I am moved most by *He Never Expected Much*, the poet's reflection on his eighty-sixth birthday, where his dialogue with the 'World' attains a resolution:

'I do not promise overmuch,
  Child; overmuch;
Just neutral-tinted haps and such,'
  You said to minds like mine.
Wise warning for your credit's sake!
Which I for one failed not to take,
And hence could stem such strain and ache
  As each year might assign.

The 'neutral-tinted haps,' so supremely hard to get into poems, are the staple of Hardy's achievement in verse, and contrast both to Wordsworth's 'sober coloring' and Shelley's 'deep autumnal tone' All through *Winter Words* the attentive reader will hear a chastened return of High Romantic Idealism, but muted into Hardy's tonality. Where Yeats malformed both himself and his High Romantic fathers, Blake and Shelley, in the violences of *Last Poems and Plays*, Hardy more effectively subdued the questing temperaments of his fathers, Shelley and Browning, in *Winter Words*. The wrestling with the great dead is subtler in Hardy, and kinder both to himself and to the fathers.

[f] Marty South, Sue Bridehead, and Angel Clare are characters in Thomas Hardy's novels, *The Woodlanders*, *Jude the Obscure* and *Tess of the Durbervilles*, respectively.

Hardy's Shelley was essentially the darker poet of *Adonais* and *The Triumph of Life*, though I find more quotations from *The Revolt of Islam* scattered through the novels than from any other single work by Shelley, and I suppose *Hellas* and *Prometheus Unbound* were even more direct, technical influences upon *The Dynasts*. But Hardy was one of those young men who went about in the 1860's carrying a volume of Shelley in his pocket. Quite simply, he identified Shelley's voice with poetry itself, and though he could allow his ironic sense to touch writers, he kept Shelley inviolate, almost as a kind of secular Christ. His misprision of Shelley, his subversion of Shelley's influence, was an unconscious defense, quite unlike the overt struggle against Shelley of Browning and Yeats.

American poets, far more than British, have rebelled overtly against ancestral voices, partly because of Whitman's example, and also because of Emerson's polemic against the very idea of influence, his insistence that going alone must mean refusing even the good models, and so entails reading primarily as an inventor. Our greater emphasis upon originality has produced inversely a more malevolent anxiety of influence, and our poets consequently misinterpret their precursors more radically than do the British. Hardy's was a gentler case of influence-anxiety than that of any other modern strong poet, for reasons allied, I think, to the astonishing ease of Hardy's initial entrance into his poethood. But Stevens was an astonishing instance of late incarnation; fifteen years had to intervene between his undergraduate verse and his first real poem, *Blanche McCarthy*, not written until 1915, when he was nearly thirty-six:

> Look in the terrible mirror of the sky
> And not in this dead glass, which can reflect
> Only the surfaces—the bending arm,
> The leaning shoulder and the searching eye.
>
> Look in the terrible mirror of the sky.
> Oh, bend against the invisible; and lean
> To symbols of descending night; and search
> The glare of revelations going by!
>
> Look in the terrible mirror of the sky.
> See how the absent moon waits in a glade
> Of your dark self, and how the wings of stars,
> Upward, from unimagined coverts, fly.

Here, at this true origin, Stevens is already an involuntary and desperate Transcendentalist, rejecting 'the dead glass' of the object-world or Not-Me, and directing his vision to the sky, 'terrible mirror' for reflecting either the Giant of one's imagination or the Dwarf of the self's disintegration. But the High Romantic, Shelleyan emblems of imagination, moon and stars, are obscured by the self's darkness and by an inventive faculty still unable to function. Yet the desire for revelations, for an inwardness that might stand up to the sky, is dominant and would prevail.

The Rock would have been Stevens' last book if he had not been persuaded to publish a *Collected Poems*. Less various than *Winter Words*, it goes beyond

251

Hardy with several works of a final sublimity: *Madame La Fleurie, To an Old Philosopher in Rome, The World as Meditation, The Rock* itself, and most of all, *The River of Rivers in Connecticut.* These last visions are all Returns of the Dead, final re-captures of priority from a complex precursor, a composite figure at once English and American, but consistently Romantic: Wordsworth, Keats, Shelley, Emerson, Whitman. Whitman is most pervasive, as large a hidden form in Stevens as Shelley was in Hardy. The poet of *The Sleepers* and of the elegy for Lincoln is so stationed in *The Rock's* cadences and gestures that a reading of Whitman now finds him shadowed by Stevens. *Madame La Fleurie*, Stevens' fearful vision of the earth's final form, is Whitman's terrible mother let loose upon the land. The ultimate revisioning of the inventors of an American Sublime—Emerson and Whitman—is most effective in the wholly solipsistic and new vitalism that rises up as the 'unnamed flowing'—of 'the river that flows nowhere, like a sea,' a river of the heightened senses with a 'propelling force' that would prevent even Charon from crossing it. In Stevens' strange, triumphantly isolated joy at the end, as in Hardy's sublimely grim and solitary refusal to sorrow in sorrow, there is the accent of a strong poet who has completed the dialectic of misprision, as Yeats could not quite complete it. Stevens and Hardy weathered their wrestling with the dead, and either could have said at the end what Stevens said, when he saw himself alone with his book as a heterocosm, a finished version of the self or *The Planet on the Table:*

> His self and the sun were one
> And his poems, although makings of his self,
> Were no less makings of the sun.

No less were they makings of the precursor, but the Wars of Eden had been fought, and the hard, partial victory had been won.

14 E. D. Hirsch Jr.

E. D. Hirsch, Jr. (b. 1928) is William R. Kenan Professor of English at the University of Virginia, where he has taught for many years. His books include *Wordsworth and Schelling: a typological study of Romanticism* (1960), *Innocence and Experience: an introduction to Blake* (1964), and *Validity in Interpretation* (1967). This last-named book is perhaps the most formidable theoretical defence of the principles and methods of traditional literary scholarship and cognitive criticism to have been written in English. Drawing on the philosophical and theological tradition of hermeneutics (the theory of interpretation), Hirsch argued that the 'meaning' of a literary text is objectively knowable, and distinguishable from the 'significance' attributed to that meaning by particular readers. His argument was directed particularly against the 'anti-intentionalist' formalism of the Anglo–American New Criticism; but it conflicts even more sharply with the theoretical and methodological principles of the post-structuralist criticism, inspired by Continental European writers like Barthes and Derrida, which attracted a considerable following in America in the decade after *Validity in Interpretation* was published.

The essay 'Faulty Perspectives', reprinted here from Hirsch's collection of essays, *The Aims of Interpretation* (1976), reflects his awareness of these new challenges to his position, without significantly revising the latter. Hirsch's use of the term 'historicism' to mean a fallacious and tendentious periodization of history perhaps owes something to Karl Popper's *The Poverty of Historicism* (1961). It is not, of course, to be confused with the historical method of scholarship, which Hirsch himself stands for.

CROSS-REFERENCES: 11. Iser
15. Abrams
19. Fish
24. Belsey

COMMENTARY: William Ray, 'E. D. Hirsch: individual meaning as shared meaning', in Ray's *Literary Meaning: from Phenomenology to Deconstruction* (1984)
Robert Crosman, 'Do Readers Make Meaning?', Susan R. Suleiman and Inge Crosman (eds), *The Reader in the Text* (1980)

Faulty perspectives

The main intellectual (and emotional) sanction for dogmatic skepticism in present-day literary theory is its assumption that all 'knowledge' is relative. This cognitive atheism, as I call it, is based mainly on the idea that everybody sees literature from his own 'angle of vision,' and responds emotionally to literature through his own system of values and associations. Individualized in this way, cognitive atheism is straightforward subjectivism. But other closely related forms in literary theory and practice are cultural relativism, historical relativism, and methodological relativism. All exhibit the same structure; all of them make truth and reality relative to a spiritual perspective. That this doctrine of critical relativity should itself be the single doctrine exempt from an otherwise universal skepticism rarely strikes its adherents as a damaging inconsistency, or even a curious paradox. Tough-minded cognitive atheism usually tends to be an emotional given rather than a developed system. But if mere inconsistency is no bar to dogmatic skepticism in literary theory, one might hope nonetheless for a conversion to agnosticism if it could be shown that the doctrine of cognitive relativity is based on premises that are empirically wrong.

I. *The metaphor of perspective*

Words concerning the changing appearances of an object, when it is seen from different points in space, came to the lexical scene rather late in modern European languages. Perspective-words are not found at all in the lexicons of ancient Greece and Rome. The Orient was apparently more precocious. Evidence from the actual practice of early Chinese painters shows that they understood systematically the distorted appearance of objects when viewed by monocular vision from a single location in space. But in the West, the 'laws of perspective,' which is to say the systematic distortions of spatially located vision, were not understood until the fifteenth century, the period when painters worked out the principles for representing monocular perspectives on two-dimensional surfaces.

Why did Western painters take so long to discover elemental principles of their illusionist art? The answer is probably to be found in developmental psychology, especially in Piaget's experiments with young children.[1] In learning to interpret the world visually, every child must go through a long, tedious, error-filled process before he learns to compensate for perspective-effects. In going through this learning process, the normal child is, of course, greatly assisted by a built-in perspective-compensator which he possesses at birth: his binocular vision. The child from the start has a double perspective; he constantly looks at the world from two points of view. Because the distance between these two points is a constant, he gradually learns to reinterpret the distortions of a one-eyed view of the world. That is why the 'laws of perspective' were so difficult, so unnatural, and so late to be discovered. To learn them meant to unlearn the basic and arduous lessons of childhood, as documented by Piaget. So wayward is this process of deconstruction that early researches into perspective-effects required special devices like the *camera oscura* and the instruments that Dürer depicted in his 'Demonstration of Perspective.'

It has taken Western culture an even longer time to discover the spiritual analogues to perspective-effects as represented in such metaphors as *viewpoint* (1856), *standpoint* (1836), *mental perspective* (1841), and *attitude* (1837), the dates in parentheses representing the first occasion of such figurative usage recorded in the *New English Dictionary*. If Renaissance painters required the *camera oscura*, the Victorians, in making their spiritual analogue, apparently required Kant.[2] To assume that one's own sense of reality is distorted by one's spiritual location, on the analogy of monocular vision, required the Copernican revolution of the Kantian philosophy.

But the implied relativism in that analogue is a supreme irony, since the purpose of the critical philosophy was to defend the validity and universality of knowledge, not its dependence on a spiritual perspective. It is not only an irony, it is a total vulgarization of the great Kantian insight. This chapter is a sketch of some of these vulgarizations in the domain of hermeneutic theory, and an argument against their uncritical and facile application.

II. The perspective of history: three relativistic fallacies

It was chiefly Herder[a] in the late eighteenth century who challenged the assumption that the perspective of human nature is essentially the same in all times and places. Herder's contrary view of history has been called 'historicism' by Meinecke[b], who judges it to be 'one of the greatest revolutions that Western thought has experienced.'[3] Undoubtedly Meinecke is right. And one effect of this revolution was to introduce the metaphor of perspective into the domain of historical description. Not until historians began to assume that men's perspectives are essentially different in different eras did they begin to write monographs on the Romantic *Zeitgeist* or the Medieval Mind. In various degrees of sophistication, such perspectival concepts are now the staple of literary history.

According to Meinecke, the chief feature of historicism 'is the replacing of a generalizing mode of thinking about human phenomena with an individualizing mode of thinking.' But Meinecke's description is only partly accurate for modern historicism (or cultural perspectivism) in its uncritical forms. Literary history often stresses the individuality of a period without placing a correspondent stress on

[a] Johann Gottfried von Herder (1744–1803), German philosopher, poet and critic. Author of *Outlines of The Philosophy of Man* (1784–91)

[b] Friedrich Meinecke (1862–1954), German historian.

discordant individualities within a period. And this is odd, since those who understand the sameness of individuals within a period do not very often perceive sameness among individuals across different periods. Meinecke is himself an historian, a distinguished one, who avoids this inconsistency. History of any sort, including literary history, he asserts, would be impossible on the assumption that man's perspective changes radically in history; and it would be empty if it assumed that human nature remained everywhere the same. Uncritical dogma in either direction deserves to be called a fallacy. It is not, of course, a logical fallacy, only an offence against experience and common sense.

The first historicist fallacy on my list of three I call the fallacy of the inscrutable past, since under it, one regards persons of the past in the way Englishmen in novels used to regard inscrutable Orientals. Literary historians of this style infer from the past a state of mind so different from our own that its texts can be understood only by an initiated few, from whom an act of 'historical sympathy' is required to understand a distant era that seems to be populated by beings who might have come from Mars. I will take as illustration the following inferences of Professor Bruno Snell. After an impressive lexical analysis of the *Odyssey* and *Iliad*, Professor Snell concludes that the Greeks of Homer's day possessed no conscious idea of a unified human self; in the Homeric poems he finds no word for such a concept. By the same process of lexical inference he finds that the Greeks possessed no concept of a unified human body. The Homeric poems refer only to parts of the body, never to the whole.[4] Habitually, then, Greeks must have regarded the human body as merely a congeries of parts. I do not deny that Professor Snell could be right, I only assert that it is exceedingly improbable he is right. I doubt that he would have advanced his theories if he had not studied in a tradition which honored the perspectivist fallacy of the inscrutable past.

Snell's book has been influential, but one could not condemn its interesting improbabilities if these and similar ones by literary scholars had not produced a very damaging reaction among present-day theorists. Theorists like Gadamer[c], for instance, or like Barthes, rightly object to the cultural narcosis induced by such 'reconstructions' of the past.[5] But as an antidote, they recommend that we vitalize the inscrutable texts of the past by distorting them to our own perspective. In other words, they accept the fallacy of the inscrutable past as the premise on which they base their skeptical counterproposal. It is far better to distort the past in an interesting and relevant way than to distort and deaden it under the pretense of historical reconstruction. Hence, both Snell in his historical reconstruction and Gadamer in his historical vitalization are extreme historicists and perspectivists. They are brothers under the skin. Both assume that the perspective-ridden meanings of the past are irremediably alien to us. In the one case we are asked to join in a perspective that yields a humanity and a reality unlike our own. In the other case we are advised to ignore such alien reality as irrelevant to our concerns and to construct instead a usable past out of our own perspective. If we were truly required to choose between Snell and Gadamer on this point, the ethical preference would lie with Gadamer, since a useful distortion

[c] Hans-Georg Gadamer, German philosopher, author of *Truth and Method* (1960).

would be superior to a useless one. But we are not required to make a choice based on fallacious premises.

My second fallacy of historicism is the fallacy of the homogeneous past. Obviously, it is often accompanied by the fallacy of the inscrutable past, as in the case of Snell, who seems to assert that *all* the Greeks of Homer's day lacked a concept of a unified human self. Under this fallacy, everybody who composed texts in the Elizabethan Age, or the Romantic Age, or the Periclean Age shared in each case a common perspective imposed by their shared culture. Literary historians who write on this premise are content to apply it in the following sort of syllogism:

> Medieval Man believed in alchemy.
> Chaucer was a Medieval Man.
> Chaucer believed in alchemy.

The most distinguished exemplar of this monolithic cultural perspectivism is no doubt D. W. Robertson. Certainly he represents a convenient example, since, like Snell, he exhibits the fallacy so very purely. Of course the fallacy of the homogeneous past lies not in its logic, which is quite unassailable, but in the implausibility of its major premise about the Medieval Mind, or the Greek Mind, or the Victorian Frame of Mind.

Used critically, such concepts as the Victorian frame of mind are, of course, entirely reasonable. A shared culture does indeed mean a shared spiritual perspective—where the culture and the perspective are shared. Even odd-seeming generalizations about the medieval mind are reasonable tools, so long as they remain tools—heuristic devices that pave the way into another cultural environment. But to assume that *any* cultural environment is homogeneous, even on the very abstract level at which literary history is conducted, is to make an assumption about human communities which experience contradicts.

Finally my third historicistic fallacy. It is the one I wish chiefly to expose. It now lurks behind many a critical bush. It is the fallacy of the homogeneous present-day perspective. Only by accepting this additional fallacy, for example, can Gadamer offer an alternative to Snell. For when Gadamer attacks the 'deadness' of pretended historical reconstruction, he assumes a present that has its own peculiar deadness. To whom, for instance, is historical reconstruction dead? Why, to the homogeneous 'us.' Jan Kott[d] invites 'us' to meet Shakespeare, 'our contemporary.' Roland Barthes invites 'us' to meet 'our' contemporary, Racine, to make him speak to 'us.' But this homogeneity in our present perspective is a construction as artificial as any of the despised 'reconstructions' of the past. It is entirely false to Herder's genial insight into the great multifariousness of human-being, both past and present—the original insight of historicism in which all its later fallacies are grounded.

In such later theories, then, Herder's insight into the individuality of men and cultures has been vulgarized. A complementary insight by his contemporary Vico

---

[d] Jan Kott is a Polish emigré critic and theatrical producer, author of *Shakespeare Our Contemporary* (1964).

has been repudiated. Erich Auerbach has phrased Vico's idea as follows: 'The entire development of human history as made by men is potentially contained in the human mind, and may, therefore, by a process of research and re-evocation be understood by men.'[6] To say with Herder that men and cultures are often very different from one another is not to deny that a man can understand someone with a perspective very different from his own. Vico's conception, later elaborated by Dilthey[e], was that men share a common potential to be other than they are.[7] The distance between one culture and another may not in every instance be bridgeable, but the same is true between persons who inhabit the same culture. Cultural perspectivism, of the sort I have been attacking, forgets that the distance between one historical period and another is a very small step in comparison to the huge metaphysical gap we must leap to understand the perspective of another person in any time or place.

III What is an approach?

Dilthey's psychological model for our potential ability to understand the past is persuasive and balanced. But Dilthey himself did not always manage to preserve this balance in his writings. It is mainly to him that we owe the word *Weltan-schauung*, that is, the spiritual perspective of a person or a culture. In the domain of literary criticism, the critic's *Weltanschauung* is sometimes called his 'approach,' a term first used in this perspectival sense in the twentieth century. The critic's interpretation of literature depends on his 'approach.' What the scholar discovers depends on his 'approach.' The term implies a methodological perspectivism.

Dilthey tells the story of a nightmare that visited him sometime after he had begun to use the term *Weltanschauung*. As a guest in a friend's house, he had seen assigned a bed near a reproduction of Raphael's *School of Athens*, and as he slept he dreamt that the picture had come to life. All the famous thinkers of antiquity began to rearrange themselves in groups according to their *Weltan-schauungen*. Slowly into the dream composition came later thinkers: Kant, Schiller, Carlyle, Ranke, Guizot—each of whom was drawn to one of the groups that had formed around Plato or Heraclitus or Archimedes. Wandering back and forth among the groups were other thinkers who tried to mediate between them, but without success. In fact, the groups only moved farther and farther apart, until they could communicate only among themselves. The thinkers had become isolated in their separate approaches to reality. Then Dilthey awoke from his dream, which he interpreted as follows: No man can see any reality steadily and see it whole. Each approach is partial and incommensurate with other approaches. 'To contemplate all the aspects in their totality is denied to us.'[8] But in his waking state there was for Dilthey a consolation: each approach may be partial and confined, but each does disclose its own particular element of truth.

The history of literary criticism and scholarship yields its own version of Dilthey's nightmare. One need only paste different faces on Raphael's draped

[e] Wilhelm Dilthey (1833–1911), German philosopher and social scientist.

figures. On the far left, a group surrounds Freud, but refuses to converse with a nearby group surrounding Jung. Also on the left, of course, is another bearded German, Marx, with his numerous adherents; and still another German on the far right, Schleiermacher, is surrounded by a swarm of philologists, some of them with badges marked MLA. In the center, Plato and Aristotle cannot manage to hold their adherents together. Winters and Leavis move back and forth between them, following Coleridge, Arnold, and Johnson. Many other figures enter the composition. One group of them hesitates. They part, going towards different masters. They join again in puzzlement; they speak rapidly in French. At this point the restless dreamer wakes up.

What does the nightmare mean? Is Dilthey's mournful interpretation right? Does each critical approach present a partial truth forever trapped within its sponsoring perspective? Or worse, does each approach present a complete version of literature, as seen (and distorted) by its own perspective? To anyone desiring knowledge, either interpretation of the dream is a nightmare. Critical approaches cannot complement and support one another if they sponsor different meanings. We cannot look at a blackbird thirteen ways and thereby expect to come up with a truer blackbird—if our model assumes that each way of looking gives us a different blackbird. The net result would be thirteen blackbirds, and by analogy, thirteen interpretations of the same text. The perspectival implications of the word 'approach' lead us logically to the skeptical conclusion that scholars and critics who use different approaches are just not perceiving or talking about the same reality.

Occasionally this impasse brings to somebody's mind the parable about the blind men and the elephant—the Anglo-Saxon version of Dilthey's nightmare. The blind man at the tail thinks the elephant is a snake, but the blind man at a leg thinks the elephant is a tree. But the parable itself is far more rational and comforting than the inference it is supposed to support in literary criticism. An intelligent and energetic blind man could conceivably move about and touch different parts of the creature and conclude that he was touching an elephant. But the word 'approach' implies a different version of the story in which such a resolution would be impossible. In that story, several blind men are standing in different positions around one of the elephant's legs, yet they persist in their disagreement about what they are touching.

The story has to be told this way because no critic can approach textual meaning from any direction at all before there exists for him a meaning to be approached. Textual meaning is not like an elephant or a tree; it is not something out there to be approached from different points of view. It is not *there* for the critic in any sense until he has construed it. If a Marxist critic construes a text differently from a formalist critic, that is an irrelevant accident. No perspectival necessity requires him to do so. Marxist critics and formalist critics may be equally able to understand what a text means. What they usually differ in is the significance they give to that meaning.

Whatever a critic's approach may be, it must necessarily follow upon his understanding. An approach must be subsequent to a construing of what the written symbols mean. Nor is a construction of meaning something that is altered by different critical approaches. It is not a physical object that shows different configurations when viewed from different positions. Meaning is an object that exists *only* by virtue of a single, privileged, precritical approach. No matter how much critics may differ in critical approach, they must understand a text through the same precritical approach if they are to understand it at all. Why this must be so is the burden of the final part of this essay.

IV The Paradoxes of Perspectivism

I have argued that perspectivism, the theory that interpretation varies with the standpoint of the interpreter, is a root form of critical skepticism. Implicitly it rejects the possibility of an interpretation that is independent of the interpreter's own values and preconceptions; ultimately it repudiates correctness of interpretation as a possible goal. Since all interpretations are perspective-ridden, disparate interpretations can be equally correct, or what is the same thing, equally incorrect. But in that case what is left as an acceptable critical standard? Authenticity. A valid interpretation is one that represents an authentic realization of meaning through one's own perspective, or through that of one's time and culture. The practical aim of perspectivism can be expressed in positive terms as an attempt to replace the meaningless criterion of correctness with the presumably meaningful criterion of authenticity.

This explains why the issue was not entirely resolvable when conservative scholars attacked Roland Barthes's perspectivist interpretations of Racine; the terms of the debate were incommensurate. An 'authentic' interpretation is not diminished in its authenticity just because it is 'incorrect.' This same irreconcilable clash of standards rendered inconclusive the similar polemics in biblical studies between 'correct' interpreters like Karl Barth and 'authentic' interpreters like Rudolph Bultmann. Obviously, debates about concrete interpretations cannot be settled before having resolved this fundamental conflict of criteria. For perspectivists, validity is entirely a function of the encounter between a text and one's inescapable cultural self.

But what, after all, is a perspective? The metaphor is spatial and visual, while the matter at hand is neither. If we were required momentarily to abandon the metaphor in favor of more descriptive terms, we would be forced to the realization that the visual metaphor refers to Kant's Copernican revolution in philosophy. Perspectivism is a version of the Kantian insight that man's experience is pre-accommodated to his categories of experience. The contribution to modern thought of Dilthey and others was in extending the Kantian insight beyond the abstract, universal realms of science and mathematics into the richer, more complex domains of cultural experience. Conscious of his debt to Kant, Dilthey conceived his theoretical work on interpretation as part of a larger program which he called the 'Critique of Historical Reason.'

What is popularly called a 'perspective' refers to a theory which in its classical and adequate form had nothing to do with the visual metaphor. Hence, at this point, my exposition must itself become less metaphorical and philosophically more serious. Kant postulated a universal structure in human subjectivity which constitutes experience, and which thereby guarantees the possibility of scientific knowledge. Dilthey and others postulated that, beyond this universal subjectivity, there exists a cultural subjectivity, structured by further categories which are analogously constitutive of all cultural experience. Since Dilthey and his fellow theorists were intimately aware that, under this conception, verbal meaning is entirely relative to cultural subjectivity, it may be instructive to ask more particularly how they managed to eschew the skeptical conclusions of Dilthey's nightmare.

The problem is certainly a grave one. If all interpretation is constituted by the interpreter's own cultural categories, how can he possibly understand meanings that are constituted by different cultural categories? Dilthey's answer was straightforward and perfectly within the sponsoring Kantian tradition. We can understand culturally alien meanings because we are able to adopt culturally alien categories. Admittedly, we can understand Racine only through those alien categories that are constitutive of his meaning—only through his perspective. Yet we *can* adopt his categories; for cultural subjectivity is not an epistemological ultimate, comparable to Kant's universal system of categories. Cultural subjectivity is not innate, but acquired; it derives from a potential, present in every man, that is capable of sponsoring an indefinite number of culturally conditioned categorial systems. It is within the capacity of every individual to imagine himself other than he is, to realize in himself another human or cultural possibility.

But the metaphor of perspective compels a different conclusion. Since every man sees the world from a different perspective, each one of us would have to misunderstand the other in his own way. That is the lesson taught by the analogy of visual perception. Misleading as it is, the analogy is with us and must be recognized as one of *our* cultural categories. Let me therefore introduce the first of my two paradoxes by taking the visual analogy seriously. I am led to the following skeptical argument:

1. Every object appears differently from different perspectives.
2. An interpreter always views a text in a perspective that is different from the author's.
3. Therefore, the meaning perceived by an interpreter must be at best subtly different from the meaning perceived by the author.

Yet even as a description of spatial-visual perception the argument is not empirically accurate. For instance, if I observe a building from one street and a friend looks at it from another street, the differences in what we see are indeed attributable to our different perspectives. Even if we were standing on the same street, just a few feet apart, differences would exist. The paradox is that, despite these differences, both of us perceive (i.e., visually interpret) the very same building. We see, that is, an object which is not entirely visible from *any* perspective, yet nevertheless we perceive it, know it, recognize it together; for by an imaginative extension we are always visually completing and correcting the partial view we get from a single perspective, just as binocular vision completes and corrects monocular perspective effects. If I see only one side of the building, I still know that it has other sides, and that the object of my perception is a whole building, not just the side that I see. My separated friend and I are therefore quite correct when we agree that we are seeing the same thing, and equally correct in assuming that the explicit components of our perception are nonetheless different. The paradox involved here is that of the intentionality of consciousness—as explored in the work of Brentano, Meinong and Husserl. And it is a paradox which completely subverts the naiver assumptions of popular perspectivism. Perspective-effects do not necessarily distort and relativize what we understand. Anyone who takes the perspectivist metaphor seriously is forced by the empirical facts of visual perception to reverse his original inference, and conclude that a diversity of perspectives does not necessarily compel a diversity of understood meanings.

The skeptical perspectivist does better, therefore, if he retreats to the more adequate premises of the Kantian argument. This is his most powerful line of defense, and from it he can argue quite correctly that my building can be quite different from my friend's even if we trade places and view it from an identical physical perspective. My building is not a mere physical given but an object constituted by my own special categorial system. By the same token, every interpretation of verbal meaning is constituted by the categories through which it is construed. Yet, for everyone who looks at it, a building stands there as an object of some sort. Verbal meaning is not an object like that. As a construction from a mute text, meaning has existence only in consciousness. Apart from the categories through which it is construed, meaning can have no existence at all. This, then, is the second and more important paradox of perspectivism. By an extension of the great Kantian insight on which it is ultimately based, interpretive perspectivism argues for the constitutive nature of cultural categories. In its deepest significance therefore, perspectivism implies that verbal meaning exists *only* by virtue of the perspective which gives it existence. And this compels the conclusion that verbal meaning can exist only from one perspective. Again, under this second paradox, perspectivism once more has to repudiate its naive skeptical conclusions. No longer can it suppose that a meaning appears differently from different perspectives, but is compelled to concede the absolute impossibility of viewing *meaning* from different perspectives.

It is an evasion at best to argue that the interpreter's alien perspective distorts meaning, for it is impossible to distort something that cannot even exist by means of an alien perspective. The radical perspectivists are not radical enough by half. When, for instance, H. G. Gadamer speaks of a fusion of perspectives, a *Horizontverschmelzung*, he overlooks the paradox that this intermediate perspective can no longer possess the meaning it pretends to carry into the contemporary world. Of course, the words of a text can be respoken from a new perspective and a new meaning formulated. Of course, as some critics insist, the reader can become a self-imaging author. But a text cannot be *interpreted* from a perspective different from the original author's. Meaning is understood from the perspective that lends existence to meaning. Any other procedure is not interpretation but authorship.

Every act of interpretation involves, therefore, at least two perspectives, that of the author and that of the interpreter. The perspectives are entertained both at once, as in normal binocular vision. Far from being an extraordinary or illusory feat, this entertaining of two perspectives at once is the ground of all human intercourse, and a universal fact of speech which the linguists have called the 'doubling of personality.'[9] When we speak or interpret speech, we are never trapped in a single matrix of spiritual categories; we are never merely listeners or merely speakers; we are both at once. Readers of this essay—emphatically those who are disagreeing with my argument—are here and now practicing both interpretation and criticism, are entertaining two perspectives at once. For, my meaning exists and is construed only from my perspective, while the simultaneous criticism of that meaning implies a different perspective. The empirical actuality of this double perspective, universal in verbal intercourse, calls in doubt a basic premise of hermeneutical relativism and, with it, most of the presently fashionable forms of cognitive atheism.

NOTES

1. Jean Piaget, *The Construction of Reality in the Child* (New York, 1971).
2. The inference that Kant's philosophy lay behind this conception is further supported by the suggestive fact that S. T. Coleridge, one of the first Englishmen to read Kant, was also the first author recorded in the *NED* to use the phrase 'point of view' as a spiritual metaphor. On the other hand, David Hume showed himself to be a proto-Kantian in ways beyond those recognized by Kant, in the following use of the phrase, not recorded in the *NED:* 'Every work of art in order to produce its due effect on the mind, must be surveyed in a certain point of view, and cannot be fully relished by persons whose situation, real or imaginary, is not conformable to that which is required by the performance' ('Of the Standard of Taste,' 1757).
3. F. Meinecke, *Die Entstehung des Historismus* (Munich, 1947).
4. Bruno Snell, *The Discovery of the Mind*, trans. Rosenmeyer (Cambridge, Mass., 1953): 'Homer's men had as yet no knowledge of the intellect or of the soul' (p. ix); 'The Homeric man had a body exactly like the later Greeks, but he did not know it *qua* body, but merely as the sum total of his limbs. This is another way of saying that the Homeric Greeks did not yet have a body in the modern sense of the word' (p. 8).
5. H. G. Gadamer, *Wahrheit und Methode* (Tübingen, 1960), esp. pp. 290–324, and Roland Barthes, *Sur Racine* (Paris 1960).
6. Erich Auerbach, 'Vico and Aesthetic Historicism,' in *Scenes from the Drama of European Literature* (New York, 1959).
7. W. Dilthey, *Zergliedende und Beschreibende Psychologie*, vol. 5 in Gesammelete Schriften, 8 vols. (Berlin, 1921–31).
8. W. Dilthey 'The Dream,' in W. Kluback, *Wilhelm Dilthey's Philosophy of History*, pp. 103–9.
9. Ch. Balley, *Linguistique générale et linguistique française* (Bern, 1944), p. 37. See also P. F. Strawson, 'Intention and Convention in Speech Acts,' *Philosophical Review* 73 (1964): 439–60.

15 M. H. Abrams

M. H. Abrams (b. 1912) was educated at Harvard and has taught for many years at Cornell University, where he is at present Class of 1916 Professor. His study of Romantic poetics, _The Mirror and the Lamp_ (1953) is a classic of modern literary scholarship. His other publications include _A Glossary of Literary Terms_ (1957, extensively revised 1981), probably the best reference book of its kind, and _Natural Supernaturalism_ (1971), which led indirectly to the writing of 'The Deconstructive Angel', reprinted below.

This paper was originally delivered at a session of the Modern Language Association in December 1976, which, under the chairmanship of Sheldon Sacks, brought together Abrams, J. Hillis Miller and Wayne Booth, all of whom had previously debated the theoretical and methodological implications of _Natural Supernaturalism_ in the pages of _Critical Inquiry_, to pursue these matters under the general heading of 'The Limits of Pluralism'. Their papers were subsequently published in _Critical Inquiry_ 3 (1977). Abrams' contribution, 'The Deconstructive Angel' is both a lucid exposition of the deconstructionist theory of discourse, and a trenchant attack on it from the standpoint of traditional humanist scholarship. Abrams' most telling argument is perhaps his claim that, in their own discursive practice, deconstructionists rely on the communicative power of language which they theoretically deny. (The deconstructionists' reply is that such paradoxes and contradictions are to be found everywhere in language as soon as one probes beneath its surface: see the following item by J. Hillis Miller.)

CROSS-REFERENCES: 6. Derrida
                         14. Hirsch
                         16. Miller
                         21. De Man

COMMENTARY: Morse Peckham, 'The Infinitude of Pluralism', _Critical Inquiry_ 3 (1977) pp. 803–16 [See also Abrams' 'Behaviourism and Deconstruction: a comment on Morse Peckham's "The Infinitude of Pluralism"', _Critical Inquiry_ 4 (1977) pp. 181–93]

The deconstructive angel

> Demogorgon.　　—If the Abysm
> Could vomit forth its secrets:—but a voice
> Is wanting ...
> 　　　　—Shelley, *Prometheus Unbound*

We have been instructed these days to be wary of words like 'origin,' 'center,' and 'end,' but I will venture to say that this session had its origin in the dialogue between Wayne Booth[a] and myself which centered on the rationale of the historical procedures in my book, *Natural Supernaturalism*. Hillis Miller had, in all innocence, written a review of that book; he was cited and answered by Booth, then re-cited and re-answered by me, and so was sucked into the vortex of our exchange to make it now a dialogue of three. And given the demonstrated skill of our chairman in fomenting debates, who can predict how many others will be drawn into the vortex before it comes to an end?

I shall take this occasion to explore the crucial issue that was raised by Hillis Miller in his challenging review. I agreed with Wayne Booth that pluralism—the bringing to bear on a subject of diverse points of view, with diverse results—is not only valid, but necessary to our understanding of literary and cultural history: in such pursuits the convergence of diverse points of view is the only way to achieve a vision in depth. I also said, however, that Miller's radical statement, in his review, of the principles of what he calls deconstructive interpretation goes beyond the limits of pluralism, by making impossible anything that we would account as literary and cultural history.[1] The issue would hardly be worth pursuing on this public platform if it were only a question of the soundness of the historical claims in a single book. But Miller considered *Natural Supernaturalism* as an example 'in the grand tradition of modern humanistic scholarship, the tradition of Curtius, Auerbach. Lovejoy, C. S. Lewis,'[2] and he made it clear that what is at stake is the validity of the premises and procedures of the entire body of traditional inquiries in the human sciences. And that is patently a matter important enough to warrant our discussion.

Let me put as curtly as I can the essential, though usually implicit, premises that I share with traditional historians of Western culture, which Miller puts in question and undertakes to subvert:

---

[a] Wayne Booth is a distinguished American critic of the Chicago School, author of *The Rhetoric of Fiction* and several other books. See section 42 of *20th Century Literary Criticism*.

1. The basic materials of history are written texts; and the authors who wrote these texts (with some off-center exceptions) exploited the possibilities and norms of their inherited language to say something determinate, and assumed that competent readers, insofar as these shared their own linguistic skills, would be able to understand what they said.
2. The historian is indeed for the most part able to interpret not only what the passages that he cites might mean now, but also what their writers meant when they wrote them. Typically, the historian puts his interpretation in language which is partly his author's and partly his own; if it is sound, this interpretation approximates, closely enough for the purpose at hand, what the author meant.
3. The historian presents his interpretation to the public in the expectation that the expert reader's interpretation of a passage will approximate his own and so confirm the 'objectivity' of his interpretation. The worldly-wise author expects that some of his interpretations will turn out to be mistaken, but such errors, if limited in scope, will not seriously affect the soundness of his overall history. If, however, the bulk of his interpretations are misreadings, his book is not to be accounted a history but an historical fiction.

Notice that I am speaking here of linguistic interpretation, not of what is confusingly called 'historical interpretation'—that is, the categories, topics, and conceptual and explanatory patterns that the historian brings to his investigation of texts, which serve to shape the story within which passages of texts, with their linguistic meanings, serve as instances and evidence. The differences among these organizing categories, topics, and patterns effect the diversity in the stories that different historians tell, and which a pluralist theory finds acceptable. Undeniably, the linguistic meanings of the passages cited are in some degree responsive to differences in the perspective that a historian brings to bear on them; but the linguistic meanings are also in considerable degree recalcitrant to alterations in perspective, and the historian's fidelity to these meanings, without his manipulating and twisting them to fit his preconceptions, serves as a prime criterion of the soundness of the story that he undertakes to tell.

One other preliminary matter: I don't claim that my interpretation of the passages I cite exhausts everything that these passages mean. In his review, Hillis Miller says that 'a literary or philosophical text, for Abrams, has a single unequivocal meaning "corresponding" to the various entities it "represents" in a more or less straightforward mirroring.' I don't know how I gave Miller the impression that my 'theory of language is implicitly mimetic,' a 'straightforward mirror' of the reality it reflects,[3] except on the assumption he seems to share with Derrida, and which seems to me obviously mistaken, that all views of language which are not in the deconstructive mode are mimetic views. My view of language, as it happens, is by and large functional and pragmatic: language, whether spoken or written, is the use of a great variety of speech-acts to accomplish a great diversity of human purposes; only one of these many purposes is to assert something about a state of affairs; and such a linguistic assertion does not mirror, but serves to direct attention to selected aspects of that state of affairs.

At any rate, I think it is quite true that many of the passages I cite are equivocal and multiplex in meaning. All I claim—all that any traditional historian needs to claim—is that, whatever else the author also meant, he meant, at a sufficient approximation, at least *this*, and that the 'this' that I specify is sufficient to the story I undertake to tell. Other historians, having chosen to tell a different story, may in their interpretation identify different aspects of the meanings conveyed by the same passage.

That brings me to the crux of my disagreement with Hillis Miller. His central contention is not simply that I am sometimes, or always, wrong in my interpretation, but instead that I—like other traditional historians—can never be right in my interpretation. For Miller assents to Nietzsche's challenge of 'the concept of "rightness" in interpretation,' and to Nietzsche's assertion that 'the same text authorizes innumerable interpretations (*Auslegungen*): there is no "correct" interpretation.'[4] Nietzsche's views of interpretation, as Miller says, are relevant to the recent deconstructive theorists, including Jacques Derrida and himself, who have 'reinterpreted Nietzsche' or have written 'directly or indirectly under his aegis.' He goes on to quote a number of statements from Nietzsche's *The Will to Power* to the effect, as Miller puts it, 'that reading is never the objective identifying of a sense but the importation of meaning into a text which has no meaning "in itself."' For example: 'Ultimately, man finds in things nothing but what he himself has imported into them.' 'In fact interpretation is itself a means of becoming master of something.'[5] On the face of it, such sweeping deconstructive claims might suggest those of Lewis Carroll's linguistic philosopher, who asserted that meaning is imported into a text by the interpreter's will to power:

'The question is,' said Alice, 'whether you *can* make words mean so many different things.'
'The question is,' said Humpty Dumpty, 'which is to be master—that's all.'

But of course I don't at all believe that such deconstructive claims are, in Humpty Dumpty fashion, simply dogmatic assertions. Instead, they are conclusions which are derived from particular linguistic premises. I want, in the time remaining, to present what I make out to be the elected linguistic premises, first of Jacques Derrida, then of Hillis Miller, in the confidence that if I misinterpret these theories, my errors will soon be challenged and corrected. Let me eliminate suspense by saying at the beginning that I don't think that their radically skeptical conclusions from these premises are wrong. On the contrary, I believe that their conclusions are right—in fact, they are *infallibly* right, and that's where the trouble lies.

1

It is often said that Derrida and those who follow his lead subordinate all inquiries to a prior inquiry into language. This is true enough, but not specific enough, for it does not distinguish Derrida's work from what Richard Rorty calls 'the linguistic turn'[6] which characterizes modern Anglo–American philosophy and also a great part of Anglo–American literary criticism, including the 'New Criticism,' of the last half-century. What is distinctive about Derrida is first that, like other French structuralists, he shifts his inquiry from language to *écriture*, the written or printed text; and second that he conceives a text in an extraordinarily limited fashion.

Derrida's initial and decisive strategy is to disestablish the priority, in traditional views of language, of speech over writing. By priority I mean the use of oral discourse as the conceptual model from which to derive the semantic and other features of written language and of language in general. And Derrida's shift to elementary reference is to a written text which consists of what we find when we look at it—to 'un texte déjà écrit, noir sur blanc. [a text already written, black on white]'[7] In the dazzling play of Derrida's expositions, his ultimate recourse is to these black marks on white paper as the sole things that are actually present in reading, and so are not fictitious constructs, illusions, phantasms; the visual features of these black-on-blanks he expands in multiple dimensions of elaborately figurative significance, only to contract them again, at telling moments, to their elemental status. The only things that are patently there when we look at a text are 'marks' that are demarcated, and separated into groups, by 'blanks'; there are also 'spaces,' 'margins,' and the 'repetitions' and 'differences' that we find when we compare individual marks and groups of marks. By his rhetorical mastery Derrida solicits us to follow him in his move to these new premises, and to allow ourselves to be locked into them. This move is from what he calls the closed 'logocentric' model of all traditional or 'classical' views of language (which, he maintains, is based on the illusion of a Platonic or Christian transcendent being or presence, serving as the origin and guarantor of meanings) to what I shall call his own graphocentric model, in which the sole presences are marks-on-blanks.

By this bold move Derrida puts out of play, before the game even begins, every source of norms, controls, or indicators which, in the ordinary use and experience of language, set a limit to what we can mean and what we can be understood to mean. Since the only givens are already-existing marks, 'déjà écrit,' we are denied recourse to a speaking or writing subject, or ego, or cogito, or consciousness, and so to any possible agency for the intention of meaning something ('vouloir dire'); all such agencies are relegated to the status of fictions generated by language, readily dissolved by deconstructive analysis. By this move he leaves us no place for referring to how we learn to speak, understand, or read language, and how, by interaction with more competent users and by our own developing experience with language, we come to recognize and correct our mistakes in speaking or understanding. The author is translated by Derrida (when he's not speaking in the momentary shorthand of traditional fictions) to a status as one more mark among other marks, placed at the head or the end of a text or set of texts, which are denominated as 'bodies of work identified according to the "proper name" of a signature.'[8] Even syntax, the organization of words into a significant sentence, is given no role in determining the meanings of component words, for according to the graphocentric model, when we look at a page we see no organization but only a 'chain' of grouped marks, a sequence of individual signs.

It is the notion of 'the sign' that allows Derrida a limited opening-out of his premises. For he brings to a text the knowledge that the marks on a page are not random markings, but signs, and that a sign has a dual aspect as signifier and signified, signal and concept, or mark-with-meaning. But these meanings, when we look at a page, are not there, either as physical or mental presences. To account for significance, Derrida turns to a highly specialized and elaborated use of Saussure's notion that the identity either of the sound or of the significance of a sign does not consist in a positive attribute, but in a negative (or relational) attribute—that is, its 'difference,' or differentiability, from other sounds and other significations within a particular linguistic system.[9] This notion of difference is readily available to Derrida, because inspection of the printed page shows that some marks and sets of marks repeat each other, but that others differ from each other. In Derrida's theory 'difference'—not 'the difference between a and b and c . . .' but simply 'difference' in itself—supplements the static elements of a text with an essential operative term, and as such (somewhat in the fashion of the term 'negativity' in the dialectic of Hegel) it performs prodigies. For 'difference' puts into motion the incessant play (*jeu*) of signification that goes on within the seeming immobility of the marks on the printed page.

To account for what is distinctive in the signification of a sign Derrida puts forward the term 'trace,' which he says is not a presence, though it functions as a kind of 'simulacrum' of a signified presence. Any signification that difference has activated in a signifier in the past remains active as a 'trace' in the present instance as it will in the future,[10] and the 'sedimentation' of traces which a signifier has accumulated constitutes the diversity in the play of its present significations. This trace is an elusive aspect of a text which is not, yet functions as though it were; it plays a role without being 'present', it 'appears/disappears'; 'in presenting itself it effaces itself.'[11] Any attempt to define or interpret the significance of a sign or chain of signs consists in nothing more than the interpreter's putting in its place another sign or chain of signs, 'sign-substitutions,' whose self-effacing traces merely defer laterally, from substitution to substitution, the fixed and present meaning (or the signified 'presence') we vainly pursue. The promise that the trace seems to offer of a presence on which the play of signification can come to rest in a determinate reference is thus never realizable, but incessantly deferred, put off, delayed. Derrida coins what in French is the portmanteau term *différance* (spelled -*a*nce, and fusing the notions of differing and deferring) to indicate the endless play of generated significances, in which the reference is interminably postponed.[12] The conclusion, as Derrida puts it, is that 'the central signified, the originating or transcendental signified' is revealed to be 'never absolutely present outside a system of differences,' and this 'absence of an ultimate signified extends the domain and play of signification to infinity.'[13]

What Derrida's conclusion comes to is that no sign or chain of signs can have a determinate meaning. But it seems to me that Derrida reaches this conclusion by a process which, in its own way, is no less dependent on an origin, ground, and end, and which is no less remorselessly 'teleological,' than the most rigorous of the metaphysical systems that he uses his conclusions to deconstruct. His origin and ground are his graphocentric premises, the closed chamber of texts for which he invites us to abandon our ordinary realm of experience in speaking, hearing, reading, and understanding language. And from such a beginning we move to a foregone conclusion. For Derrida's chamber of texts is a sealed echo-chamber in which meanings are reduced to a ceaseless echolalia, a vertical and lateral reverberation from sign to sign of ghostly non-presences emanating from no voice, intended by no one, referring to nothing, bombinating in a void.

For the mirage of traditional interpretation, which vainly undertakes to determine what an author meant, Derrida proposes the alternative that we deliver ourselves over to a free participation in the infinite free-play of signification opened out by the signs in a text. And on this cheerless prospect of language and the cultural enterprise in ruins Derrida bids us to try to gaze, not with a Rousseauistic nostalgia for a lost security as to meaning which we never in fact possessed, but instead with 'a Nietzschean *affirmation*, the joyous affirmation of the play of the world and of the innocence of becoming, the affirmation of a world of signs without error [*faute*], without truth, without origin, which is offered to an active interpretation. . . . And it plays without security. . . . In absolute chance, affirmation also surrenders itself to *genetic* indeterminacy, to the *seminal* chanciness [*aventure*] of the trace.'[14] The graphocentric premises eventuate in what is patently a metaphysics, a world-view of the free and unceasing play of *différance* which (since we can only glimpse this world by striking free of language, which inescapably implicates the entire metaphysics of presence that this view replaces) we are not able even to name. Derrida's vision is thus, as he puts it, of an 'as yet unnamable something which cannot announce itself except . . . under the species of a non-species, under the formless form, mute, infant, and terrifying, of monstrosity.'[15]

2

Hillis Miller sets up an apt distinction between two classes of current structuralist critics, the 'canny critics' and the 'uncanny critics.' The canny critics cling still to the possibility of 'a structuralist-inspired criticism as a rational and rationalizable activity, with agreed-upon rules of procedure, given facts, and measurable results.' The uncanny critics have renounced such a nostalgia for impossible certainties.[16] And as himself an uncanny critic, Miller's persistent enterprise is to get us to share, in each of the diverse works that he criticizes, its self-deconstructive revelation that in default of any possible origin, ground, presence, or end, it is an interminable free-play of indeterminable meanings.

Like Derrida, Miller sets up as his given the written text, 'innocent black marks on a page'[17] which are endowed with traces, or vestiges of meaning; he then employs a variety of strategies that maximize the number and diversity of the possible meanings while minimizing any factors that might limit their free-play. It is worthwhile to note briefly two of those strategies.

For one thing Miller applies the terms 'interpretation' and 'meaning' in an extremely capacious way, so as to conflate linguistic utterance or writing with any metaphysical representation of theory or of 'fact' about the physical world. These diverse realms are treated equivalently as 'texts' which are 'read' or 'interpreted.' He thus leaves no room for taking into account that language, unlike the physical world, is a cultural institution that developed expressly in order to mean something and to convey what is meant to members of a community who have learned how to use and interpret language. And within the realm of explicitly verbal texts, Miller allows for no distinction with regard to the kinds of norms that may obtain or may not obtain for the 'interpretation' of the entire corpus of an individual author's writings, or of a single work in its totality, or of a particular passage, sentence, or word within that work. As a critical pluralist, I would agree that there are a diversity of sound (though not equally adequate) interpretations of the play *King Lear*, yet I claim to know precisely what Lear meant when he said, 'Pray you undo this button.'

A second strategy is related to Derrida's treatment of the 'trace.' Like Derrida, Miller excludes by his elected premises any control or limitation of signification by reference to the uses of a word or phrase that are current at the time an author writes, or to an author's intention, or to the verbal or generic context in which a word occurs. Any word within a given text—or at least any 'key word,' as he calls it, that he picks out for a special scrutiny—can thus be claimed to signify any and all of the diverse things it has signified in the varied forms that the signifier has assumed through its recorded history; and not only in a particular language, such as English or French, but back through its etymology in Latin and Greek all the way to its postulated Indo–European root. Whenever and by whomever and in whatever context a printed word is used, therefore, the limits of what it can be said to mean in that use are set only by what the interpreter can find in historical and etymological dictionaries, supplemented by any further information that the interpreter's own erudition can provide. Hence Miller's persistent recourse to etymology—and even to the significance of the shapes of the printed letters in the altering form of a word—in expounding the texts to which he turns his critical attention.[18]

Endowed thus with the sedimented meanings accumulated over its total history, but stripped of any norms of selecting some of these and rejecting others, a key word—like the larger passage or total text of which the word is an element—becomes (in the phrase Miller cites from Mallarmé) a *suspens vibratoire*,[19] a vibratory suspension of equally likely meanings, and these are bound to include 'incompatible' or 'irreconcilable' or 'contradictory' meanings. The conclusion from these views Miller formulates in a variety of ways: a key word, or a passage, or a text, since it is a ceaseless play of anomalous meanings, is 'indeterminable,' 'undecipherable,' 'unreadable,' 'undecidable.'[20] Or more bluntly: 'All reading is misreading.' 'Any reading can be shown to be a misreading on evidence drawn from the text itself.' But in misreading a text, the interpreter is merely repeating what the text itself has done before him, for 'any literary text, with more or less explicitness or clarity, already reads or misreads itself.'[21] To say that this concept of interpretation cuts the ground out from under the kind of history I undertook

271

to write is to take a very parochial view of what is involved; for what it comes to is that no text, in part or whole, can mean anything in particular, and that we can never say just what anyone means by anything he writes.

But if all interpretation is misinterpretation, and if all criticism (like all history) of texts can engage only with a critic's own misconstruction, why bother to carry on the activities of interpretation and criticism? Hillis Miller poses this question more than once. He presents his answers in terms of his favorite analogues for the interpretive activity, which he explores with an unflagging resourcefulness. These analogues figure the text we read as a Cretan labyrinth, and also as the texture of a spider's web; the two figures, he points out, have been fused in earlier conflations in the myth of Ariadne's thread, by which Theseus retraces the windings of the labyrinth, and of Arachne's thread, with which she spins her web.[22] Here is one of Miller's answers to the question, why pursue the critical enterprise?

> Pater's writings, like those of other major authors in the Occidental tradition, are at once open to interpretation and ultimately indecipherable, unreadable. His texts lead the critic deeper and deeper into a labyrinth until he confronts a final aporia. This does not mean, however, that the reader must give up from the beginning the attempt to understand Pater. Only by going all the way into the labyrinth, following the thread of a given clue, can the critic reach the blind alley, vacant of any Minotaur, that impasse which is the end point of interpretation.[23]

Now, I make bold to claim that I understand Miller's passage, and that what it says, in part, is that the deconstructive critic's act of interpretation has a beginning and an end; that it begins as an intentional, goal-oriented quest; and that this quest is to end in an impasse.

The reaching of the interpretive aporia or impasse precipitates what Miller calls 'the uncanny moment'—the moment in which the critic, thinking to deconstruct the text, finds that he has simply participated in the ceaseless play of the text as a self-deconstructive artefact. Here is another of Miler's statements, in which he describes both his own and Derrida's procedure:

> Deconstruction as a mode of interpretation works by a careful and circumspect entering of each textual labyrinth. . . . The deconstructive critic seeks to find, by this process of retracing, the element in the system studied which is alogical, the thread in the text in question which will unravel it all, or the loose stone which will pull down the whole building. The deconstruction, rather, annihilates the ground on which the building stands by showing that the text has already annihilated that ground, knowingly or unknowingly. Deconstruction is not a dismantling of the structure of a text but a demonstration that it has already dismantled itself.[24]

The uncanny moment in interpretation, as Miller phrases it elsewhere, is a sudden '*mise en abyme*' in which the bottom drops away and, in the endless regress of the self-baffling free-play of meanings in the very signs which both reveal an abyss and, by naming it, cover it over, we catch a glimpse of the abyss itself in a 'vertigo of the underlying nothingness.'[25]

The 'deconstructive critic,' Miller has said, '*seeks* to find' the alogical element in a text, the thread which, when pulled, will unravel the whole texture. Given the game Miller has set up, with its graphocentric premises and freedom of interpretive maneuver, the infallible rule of the deconstructive quest is, 'Seek and ye shall find.' The deconstructive method works, because it can't help working; it is a can't-fail enterprise; there is no complex passage of verse or prose which could possibly serve as a counter-instance to test its validity or limits. And the uncanny critic, whatever the variousness and distinctiveness of the texts to which he applies his strategies, is bound to find that they all reduce to one thing and one thing only. In Miller's own words: each deconstructive reading, 'performed on any literary, philosophical, or critical text . . . reaches, in the particular way the given text allows it, the "same" moment of an aporia. . . . The reading comes back again and again, with different texts, to the "same" impasse.'[26]

It is of no avail to point out such criticism has nothing whatever to do with our common experience of the uniqueness, the rich variety, and the passionate human concerns in works of literature, philosophy, or criticism—these are matters which are among the linguistic illusions that the criticism dismantles. There are, I want to emphasize, rich rewards in reading Miller, as in reading Derrida, which include a delight in his resourceful play of mind and language and the many and striking insights yielded by his wide reading and by his sharp eye for unsuspected congruities and differences in our heritage of literary and philosophical writings. But these rewards are yielded by the way, and that way is always to the ultimate experience of vertigo, the uncanny *frisson* at teetering with him on the brink of the abyss; and even the shock of this discovery is soon dulled by its expected and invariable recurrence.

I shall cite a final passage to exemplify the deft and inventive play of Miller's rhetoric, punning, and figuration, which give his formulations of the *mise en abyme* a charm that is hard to resist. In it he imposes his fused analogues of labyrinth and web and abyss on the black-on-blanks which constitute the elemental given of the deconstructive premises:

> Far from providing a benign escape from the maze, Ariadne's thread makes the labyrinth, is the labyrinth. The interpretation or solving of the puzzles of the textual web only adds more filaments to the web. One can never escape from the labyrinth because the activity of escaping makes more labyrinth, the thread of a linear narrative or story. Criticism is the production of more thread to embroider the texture or textile already there. This thread is like a filament of ink which flows from the pen of the writer, keeping him in the web but suspending him also over the chasm, the blank page that thin line hides.[27]

To interpret: Hillis Miller, suspended by the labyrinthine lines of a textual web over the abyss that those black lines demarcate on the blank page, busies himself to unravel the web that keeps him from plunging into the blank-abyss, but finds he can do so only by an act of writing which spins a further web of lines, equally vulnerable to deconstruction, but only by another movement of the pen that will trace still another inky net over the ever-receding abyss. As Miller remarks, I suppose ruefully, at the end of the passage I quoted, 'In one version of Ariadne's story she is said to have hanged herself with her thread in despair after being abandoned by Theseus.'

3

What is one to say in response to this abysmal vision of the textual world of literature, philosophy, and all the other achievements of mankind in the medium of language? There is, I think, only one adequate response, and that is the one that William Blake made to the Angel in *The Marriage of Heaven and Hell*. After they had groped their way down a 'winding cavern,' the Angel revealed to Blake a ghastly vision of hell as an 'infinite Abyss'; in it was 'the sun, black but shining,' around which were 'fiery tracks on which revolv'd vast spiders.' But no sooner, says Blake, had 'my friend the Angel' departed, 'than this appearance was no more, but I found myself sitting on a pleasant bank beside a river by moon light, hearing a harper who sung to a harp.' The Angel, 'surprised asked me how I escaped? I answered: "All that we saw was owing to your metaphysics."'

As a deconstructive Angel, Hillis Miller, I am happy to say, is not serious about deconstruction, in Hegel's sense of 'serious'; that is, he does not entirely and consistently commit himself to the consequences of his premises. He is in fact, fortunately for us, a double agent who plays the game of language by two very different sets of rules. One of the games he plays is that of a deconstructive critic of literary texts. The other is the game he will play in a minute or two when he steps out of his graphocentric premises onto this platform and begins to talk to us.

I shall hazard a prediction as to what Miller will do then. He will have determinate things to say and will masterfully exploit the resources of language to express these things clearly and forcibly, addressing himself to us in the confidence that we, to the degree that we have mastered the constitutive norms of this kind of discourse, will approximate what he means. He will show no inordinate theoretical difficulties about beginning his discourse or conducting it through its middle to an end. What he says will manifest, by immediate inference, a thinking subject or ego and a distinctive and continuant ethos, so that those of you who, like myself, know and admire his recent writings will be surprised and delighted by particularities of what he says, but will correctly anticipate both its general tenor and its highly distinctive style and manner of proceeding. What he says, furthermore, will manifest a feeling as well as thinking subject; and unless it possesses a superhuman forbearance, this subject will express some natural irritation that I, an old friend, should so obtusely have misinterpreted what he has said in print about his critical intentions.

Before coming here, Miller worked his thoughts (which involved inner speech) into the form of writing. On this platform, he will proceed to convert this writing to speech; and it is safe to say—since our chairman is himself a double agent, editor of a critical journal as well as organizer of this symposium—that soon his speech will be reconverted to writing and presented to the public. This substitution of *écriture* for *parole* will certainly make a difference, but not an absolute difference; what Miller says here, that is, will not jump an ontological gap to the printed page, shedding on the way all the features that made it intelligible as discourse. For each of his readers will be able to reconvert the black-on-blanks back into speech, which he will hear in his mind's ear; he will perceive the words not simply as marks nor as sounds, but as already invested with meaning; also, by immediate inference, he will be aware in his reading of an intelligent subject, very similar to the one we will infer while listening to him here, who organizes the well-formed and significant sentences and marshals the argument conveyed by the text.

There is no linguistic or any other law we can appeal to that will prevent a deconstructive critic from bringing his graphocentric procedures to bear on the printed version of Hillis Miller's discourse—or of mine, or of Wayne Booth's— and if he does, he will infallibly be able to translate the text into a vertiginous *mise en abyme*. But those of us who stubbornly refuse to substitute the rules of the deconstructive enterprise for our ordinary skill and tact at language will find that we are able to understand this text very well. In many ways, in fact, we will understand it better than while hearing it in the mode of oral discourse, for the institution of print will render the fleeting words of his speech by a durable graphic correlate which will enable us to take our own and not the speaker's time in attending to it, as well as to re-read it, to collocate, and to ponder until we are satisfied that we have approximated the author's meaning.

After Hillis Miller and I have pondered in this way over the text of the other's discourse, we will probably, as experience in such matters indicates, continue essentially to disagree. By this I mean that neither of us is apt to find the other's reasons so compelling as to get him to change his own interpretive premises and aims. But in the process, each will have come to see more clearly what the other's reasons are for doing what he does, and no doubt come to discover that some of these reasons are indeed good reason in that, however short of being compelling, they have a bearing on the issue in question. In brief, insofar as we set ourselves, in the old-fashioned way, to make out what the other means by what he says, I am confident that we shall come to a better mutual understanding. After all, without that confidence that we can use language to say what we mean and can interpret language so as to determine what was meant, there is no rationale for the dialogue in which we are now engaged.

NOTES

1. 'Rationality and Imagination in Cultural History: A Reply to Wayne Booth,' *Critical Inquiry* 2 (Spring 1976): 456–60.
2. 'Tradition and Difference,' *Diacritics* 2 (Winter 1972): 6.
3. Ibid., pp. 10–11.
4. Ibid., pp. 8, 12.
5. Ibid.
6. Richard Rorty, ed., *The Linguistic Turn* (Chicago and London, 1967).

7. Jacques Derrida, 'La Double séance,' in *La Dissémination* (Paris, 1972), p. 203.
8. Derrida, 'La Mythologie blanche: la métaphore dans le texte philosophique,' in *Marges de la philosophie* (Paris, 1972), p. 304. Translations throughout are my own.
9. Ferdinand de Saussure, *Course in General Linguistics*, trans. Wade Baskin (New York, 1959), pp. 117–21.
10. Derrida, 'La Différance,' in *Marges de la philosophie*, pp. 12–14, 25.
11. Ibid., pp. 23–24.
12. In the traditional or 'classical' theory of signs, as Derrida describes the view that he dismantles, the sign is taken to be 'a deferred presence ... the circulation of signs defers the moment in which we will be able to encounter the thing itself, to get hold of it, consume or expend it, touch it, see it, have a present intuition of it' (ibid., p. 9). See also 'Hors livre' in *La Dissémination*, pp. 10–11.
13. Derrida, 'La Structure, le signe et le jeu dans le discours des sciences humaines,' in *L'Écriture et la différance* (Paris, 1967), p. 411.
14. Ibid., p. 427. Derrida adds that this 'interpretation of interpretation,' which affirms free-play ... tries to pass beyond man and humanism. ...' On the coming 'monstrosity,' see also *De la grammatologie* (Paris, 1967), p. 14.
15. Derrida, 'La Structure, le signe,' p. 428. 'We possess no language ... which is alien to this history: we cannot express a single destructive proposition which will not already have slipped into the form, the logic, and the implicit postulates of that very thing that it seeks to oppose.' 'Each limited borrowing drags along with it all of metaphysics' (pp. 412–13).
16. J. Hillis Miller, 'Stevens' Rock and Criticism as Cure, II,' *The Georgia Review* 30 (Summer 1976): 335–36.
17. Miller, 'Walter Pater: A Partial Portrait,' *Daedalus* 105 (Winter 1976): 107.
18. See, for example, his unfolding of the meanings of 'cure' and 'absurd' in 'Stevens' Rock and Criticism as Cure,' I, *The Georgia Review* 30 (Spring 1976): 6–11. For his analysis of significance in the altering shapes, through history, of the printed form of a word see his exposition of *abyme*, ibid., p. 11; also his exposition of the letter x in 'Ariadne's Thread: Repetition and the Narrative Line,' *Critical Inquiry* 3 (Autumn 1976): 75–76.
19. 'Tradition and Difference,' p. 12.
20. See, e.g., 'Stevens' Rock,' I, pp. 9–11; 'Walter Pater,' p. 111.
21. 'Walter Pater,' p. 98; 'Stevens' Rock, II,' p. 333.
22. 'Ariadne's Thread,' p. 66.
23. 'Walter Pater,' p. 112.
24. 'Stevens' Rock, II,' p. 341. See also 'Walter Pater,' p. 101, and 'Ariadne's Thread,' p. 74.
25. Stevens' Rock,' I, pp. 11–12. The unnamable abyss which Miller glimpses has its parallel in the unnamable and terrifying monstrosity which Derrida glimpses; see above, p. 432.
26. 'Deconstructing the Deconstructors.' *Diacritics* 5 (Summer 1975): 30.
27. 'Stevens' Rock, II,' p. 337.

16 J. Hillis Miller

J. Hillis Miller (b. 1928) has taught at several American universities, including Johns Hopkins and Yale, where he is now Professor of English. His early work on nineteenth- and twentieth-century literature, such as *The Disappearance of God* (1963), *Poets of Reality* (1965) and *Thomas Hardy: distance and desire* (1970) was influenced by the Geneva School of phenomenological criticism (see headnote on Iser, above) on whom Miller wrote a much-cited article ('The Geneva School', *Critical Quarterly* 8 [1966]). Later, Miller became an enthusiastic disciple of Jacques Derrida (see pp. 107–23, above), applying the French philosopher's theory and method to interpretive literary criticism in numerous books and articles of great intellectual brilliance (for example, *Fiction and Repetition* [1982] and *Ariadne's Thread* [1985]).

Like his colleagues at Yale, Harold Bloom and Geoffrey Hartman, Miller has been accused by traditional literary scholars of perversely indulging his own hermeneutic ingenuity at the expense of the texts and authors he discusses; and the paper reprinted below was originally occasioned by such an attack (see headnote to the preceding essay by M. H. Abrams.)

'The Critic as Host' was delivered at the same session of the MLA as Abrams' 'The Deconstructive Angel', and is not therefore a direct reply to the latter, though it can be read as such. Citing previous remarks by Wayne Booth and Abrams, asserting that deconstructive criticism is 'parasitic' upon the 'obvious and univocal' meaning of a literary text, Miller subjects these words to a characteristically brilliant and labyrinthine investigation, revealing paradox and internal contradiction where commonsense sees only simple concepts defined by their opposites. The aim is to demonstrate by a kind of practical criticism the poststructuralist axiom that 'language is not an instrument or tool in man's hands, a submissive means of thinking. Language rather thinks man and his "world", including poems.' A poem, like Shelley's *The Triumph of Time*, is only a special case of the intertextuality of all discourse.

'The Critic as Host' is reprinted here from *Critical Inquiry*, 3 (1977). A revised and expanded version of this paper, with more extensive discussion of *The Triumph of Time*, was published in *Deconstruction and Criticism* (1979) by Harold Bloom and others.

CROSS-REFERENCES: 6. Derrida
15. Abrams
21. De Man
25. Hartman

COMMENTARY: Christopher Norris, *Deconstruction: theory and practice* (1982) [Ch. 6, 'The American Connection']

The critic as host

> '*Je meurs où je m'attache*,'[a] Mr. Holt said with a polite grin. 'The ivy
> says so in the picture, and clings to the oak like a fond parasite as it is.'
> 'Parricide, sir!' cries Mrs. Tusher.
>
> —*Henry Esmond*, bk. 1, chap. 3

At one point in 'Rationality and Imagination in Cultural History' M. H. Abrams cites Wayne Booth's assertion that the 'deconstructionist' reading of a given work 'is plainly and simply parasitical' on 'the obvious or univocal reading.'[1] The latter is Abrams' phrase, the former Booth's. My citation of a citation is an example of a kind of chain which it will be part of any intention here to interrogate. What happens when a critical essay extracts a 'passage' and 'cites' it? Is this different from a citation, echo, or allusion within a poem? Is a citation an alien parasite within the body of its host, the main text, or is it the other way around, the interpretative text the parasite which surrounds and strangles the citation which is its host? The host feeds the parasite and makes its life possible, but at the same time is killed by it, as 'criticism' is often said to kill 'literature.' Or can host and parasite live happily together, in the domicile of the same text, feeding each other or sharing the food?

Abrams, in any case, goes on to add 'a more radical reply.' If 'deconstructionist principles' are taken seriously, he says, 'any history which relies on written texts becomes an impossibility.'[2] So be it. That is not much of an argument. A certain notion of history or of literary history, like a certain notion of determinable reading, might indeed be an impossibility, and if so, it might be better to know that, and not to fool oneself or be fooled. It might, or it might not. That something in the realm of interpretation is a demonstrable impossibility does not prevent it from being 'done,' as the abundance of histories, literary histories, and readings demonstrates. On the other hand, I should agree that 'the impossibility of reading should not be taken too lightly.'[3] It has consequences, for life and death, since it is inscribed, incorporated, in the bodies of individual human beings and in the body politic of our cultural life and death together.

'Parasitical'—the word is an interesting one. It suggests the image of 'the obvious or univocal reading' as the mighty, masculine oak or ash, rooted in the solid ground, endangered by the insidious twining around it of ivy, English or maybe poison, somehow feminine, secondary, defective, or dependent, a clinging vine, able to live in no other way but by drawing the life sap of its host, cutting

---

[a] 'I die where I attach myself.'

off its light and air. I think of the end of Thackeray's *Vanity Fair*: 'God bless you, honest William!—Farewell, dear Amelia—Grow green again, tender little parasite, round the rugged old oak to which you cling!' Or of Hardy's 'The Ivy-Wife,' of which here are the last two stanzas:

> In new affection next I strove
>> To coll an ash I saw,
> And he in trust received my love;
>> Till with my soft green claw
> I cramped and bound him as I wove . . .
>> Such was my love: ha-ha!
>
> By this I gained his strength and height
>> Without his rivalry.
> But in my triumph I lost sight
>> Of afterhaps. Soon he,
> Being bark-bound, flagged, snapped, fell outright,
>> And in his fall felled me!

These sad love stories of a domestic affection which nevertheless introduces the uncanny, the alien, the parasitical into the closed economy of the home, the *Unheimlich* into the *Heimlich*,[b] no doubt describe well enough the way some people may feel about the relation of a 'deconstructive' interpretation to 'the obvious or univocal reading.' The parasite is destroying the host. The alien has invaded the house, perhaps to kill the father of the family, in an act which does not look like parricide, but is. Is that 'obvious' reading in fact, however, so 'obvious' or even so 'univocal'? May it not be already that uncanny alien which is so close that it cannot be seen as strange, as host in the sense of enemy rather than host in the sense of open-handed dispenser of hospitality? Equivocal rather than univocal and most equivocal in its intimate familiarity and in its ability to have got itself taken for granted as 'obvious' and 'univocal,' one-voiced?

'Parasite' is one of those words which calls up its apparent 'opposite.' It has no meaning without that counterpart. There is no parasite without its host. At the same time both word and counterword subdivide and reveal themselves each to be fissured already within themselves and to be, like *Unheimlich, unheimlich*, an example of a double antithetical word. Words in 'para,' like words in 'ana,' have this as an intrinsic property, capability, or tendency. 'Para' as a prefix in English (sometimes 'par') indicates alongside, near or beside, beyond, incorrectly, resembling or similar to, subsidiary to, isomeric or polymeric to. In borrowed Greek compounds 'para' indicates beside, to the side of, alongside, beyond, wrongfully, harmfully, unfavorably, and among.[4] The words in 'para' form one branch of the tangled labyrinth of words using some form of the Indo-European root *per*, which is the 'base of prepositions and pre-verbs with the basic meaning

---

[b] *Unheimlich* is the German word for 'uncanny'. Miller implies that *Heimlich* means 'homely'. *Heim* is indeed the German word for 'home', but *heimlich* means 'secret'. For once Miller seems to have underestimated the duplicity of language.

of "forward," "through," and a wide range of extended senses such as "in front of," "before," "early," "first," "chief," "toward," "against," "near," "at," "around."'

I said words in 'para' are one branch of the labyrinth of 'pers,' but it is easy to see that the branch is itself a miniature labyrinth. 'Para' is an 'uncanny' double antithetical prefix signifying at once proximity and distance, similarity and difference, interiority and exteriority, something at once inside a domestic economy and outside it, something simultaneously this side of the boundary line, threshold, or margin, and at the same time beyond it, equivalent in status and at the same time secondary or subsidiary, submissive, as of guest to host, slave to master. A thing in 'para' is, moreover, not only simultaneously on both sides of the boundary line between inside and outside. It is also the boundary itself, the screen which is at once a permeable membrane connecting inside and outside, confusing them with one another, allowing the outside in, making the inside out, dividing them but also forming an ambiguous transition between one and the other. Though any given word in 'para' may seem to choose unequivocally or univocally one of these possibilities, the other meanings are always there as a shimmering or wavering in the word which makes it refuse to stay still in a sentence, like a slightly alien guest within the syntactical closure where all the words are family friends together. Words in 'para' include: parachute, paradigm, parasol, the French *paravent* (screen protecting against the wind), and *parapluie* (umbrella), paragon, paradox, parapet, parataxis, parapraxis, parabasis, paraphrase, paragraph, paraph, paralysis, paranoia, paraphernalia, parallel, parallax, parameter, parable, paresthesia, paramnesia, paregoric, parergon, paramorph, paramecium, Paraclete, paramedical, paralegal—and parasite.

'Parasite' comes from the Greek, *parasitos*, etymologically: 'beside the grain,' *para*, beside (in this case) plus *sitos*, grain, food. 'Sitology' is the science of foods, nutrition, and diet. 'Parasite' was originally something positive, a fellow guest, someone sharing the food with you, there with you beside the grain. Later on, 'parasite' came to mean a professional dinner guest, someone expert at cadging invitations without ever giving dinners in return. From this developed the two main modern meanings in English, the biological and the social. A parasite is (1) 'Any organism that grows, feeds, and is sheltered on or in a different organism while contributing nothing to the survival of its host'; (2) 'A person who habitually takes advantage of the generosity of others without making any useful return.' To call a kind of criticism 'parasitical' is, in either case, strong language.

A curious system of thought, or of language, or of social organization (in fact all three at once) is implicit in the word parasite. There is no parasite without a host. The host and the somewhat sinister or subversive parasite are fellow guests beside the food, sharing it. On the other hand, the host is himself the food, his substance consumed without recompense, as when one says, 'He is eating me out of house and home.' The host may then become the host in another sense, not etymologically connected. The word 'Host' is of course the name for the consecrated bread or wafer of the Eucharist, from Middle English *oste*, from Old French *oiste*, from Latin *hostia*, sacrifice, victim.

If the host is both eater and eaten, he also contains in himself the double antithetical relation of host and guest, guest in the bifold sense of friendly presence and alien invader. The words 'host' and 'guest' go back in fact to the same etymological root: *ghos-ti*, stranger, guest, host, properly 'someone with whom one has reciprocal duties of hospitality.' The modern English word 'host' in this alternative sense comes from the Middle English (*h*)*oste*, from Old French, host, guest, from Latin *hospes* (stem *hospit-*), guest, host, stranger. The 'pes' or 'pit' in the Latin words and in such modern English words as 'hospital' and 'hospitality' is from another root, *pot*, meaning 'master.' The compound or bifurcated root *ghos-pot* meant 'master of guests,' 'one who symbolizes the relationship of reciprocal hospitality,' as in the Slavic *gospodi*, Lord, sir, master. 'Guest,' on the other hand, is from Middle English *gest*, from Old Norse *gestr*, from *ghos-ti*, the same root as for 'host.' A host is a guest, and a guest is a host. A host is a host. The relation of household master offering hospitality to a guest and the guest receiving it, of host and parasite in the original sense of 'fellow guest,' is inclosed within the word 'host' itself. A host in the sense of a guest, moreover, is both a friendly visitor in the house and at the same time an alien presence who turns the home into a hotel, a neutral territory. Perhaps he is the first emissary of a host of enemies (from Latin *hostis* [stranger, enemy]), the first foot in the door, to be followed by a swarm of hostile strangers, to be met only by our own host, as the Christian deity is the Lord God of Hosts. The uncanny antithetical relation exists not only between pairs of words in this system, host and parasite, host and guest, but within each word in itself. It reforms itself in each polar opposite when that opposite is separated out, and it subverts or nullifies the apparently unequivocal relation of polarity which seems the conceptual scheme appropriate for thinking through the system. Each word in itself becomes separated by the strange logic of the 'para,' membrane which divides inside from outside and yet joins them in a hymeneal bond, or allows an osmotic mixing, making the strangers friends, the distant near, the dissimilar similar, the *Unheimlich heimlich*, the homely homey, without, for all its closeness and similarity, ceasing to be strange, distant, dissimilar.

What does all this have to do with poems and with the reading of poems? It is meant, first, as an 'example' of the deconstructive strategy of interpretation, applied, in this case, not to the text of a poem but to the cited fragment of a critical essay containing within itself a citation from another essay, like a parasite within its host. The 'example' is a fragment like those miniscule bits of some substance which are put in a tiny test tube and explored by certain techniques of analytical chemistry. To get so far or so much out of a little piece of language (and I have only begun to go as far as I mean to go), context after context widening out from these few phrases to include as their necessary milieux all the family of Indo-European languages, all the literature and conceptual thought within those languages, and all the permutations of our social structures of household economy, gift-giving and gift-receiving—this is a polemical implication of what I have said. It is an argument for the value of recognizing the great complexity and equivocal richness of apparently obvious or univocal language, even the language of criticism, which is in this respect continuous with the language of literature. This complexity and equivocal richness, my discussion of 'parasite' implies, resides in part in the fact that there is no conceptual expression without figure, and no intertwining of concept and figure without an implied story, narrative, or myth, in this case the story of the alien guest in the home. Deconstruction is an investigation of what is implied by this inherence of figure, concept, and narrative in one another. Deconstruction is therefore a rhetorical discipline.

My little example of a deconstructive strategy at work is meant, moreover, to indicate, no doubt inadequately, the hyperbolic exuberance, the letting language go as far as it will take one, or the going with a given text as far as it will go, to its limits, which is an essential part of the procedure. Its motto might be Wallace Stevens' couplet, his version of the way the prison-house of language may be a place of joy, even of expansion, in spite of remaining an enclosure and a place of suffering and deprivation: 'Natives of poverty, children of malheur,/ The gaiety of language is our seigneur.'[5] My little example is, finally, about what it exemplifies. It provides a model for the relation of critic to critic, for the incoherence within a single critic's language, for the asymmetrical relation of critical text to poem, for the incoherence within any single literary text, and for the skewed relation of a poem to its predecessors.

To speak of the 'deconstructive' reading of a poem as 'parasitical' on the 'obvious or univocal reading' is to enter, perhaps unwittingly, into the strange logic of the parasite, to make the univocal equivocal in spite of oneself, according to the law that language is not an instrument or tool in man's hands, a submissive means of thinking. Language rather thinks man and his 'world,' including poems, if he will allow it to do so. As Martin Heidegger, in 'Building Dwelling Thinking,' puts it: 'It is language that tells us about the nature of a thing, provided that we respect language's own nature.'[6]

The system of figurative thought (but what thought is not figurative?) inscribed within the word parasite and its associates, host and guest, invites us to recognize that the 'obvious or univocal reading' of a poem is not identical with the poem itself, as perhaps it may be easy to assume. Both readings, the 'univocal' one and the 'deconstructive' one, are fellow guests 'beside the grain,' host and guest, host and host, host and parasite, parasite and parasite. The relation is a triangle, not a polar opposition. There is always a third to whom the two are related, something before them or between them, which they divide, consume, or exchange, across which they meet. Or rather, the relation in question is always a chain, that strange sort of chain without beginning or end in which no commanding element (origin, goal, or underlying principle) may be identified, but in which there is always something earlier or something later to which any part of the chain on which one focuses refers and which keeps the chain open, undecidable. The relation between any two contiguous elements in this chain is that strange opposition which is of intimate kinship and at the same time of enmity. It is therefore not able to be encompassed in the ordinary logic of polar opposition, nor is it open to dialectical synthesis.

Moreover, each 'single element,' far from being unequivocally what it is, subdivides within itself to recapitulate the relation of parasite and host of which, on the large scale, it appears to be one or the other pole. On the one hand, the 'obvious or univocal reading' always contains the 'deconstructive reading' as a parasite encrypted within itself, as part of itself, and, on the other hand, the 'deconstructive' reading can by no means free itself from the metaphysical, logocentric reading which it means to contest. The poem in itself, then, is neither the host nor the parasite but the food they both need, host in another sense, the third element in this particular triangle. Both readings are at the same table together, bound by that strange relation of reciprocal obligation, of gift- or food-giving and gift- or food-receiving, which Marcel Mauss has analyzed in *The Gift*. The word 'gift,' in fact, in various languages, contains puns or figures which reform the logic or alogic of the relation of parasite and host I am exploring here. *Gift* in German means poison. To receive or give a gift is a profoundly dangerous or equivocal act. One of the French words for gift, *cadeau*, comes from the Latin *catena*, little chain, rings bound together in a series. Every gift is a ring or a chain,[7] and the gift-giver or gift-receiver enters into the endless ring or chain of reciprocal obligation which Mauss has identified as universally present in 'archaic' or 'civilized' societies. Martin Heidegger has appropriated this image in one of his most splendidly exuberant word plays as the necessary figure for the formulation of the perpetual interchange or mirror play among the fourfold entities making up 'the world': earth, sky, man, and the gods. The gift is the thing mirrored, passed back and forth among these, so brought into existence as a thing, as a present, as present, as a ring becomes a gift, currency, when it passes current between one person and another, for example as a wedding present:

> Nestling, malleable, pliant, compliant, nimble—in Old German these are
> called *ring* and *gering*. The mirror-play of the worlding world, as the
> ringing of the ring, wrests free the united four into their own compliancy,
> the circling compliancy of their presence. Out of the ringing mirror-play
> the thinging of the thing takes place.[8]

A chain, however, is precisely not a ring, but a series of rings, each ring open to receive the next, enclosed by the next, and the whole possibly open-ended, always open to the possibility of having another link added. The play between the enclosed exchange within the ring of like for like, in intimate 'nestling' domesticity, and the chain which opens the ring of the domestic enclosure to the alien, to the host in the sense of hostile, is my subject here. My argument is that the parasite is always already present within the host, the enemy always already within the house, the ring always an open chain.

That ring of gift-giving and gift-receiving, the mutual obligation to give and to take certain kinds of gifts at certain times, at weddings, at birthdays, at 'coming-out' or 'growing-up' parties, or when one is a guest in another man's house (what is called a 'bread-and-butter' present), operates in its own way as strongly in 'advanced' societies like our own as in the more 'archaic' ones Mauss discusses, for example in the highly formalized social relations represented so splendidly in the Norse Sagas. Gift-giving is the binding or sealing of that relation of reciprocal obligation expressed in the word 'host,' but it is also apotropaic, the warding off of the evil the parasite may do you or the evil your host may somehow do you if you do not recompense him for feeding you. A parasite in the wholly negative sense is the one who does not make this recompense and so goes through the world blocking the endless chain of gifting, so keeping it going. At the same time the gift itself may be the poison, the dangerous parasite, the paying back for an injury, even if that injury is no more serious than putting your friend, your guest, or your host in possession of what is known as a 'white elephant,' the sort of useless present which gathers dust in the attic. It is the gift itself which is the blocking agent, keeping the chain in perpetual self-generation. The gift is the thing always left over which obliges someone to give yet another gift, and its recipient yet another, and so on and on, the balance never coming right, as a poem invites an endless sequence of commentaries which never succeed in 'getting the poem right.'

The poem, in my figure, is that ambiguous gift, food, host in the sense of victim, sacrifice, that which is broken, divided, passed around, consumed by the critics canny and uncanny who are in that odd relation to one another of host and parasite. The poem, however, any poem, is, it is easy to see, parasitical in its turn on earlier poems, or contains earlier poems as enclosed parasites within itself, in another version of the perpetual reversal of parasite and host. If the poem is food and poison for the critics, it must in its turn have eaten. It must have been a cannibal consumer of earlier poems.

Take, for example, Shelley's 'The Triumph of Life.' It is inhabited, as its critics have shown, by a long chain of parasitical presences, echoes, allusions guests, ghosts of previous texts. These are present within the domicile of the poem in that curious phantasmal way, affirmed, negated, sublimated, twisted, straightened out, travestied, which Harold Bloom has begun to study and which it is one major task of literary interpretation today to investigate further and to define. The previous text is both the ground of the new one and something the new poem must annihilate by incorporating it, turning it into ghostly insubstantiality, so that it may perform its possible–impossible task of becoming its own ground. The new poem both needs the old texts and must destroy them. It is both parasitical on them, feeding ungraciously on their substance, and at the same time it is the sinister host which unmans them by inviting them into its home, as the Green Knight invites Gawain. Each previous link in the chain, in its turn, played the same role, as host and parasite, in relation to its predecessors. From the Old to the New Testament, from Ezekiel to Revelation, to Dante, to Ariosto and Spenser, to Milton, to Rousseau, to Wordsworth and Coleridge, the chain leads ultimately to 'The Triumph of Life.' That poem, in its turn, or Shelley's work generally, is present within the work of Hardy or Yeats or Stevens and forms part of a sequence in the major texts of Romantic nihilism including Nietzsche, Freud, Heidegger, and Blanchot, in a perpetual re-expression of the relation of host and parasite which forms itself again today in current criticism. It is present, for example, in the relation between 'univocal' and 'deconstructionist' readings of 'The Triumph of Life,' between the readings of Meyer Abrams and Harold Bloom, or between Abrams' reading of 'The Triumph of Life' and the one I have implicitly proposed here, or, in a perhaps more problematic way, between Harold Bloom and Jacques Derrida, or between Jacques Derrida and Paul de Man, or within the work of each one of these critics taken separately.

The inexorable law which makes the uncanny, 'undecidable,' or 'alogical' relation of host and parasite, heterogeneity within homogeneity, enemy within the home, re-form itself within each separate entity which had seemed, on the larger scale, to be one or the other, applies as much to critical essays as to the texts they treat. 'The Triumph of Life,' as I hope to show in another essay, contains within itself, jostling irreconcilably with one another, both logocentric metaphysics and nihilism. It is no accident that critics have disagreed about it. The meaning of 'The Triumph of Life' can never be reduced to any one 'univocal' reading, neither the 'obvious' one nor a single-minded deconstructionist one, if there could be such a thing, which there cannot. The poem, like all texts, is 'unreadable,' if by 'readable' one means open to a single, definitive, univocal interpretation. In fact, neither the 'obvious' reading nor the 'deconstructionist' reading is 'univocal.' Each contains, necessarily, its enemy within itself, is itself both host and parasite. The deconstructionist reading contains the obvious one and vice versa. Nihilism is an inalienable alien presence within Occidental metaphysics, both in poems and in the criticism of poems.

NOTES

1. *Critical Inquiry* 2, no. 3 (Spring 1976): 457–58. The first phrase is quoted from Wayne Booth, 'M. H. Abrams: Historian as Critic, Critic as Pluralist,' ibid., p. 441.
2. Ibid., p. 458.
3. Paul de Man, 'The Timid God,' *The Georgia Review* 29, no. 3 (Fall 1975): 558.
4. All definitions and etymologies in this essay come from *The American Heritage Dictionary of the English Language*, ed. William Morris (Boston, 1969).
5. 'Esthétique du Mal,' XI, 10–11.
6. *Poetry, Language, Thought*, trans. Albert Hofstadter (New York, 1971) p. 146; from 'Bauen Wohnen Denken,' *Vorträge und Aufsätze* (Pfullingen, 1967), 2:20: 'Der Zuspruch über das Wesen einer Sache kommt zu uns aus der Sprache, vorausgesetzt, dass wir deren eigenes Wesen achten.'
7. On the chain linking chain, gift, ring, anniversary, party, festival or feast, present (in both senses), and paraph or flourish of the pen, see Jacques Derrida, *Glas* (Paris, 1974), p. 271a.
8. 'The Thing,' *Poetry, Language, Thought*, p. 180; from 'Das Ding,' *Vorträge und Aufsätze*, 2:53: 'Schmiegsam, schmiedbar, geschmeidig, fügsam, leicht heisst in unserer alten deutschen Sprache 'ring' und 'gering.' Das Spiegel-Spiel der weltenden Welt entringt als das Gering des Ringes die einigen Vier in das eigene Fügsame, das Ringe ihres Wesens. Aus dem Spiegel-Spiel des Gerings des Ringen ereignet sich das Dingen des Dinges.'

17 Hélène Cixous

Hélène Cixous (b. 1938) was born in Algeria and teaches at the University of Paris, Vincennes. A sophisticated literary critic in the post-structuralist mode, and the author of a major study of James Joyce which has been translated into English (*The Exile of James Joyce* [1976]), Hélène Cixous is also the author of novels and plays. These two aspects of her life and work, the critical and the creative, converge in the radical feminist writing exemplified by 'Sorties', reprinted below. Although Hélène Cixous has, on occasion, repudiated the label 'feminist', on the grounds that it perpetuates the hierarchical opposition of masculine/feminine which she is trying to deconstruct, the import of her work is consistent with that of many self-styled feminist writers.

Hélène Cixous represents a distinctively French brand of radical feminism which centres on the concept of *écriture feminine*, or feminine writing—'the inscription of the female body and female difference in language and text', as Elaine Showalter defines it (see below, pp. 331–37). Though it has affinities with the criticism that arose out of the Anglo-American Women's Liberation Movement of the late 1960s and 70s, it is perhaps more directly indebted to the work of Simone de Beauvoir and the intellectual ferment generated by *les événements* of 1968 in Paris. Its emphasis is psychological rather than sociological, theoretical rather than pragmatic.

Lacan's revisionist reading of Freud, and Derrida's critique of logocentrism, are enlisted and to some extent implicated in Cixous' attack on patriarchal culture: Lacan's symbolic 'phallus' and Derrida's logocentrism are seen as two aspects of a pervasive and oppressive 'phallocentrism'.

'Sorties', which can mean in French, escapes, departures, outcomings, as well as having the military meaning which it has in English, was originally published in *La Jeune Neé* ('The Newly Born Woman') in 1975. This extract, translated by Ann Liddle, is reprinted from *New French Feminisms*, edited by Elaine Marks and Isabelle de Courtivron (1980).

CROSS-REFERENCES: 5. Lacan
                   20. Showalter
                   26. Mitchell
COMMENTARY: Toril Moi, *Sexual/Textual Politics* (1985) [Ch. 6, 'Hélène Cixous: an imaginary utopia']

Sorties

Where is she?

Activity/passivity,
Sun/Moon,
Culture/Nature,
Day/Night,

Father/Mother,
Head/heart,
Intelligible/sensitive,
Logos/Pathos.

Form, convex, step, advance, seed, progress.
Matter, concave, ground—which supports the step, receptacle.

Man
Woman

Always the same metaphor: we follow it, it transports us, in all of its forms, wherever a discourse is organized. The same thread, or double tress leads us, whether we are reading or speaking, through literature, philosophy, criticism, centuries of representation, of reflection.

Thought has always worked by opposition,
Speech/Writing
High/Low

By dual, *hierarchized*[1] oppositions. Superior/Inferior. Myths, legends, books. Philosophical systems. Wherever an ordering intervenes, a law organizes the thinkable by (dual, irreconcilable; or mitigable, dialectical) oppositions. And all the couples of oppositions are *couples*. Does this mean something? Is the fact that logocentrism subjects thought—all of the concepts, the codes, the values—to a two-term system, related to 'the' couple man/woman?

Nature/History,
Nature/Art,
Nature/Mind,
Passion/Action.

Theory of culture, theory of society, the ensemble of symbolic systems—art, religion, family, language,—everything elaborates the same systems. And the movement by which each opposition is set up to produce meaning is the movement

287

by which the couple is destroyed. A universal battlefield. Each time a war breaks out. Death is always at work.

Father/son   Relationships of authority, of privilege, of force.
Logos/writing Relationships: opposition, conflict, relief, reversion.
Master/slave   Violence. Repression.

And we perceive that the 'victory' always amounts to the same thing: it is hierarchized. The hierarchization subjects the entire conceptual organization to man. A male privilege, which can be seen in the opposition by which it sustains itself, between *activity* and *passivity*. Traditionally, the question of sexual difference is coupled with the same opposition: activity/passivity.

That goes a long way. If we examine the history of philosophy—in so far as philosophical discourse orders and reproduces all thought—we perceive[2] that: it is marked by an absolute constant, the orchestrator of values, which is precisely the opposition activity/passivity.

In philosophy, woman is always on the side of passivity. Every time the question comes up; when we examine kinship structures; whenever a family model is brought into play; in fact as soon as the ontological question is raised; as soon as you ask yourself what is meant by the question 'What is it?'; as soon as there is a will to say something. A will: desire, authority, you examine that, and you are led right back—to the father. You can even fail to notice that there's no place at all for women in the operation! In the extreme the world of 'being' can function to the exclusion of the mother. No need for mother—provided that there is something of the maternal: and it is the father then who acts as—is—the mother. Either the woman is passive; or she doesn't exist. What is left is unthinkable, unthought of. She does not enter into the oppositions, she is not coupled with the father (who is coupled with the son).

There is Mallarmé's[3] tragic dream, a father lamenting the mystery of paternity, which mourning tears out of the poet, the mourning of mournings, the death of the beloved son: this dream of a union between the father and the son—and no mother then. Man's dream is the face of death. Which always threatens him differently than it threatens woman.

'an alliance
a union, superb   And dream of masculine
—and the life   filiation, dream of God the father
remaining in me   emerging from himself
I shall use it   in his son,—and
to—   no mother then
so no mother then?'

She does not exist, she may be nonexistent; but there must be something of her. Of woman, upon whom he no longer depends, he retains only this space, always virginal, matter subjected to the desire that he wishes to imprint.

And if you examine literary history, it's the same story. It all refers back to man to *his* torment, his desire to be (at) the origin. Back to the father. There is an intrinsic bond between the philosophical and the literary (to the extent that it signifies, literature is commanded by the philosophical) and phallocentrism. The philosophical constructs itself starting with the abasement of woman. Subordination of the feminine to the masculine order which appears to be the condition for the functioning of the machine.

The challenging of this solidarity of logocentrism and phallocentrism has today become insistent enough—the bringing to light of the fate which has been imposed upon woman, of her burial—to threaten the stability of the masculine edifice which passed itself off as eternalnatural; by bringing forth from the world of femininity reflections, hypotheses which are necessarily ruinous for the bastion which still holds the authority. What would become of logocentrism, of the great philosophical systems, of world order in general if the rock upon which they founded their church were to crumble?

If it were to come out in a new day that the logocentric project had always been, undeniably, to *found* (fund)[4] phallocentrism, to insure for masculine order a rationale equal to history itself?

Then all the stories would have to be told differently, the future would be incalculable, the historical forces would, will, change hands, bodies; another thinking as yet not thinkable will transform the functioning of all society. Well, we are living through this very period when the conceptual foundation of a millenial culture is in process of being undermined by millions of a species of mole as yet not recognized.

When they awaken from among the dead, from among the words, from among the laws. . . .

What does one give?

The specific difference that has determined the movement of history as a movement of property is articulated between two economies that define themselves in relation to the problematics of giving.

The (political) economy of the masculine and of the feminine is organized by different requirements and constraints, which, when socialized and metaphorized, produce signs, relationships of power, relationships of production and of reproduction, an entire immense system of cultural inscription readable as masculine or feminine.

I am careful here to use the *qualifiers* of sexual difference, in order to avoid the confusion man/masculine, woman/feminine: for there are men who do not repress their femininity, women who more or less forcefully inscribe their masculinity. The difference is not, of course, distributed according to socially determined 'sexes.' Furthermore, when I speak of political economy and of libidinal economy, in putting the two together, I am not bringing into play the false question of origin, that tall tale sustained by male privilege. We must guard against falling complacently or blindly into the essentialist ideological interpretation, as, for example, Freud and Jones, in different ways, ventured to do; in their quarrel over the subject of feminine sexuality, both of them, starting from opposite points of view, came to support the awesome thesis of a 'natural,' anatomical determination of sexual difference-opposition. And from there on, both implicitly support phallocentrism's position of power.

Let us review the main points of the opposing positions: [Ernest] Jones (in *Early Feminine Sexuality*), using an ambiguous approach, attacks the Freudian theses that make of woman an imperfect man.

For Freud:

(1) the 'fatality' of the feminine situation is a result of an anatomical 'defectiveness.'

(2) there is only one libido, and its essence is male; the inscription of sexual difference begins only with a phallic phase which both boys and girls go through. Until then, the girl has been a sort of little boy: the genital organization of the infantile libido is articulated by the equivalence activity/masculinity; the vagina has not as yet been 'discovered.'

(3) the first love object being, for both sexes, the mother, it is only for the boy that love of the opposite sex is 'natural.'

For Jones: femininity is an autonomous 'essence.'

From the outset (starting from the age of six months) the girl has a *feminine* desire for her father; an analysis of the little girl's earliest fantasms would in fact show that, in place of the breast which is perceived as disappointing, it is the penis that is desired, or an object of the same form (by an analogical displacement). It follows, since we are already into the chain of substitutions, that in the series of partial objects, in place of the penis, would come the child—for in order to counter Freud, Jones docilely returns to the Freudian terrain. And then some. From the equation breast–penis–child, he concludes that the little girl experiences with regard to the father a primary desire. (And this would include the desire to have a child by the father as well.) And, of course, the girl also has a primary love for the opposite sex. She too, then, has a right to her Oedipal complex as a primary formation, and to the threat of mutilation by the mother. At last she is a woman, anatomically, without defect: her clitoris is not a minipenis. Clitoral masturbation is not, as Freud claims, a masculine practice. And it would seem in light of precocious. fantasms that the vagina is discovered very early.

In fact, in affirming that there is a specific femininity (while in other respects preserving the theses of an orthodoxy) it is still phallocentrism that Jones re-inforces, on the pretext of taking the part of femininity (and of God, who he recalls created them male and female—!). And bisexuality vanishes into the unbridged abyss that separates the opponents here.

As for Freud, if we subscribe to what he sets forth when he identifies with Napoleon in his article of 1933 on *The Disappearance of the Oedipus Complex*:

'anatomy is destiny,' then we participate in the sentencing to death of woman. And in the completion of all History.

That the difference between the sexes may have psychic consequences is undeniable. But they are surely not reducible to those designated by a Freudian analysis. Starting with the relationship of the two sexes to the Oedipal complex, the boy and the girl are oriented toward a division of social roles so that women 'inescapably' have a lesser productivity, because they 'sublimate' less than men and because symbolic activity, hence the production of culture, is men's doing.[5]

Freud moreover starts from what he calls the *anatomical* difference between the sexes. And we know how that is pictured in his eyes: as the difference between having/not having the phallus. With reference to these precious parts. Starting from what will be specified, by Lacan, as the transcendental signifier.

But *sexual difference* is not determined merely by the fantasized relationship to anatomy, which is based, to a great extent, upon the point of *view*, therefore upon a strange importance accorded [by Freud and Lacan] to exteriority and to the specular in the elaboration of sexuality. A voyeur's theory, of course.

No, it is at the level of sexual pleasure [*jouissance*][6] in my opinion that the difference makes itself most clearly apparent in as far as woman's libidinal economy is neither identifiable by a man nor referable to the masculine economy.

For me, the question 'What does she want?' that they ask of woman, a question that in fact woman asks herself because they ask it of her, because precisely there is so little place in society for her desire that she ends up by dint of not knowing what to do with it, no longer knowing where to put it, or if she has any, conceals the most immediate and the most urgent question: 'How do I experience sexual pleasure?' What is feminine *sexual pleasure*, where does it take place, how is it inscribed at the level of her body, of her unconscious? And then how is it put into writing?

We can go on at length about a hypothetical prehistory and about a matriarchal era. Or we can, as did Bachofen,[7] attempt to reconstitute a gynecocratic society, and to deduce from it poetic and mythical effects that have a powerfully subversive import with regard to the family and to male power.

All the other ways of depicting the history of power, property, masculine domination, the constitution of the State, the ideological apparatus have their effectiveness. But the change taking place has nothing to do with questions of 'origin'. Phallocentrism *is*. History has never produced, recorded anything but that. Which does not mean that this form is inevitable or natural. Phallocentrism is the enemy. Of *everyone*. Men stand to lose by it, differently but as seriously as women. And it is time to transform. To invent the other history.

There is no such thing as 'destiny,' 'nature,' or essence, but living structures, caught up, sometimes frozen within historicocultural limits which intermingle with the historical scene to such a degree that it has long been impossible and is still difficult to think or even to imagine something else. At present, we are living through a transitional period—where the classical structure appears as if it might crack.

To predict what will happen to sexual difference—in another time (in two or three hundred years?) is impossible. But there should be no misunderstanding:

men and women are caught up in a network of millenial cultural determinations of a complexity that is practically unanalyzable: we can no more talk about 'woman' than about 'man' without getting caught up in an ideological theater where the multiplication of representations, images, reflections, myths, identifications constantly transforms, deforms, alters each person's imaginary order and in advance, renders all conceptualization null and void.[8]

There is no reason to exclude the possibility of radical transformations of behaviour, mentalities, roles, and political economy. The effects of these transformations on the libidinal economy are unthinkable today. Let us imagine simultaneously a *general* change in all of the structure of formation, education, framework, hence of reproduction, of ideological effects, and let us imagine a real liberation of sexuality, that is, a transformation of our relationship to our body (—and to another body), an approximation of the immense material organic sensual universe that we are, this not being possible, of course, without equally radical political transformations (imagine!). Then 'femininity,' 'masculinity,' would inscribe their effects of difference, their economy, their relationships to expenditure, to deficit, to giving, quite differently. That which appears as 'feminine' or 'masculine' today would no longer amount to the same thing. The general logic of difference would no longer fit into the opposition that still dominates. The difference would be a crowning display of new differences.

But we are still floundering about—with certain exceptions—in the Old order.

The masculine future:

There are exceptions. There always have been those uncertain, poetic beings, who have not let themselves be reduced to the state of coded mannequins by the relentless repression of the homosexual component. Men or women, complex, mobile, open beings. Admitting the component of the other sex makes them at once much richer, plural, strong, and to the extent of this mobility, very fragile. We invent only on this condition: thinkers, artists, creators of new values, 'philosophers' of the mad Nietzschean sort, inventors and destroyers of concepts, of forms, the changers of life cannot but be agitated by singularities—complementary or contradictory. This does not mean that in order to create you must be homosexual. But there is no *invention* possible, whether it be philosophical or poetic, without the presence in the inventing subject of an abundance of the other, of the diverse: persons-detached, persons-thought, peoples born of the unconscious, and in each desert, suddenly animated, a springing forth of self that we did not know about—our women, our monsters, our jackals, our Arabs, our fellow-creatures, our fears.[9] But there is no invention of other I's, no poetry, no fiction without a certain homosexuality (interplay therefore of bisexuality) making in me a crystallized work of my ultrasubjectivities.[10] I is this matter, personal, exuberant, lively masculine, feminine, or other in which I delights me and distresses me. And in the concert of personalizations called I, at the same time that you repress a certain homosexuality, symbolically, substitutively, it comes out through various signs—traits, comportments, manners, gestures—and it is seen still more clearly in writing.

Thus, under the name of Jean Genet,[11] what is inscribed in the movement of a text which divides itself, breaks itself into bits, regroups itself, is an abundant, maternal, pederastic femininity. A phantasmatical mingling of men, of males, of messieurs, of monarchs, princes, orphans, flowers, mothers, breasts, gravitates around a marvelous 'sun of energy' love, which bombards and disintegrates these ephemeral amorous singularities so that they may recompose themselves in other bodies for new passions. . . .

NOTES

1. The translation is faithful to Hélène Cixous's many neologisms.—Tr.
2. This is what all of Derrida's work traversing—investigating the history of philosophy—seeks to make apparent. In Plato, Hegel, Nietzsche, the same process goes on, repression, exclusion, distancing of woman. Murder which intermingles with history as a manifestation and representation of masculine power.
3. *Pour un tombeau d'Anatole* (Editions du Seuil, 1961, p. 138) tomb in which Mallarmé preserves his son, guards him, he himself the mother, from death.
4. *Fonder* in French means both 'to found' and 'to fund.'—Tr.
5. Freud's thesis is the following: when the Oedipal complex disappears the superego becomes its heir. At the moment when the boy begins to feel the threat of castration, he begins to overcome the Oedipus complex, with the help of a very severe superego. The Oedipus complex for the boy is a primary process: his first love object, as for the girl, is the mother. But the girl's development is inevitably controlled by the pressure of a less severe superego: the discovery of her castration results in a less vigorous superego. She never completely overcomes the Oedipus complex. The feminine Oedipus complex is not a primary process: the pre-Oedipal attachment to the mother entails for the girl a difficulty from which, says Freud, she never recovers: the necessity of changing objects (to love the father), in mid-stream is a painful conversion, which is accompanied by an additional renunciation: the passage from pre-Oedipal sexuality to 'normal' sexuality implies the abandonment of the clitoris in order to move on to the vagina. When this 'destiny' is fulfilled, women have a reduced symbolic activity: they have nothing to lose, to gain, to defend.
6. *Jouissance* is a word used by Hélène Cixous to refer to that intense, rapturous pleasure which women know and which men fear.—Ed.
7. J. J. Bachofen (1815–1887) Swiss historian of 'gynecocracy,' 'historian' of a nonhistory. His project is to demonstrate that the nations (Greek, Roman, Hebrew) went through an age of 'gynecocracy,' the reign of the Mother, before arriving at a patriarchy. This epoch can only be deduced, as it has no history. Bachofen advances that this state of affairs, humiliating for men, must have been repressed, covered over by historical forgetfulness. And he attempts to create (in *Das Mutterrecht* in particular, 1861) an archeology of the matriarchal system, of great beauty, starting with a reading of the first historical texts, at the level of the symptom, of their unsaid. Gynecocracy, he says, is well-ordered materialism.
8. There are coded paradigms, symptomatic of a repeated consensus, which project the man/woman robot couple as seen by contemporary societies. See the 1975 issue of UNESCO consecrated to the International Year of Woman.
9. The French here, *nos semblables, nos frayeurs*, plays on and with the last line of Baudelaire's famous poem 'Au lecteur' [To the reader]: 'Hypocrite lecteur,—mon semblable,—mon frère.'—Tr.
10. Hélène Cixous, *Prénoms de personne* (Editions du Seuil, 1974) 'Tales of Hoffman,' p. 112 passim.
11. Jean Genet, French novelist and playwright, to whose writing Hélène Cixous refers when she gives examples of the inscription of pederastic femininity.—Tr.

18 Edward Said

Edward Said (b. 1935) is a Palestinian, who was educated in Palestine and Egypt when those countries were under British jurisdiction, and subsequently in the United States. He is Parr Professor of English and Comparative Literature at Columbia University, New York. Said's first book was a critical study of Conrad, *Joseph Conrad and the Fiction of Autobiography* (1966), that took a phenomenological approach to its subject, but was recognizably within the tradition of Anglo–American 'New Criticism'. Said was one of the first critics in America to respond to the challenge of European structuralist and post-structuralist theory, and his thoughtful, sometimes anxious reflections upon these developments may be traced in his books *Beginnings* (1975) and *The World, the Text and the Critic* (1983). Said has disliked the increasing hermeticism of deconstructive criticism, and has been drawn to Marxist and Foucauldian analyses of literature and culture as sites of political and ideological struggle. In *Orientalism* (1978) he found a rewarding subject for such an approach.

Orientalism is the discourse of the West about the East, a huge body of texts—literary, topographical, anthropological, historical, sociological—that has been accumulating since the Renaissance. Said, concentrating his attention on writing about the Near East, is concerned to show how this discourse is at once self-validating, constructing certain stereotypes which become accepted as self-evident facts, and also in conscious or unconscious collusion with political and economic imperialism. 'Taking the late eighteenth century as a very roughly defined starting point,' says Said, in the introduction to his book, 'Orientalism can be discussed and analyzed as the corporate institution for dealing with the Orient—dealing with it by making statements about it, authorizing views of it, describing it, by teaching it, settling it, ruling over it: in short, Orientalism as a Western style for dominating, restructuring, and having authority over the Orient.' Said is uniquely qualified to undertake such a study, and *Orientalism* impressively combines political passion with wide-ranging scholarship.

The following extract, called simply 'Crisis' in the original text, concludes the first section of the book, entitled 'The Scope of Orientalism'.

CROSS-REFERENCES: 10. Foucault
COMMENTARY: Dennis Porter, 'Orientalism and its Problems', in Francis Barker *et al.* (eds) *The Politics of Theory* (Essex Sociology of Literature Conference, 1982)

Crisis [in orientalism]

It may appear strange to speak about something or someone as holding a *textual* attitude, but a student of literature will understand the phrase more easily if he will recall the kind of view attacked by Voltaire in *Candide,* or even the attitude to reality satirized by Cervantes in *Don Quixote.* What seems unexceptionable good sense to these writers is that it is a fallacy to assume that the swarming, unpredictable, and problematic mess in which human beings live can be under-stood on the basis of what books—texts—say; to apply what one learns out of a book literally to reality is to risk folly or ruin. One would no more think of using *Amadis of Gaul*[a] to understand sixteenth-century (or present-day) Spain than one would use the Bible to understand, say, the House of Commons. But clearly people have tried and do try to use texts in so simple-minded a way, for otherwise *Candide* and *Don Quixote* would not still have the appeal for readers that they do today. It seems a common human failing to prefer the schematic auth-ority of a text to the disorientations of direct encounters with the human. But is this failing constantly present, or are there circumstances that, more than others, make the textual attitude likely to prevail?

Two situations favor a textual attitude. One is when a human being confronts at close quarters something relatively unknown and threatening and previously distant. In such a case one has recourse not only to what in one's previous experience the novelty resembles but also to what one has read about it. Travel books or guidebooks are about as 'natural' a kind of text, as logical in their composition and in their use, as any book one can think of, precisely because of this human tendency to fall back on a text when the uncertainties of travel in strange parts seem to threaten one's equanimity. Many travelers find themselves saying of an experience in a new country that it wasn't what they expected, meaning that it wasn't what a book said it would be. And of course many writers of travel books or guidebooks compose them in order to say that a country *is* like this, or better, that it *is* colorful, expensive, interesting, and so forth. The idea in either case is that people, places, and experiences can always be described by a book, so much so that the book (or text) acquires a greater authority, and use, even than the actuality it describes. The comedy of Fabrice del Dongo's search for the battle of Waterloo[b] is not so much that he fails to find the battle, but that he looks for it as something texts have told him about.

---

[a] A Spanish romance of uncertain origin, first printed in the sixteenth century.
[b] The reference is to the hero of Stendhal's novel, *La Chartreuse de Parme* (1839).

A second situation favoring the textual attitude is the appearance of success. If one reads a book claiming that lions are fierce and then encounters a fierce lion (I simplify, of course), the chances are that one will be encouraged to read more books by that same author, and believe them. But if, in addition, the lion book instructs one how to deal with a fierce lion, and the instructions work perfectly, then not only will the author be greatly believed, he will also be impelled to try his hand at other kinds of written performance. There is a rather complex dialectic of reinforcement by which the experiences of readers in reality are determined by what they have read, and this in turn influences writers to take up subjects defined in advance by readers' experiences. A book on how to handle a fierce lion might then cause a series of books to be produced on such subjects as the fierceness of lions, the origins of fierceness, and so forth. Similarly, as the focus of the text centers more narrowly on the subject—no longer lions but their fierceness—we might expect that the ways by which it is recommended that a lion's fierceness be handled will actually *increase* its fierceness, force it to be fierce since that is what it is, and that is what in essence we know or can *only* know about it.

A text purporting to contain knowledge about something actual, and arising out of circumstances similar to the ones I have just described, is not easily dismissed. Expertise is attributed to it. The authority of academics, institutions, and governments can accrue to it, surrounding it with still greater prestige than its practical successes warrant. Most important, such texts can *create* not only knowledge but also the very reality they appear to describe. In time such knowledge and reality produce a tradition, or what Michel Foucault calls a discourse, whose material presence or weight, not the originality of a given author, is really responsible for the texts produced out of it. This kind of text is composed out of those pre-existing units of information deposited by Flaubert in the catalogue of *idées reçues.*[c]

In the light of all this, consider Napoleon and de Lesseps.[d] Everything they knew, more or less, about the Orient came from books written in the tradition of Orientalism, placed in its library of *idées reçues*; for them the Orient, like the fierce lion, was something to be encountered and dealt with to a certain extent *because* the texts made that Orient possible. Such an Orient was silent, available to Europe for the realization of projects that involved but were never directly responsible to the native inhabitants, and unable to resist the projects, images, or mere descriptions devised for it. Earlier I called such a relation between Western writing (and its consequences) and Oriental silence the result of and the sign of the West's great cultural strength, its will to power over the Orient. But there is another side to the strength, a side whose existence depends on the

[c] The Catalogue or Dictionary of Received Ideas is an ironic appendix to Gustave Flaubert's novel *Bouvard et Pécuchet*, published posthumously in 1881.

[d] Napoleon Bonaparte led a military expedition to Egypt in 1798 and initiated an academic study of that country whose findings were published in twenty-three volumes between 1809 and 1828 under the title, *Description de l'Egypte*. Ferdinand de Lesseps (1805–94) was a French diplomat and engineer who designed and supervised the construction of the Suez canal in 1859–69.

pressures of the Orientalist tradition and its textual attitude to the Orient; this side lives its own life, as books about fierce lions will do until lions can talk back. The perspective rarely drawn on Napoleon and de Lesseps—to take two among the many projectors who hatched plans for the Orient—is the one that sees them carrying on in the dimensionless silence of the Orient mainly because the discourse of Orientalism, over and above the Orient's powerlessness to do anything about them, suffused their activity with meaning, intelligibility, and reality. The discourse of Orientalism and what made it possible—in Napoleon's case, a West far more powerful militarily than the Orient—gave them Orientals who could be described in such works as the *Description de l'Égypte* and an Orient that could be cut across as de Lesseps cut across Suez. Moreover, Orientalism gave them their success—at least from their point of view, which had nothing to do with that of the Oriental. Success, in other words, had all the actual human interchange between Oriental and Westerner of the Judge's 'said I to myself, said I' in *Trial by Jury*.[e]

Once we begin to think of Orientalism as a kind of Western projection onto and will to govern over the Orient, we will encounter few surprises. For if it is true that historians like Michelet, Ranke, Tocqueville, and Burckhardt *emplot* their narratives 'as a story of a particular kind,'[1] the same is also true of Orientalists who plotted Oriental history, character, and destiny for hundreds of years. During the nineteenth and twentieth centuries the Orientalists became a more serious quantity, because by then the reaches of imaginative and actual geography had shrunk, because the Oriental-European relationship was determined by an unstoppable European expansion in search of markets, resources, and colonies, and finally, because Orientalism had accomplished its self-metamorphosis from a scholarly discourse to an imperial institution. Evidence of this metamorphosis is already apparent in what I have said of Napoleon, de Lesseps, Balfour, and Cromer.[f] Their projects in the Orient are understandable on only the most rudimentary level as the efforts of men of vision and genius, heroes in Carlyle's sense. In fact Napoleon, de Lesseps, Cromer, and Balfour are far more *regular*, far less unusual, if we recall the schemata of d'Herbelot and Dante[g] and add to them both a modernized, efficient engine (like the nineteenth-century European empire) and a positive twist: since one cannot ontologically obliterate the Orient (as d'Herbelot and Dante perhaps realized), one does have the means to capture it, treat it, describe it, improve it, radically alter it.

The point I am trying to make here is that the transition from a merely textual apprehension, formulation, or definition of the Orient to the putting of all this into practice in the Orient did take place, and that Orientalism had much to do

---

[e] A comic opera by Gilbert and Sullivan, first performed in 1875.

[f] James Arthur Balfour (1848–1930), as British Foreign Secretary in 1917, issued the Balfour Declaration, pledging support for the establishment of a Jewish National Home in Palestine (the forerunner of the modern state of Israel). Lord Cromer (1841–1917) was the British administrator and diplomat who virtually ruled Egypt in the period 1883–1917.

[g] Barthélmyd d'Herbelot's *Bibliothèque Orientale* (1697) was the standard European reference book on the subject until the early nineteenth century. Dante included Mohammed and other Muslims in his Inferno.

with that—if I may use the word in a literal sense—*preposterous* transition. So far as its strictly scholarly work was concerned (and I find the idea of strictly scholarly work as disinterested and abstract hard to understand: still, we can allow it intellectually), Orientalism did a great many things. During its great age in the nineteenth century it produced scholars; it increased the number of languages taught in the West and the quantity of manuscripts edited, translated, and commented on; in many cases, it provided the Orient with sympathetic European students, genuinely interested in such matters as Sanskrit grammar, Phoenician numismatics, and Arabic poetry. Yet—and here we must be very clear—Orientalism overrode the Orient. As a system of thought about the Orient, it always rose from the specifically human detail to the general transhuman one; an observation about a tenth-century Arab poet multiplied itself into a policy towards (and about) the Oriental mentality in Egypt, Iraq, or Arabia. Similarly a verse from the Koran would be considered the best evidence of an ineradicable Muslim sensuality. Orientalism assumed an unchanging Orient, absolutely different (the reasons change from epoch to epoch) from the West. And Orientalism, in its post-eighteenth-century form, could never revise itself. All this makes Cromer and Balfour, as observers and administrators of the Orient, inevitable.

The closeness between politics and Orientalism, or to put it more circumspectly, the great likelihood that ideas about the Orient drawn from Orientalism can be put to political use, is an important yet extremely sensitive truth. It raises questions about the predisposition towards innocence or guilt, scholarly disinterest or pressure-group complicity, in such fields as black or women's studies. It necessarily provokes unrest in one's conscience about cultural, racial, or historical generalizations, their uses, value, degree of objectivity, and fundamental intent. More than anything else, the political and cultural circumstances in which Western Orientalism has flourished draw attention to the debased position of the Orient or Oriental as an object of study. Can any other than a political master-slave relation produce the Orientalized Orient perfectly characterized by Anwar Abdel Malek?

a) On the level of the *position of the problem*, and the problematic . . . the Orient and Orientals [are considered by Orientalism] as an 'object' of study, stamped with an otherness—as all that is different, whether it be 'subject' or 'object'—but of a constitutive otherness, of an essentialist character. . . . This 'object' of study will be, as is customary, passive, non-participating, endowed with a 'historical' subjectivity, above all, non-active, non-autonomous, non-sovereign with regard to itself: the only Orient or Oriental or 'subject' which could be admitted, at the extreme limit, is the alienated being, philosophically, that is, other than itself in relationship to itself, posed, understood, defined—and acted—by others.

b) On the level of the *thematic*, [the Orientalists] adopt an essentialist conception of the countries, nations and peoples of the Orient under study, a conception which expresses itself through a characterized ethnist typology . . . and will soon proceed with it towards racism.

According to the traditional orientalists, an essence should exist—sometimes even clearly described in metaphysical terms—which constitutes the inalienable and common basis of all the beings considered; this essence is both 'historical,' since it goes back to the dawn of history, and fundamentally a-historical, since it transfixes the being, 'the object' of study, within its inalienable and non-evolutive specificity, instead of defining it as all other beings, states, nations, peoples, and cultures—as a product, a resultant of the vection of the forces operating in the field of historical evolution.

Thus one ends with a typology—based on a real specificity, but detached from history, and, consequently, conceived as being intangible, essential—which makes of the studied 'object' another being with regard to whom the studying subject is transcendent; we will have a homo Sinicus, a homo Arabicus (and why not a homo Aegypticus, etc.), a homo Africanus, the man—the 'normal man,' it is understood—being the European man of the historical period, that is, since Greek antiquity. One sees how much, from the eighteenth to the twentieth century, the hegemonism[h] of possessing minorities, unveiled by Marx and Engels, and the anthropocentrism dismantled by Freud are accompanied by europocentrism in the area of human and social sciences, and more particularly in those in direct relationship with non-European peoples.[2]

Abdel Malek sees Orientalism as having a history which, according to the 'Oriental' of the late twentieth century, led it to the impasse described above. Let us now briefly outline that history as it proceeded through the nineteenth century to accumulate weight and power, 'the hegemonism of possessing minorities,' and anthropocentrism in alliance with Europocentrism. From the last decades of the eighteenth century and for at least a century and a half, Britain and France dominated Orientalism as a discipline. The great philological discoveries in comparative grammar made by Jones, Franz Bopp, Jakob Grimm, and others were originally indebted to manuscripts brought from the East to Paris and London. Almost without exception, every Orientalist began his career as a philologist, and the revolution in philology that produced Bopp, Sacy, Burnouf, and their students was a comparative science based on the premise that languages belong to families, of which the Indo-European and the Semitic are two great instances. From the outset, then, Orientalism carried forward two traits: (1) a newly found scientific self-consciousness based on the linguistic importance of the Orient to Europe, and (2) a proclivity to divide, subdivide, and redivide its subject matter without ever changing its mind about the Orient as being always the same, unchanging, uniform and radically peculiar object.

Friedrich Schlegel, who learned his Sanskrit in Paris, illustrates these traits together. Although by the time he published his *Über die Sprache und Weisheit*

---

[h] The concept of 'hegemony'—cultural or ideological domination of the majority by a minority that is accepted as 'natural' by both groups—derives from the Italian Marxist Antonio Gramsci (1891–1937).

der Indier [On The Language and Wisdom of India] in 1808 Schlegel had practically renounced his Orientalism, he still held that Sanskrit and Persian on the one hand and Greek and German on the other had more affinities with each other than with the Semitic, Chinese, American, or African languages. Moreover, the Indo-European family was artistically simple and satisfactory in a way the Semitic, for one, was not. Such abstractions as this did not trouble Schlegel, for whom nations, races, minds, and peoples as things one could talk about passionately—in the ever-narrowing perspective of populism first adumbrated by Herder—held a lifelong fascination. Yet nowhere does Schlegel talk about the living, contemporary Orient. When he said in 1800, 'It is in the Orient that we must search for the highest Romanticism ,' he meant the Orient of the *Sakuntala,* the Zend-Avesta, and the Upanishads.*ⁱ* As for the Semites, whose language was agglutinative, unaesthetic, and mechanical, they were different, inferior, backward. Schlegel's lectures on language and on life, history, and literature are full of these discriminations, which he made without the slightest qualification. Hebrew, he said, was made for prophetic utterance and divination; the Muslims, however, espoused a 'dead empty Theism, a merely negative Unitarian faith.'[3]

Much of the racism in Schlegel's strictures upon the Semites and other 'low' Orientals was widely diffused in European culture. But nowhere else, unless it be later in the nineteenth century among Darwinian anthropologists and phrenologists, was it made the basis of a scientific subject matter as it was in comparative linguistics or philology. Language and race seemed inextricably tied, and the 'good' Orient was invariably a classical period somewhere in a long-gone India, whereas the 'bad' Orient lingered in present-day Asia, parts of North Africa, and Islam everywhere. 'Aryans,' were confined to Europe and the ancient Orient; as Léon Poliakov has shown (without once remarking, however, that 'Semites' were not only the Jews but the Muslims as well[4]), the Aryan myth dominated historical and cultural anthropology at the expense of the 'lesser' peoples.

The official intellectual genealogy of Orientalism would certainly include Gobineau, Renan, Humboldt, Steinthal, Burnouf, Remusat, Palmer, Weil, Dozy, Muir, to mention a few famous names almost at random from the nineteenth century. It would also include the diffusive capacity of learned societies: the Société asiatique, founded in 1822; the Royal Asiatic Society, founded in 1823; the American Oriental Society, founded in 1842; and so on. But it might perforce neglect the great contribution of imaginative and travel literature, which strengthened the divisions established by Orientalists between the various geographical, temporal, and racial departments of the Orient. Such neglect would be incorrect, since for the Islamic Orient this literature is especially rich and makes a significant contribution to building the Orientalist discourse. It includes work by Goethe, Hugo, Lamartine, Chateaubriand, Kinglake, Nerval, Flaubert, Lane, Burton, Scott, Byron, Vigny, Disraeli, George Eliot, Gautier. Later, in the late nineteenth and early twentieth centuries, we could add Doughty, Barrès, Loti, T. E. Lawrence, Forster. All these writers give a bolder outline to Disraeli's

---

ⁱ Sakuntala is a Sanskrit verse drama by the Indian fifth century poet Kalidasa. The Zend-Avesta is the scripture of Zoroastrianism. The Upanishads belong to Hindu scripture.

'great Asiatic mystery.' In this enterprise there is considerable support not only from the unearthing of dead Oriental civilizations (by European excavators) in Mesopotamia, Egypt, Syria, and Turkey, but also from major geographical surveys done all through the Orient.

By the end of the nineteenth century these achievements were materially abetted by the European occupation of the entire Near Orient (with the exception of parts of the Ottoman Empire, which was swallowed up after 1918). The principal colonial powers once again were Britain and France, although Russia and Germany played some role as well.[5] To colonize meant at first the identification—indeed, the creation—of interests; these could be commercial, communicational, religious, military, cultural. With regard to Islam and the Islamic territories, for example, Britain felt that it had legitimate interests, as a Christian power, to safeguard. A complex apparatus for tending these interests developed. Such early organizations as the Society for Promoting Christian Knowledge (1698) and the Society for the Propagation of the Gospel in Foreign Parts (1701) were succeeded and later abetted by the Baptist Missionary Society (1792), the Church Missionary Society (1799), the British and Foreign Bible Society (1804), the London Society for Promoting Christianity Among the Jews (1808). These missions 'openly joined the expansion of Europe.'[6] Add to these the trading societies, learned societies, geographical exploration funds, translation funds, the implantation in the Orient of schools, missions, consular offices, factories, and sometimes large European communities, and the notion of an 'interest' will acquire a good deal of sense. Thereafter interests were defended with much zeal and expense.

So far my outline is a gross one. What of the typical experiences and emotions that accompany both the scholarly advances of Orientalism and the political conquests aided by Orientalism? First, there is disappointment that the modern Orient is not at all like the texts. Here is Gérard de Nerval writing to Théophile Gautier at the end of August 1843:

> I have already lost, Kingdom after Kingdom, province after province, the
> more beautiful half, of the universe, and soon I will know of no place in
> which I can find a refuge for my dreams; but it is Egypt that I most
> regret having driven out of my imagination, now that I have sadly placed
> it in my memory.[7]

This is by the author of a great *Voyage en Orient*. Nerval's lament is a common topic of Romanticism (the betrayed dream, as described by Albert Béguin in *L'Ame romantique et le rêve* [*The Romantic Spirit and Dream*]) and of travelers in the Biblical Orient, from Chateaubriand to Mark Twain. Any direct experience of the mundane Orient ironically comments on such valorizations of it as were to be found in Goethe's 'Mahometsgesang' or Hugo's 'Adieux de l'hôtesse arabe.' Memory of the modern Orient disputes imagination, sends one back to the imagination as a place preferable, for the European sensibility, to the real Orient. For a person who has never seen the Orient, Nerval once said to Gautier, a lotus is still a lotus; for me it is only a kind of onion. To write about the modern Orient is either to reveal an upsetting demystification of images culled from texts, or to confine oneself to the Orient of which Hugo spoke in his original preface to *Les Orientales*, the Orient as 'image' or 'pensée,' symbols of 'une sorte de préoccupation générale [a kind of general preoccupation].'[8]

If personal disenchantment and general preoccupation fairly map the Orientalist sensibility at first, they entail certain other more familiar habits of thought, feeling, and perception. The mind learns to separate a general apprehension of the Orient from a specific experience of it; each goes its separate way, so to speak. In Scott's novel *The Talisman* (1825), Sir Kenneth (of the Crouching Leopard) battles a single Saracen to a standoff somewhere in the Palestinian desert; as the Crusader and his opponent, who is Saladin in disguise, later engage in conversation, the Christian discovers his Muslim antagonist to be not so bad a fellow after all. Yet he remarks:

> I well thought . . . that your blinded race had their descent from the foul fiend, without whose aid you would never have been able to maintain this blessed land of Palestine against so many valiant soldiers of God. I speak not thus of thee in particular, Saracen, but generally of thy people and religion. Strange is it to me, however, not that you should have the descent from the Evil One, but that you should boast of it.[9]

For indeed the Saracen does boast of tracing his race's line back to Eblis, the Muslim Lucifer. But what is truly curious is not the feeble historicism by which Scott makes the scene 'medieval,' letting Christian attack Muslim theologically in a way nineteenth-century Europeans would not (they would, though); rather, it is the airy condescension of damning a whole people 'generally' while mitigating the offense with a cool 'I don't mean you in particular.'

Scott, however, was no expert on Islam (although H. A. R. Gibb, who was, praised *The Talisman* for its insight into Islam and Saladin[10]), and he was taking enormous liberties with Eblis's role by turning him into a hero for the faithful. Scott's knowledge probably came from Byron and Beckford, but it is enough for us here to note how strongly the general character ascribed to things Oriental could withstand both the rhetorical and the existential force of obvious exceptions. It is as if, on the one hand, a bin called 'Oriental' existed into which all the authoritative, anonymous, and traditional Western attitudes to the East were dumped unthinkingly, while on the other, true to the anecdotal tradition of storytelling, one could nevertheless tell of experiences with or in the Orient that had little to do with the generally serviceable bin. But the very structure of Scott's prose shows a closer intertwining of the two than that. For the general category in advance offers the specific instance a limited terrain in which to operate: no matter how deep the specific exception, no matter how much a single Oriental can escape the fences placed around him, he is *first* an Oriental, *second* a human being, and *last* again an Oriental.

So general a category as 'Oriental' is capable of quite interesting variations. Disraeli's enthusiasm for the Orient appeared first during a trip East in 1831. In Cairo he wrote, 'My eyes and mind yet ache with a grandeur so little in unison with our own likeness'.[11] General grandeur and passion inspired a transcendent sense of things and little patience for actual reality. His novel *Tancred* is steeped in racial and geographical platitudes; everything is a matter of race, Sidonia states, so much so that salvation can only be found in the Orient and amongst its races. There, as a case in point, Druzes, Christians, Muslims, and Jews hobnob easily because—someone quips—Arabs are simply Jews on horseback, and all are Orientals at heart. The unisons are made between general categories, not between categories and what they contain. An Oriental lives in the Orient, he lives a life of Oriental ease, in a state of Oriental despotism and sensuality, imbued with a feeling of Oriental fatalism. Writers as different as Marx, Disraeli, Burton, and Nerval could carry on a lengthy discussion between themselves, as it were, using all those generalities unquestioningly and yet intelligibly.

With disenchantment and a generalized—not to say schizophrenic—view of the Orient, there is usually another peculiarity. Because it is made into a general object, the whole Orient can be made to serve as an illustration of a particular form of eccentricity. Although the individual Oriental cannot shake or disturb the general categories that make sense of his oddness, his oddness can never- theless be enjoyed for its own sake. Here, for example, is Flaubert describing the spectacle of the Orient:

> To amuse the crowd, Mohammed Ali's jester took a woman in a Cairo bazaar one day, set her on the counter of a shop, and coupled with her publicly while the shopkeeper calmly smoked his pipe.
> On the road from Cairo to Shubra some time ago a young fellow had himself publicly buggered by a large monkey—as in the story above, to create a good opinion of himself and make people laugh.
> A marabout died a while ago—an idiot—who had long passed as a saint marked by God; all the Moslem women came to see him and masturbated him—in the end he died of exhaustion—from morning to night it was a perpetual jacking-off. . . .
> *Quid dicis* [what say you?] of the following fact: some time ago a *santon* (ascetic priest) used to walk through the streets of Cairo completely naked except for a cap on his head and another on his prick. To piss he would doff the prick-cap, and sterile women who wanted children would run up, put themselves under the parabola of his urine and rub themselves with it.[12]

Flaubert frankly acknowledges that this is grotesquerie of a special kind. 'All the old comic business'—by which Flaubert meant the well-known conventions of 'the cudgeled slave . . . the coarse trafficker in women . . . the thieving merchant'—acquire a new, 'fresh . . . genuine and charming' meaning in the Orient. This meaning cannot be reproduced; it can only be enjoyed on the spot and 'brought back' very approximately. The Orient is *watched*, since its almost (but never quite) offensive behavior issues out of a reservoir of infinite pecu- liarity; the European, whose sensibility tours the Orient, is a watcher, never involved, always detached, always ready for new examples of what the *Description de l'Égypte* called 'bizarre jouissance.' The Orient becomes a living tableau of queerness.

And this tableau quite logically becomes a special topic for texts. Thus the circle is completed; from being exposed as what texts do not prepare one for, the Orient can return as something one writes about in a disciplined way. Its foreignness can be translated, its meanings decoded, its hostility tamed; yet the *generality* assigned to the Orient, the disenchantment that one feels after encountering it, the unresolved eccentricity it displays, are all redistributed in what is said or written about it. Islam, for example, was typically Oriental for Orientalists of the late nineteenth and early twentieth centuries. Carl Becker argued that although 'Islam' (note the vast generality) inherited the Hellenic tradition, it could neither grasp nor employ the Greek, humanistic tradition; moreover, to understand Islam one needed above all else to see it, not as an 'original' religion, but as a sort of failed Oriental attempt to employ Greek philosophy without the creative inspiration that we find in Renaissance Europe.[13] For Louis-Massignon, perhaps the most renowned and influential of modern French Orientalists, Islam was a systematic rejection of the Christian incarnation, and its greatest hero was not Mohammed or Averroës but al-Hallaj, a Muslim saint who was crucified by the orthodox Muslims for having dared to personalize Islam.[14] What Becker and Massignon explicitly left out of their studies was the eccentricity of the Orient, which they backhandedly acknowledged by trying so hard to regularize it in Western terms. Mohammed was thrown out, but al-Hallaj was made prominent because he took himself to be a Christ-figure.

As a judge of the Orient, the modern Orientalist does not, as he believes and even says, stand apart from it objectively. His human detachment, whose sign is the absence of sympathy covered by professional knowledge, is weighted heavily with all the orthodox attitudes, perspectives, and moods of Orientalism that I have been describing. His Orient is not the Orient as it is, but the Orient as it has been Orientalized. An unbroken arc of knowledge and power connects the European or Western statesman and the Western Orientalists; it forms the rim of the stage containing the Orient. By the end of World War I both Africa and the Orient formed not so much an intellectual spectacle for the West as a privileged terrain for it. The scope of Orientalism exactly matched the scope of empire, and it was this absolute unanimity between the two that provoked the only crisis in the history of Western thought about and dealings with the Orient. And this crisis continues now.

Beginning in the twenties, and from one end of the Third World to the other, the response to empire and imperialism has been dialectical. By the time of the Bandung Conference in 1955[j] the entire Orient had gained its political independence from the Western empires and confronted a new configuration of imperial powers, the United States and the Soviet Union. Unable to recognize 'its' Orient in the new Third World, Orientalism now faced a challenging and politically armed Orient. Two alternatives opened before Orientalism. One was to carry on as if nothing had happened. The second was to adapt the old ways to the new. But to the Orientalist, who believes the Orient never changes, the new is simply the old betrayed by new, misunderstanding *dis-Orientals* (we can

---

[j] At this conference, held in Bandung, Indonesia, twenty-nine nations of Africa and Asia (including Communist China) planned economic and cultural co-operation, and opposed colonialism.

permit ourselves the neologism). A third, revisionist alternative, to dispense with Orientalism altogether, was considered by only a tiny minority.

One index of the crisis, according to Abdel Malek, was not simply that 'national liberation movements in the ex-colonial' Orient worked havoc with Orientalist conceptions of passive, fatalistic 'subject races'; there was in addition the fact that 'specialists and the public at large became aware of the time-lag, not only between orientalist science and the material under study, but also—and this was to be determining—between the conceptions, the methods and the instruments of work in the human and social sciences and those of orientalism.[15] The Orientalists—from Renan to Goldziher to Macdonald to von Grunebaum, Gibb, and Bernard Lewis—saw Islam, for example, as a 'cultural synthesis' (the phrase is P. M. Holt's) that could be studied apart from the economics, sociology, and politics of the Islamic peoples. For Orientalism, Islam had a meaning which, if one were to look for its most succinct formulation, could be found in Renan's first treatise: in order best to be understood Islam had to be reduced to 'tent and tribe.' The impact of colonialism, of worldly circumstances, of historical development: all these were to Orientalists as flies to wanton boys, killed—or disregarded—for their sport, never taken seriously enough to complicate the essential Islam.

The career of H. A. R. Gibb illustrates within itself the two alternative approaches by which Orientalism has responded to the modern Orient. In 1945 Gibb delivered the Haskell Lectures at the University of Chicago. The world he surveyed was not the same one Balfour and Cromer knew before World War I. Several revolutions, two world wars, and innumerable economic, political, and social changes made the realities of 1945 an unmistakably, even cataclysmically, new object. Yet we find Gibb opening the lectures he called *Modern Trends in Islam* as follows:

> The student of Arabic civilization is constantly brought up against the striking contrast between the imaginative power displayed, for example, in certain branches of Arabic literature and the literalism, the pedantry, displayed in reasoning and exposition, even when it is devoted to these same productions. It is true that there have been great philosophers among the Muslim peoples and that some of them were Arabs, but they were rare exceptions. The Arab mind, whether in relation to the outer world or in relation to the processes of thought, cannot throw off its intense feeling for the separateness and the individuality of the concrete events. This is, I believe, one of the main factors lying behind that 'lack of a sense of law' which Professor Macdonald regarded as the characteristic difference in the Oriental.
>
> It is this, too, which explains—what is so difficult for the Western student to grasp [until it is explained to him by the Orientalist][k]—the aversion of the Muslims from the thought-processes of rationalism. . . . The rejection of rationalist modes of thought and of the utilitarian ethic which is inseparable from them has its roots, therefore, not in the so-

[k] Said's parenthesis.

called 'obscurantism' of the Muslim theologians but in the atomism and discreteness of the Arab imagination.[16]
This is pure Orientalism, of course, but even if one acknowledges the exceeding knowledge of institutional Islam that characterizes the rest of the book, Gibb's inaugural biases remain a formidable obstacle for anyone hoping to understand modern Islam. What is the meaning of 'difference' when the preposition 'from' has dropped from sight altogether? Are we not once again being asked to inspect the Oriental Muslim as if his world, unlike ours—'differently' from it—had never ventured beyond the seventh century? As for modern Islam itself, despite the complexities of his otherwise magisterial understanding of it, why must it be regarded with so implacable a hostility as Gibb's? If Islam is flawed from the start by virtue of its permanent disabilities, the Orientalist will find himself opposing any Islamic attempts to reform Islam, because, according to his views, reform is a betrayal of Islam: this is exactly Gibb's argument. How can an Oriental slip out from these manacles into the modern world except by repeating with the Fool in *King Lear*, 'They'll have me whipp'd for speaking true, thou'lt have me whipp'd for lying; and sometimes I am whipp'd for holding my peace.'

Eighteen years later Gibb faced an audience of English compatriots, only now he was speaking as the director of the Center for Middle Eastern Studies at Harvard. His topic was 'Area Studies Reconsidered,' in which, among other *aperçus*, he agreed that 'the Orient is much too important to be left to the Orientalists.' The new, or second alternative, approach open to Orientalists was being announced, just as *Modern Trends* exemplified the first, or traditional, approach. Gibb's formula is well-intentioned in 'Area Studies Reconsidered,' so far, of course, as the Western experts on the Orient are concerned, whose job it is to prepare students for careers 'in public life and business.' What we now need, said Gibb, is the traditional Orientalist *plus* a good social scientist working together: between them the two will do 'interdisciplinary' work. Yet the traditional Orientalist will not bring outdated knowledge to bear on the Orient; no, his expertise will serve to remind his uninitiated colleagues in area studies that 'to apply the psychology and mechanics of Western political institutions to Asian or Arab situations is pure Walt Disney'.[17]

In practice this notion has meant that when Orientals struggle against colonial occupation, you must say (in order not to risk a Disneyism) that Orientals have never understood the meaning of self-government the way 'we' do. When some Orientals oppose racial discrimination while others practice it, you say 'they're all Orientals at bottom' and class interest, political circumstances, economic factors are totally irrelevant. Or with Bernard Lewis, you say that if Arab Palestinians oppose Israeli settlement and occupation of their lands, then that is merely 'the return of Islam,' or, as a renowned contemporary Orientalist defines it, Islamic opposition to non-Islamic peoples,[18] a principle of Islam enshrined in the seventh century. History, politics, and economics do not matter. Islam is Islam, the Orient is Orient, and please take all your ideas about a left and a right wing, revolutions, and change back to Disneyland.

If such tautologies, claims, and dismissals have not sounded familiar to historians, sociologists, economists, and humanists in any other field except

Orientalism, the reason is patently obvious. For like its putative subject matter, Orientalism has not allowed ideas to violate its profound serenity. But modern Orientalists—or area experts, to give them their new name—have not passively sequestered themselves in language departments. On the contrary, they have profited from Gibb's advice. Most of them today are indistinguishable from other 'experts' and 'advisers' in what Harold Lasswell has called the policy sciences.[19] Thus the military—national-security possibilities of an alliance, say, between a specialist in 'national character analysis' and an expert in Islamic institutions were soon recognized, for expediency's sake if for nothing else. After all, the 'West' since World War II had faced a clever totalitarian enemy who collected allies for itself among gullible Oriental (African, Asian, undeveloped) nations. What better way of outflanking that enemy than by playing to the Oriental's illogical mind in ways only an Orientalist could devise? Thus emerged such masterful ploys as the stick-and-carrot technique, the Alliance for Progress, SEATO, and so forth, all of them based on traditional 'knowledge' retooled for better manipulation of its supposed object.

Thus as revolutionary turmoil grips the Islamic Orient, sociologists remind us that Arabs are addicted to 'oral functions,'[20] while economists—recycled Orientalists—observe that for modern Islam neither capitalism nor socialism is an adequate rubric.[21] As anticolonialism sweeps and indeed unifies the entire Oriental world, the Orientalist damns the whole business not only as a nuisance but as an insult to the Western democracies. As momentous, generally important issues face the world—issues involving nuclear destruction, catastrophically scarce resources, unprecedented human demands for equality, justice, and economic parity—popular caricatures of the Orient are exploited by politicians whose source of ideological supply is not only the half-literate technocrat but the superliterate Orientalist. The legendary Arabists in the State Department warn of Arab plans to take over the world. The perfidious Chinese, half-naked Indians, and passive Muslims are described as vultures for 'our' largesse and are damned when 'we lose them' to communism, or to their unregenerate Oriental instincts: the difference is scarcely significant.

These contemporary Orientalist attitudes flood the press and the popular mind. Arabs, for example, are thought of as camel-riding, terroristic, hook-nosed, venal lechers whose undeserved wealth is an affront to real civilization. Always there lurks the assumption that although the Western consumer belongs to a numerical minority, he is entitled either to own or to expend (or both) the majority of the world resources. Why? Because he, unlike the Oriental, is a true human being. No better instance exists today of what Anwar Abdel Malek calls 'the hegemonism of possessing minorities' and anthropocentrism allied with Europocentrism: a white middle-class Westerner believes it his human prerogative not only to manage the nonwhite world but also to own it, just because by definition 'it' is not quite as human as 'we' are. There is no purer example than this of dehumanized thought.

In a sense the limitations of Orientalism are, as I said earlier, the limitations that follow upon disregarding, essentializing, denuding the humanity of another culture, people, or geographical region. But Orientalism has taken a further step than that: it views the Orient as something whose existence is not only displayed but has remained fixed in time and place for the West. So impressive have the descriptive and textual successes of Orientalism been that entire periods of the Orient's cultural, political, and social history are considered mere responses to the West. The West is the actor, the Orient a passive reactor. The West is the spectator, the judge and jury, of every facet of Oriental behaviour. Yet if history during the twentieth century has provoked intrinsic change in and for the Orient, the Orientalist is stunned: he cannot realize that to some extent

> the new [Oriental] leaders, intellectuals or policy-makers, have learned many lessons from the travail of their predecessors. They have also been aided by the structural and institutional transformations accomplished in the intervening period and by the fact that they are to a great extent more at liberty to fashion the future of their countries. They are also much more confident and perhaps slightly aggressive. No longer do they have to function hoping to obtain a favorable verdict from the invisible jury of the West. Their dialogue is not with the West, it is with their fellow-citizens[22]

Moreover, the Orientalist assumes that what his texts have not prepared him for is the result either of outside agitation in the Orient or of the Orient's misguided inanity. None of the innumerable Orientalist texts on Islam, including their summa, *The Cambridge History of Islam*, can prepare their reader for what has taken place since 1948 in Egypt, Palestine, Iraq, Syria, Lebanon, or the Yemens. When the dogmas about Islam cannot serve, not even for the most Panglossian Orientalist, there is recourse to an Orientalized social-science jargon, to such marketable abstractions as élites, political stability, modernization, and institutional development, all stamped with the cachet of Orientalist wisdom. In the meantime a growing, more and more dangerous rift separates Orient and Occident.

The present crisis dramatizes the disparity between texts and reality. Yet in this study of Orientalism I wish not only to expose the sources of Orientalism's views but also to reflect on its importance, for the contemporary intellectual rightly feels that to ignore a part of the world now demonstrably encroaching upon him is to avoid reality. Humanists have too often confined their attention to departmentalized topics of research. They have neither watched nor learned from disciplines like Orientalism whose unremitting ambition was to master *all* of a world, not some easily delimited part of it such as an author or a collection of texts. However, along with such academic security-blankets as 'history,' 'literature,' or 'the humanities,' and despite its overreaching aspirations, Orientalism is involved in worldly, historical circumstances which it has tried to conceal behind an often pompous scientism and appeals to rationalism. The contemporary intellectual can learn from Orientalism how, on the one hand, either to limit or to enlarge realistically the scope of his discipline's claims, and on the other, to see the human ground (the foul-rag-and-bone shop of the heart, Yeats called it) in which texts, visions, methods, and disciplines begin, grow, thrive, and degenerate. To investigate Orientalism is also to propose intellectual ways for handling the methodological problems that history has brought forward, so to speak, in its subject matter, the Orient. But before that we must virtually see the humanistic values that Orientalism, by its scope, experiences, and structures, has all but eliminated.

NOTES

1. Hayden White, *Metahistory: The Historical Imagination in Nineteenth Century Europe* (Baltimore: Johns Hopkins University Press, 1973), p. 12.
2. Anwar Abdel Malek, 'Orientalism in Crisis,' *Diogenes* 44 (Winter 1963): 107–8.
3. Friedrich Schlegel, *Über die Sprache und Weisheit der Indier: Ein Beitrag zur Begrundung der Altertumstunde* (Heidelberg: Mohr & Zimmer, 1808), pp. 44–59; Schlegel, *Philosophie der Geschichte: In achtzehn Vorlesungen gehalten zu Wien im Jahre 1828*, ed. Jean-Jacques Anstett, vol. 9 of *Kritische Friedrich-Schlegel-Ausgabe*, ed. Ernest Behler (Munich: Ferdinand Schöningh, 1971), p. 275.
4. Léon Poliakov, *The Aryan Myth: A History of Racist and Nationalist Ideas in Europe*, trans. Edmund Howard (New York: Basic Books, 1974).
5. See Derek Hopwood, *The Russian Presence in Syria and Palestine, 1843–1943: Church and Politics in the Near East* (Oxford: Clarendon Press, 1969).
6. A. L. Tibawi, *British Interests in Palestine, 1800–1901* (London: Oxford University Press, 1961), p. 5.
7. Gérard de Nerval, *Oeuvres*, ed. Albert Béguin and Jean Richet (Paris: Gallimard, 1960), 1:933.
8. Hugo, *Oeuvres poétiques*, 1:580.
9. Sir Walter Scott, *The Talisman* (1825; reprint ed., London: J. M. Dent, 1914), pp. 38–9.
10. See Albert Hourani, 'Sir Hamilton Gibb, 1895–1971,' *Proceedings of the British Academy* 58 (1972):495.
11. Quoted by B. R. Jerman, *The Young Disraeli* (Princeton, N. J.: Princeton University Press, 1960), p. 126. See also Robert Blake, *Disraeli* (London: Eyre & Spottiswoode, 1966), pp. 59–70.
12. *Flaubert in Egypt: A Sensibility on Tour*, trans. and ed. Francis Steegmuller (Boston: Little, Brown & Co., 1973), pp. 44–5. See Gustave Flaubert, *Correspondance*, ed. Jean Bruneau (Paris: Gallimard, 1973), 1:542.
13. This is the argument presented in Carl H. Becker, *Das Erbe der Antike Im Orient und Okzident* (Leipzig: Quelle & Meyer, 1931).
14. See Louis Massignon, *La Passion d'al-Hosayn-ibn-Mansour al-Hallaj* (Paris: Paul Geuthner, 1922).
15. Abdel Malek, 'Orientalism in Crisis,' p. 112.
16. H. A. R. Gibb, *Modern Trends in Islam* (Chicago: University of Chicago Press, 1947), p. 7.
17. Gibb, *Area Studies Reconsidered*, pp. 12, 13.
18. Bernard Lewis, 'The Return of Islam,' *Commentary*, January 1976, pp. 39–49.
19. See Daniel Lerner and Harold Lasswell, eds., *The Policy Sciences: Recent Developments in Scope and Method* (Stanford, Calif.: Stanford University Press, 1951).
20. Morroe Berger, *The Arab World Today* (Garden City, N. Y.: Doubleday & Co., 1962), p. 158.
21. There is a compendium of such attitudes listed and criticized in Maxime Rodinson, *Islam and Capitalism*, trans. Brian Pearce (New York: Pantheon Books, 1973).
22. Ibrahim Abu-Lughod, 'Retreat from the Secular Path? Islamic Dilemmas of Arab Politics,' *Review of Politics* 28, no. 4 (October 1966):475.

19 Stanley Fish

Stanley Fish (b. 1938) has taught at several American universities, including the University of California at Berkeley and Johns Hopkins. He is at present Arts and Sciences Distinguished Professor of English and Law at Duke University. Originally a Renaissance scholar trained in the explicatory techniques of the New Criticism (his first two books were critical studies of Skelton and Milton, respectively), he has become increasingly interested in questions of literary theory, and a leading exponent of American 'reader-response' criticism. This development was entirely logical and self-consistent. His book on Milton, *Surprised by Sin* (1967), was subtitled, 'The Reader in *Paradise Lost*', and argued that the reader of that poem is constantly lured into mistakes of interpretation by the ambiguities of Milton's syntax, and thus compelled to recognize his own 'fallen' state. *Self-Consuming Artefacts* (1972) adopted a similar approach to other seventeenth-century texts, and included an appendix entitled 'Affective Stylistics' in which Fish expounded the theoretical basis of his critical method.

Fish's work starts from and questions the New Criticism's effort to locate literary meaning in the formal features of the text, rather than in the author's intention or the reader's response (see 'The Intentional Fallacy' and 'The Affective Fallacy' by W. K. Wimsatt Jr and Monroe C. Beardsley, section 26 of *20th Century Literary Criticism*). In 'Interpreting the *Variorum*' Fish argues that both authorial intention and formal features are produced by the interpretive assumptions and procedures the reader brings to the text, and that they have no prior or objective existence outside the reading experience.

This argument has affinities with the reception theory of Wolfgang Iser (see pp. 212–28 above) and with Derridean theories of discourse; but Fish arrived at it by an independent, more pragmatic route, and is at once more radical than Iser and less radical than Derrida, rescuing criticism from the *abîme* of total relativism by the concept of the 'interpretive community'. He has defended, and elaborated on, his views in a number of essays and lectures collected in *Is There a Text in This Class?* (1980), dealing wittily and incisively with such topics as stylistics and speech act theory in the process. 'Interpreting the *Variorum*', first published in *Critical Inquiry* in 1976, is reprinted here from *Is There a Text in This Class?*, and like all the items in that book is prefaced by a retrospective commentary by the author.

CROSS-REFERENCES: 11. Wolfgang Iser
21. De Man

COMMENTARY: William E. Ray, 'Stanley Fish: supersession and transcendence', in Ray's *Literary Meaning: from phenomenology to deconstruction* (1984)

Interpreting the Variorum

[This essay was written in three stages and, as it finally stands, is something of a self-consuming artifact. The original version was prepared in 1973 for a Modern Language Association forum organized by Fredric Jameson and was intended as a brief for reader-oriented criticism. I seized upon the publication of the Milton *Variorum* because it greatly facilitated what had long since become my method, the surveying of the critical history of a work in order to find disputes that rested upon a base of agreement of which the disputants were unaware. I then identified that base with the experience of a work, and argued that formalist criticism, because it is spatial rather than temporal in its emphasis, either ignored or suppressed what is really happening in the act of reading. Thus, in the case of three sonnets by Milton, what is really happening depends upon a moment of hesitation or syntactic slide, when a reader is invited to make a certain kind of sense only to discover (at the beginning of the next line) that the sense he has made is either incomplete or simply wrong. 'In a formalist analysis,' I complain, 'that moment will disappear, either because it has been flattened out and made into an (insoluble) crux or because it has been eliminated in the course of a procedure that is incapable of finding value in temporal phenomena.'

What I did not then see is that the moment that disappears in a formalist analysis is the moment that has been made to appear in another kind of analysis, the kind of analysis I was urging in this essay. This is the point of the second stage of the essay, which begins by declaring that formal features do not exist independently of the reader's experience and ends by admitting that my account of the reader's experience is itself the product of a set of interpretive assumptions. In other words, the facts that I cite as ones ignored by a formalist criticism (premature conclusions, double syntax, misidentification of speakers) are not discovered but *created* by the criticism I was myself practicing. The indictment of the first two sections—that a bad (because spatial) model had suppressed what was really happening—loses its force because of my realization that the notion 'really happening' is just one more interpretation. This realization immediately presented me with the problem that led me in the fall of 1975 to write the final section, the problem of accounting for the agreement readers often reach and for the principled ways in which they disagree. It was at this point that I elaborated the notion of interpretive communities as an explanation both for the difference we see—and, by seeing, make—and for the fact that those differences are not random or idiosyncratic but systematic and conventional. The essay thus

311

concludes with a perspective that is not at all the perspective with which it began, and it is from that perspective that the essays subsequent to this one are written.]

The Case for Reader-Response Analysis

The first two volumes of the Milton *Variorum Commentary* have now appeared, and I find them endlessly fascinating. My interest, however, is not in the questions they manage to resolve (although these are many) but in the theoretical assumptions which are responsible for their occasional failures. These failures constitute a pattern, one in which a host of commentators—separated by as much as two hundred and seventy years but contemporaries in their shared concerns— are lined up on either side of an interpretive crux. Some of these are famous, even infamous: what is the two-handed engine in *Lycidas*? what is the meaning of Haemony in *Comus*? Others, like the identity of whoever or whatever comes to the window in *L'Allegro*, line 46, are only slightly less notorious. Still others are of interest largely to those who make editions: matters of pronoun referents, lexical ambiguities, punctuation. In each instance, however, the pattern is consistent: every position taken is supported by wholly convincing evidence—in the case of *L'Allegro* and the coming to the window there is a persuasive champion for every proper noun within a radius of ten lines—and the editorial procedure always ends either in the graceful throwing up of hands or in the recording of a disagreement between the two editors themselves. In short, these are problems that apparently cannot be solved, at least not by the methods traditionally brought to bear on them. What I would like to argue is that they are not *meant* to be solved but to be experienced (they signify), and that consequently any procedure that attempts to determine which of a number of readings is correct will necessarily fail. What this means is that the commentators and editors have been asking the wrong questions and that a new set of questions based on new assumptions must be formulated. I would like at least to make a beginning in that direction by examining some of the points in dispute in Milton's sonnets. I choose the sonnets because they are brief and because one can move easily from them to the theoretical issues with which this paper is finally concerned.

Milton's twentieth sonnet—'Lawrence of virtuous father virtuous son'—has been the subject of relatively little commentary. In it the poet invites a friend to join him in some distinctly Horatian pleasures—a neat repast intermixed with conversation, wine, and song, a respite from labor all the more enjoyable because outside the earth is frozen and the day sullen. The only controversy the sonnet has inspired concerns its final two lines:

> Lawrence of virtuous father virtuous son,
>   Now that the fields are dank, and ways are mire,
>   Where shall we sometimes meet, and by the fire
>   Help waste a sullen day; what may be won
> From the hard season gaining; time will run   5
>   On smoother, till Favonius reinspire

> The frozen earth; and clothe in fresh attire
> The lily and rose, that neither sowed nor spun.
> What neat repast shall feast us, light and choice,
> Of Attic taste, with wine, whence we may rise   10
> To hear the lute well touched, or artful voice
> Warble immortal notes and Tuscan air?
> He who of those delights can judge, and spare
> To interpose them oft, is not unwise.[1]

The focus of the controversy is the word 'spare,' for which two readings have been proposed: leave time for and refrain from. Obviously the point is crucial if one is to resolve the sense of the lines. In one reading 'those delights' are being recommended—he who can leave time for them is not unwise; in the other, they are the subject of a warning—he who knows when to refrain from them is not unwise. The proponents of the two interpretations cite as evidence both English and Latin syntax, various sources and analogues, Milton's 'known attitudes' as they are found in his other writings, and the unambiguously expressed sentiments of the following sonnet on the same question. Surveying these arguments, A. S. P. Woodhouse roundly declares: 'It is plain that all the honours rest with' the meaning 'refrain from' or 'forbear to.' This declaration is followed immediately by a bracketed paragraph initialled D. B. for Douglas Bush, who, writing presumably after Woodhouse has died, begins 'In spite of the array of scholarly names the case for "forbear to" may be thought much weaker, and the case for "spare time for" much stronger, than Woodhouse found them.'[2] Bush then proceeds to review much of the evidence marshaled by Woodhouse and to draw from it exactly the opposite conclusion. If it does nothing else, this curious performance anticipates a point I shall make in a few moments: evidence brought to bear in the course of formalist analyses—that is, analyses generated by the assumption that meaning is embedded in the artifact—will always point in as many directions as there are interpreters; that is, not only will it prove something, it will prove anything.

It would appear then that we are back at square one, with a controversy that cannot be settled because the evidence is inconclusive. But what if that controversy is *itself* regarded as evidence, not of ambiguity that must be removed, but of an ambiguity that readers have always experienced? What, in other words, if for the question 'what does "spare" mean?' we substitute the question 'what does the fact that the meaning of "spare" has always been an issue mean'? The advantage of this question is that it can be answered. Indeed it has already been answered by the readers who are cited in the *Variorum Commentary*. What these readers debate is the judgment the poem makes on the delights of recreation; what their debate indicates is that the judgment is blurred by a verb that can be made to participate in contradictory readings. (Thus the important thing about the evidence surveyed in the *Variorum* is not how it is marshaled but that it could be marshaled at all, because it then becomes evidence of the equal availability of both interpretations.) In other words, the lines first generate a pressure for judgment—'he who of those delights can judge'—and then decline to deliver it; the pressure, however, still exists, and it is transferred from the words on the page to the reader (the reader is 'he who'), who comes away from the poem not with a statement but with a responsibility, the responsibility of deciding when and how often—if at all—to indulge in 'those delights' (they remain delights in either case). This transferring of responsibility from the text to its readers is what the lines ask us to do—it is the essence of their experience—and in my terms it is therefore what the lines *mean*. It is a meaning the *Variorum* critics attest to even as they resist it, for what they are laboring so mightily to do by fixing the sense of the lines is to give the responsibility back. The text, however, will not accept it and remains determinedly evasive, even in its last two words, 'not unwise.' In their position these words confirm the impossibility of extracting from the poem a moral formula, for the assertion (certainly too strong a word) they complete is of the form, 'He who does such and such, of him it cannot be said that he is unwise'; but of course neither can it be said that he is wise. Thus what Bush correctly terms the 'defensive' 'not unwise' operates to prevent us from attaching the label 'wise' to any action, including *either* of the actions—leaving time for or refraining from—represented by the ambiguity of 'spare.' Not only is the pressure of judgment taken off the poem, it is taken off the activity the poem at first pretended to judge. The issue is finally not the moral status of 'those delights'—they become in seventeenth-century terms 'things indifferent'—but on the good or bad uses to which they can be put by readers who are left, as Milton always leaves them, to choose and manage by themselves.

Let us step back for a moment and see how far we've come. We began with an apparently insoluble problem and proceeded, not to solve it, but to make it signify, first by regarding it as evidence of an experience and then by specifying for that experience a meaning. Moreover, the configurations of that experience, when they are made available by a reader-oriented analysis, serve as a check against the endlessly inconclusive adducing of evidence which characterizes formalist analysis. That is to say, any determination of what 'spare' means (in a positivist or literal sense) is liable to be upset by the bringing forward of another analogue, or by a more complete computation of statistical frequencies, or by the discovery of new biographical information, or by anything else; but if we first determine that everything in the line before 'spare' creates the expectation of an imminent judgment then the ambiguity of 'spare' can be assigned a significance in the context of that expectation. (It disappoints it and transfers the pressure of judgment to us.) That context is experiential, and it is within its contours and constraints that significances are established (both in the act of reading and in the analysis of that act). In formalist analyses the only constraints are the notoriously open-ended possibilities and combination of possibilities that emerge when one begins to consult dictionaries and grammars and histories; to consult dictionaries, grammars, and histories is to assume that meanings can be specified independently of the activity of reading; what the example of 'spare' shows is that it is in and by that activity that meanings—experiential, not positivist—are created.

In other words, it is the structure of the reader's experience rather than any structures available on the page that should be the object of description. In the case of Sonnet 20, that experiential structure was uncovered when an examination of formal structures led to an impasse; and the pressure to remove that impasse led to the substitution of one set of questions for another. It will more often be the case that the pressure of a spectacular failure will be absent. The sins of formalist-positivist analysis are primarily sins of omission, not an inability to explain phenomena but an inability to see that they are there because its assumptions make it inevitable that they will be overlooked or suppressed. Consider, for example, the concluding lines of another of Milton's sonnets, 'Avenge O Lord thy slaughtered saints.'

> Avenge O Lord thy slaughtered saints, whose bones
>   Lie scattered on the Alpine mountains cold,
>   Even them who kept thy truth so pure of old
>   When all our fathers worshipped stocks and stones,
> Forget not: in thy book record their groans
>   Who were thy sheep and in their ancient fold
>   Slain by the bloody Piedmontese that rolled
>   Mother with infant down the rocks. Their moans
> The vales redoubled to the hills, and they
>   To heaven. Their martyred blood and ashes sow
>   O'er all the Italian fields where still doth sway
> The triple Tyrant: that from these may grow
>   A hundredfold, who having learnt thy way
>   Early may fly the Babylonian woe.

In this sonnet, the poet simultaneously petitions God and wonders aloud about the justice of allowing the faithful—'Even them who kept thy truth'—to be so brutally slaughtered. The note struck is alternately one of plea and complaint, and there is more than a hint that God is being called to account for what has happened to the Waldensians. It is generally agreed, however, that the note of complaint is less and less sounded and that the poem ends with an affirmation of faith in the ultimate operation of God's justice. In this reading, the final lines are taken to be saying something like this: From the blood of these martyred, O God, raise up a new and more numerous people, who, by virtue of an early education in thy law, will escape destruction by fleeing the Babylonian woe. Babylonian woe has been variously glossed;[3] but whatever it is taken to mean it is always read as part of a statement that specifies a set of conditions for the escaping of destruction or punishment; it is a warning to the reader as well as a petition to God. As a warning, however, it is oddly situated since the conditions it seems to specify were in fact met by the Waldensians, who of all men most followed God's laws. In other words, the details of their story would seem to undercut the affirmative moral the speaker proposes to draw from it. It is further undercut by a reading that is fleetingly available, although no one has acknowledged it because it is a function not of the words on the page but of the experience of the reader. In that experience, line 13 will for a moment be accepted as a complete sense unit and the emphasis of the line will fall on 'thy way' (a phrase that has received absolutely no attention in the commentaries). At this

315

point 'thy way' can refer only to the way in which God has dealt with the Waldensians. That is, 'thy way' seems to pick up the note of outrage with which the poem began, and if we continue to so interpret it, the conclusion of the poem will be a grim one indeed: since by this example it appears that God rains down punishment indiscriminately, it would be best perhaps to withdraw from the arena of his service, and thereby hope at least to be safely out of the line of fire. This is not the conclusion we carry away, because as line 14 unfolds, another reading of 'thy way' becomes available, a reading in which 'early' qualifies 'learnt' and refers to something the faithful should do (learn thy way at an early age) rather than to something God has failed to do (save the Waldensians). These two readings are answerable to the pulls exerted by the beginning and ending of the poem: the outrage expressed in the opening lines generates a pressure for an explanation, and the grimmer reading is answerable to that pressure (even if it is also disturbing); the ending of the poem, the forward and upward movement of lines 10–14, creates the expectation of an affirmation, and the second reading fulfills that expectation. The criticism shows that in the end we settle on the more optimistic reading—it feels better—but even so the other has been a part of our experience, and because it has been a part of our experience, it *means*. What it means is that while we may be able to extract from the poem a statement affirming God's justice, we are not allowed to forget the evidence (of things seen) that makes the extraction so difficult (both for the speaker and for us). It is a difficulty we experience in the act of reading, even though a criticism which takes no account of that act has, as we have seen, suppressed it.

In each of the sonnets we have considered, the significant word or phrase occurs at a line break where a reader is invited to place it first in one and then in another structure of syntax and sense. This moment of hesitation, of semantic or syntactic slide, is crucial to the experience the verse provides, but in a formalist analysis that moment will disappear, either because it has been flattened out and made into an (insoluble) interpretive crux or because it has been eliminated in the course of a procedure that is incapable of finding value in temporal phenomena. In the case of 'When I consider how my light is spent,' these two failures are combined.

> When I consider how my light is spent,
> Ere half my days, in this dark world and wide,
> And that one talent which is death to hide,
> Lodged with me useless, though my soul more bent
> To serve therewith my maker, and present
> My true account, lest he returning chide,
> Doth God exact day-labour, light denied,
> I fondly ask; but Patience to prevent
> That murmur, soon replies, God doth not need
> Either man's work or his own gifts, who best
> Bear his mild yoke, they serve him best, his state
> Is kingly. Thousands at his bidding speed

> And post o'er land and ocean without rest:
> They also serve who only stand and wait.

The interpretive crux once again concerns the final line: 'They also serve who only stand and wait.' For some this is an unqualified acceptance of God's will, while for others the note of affirmation is muted or even forced. The usual kinds of evidence are marshaled by the opposing parties, and the usual inconclusiveness is the result. There are some areas of agreement. 'All the interpretations,' Woodhouse remarks, 'recognize that the sonnet commences from a mood of depression, frustration [and] impatience.'[4] The object of impatience is a God who would first demand service and then take away the means of serving, and the oft noted allusion to the parable of the talents lends scriptural support to the accusation the poet is implicitly making: you have cast the wrong servant into unprofitable darkness. It has also been observed that the syntax and rhythm of these early lines, and especially of lines 6–8, are rough and uncertain; the speaker is struggling with his agitated thoughts and he changes directions abruptly, with no regard for the line as a unit of sense. The poem, says one critic, 'seems almost out of control.'[5]

The question I would ask is 'whose control?' For what these formal descriptions point to (but do not acknowledge) is the extraordinary number of adjustments required of readers who would negotiate these lines. The first adjustment is the result of the expectations created by the second half of line 6—'lest he returning chide.' Since there is no full stop after 'chide,' it is natural to assume that this will be an introduction to reported speech, and to assume further that what will be reported is the poet's anticipation of the voice of God as it calls him, to an unfair accounting. This assumption does not survive line 7—'Doth God exact day-labour, light denied'—which, rather than chiding the poet for his inactivity, seems to rebuke him for having expected that chiding. The accents are precisely those heard so often in the Old Testament when God answers a reluctant Gideon, or a disputatious Moses, or a self-justifying Job: do you presume to judge my ways or to appoint my motives? Do you think I would exact day labor, light denied? In other words, the poem seems to turn at this point from a questioning of God to a questioning of that questioning; or, rather, the reader turns from the one to the other in the act of revising his projection of what line 7 will say and do. As it turns out, however, that revision must itself be revised because it had been made within the assumption that what we are hearing is the voice of God. This assumption falls before the very next phrase. 'I fondly ask,' which requires not one but two adjustments. Since the speaker of line 7 is firmly identified as the poet, the line must be reinterpreted as a continuation of his complaint—Is that the way you operate, God, denying light, but exacting labor?—but even as that interpretation emerges, the poet withdraws from it by inserting the adverb 'fondly,' and once again the line slips out of the reader's control.

In a matter of seconds, then, line 7 has led four experiential lives, one as we anticipate it, another as that anticipation is revised, a third when we retroactively identify its speaker, and a fourth when that speaker disclaims it. What changes in each of these lives is the status of the poet's murmurings—they are alternately expressed, rejected, reinstated, and qualified—and as the sequence ends, the reader is without a firm perspective on the question of record: does God deal justly with his servants?

A firm perspective appears to be provided by Patience, whose entrance into the poem, the critics tell us, gives it both argumentative and metrical stability. But in fact the presence of Patience in the poem finally assures its continuing instability by making it impossible to specify the degree to which the speaker approves, or even participates in, the affirmation of the final line: 'They also serve who only stand and wait.' We know that Patience to prevent the poet's murmur soon replies (not soon enough however to prevent the murmur from registering), but we do not know when that reply ends. Does Patience fall silent in line 12, after 'kingly'? or at the conclusion of line 13? or not at all? Does the poet appropriate these lines or share them or simply listen to them, as we do? These questions are unanswerable, and it is because they remain unanswerable that the poem ends uncertainly. The uncertainty is not in the statement it makes—in isolation line 14 is unequivocal—but in our inability to assign that statement to either the poet or to Patience. Were the final line marked unambiguously for the poet, then we would receive it as a resolution of his earlier doubts; and were it marked for Patience, it would be a sign that those doubts were still very much in force. It is marked for neither, and therefore we are without the satisfaction that a firmly conclusive ending (in *any* direction) would have provided. In short, we leave the poem unsure, and our unsureness is the realization (in our experience) of the unsureness with which the affirmation of the final line is, or is not, made. (This unsureness also operates to actualize the two possible readings of 'wait': wait in the sense of expecting, that is waiting for an opportunity to serve actively or wait in the sense of waiting *in* service, a waiting that is itself fully satisfying because the impulse to self-glorifying action has been stilled.)

The question debated in the *Variorum Commentary* is, how far from the mood of frustration and impatience does the poem finally move? The answer given by an experiential analysis is that you can't tell, and the fact that you can't tell is responsible for the uneasiness the poem has always inspired. It is that uneasiness which the critics inadvertently acknowledge when they argue about the force of the last line, but they are unable to make analytical use of what they acknowledge because they have no way of dealing with or even recognizing experiential (that is, temporal) structures. In fact, more than one editor has eliminated those structures by punctuating them out of existence: first by putting a full stop at the end of line 6 and thereby making it unlikely that the reader will assign line 7 to God (there will no longer be an expectation of reported speech), and then by supplying quotation marks for the sestet in order to remove any doubts one might have as to who is speaking. There is of course no warrant for these emendations, and in 1791 Thomas Warton had the grace and honesty to admit as much. 'I have,' he said, 'introduced the turned commas both in the question and answer, not from any authority, but because they seem absolutely necessary to the sense'.[6]

Undoing the case for reader-response analysis

Editorial practices like these are only the most obvious manifestations of the assumptions to which I stand opposed: the assumption that there *is* a sense, that it is embedded or encoded in the text, and that it can be taken in at a single glance. These assumptions are, in order, positivist, holistic, and spatial, and to have them is to be committed both to a goal and to a procedure. The goal is to settle on a meaning, and the procedure involves first stepping back from the text, and then putting together or otherwise calculating the discrete units of significance it contains. My quarrel with this procedure (and with the assumptions that generate it) is that in the course of following it through the reader's activities are at once ignored and devalued. They are ignored because the text is taken to be self-sufficient—everything is *in* it—and they are devalued because when they are thought of at all, they are thought of as the disposable machinery of extraction. In the procedures I would urge, the reader's activities are at the center of attention, where they are regarded not as leading to meaning but as *having* meaning. The meaning they have is a consequence of their not being empty; for they include the making and revising of assumptions, the rendering and regretting of judgments, the coming to and abandoning of conclusions, the giving and withdrawing of approval, the specifying of causes, the asking of questions, the supplying of answers, the solving of puzzles. In a word, these activities are interpretive—rather than being preliminary to questions of value, they are at every moment settling and resettling questions of value—and because they are interpretive, a description of them will also be, and without any additional step, an interpretation, not after the fact but of the fact (of experiencing). It will be a description of a moving field of concerns, at once wholly present (not waiting for meaning but constituting meaning) and continually in the act of reconstituting itself.

As a project such a description presents enormous difficulties, and there is hardly time to consider them here;[7] but it should be obvious from my brief examples how different it is from the positivist-formalist project. Everything depends on the temporal dimension, and as a consequence the notion of a mistake, at least as something to be avoided, disappears. In a sequence where a reader first structures the field he inhabits and then is asked to restructure it (by changing an assignment of speaker or realigning attitudes and positions) there is no question of priority among his structurings; no one of them, even if it is the last, has privilege; each is equally legitimate, each equally the proper object of analysis, because each is equally an event in his experience.

The firm assertiveness of this paragraph only calls attention to the questions it avoids. Who is this reader? How can I presume to describe his experiences, and what do I say to readers who report that they do not have the experiences I describe? Let me answer these questions or rather make a beginning at answering them in the context of another example, this time from Milton's *Comus*. In line 46 of *Comus* we are introduced to the villain by way of a genealogy:

> Bacchus that first from out the purple grape,
> Crushed the sweet poison of misused wine.

In almost any edition of this poem, a footnote will tell you that Bacchus is the god of wine. Of course most readers already know that, and because they know it, they will be anticipating the appearance of 'wine' long before they come upon it in the final position. Moreover, they will also be anticipating a negative judgment on it, in part because of the association of Bacchus with revelry and excess, and especially because the phrase 'sweet poison' suggests that the judgment has already been made. At an early point then, we will have both filled in the form of the assertion and made a decision about its moral content. That decision is upset by the word 'misused'; for what 'misused' asks us to do is transfer the pressure of judgment from wine (where we have already placed it) to the abusers of wine, and therefore when 'wine' finally appears, we must declare it innocent of the charges we have ourselves made.

This, then, is the structure of the reader's experience—the transferring of a moral label from a thing to those who appropriate it. It is an experience that depends on a reader for whom the name Bacchus has precise and immediate associations; another reader, a reader for whom those associations are less precise will not have that experience because he will not have rushed to a conclusion in relation to which the word 'misused' will stand as a challenge. Obviously I am discriminating between these two readers and between the two equally real experiences they will have. It is not a discrimination based simply on information, because what is important is not the information itself, but the action of the mind which its possession makes possible for one reader and impossible for the other. One might discriminate further between them by noting that the point at issue— whether value is a function of objects and actions or of intentions—is at the heart of the seventeenth-century debate over 'things indifferent.' A reader who is aware of that debate will not only *have* the experience I describe; he will recognize at the end of it that he has been asked to take a position on one side of a continuing controversy; and that recognition (also a part of his experience) will be part of the disposition with which he moves into the lines that follow.

It would be possible to continue with this profile of the optimal reader, but I would not get very far before someone would point out that what I am really describing is the intended reader, the reader whose education, opinions, concerns, linguistic competences, and so on make him capable of having the experience the author wished to provide. I would not resist this characterization because it seems obvious that the efforts of readers are always efforts to discern and therefore to realize (in the sense of becoming) an author's intention. I would only object if that realization were conceived narrowly, as the single act of comprehending an author's purpose, rather than (as I would conceive it) as the succession of acts readers perform in the continuing assumption that they are dealing with intentional beings. In this view discerning an intention is no more or less than understanding, and understanding includes (is constituted by) all the activities which make up what I call the structure of the reader's experience. To describe that experience is therefore to describe the reader's efforts at understanding, and to describe the reader's efforts at understanding is to describe his realization (in two senses) of an author's intention. Or to put it another way, what my analyses amount to are descriptions of a succession of decisions made by readers about an author's intention—decisions that are not limited to the specifying of purpose but include the specifying of every aspect of successively intended worlds, decisions that are precisely the shape, because they are the content, of the reader's activities.

Having said this, however, it would appear that I am open to two objections. The first is that the procedure is a circular one. I describe the experience of a reader who in his strategies is answerable to an author's intention, and I specify the author's intention by pointing to the strategies employed by that same reader. But this objection would have force only if it were possible to specify one independently of the other. What is being specified from either perspective are the conditions of utterance, of what could have been understood to have been meant by what was said. That is, intention and understanding are two ends of a conventional act, each of which necessarily stipulates (includes, defines, specifies) the other. To construct the profile of the informed or at-home reader is at the same time to characterize the author's intention and vice versa, because to do either is to specify the *contemporary* conditions of utterance, to identify, by becoming a member of, a community made up of those who share interpretive strategies.

The second objection is another version of the first: if the content of the reader's experience is the succession of acts he performs in search of an author's intentions, and if he performs those acts at the bidding of the text, does not the text then produce or contain everything—intention *and* experience—and have I not compromised my antiformalist position? This objection will have force only if the formal patterns of the text are assumed to exist independently of the reader's experience, for only then can priority be claimed for them. Indeed, the claims of independence and priority are one and the same; when they are separated it is so that they can give circular and illegitimate support to each other. The question 'do formal features exist independently?' is usually answered by pointing to their priority: they are 'in' the text before the reader comes to it. The question 'are formal features prior?' is usually answered by pointing to their independent status: they are 'in' the text before the reader comes to it. What looks like a step in an argument is actually the spectacle of an assertion supporting itself. It follows then that an attack on the independence of formal features will also be an attack on their priority (and vice versa), and I would like to mount such an attack in the context of two short passages from *Lycidas*.

The first passage (actually the second in the poem's sequence) begins at line 42:

> The willows and the hazel copses green
> Shall now no more be seen,
> Fanning their joyous leaves to thy soft lays.

It is my thesis that the reader is always making sense (I intend 'making' to have its literal force), and in the case of these lines the sense he makes will involve the assumption (and therefore the creation) of a completed assertion after the word 'seen,' to wit, the death of Lycidas has so affected the willows and the hazel copses green that, in sympathy, they will wither and die (will no more be seen by *anyone*). In other words, at the end of line 43 the reader will have hazarded an interpretation, or performed an act of perceptual closure, or made a decision as to what is being asserted. I do not mean that he has done four things, but that he has done one thing the description of which might take any one of four forms—making sense, interpreting, performing perceptual closure, deciding about what is intended. (The importance of this point will become clear later.) Whatever he has done (that is, however we characterize it), he will undo it in the act of reading the next line, for here he discovers that his closure, or making of sense, was premature and that he must make a new one in which the relationship between man and nature is exactly the reverse of what was first assumed. The willows and the hazel copses green will in fact be seen, but they will not be seen by Lycidas. It is he who will be no more, while they go on as before, fanning their joyous leaves to someone else's soft lays (the whole of line 44 is now perceived as modifying and removing the absoluteness of 'seen'). Nature is not sympathetic, but indifferent, and the notion of her sympathy is one of those 'false surmises' that the poem is continually encouraging and then disallowing.

The previous sentence shows how easy it is to surrender to the bias of our critical language and begin to talk as if poems, not readers or interpreters, did things. Words like 'encourage' and 'disallow' (and others I have used in this essay) imply agents, and it is only 'natural' to assign agency first to an author's intentions and then to the forms that assumedly embody them. What really happens, I think, is something quite different: rather than intention and its formal realization producing interpretation (the 'normal' picture), interpretation creates intention and its formal realization, by creating the conditions in which it becomes possible to pick them out. In other words, in the analysis of these lines from *Lycidas* I did what critics always do: I 'saw' what my interpretive principles permitted or directed me to see, and then I turned around and attributed what I had 'seen' to a text and an intention. What my principles direct me to 'see' are readers performing acts; the points at which I find (or to be more precise, declare) those acts to have been performed become (by a sleight of hand) demarcations *in* the text; those demarcations are then available for the designation 'formal features,' and as formal features they can be (illegitimately) assigned the responsibility for producing the interpretation which in fact produced them. In this case, the demarcation my interpretation calls into being is placed at the end of line 42; but of course the end of that (or any other) line is worth noticing or pointing out only because my model *demands* (the word is not too strong) perceptual closures and therefore locations at which they occur; in that model this point will be one of those locations, although (1) it need not have been (not every line ending occasions a closure) and (2) in another model, one that does not give value to the activities of readers, the possibility of its being one would not have arisen

What I am suggesting is that formal units are always a function of the inter-pretative model one brings to bear; they are not 'in' the text, and I would make the same argument for intentions. That is, intention is no more embodied 'in' the text than are formal units; rather an intention, like a formal unit, is made when perceptual or interpretive closure is hazarded; it is verified by an interpretive act, and I would add, it is not verifiable in any other way. This last assertion is too large to be fully considered here, but I can sketch out the argumentative sequence I would follow were I to consider it: intention is known when and only when it is recognized; it is recognized as soon as you decide about it; you decide about it as soon as you make a sense; and you make a sense (or so my model claims) as soon as you can.

Let me tie up the threads of my argument with a final example from *Lycidas*:

> He must not float upon his wat'ry bier
> Unwept . . .

Here the reader's experience has much the same career as it does in lines 42–44: at the end of line 13 perceptual closure is hazarded, and a sense is made in which the line is taken to be a resolution bordering on a promise: that is, there is now an expectation that something will be done about this unfortunate situation, and the reader anticipates a call to action, perhaps even a program for the undertaking of a rescue mission. With 'Unwept,' however, that expectation and anticipation are disappointed, and the realization of that disappointment will be inseparable from the making of a new (and less comforting) sense: nothing will be done; Lycidas will continue to float upon his wat'ry bier, and the only action taken will be the lamenting of the fact that no action will be efficacious, including the actions of speaking and listening to this lament (which in line 15 will receive the meretricious and self-mocking designation 'melodious tear'). Three 'structures' come into view at precisely the same moment, the moment when the reader having resolved a sense unresolves it and makes a new one; that moment will also be the moment of picking out a formal pattern or unit, end of line/beginning of line, and it will also be the moment at which the reader, having decided about the speaker's intention, about what is meant by what has been said, will make the decision again and in so doing will make another intention.

This, then, is my thesis: that the form of the reader's experience, formal units, and the structure of intention are one, that they come into view simultaneously, and that therefore the questions of priority and independence do not arise. What does arise is another question: what produces *them*? That is, if intention, form, and the shape of the reader's experience are simply different ways of referring to (different perspectives on) the same interpretive act, what is that act an interpretation *of*? I cannot answer that question, but neither, I would claim, can anyone else, although formalists try to answer it by pointing to patterns and claiming that they are available independently of (prior to) interpretation. These patterns vary according to the procedures that yield them: they may be statistical (number of two-syllable words per hundred words), grammatical (ratio of passive to active constructions, or of right-branching to left-branching sentences, or of anything else); but whatever they are I would argue that they do not lie innocently in the world but are themselves constituted by an interpretive act, even if, as is often the case, that act is unacknowledged. Of course, this is as true of my analyses as it is of anyone else's. In the examples offered here I appropriate the notion 'line ending' and treat it as a fact of nature; and one might conclude that as a fact it is responsible for the reading experience I describe. The truth I think is exactly the reverse: line endings exist by virtue of perceptual strategies rather than the other way around. Historically, the strategy that we know as 'reading (or hearing) poetry' has included paying attention to the line as a unit, but it is precisely that attention which has made the line as a unit (either of print or of aural duration) available. A reader so practiced in paying that attention that he regards the line as a brute fact rather than as a convention will have a great deal of difficulty with concrete poetry; if he overcomes that difficulty, it will not be because he has learned to ignore the line as a unit but because he will have acquired a new set of interpretive strategies (the strategies constitutive of 'concrete poetry reading') in the context of which the line as a unit no longer exists. In short, what is noticed is what has been *made* noticeable, not by a clear and undistorting glass, but by an interpretive strategy.

This may be hard to see when the strategy has become so habitual that the forms it yields seem part of the world. We find it easy to assume that alliteration as an effect depends on a 'fact' that exists independently of any interpretive 'use' one might make of it, the fact that words in proximity begin with the same letter. But it takes only a moment's reflection to realize that the sameness, far from being natural, is enforced by an orthographic convention; that is to say, it is the product of an interpretation. Were we to substitute phonetic conventions for orthographic ones (a 'reform' traditionally urged by purists), the supposedly 'objective' basis for alliteration would disappear because a phonetic transcription would require that we distinguish between the initial sounds of those very words that enter into alliterative relationships; rather than conforming to those relationships, the rules of spelling make them. One might reply that, since alliteration is an aural rather than a visual phenomenon when poetry is heard, we have unmediated access to the physical sounds themselves and hear 'real' similarities. But phonological 'facts' are no more uninterpreted (or less conventional) than the 'facts' of orthography; the distinctive features that make articulation and reception possible are the product of a system of differences that must be *imposed* before it can be recognized; the patterns the ear hears (like the patterns the eye sees) are the patterns its perceptual habits make available.

One can extend this analysis forever, even to the 'facts' of grammar. The history of linguistics is the history of competing paradigms, each of which offers a different account of the constituents of language. Verbs, nouns, cleft sentences, transformations, deep and surface structures, semes, rhemes, tagmemes—now you see them, now you don't, depending on the descriptive apparatus you employ. The critic who confidently rests his analyses on the bedrock of syntactic descriptions is resting on an interpretation; the facts he points to *are* there, but only as a consequence of the interpretive (man-made) model that has called them into being.

The moral is clear: the choice is never between objectivity and interpretation but between an interpretation that is unacknowledged as such and an interpretation that is at least aware of itself. It is this awareness that I am claiming for myself, although in doing so I must give up the claims implicitly made in the first part of this essay. There I argue that a bad (because spatial) model had suppressed what was really happening, but by my own declared principles the notion 'really happening' is just one more interpretation.

Interpretive communities

It seems then that the price one pays for denying the priority of either forms or intentions is an inability to say how it is that one ever begins. Yet we do begin, and we continue, and because we do there arises an immediate counterobjection to the preceding pages. If interpretive acts are the source of forms rather than the other way around, why isn't it the case that readers are always performing the same acts or a sequence of random acts, and therefore creating the same forms or a random succession of forms? How, in short, does one explain these two 'facts' of reading? (1) The same reader will perform differently when reading two 'different' (the word is in quotation marks because its status is precisely what is at issue) texts; and (2) different readers will perform similarly when reading the 'same' (in quotes for the same reason) text. That is to say, both the stability of interpretation among readers and the variety of interpretation in the career of a single reader would seem to argue for the existence of something independent of and prior to interpretive acts, something which produces them. I will answer this challenge by asserting that both the stability and the variety are functions of interpretive strategies rather than of texts.

Let us suppose that I am reading *Lycidas*. What is it that I am doing? First of all, what I am not doing is 'simply reading,' an activity in which I do not believe because it implies the possibility of pure (that is, disinterested) perception. Rather, I am proceeding on the basis of (at least) two interpretive decisions. (1) That *Lycidas* is a pastoral (2) that it was written by Milton. (I should add that the notions 'pastoral' and 'Milton' are also interpretations; that is, they do not stand for a set of indisputable, objective facts; if they did, a great many books would not now be getting written.) Once these decisions have been made (and if I had not made these I would have made others, and they would be consequential in the same way), I am immediately predisposed to perform certain acts, to 'find,' by looking for, themes (the relationship between natural processes and the careers of men, the efficacy of poetry or of any other action), to confer significances (on flowers, streams, shepherds, pagan deities), to mark out 'formal' units (the lament, the consolation, the turn, the affirmation of faith, and so on). My disposition to perform these acts (and others; the list is not meant to be exhaustive) constitutes a set of interpretive strategies, which, when they are put into execution, become the large act of reading. This is to say, interpretive strategies are not put into execution after reading (the pure act of perception in which I do not believe); they are the shape of reading, and because they are the shape of reading, they give texts their shape, making them rather than, as it is usually assumed, arising from them. Several important things follow from this account:
(1) I did not have to execute this particular set of interpretive strategies

because I did not have to make those particular interpretive (pre-reading) decisions. I could have decided, for example, that *Lycidas* was a text in which a set of fantasies and defenses find expression. These decisions would have entailed the assumption of another set of interpretive strategies (perhaps like that put forward by Norman Holland in *The Dynamics of Literary Response*) and the execution of that set would have made another text.

(2) I could execute this same set of strategies when presented with texts that did not bear the title (again a notion which is itself an interpretation) *Lycidas, A Pastoral Monody*. I could decide (it is a decision some have made) that *Adam Bede* is a pastoral written by an author who consciously modeled herself on Milton (still remembering that 'pastoral' and 'Milton' are interpretations, not facts in the public domain); or I could decide, as Empson did, that a great many things not usually considered pastoral were in fact to be so read; and either decision would give rise to a set of interpretive strategies, which, when put into action, would *write* the text I write when reading *Lycidas*. (Are you with me?)

(3) A reader other than myself who, when presented with *Lycidas*, proceeds to put into execution a set of interpretive strategies similar to mine (how he could do so is a question I will take up later), will perform the same (or at least a similar) succession of interpretive acts. He and I then might be tempted to say that we agree about the poem (thereby assuming that the poem exists independently of the acts either of us performs); but what we really would agree about is the way to write it.

(4) A reader other than myself who, when presented with *Lycidas* (please keep in mind that the status of *Lycidas* is what is at issue), puts into execution a different set of interpretive strategies, will perform a different succession of interpretive acts. (I am assuming, it is the article of my faith, that a reader will always execute some set of interpretive strategies and therefore perform some succession of interpretive acts.) One of us might then be tempted to complain to the other that we could not possibly be reading the same poem (literary criticism is full of such complaints) and he would be right; for each of us would be reading the poem he had made.

The large conclusion that follows from these four smaller ones is that the notions of the 'same' or 'different' texts are fictions. If I read *Lycidas* and *The Waste Land* differently (in fact I do not), it will not be because the formal structures of the two poems (to term them such is also an interpretive decision) call forth different interpretive strategies but because my predisposition to execute different interpretive strategies will *produce* different formal structures. That is, the two poems are different because I have decided that they will be. The proof of this is the possibility of doing the reverse (that is why point 2 is so important). That is to say, the answer to the question 'why do different texts give rise to different sequences of interpretive acts?' is that *they don't have to*, an answer which implies strongly that 'they' don't exist. Indeed, it has always been possible to put into action interpretive strategies designed to make all texts one, or to put it more accurately, to be forever making the same text. Augustine urges just such a strategy, for example, in *On Christian Doctrine* where he delivers the 'rule of faith' which is of course a rule of interpretation. It is dazzlingly simple: everything in the Scriptures, and indeed in the world when it is properly read, points to (bears the meaning of) God's love for us and our answering responsibility to love our fellow creatures for His sake. If only you should come upon something which does not at first seem to bear this meaning, that 'does not literally pertain to virtuous behavior or to the truth of faith,' you are then to take it 'to be figurative' and proceed to scrutinize it 'until an interpretation contributing to the reign of charity is produced.' This is then both a stipulation of what meaning there is and a set of directions for finding it, which is of course a set of directions—of interpretive strategies—for making it, that is, for the endless reproduction of the same text. Whatever one may think of this interpretive program, its success and ease of execution are attested to by centuries of Christian exegesis. It is my contention that any interpretive program, any set of interpretive strategies, can have a similar success, although few have been as spectacularly successful as this one. (For some time now, for at least three hundred years, the most successful interpretive program has gone under the name 'ordinary language.') In our own discipline programs with the same characteristic of always reproducing one text include psychoanalytic criticism, Robertsonianism[a] (always threatening to extend its sway into later and later periods), numerology (a sameness based on the assumption of innumerable fixed differences).

The other challenging question—'why will different readers execute the same interpretive strategy when faced with the "same" text?'—can be handled in the same way. The answer is again that *they don't have to*, and my evidence is the entire history of literary criticism. And again this answer implies that the notion 'same text' is the product of the possession by two or more readers of similar interpretive strategies.

But why should this ever happen? Why should two or more readers ever agree, and why should regular, that is, habitual, differences in the career of a single reader ever occur? What is the explanation on the one hand of the stability of interpretation (at least among certain groups at certain times) and on the other of the orderly variety of interpretation if it is not the stability and variety of texts? The answer to all of these questions is to be found in a notion that has been implicit in my argument, the notion of *interpretive communities*. Interpretive communities are made up of those who share interpretive strategies not for reading (in the conventional sense) but for writing texts, for constituting their properties and assigning their intentions. In other words, these strategies exist prior to the act of reading and therefore determine the shape of what is read rather than, as is usually assumed, the other way around. If it is an article of faith in a particular community that there are a variety of texts, its members will boast a repertoire of strategies for making them. And if a community believes in the existence of only one text, then the single strategy its members employ will be forever writing it. The first community will accuse the members of the second of being reductive, and they in turn will call their accusers superficial. The assumption in each community will be that the other is not correctly perceiving the 'true text,' but the truth will be that each perceives the text (or texts) its

[a] A reference to the medievalist, D. W. Robertson.

327

interpretive strategies demand and call into being. This, then, is the explanation both for the stability of interpretation among different readers (they belong to the same community) and for the regularity with which a single reader will employ different interpretive strategies and thus make different texts (he belongs to different communities). It also explains why there are disagreements and why they can be debated in a principled way: not because of a stability in texts, but because of a stability in the makeup of interpretive communities and therefore in the opposing positions they make possible. Of course this stability is always temporary (unlike the longed for and timeless stability of the text). Interpretive communities grow and decline, and individuals move from one to another; thus, while the alignments are not permanent, they are always there, providing just enough stability for the interpretive battles to go on, and just enough shift and slippage to assure that they will never be settled. The notion of interpretive communities thus stands between an impossible ideal and the fear which leads so many to maintain it. The ideal is of perfect agreement and it would require texts to have a status independent of interpretation. The fear is of interpretive anarchy, but it would only be realized if interpretation (text making) were completely random. It is the fragile but real consolidation of interpretive communities that allows us to talk to one another, but with no hope or fear of ever being able to stop.

In other words interpretive communities are no more stable than texts because interpretive strategies are not natural or universal, but learned. This does not mean that there is a point at which an individual has not yet learned any. The ability to interpret is not acquired; it is constitutive of being human. What is acquired are the ways of interpreting and those same ways can also be forgotten or supplanted, or complicated or dropped from favor ('no one reads that way anymore'). When any of these things happens, there is a corresponding change in texts, not because they are being read differently, but because they are being written differently.

The only stability, then, inheres in the fact (at least in my model) that interpretive strategies are always being deployed, and this means that communication is a much more chancy affair than we are accustomed to think it. For if there are no fixed texts, but only interpretive strategies making them, and if interpretive strategies are not natural, but learned (and are therefore unavailable to a finite description), what is it that utterers (speakers, authors, critics, me, you) do? In the old model utterers are in the business of handing over ready-made or prefabricated meanings. These meanings are said to be encoded, and the code is assumed to be in the world independently of the individuals who are obliged to attach themselves to it (if they do not they run the danger of being declared deviant). In my model, however, meanings are not extracted but made and made not by encoded forms but by interpretive strategies that call forms into being. It follows then that what utterers do is give hearers and readers the opportunity to make meanings (and texts) by inviting them to put into execution a set of strategies. It is presumed that the invitation will be recognized, and that presumption rests on a projection on the part of a speaker or author of the moves *he* would make if confronted by the sounds or marks he is uttering or setting down.

It would seem at first that this account of things simply reintroduces the old objection; for isn't this an admission that there is after all a formal encoding, not perhaps of meanings, but of the directions for making them, for executing interpretive strategies? The answer is that they will only *be* directions to those who already have the interpretive strategies in the first place. Rather than producing interpretive acts, they are the product of one. An author hazards his projection, not because of something 'in' the marks, but because of something he assumes to be in his reader. The very existence of the 'marks' is a function of an interpretive community, for they will be recognized (that is, made) only by its members. Those outside that community will be deploying a different set of interpretive strategies (interpretation cannot be withheld) and will therefore be making different marks.

So once again I have made the text disappear, but unfortunately the problems do not disappear with it. If everyone is continually executing interpretive strategies and in that act constituting texts, intentions, speakers, and authors, how can any one of us know whether or not he is a member of the same interpretive community as any other of us? The answer is that he can't, since any evidence brought forward to support the claim would itself be an interpretation (especially if the 'other' were an author long dead). The only 'proof' of membership is fellowship, the nod of recognition from someone in the same community, someone who says to you what neither of us could ever prove to a third party: 'we know.' I say it to you now, knowing full well that you will agree with me (that is, understand) only if you already agree with me.

NOTES

1. All references are to *The Poems of John Milton*, ed. John Carey and Alastair Fowler (London: Longman, 1968).
2. *A Variorum Commentary on the Poems of John Milton*, vol. 2, pt. 2, ed. A. S. P. Woodhouse and Douglas Bush (New York: Columbia University Press, 1972), p. 475.
3. It is first of all a reference to the city of iniquity from which the Hebrews are urged to flee in Isaiah and Jeremiah. In Protestant polemics Babylon is identified with the Roman Church whose destruction is prophesied in the book of Revelation. And in some Puritan tracts Babylon is the name for Augustine's earthly city, from which the faithful are to flee inwardly in order to escape the fate awaiting the unregenerate. See *Variorum Commentary*, pp. 440–441.
4. *Variorum Commentary*, p. 469.
5. Ibid., p. 457.
6. *Poems upon Several Occasions, English, Italian, and Latin, with Translations, by John Milton*, ed. Thomas Warton (London, 1791), p. 352.
7. See my *Surprised by Sin: The Reader in Paradise Lost* (London and New York: Macmillan, 1967); *Self-Consuming Artifacts: The Experience of Seventeenth-Century Literature* (Berkeley: University of California Press, 1972); 'What Is Stylistics and Why Are They Saying Such Terrible Things About It?'; 'How Ordinary Is Ordinary Language?'; 'Facts and Fictions: A Reply to Ralph Rader' in *Is there a Text in This Class?* (Cambridge Mass.: Harvard University Press, 1980).

20 Elaine Showalter

Elaine Showalter (b. 1941) taught English and Women's Studies for many years at Rutgers University, and is now Professor of English at Princeton. Her book, *A Literature of Their Own: British women novelists from Brontë to Lessing* (1977) quickly established itself as an authoritative study of its subject, and a standard textbook in the rapidly burgeoning field of women's studies.

Contemporary feminist criticism obviously derived its original impetus from the Women's Liberation Movement of the late 1960s, Mary Ellman's *Thinking About Women* (1968) and Kate Millett's *Sexual Politics* (1970) being pioneering books in this respect. The initial effort of feminist critics was to revise orthodox 'male' literary history, exposing sexual stereotyping in canonical texts and reinterpreting or reviving the work of women writers. Elaine Showalter's *A Literature of Their Own* was a major contribution to this project, but by the late 1970s it seemed to her that feminist criticism had reached 'a theoretical impasse'. In a lecture delivered in 1978, entitled 'Towards a Feminist Poetics' (published in *Women's Writing and Writing About Women*, ed. Mary Jacobus [1979], reprinted in *The New Feminist Criticism*, ed. Showalter [1985]), she attributed this impasse to the essentially male character of 'theory' itself, as practised and professionally institutionalized in the academy.

In 'Feminist Criticism in the Wilderness', first published in *Critical Inquiry* in 1981, she finds feminist criticism no more unified, but more adventurous in assimilating and engaging with theory: 'it now appears that what looked like a theoretical impasse was actually an evolutionary phase'. This lucid and informative survey of contemporary feminist criticism is backed up with notes that constitute a valuable bibliography of the field. It is reprinted here from *The New Feminist Criticism*, edited by Elaine Showalter (1985).

CROSS-REFERENCE: 17. Cixous
26. Mitchell

COMMENTARY: K. K. Ruthven, *Feminist Literary Studies: an Introduction* (1984)
Sydney Kaplan, 'Varieties of feminist criticism,' in *Making a Difference: Feminist Literary Criticism* (1985)

Feminist criticism in the wilderness

Pluralism and the feminist critique

> Women have no wilderness in them,
> They are provident instead
> Content in the tight hot cell of
>   their hearts
> To eat dusty bread.
>   Louise Bogan, 'Women'

In a splendidly witty dialogue of 1975, Carolyn Heilbrun and Catharine Stimpson identified two poles of feminist literary criticism. The first of these modes, righteous, angry, and admonitory, they compared to the Old Testament, 'looking for the sins and errors of the past.' The second mode, disinterested and seeking 'the grace of imagination,' they compared to the New Testament. Both are necessary, they concluded, for only the Jeremiahs of ideology can lead us out of the 'Egypt of female servitude' to the promised land of humanism.[1] Matthew Arnold also thought that literary critics might perish in the wilderness before they reached the promised land of disinterestedness. Heilbrun and Stimpson were neo-Arnoldian as befitted members of the Columbia and Barnard faculties. But if, in the 1980s, feminist literary critics are still wandering in the wilderness, we are in good company; for, as Geoffrey Hartman tells us, *all* criticism is in the wilderness.[2] Feminist critics may be startled to find ourselves in this band of theoretical pioneers, since in the American literary tradition the wilderness has been an exclusively masculine domain. Yet between feminist ideology and the liberal ideal of disinterestedness lies the wilderness of theory, which we too must make our home.

Until very recently, feminist criticism has not had a theoretical basis; it has been an empirical orphan in the theoretical storm. In 1975, I was persuaded that no theoretical manifesto could adequately account for the varied methodologies and ideologies which called themselves feminist reading or writing.[3] By the next year, Annette Kolodny had added her observation that feminist literary criticism appeared 'more like a set of interchangeable strategies than any coherent school or shared goal orientation.'[4] Since then, the expressed goals have not been notably unified. Black critics protest the 'massive silence' of feminist criticism about black and Third-World women writers and call for a black feminist aesthetic that would deal with both racial and sexual politics. Marxist feminists wish to focus on class along with gender as a crucial determinant of literary production.[5] Literary historians want to uncover a lost tradition. Critics trained in deconstructionist methodologies wish to 'synthesize a literary criticism that is both textual and feminist.'[6] Freudian and Lacanian critics want to theorize about women's relationship to language and signification.

An early obstacle to constructing a theoretical framework for feminist criticism was the unwillingness of many women to limit or bound an expressive and dynamic enterprise. The openness of feminist criticism appealed particularly to Americans who perceived the structuralist, post-structuralist, and deconstructionist debates of the 1970s as arid and falsely objective, the epitome of a pernicious masculine discourse from which many feminists wished to escape. Recalling in *A Room of One's Own* how she had been prohibited from entering the university library, the symbolic sanctuary of the male *logos*, Virginia Woolf wisely observed that while it is 'unpleasant to be locked out . . . it is worse, perhaps, to be locked in.' Advocates of the antitheoretical position traced their descent from Woolf and from other feminist visionaries, such as Mary Daly, Adrienne Rich and Marguerite Duras, who had satirized the sterile narcissism of male scholarship and celebrated women's fortunate exclusion from its patriarchal methodolatry. Thus for some, feminist criticism was an act of resistance to theory, a confrontation with existing canons and judgments, what Josephine Donovan calls 'a mode of negation within a fundamental dialectic.' As Judith Fetterley declared in her book, *The Resisting Reader*, feminist criticism has been characterized by 'a resistance to codification and a refusal to have its parameters prematurely set.' I have discussed elsewhere, with considerable sympathy, the suspicion of monolithic systems and the rejection of scientism in literary study that many feminist critics have voiced. While scientific criticism struggled to purge itself of the subjective, feminist criticism reasserted the authority of experience.[7]

Yet it now appears that what looked like a theoretical impasse was actually an evolutionary phase. The ethics of awakening have been succeeded, at least in the universities, by a second stage characterized by anxiety about the isolation of feminist criticism from a critical community increasingly theoretical in its interests and indifferent to women's writing. The question of how feminist criticism should define itself with relation to the new critical theories and theorists has occasioned sharp debate in Europe and the United States. Nina Auerbach has noted the absence of dialogue and asks whether feminist criticism itself must accept responsibility:

> Feminist critics seem particularly reluctant to define themselves to the uninitiated. There is a sense in which our sisterhood has become too powerful; as a school, our belief in ourself is so potent that we decline communication with the networks of power and respectability we say we want to change.[8]

But rather than declining communication with these networks, feminist criticism has indeed spoken directly to them, in their own media: *PMLA*, *Diacritics*, *Glyph*, *Tel Quel*, *New Literary History*, and *Critical Inquiry*. For the feminist critic seeking clarification, the proliferation of communiqués may itself prove confusing.

There are two distinct modes of feminist criticism, and to conflate them (as most commentators do) is to remain permanently bemused by their theoretical potentialities. The first mode is ideological; it is concerned with the feminist as *reader*, and it offers feminist readings of texts which consider the images and stereotypes of women in literature, the omissions and misconceptions about women in criticism, and woman-as-sign in semiotic systems. This is not all feminist reading can do; it can be a liberating intellectual act, as Adrienne Rich proposes:

A radical critique of literature, feminist in its impulse, would take the work first of all as a clue to how we live, how we have been living, how we have been led to imagine ourselves, how our language has trapped as well as liberated us, how the very act of naming has been till now a male prerogative, and how we can begin to see and name—and therefore live—afresh.[9]

This invigorating encounter with literature, which I will call *feminist reading* or the *feminist critique*, is in essence a mode of interpretation, one of many which any complex text will accommodate and permit. It is very difficult to propose theoretical coherence in an activity which by its nature is so eclectic and wide-ranging, although as a critical practice feminist reading has certainly been influential. But in the free play of the interpretive field, the feminist critique can only compete with alternative readings, all of which have the built-in obsolescence of Buicks, cast away as newer readings take their plase. As Kolodny, the most sophisticated theorist of feminist interpretation, has conceded:

All the feminist is asserting, then, is her own equivalent right to liberate new (and perhaps different) significances from these same texts; and, at the same time, her right to choose which features of a text she takes as relevant because she is, after all, asking new and different questions of it. In the process, she claims neither definitiveness nor structural completeness for her different readings and reading systems, but only their usefulness in recognizing the particular achievements of woman-as-author and their applicability in conscientiously decoding woman-as-sign.

Rather than being discouraged by these limited objectives, Kolodny found them the happy cause of the 'playful pluralism' of feminist critical theory, a pluralism which she believes to be 'the only critical stance consistent with the current status of the larger women's movement.'[10] Her feminist critic dances adroitly through the theoretical minefield.

Keenly aware of the political issues involved and presenting brilliant arguments, Kolodny nonetheless fails to convince me that feminist criticism must altogether abandon its hope 'of establishing some basic conceptual model.' If we see our critical job as interpretation and reinterpretation, we must be content with pluralism as our critical stance. But if we wish to ask questions about the process and the contexts of writing, if we genuinely wish to define ourselves to the uninitiated, we cannot rule out the prospect of theoretical consensus at this early stage.

All feminist criticism is in some sense revisionist, questioning the adequacy of accepted conceptual structures, and indeed most contemporary American criticism claims to be revisionist too. The most exciting and comprehensive case for this

333

'revisionary imperative' is made by Sandra Gilbert: at its most ambitious, she asserts, feminist criticism 'wants to decode and demystify all the disguised questions and answers that have always shadowed the connections between textuality and sexuality, genre and gender, psychosexual identity and cultural authority.'[11] But in practice, the revisionary feminist critique is redressing a grievance and is built upon existing models. No one would deny that feminist criticism has affinities to other contemporary critical practices and methodologies and that the best work is also the most fully informed. Nonetheless, the feminist obsession with correcting, modifying, supplementing, revising, humanizing, or even attacking male critical theory keeps us dependent upon it and retards our progress in solving our own theoretical problems. What I mean here by 'male critical theory' is a concept of creativity, literary history, or literary interpretation based entirely on male experience and put forward as universal. So long as we look to androcentric models for our most basic principles—even if we revise them by adding the feminist frame of reference—we are learning nothing new. And when the process is so one-sided, when male critics boast of their ignorance of feminist criticism, it is disheartening to find feminist critics still anxious for approval from the 'white fathers' who will not listen or reply. Some feminist critics have taken upon themselves a revisionism which becomes a kind of homage; they have made Lacan the ladies' man of *Diacritics* and have forced Pierre Macherey into those dark alleys of the psyche where Engels feared to tread. According to Christiane Makward, the problem is even more serious in France than in the United States: 'If neofeminist thought in France seems to have ground to a halt,' she writes, 'it is because it has continued to feed on the discourse of the masters.'[12]

It is time for feminist criticism to decide whether between religion and revision we can claim any firm theoretical ground of our own. In calling for a feminist criticism that is genuinely women centered, independent, and intellectually coherent, I do not mean to endorse the separatist fantasies of radical feminist visionaries or to exclude from our critical practice a variety of intellectual tools. But we need to ask much more searchingly what we want to know and how we can find answers to the questions that come from *our* experience. I do not think that feminist criticism can find a usable past in the androcentric critical tradition. It has more to learn from women's studies than from English studies, more to learn from international feminist theory than from another seminar on the masters. It must find its own subject, its own system, its own theory, and its own voice. As Rich writes of Emily Dickinson, in her poem 'I Am in Danger—Sir—,' we must choose to have the argument out at last on our own premises.

Defining the feminine: gynocritics and the woman's test

A woman's writing is always feminine; it cannot help being feminine; at its best it is most feminine; the only difficulty lies in defining what we mean by feminine.

Virginia Woolf

It is impossible to define a feminine practice of writing, and this is an impossibility that will remain, for this practice will never be theorized, enclosed, encoded—which doesn't mean that it doesn't exist.

Hélène Cixous, 'The Laugh of the Medusa'

In the past decade, I believe, this process of defining the feminine has started to take place. Feminist criticism has gradually shifted its center from revisionary readings to a sustained investigation of literature by women. The second mode of feminist criticism engendered by this process is the study of women *as writers*, and its subjects are the history, styles, themes, genres, and structures of writing by women; the psychodynamics of female creativity; the trajectory of the individual or collective female career; and the evolution and laws of a female literary tradition. No English term exists for such a specialized critical discourse, and so I have invented the term 'gynocritics.' Unlike the feminist critique, gynocritics offers many theoretical opportunities. To see women's writing as our primary subject forces us to make the leap to a new conceptual vantage point and to redefine the nature of the theoretical problem before us. It is no longer the ideological dilemma of reconciling revisionary pluralisms but the essential question of difference. How can we constitute women as a distinct literary group? What is *the difference* of women's writing?

Patricia Meyer Spacks, I think, was the first academic critic to notice this shift from an androcentric to a gynocentric feminist criticism. In *The Female Imagination* (1975), she pointed out that few feminist theorists had concerned themselves with women's writing. Simone de Beauvoir's treatment of women writers in *The Second Sex* 'always suggests an a priori tendency to take them less seriously than their masculine counterparts'; Mary Ellmann, in *Thinking about Women*, characterized women's literary success as escape from the categories of womanhood; and, according to Spacks, Kate Millett, in *Sexual Politics*, 'has little interest in women imaginative writers.'[13] Spacks's wideranging study inaugurated a new period of feminist literary history and criticism which asked, again and again, how women's writing had been different, how womanhood itself shaped women's creative expression. In such books as Ellen Moers's *Literary Women* (1976), my *A Literature of Their Own* (1977), Nina Baym's *Woman's Fiction* (1978), Sandra Gilbert and Susan Gubar's *The Madwoman in the Attic* (1979), and Margaret Homans's *Women Writers and Poetic Identity* (1980), and in hundreds of essays and papers, women's writing asserted itself as the central project of feminist literary study.

This shift in emphasis has also taken place in European feminist criticism. To date, most commentary on French feminist critical discourse has stressed its fundamental dissimilarity from the empirical American orientation, its unfamiliar intellectual grounding in linguistics, Marxism, neo-Freudian and Lacanian psychoanalysis, and Derridean deconstruction. Despite these differences, however, the new French feminisms have much in common with radical American feminist theories in terms of intellectual affiliations and rhetorical energies. The concept of *écriture féminine*, the inscription of the female body and female difference in language and text, is a significant theoretical formulation in French feminist criticism, although it describes a Utopian possibility rather than a literary practice. Hélène Cixous, one of the leading advocates of *écriture féminine*, has admitted that, with only a few exceptions, 'there has not yet been any writing that inscribes femininity,' and Nancy Miller explains that *écriture féminine* 'privileges a textuality of the avant-garde, a literary production of the late twentieth century, and it is therefore fundamentally a hope, if not a blueprint, for the future.'[14] Nonetheless, the concept of *écriture féminine* provides a way of talking about women's writing which reasserts the *value* of the feminine and identifies the theoretical project of feminist criticism as the analysis of difference. In recent years, the translations of important work by Julia Kristeva, Cixous, and Luce Irigaray and the excellent collection *New French Feminisms* have made French criticism much more accessible to American feminist scholars.[15]

English feminist criticism, which incorporates French feminist and Marxist theory but is more traditionally oriented to textual interpretation, is also moving toward a focus on women's writing.[16] The emphasis in each country falls somewhat differently: English feminist criticism, essentially Marxist, stresses oppression; French feminist criticism, essentially psychoanalytic, stresses repression; American feminist criticism, essentially textual, stresses expression. All, however, have become gynocentric. All are struggling to find a terminology that can rescue the feminine from its stereotypical associations with inferiority.

Defining the unique difference of women's writing, as Woolf and Cixous have warned, must present a slippery and demanding task. Is difference a matter of style? Genre? Experience? Or is it produced by the reading process, as some textual critics would maintain? Spacks calls the difference of women's writing a 'delicate divergency' testifying to the subtle and elusive nature of the feminine practice of writing. Yet the delicate divergency of the woman's text challenges us to respond with equal delicacy and precision to the small but crucial deviations, the cumulative weightings of experience and exclusion, that have marked the history of women's writing. Before we can chart this history, we must uncover it, patiently and scrupulously; our theories must be firmly grounded in reading and research. But we have the opportunity, through gynocritics, to learn something solid, enduring, and real about the relation of women to literary culture.

Theories of women's writing presently make use of four models of difference: biological, linguistic, psychoanalytic, and cultural. Each is an effort to define and differentiate the qualities of the woman writer and the woman's text; each model also represents a school of gynocentric feminist criticism with its own favorite texts, styles, and methods. They overlap but are roughly sequential in that each incorporates the one before. I shall try now to sort out the various terminologies and assumptions of these four models of difference and evaluate their usefulness.

Women's writing and woman's body

> *More body, hence more writing.*
> Cixous, 'The Laugh of the Medusa'

Organic or biological criticism is the most extreme statement of gender difference, of a text indelibly marked by the body: anatomy is textuality. Biological criticism is also one of the most sibylline and perplexing theoretical formulations of feminist criticism. Simply to invoke anatomy risks a return to the crude essentialism, the phallic and ovarian theories of art, that oppressed women in the past. Victorian physicians believed that women's physiological functions diverted about twenty percent of their creative energy from brain activity. Victorian anthropologists believed that the frontal lobes of the male brain were heavier and more developed than female lobes and thus that women were inferior in intelligence.

While feminist criticism rejects the attribution of literal biological inferiority, some theorists seem to have accepted the *metaphorical* implications of female biological difference in writing. In *The Madwoman in the Attic*, for example, Gilbert and Gubar structure their analysis of women's writing around metaphors of literary paternity. 'In patriarchal western culture,' they maintain, '. . . the text's author is a father, a progenitor, a procreator, an aesthetic patriarch whose pen is an instrument of generative power like his penis.' Lacking phallic authority, they go on to suggest, women's writing is profoundly marked by the anxieties of this difference: 'If the pen is a metaphorical penis, from what organ can females generate texts?'[17]

To this rhetorical question Gilbert and Gubar offer no reply; but it is a serious question of much feminist theoretical discourse. Those critics who, like myself, would protest the fundamental analogy might reply that women generate texts from the brain or that the word-processor, with its compactly coded microchips, its inputs and outputs, is a metaphorical womb. The metaphor of literary paternity, as Auerbach has pointed out in her review of *The Madwoman*, ignores 'an equally timeless and, for me, even more oppressive metaphorical equation between literary creativity and childbirth.'[18] Certainly metaphors of literary *maternity* predominated in the eighteenth and nineteenth centuries; the process of literary creation is analogically much more similar to gestation, labor, and delivery than it is to insemination. Describing Thackeray's plan for *Henry Esmond*, for example, Douglas Jerrold jovially remarked, 'You have heard, I suppose, that Thackeray is big with twenty parts, and unless he is wrong in his time, expects the first installment at Christmas.'[19] (If to write is metaphorically to give birth, from what organ can males generate texts?)

Some radical feminist critics, primarily in France but also in the United States, insist that we must read these metaphors as more than playful; that we must seriously rethink and redefine biological differentiation and its relation to women's writing. They argue that 'women's writing proceeds from the body, that our sexual differentiation is also our source.'[20] In *Of Woman Born*, Rich explains her belief that

> female biology . . . has far more radical implications than we have yet come
> to appreciate. Patriarchal thought has limited female biology to its own
> narrow specifications. The feminist vision has recoiled from female biology
> for these reasons; it will, I believe, come to view our physicality as a
> resource rather than a destiny. In order to live a fully human life, we
> require not only *control* of our bodies . . . we must touch the unity and
> resonance of our physicality, the corporeal ground of our intelligence.[21]

Feminist criticism written in the biological perspective generally stresses the importance of the body as a source of imagery. Alicia Ostriker, for example, argues that contemporary American women poets use a franker, more pervasive anatomical imagery than their male counterparts and that this insistent body language refuses the spurious transcendence that comes at the price of denying the flesh. In a fascinating essay on Whitman and Dickinson, Terence Diggory shows that physical nakedness, so potent a poetic symbol of authenticity for Whitman and other male poets, had very different connotations for Dickinson and her successors, who associated nakedness with the objectified or sexually exploited female nude and who chose instead protective images of the armored self.[22]

Feminist criticism which itself tries to be biological, to write from the critic's body, has been intimate, confessional, often innovative in style and form. Rachel Blau DuPlessis's 'Washing Blood,' the introduction to a special issue of *Feminist Studies* on the subject of motherhood, proceeds, in short lyrical paragraphs, to describe her own experience in adopting a child, to recount her dreams and nightmares, and to meditate upon the 'healing unification of body and mind based not only on the lived experiences of motherhood as a social institution . . . but also on a biological power speaking through us.'[23] Such criticism makes itself defiantly vulnerable, virtually bares its throat to the knife, since our professional taboos against self-revelation are so strong. When it succeeds, however, it achieves the power and the dignity of art. Its existence is an implicit rebuke to women critics who continue to write, according to Rich, 'from somewhere outside their female bodies.' In comparison to this flowing confessional criticism, the tight-lipped Olympian intelligence of such texts as Elizabeth Hardwick's *Seduction and Betrayal* or Susan Sontag's *Illness as Metaphor* can seem arid and strained.

Yet in its obsessions with the 'corporeal ground of our intelligence,' feminist biocriticism can also become cruelly prescriptive. There is a sense in which the exhibition of bloody wounds becomes an initiation ritual quite separate and disconnected from critical insight. And as the editors of the journal *Questions féministes* point out, 'it is . . . dangerous to place the body at the center of a search for female identity. . . . The themes of otherness and of the Body merge together, because the most visible difference between men and women, and the only one we know for sure to be permanent . . . is indeed the difference in body. This difference has been used as a pretext to "justify" full power of one sex over the other' (trans. Yvonne Rochette-Ozzello, *NFF*, p. 218). The study of biological imagery in women's writing is useful and important as long as we understand that factors other than anatomy are involved in it. Ideas about the body are fundamental to understanding how women conceptualize their situation in society; but there can be no expression of the body which is unmediated by linguistic, social, and literary structures. The difference of woman's literary practice, therefore, must be sought (in Miller's words) in 'the body of her writing and not the writing of her body.'[24]

Women's writing and women's language

The women say, the language you speak poisons your glottis tongue
palate lips. They say, the language you speak is made up of words that
are killing you. They say, the language you speak is made up of signs
that rightly speaking designate what men have appropriated.

Monique Wittig, Les Guérillères

Linguistic and textual theories of women's writing ask whether men and women use language differently; whether sex differences in language use can be theorized in terms of biology, socialization, or culture; whether women can create new languages of their own; and whether speaking, reading, and writing are all gender marked. American, French, and British feminist critics have all drawn attention to the philosophical, linguistic, and practical problems of women's use of language, and the debate over language is one of the most exciting areas in gynocritics. Poets and writers have led the attack on what Rich calls 'the oppressor's language,' a language sometimes criticized as sexist, sometimes as abstract. But the problem goes well beyond reformist efforts to purge language of its sexist aspects. As Nelly Furman explains 'It is through the medium of language that we define and categorize areas of difference and similarity, which in turn allow us to comprehend the world around us. Male-centred categorizations predominate in American English and subtly shape our understanding and perception of reality; this is why attention is increasingly directed to the inherently oppressive aspects for women of a male-constructed language system.'[25] According to Carolyn Burke, the language system is at the centre of French feminist theory:

> The central issue in much recent women's writing in France is to find
> and use an appropriate female language. Language is the place to begin:
> a *prise de conscience* [capture of consciousness] must be followed by a *prise*
> *de la parole* [capture of speech]. . . . In this view, the very forms of the
> dominant mode of discourse show the mark of the dominant masculine
> ideology. Hence, when a woman writes or speaks herself into existence,
> she is forced to speak in something like a foreign tongue, a language with
> which she may be uncomfortable.[26]

Many French feminists advocate a revolutionary linguism, an oral break from the dictatorship of patriarchal speech. Annie Leclerc, in *Parole de femme*, calls on women 'to invent a language that is not oppressive, a language that does not leave speechless but that loosens the tongue' (trans. Courtivron, *NFF*, p. 179). Chantal Chawaf, in an essay on 'La chair linguistique,' connects biofeminism and linguism in the view that women's language and a genuinely feminine practice of writing will articulate the body:

> In order to reconnect the book with the body and with pleasure, we must
> disintellectualize writing. . . . And this language, as it develops, will not
> degenerate and dry up, will not go back to the fleshless academicism, the
> stereotypical and servile discourses that we reject.

> ... Feminine language must, by its very nature, work on life
> passionately, scientifically, poetically, politically in order to make it
> invulnerable. [Trans. Rochette-Ozzello, *NFF*, pp. 177–78]

But scholars who want a women's language that *is* intellectual and theoretical, that works *inside* the academy, are faced with what seems like an impossible paradox, as Xavière Gauthier has lamented: 'As long as women remain silent, they will be outside the historical process. But, if they begin to speak and write *as men do*, they will enter history subdued and alienated; it is a history that, logically speaking, their speech should disrupt' (trans. Marilyn A. August, *NFF*, pp. 162–63). What we need, Mary Jacobus has proposed, is a women's writing that works within 'male' discourse but works 'ceaselessly to deconstruct it: to write what cannot be written,' and according to Shoshana Felman, 'the challenge facing the woman today is nothing less than to "reinvent" language, ... to speak not only against, but outside of the specular phallogocentric structure, to establish the status of which would no longer be defined by the phallacy of masculine meaning.'[27]

Beyond rhetoric, what can linguistic, historical, and anthropological research tell us about the prospects for a women's language? First of all, the concept of a women's language is not original with feminist criticism; it is very ancient and appears frequently in folklore and myth. In such myths, the essence of women's language is its secrecy; what is really being described is the male fantasy of the enigmatic nature of the feminine. Herodotus, for example, reported that the Amazons were able linguists who easily mastered the languages of their male antagonists, although men could never learn the women's tongue. In *The White Goddess*, Robert Graves romantically argues that a women's language existed in a matriarchal stage of prehistory; after a great battle of the sexes, the matriarchy was overthrown and the women's language went underground, to survive in the mysterious cults of Eleusis and Corinth and the witch covens of Western Europe. Travelers and missionaries in the seventeenth and eighteenth centuries brought back accounts of 'women's languages' among American Indians, Africans, and Asians (the differences in linguistic structure they reported were usually superficial). There is some ethnographic evidence that in certain cultures women have evolved a private form of communication out of their need to resist the silence imposed upon them in public life. In ecstatic religions, for example, women, more frequently than men, speak in tongues, a phenomenon attributed by anthropologists to their relative inarticulateness in formal religious discourse. But such ritualized and unintelligible female 'languages' are scarcely cause for rejoicing; indeed, it was because witches were suspected of esoteric knowledge and possessed speech that they were burned.[28]

From a political perspective, there are interesting parallels between the feminist problem of a women's language and the recurring 'language issue' in the general history of decolonization. After a revolution, a new state must decide which language to make official: the language that is 'psychologically immediate,' that allows 'the kind of force that speaking one's mother tongue permits'; or the language that 'is an avenue to the wider community of modern culture,' a community to whose movements of thought only 'foreign' languages can give access.[29] The language issue in feminist criticism has emerged, in a sense, after our revolution, and it reveals the tensions in the women's movement between those who would stay outside the academic establishments and the institutions of criticism and those who would enter and even conquer them.

The advocacy of a women's language is thus a political gesture that also carries tremendous emotional force. But despite its unifying appeal, the concept of a women's language is riddled with difficulties. Unlike Welsh, Breton, Swahili, or Amharic, that is, languages of minority or colonized groups, there is no mother tongue, no genderlect spoken by the female population in a society, which differs significantly from the dominant language. English and American linguists agree that 'there is absolutely no evidence that would suggest the sexes are preprogrammed to develop structurally different linguistic systems.' Furthermore, the many specific differences in male and female speech, intonation, and language use that have been identified cannot be explained in terms of 'two separate sex-specific languages' but need to be considered instead in terms of styles, strategies, and contexts of linguistic performance.[30] Efforts at quantitative analysis of language in texts by men or women, such as Mary Hiatt's computerized study of contemporary fiction, *The Way Women Write* (1977), can easily be attacked for treating words apart from their meanings and purposes. At a higher level, analyses which look for 'feminine style' in the repetition of stylistic devices, image patterns, and syntax in women's writing tend to confuse innate forms with the overdetermined results of literary choice. Language and style are never raw and instinctual but are always the products of innumerable factors, of genre, tradition, memory, and context.

The appropriate task for feminist criticism, I believe, is to concentrate on women's access to language, on the available lexical range from which words can be selected, on the ideological and cultural determinants of expression. The problem is not that language is insufficient to express women's consciousness but that women have been denied the full resources of language and have been forced into silence, euphemism, or circumlocution. In a series of drafts for a lecture on women's writing (drafts which she discarded or suppressed), Woolf protested against the censorship which cut off female access to language. Comparing herself to Joyce, Woolf noted the differences between their verbal territories: 'Now men are shocked if a woman says what she feels (as Joyce does). Yet literature which is always pulling down blinds is not literature. All that we have ought to be expressed—mind and body—a process of incredible difficulty and danger.'[31]

'All that we have ought to be expressed—mind and body.' Rather than wishing to limit women's linguistic range, we must fight to open and extend it. The holes in discourse, the blanks and gaps and silences, are not the spaces where female consciousness reveals itself but the blinds of a 'prison-house of language.' Women's literature is still haunted by the ghosts of repressed language, and until we have exorcised those ghosts, it ought not to be in language that we base our theory of difference.

Women's writing and woman's psyche

Psychoanalytically oriented feminist criticism locates the difference of women's writing in the author's psyche and in the relation of gender to the creative process. It incorporates the biological and linguistic models of gender difference in a theory of the female psyche or self, shaped by the body, by the development of language, and by sex-role socialization. Here too there are many difficulties to overcome; the Freudian model requires constant revision to make it gynocentric. In one grotesque early example of Freudian reductivism, Theodor Reik suggested that women have fewer writing blocks than men because their bodies are constructed to facilitate release: 'Writing, as Freud told us at the end of his life, is connected with urinating, which physiologically is easier for a woman— they have a wider bladder.'[32] Generally, however, psychoanalytic criticism has focused not on the capacious bladder (could this be the organ from which females generate texts?) but on the absent phallus. Penis envy, the castration complex, and the Oedipal phase have become the Freudian coordinates defining women's relationship to language, fantasy, and culture. Currently the French psychoanalytic school dominated by Lacan has extended castration into a total metaphor for female literary and linguistic disadvantage. Lacan theorizes that the acquisition of language and the entry into its symbolic order occurs at the Oedipal phase in which the child accepts his or her gender identity. This stage requires an acceptance of the phallus as a privileged signification and a consequent female displacement, as Cora Kaplan has explained:

> The phallus as signifier has a central, crucial position in language, for if language embodies the patriarchal law of the culture, its basic meanings refer to the recurring process by which sexual difference and subjectivity are acquired. . . . Thus the little girl's access to the Symbolic, i.e., to language and its laws, is always negative and/or mediated by introsubjective relation to a third term, for it is characterized by an identification with lack.[33]

In psychoanalytic terms, 'lack' has traditionally been associated with the feminine, although Lac(k)anian critics can now make their statements linguistically. Many feminists believe that psychoanalysis could become a powerful tool for literary criticism, and recently there has been a renewed interest in Freudian theory. But feminist criticism based in Freudian or post-Freudian psychoanalysis must continually struggle with the problem of feminine disadvantage and lack. In *The Madwoman in the Attic*, Gilbert and Gubar carry out a feminist revision of Harold Bloom's Oedipal model of literary history as a conflict between fathers and sons and accept the essential psychoanalytic definition of the woman artist as displaced, disinherited, and excluded. In their view, the nature and 'difference' of women's writing lies in its troubled and even tormented relationship to female identity; the woman writer experiences her own gender as 'a painful obstacle or even a debilitating inadequacy.' The nineteenth-century woman writer inscribed her own sickness, her madness, her anorexia, her agoraphobia, and her paralysis in her texts; and although Gilbert and Gubar are dealing specifically with the nineteenth century, the range of their allusion and quotation suggests a more general thesis:

> Thus the loneliness of the female artist, her feelings of alienation from male predecessors coupled with her need for sisterly precursors and successors, her urgent sense of her need for a female audience together with her fear of the antagonism of male readers, her culturally conditioned timidity about self-dramatization, her dread of the patriarchal authority of art, her anxiety about the impropriety of female invention—all these phenomena of 'inferiorization' mark the woman writer's struggle for artistic self-definition and differentiate her efforts at self-creation from those of her male counterpart.[34]

In 'Emphasis Added,' Miller takes another approach to the problem of negativity in psychoanalytic criticism. Her strategy is to expand Freud's view of female creativity and to show how criticism of women's texts has frequently been unfair because it has been based in Freudian expectations. In his essay 'The Relation of the Poet to Daydreaming' (1908),[a] Freud maintained that the unsatisfied dreams and desires of women are chiefly erotic; these are the desires that shape the plots of women's fiction. In contrast, the dominant fantasies behind men's plots are egoistic and ambitious as well as erotic. Miller shows how women's plots have been granted or denied credibility in terms of their conformity to this phallocentric model and that a gynocentric reading reveals a repressed egoistic/ambitious fantasy in women's writing as well as in men's. Women's novels which are centrally concerned with fantasies of romantic love belong to the category disdained by George Eliot and other serious women writers as'silly novels'; the smaller number of women's novels which inscribe a fantasy of power imagine a world for women outside of love, a world, however, made impossible by social boundaries.

There has also been some interesting feminist literary criticism based on alternatives to Freudian psychoanalytic theory: Annis Pratt's Jungian history of female archetypes, Barbara Rigney's Laingian study of the divided self in women's fiction, and Ann Douglas's Eriksonian analysis of inner space in nineteenth-century women's writing.[35] And for the past few years, critics have been thinking about the possibilities of a new feminist psychoanalysis that does *not* revise Freud but instead emphasizes the development and construction of gender identities.

The most dramatic and promising new work in feminist psychoanalysis looks at the pre-Oedipal phase and at the process of psychosexual differentiation. Nancy Chodorow's *The Reproduction of Mothering: Psychoanalysis and the Sociology of Gender* (1978) has had an enormous influence on women's studies. Chodorow revises traditional psychoanalytic concepts of differentiation, the process by which the child comes to perceive the self as separate and to develop ego and body boundaries. Since differentiation takes place in relation to the mother (the primary caretaker), attitudes toward the mother 'emerge in the earliest differen-

---

[a] See *20th Century Literary Criticism*, Section 3.

tiation of the self'; 'the mother, who is a woman becomes and remains for children of both genders the other, or object'[36] The child develops core gender identity concomitantly with differentiation, but the process is not the same for boys and girls. A boy must learn his gender identity negatively as being not-female, and this difference requires continual reinforcement. In contrast, a girl's core gender identity is positive and built upon sameness, continuity, and identification with the mother. Women's difficulties with feminine identity come after Oedipal phase, in which male power and cultural hegemony give sex differences a transformed value. Chodorow's work suggests that shared parenting, the involvement of men as primary caretakers of children, will have a profound effect on our sense of sex difference, gender identity, and sexual preference.

But what is the significance of feminist psychoanalysis for literary criticism? One thematic carry-over has been a critical interest in the mother-daughter configuration as a source of female creativity.[37] Elizabeth Abel's bold investigation of female friendship in contemporary women's novels uses Chodorow's theory to show how not only the relationships of women characters but also the relationship of women writers to each other are determined by the psychodynamics of female bonding. Abel too confronts Bloom's paradigm of literary history, but unlike Gilbert and Gubar she sees a 'triadic female pattern' in which the Oedipal relation to the male tradition is balanced by the women writer's pre-Oedipal relation to the female tradition. 'As the dynamics of female friendship differ from those of male', Abel concludes, 'the dynamics of female literary influence also diverge and deserve a theory of influence attuned to female psychology and to women's dual position in literary history.'[38]

Like Gilbert, Gubar, and Miller, Abel brings together women's texts from a variety of national literatures, choosing to emphasize 'the constancy of certain emotional dynamics depicted in diverse cultural situations.' Yet the privileging of gender implies not only the constancy but also the immutability of these dynamics. Although psychoanalytically based models of feminist criticism can now offer us remarkable and persuasive readings of individual texts and can highlight extraordinary similarities between women writing in a variety of cultural circumstances, they cannot explain historical change, ethnic difference, or the shaping force of generic and economic factors. To consider these issues, we must go beyond psychoanalysis to a more flexible and comprehensive model of women's writing which places it in the maximum context of culture.

Women's writing and women's culture

I consider women's literature as a specific category, not because of biology, but because it is, in a sense, the literature of the colonized.

Christiane Rochefort,
'The Privilege of Consciousness'

A theory based on a model of women's culture can provide, I believe, a more complete and satisfying way to talk about the specificity and difference of women's writing than theories based in biology, linguistics, or psychoanalysis. Indeed, a theory of culture incorporates ideas about women's body, language, and psyche but interprets them in relation to the social contexts in which they occur. The ways in which women conceptualize their bodies and their sexual and reproductive functions are intricately linked to their cultural environments. The female psyche can be studied as the product or construction of cultural forces. Language, too, comes back into the picture, as we consider the social dimensions and determinants of language use, the shaping of linguistic behaviour and cultural ideals. A cultural theory acknowledges that there are important differences between women as writers: class, race, nationality, and history are literary determinants as significant as gender. Nonetheless, women's culture forms a collective experience within the cultural whole, an experience that binds women writers to each other over time and space. It is in the emphasis on the binding force of women's culture that this approach differs from Marxist theories of cultural hegemony.

Hypotheses of women's culture have been developed over the last decade primarily by anthropologists, sociologists, and social historians in order to get away from masculine systems, hierarchies, and values and to get at the primary and self-defined nature of female cultural experience. In the field of women's history, the concept of women's culture is still controversial, although there is agreement on its significance as a theoretical formulation. Gerda Lerner explains the importance of examining women's experience in its own terms:

> Women have been left out of history not because of the evil conspiracies of men in general or male historians in particular, but because we have considered history only in male-centered terms. We have missed women and their activities, because we have asked questions of history which are inappropriate to women. To rectify this, and to light up areas of historical darkness we must, for a time, focus on a *woman-centered* inquiry, considering the possibility of the existence of a female culture *within* the general culture shared by men and women. History must include an account of the female experience over time and should include the development of feminist consciousness as an essential aspect of women's past. This is the primary task of women's history. The central question it raises is: What would history be like if it were seen through the eyes of women and ordered by values they define?[39]

In defining female culture, historians distinguish between the roles, activities, tastes, and behaviors prescribed and considered appropriate for women and those activities, behaviors, and functions actually generated out of women's lives. In the late-eighteenth and nineteenth centuries, the term 'woman's sphere' expressed the Victorian and Jacksonian vision of separate roles for men and women, with little or no overlap and with women subordinate. Woman's sphere was defined and maintained by men, but women frequently internalized its precepts in the American 'cult of true womanhood' and the English 'feminine ideal'. Women's culture, however, redefines women's 'activities and goals from a woman-centered point of view. . . . The term implies an assertion of equality and an awareness of sisterhood, the communality of women.' Women's culture refers to 'the broad-based communality of values, institutions, relationships, and methods of communication' unifying nineteenth-century female experience, a culture nonetheless with significant variants by class and ethnic group (*MFP*, pp. 52, 54).

Some feminist historians have accepted the model of separate spheres and have seen the movement from woman's sphere to women's culture to women's-rights activism as the consecutive stages of an evolutionary political process. Others see a more complex and perpetual negotiation taking place between women's culture and the general culture. As Lerner has argued:

> It is important to understand that 'woman's culture' is not and should not be seen as a subculture. It is hardly possible for the majority to live in a subculture. . . . Women live their social existence within the general culture and, whenever they are confined by patriarchal restraint or segregation into separateness (which always has subordination as its purpose), they transform this restraint into complementarity (asserting the importance of woman's function, even its 'superiority') and redefine it. Thus, women live a duality—as members of the general culture and as partakers of women's culture. [*MFP*, p. 52]

Lerner's views are similar to those of some cultural anthropologists. A particularly stimulating analysis of female culture has been carried out by two Oxford anthropologists, Shirley and Edwin Ardener. The Ardeners have tried to outline a model of women's culture which is not historically limited and to provide a terminology for its characteristics. Two essays by Edwin Ardener, 'Belief and the Problem of Women' (1972) and 'The "Problem" Revisited' (1975), suggest that women constitute a *muted group*, the boundaries of whose culture and reality overlap, but are not wholly contained by, the *dominant (male) group*. A model of the cultural situation of women is crucial to understanding both how they are perceived by the dominant group and how they perceive themselves and others. Both historians and anthropologists emphasize the incompleteness of androcentric models of history and culture and the inadequacy of such models for the analysis of female experience. In the past, female experience which could not be accommodated by androcentric models was treated as deviant or simply ignored. Observation from an exterior point of view could never be the same as comprehension from within. Ardener's model also has many connections to and implications for current feminist literary theory, since the concepts of perception, silence, and silencing are so central to discussions of women's participation in literary culture.[40]

By the term 'muted,' Ardener suggests problems both of language and of power. Both muted and dominant groups generate beliefs or ordering ideas of social reality at the unconscious level, but dominant groups control the forms or structures in which consciousness can be articulated. Thus muted groups must mediate their beliefs through the allowable forms of dominant structures. Another way of putting this would be to say that all language is the language of the dominant order, and women, if they speak at all, must speak through it. How then,

Ardener asks, 'does the symbolic weight of that other mass of persons express itself?' In his view, women's beliefs find expression through ritual and art, expressions which can be deciphered by the ethnographer, either female or male, who is willing to make the effort to perceive beyond the screens of the dominant structure.[41]

Let us now look at Ardener's diagram of the relationship of the dominant and the muted group:

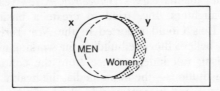

Unlike the Victorian model of complementary spheres, Ardener's groups are represented by intersecting circles. Much of muted circle Y falls within the boundaries of dominant circle X; there is also a crescent of Y which is outside the dominant boundary and therefore (in Ardener's terminology) 'wild.' We can think of the 'wild zone' of women's culture spatially, experientially, or meta-physically. Spatially it stands for an area which is literally no-man's-land, a place forbidden to men, which corresponds to the zone in X which is off limits to women. Experientially it stands for the aspects of the female life-style which are outside of and unlike those of men; again, there is a corresponding zone of male experience alien to women. But if we think of the wild zone metaphysically, or in terms of consciousness, it has no corresponding male space since all of male consciousness is within the circle of the dominant structure and thus accessible to or structured by language. In this sense, the 'wild' is always imaginary; from the male point of view, it may simply be the projection of the unconscious. In terms of cultural anthropology, women know what the male crescent is like, even if they have never seen it, because it becomes the subject of legend (like the wilderness). But men do not know what is in the wild.

For some feminist critics, the wild zone, or 'female space,' must be the address of a genuinely women-centered criticism, theory, and art, whose shared project is to bring into being the symbolic weight of female consciousness, to make the invisible visible, to make the silent speak. French feminist critics would like to make the wild zone the theoretical base of women's difference. In their texts, the wild zone becomes the place for the revolutionary women's language, the language of everything that is repressed, and for the revolutionary women's writing in 'white ink.' It is the Dark Continent in which Cixous's laughing Medusa and Wittig's *guérillères* reside. Through voluntary entry into the wild zone, other feminist critics tell us, a woman can write her way out of the 'cramped confines of patriarchal space.'[42] The images of this journey are now familiar in feminist quest fictions and in essays about them. The writer/heroine, often guided by another woman, travels to the 'mother country' of liberated desire and female authenticity; crossing to the other side of the mirror, like Alice in Wonderland, is often a symbol of the passage.

Many forms of American radical feminism also romantically assert that women are closer to nature, to the environment, to a matriarchal principle at once biological and ecological. Mary Daly's *Gyn/Ecology* and Margaret Atwood's novel *Surfacing* are texts which create this feminist mythology. In English and American literature, women writers have often imagined Amazon Utopias, cities or countries situated in the wild zone or on its border: Elizabeth Gaskell's gentle *Cranford* is probably an Amazon Utopia; so is Charlotte Perkins Gilman's *Herland* or, to take a recent example, Joanna Russ's *Whileaway*. A few years ago, the feminist publishing house Daughters, Inc. tried to create a business version of the Amazon Utopia; as Lois Gould reported in the *New York Times Magazine* (2 January 1977), 'They believe they are building the working models for the critical next stage of feminism: full independence from the control and influence of "male-dominated" institutions—the news media, the health, education, and legal systems, the art, theater, and literary worlds, the banks.'

These fantasies of an idyllic enclave represent a phenomenon which feminist criticism must recognize in the history of women's writing. But we must also understand that there can be no writing or criticism totally outside of the dominant structure; no publication is fully independent from the economic and political pressures of the male-dominated society. The concept of a woman's text in the wild zone is a playful abstraction; in the reality to which we must address ourselves as critics, women's writing is a 'double-voiced discourse' that always embodies the social, literary, and cultural heritages of both the muted and the dominant.[43] And insofar as most feminist critics are also women writing, this precarious heritage is one we share; every step that feminist criticism takes toward defining women's writing is a step toward self-understanding as well; every account of a female literary culture and a female literary tradition has parallel significance for our own place in critical history and critical tradition.

Women writing are not, then, *inside* and *outside* of the male tradition; they are inside two traditions simultaneously, 'undercurrents,' in Ellen Moers's metaphor, of the mainstream. To mix metaphors again, the literary estate of women, as Myra Jehlen says, 'suggests . . . a more fluid imagery of interacting juxtapositions, the point of which would be to represent not so much the territory, as its defining borders. Indeed, the female territory might well be envisioned as one long border, and independence for women, not as a separate country, but as open access to the sea.' As Jehlen goes on to explain, an aggressive feminist criticism must poise itself on this border and must see women's writing in its changing historical and cultural relation to that other body of texts identified by feminist criticism not simply as literature but as 'men's writing.'[44]

The difference of women's writing, then, can only be understood in terms of this complex and historically grounded cultural relation. An important aspect of Ardener's model is that there are muted groups other than women; a dominant structure may determine many muted structures. A black American woman poet, for example, would have her literary identity formed by the dominant (white male) tradition, by a muted women's culture, and by a muted black culture. She would be affected by both sexual and racial politics in a combination unique to her case; at the same time, as Barbara Smith points out, she shares an experience specific to her group: 'Black women writers constitute an identifiable literary tradition . . . thematically, stylistically, aesthetically, and conceptually. Black women writers manifest common approaches to the act of creating literature as a direct result of the specific political, social, and economic experience they have been obliged to share.'[45] Thus the first task of a gynocentric criticism must be to plot the precise cultural locus of female literary identity and to describe the forces that intersect an individual woman writer's cultural field. A gynocentric criticism would also situate women writers with respect to the variables of literary culture, such as modes of production and distribution, relations of author and audience, relations of high to popular art, and hierarchies of genre.

Insofar as our concepts of literary periodization are based on men's writing, women's writing must be forcibly assimilated to an irrelevant grid; we discuss a Renaissance which is not a renaissance for women, a Romantic period in which women played very little part, a modernism with which women conflict. At the same time, the ongoing history of women's writing has been suppressed, leaving large and mysterious gaps in accounts of the development of genre. Gynocentric criticism is already well on the way to providing us with another perspective on literary history. Margaret Anne Doody, for example, suggests that 'the period between the death of Richardson and the appearance of the novels of Scott and Austen' which has 'been regarded as a dead period, a dull blank' is in fact the period in which late eighteenth-century women writers were developing 'the paradigm for women's fiction of the nineteenth century—something hardly less than the paradigm of the nineteenth-century novel itself.'[46] There has also been a feminist rehabilitation of the female gothic, a mutation of a popular genre once believed marginal but now seen as part of the great tradition of the novel.[47] In American literature, the pioneering work of Ann Douglas, Nina Baym, and Jane Tompkins, among others, has given us a new view of the power of women's fiction to feminize nineteenth-century American culture.[48] And feminist critics have made us aware that Woolf belonged to a tradition other than modernism and that this tradition surfaces in her work precisely in those places where criticism has hitherto found obscurities, evasions, implausibilities, and imperfections.[49]

Our current theories of literary influence also need to be tested in terms of women's writing. If a man's text, as Bloom and Edward Said have maintained, is fathered, then a woman's text is not only mothered but parented, it confronts both paternal and maternal precursors and must deal with the problems and advantages of both lines of inheritance. Woolf says in *A Room of One's Own* that 'a woman writing thinks back through her mothers.' But a woman writing unavoidably thinks back through her fathers as well; only male writers can forget or mute half of their parentage. The dominant culture need not consider the muted, except to rail against 'the woman's part' in itself. Thus we need more subtle and supple accounts of influence, not just to explain women's writing but also to understand how men's writing has resisted the acknowledgment of female precursors.

We must first go beyond the assumption that women writers either imitate their male predecessors or revise them and that this simple dualism is adequate to describe the influences on the woman's text. I. A. Richards once commented that the influence of G. E. Moore had had an enormous negative impact on his work: 'I feel like an obverse of him. Where there's a hole in him, there's bulge in me.'[50] Too often women's place in literary tradition is translated into the crude topography of hole and bulge, with Milton, Byron, or Emerson the bulging bogeys on one side and women's literature from Aphra Behn to Adrienne Rich a pocked moon surface of revisionary lacunae on the other. One of the great advantages of the women's-culture model is that it shows how the female tradition can be a positive source of strength and solidarity as well as a negative source of powerlessness; it can generate its own experiences and symbols which are not simply the obverse of the male tradition.

How can a cultural model of women's writing help us to read a woman's text? One implication of this model is that women's fiction can be read as a double-voiced discourse, containing a 'dominant' and a 'muted' story, what Gilbert and Gubar call a 'palimpsest.' I have described it elsewhere as an object/field problem in which we must keep two alternative oscillating texts simultaneously in view: 'In the purest feminist literary criticism we are . . . presented with a radical alteration of our vision, a demand that we see meaning in what has previously been empty space. The orthodox plot recedes, and another plot, hitherto submerged in the anonymity of the background, stands out in bold relief like a thumbprint.' Miller too sees 'another text' in women's fiction, 'more or less muted from novel to novel' but 'always there to be read.'[51]

Another interpretative strategy for feminist criticism might be the contextual analysis that the cultural anthropologist Clifford Geertz calls 'thick description.' Geertz calls for descriptions that seek to understand the meaning of cultural phenomena and products by 'sorting out the structures of signification . . . and determining their social ground and import.'[52] A genuinely 'thick' description of women's writing would insist upon gender and upon a female literary tradition among the multiple strata that make up the force of meaning in a text. No description, we must concede, could ever be thick enough to account for all the factors that go into the work of art. But we could work toward completeness, even as an unattainable ideal.

In suggesting that a cultural model of women's writing has considerable usefulness for the enterprise of feminist criticism, I don't mean to replace psychoanalysis with cultural anthropology as the answer to all our theoretical problems or to enthrone Ardener and Geertz as the new white father in place of Freud, Lacan, and Bloom. No theory, however suggestive, can be a substitute for the close and extensive knowledge of women's texts which constitutes our essential subject. Cultural anthropology and social history can perhaps offer us a terminology and a diagram of women's cultural situation. But feminist critics must use this concept in relation to what women actually write, not in relation to a theoretical, political, metaphoric, or visionary ideal of what women ought to write.

I began by recalling that a few years ago feminist critics thought we were on a pilgrimage to the promised land in which gender would lose its power, in which all texts would be sexless and equal, like angels. But the more precisely we understand the specificity of women's writing not as a transient by-product of sexism but as fundamental and continually determining reality, the more clearly we realize that we have misperceived our destination. We may never reach the promised land at all; for when feminist critics see our task as the study of women's writing, we realize that the land promised to us is not the serenely undifferentiated universality of texts but the tumultuous and intriguing wilderness of difference itself.

NOTES [References to 'this volume' are to *The New Feminist Criticism* (1985), ed. Showalter.]

1. Carolyn G. Heilbrun and Catharine R. Stimpson, 'Theories of Feminist Criticism: A Dialogue,' in *Feminist Literary Criticism*, ed. Josephine Donovan (Lexington: University Press of Kentucky, 1975), p. 64. I also discuss this distinction in my 'Toward a Feminist Poetics,' in this volume, pp. 125–143; a number of the ideas in the first part of the present essay are raised more briefly in the earlier piece.
2. No women critics are discussed in Geoffrey Hartman's *Criticism in the Wilderness: The Study of Literature Today* (New Haven, Conn.; Yale University Press, 1980), but he does describe a feminine spirit called 'the Muse of Criticism': 'more a governess than a Muse, the stern daughter of books no longer read under trees and in the fields' (p. 175).
3. See my 'Literary Criticism,' Review Essay, *Signs* I (Winter 1975): 435–60.
4. Annette Kolodny, 'Literary Criticism,' Review Essay, *Signs* 2 (Winter 1976): 420.
5. On black criticism, see Barbara Smith, 'Toward a Black Feminist Criticism,' in this volume, pp. 168–85, and Mary Helen Washington, 'New Lives and New Letters: Black Women Writers at the End of the Seventies,' *College English* 43 (January 1981): 1–11. On Marxist criticism, see the Marxist-Feminist Literature Collective's 'Women's Writing,' *Ideology and Consciousness* 3 (Spring 1978): 27–48, a collectively written analysis of several nineteenth-century women's novels which gives equal weight to gender, class, and literary production as textual determinants.
6. Margaret Homans, *Women Writers and Poetic Identity: Dorothy Wordsworth, Emily Brontë, and Emily Dickinson* (Princeton, N.J.: Princeton University Press, 1980), p. 10.
7. Josephine Donovan, 'Afterward: Critical Revision,' *Feminist Literary Criticism*, p. 74. Judith Fetterley, *The Resisting Reader: A Feminist Approach to American Fiction* (Bloomington: Indiana University Press, 1978), p. viii. See my 'Toward a Feminist Poetics,' pp. 125–43. *The Authority of Experience* is the title of an anthology edited by Arlyn Diamond and Lee R. Edwards (Amherst, Mass.: University of Massachusetts Press, 1977).
8. Nina Auerbach, 'Feminist Criticism Reviewed,' in *Gender and Literary Voice*, ed. Janet Todd (New York: Holmes & Meier, 1980), p. 258.
9. Adrienne Rich, 'When We Dead Awaken: Writing as Re-Vision,' *On Lies, Secrets, and Silence* (New York: W. W. Norton, 1979), p. 35.
10. Annette Kolodny, 'Dancing through the Minefield: Some Observations on the Theory, Practice, and Politics of a Feminist Literary Criticism,' in this volume. The complete theoretical case for a feminist hermeneutics is outlined in Kolodny's essays, including 'Some Notes on Defining a "Feminist Literary Criticism,"' *Critical Inquiry* 2 (Autumn 1975): 75–92; 'A Map for Rereading; or, Gender and the Interpretation of Literary Texts,' in this volume, pp. 46–62; and 'The Theory of Feminist Criticism' (paper delivered at the National Center for the Humanities Conference on Feminist Criticism, Research Triangle Park, N.C., March 1981).
11. Sandra M. Gilbert, 'What Do Feminist Critics Want? A Postcard from the Volcano,' in this volume, p. 36.
12. Christiane Makward, 'To Be or Not to Be. . . . A Feminist Speaker,' in *The Future of Difference*, ed. Hester Eisenstein and Alice Jardine (Boston: G. K. Hall, 1980), p. 102. On Lacan, see Jane Gallop, 'The Ladies' Man,' *Diacritics* 6 (Winter 1976): 28–34; on Macherey, see the Marxist-Feminist Literature Collective's 'Women's Writing.'
13. Patricia Meyer Spacks, *The Female Imagination* (New York: Alfred A. Knopf, 1975), pp. 19, 32.
14. Hélène Cixous, 'The Laugh of the Medusa,' trans. Keith and Paula Cohen, *Signs* 1 (Summer 1976): 878. Nancy K. Miller, 'Emphasis Added: Plots and Plausibilities in Women's Fiction,' in this volume, pp. 339–60.
15. For an overview, see Domna C. Staunton, 'Language and Revolution: The Franco-American Dis-Connection,' in Eisenstein and Jardine, *Future of Difference*, pp. 73–87, and Elaine Marks and Isabelle de Courtivron, eds., *New French Feminisms* (Amherst: University of Massachusetts Press,

1979); all further references to *New French Feminisms*, abbreviated *NFF*, will hereafter be included with translator's name parenthetically in the text.

16. Two major works are the manifesto of the Marxist-Feminist Literature Collective, 'Women's Writing,' and the papers from the Oxford University lectures on women and literature, Mary Jacobus, ed., *Women Writing and Writing about Women* (New York: Barnes & Noble Imports, 1979).

17. Sandra M. Gilbert and Susan Gubar, *The Madwoman in the Attic: The Woman Writer and the Nineteenth-Century Literary Imagination* (New Haven, Conn.: Yale University Press, 1979), pp. 6, 7.

18. Nina Auerbach, review of *Madwoman*, *Victorian Studies* 23 (Summer 1980): 506.

19. Douglas Jerrold, quoted in Kathleen Tillotson, *Novels of the Eighteen-Forties* (London: Oxford University Press, 1961), p. 39 n. James Joyce imagined the creator as female and literary creation as a process of gestation; see Richard Ellmann, *James Joyce: A Biography* (London: Oxford University Press, 1959), pp. 306–8.

20. Carolyn G. Burke, 'Report from Paris: Women's Writing and the Women's Movement,' *Signs* 3 (Summer 1978): 851.

21. Adrienne Rich, *Of Woman Born: Motherhood as Experience and Institution* (New York: W. W. Norton, 1976), p. 62. Biofeminist criticism has been influential in other disciplines as well: e.g., art critics, such as Judy Chicago and Lucy Lippard, have suggested that women artists are compelled to use a uterine or vaginal iconography of centralized focus, curved lines, and tactile or sensuous forms. See Lippard, *From the Center: Feminist Essays on Women's Art* (New York: E. P. Dutton, 1976).

22. See Alicia Ostriker, 'Body Language: Imagery of the Body in Women's Poetry,' in *The State of the Language*, ed. Leonard Michaels and Christopher Ricks (Berkeley: University of California Press, 1980), pp. 247–63, and Terence Diggory, 'Armoured Women, Naked Men: Dickinson, Whitman, and Their Successors,' in *Shakespeare's Sisters: Feminist Essays on Women Poets*, ed. Sandra M. Gilbert and Susan Gubar (Bloomington: Indiana University Press, 1979), pp. 135–50.

23. Rachel Blau DuPlessis, 'Washing Blood,' *Feminist Studies* 4 (June 1978): 10. The entire issue is an important document of feminist criticism.

24. Nancy K. Miller, 'Women's Autobiography in France: For a Dialectics of Identification,' in *Women and Language in Literature and Society*, ed. Sally McConnell-Ginet, Ruth Borker, and Nelly Furnam (New York: Praeger, 1980), p. 271.

25. Nelly Furnam, 'The Study of Women and Language: Comment Vol. 3, No. 3,' *Signs* 4 (Autumn 1978): 182.

26. Burke, 'Report from Paris,' p. 844.

27. Jacobus, 'The Difference of View,' in *Women's Writing and Writing about Women*, pp. 12–13. Shoshana Felman, 'Women and Madness: The Critical Phallacy,' *Diacritics* 5 (Winter 1975): 10.

28. On women's language, see Sarah B. Pomeroy, *Goddesses, Whores, Wives, and Slaves: Women in Classical Antiquity* (New York: Schocken Books, 1976), p. 24; Sally McConnell-Ginet, 'Linguistics and the Feminist Challenge,' in *Women and Language*, p. 14; and Joan M. Lewis, *Ecstatic Religion* (1971), cited in Shirley Ardener, ed., *Perceiving Women* (New York: Halsted Press, 1978), p. 50.

29. Clifford Geertz, *The Interpretation of Cultures* (New York: Basic Books, 1973), pp. 241–42.

30. McConnell-Ginet, 'Linguistics and the Feminist Challenge,' pp. 13, 16.

31. Virginia Woolf, 'Speech, Manuscript Notes,' *The Pargiters: The Novel-Essay Portion of the Years 1882–1941*, ed. Mitchell A. Leaska (New York: New York Public Library, 1977), p. 164.

32. Quoted in Erika Freeman, *Insights: Conversations with Theodor Reik* (Englewood Cliffs, N.J.: Prentice-Hall, 1971), p. 166. Reik goes on, 'But what the hell, writing! The great task of a woman is to bring a child into the world.'

33. Cora Kaplan, 'Language and Gender,' unpublished paper, University of Sussex, 1977, p. 3.

34. Gilbert and Gubar, *Madwoman in the Attic*, p. 50.

35. See Annis Pratt, 'The New Feminist Criticisms,' in *Beyond Intellectual Sexism: A New Woman, a New Reality*, ed. Joan I. Roberts (New York: Longman, 1976); Barbara H. Rigney, *Madness and Sexual Politics in the Feminist Novel: Studies in Brontë, Woolf, Lessing, and Atwood* (Madison: University of Wisconsin Press, 1978); and Ann Douglas, 'Mrs. Sigourney and the Sensibility of the Inner Space', *New England Quarterly* 45 (June 1972): 163–81.

36. Nancy Chodorow, 'Gender, Relation, and Difference in Psychoanalytic Perspective,' in Eisenstein and Jardine, *Future of Difference*, p. 11. See also Chodorow et al., 'On *The Reproduction of Mothering*: A methodological Debate,' *Signs* 6 (Spring 1981): 482–514.

37. See, e.g., *The Lost Tradition: Mothers and Daughters in Literature*, ed. Cathy M. Davidson and E. M. Broner (New York: Frederick Ungar, 1980); this work is more engaged with myths and images of matrilineage than with redefining female identity.

38. Elizabeth Abel, '(E)Merging Identities: The Dynamics of Female Friendship in Contemporary Fiction by Women,' *Signs* 6 (Spring 1981): 434.

39. Gerda Lerner, 'The Challenge of Women's History,' *The Majority Finds Its Past: Placing Women in History* (New York: Oxford University Press, 1979); all further references to this book, abbreviated *MFP*, will hereafter be included parenthetically in the text.

40. See, e.g., Tillie Olsen, *Silences* (New York: Delacorte Press, 1978); Sheila Rowbotham, *Woman's Consciousness, Man's World* (New York: Penguin Books, 1974), pp. 31–37; and Marcia Landy, 'The Silent Woman: Towards a Feminist Critique,' in Diamond and Edwards, *Authority of Experience* (n. 7 above), pp. 16–27.

41. Edwin Ardener, 'Belief and the Problem of Women,' in S. Ardener, *Perceiving Women* (note 28 above), p. 3.

42. Mari McCarty, 'Possessing Female Space: "The Tender Shoot,"' *Women's Studies* 8 (1981): 368.

43. Susan Lanser and Evelyn Torton Beck, '[Why] Are There No Great Women Critics? And What Difference Does It Make?' in *The Prism of Sex: Essays in the Sociology of Knowledge*, ed. Beck and Julia A. Sherman (Madison: University of Wisconsin Press, 1979), p. 86.

44. Myra Jehlen, 'Archimedes and the Paradox of Feminist Criticism,' *Signs* 6 (Fall 1981): 582.

45. Smith, 'Black Feminist Criticism.' See also Gloria T. Hull, 'Afro-American Women Poets: A Bio-Critical Survey,' in Gilbert and Gubar, *Shakespeare's Sisters*, pp. 165–82, and Elaine Marks, 'Lesbian Intertextuality,' in *Homosexualities and French Literature*, ed. Marks and George Stambolian (Ithaca, N.Y.: Cornell University Press, 1979).

46. Margaret Anne Doody, 'George Eliot and the Eighteenth-Century Novel,' *Nineteenth-Century Fiction* 35 (December 1980): 267–68.

47. See, e.g., Judith Wilt, *Ghosts of the Gothic: Austen, Eliot, and Lawrence* (Princeton, N.J.: Princeton University Press, 1980).

48. See Ann Douglas, *The Feminization of American Culture* (New York: Alfred A. Knopf, 1977); Nina Baym, *Woman's Fiction: A Guide to Novels by and about Women in America, 1820–1870* (Ithaca, N.Y.: Cornell Unviersity Press, 1978); and Jane P. Tompkins, 'Sentimental Power: *Uncle Tom's Cabin* and the Politics of Literary History,' in this volume.

49. See, e.g., the analysis of Woolf in Sandra M. Gilbert, 'Costumes of the Mind: Transvestism as Metaphor in Modern Literature,' *Critical Inquiry* 7 (Winter 1980): 391–417.

50. I. A. Richards, quoted in John Paul Russo, 'A Study in Influence: The Moore-Richards Paradigm,' *Critical Inquiry* 5 (Summer 1979): 687.

51. Showalter, 'Literary Criticism,' p. 435; Miller, 'Emphasis Added'. To take one example, whereas *Jane Eyre* had always been read in relation to an implied 'dominant' fictional and social mode and had thus been perceived as flawed, feminist readings foreground its muted symbolic strategies and explore its credibility and coherence in its own terms. Feminist critics revise views like those of Richard Chase, who describes Rochester as castrated, thus implying that Jane's neurosis is penis envy, and G. Armour Craig, who sees the novel as Jane's struggle for superiority, to see Jane instead as healthy within her own system, that is, a *women's* society. See Chase, 'The Brontës; or, Myth Domesticated,' in *Jane Eyre* (New York: W. W. Norton, 1971), pp. 462–71; Craig, 'The Unpoetic Compromise: On the Relation between Private vision and Social Order in Nineteenth-Century English Fiction,' in *Self and Society*, ed. Mark Schorer (New York, 1956), pp. 30–41; Nancy Pell, 'Resistance, Rebellion, and Marriage: The Economics of *Jane Eyre*,' *Nineteenth-Century Fiction* 31 (March 1977): 397–420; Helene Moglen, *Charlotte Brontë: The Self Conceived* (New York: W. W. Norton, 1977); Adrienne Rich, '*Jane Eyre*: The Temptations of a Motherless Woman,' *MS*, October 1973; and Maurianne Adams, '*Jane Eyre*: Woman's Estate,' in Diamond and Edwards, *Authority of Experience*, pp. 137–59.

52. Geertz, *Interpretation of Cultures*, p. 9.

21 Paul de Man

Paul de Man (1919–83) was born in Belgium and educated in Europe. For most of his professional life, however, he taught in North American universities, and at the time of his death he was Stirling Professor of the Humanities at Yale. He was widely regarded as the most powerful and profound mind in the group of literary critics and theorists who, inspired in part by the work of Jacques Derrida, made Yale a centre of deconstruction in the 1970s. He was certainly, compared with the other leading members, J. Hillis Miller, Geoffrey Hartman, and Harold Bloom, the least playful, the most austerely intellectual. He was greatly revered by his colleagues and students, and his untimely death was widely mourned in the scholarly community.

Paul de Man's work consists mostly of long essays on some of the fundamental texts and problems of the interdisciplinary mix of literature, philosophy, and linguistics that has become known as Theory. The most important were collected in *Blindness and Insight*: *essays in the rhetoric of contemporary criticism* (1971; revised 1985) and *Allegories of Reading: figural language in Rousseau, Nietzsche, Rilke, and Proust* (1979). His work is difficult to summarize, dedicated as it is to showing that the effort to pin down truth in language is both inevitable and impossible. This double bind, which other deconstructionists take as a licence to pursue meaning as far as their own hermeneutic ingenuity will carry them, is accepted by de Man in a spirit of stoical irony. That spirit is very clearly manifested in 'The Resistance to Theory', a late essay selected here because it both describes de Man's position clearly and economically, and because it engages directly (and historically) with the underlying theme of this Reader: the relations between theory and practice in literary studies ('practice' in the multiple sense of criticism, scholarship, teaching).

What makes language such an unreliable medium for stating simple truths, in de Man's view (and that of Nietzsche, a writer to whom he is much indebted), is its rhetorical or figural component. Rhetoric is continually undermining the abstract systems of grammar and logic (de Man adopts the scholastic division of language into these three spheres). Literature, which flaunts its rhetoricity, avoids the bad faith of other discourses that try to repress or deny it—including the discourse of traditional literary criticism and literary history. If 'it is not *a priori* certain that literature is a reliable source of information about anything but its own language', then the traditional concern of literary studies to trace the connection between the world and the book is vain. The resistance to theory manifested by traditional scholars is shown to be a symptom of anxiety caused by their subscription to a false concept of representation. But having scornfully dismissed the opposition, de Man, in a characteristic move, turns the argument against himself: the resistance to theory is only a displacement of a much deeper resistance, or contradiction, in theory itself. However, 'to claim that this would be a sufficient reason not to envisage doing literary theory', de Man dryly remarks, 'would be like rejecting anatomy because it has failed to cure mortality.' 'The resistance to theory' is reprinted from *Yale French Studies*, 63, (1982).

CROSS-REFERENCES: 4. Genette
15. Abrams
16. Miller
23. Eagleton

COMMENTARY: William Ray, 'Paul de Man: the irony of deconstruction/the deconstruction of irony', in Ray's *Literary Meaning: from phenomenology to deconstruction* (1984)
Stephano Rosso, 'An Interview with Paul de Man', *Critical Inquiry* 12 (1986) pp. 788–95

The resistance to theory

This essay was not originally intended to address the question of teaching directly, although it was supposed to have a didactic and an educational function—which it failed to achieve. It was written at the request of the Committee on the Research Activities of the Modern Language Association as a contribution to a collective volume entitled *Introduction to Scholarship in Modern Languages and Literatures*. I was asked to write the section on literary theory. Such essays are expected to follow a clearly determined program: they are supposed to provide the reader with a select but comprehensive list of the main trends and publications in the field, to synthesize and classify the main problematic areas and to lay out a critical and programmatic projection of the solutions which can be expected in the foreseeable future. All this with a keen awareness that, ten years later, someone will be asked to repeat the same exercise.

I found it difficult to live up, in minimal good faith, to the requirements of this program and could only try to explain, as concisely as possible, why the main theoretical interest of literary theory consists in the impossibility of its definition. The Committee rightly judged that this was an inauspicious way to achieve the pedagogical objectives of the volume and commissioned another article. I thought their decision altogether justified, as well as interesting in its implications for the teaching of literature.

I tell this for two reason. First, to explain the traces in the article of the original assignment which account for the awkwardness of trying to be more retrospective and more general than one can legitimately hope to be. But secondly, because the predicament also reveals a question of general interest: that

355

of the relationship between the scholarship (the key word in the title of the MLA volume), the theory, and the teaching of literature.

Overfacile opinion notwithstanding, teaching is not primarily an intersubjective relationship between people but a cognitive process in which self and other are only tangentially and contiguously involved. The only teaching worthy of the name is scholarly, not personal; analogies between teaching and various aspects of show business or guidance counselling are more often than not excuses for having abdicated the task. Scholarship has, in principle, to be eminently teachable. In the case of literature, such scholarship involves at least two complementary areas: historical and philological facts as the preparatory condition for understanding, and methods of reading or interpretation. The latter is admittedly an open discipline, which can, however, hope to evolve by rational means, despite internal crises, controversies and polemics. As a controlled reflection on the formation of method, theory rightly proves to be entirely compatible with teaching, and one can think of numerous important theoreticians who are or were also prominent scholars. A question arises only if a tension develops between methods of understanding and the knowledge which those methods allow one to reach. If there is indeed something about literature, as such, which allows for a discrepancy between truth and method, between *Wahrheit* and *Methode*, then scholarship and theory are no longer necessarily compatible; as a first casualty of this complication, the notion of 'literature as such' as well as the clear distinction between history and interpretation can no longer be taken for granted. For a method that cannot be made to suit the 'truth' of its object can only teach delusion. Various developments, not only in the contemporary scene but in the long and complicated history of literary and linguistic instruction, reveal symptoms that suggest that such a difficulty is an inherent focus of the discourse about literature. These uncertainties are manifest in the hostility directed at theory in the name of ethical and aesthetic values, as well as in the recuperative attempts of theoreticians to reassert their own subservience to these values. The most effective of these attacks will denounce theory as an obstacle to scholarship and, consequently, to teaching. It is worth examining whether, and why, this is the case. For if this is indeed so, then it is better to fail in teaching what should not be taught than to succeed in teaching what is not true.

A general statement about literary theory should not, in theory, start from pragmatic considerations. It should address such questions as the definition of literature (what is literature?) and discuss the distinction between literary and non-literary uses of language, as well as between literary and non-verbal forms of art. It should then proceed to the descriptive taxonomy of the various aspects and species of the literary genus and to the normative rules that are bound to follow from such a classification. Or, if one rejects a scholastic for a phenomenological model, one should attempt a phenomenology of the literary activity as writing, reading or both, or of the literary work as the product, the correlate of such an activity. Whatever the approach taken (and several other theoretically justifiable starting-points can be imagined) it is certain that considerable difficulties will arise at once, difficulties that cut so deep that even the most elementary task of scholarship, the delimitation of the corpus and the *état présent* of the question, is bound to end in confusion, not necessarily because the bibliography is so large but because it is impossible to fix its borderlines. Such predictable difficulties have not prevented many writers on literature from proceeding along theoretical rather than pragmatic lines, often with considerable success. It can be shown however that, in all cases, this success depends on the power of a system (philosophical, religious or ideological) that may well remain implicit but that determines an *a priori* conception of what is 'literary' by starting out from the premises of the system rather than from the literary thing itself—if such a 'thing' indeed exists. This last qualification is of course a real question which in fact accounts for the predictability of the difficulties just alluded to: if the condition of existence of an entity is itself particularly critical, then the theory of this entity is bound to fall back into the pragmatic. The difficult and inconclusive history of literary theory indicates that this is indeed the case for literature in an even more manifest manner than for other verbalized occurrences such as jokes, for example, or even dreams. The attempt to treat literature theoretically may as well resign itself to the fact that it has to start out from empirical considerations.

Pragmatically speaking, then, we know that there has been, over the last fifteen to twenty years, a strong interest in something called literary theory and that, in the United States, this interest has at times coincided with the importation and reception of foreign, mostly but not always continental influences. We also know that this wave of interest now seems to be receding as some satiation or disappointment sets in after the initial enthusiasm. Such an ebb ·and flow is natural enough, but it remains interesting, in this case, because it makes the depth of the resistance to literary theory so manifest. It is a recurrent strategy of any anxiety to defuse what it considers threatening by magnification or minimization, by attributing to it claims to power of which it is bound to fall short. If a cat is called a tiger it can easily be dismissed as a paper tiger; the question remains however why one was so scared of the cat in the first place. The same tactic works in reverse: calling the cat a mouse and then deriding it for its pretense to be mighty. Rather than being drawn into this polemical whirlpool, it might be better to try to call the cat a cat and to document, however briefly, the contemporary version of the resistance to theory in this country.

The predominant trends in North American literary criticism, before the nineteen sixties, were certainly not averse to theory, if by theory one understands the rooting of literary exegesis and of critical evaluation in a system of some conceptual generality. Even the most intuitive, empirical and theoretically low-key writers on literature made use of a minimal set of concepts (tone, organic form, allusion, tradition, historical situation, etc.) of at least some general import. In several other cases, the interest in theory was publicly asserted and practised. A broadly shared methodology, more or less overtly proclaimed, links together such influential text books of the era as *Understanding Poetry* (Brooks and Warren), *Theory of Literature* (Wellek and Warren) and *The Fields of Light* (Reuben Brower) or such theoretically oriented works as *The Mirror and the*

Lamp, Language as Gesture, and *The Verbal Icon*[a].

Yet, with the possible exception of Kenneth Burke and, in some respects, Northrop Frye, none of these authors would have considered themselves theoreticians in the post-1960 sense of the term, nor did their work provoke as strong reactions, positive or negative, as that of later theoreticians. There were polemics, no doubt, and differences in approach that cover a wide spectrum of divergencies, yet the fundamental curriculum of literary studies as well as the talent and training expected for them were not being seriously challenged. New Critical approaches experienced no difficulty fitting into the academic establishments without their practitioners having to betray their literary sensibilities in any way; several of its representatives pursued successful parallel careers as poets or novelists next to their academic functions. Nor did they experience difficulties with regard to a national tradition which, though certainly less tyrannical than its European counterparts, is nevertheless far from powerless. The perfect embodiment of the New Criticism remains, in many respects, the personality and the ideology of T. S. Eliot, a combination of original talent, traditional learning, verbal wit and moral earnestness, an Anglo-American blend of intellectual gentility not so repressed as not to afford tantalizing glimpses of darker psychic and political depths, but without breaking the surface of an ambivalent decorum that has its own complacencies and seductions. The normative principles of such a literary ambiance are cultural and ideological rather than theoretical, oriented towards the integrity of a social and historical self rather than towards the impersonal consistency that theory requires. Culture allows for, indeed advocates, a degree of cosmopolitanism, and the literary spirit of the American Academy of the fifties was anything but provincial. It had no difficulty appreciating and assimilating outstanding products of a kindred spirit that originated in Europe: Curtius, Auerbach, Croce, Spitzer, Alonso, Valéry and also, with the exception of some of his works, J. P. Sartre. The inclusion of Sartre in this list is important, for it indicates that the dominant cultural code we are trying to evoke cannot simply be assimilated to a political polarity of the left and the right, of the academic and the non-academic, of Greenwich Village and Gambier, Ohio. Politically oriented and predominently non-academic journals, of which the *Partisan Review* of the fifties remains the best example, did not (after due allowance is made for all proper reservations and distinctions) stand in any genuine opposition to the New Critical approaches. The broad, though negative, consensus that brings these extremely diverse trends and individuals together is their shared resistance to theory. This diagnosis is borne out by the arguments and complicities that have since come to light in a more articulate opposition to the common opponent.

The interest of these considerations would be at most anecdotal (the historical impact of twentieth-century literary discussion being so slight) if it were not for the theoretical implications of the resistance to theory. The local manifestations of this resistance are themselves systematic enough to warrant one's interest.

---

[a] These titles are the work of M. H. Abrams, R. P. Blackmur and W. K. Wimsatt (with Monroe C. Beardsley), respectively.

What is it that is being threatened by the approaches to literature that developed during the sixties and that now, under a variety of designations, make up the ill-defined and somewhat chaotic field of literary theory? These approaches cannot be simply equated with any particular method or country. Structuralism was not the only trend to dominate the stage, not even in France, and structuralism as well as semiology are inseparable from prior tendencies in the Slavic domain. In Germany, the main impulses have come from other directions, from the Frankfurt school and more orthodox Marxists, from post-Husserlian phenomenology and post-Heideggerian hermeneutics, with only minor inroads made by structural analysis. All these trends have had their share of influence in the United States, in more or less productive combinations with nationally rooted concerns. Only a nationally or personally competitive view of history would wish to hierarchize such hard-to-label movements. The possibility of doing literary theory, which is by no means to be taken for granted, has itself become a consciously reflected-upon question and those who have progressed furthest in this question are the most controversial but also the best sources of information. This certainly includes several of the names loosely connected with structuralism, broadly enough defined to include Saussure, Jakobson and Barthes as well as Greimas and Althusser, that is to say, so broadly defined as to be no longer of use as a meaningful historical term.

Literary theory can be said to come into being when the approach to literary texts is no longer based on non-linguistic, that is to say historical and aesthetic, considerations or, to put it somewhat less crudely, when the object of discussion is no longer the meaning or the value but the modalities of production and of reception of meaning and of value prior to their establishment—the implication being that this establishment is problematic enough to require an autonomous discipline of critical investigation to consider its possibility and its status. Literary history, even when considered at furthest remove from the platitudes of positivistic historicism, is still the history of an understanding of which the possibility is taken for granted. The question of the relationship between aesthetics and meaning is more complex, since aesthetics apparently has to do with the *effect* of meaning rather than with its content *per se*. But aesthetics is in fact, ever since its development just before and with Kant, a phenomenalism of a process of meaning and understanding, and it may be naive in that it postulates (as its name indicates) a phenomenology of art and of literature which may well be what is at issue. Aesthetics is part of a universal system of philosophy rather than a specific theory. In the nineteenth-century philosophical tradition, Nietzsche's challenge of the system erected by Kant, Hegel and their successors, is a version of the general question of philosophy. Nietzsche's critique of metaphysics includes, or starts out from, the aesthetic, and the same could be argued for Heidegger. The invocation of prestigious philosophical names does not intimate that the present-day development of literary theory is a by-product of larger philosophical speculations. In some rare cases, a direct link may exist between philosophy and literary theory. More frequently, however, contemporary literary theory is a relatively autonomous version of questions that also surface, in a different context, in philosophy, though not necessarily in a clearer and more rigorous form. Philosophy, in England as well as on the Continent, is less freed from traditional patterns than it sometimes pretends to believe and the prominent, though never dominant, place of aesthetics among the main components of the system is a constitutive part of this system. It is therefore not surprising that contemporary literary theory came into being from outside philosophy and sometimes in conscious rebellion against the weight of its tradition. Literary theory may now well have become a legitimate concern of philosophy but it cannot be assimilated to it, either factually or theoretically. It contains a necessarily pragmatic moment that certainly weakens it as theory but that adds a subversive element of unpredictability and makes it something of a wild card in the serious game of the theoretical disciplines.

The advent of theory, the break that is now so often being deplored and that sets it aside from literary history and from literary criticism, occurs with the introduction of linguistic terminology in the metalanguage about literature. By linguistic terminology is meant a terminology that designates reference prior to designating the referent and takes into account, in the consideration of the world, the referential function of language or, to be somewhat more specific, that considers reference as a function of language and not necessarily as an intuition. Intuition implies perception, consciousness, experience, and leads at once into the world of logic and of understanding with all its correlatives, among which aesthetics occupies a prominent place. The assumption that there can be a science of language which is not necessarily a logic leads to the development of a terminology which is not necessarily aesthetic. Contemporary literary theory comes into its own in such events as the application of Saussurian linguistics to literary texts.

The affinity between structural linguistics and literary texts is not as obvious as, with the hindsight of history, it now may seem. Peirce, Saussure, Sapir and Bloomfield were not originally concerned with literature at all but with the scientific foundations of linguistics. But the interest of philologists such as Roman Jakobson or literary critics such as Roland Barthes in semiology reveals the natural attraction of literature to a theory of linguistic signs. By considering language as a system of signs and of signification rather than as an established pattern of meanings, one displaces or even suspends the traditional barriers between literary and presumably non-literary uses of language and liberates the corpus from the secular weight of textual canonization. The results of the encounter between semiology and literature went considerably further than those of many other theoretical models—philological, psychological or classically epistemological—which writers on literature in quest of such models had tried out before. The responsiveness of literary texts to semiotic analysis is visible in that, whereas other approaches were unable to reach beyond observations that could be paraphrased or translated in terms of common knowledge, these analyses revealed patterns that could only be described in terms of their own, specifically linguistic, aspects. The linguistics of semiology and of literature apparently have something in common that only their shared perspective can detect and that pertains distinctively to them. The definition of this something, often referred to as literariness, has become the object of literary theory.

Literariness, however, is often misunderstood in a way that has provoked much of the confusion which dominates today's polemics. It is frequently assumed, for instance, that literariness is another word for, or another mode of, aesthetic response. The use, in conjunction with literariness, of such terms as style and stylistics, form or even 'poetry' (as in 'the poetry of grammar'), all of which carry strong aesthetic connotations, helps to foster this confusion, even among those who first put the term in circulation. Roland Barthes, for example, in an essay properly and revealingly dedicated to Roman Jakobson, speaks eloquently of the writer's quest for a perfect coincidence of the phonic properties of a word with its signifying function. 'We would also wish to insist on the Cratylism[b] of the name (and of the sign) in Proust... Proust sees the relationship between signifier and signified as motivated, the one copying the other and representing in its material form the signified essence of the thing (and not the thing itself) ... This realism (in the scholastic sense of the word), which conceives of names as the "copy" of the ideas, has taken, in Proust, a radical form. But one may well ask whether it is not more or less consciously present in all writing and whether it is possible to be a writer without some sort of belief in the natural relationship between names and essences. The poetic function, in the widest sense of the word, would thus be defined by a Cratylian awareness of the sign, and the writer would be the conveyor of this secular myth which wants language to imitate the idea and which, contrary to the teachings of linguistic science, thinks of signs as motivated signs.'[1] To the extent that Cratylism assumes a convergence of the phenomenal aspects of language, as sound, with its signifying function as referent, it is an aesthetically oriented conception; one could, in fact, without distortion, consider aesthetic theory, including its most systematic formulation in Hegel, as the complete unfolding of the model of which the Cratylian conception of language is a version. Hegel's somewhat cryptic reference to Plato, in the *Aesthetics*, may well be interpreted in this sense. Barthes and Jakobson often seem to invite a purely aesthetic reading, yet there is a part of their statement that moves in the opposite direction. For the convergence of sound and meaning celebrated by Barthes in Proust and, as Gérard Genette has decisively shown,[2] later dismantled by Proust himself as a seductive temptation to mystified minds, is also considered here to be a mere *effect* which language can perfectly well achieve, but which bears no substantial relationship, by analogy or by ontologically grounded imitation, to anything beyond that particular effect. It is a rhetorical rather than an aesthetic function of language, an identifiable trope (paranomasis) that operates on the level of the signifier and contains no responsible pronouncement on the nature of the world—despite its powerful potential to create the opposite illusion. The phenomenality of the signifier, as sound, is unquestionably involved in the correspondence between the name and the thing named, but the link, the relationship between word and thing is not phenomenal but conventional.

[b] The idea that there is an existential, as opposed to a merely conventional, relation between words and the things to which they refer, is mooted in Plato's dialogue, *Cratylus*.

This gives the language considerable freedom from referential restraint, but it makes it epistemologically highly suspect and volatile, since its use can no longer be said to be determined by considerations of truth and falsehood, good and evil, beauty and ugliness, or pleasure and pain. Whenever this autonomous potential of language can be revealed by analysis, we are dealing with literariness and, in fact, with literature as the place where this negative knowledge about reliability of linguistic utterance is made available. The ensuing foregrounding of material, phenomenal aspects of the signifier creates a strong illusion of aesthetic seduction at the very moment when the actual aesthetic function has been, at the very least, suspended. It is inevitable that semiology or similarly oriented methods be considered formalistic, in the sense of being aesthetically rather than semantically valorized, but the inevitability of such an interpretation does not make it less aberrant. Literature involves the voiding, rather than the affirmation, of aesthetic categories. One of the consequences of this is that, whereas we have traditionally been accustomed to reading literature by analogy with the plastic arts and with music, we now have to recognize the necessity of a non-perceptual, linguistic moment in painting and in music, and learn to *read* pictures rather than to *imagine* meaning.

If literariness is not an aesthetic quality, it is also not primarily mimetic. Mimesis becomes one trope among others, language choosing to imitate a non-verbal entity just as paranomasis 'imitates' a sound without any claim to identity (or reflection on difference) between the verbal and non-verbal elements. The most misleading representation of literariness, and also the most recurrent objection to contemporary literary theory, considers it as pure verbalism, as a denial of the reality principle in the name of absolute fictions, and for reasons that are said to be ethically and politically shameful. The attack reflects the anxiety of the aggressors rather than the guilt of the accused. By allowing for the necessity of a non-phenomenal linguistics, one frees the discourse on literature from naive oppositions between fiction and reality, which are themselves an offspring of an uncritically mimetic conception of art. In a genuine semiology as well as in other linguistically oriented theories, the referential function of language is not being denied—far from it; what is in question is its authority as a model for natural or phenomenal cognition. Literature is fiction not because it somehow refuses to acknowledge 'reality,' but because it is not *a priori* certain that language functions according to principles which are those, or which are *like* those, of the phenomenal world. It is therefore not *a priori* certain that literature is a reliable source of information about anything but its own language.

It would be unfortunate, for example, to confuse the materiality of the signifier with the materiality of what it signifies. This may seem obvious enough on the level of light and sound, but it is less so with regard to the more general phenomenality of space, time or especially of the self: no one in his right mind will try to grow grapes by the luminosity of the word 'day,' but it is very difficult not to conceive the pattern of one's past and future existence as in accordance with temporal and spatial schemes that belong to fictional narratives and not to the world. This does not mean that fictional narratives are not part of the world and of reality; their impact upon the world may well be all too strong for comfort.

What we call ideology is precisely the confusion of linguistic with natural reality, of reference with phenomenalism. It follows that, more than any other mode of inquiry, including economics, the linguistics of literariness is a powerful and indispensable tool in the unmasking of ideological aberrations, as well as a determining factor in accounting for their occurrence. Those who reproach literary theory for being oblivious to social and historical (that is to say ideological) reality are merely stating their fear at having their own ideological mystifications exposed by the tool they are trying to discredit. They are, in short, very poor readers of Marx's *German Ideology*.

In these all too summary evocations of arguments that have been much more extensively and convincingly made by others, we begin to perceive some of the answers to the initial question: what is it about literary theory that is so threatening that it provokes such strong resistances and attacks? It upsets rooted ideologies by revealing the mechanics of their workings; it goes against a powerful philosophical tradition of which aesthetics is a prominent part; it upsets the established canon of literary works and blurs the borderlines between literary and non-literary discourse. By implication, it may also reveal the links between ideologies and philosophy. All this is ample enough reason for suspicion, but not a satisfying answer to the question. For it makes the tension between contemporary literary theory and the tradition of literary studies appear as a mere historical conflict between two modes of thought that happen to hold the stage at the same time. If the conflict is merely historical, in the literal sense, it is of limited theoretical interest, a passing squall in the intellectual weather of the world. As a matter of fact, the arguments in favor of the legitimacy of literary theory are so compelling that it seems useless to concern oneself with the conflict at all. Certainly, none of the objections to theory, presented again and again, always misinformed or based on crude misunderstandings of such terms as mimesis, fiction, reality, ideology, reference and, for that matter, relevance, can be said to be of genuine rhetorical interest.

It may well be, however, that the development of literary theory is itself overdetermined by complications inherent in its very project and unsettling with regard to its status as a scientific discipline. Resistance may be a built-in constituent of its discourse, in a manner that would be inconceivable in the natural sciences and unmentionable in the social sciences. It may well be, in other words, that the polemical opposition, the systematic non-understanding and misrepresentation, the unsubstantial but eternally recurrent objections, are the displaced symptoms of a resistance inherent in the theoretical enterprise itself. To claim that this would be a sufficient reason not to envisage doing literary theory would be like rejecting anatomy because it has failed to cure mortality. The real debate of literary theory is not with its polemical opponents but rather with its own methodological assumptions and possibilities. Rather than asking why literary theory is threatening, we should perhaps ask why it has such difficulty going about its business and why it lapses so readily either into the language of self-justification and self-defense or else into the overcompensation of a programmatically euphoric utopianism. Such insecurity about its own project calls for self-analysis, if one is to understand the frustrations that attend upon its practitioners,

363

even when they seem to dwell in serene methodological self-assurance. And if these difficulties are indeed an integral part of the problem, then they will have to be, to some extent, a-historical in the temporal sense of the term. The way in which they are encountered on the present local literary scene as a resistance to the introduction of linguistic terminology in aesthetic and historical discourse about literature is only one particular version of a question that cannot be reduced to a specific historical situation and called modern, post-modern, post-classical or romantic (not even in Hegel's sense of the term), although its compulsive way of forcing itself upon us in the guise of a system of historical periodization is certainly part of its problematic nature. Such difficulties can be read in the text of literary theory at all times, at whatever historical moment one wishes to select. One of the main achievements of the present theoretical trends is to have restored some awareness of this fact. Classical, medieval and Renaissance literary theory is now often being read in a way that knows enough about what it is doing not to wish to call itself 'modern.'

We return, then, to the original question in an attempt to broaden the discussion enough to inscribe the polemics inside the question rather than having them determine it. The resistance to theory is a resistance to the use of language about language. It is therefore a resistance to language itself or to the possibility that language contains factors or functions that cannot be reduced to intuition. But we seem to assume all too readily that, when we refer to something called 'language,' we know what it is we are talking about, although there is probably no word to be found in the language that is as overdetermined, self-evasive, disfigured and disfiguring as 'language.' Even if we choose to consider it at a safe remove from any theoretical model, in the pragmatic history of 'language,' not as a concept, but as a didactic assignment that no human being can bypass, we soon find ourselves confronted by theoretical enigmas. The most familiar and general of all linguistic models, the classical *trivium*, which considers the sciences of language as consisting of grammar, rhetoric and logic (or dialectics), is in fact a set of unresolved tensions powerful enough to have generated an infinitely prolonged discourse of endless frustration of which contemporary literary theory, even at its most self-assured, is one more chapter. The difficulties extend to the internal articulations between the constituent parts as well as to the articulation of the field of language with the knowledge of the world in general, the link between the *trivium* and the *quadrivium*, which covers the non-verbal sciences of number (arithmetic), of space (geometry), of motion (astronomy) and of time (music). In the history of philosophy, this link is traditionally, as well as substantially, accomplished by way of logic, the area where the rigor of the linguistic discourse about itself matches up with the rigor of the mathematical discourse about the world. Seventeenth-century epistemology, for instance, at the moment when the relationship between philosophy and mathematics is particularly close, holds up the language of what it calls geometry (*mos geometricus*), and which in fact includes the homogeneous concatenation between space, time and number, as the sole model of coherence and economy. Reasoning *more geometrico* is said to be 'almost the only mode of reasoning that is infallible, because it is the only one to adhere to the true method, whereas all other ones are by natural necessity in a degree of confusion of which only geometrical minds can be aware.'[3] This is a clear instance of the interconnection between a science of the phenomenal world and a science of language conceived as definitional logic, the pre-condition for a correct axiomatic-deductive, synthetic reasoning. The possibility of thus circulating freely between logic and mathematics has its own complex and problematic history as well as its contemporary equivalences with a different logic and a different mathematics. What matters for our present argument is that this articulation of the sciences of language with the mathematical sciences represents a particularly compelling version of a continuity between a theory of language, as logic, and the knowledge of the phenomenal world to which mathematics give access. In such a system, the place of aesthetics is preordained and by no means alien, provided the priority of logic, in the model of the *trivium*, is not being questioned. For even if one assumes, for the sake of argument and against a great deal of historical evidence, that the link between logic and the natural sciences is secure, this leaves open the question, within the confines of the *trivium* itself, of the relationship between grammar, rhetoric and logic. And this is the point at which literariness, the use of language that foregrounds the rhetorical over the grammatical and the logical function, intervenes as a decisive but unsettling element which, in a variety of modes and aspects, disrupts the inner balance of the model and, consequently, its outward extension to the non-verbal world as well.

Logic and grammar seem to have a natural enough affinity for each other and, in the tradition of Cartesian linguistics, the grammarians of Port-Royal[c] experienced little difficulty at being logicians as well. The same claim persists today in very different methods and terminologies that nevertheless maintain the same orientation toward the universality that logic shares with science. Replying to those who oppose the singularity of specific texts to the scientific generality of the semiotic project, A. J. Greimas[d] disputes the right to use the dignity of 'grammar' to describe a reading that would not be committed to universality. Those who have doubts about the semiotic method, he writes, 'postulate the necessity of constructing a grammar for each particular text. But the essence (*le propre*) of a grammar is its ability to account for a large number of texts, and the metaphorical use of the term . . . fails to hide the fact that one has, in fact, given up on the semiotic project.'[4] There is no doubt that what is here prudently called 'a large number' implies the hope at least of a future model that would in fact be applicable to the generation of all texts. Again, it is not our present purpose to discuss the validity of this methodological optimism, but merely to offer it as an instance of the persistent symbiosis between grammar and logic. It is clear that, for Greimas as for the entire tradition to which he belongs, the grammatical and the logical function of language are co-extensive. Grammar is an isotope of logic.

---

[c] Port Royal was the base of the Jansenist religious community in seventeenth-century France to which Blaise Pascal belonged.

[d] A. J. Greimas is a distinguished French semiotician and narratologist, whose works include *Maupassant* (1976) and *Semiotique* (1979)

It follows that, as long as it remains grounded in grammar, any theory of language, including a literary one, does not threaten what we hold to be the underlying principle of all cognitive and aesthetic linguistic systems. Grammar stands in the service of logic which, in turn, allows for the passage to the knowledge of the world. The study of grammar, the first of the *artes liberales*, is the necessary pre-condition for scientific and humanistic knowledge. As long as it leaves this principle intact, there is nothing threatening about literary theory. The continuity between theory and phenomenalism is asserted and preserved by the system itself. Difficulties occur only when it is no longer possible to ignore the epistemological thrust of the rhetorical dimension of discourse, that is, when it is no longer possible to keep it in its place as a mere adjunct, a mere ornament within the semantic function.

The uncertain relationship between grammar and rhetoric (as opposed to that between grammar and logic) is apparent, in the history of the *trivium*, in the uncertain status of figures of speech or tropes, a component of language that straddles the disputed borderlines between the two areas. Tropes used to be part of the study of grammar but were also considered to be the semantic agent of the specific function (or effect) that rhetoric performs as persuasion as well as meaning. Tropes, unlike grammar, pertain primordially to language. They are text-producing functions that are not necessarily patterned on a non-verbal entity, whereas grammar is by definition capable of extra-linguistic generalization. The latent tension between rhetoric and grammar precipitates out in the problem of reading, the process that necessarily partakes of both. It turns out that the resistance to theory is in fact a resistance to reading, a resistance that is perhaps at its more effective, in contemporary studies, in the methodologies that call themselves theories of reading but nevertheless avoid the function they claim as their object.

What is meant when we assert that the study of literary texts is necessarily dependent on an act of reading, or when we claim that this act is being systematically avoided? Certainly more than the tautology that one has to have read at least some parts, however small, of a text (or read some part, however small, of a text about this text) in order to be able to make a statement about it. Common as it may be, criticism by hearsay is only rarely held up as exemplary. To stress the by no means self-evident necessity of reading implies at least two things. First of all, it implies that literature is not a transparent message in which it can be taken for granted that the distinction between the message and the means of communication is clearly established. Second, and more problematically, it implies that the grammatical decoding of a text leaves a residue of indetermination that has to be, but cannot be, resolved by grammatical means, however extensively conceived. The extension of grammar to include para-figural dimensions is in fact the most remarkable and debatable strategy of contemporary semiology, especially in the study of syntagmatic and narrative structures. The codification of contextual elements well beyond the syntactical limits of the sentence leads to the systematic study of metaphrastic[e] dimensions and has considerably refined and

Metaphrase means translation, from one language or from one form to another.

expanded the knowledge of textual codes. It is equally clear, however, that this extension is always strategically directed towards the replacement of rhetorical figures by grammatical codes. The tendency to replace a rhetorical by a grammatical terminology (to speak of hypotaxis, for instance, to designate anamorphic or metonymic tropes)*f* is part of an explicit program, a program that is entirely admirable in its intent since it tends towards the mastering and the clarification of meaning. The replacement of a hermeneutic by a semiotic model, of interpretation by decoding, would represent, in view of the baffling historical instability of textual meanings (including, of course, those of canonical texts) a considerable progress. Much of the hesitation associated with 'reading' could thus be dispelled.

The argument can be made, however, that no grammatical decoding, however refined, could claim to reach the determining figural dimensions of a text. There are elements in all texts that are by no means ungrammatical, but whose semantic function is not grammatically definable, neither in themselves nor in context. Do we have to interpret the genitive in the title of Keats' unfinished epic *The Fall of Hyperion* as meaning 'Hyperion's fall,' the case story of the defeat of an older by a newer power, the very recognizable story from which Keats indeed started out but from which he increasingly strayed away, or as 'Hyperion falling,' the much less specific but more disquieting evocation of an actual process of falling, regardless of its beginning, its end or the identity of the entity to whom it befalls to be falling. This story is indeed told in the later fragment entitled *The Fall of Hyperion*, but it is told about a character who resembles Apollo rather than Hyperion, the same Apollo who, in the first version (called *Hyperion*), should definitely be triumphantly standing rather than falling if Keats had not been compelled to interrupt, for no apparent reason, the story of Apollo's triumph. Does the title tell us that Hyperion is fallen and that Apollo stands, or does it tell us that Hyperion and Apollo (and Keats, whom it is hard to distinguish, at times, from Apollo) are interchangeable in that all of them are necessarily and constantly falling? Both readings are grammatically correct, but it is impossible to decide from the context (the ensuring narrative) which version is the right one. The narrative context suits neither and both at the same time, and one is tempted to suggest that the fact that Keats was unable to complete either version manifests the impossibility, for him as for us, of reading his own title. One could then read the word 'Hyperion' in the title *The Fall of Hyperion* figurally, or, if one wishes, intertextually, as referring not to the historical or mythological character but as referring to the title of Keats' own earlier text (*Hyperion*). But are we then telling the story of the failure of the first text as the success of the second, the Fall of *Hyperion* as the Triumph of *The Fall of Hyperion*? Manifestly yes, but not quite, since the second text also fails to be concluded. Or are we telling the story of why all texts, as texts, can always be said to be falling? Manifestly yes, but not

---

f Hypotaxis is grammatical subordination of one clause to another, as opposed to parataxis, which simply juxtaposes them. 'Anamorphic' means distorting. De Man seems to imply that hypotaxis is to metonymy and synecdoche (which distort the signified) as parataxis is to metaphor (which juxtaposes two signifieds). See Jakobson on metaphor and metonymy, pp. 57–61 above.

quite, either, since the story of the fall of the first version, as told in the second, applies to the first version only and could not legitimately be read as meaning also the fall of *The Fall of Hyperion*. The undecidability involves the figural or literal status of the proper name Hyperion as well as of the verb falling, and is thus a matter of figuration and not of grammar. In 'Hyperion's Fall,' the word 'fall' is plainly figural, the representation of a figural fall, and we, as readers, read this fall standing up. But in 'Hyperion falling,' this is not so clearly the case, for if Hyperion can be Apollo and Apollo can be Keats, then he can also be us and his figural (or symbolic) fall becomes his and our literal falling as well. The difference between the two readings is itself structured as a trope. And it matters a great deal how we read the title, as an exercise not only in semantics, but in what the text actually does to us. Faced with the ineluctable necessity to come to a decision, no grammatical or logical analysis can help us out. Just as Keats had to break off his narrative, the reader has to break off his understanding at the very moment when he is most directly engaged and summoned by the text. One could hardly expect to find solace in this 'fearful symmetry' between the author's and the reader's plight since, at this point, the symmetry is no longer a formal but an actual trap, and the question no longer 'merely' theoretical.

This undoing of theory, this disturbance of the stable cognitive field that extends from grammar to logic to a general science of man and of the phenomenal world, can in its turn be made into a theoretical project of rhetorical analysis that will reveal the inadequacy of grammatical models of non-reading. Rhetoric, by its actively negative relationship to grammar and to logic, certainly undoes the claims of the *trivium* (and by extension, of language) to be an epistemologically stable construct. The resistance to theory is a resistance to the rhetorical or tropological dimension of language, a dimension which is perhaps more explicitly in the foreground in literature (broadly conceived) than in other verbal manifestations or—to be somewhat less vague—which can be revealed in any verbal event when it is read textually. Since grammar as well as figuration is an integral part of reading, it follows that reading will be a negative process in which the grammatical cognition is undone, at all times, by its rhetorical displacement. The model of the *trivium* contains within itself the pseudo-dialectic of its own undoing and its history tells the story of this dialectic.

This conclusion allows for a somewhat more systematic description of the contemporary theoretical scene. This scene is dominated by an increased stress on reading as a theoretical problem or, as it is sometimes erroneously phrased, by an increased stress on the reception rather than on the production of texts. It is in this area that the most fruitful exchanges have come about between writers and journals of various countries and that the most interesting dialogue has developed between literary theory and other disciplines, in the arts as well as in linguistics, philosophy and the social sciences. A straightforward *report* on the present state of literary theory in the United States would have to stress the emphasis on reading, a direction which is already present, moreover, in the New Critical tradition of the forties and the fifties. The methods are now more technical, but the contemporary interest in a poetics of literature is clearly linked, traditionally enough, to the problems of reading. And since the models that are

being used certainly are no longer *simply* intentional and centered on an identifiable self, nor *simply* hermeneutic in the postulation of a single originary, pre-
figural and absolute text, it would appear that this concentration on reading
would lead to the rediscovery of the theoretical difficulties associated with rhetoric. This is indeed the case, to some extent; but not quite. Perhaps the most
instructive aspect of contemporary theory is the refinement of the techniques by
which the threat inherent in rhetorical analysis is being avoided at the very
moment when the efficacy of these techniques has progressed so far that the
rhetorical obstacles to understanding can no longer be mistranslated in thematic
and phenomenal commonplaces. The resistance to theory which, as we saw, is
a resistance to reading, appears in its most rigorous and theoretically elaborated
form among the theoreticians of reading who dominate the contemporary theoretical scene.

It would be a relatively easy, though lengthy, process to show that this is so
for theoreticians of reading who, like Greimas or, on a more refined level,
Riffaterre or, in a very different mode, H. R. Jauss or Wolfgang Iser[g]—all of
whom have a definite, though sometimes occult, influence on literary theory in
this country—are committed to the use of grammatical models or, in the case of
Rezeptionsaesthetik, to traditional hermeneutic models that do not allow for the
problematization of the phenomenalism of reading and therefore remain uncritically confined within a theory of literature rooted in aesthetics. Such an argument
would be easy to make because, once a reader has become aware of the rhetorical
dimensions of a text, he will not be amiss in finding textual instances that are
irreduceable to grammar or to historically determined meaning, provided only he
is willing to acknowledge what he is bound to notice. The problem quickly
becomes the more baffling one of having to account for the shared reluctance
to acknowledge the obvious. But the argument would be lengthy because it has
to involve a textual analysis that cannot avoid being somewhat elaborate; one can
succinctly suggest the grammatical indetermination of a title such as *The Fall of
Hyperion*, but to confront such an undecideable enigma with the critical reception
and reading of Keat's text requires some space.

The demonstration is less easy (though perhaps less ponderous) in the case
of theoreticians of reading whose avoidance of rhetoric takes another turn. We
have witnessed, in recent years, a strong interest in certain elements in language
whose function is not only not dependent on any form of phenomenalism but on
any form of cognition as well, and which thus excludes, or postpones, the
consideration of tropes, ideologies, etc., from a reading that would be primarily
performative. In some cases, a link is reintroduced between performance,
grammar, logic, and stable referential meaning, and the resulting theories (as in
the case of Ohmann) are not in essence distinct from those of avowed grammarians
or semioticians. But the most astute practitioners of a speech act theory of reading
avoid this relapse and rightly insist on the necessity to keep the actual performance of speech acts, which is conventional rather than cognitive, separate from

[g] See headnote on Wolfgang Iser, p. 211, above, and reference to Michael Riffaterre under
Commentary on Roman Jakobson, p. 32, above.

its causes and effects—to keep, in their terminology, the illocutionary force separate from its perlocutionary function. Rhetoric, understood as persuasion, is forcefully banished (like Coriolanus) from the performative moment and exiled in the affective area of perlocution. Stanley Fish, in a masterful essay, convincingly makes this point.[5] What awakens one's suspicion about this conclusion is that it relegates persuasion, which is indeed inseparable from rhetoric, to a purely affective and intentional realm and makes no allowance for modes of persuasion which are no less rhetorical and no less at work in literary texts, but which are of the order of persuasion by *proof* rather than persuasion by seduction. Thus to empty rhetoric of its epistemological impact is possible only because its tropological, figural functions are being bypassed. It is as if, to return for a moment to the model of the *trivium*, *rhetoric* could be isolated from the generality that grammar and logic have in common and considered as a mere correlative of an illocutionary power. The equation of rhetoric with psychology rather than with epistemology opens up dreary prospects of pragmatic banality, all the drearier if compared to the brilliance of the performative analysis. Speech act theories of reading in fact repeat, in a much more effective way, the grammatization of the *trivium* at the expense of rhetoric. For the characterization of the performative as sheer convention reduces it in effect to a grammatical code among others. The relationship between trope and performance is actually closer but more disruptive than what is here being proposed. Nor is this relationship properly captured by reference to a supposedly 'creative' aspect of performance, a notion with which Fish rightly takes issue. The performative power of language can be called positional, which differs considerably from conventional as well as from 'creatively' (or, in the technical sense, intentionally) constitutive. Speech act oriented theories of reading read only to the extent that they prepare the way for the rhetorical reading they avoid.

But the same is still true even if a 'truly' rhetorical reading that would stay clear of any undue phenomenalization or of any undue grammatical or performative codification of the text could be conceived—something which is not necessarily impossible and for which the aims and methods of literary theory should certainly strive. Such a reading would indeed appear as the methodical undoing of the grammatical construct and, in its systematic disarticulation of the *trivium*, will be theoretically sound as well as effective. Technically correct rhetorical readings may be boring, monotonous, predictable and unpleasant, but they are irrefutable. They are also totalizing (and potentially totalitarian) for since the structures and functions they expose do not lead to the knowledge of an entity (such as language) but are an unreliable process of knowledge production that prevents all entities, including linguistic entities, from coming into discourse as such, they are indeed universals, consistently defective models of language's impossibility to be a model language. They are, always in theory, the most elastic theoretical and dialectical model to end all models and they can rightly claim to contain within their own defective selves all the other defective models of reading-avoidance, referential, semiological, grammatical, performative, logical, or whatever. They are theory and not theory at the same, the universal theory of the impossibility of theory. To the extent however that they are theory, that is to say teachable, generalizable and highly responsive to systematization, rhetorical readings, like the other kinds, still avoid and resist the reading they advocate. Nothing can overcome the resistance to theory since theory *is* itself this resistance. The loftier the aims and the better the methods of literary theory, the less possible it becomes. Yet literary theory is not in danger of going under; it cannot help but flourish, and the more it is resisted, the more it flourishes, since the language it speaks is the language of self-resistance. What remains impossible to decide is whether this flourishing is a triumph or a fall.

NOTES

1. Roland Barthes, 'Proust et les noms' in *To honor Roman Jakobson* (The Hague, 1967) part I, pp. 157ff.
2. 'Proust et le langage indirect' in *Figures II* (Paris, 1969).
3. Pascal, 'De l'esprit géométrique et de l'art de persuader,' in *Oeuvres complètes* presented by L. Lafuma (Paris: Editions du Seuil, 1963) pp. 349ff.
4. A. J. Greimas, *Du Sens* (Paris: Edition du Seuil, 1970), p. 13.
5. Stanley Fish, 'How to do things with Austin and Searle: Speech Act Theory and Literary Criticism,' in *MLN* 91 (1976), pp. 983–1025. See especially p. 1008.

22 Fredric Jameson

Fredric Jameson (b. 1934) has taught at several American universities, including Harvard, the University of California at San Diego and Santa Cruz, and Yale. At present he is Professor of English at Duke University. Since the publication of his *Marxism and Form* (1971) he has been generally acknowledged as the leading American exponent of Marxist criticism, but his work also displays an intellectually powerful grasp of the whole range of structuralist and post-structuralist theory. *The Prison–House of Language* (1972) is a valuable exposition of structuralism and Russian Formalism, as well a critique of them from the point of view of dialectical materialism. *The Political Unconscious: Narrative as a Socially Symbolic Act* (1981) is a densely packed synthesis of structuralism, post-structuralism, Freudian psychoanalysis and various schools of Marxism. His *Fables of Aggression* (1979) is a study of fascist ideology in modernist writers such as Wyndham Lewis and Ezra Pound.

More recently Jameson has turned his attention to the topic of postmodernism, and its socio-economic context of 'late capitalism.' 'The Politics of Theory: Ideological Positions in the Postmodern Debate' is one of three influential arti-cles he has published on this theme. The others are 'Postmodernism and Consumer Society' published in *The Anti-Aesthetic*, edited by Hal Foster (1983; English edition, entitled *Postmodern Culture*, 1985) and a much expanded and elaborated version of this, entitled 'Postmodernism, or the Cultural Logic of Late Capitalism,' published in *New Left Review* (July/August 1984), where it provoked a number of interesting rejoinders from Marxists who thought Jameson was too indulgent towards, or too easily seduced by, postmodernist art. (See the essay by Terry Eagleton reprinted in the following section of this Reader.) In 'The Politics of Theory' Jameson takes a more detached view of the topic, exploring the paradox that postmodernist art seems capable of generating passionate advo-cacy and passionate opposition from politically reactionary and politically progressive critics in every possible permutation. His conclusion is 'that we are *within* the culture of postmodernism to the point where its facile repudiation is as impossible as any equally facile celebration of it is complacent and corrupt.' The essay is reprinted from *New German Critique*, where it was first published in 1984.

CROSS-REFERENCE: 23. Eagleton
        28. Eco

COMMENTARY: Dan Latimer, 'Jameson and Post-Modernism', *New Left Review*, no. 148 (Nov–Dec 1984), pp. 116–28.
William C. Dowling, *Jameson, Althusser, Marx: an introduction to 'The Political Unconscious'* (1984).

The politics of theory: Ideological positions in the postmodernism debate

The problem of postmodernism—how its fundamental characteristics are to be described, whether it even exists in the first place, whether the very *concept* is of any use, or is, on the contrary, a mystification—this problem is at one and the same time an aesthetic and a political one. The various positions which can logically be taken on it, whatever terms they are couched in, can always be shown to articulate visions of history, in which the evaluation of the social moment in which we live today is the object of an essentially political affirmation or repudiation. Indeed, the very enabling premise of the debate turns on an initial, strategic, presupposition about our social system: to grant some historic originality to a postmodernist culture is also implicitly to affirm some radical structural difference between what is sometimes called consumer society and earlier moments of the capitalism from which it emerged.

The various logical possibilities, however, are necessarily linked with the taking of a position on that other issue inscribed in the very designation 'postmodernism' itself, namely, the evaluation of what must now be called high or classical modernism itself. Indeed, when we make some initial inventory of the varied cultural artifacts that might plausibly be characterized as postmodern, the temptation is strong to seek the 'family resemblance' of such heterogeneous styles and products, not in themselves, but in some common high modernist impulse and aesthetic against which they all, in one way or another, stand in reaction.

The seemingly irreducible variety of the postmodern can be observed fully as problematically within the individual media (of arts) as between them: what affinities, besides some overall generational reaction, to establish between the elaborate false sentences and syntactic mimesis of John Ashbery and the much simpler talk poetry that began to emerge in the early 1960s in protest against the New Critical aesthetic of complex, ironic style? Both register, no doubt, but in very different ways indeed, the institutionalization of high modernism in this same period, the shift from an oppositional to a hegemonic[a] position of the classics of

---

[a] See note *h*, p. 299, above.

modernism, the latter's conquest of the university, the museum, the art gallery network and the foundations, the assimilation, in other words, of the various high modernisms, into the 'canon' and the subsequent attenuation of everything in them felt by our grandparents to be shocking, scandalous, ugly, dissonant, immoral and antisocial.

The same heterogeneity can be detected in the visual arts, between the inaugural reaction against the last high modernist school in painting—Abstract Expressionism—in the work of Andy Warhol and so-called pop art, and such quite distinct aesthetics as those of conceptual art, photorealism and the current New Figuration or neo-Expressionism. It can be witnessed in film, not merely between experimental and commercial production, but also within the former itself, where Godard's 'break' with the classical filmic modernism of the great 'auteurs' (Hitchcock, Bergman, Fellini, Kurasawa) generates a series of stylistic reactions against itself in the 1970s, and is also accompanied by a rich new development of experimental video (a new medium inspired by, but significantly and structurally distinct from, experimental film). In music also, the inaugural moment of John Cage now seems far enough from such later syntheses of classical and popular styles in composers like Phil Glass and Terry Riley, as well as from punk and New Wave rock of the type of The Clash, The Talking Heads and the Gang of Four, themselves significantly distinct from disco or glitter rock. (In film or in rock, however, a certain historical logic can be reintroduced by the hypothesis that such newer media recapitulate the evolutionary stages or breaks between realism, modernism and postmodernism, in a compressed time span, such that the Beatles and the Stones occupy the high modernist moment embodied by the 'auteurs' of 1950s and 1960s art films.)

In narrative proper, the dominant conception of a dissolution of linear narrative, a repudiation of representation, and a 'revolutionary' break with the (repressive) ideology of storytelling generally, does not seem adequate to encapsulate such very different work as that of Burroughs, but also of Pynchon and Ishmael Reed; of Beckett, but also of the French *nouveau roman* and its own sequels, and of the 'non-fiction novel' as well, and the New Narrative. Meanwhile, a significantly distinct aesthetic has seemed to emerge both in commercial film and in the novel with the production of what may be called nostalgia art (or *la mode rétro*).

But it is evidently architecture which is the privileged terrain of struggle of postmodernism and the most strategic field in which this concept has been debated and its consequences explored. Nowhere else has the 'death of modernism' been felt so intensely, or pronounced more stridently; nowhere else have the theoretical and practical stakes in the debate been articulated more programmatically. Of a burgeoning literature on the subject, Robert Venturi's *Learning from Las Vegas* (1971), a series of discussions by Christopher Jencks, and Pier Paolo Portoghesi's Biennale presentation, *After Modern Architecture*, may be cited as usefully illuminating the central issues in the attack on the architectural high modernism of the International Style (Le Corbusier, Wright, Mies): namely, the bankruptcy of the monumental (buildings which, as Venturi puts it, are really *sculptures*), the failure of its protopolitical or Utopian program (the transformation of all of social life by way of the transformation of space), its elitism including the authoritarianism of the charismatic leader, and finally its virtual destruction of the older city fabric by a proliferation of glass boxes and of high rises that, disjoining themselves from their immediate contexts, turn these last into the degraded public space of an urban no-man's-land.

Still, architectural postmodernism is itself no unified or monolithic period style, but spans a whole gamut of allusions to styles of the past, such that within it can be distinguished a baroque postmodernism, (say, Michael Graves), a rococo postmodernism (Charles Moore or Venturi), a classical and a neoclassical postmodernism (Rossi and De Porzemparc respectively), and perhaps even a Mannerist and a Romantic variety, not to speak of a High Modernist postmodernism itself. This complacent play of historical allusion and stylistic pastiche (termed 'historicism' in the architectural literature) is a central feature of postmodernism more generally.

Yet the architectural debates have the merit of making the political resonance of these seemingly aesthetic issues inescapable, and allowing it to be detectable in the sometimes more coded or veiled discussions in the other arts. On the whole, four general positions on postmodernism may be disengaged from the variety of recent pronouncements on the subject; yet even this relatively neat scheme or *combinatoire* is further complicated by one's impression that each of these possibilities is susceptible of either a politically progressive or a politically reactionary expression (speaking now from a Marxist or more generally left perspective).

One can, for example, salute the arrival of postmodernism from an essentially anti-modernist standpoint.[1] A somewhat earlier generation of theorists (most notably Ihab Hassan) seems already to have done something like this when they dealt with the postmodernist aesthetic in terms of a more properly poststructuralist thematics (the *Tel quel*[b] attack on the ideology of representation, the Heideggerian or Derridean 'end of Western metaphysics'): here what is often not yet called postmodernism (see the Utopian prophecy at the end of Foucault's *The Order of Things*) is saluted as the coming of a whole new way of thinking and being in the world. But since Hassan's celebration also includes a number of the more extreme monuments of high modernism (Joyce, Mallarmé), this would be a relatively more ambiguous stance, were it not for the accompanying celebration of a new information high technology which marks the affinity between such evocations and the political thesis of a properly *postindustrial society*.

All of which is largely disambiguated in Tom Wolfe's *From Bauhaus to Our House*, an otherwise undistinguished book report on the recent architectural debates by a writer whose own New Journalism itself constitutes one of the varieties of postmodernism. What is interesting and symptomatic about this book is however the absence of any Utopian celebration of the postmodern and—far more strikingly—the passionate hatred of the Modern that breathes through the

---

[b] See headnote, p. 229, above.

otherwise obligatory camp[c] sarcasm of the rhetoric; and this is not a new, but a dated and archaic passion. It is as though the original horror of the first middle class spectators of the very emergence of the Modern itself—the first Corbusiers, as white as the first freshly built cathedrals of the 12th century, the first scandalous Picasso heads, with two eyes on one profile like a flounder, the stunning 'obscurity' of the first editions of *Ulysses* or *The Waste Land*: as though this disgust of the original philistines, Spiessbürger[d], bourgeois or Main Street Babbitry[e], had suddenly come back to life, infusing the newer critiques of modernism with an ideologically very different spirit, whose effect is on the whole to reawaken in the reader an equally archaic sympathy with the protopolitical, Utopian, anti-middle-class impulses of a now extinct high modernism itself. Wolfe's diatribe thus offers a stunning example of the way in which a reasoned and contemporary, theoretical repudiation of the modern—much of whose progressive force springs from a new sense of the urban and a now considerable experience of the destruction of older forms of communal and urban life in the name of a high modernist orthodoxy—can be handily reappropriated and pressed into the service of an explicitly reactionary cultural politics.

These positions—anti-modern, pro-postmodern—then find their opposite number and structural inversion in a group of counter-statements whose aim is to discredit the shoddiness and irresponsibility of the postmodern in general by way of a reaffirmation of the authentic impulse of a high modernist tradition still considered to be alive and vital. Hilton Kramer's twin manifestoes in the inaugural issue of his new journal, *The New Criterion*, articulate these views with force, contrasting the moral responsibility of the 'masterpieces' and monuments of classical modernism with the fundamental irresponsibility and superficiality of a postmodernism associated with camp and with the 'facetiousness' of which the Wolfe style is a ripe and obvious example.

What is more paradoxical is that politically Wolfe and Kramer have much in common; and there would seem to be a certain inconsistency in the way in which Kramer must seek to eradicate from the 'high seriousness' of the classics of the modern their fundamentally anti-middle-class stance and the protopolitical passion which informs the repudiation, by the great modernists, of Victorian taboos and family life, of commodification, and of the increasing asphyxiation of a desacralizing capitalism, from Ibsen to Lawrence, from Van Gogh to Jackson Pollock. Kramer's ingenious attempt to assimilate this ostensibly anti-bourgeois stance of the great modernists to a 'loyal opposition' secretly nourished, by way of foundations and grants, by the bourgeoisie itself—while most unconvincing indeed—is surely itself enabled by the contradictions of the cultural politics of modernism proper, whose negations depend on the persistence of what they

[c] 'Camp' here refers to a mannered, exaggerated, tongue-in-cheek style of expressing aesthetic preferences. For further elucidation, see Susan Sontag's 'Notes on Camp' in *Against Interpretation* (1967).

[d] German word for a middle-class person hostile to high culture.

[e] A reference to Sinclair Lewis's novel *Babbit* (1922), a portrait of a philistine small-town businessman.

repudiate and entertain—when they do not, very rarely indeed (as in Brecht), attain some genuine political self-consciousness—a symbiotic relationship with capital.

It is, however, easier to understand Kramer's move here when the political project of *The New Criterion* is clarified: for the mission of the journal is clearly to eradicate the 1960s and what remains of that legacy, to consign that whole period to the kind of oblivion which the 1950s were able to devise for the 1930s, or the 1920s for the rich political culture of the pre-World-War-I era. *The New Criterion* therefore inscribes itself in the effort, on-going and at work everywhere today, to construct some new conservative cultural counter-revolution, whose terms range from the aesthetic to the ultimate defense of the family and of religion. It is therefore paradoxical that this essentially political project should explicitly deplore the omnipresence of politics in contemporary culture—an infection largely spread during the 1960s, but which Kramer holds responsible for the moral imbecility of the post-modernism of our own period.

The problem with the operation—an obviously indispensible one from the conservative viewpoint—is that for whatever reason its paper-money rhetoric does not seem to have been backed by the solid gold of state power, as was the case with McCarthyism[f] or in the period of the Palmer raids[g]. The failure of the Vietnam War seems, at least for the moment, to have made the naked exercise of repressive power impossible,[2] and endowed the 1960s with a persistence in collective memory and experience which it was not given to the traditions of the 1930s or the pre-World-War-I period to know. Kramer's 'cultural revolution' therefore tends most often to lapse into a feebler and sentimental nostalgia for the 1950s and the Eisenhower era.

It will not be surprising, in the light of what has been shown for an earlier set of positions on modernism and postmodernism, that in spite of the openly conservative ideology of this second evaluation of the contemporary cultural scene, the latter can also be appropriated for what is surely a far more progressive line on the subject. We are indebted to Jürgen Habermas[3] for this dramatic reversal and rearticulation of what remains the affirmation of the supreme value of the Modern and the repudiation of the theory, as well as the practice, of postmodernism. For Habermas, however, the vice of postmodernism consists very centrally in its politically reactionary function, as the attempt everywhere to discredit a modernist impulse Habermas himself associates with the bourgeois Enlightenment and with the latter's still universalizing and Utopian spirit. With Adorno[h] himself, Habermas seeks to rescue and to recommemorate what both see

[f] A reference to Senator Joseph McCarthy, who led a witch-hunt against alleged Communists in America in the 1950s.

[g] A reference to A. Mitchell Palmer, U. S. Attorney General 1919–21, who zealously prosecuted those suspected of disloyalty to America.

[h] Theodor Adorno (1903–60) and Max Horkheimer (1895–1973) were among the earliest and most distinguished members of the 'Frankfurt School' of Marxist social scientists. Exiled to America in the Nazi period, the group returned to Germany in 1949. Jürgen Habermas (b. 1929) is the most distinguished member of its 'second generation'.

as the essentially negative, critical and Utopian power of the great high modernisms. On the other hand, his attempt to associate these last with the spirit of the 18th century Enlightenment marks a decisive break indeed with Adorno and Horkheimer's somber *Dialectic of Enlightenment*, in which the scientific ethos of the *philosophes*[i] is dramatized as a misguided will to power and domination over nature, and their own desacralizing program as the first stage in the development of a sheerly instrumentalizing world view which will lead straight to Auschwitz. This very striking divergence can be accounted for by Habermas' own vision of history, which seeks to maintain the promise of 'liberalism' and the essentially Utopian content of the first, universalizing bourgeois ideology (equality, civil rights, humanitarianism, free speech and open media) over against the failure of those ideals to be realized in the development of capital itself.

As for the aesthetic terms of the debate, however, it will not be adequate to respond to Habermas' resuscitation of the modern by some mere empirical certification of the latter's extinction. We need to take into account the possibility that the national situation in which Habermas thinks and writes is rather different from our own: McCarthyism and repression are, for one thing, realities in the Federal Republic today, and the intellectual intimidation of the Left and the silencing of a left culture (largely associated, by the West German right, with 'terrorism') has been on the whole a far more successful operation than elsewhere in the West.[4] The triumph of a new McCarthyism and of the culture of the Spiessbürger and the philistine suggests the possibility that in this particular national situation Habermas may well be right, and the older forms of high modernism may still retain something of the subversive power which they have lost elsewhere. In that case, a postmodernism which seeks to enfeeble and to undermine that power may well also merit his ideological diagnosis in a local way, even though the assessment remains ungeneralizable.

Both of the previous positions—antimodern/propostmodern, and promodern/antipostmodern—are characterized by an acceptance of the new term which is tantamount to an agreement on the fundamental nature of some decisive 'break' between the modern and the postmodern moments, however these last are evaluated. There remain, however, two final logical possibilities both of which depend on the repudiation of any conception of such a historical break and which therefore, implicitly or explicitly, call into question the usefulness of the very category of postmodernism. As for the works associated with the latter, they will then be assimilated back into classical modernism proper, so that the 'postmodern' becomes little more than the form taken by the authentically modern in our own period, and a mere dialectical intensification of the old modernist impulse towards innovation. (I must here omit yet another series of debates, largely academic, in which the very continuity of modernism as it is here reaffirmed is itself called into question by some vaster sense of the profound continuity of Romanticism itself, from the late 18th century on, of which both the modern and the postmodern will be seen as mere organic stages.)

---

[i] The French rationalist philosophers of the eighteenth century.

The two final positions on the subject thus logically prove to be a positive and negative assessment respectively of a postmodernism now assimilated back into the high modernist tradition. Jean-Francois Lyotard[5] thus proposes that his own vital commitment to the new and the emergent, to a contemporary or postcontemporary cultural production now widely characterized as 'postmodern,' be grasped as part and parcel of a reaffirmation of the authentic older high modernisms very much in Adorno's spirit. The ingenious twist or swerve in his own proposal involves the proposition that something called 'postmodernism' does not *follow* high modernism proper, as the latter's waste product, but rather very precisely *precedes* and prepares it, so that the contemporary postmodernisms all around us may be seen as the promise of the return and the reinvention, the triumphant reappearance, of some new high modernism endowed with all its older power and with fresh life. This is a prophetic stance, whose analyses turn on the anti-representational thrust of modernism and postmodernism; Lyotard's aesthetic positions, however, cannot be adequately evaluated in aesthetic terms, since what informs them is an essentially social and political conception of a new social system beyond classical capitalism (our old friend, 'postindustrial society'): the vision of a regenerated modernism is in that sense inseparable from a certain prophetic faith in the possibilities and the promise of the new society itself in full emergence.

The negative inversion of this position will then clearly involve an ideological repudiation of modernism of a type which might conceivably range from Lukács'[j] older analysis of modernist forms as the replication of the reification of capitalist social life all the way to some of the more articulated critiques of high modernism of the present day. What distinguishes this final position from the antimodernisms already outlined above is, however, that it does not speak from the security of an affirmation of some new postmodernist culture, but rather sees even the latter itself as a mere degeneration of the already stigmatized impulses of high modernism proper. This particular position, perhaps the bleakest of all and the most implacably negative, can be vividly confronted in the works of the Venetian architecture historian Manfredo Tafuri, whose extensive analyses[6] constitute a powerful indictment of what we have termed the 'protopolitical' impulses in high modernism (the 'Utopian' substitution of cultural politics for politics proper, the vocation to transform the world by transforming its forms, space or language). Tafuri is however no less harsh in his anatomy of the negative, demystifying, 'critical' vocation of the various modernisms, whose function he reads as a kind of Hegelian 'ruse of History,' whereby the instrumentalizing and desacralizing tendencies of capital itself are ultimately realized through just such demolition work by the thinkers and artists of the modern movement. Their 'anticapitalism' therefore ends up laying the basis for the 'total' bureaucratic organization and control of late capitalism, and it is only logical that Tafuri should conclude by positing the impossibility of any radical transformation of culture before a radical transformation of social relations themselves.

[j] Georg Lukács (1885–1971), Hungarian Marxist critic. (See section 35 of *20th Century Literary Criticism*.)

The political ambivalence demonstrated in the earlier two positions seems to me to be maintained here, but *within* the positions of both of these very complex thinkers. Unlike many of the previously mentioned theorists, Tafuri and Lyotard are both explicitly political figures, with an overt commitment to the values of an older revolutionary tradition. It is clear, for example, that Lyotard's embattled endorsement of the supreme value of aesthetic innovation is to be understood as the figure for a certain kind of revolutionary stance; while Tafuri's whole conceptual framework is largely consistent with the classical Marxist tradition. Yet both are also, implicitly, and more openly at certain strategic moments, rewritable in terms of a post-Marxism which at length becomes indistinguishable from anti-Marxism proper. Lyotard has for example very frequently sought to distinguish his 'revolutionary' aesthetic from the older ideals of political revolution, which he sees as either being Stalinist, or as archaic and incompatible with the conditions of the new postindustrial social order; while Tafuri's apocalyptic notion of the total social revolution implies a conception of the 'total system' of capitalism which, in a period of depolitization and reaction, is only too fatally destined for the kind of discouragement which has so often led Marxists to a renunciation of the political altogether (Adorno and Merleau-Ponty[k] come to mind, along with many of the ex-Trotskyists of the 1930s and 1940s and the ex-Maoists of the 1960s and 1970s).

The combination scheme outlined above can now be schematically represented as follows; the plus and minus signs designating the politically progressive or reactionary functions of the positions in question:

	ANTI-MODERNIST	PRO-MODERNIST
PRO-POSTMODERNIST	Wolfe $-$ Jencks $+$	Lyotard $\{^+_-$
ANTI-POSTMODERNIST	Tafuri $\{^-_+$	Kramer $-$ Habermas $+$

With these remarks we come full circle and may now return to the more positive potential political content of the first position in question, and in particular to the question of a certain *populist* impulse in postmodernism which it has been the

[k] Maurice Merleau-Ponty (1900–61), French existentialist philosopher who supported Stalinist Communism in the immediate postwar period but disengaged himself from politics after the Korean War.

merit of Charles Jencks (but also of Venturi and others) to have underscored—
a question which will also allow us to deal a little more adequately with the
absolute pessimism of Tafuri's Marxism itself. What must first be observed,
however, is that most of the political positions which we have found to inform
what is most often conducted as an aesthetic debate are in reality moralizing ones,
which seek to develop final judgments on the phenomenon of postmodernism,
whether the latter is stigmatized as corrupt or on the other hand saluted as a
culturally and aesthetically healthy and positive form of innovation. But a
genuinely historical and dialectical analysis of such phenomena—particularly
when it is a matter of a present of time and of history in which we ourselves exist
and struggle—cannot afford the impoverished luxury of such absolute moralizing
judgements: the dialectic is 'beyond good and evil' in the sense of some easy
taking of sides, whence the glacial and inhuman spirit of its historical vision
(something that already disturbed contemporaries about Hegel's original system).
The point is that we are *within* the culture of postmodernism to the point where
its facile repudiation is as impossible as any equally facile celebration of it is
complacent and corrupt. Ideological judgment on postmodernism today necessarily
implies, one would think, a judgment on ourselves as well as on the artifacts in
question; nor can an entire historical period, such as our own, be grasped in
any adequate way by means of global moral judgments or their somewhat degraded
equivalent, pop-psychological diagnosis (such as those of Lasch's *Culture of
Narcissism*). On the classical Marxian view, the seeds of the future already exist
within the present and must be conceptually disengaged from it, both through
analysis and through political praxis (the workers of the Paris Commune, Marx
once remarked in a striking phrase, *'have no ideals to realize'*; they merely sought
to disengage emergent forms of new social relations from the older capitalist social
relations in which the former had already begun to stir). In place of the temptation either to denounce the complacencies of postmodernism as some final
symptom of decadence, or to salute the new forms as the harbingers of a new
technological and technocratic Utopia, it seems more appropriate to assess the
new cultural production within the working hypothesis of a general modification
of culture itself within the social restructuration of late capitalism as a system.[7]

As for emergence, however, Jencks' assertion that postmodern architecture
distinguishes itself from that of high modernism through its populist priorities[8]
may serve as the starting point for some more general discussion. What is meant,
in the specifically architectural context, is that where the now more classical high
modernist space of a Corbusier or a Wright sought to differentiate itself radically
from the fallen city fabric in which it appears—its forms thus dependent on an
act of radical disjunction from its spatial context (the great *pilotis* dramatizing
separation from the ground and safeguarding the *Novum* of the new space)—
postmodernist buildings on the contrary celebrate their insertion into the heterogeneous fabric of the commercial strip and the motel and fast-food landscape
of the post-superhighway American city. Meanwhile a play of allusion and formal
echoes ('historicism') secures the kinship of these new art buildings with the
surrounding commercial icons and spaces, thereby renouncing the high modernist
claim to radical difference and innovation.

Whether this undoubtedly significant feature of the newer architecture is to be characterized as *populist* must remain an open question: since it would seem essential to distinguish the emergent forms of a new commercial culture—beginning with advertisements and spreading on to formal *packaging* of all kinds, from products to buiidings and not excluding artistic commodities such as television shows (the 'logo') and bestsellers and films—from the older kinds of folk and genuinely 'popular' culture which flourished when the older social classes of a peasantry and an urban *artisanat* still existed and which, from the mid-19th century on, have gradually been colonized and extinguished by commodification and the market system.

What can at least be admitted is the more universal presence of this particular feature, which appears more unambiguously in the other arts as an effacement of the older distinction between high and so-called mass culture, a distinction on which modernism depended for its specificity, its Utopian function consisting at least in part in the securing of a realm of authentic experience over against the surrounding environment of philistinism, of schlock and kitsch, of commodification and of Reader's Digest culture. Indeed, it can be argued that the emergence of high modernism is itself contemporaneous with the first great expansion of a recognizable mass culture (Zola may be taken as the marker for the last coexistence of the art novel and the bestseller to be within a single text).

It is now this constitutive differentiation which seems on the point of disappearing: we have already mentioned the way in which, in music, after Schönberg and even after Cage, the two antithetical traditions of the 'classical' and the 'popular' once again begin to merge. In a more general way, it seems clear that the artists of the 'postmodern' period have been fascinated precisely by the whole new object world, not-merely of the Las Vegas strip, but also of the late show and the grade-B Hollywood film, of so-called paraliterature with its airport paperback categories of the gothic and the romance, the popular biography, the murder mystery and the science-fiction or fantasy novel (in such a way that the older generic categories discredited by modernism seem on the point of living an unexpected reappearance). In the visual arts, the renewal of photography as a significant medium in its own right and also as the 'plane of substance' in pop art or photorealism is a crucial symptom of the same process. At any rate, it becomes minimally obvious that the newer artists no longer 'quote' the materials, the fragments and motifs, of a mass or popular culture, as Joyce (and Flaubert) began to do, or Mahler; they somehow incorporate them to the point where many of our critical and evaluative categories (founded precisely on the radical differentiation of modernist and mass culture) no longer seem functional.

But if this is the case, then it seems at least possible that what wears the mask and makes the gestures of 'populism' in the various postmodernist apologias and manifestoes is in reality a mere reflex and symptom of a (to be sure momentous) cultural mutation, in which what used to be stigmatized as mass or commercial culture is now received into the precincts of a new and enlarged cultural realm. In any case, one would expect a term drawn from the typology of political ideologies to undergo basic semantic readjustments when its initial referent (that

Popular-front class coalition of workers, peasants and petty bourgeois generally called 'the people') has disappeared.

Perhaps, however, this is not so new a story after all: one remembers, indeed, Freud's delight at discovering an obscure tribal culture, which alone among the multitudinous traditions of dream-analysis on the earth had managed to hit on the notion that all dreams had hidden sexual meanings—except for sexual dreams, which meant something else! So also it would seem in the postmodernist debate, and the depoliticized bureaucratic society to which it corresponds, where all seemingly cultural positions turn out to be symbolic forms of political moralizing, except for the single overtly political note, which suggests a slippage from politics back into culture again. I have the feeling that the only adequate way out of this vicious circle, besides praxis itself, is a historical and dialectical view which seeks to grasp the present as History.

NOTES

1. The following analysis does not seem to me applicable to the work of the *boundary two* group, who early on appropriated the term 'postmodernism' in the rather different sense of a critique of establishment 'modernist' thought.
2. Written in spring, 1982.
3. See his 'Modernity—An Incomplete Project,' in Hal Foster, ed., *The Anti-Aesthetic* (Port Townsend, Washington: Bay Press, 1983), pp. 3–15. The essay was first published in *New German Critique*, 22 (Winter 1981), 3–14, under the different title 'Modernity versus Postmodernity.'
4. The specific politics associated with the 'Greens' would seem to constitute a reaction to this situation, rather than an exception from it.
5. See 'Answering the Questions: What is Postmodernism?' in J.-F. Lyotard, *The Postmodern Condition* (Minneapolis: University of Minnesota Press, 1984), pp. 71–82; the book itself focusses primarily on science and epistemology rather than on culture.
6. See in particular *Architecture and Utopia* (Cambridge: MIT Press, 1976) and *Modern Architecture*, with Francesco Dal Co (New York: Abrams, 1979); and also my 'Architecture and the Critique of Ideology,' in *Revisions: Papers in Architectural Theory and Criticism*, 1–1 (Winter, 1984).
7. I have tried to do this in 'Postmodernism, Or, The Cultural Logic of Late Capitalism,' *New Left Review*, 146 (July–Auguest, 1984), 53–92; my contribution to *The Anti-Aesthetic*, op.cit., is a fragment of this definitive version.
8. See, for example, Charles Jencks, *Late-Modern Architecture* (New York: Rizzoli, 1980); Jencks here however shifts his usage of the term from the designation for a cultural dominant or period style to the name for one aesthetic movement among others.

23 *Terry Eagleton*

Terry Eagleton (b. 1943), Fellow and Tutor at Wadham College, Oxford, is, after Raymond Williams, the leading British Marxist critic. His Marxism is considerably more overt, and less equivocal, than that of Williams, who taught him at Cambridge, and with whom Eagleton has had a somewhat Oedipal intellectual relationship, attacking him at times, paying homage at others. Eagleton is of Catholic working-class origins, and in the 1960s was involved in a project to reconcile Marxism and Catholicism, for which a short-lived but interesting magazine called *Slant* provided a platform. The work for which he is best known is wholly secular in its underlying political philosophy, but exhibits considerable change and variety in style and method.

Starting off in the British New Left critical tradition of Leavis-and-Marx (see, for instance, his *Exiles and Emigrés: studies in modern literature* [1970]), Eagleton later responded eagerly to the stimulus of European structuralist and post-structuralist theory, especially the work of Louis Althusser and Pierre Macherey. His *Criticism and Ideology* (1976) and *Marxism and Literary Criticism* (1976) reflect his engagement with the debates within Marxist literary theory generated by these writers. Althusser particularly fascinated Marxist literary intellectuals at this time by his assertion of the 'relative autonomy' (*i.e.*, freedom from economic determination) of cultural institutions, such as literature, and the promise of achieving a 'scientific' knowledge about them. In an interesting introduction to his latest collection of essays, *Against the Grain* (1986), Eagleton explains how his disillusionment with the Althusserian project, and dismay at the political drift to the Right in the Western democracies in the late 1970s, led him to produce works 'more preoccupied with questions of experience and the subject, with that difference or heterogeneity which escapes formalization, with humour, the body and the "carnivalesque", with cultural politics rather than textual science.' *Walter Benjamin* (1981), *The Rape of Clarissa* (1982) and *Literary Theory: an Introduction* (1983) exhibit these qualities in various ways and combinations.

'Capitalism, Modernism and Postmodernism' was originally published in *New Left Review* in 1985, as a response to Fredric Jameson's essay in the same journal, 'Postmodernism, or the Cultural Logic of Late Capitalism' (see headnote on Jameson in the preceding section). Eagleton's piece takes up by implication the question raised by Jameson—is postmodernism in any significant sense a critique of contemporary society—and answers it emphatically in the negative. Eagleton's scorn for postmodernist art derives partly from respect for the achievement of classic modernist and avant-garde art, partly from his commitment to practical socialism, and partly, it is interesting to note, from a lingering nostalgia for the 'unified subject' of bourgeois humanism, which, he suggests, late capitalism is deconstructing rather more effectively than postmodernism or poststructuralism. 'Capitalism, Modernism and Postmodernism' is reprinted here from *Against the Grain*.

CROSS-REFERENCES: 21. De Man
22. Jameson
28. Eco

COMMENTARY: Bernard Bergonzi, 'The Terry Eagleton Story', in Bergonzi's *The Myth of Modernism and Twentieth Century Literature*, 1986.
Richard Aczel, 'Eagleton and English', *New Left Review* No. 154 (Nov/Dec 1985) pp 113–123.

Capitalism, modernism and postmodernism

In his article 'Postmodernism, or the Cultural Logic of Late Capitalism' (*New Left Review* 146), Fredric Jameson argues that pastiche, rather than parody, is the appropriate mode of postmodernist culture. 'Pastiche', he writes, 'is, like parody, the imitation of a peculiar mask, speech in a dead language; but it is a neutral practice of such mimicry, without any of parody's ulterior motives, amputated of the satiric impulse, devoid of laughter and of any conviction that alongside the abnormal tongue you have momentarily borrowed, some healthy linguistic normality still exists.' This is an excellent point; but I want to suggest here that parody of a sort is not wholly alien to the culture of postmodernism, though it is not one of which it could be said to be particularly conscious. What is parodied by postmodernist culture, with its dissolution of art into the prevailing forms of commodity production, is nothing less than the revolutionary art of the twentieth-century avant-garde. It is as though postmodernism is among other things a sick joke at the expense of such revolutionary avant-gardism, one of whose major impulses, as Peter Bürger has convincingly argued in his *Theory of the Avant-Garde*, was to dismantle the institutional autonomy of art, erase the frontiers between culture and political society and return aesthetic production to its humble, unprivileged place within social practices as a whole.[1] In the commodified artefacts of postmodernism, the avant-gardist dream of an integration of art and society returns in monstrously caricatured form; the tragedy of a Mayakovsky is played through once more, but this time as farce. It is as though postmodernism represents the cynical belated revenge wreaked by bourgeois culture upon its revolutionary antagonists, whose utopian desire for a fusion of art and social praxis is seized, distorted and jeeringly turned back upon them as dystopian reality. Postmodernism, from this perspective, mimes the formal resolution of art and social life attempted by the avant-garde while remorselessly emptying it of its political content; Mayakovsky's poetry readings in the factory yard become Warhol's shoes and soup-cans[a].

I say it is *as though* postmodernism effects such a parody, because Jameson is surely right to claim that in reality it is sometimes blankly innocent of any such devious satirical impulse, and is entirely devoid of the kind of historical memory which might make such a disfiguring self-conscious. To place a pile of bricks in the Tate gallery once might be considered ironic; to repeat the gesture endlessly is sheer carelessness of any such ironic intention, as its shock value is inexorably drained away to leave nothing beyond brute fact. The depthless, styleless, dehistoricized, decathected surfaces of postmodernist culture are not meant to signify an alienation, for the very concept of alienation must secretly posit a dream of authenticity which postmodernism finds quite unintelligible. Those flattened surfaces and hollowed interiors are not 'alienated' because there is no longer any subject to be alienated and nothing to be alienated from, 'authenticity' having been less rejected than merely forgotten. It is impossible to discern in such forms, as it is in the artefacts of modernism proper, a wry, anguished or derisive awareness of the normative traditional humanism they deface. If depth is metaphysical illusion, then there can be nothing 'superficial' about such art-forms, for the very term has ceased to have force. Postmodernism is thus a grisly parody of socialist utopia, having abolished all alienation at a stroke. By raising alienation to the second power, alienating us even from our own alienation, it persuades us to recognize that utopia not as some remote *telos* [end] but, amazingly, as nothing less than the present itself, replete as it is in its own brute positivity and scarred through with not the slightest trace of lack. Reification, once it has extended its empire across the whole of social reality, effaces the very criteria by which it can be recognized for what it is and so triumphantly abolishes itself, returning everything to normality. The traditional metaphysical mystery was a question of depths, absences, foundations, abysmal explorations; the mystery of some modernist art is just the mind-bending truth that things are what they are, intriguingly self-identical, utterly shorn of cause, motive or ratification; postmodernism preserves this self-identity, but erases its modernist scandalousness. The dilemma of David Hume[b] is surpassed by a simple conflation: fact *is* value. Utopia cannot belong to the future because the future, in the shape of technology, is already here, exactly synchronous with the present. William Morris, in dreaming that art might dissolve into social life, turns out, it would seem, to have been a true prophet of late capitalism: by anticipating such a desire, bringing it about with premature haste, late capitalism deftly inverts its own logic and proclaims that if the artefact is a commodity, the commodity can

[a] For a note on Mayakovsky, see p. 231 above. The American Andy Warhol is the most famous, or notorious, exponent of 'Pop Art', exemplified by his paintings of Campbell's soup cans.

[b] David Hume (1711–76), British empiricist philosopher.

386

always be an artefact. 'Art' and 'life' indeed interbreed—which is to say that art models itself upon a commodity form which is already invested with aesthetic allure, in a sealed circle. The *eschaton* [end], it would appear, is already here under our very noses, but so pervasive and immediate as to be invisible to those whose eyes are still turned stubbornly away to the past or the future.

The productivist aesthetics of the early twentieth-century avant-garde spurned the notion of artistic 'representation' for an art which would be less 'reflection' than material intervention and organizing force. The aesthetics of postmodernism is a dark parody of such anti-representationalism: if art no longer reflects, it is not because it seeks to change the world rather than mimic it, but because there is in truth nothing there to be reflected, no reality which is not itself already image, spectacle, simulacrum, gratuitous fiction. To say that social reality is pervasively commodified is to say that it is always already 'aesthetic'—textured, packaged, fetishized, libidinalized; and for art to reflect reality is then for it to do no more than mirror itself, in a cryptic self-referentiality which is indeed one of the inmost structures of the commodity fetish. The commodity is less an image in the sense of a 'reflection' than an image of itself, its entire material being devoted to its own self-presentation; and in such a condition the most authentically representational art becomes, paradoxically, the anti-representational artefact whose contingency and facticity figures the fate of all late capitalist objects. If the unreality of the artistic image mirrors the unreality of its society as a whole, then this is to say that it mirrors nothing real and so does not really mirror at all. Beneath this paradox lies the historical truth that the very autonomy and brute self-identity of the postmodernist artefact is the effect of its thorough *integration* into an economic system where such autonomy, in the form of the commodity fetish, is the order of the day.

To see art in the manner of the revolutionary avant-garde, not as institutionalized object but as practice, strategy, performance, production: all of this, once again, is grotesquely caricatured by late capitalism, for which, as Jean-François Lyotard has pointed out, the 'performativity principle' is really all that counts. In his *The Postmodern Condition*, Lyotard calls attention to capitalism's 'massive subordination of cognitive statements to the finality of the best possible performance'; 'The games of scientific language', he writes, 'become the games of the rich, in which whoever is wealthiest has the best chance of being right.'[2] It is not difficult, then, to see relation between the philosophy of J. L. Austin and IBM[c], or between the various neo-Nietzscheanisms of a post-structuralist epoch and Standard Oil. It is not surprising that classical models of truth and cognition are increasingly out of favour in a society where what matters is whether you deliver the commercial or rhetorical goods. Whether among discourse theorists or the Institute of Directors, the goal is no longer truth but performativity, not reason but power. The CBI[d] are in this sense spontaneous post-structuralists to a man, utterly disenchanted (did they but know it) with epistemological realism

---

[c] J. L. Austin (1911–60) was an Oxford linguistic philosopher, the originator of 'speech act theory'. IBM is the multinational corporation that dominates the market in information technology.

[d] Confederation of British Industry (an association of employers).

and the correspondence theory of truth. That this is so is no reason for pretending that we can relievedly return to John Locke or Georg Lukács[e]; it is simply to recognize that it is not always easy to distinguish politically radical assaults on classical epistemology (among which the early Lukács must himself be numbered, alongside the Soviet avant-garde) from flagrantly reactionary ones. Indeed it is a sign of this difficulty that Lyotard himself, having grimly outlined the most oppressive aspects of the capitalist performativity principle, has really nothing to offer in its place but what amounts in effect to an anarchist version of that very same epistemology, namely the guerrilla skirmishes of a 'paralogism' which might from time to time induce ruptures, instabilities, paradoxes and micro-catastrophic discontinuities into this terroristic techno-scientific system. A 'good' pragmatics, in short, is turned against a 'bad' one; but it will always be a loser from the outset, since it has long since abandoned the Enlightenment's grand narrative of human emancipation, which we all now know to be disreputably metaphysical. Lyotard is in no doubt that '[socialist] struggles and their instruments have been transformed into regulators of the system' in all the advanced societies, an Olympian certitude which, as I write, Mrs Thatcher might at once envy and query. (Lyotard is wisely silent on the class struggle outside the advanced capitalist nations.) It is not easy to see how, if the capitalist system has been effective enough to negate all class struggle entirely, the odd unorthodox scientific experiment is going to give it much trouble. 'Postmodernist science', as Fredric Jameson suggests in his introduction to Lyotard's book, is here playing the role once assumed by high modernist art, which was similarly an experimental disruption of the given system; and Lyotard's desire to see modernism and post-modernism as continuous with one another is in part a refusal to confront the disturbing fact that modernism proved prey to institutionalization. Both cultural phases are for Lyotard manifestations of that which escapes and confounds history with the explosive force of the Now, the 'paralogic' as some barely possible, mind-boggling leap into free air which gives the slip to the nightmare of temporality and global narrative from which some of us are trying to awaken.[f] Paralogism, like the poor, is always with us, but just because the system is always with us too. The 'modern' is less a particular cultural practice or historical period, which may then suffer defeat or incorporation, than a kind of permanent ontological possibility of disrupting all such historical periodization, an essentially timeless gesture which cannot be recited or reckoned up within historical narrative because it is no more than an atemporal force which gives the lie to all such linear categorization. As with all such anarchistic or Camusian revolt, modernism can thus never really die—it has resurfaced in our own time as paralogical science—but the reason why it can never be worsted—the fact that it does not occupy the same temporal terrain or logical space as its antagonists— is precisely the reason why it can never defeat the system either. The characteristic post-structuralist blend of pessimism and euphoria springs precisely from

[e] John Locke (1632–1704), British empiricist philosopher. Georg Lukács (1885–1971) was a Hungarian Marxist critic (see *20th Century Literary Criticism*, section 35).

[f] 'History is a nightmare from which I am trying to awake.' Stephen Daedalus in James Joyce's *Ulysses*.

this paradox. History and modernity play a ceaseless cat-and-mouse game in and out of time, neither able to slay the other because they occupy different onto-logical sites. 'Game' in the positive sense—the ludic disportings of disruption and desire—plays itself out in the crevices of 'game' in the negative sense—game theory, the techno-scientific system—in an endless conflict and collusion. Modernity here really means a Nietzschean 'active forgetting' of history: the healthy spontaneous amnesia of the animal who has wilfully repressed its own sordid determinations and so is free.[g] It is thus the exact opposite of Walter Benjamin's[h] 'revolutionary nostalgia': the power of active remembrance as a ritual summoning and invocation of the traditions of the oppressed in violent constel-lation with the political present. It is no wonder that Lyotard is deeply opposed to any such historical consciousness, with his reactionary celebrations of narrative as an eternal present rather than a revolutionary recollection of the unjustly quelled. If he could remember in this Benjaminesque mode, he might be less confident that the class struggle could be merely extirpated. Nor, if he had adequately engaged Benjamin's work, could he polarize in such simplistic binary opposition—one typical of much post-structuralist thought—the grand totalizing narratives of the Enlightenment on the one hand and the micropolitical or paralogistic on the other (postmodernism as the death of metanarrative). For Benjamin's unfathomably subtle meditations on history throw any such binary poststructuralist schema into instant disarray. Benjamin's 'tradition' is certainly a totality of a kind, but at the same time a ceaseless detotalization of a tri-umphalistic ruling-class history; it is in some sense a given, yet is always constructed from the vantage point of the present; it operates as a deconstructive force within hegemonic ideologies of history, yet can be seen too as a totalizing movement within which sudden affinities, correspondences and constellations may be fashioned between disparate struggles.

A Nietzschean sense of the 'modern' also informs the work of the most influ-ential of American deconstructionists, Paul de Man, though with an added twist of irony. For 'active forgetting', de Man argues, can never be entirely successful: the distinctively modernist act, which seeks to erase or arrest history, finds itself surrendered in that very moment to the lineage it seeks to repress, perpetuating rather than abolishing it. Indeed literature for de Man is nothing less than this constantly doomed, ironically self-undoing attempt to make it new, this ceaseless incapacity ever quite to awaken from the nightmare of history: 'The continuous appeal of modernity, the desire to break out of literature toward the reality of the moment, prevails and, in its turn, folding back upon itself, engenders the repetition and the continuation of literature.'[3] Since action and temporality are indissociable, modernism's dream of self-origination, its hunger for some his-

---

[g] 'The animal lives unhistorically: it hides nothing and coincides at all moments with that which it is; it is bound to be truthful at all times, unable to be anything else . . . we will therefore have to consider the ability to experience life in a non-historical way as the most important and original of experiences, as the foundation on which right, health, greatness and anything truly human can be erected.' Friedrich Nietzsche, *Thoughts Out of Season*.

[h] Walter Benjamin (1892–1940) was a German Jewish critic and cultural theorist of unorthodox Marxist views. Terry Eagleton has written a study of him (see headnote).

torically unmediated encounter with the real, is internally fissured and self-thwarting: to write is to disrupt a tradition which depends on such disruption for its very self-reproduction. We are all, simultaneously and inextricably, modernists and traditionalists, terms which for de Man designate neither cultural movements nor aesthetic ideologies but the very structure of that duplicitous phenomenon, always in and out of time simultaneously, named literature, where this common dilemma figures itself with rhetorical self-consciousness. Literary history here, de Man contends, 'could in fact be paradigmatic for history in general'; and what this means, translated from de-Manese, is that though we will never abandon our radical political illusions (the fond fantasy of emancipating ourselves from tradition and confronting the real eyeball-to-eyeball being, as it were, a permanent pathological state of human affairs), such actions will always prove self-defeating, will always be incorporated by a history which has foreseen them and seized upon them as ruses for its own self-perpetuation. The daringly 'radical' recourse to Nietzsche, that is to say, turns out to land one in a maturely liberal Democrat position, wryly sceptical but genially tolerant of the radical antics of the young.

What is at stake here, under the guise of a debate about history and modernity, is nothing less than the dialectical relation of theory and practice. For if practice is defined in neo-Nietzschean style as spontaneous error, productive blindness or historical amnesia, then theory can of course be no more than a jaded reflection upon its ultimate impossibility. Literature, that aporetic spot in which truth and error indissolubly entwine, is at once practice and the deconstruction of practice, spontaneous act and theoretical fact, a gesture which in pursuing an unmediated encounter with reality in the same instant interprets that very impulse as metaphysical fiction. Writing is both action and a reflection upon that action, but the two are ontologically disjunct; and literature is the privileged place where practice comes to know and name its eternal difference from theory. It is not surprising, then, that the last sentence of de Man's essay makes a sudden swerve to the political: 'If we extend this notion beyond literature, it merely confirms that the bases for historical knowledge are not empirical facts but written texts, even if these texts masquerade in the guise of wars and revolutions.' A text which starts out with a problem in literary history ends up as an assault on Marxism. For it is of course Marxism above all which has insisted that actions may be theoretically informed and histories emancipatory, notions capable of scuppering de Man's entire case. It is only by virtue of an initial Nietzschean dogmatism—practice is necessarily self-blinded, tradition necessarily impeding—that de Man is able to arrive at his politically quietistic aporias.[4] Given these initial definitions, a certain judicious deconstruction of their binary opposition is politically essential, if the Nietzschean belief in affirmative action is not to license a radical politics; but such deconstruction is not permitted to transform the metaphysical trust that there is indeed a single dominant structure of action (blindness, error), and a single form of tradition (obfuscating rather than enabling an encounter with the 'real'). The Marxism of Louis Althusser comes close to this Nietzscheanism: practice is an 'imaginary' affair which thrives upon the repression of truly theoretical understanding, theory a reflection upon the necessary fictionality of such action. The two, as with Nietzsche and de Man, are ontologically disjunct, necessarily non-synchronous.

De Man, then, is characteristically rather more prudent about the possibilities of modernist experiment than the somewhat rashly celebratory Lyotard. All literature for de Man is a ruined or baffled modernism, and the institutionalization of such impulses is a permanent rather than political affair. Indeed it is part of what brings literature about in the first place, constitutive of its very possibility. It is as though, in an ultimate modernist irony, literature masters and pre-empts its own cultural institutionalization by textually introjecting it, hugging the very chains which bind it, discovering its own negative form of transcendence in its power of rhetorically naming, and thus partially distantiating, its own chronic failure to engage the real. The modernist work—and all cultural artefacts are such—is the one which knows that modernist (for which read also 'political') experiment is finally impotent. The mutual parasitism of history and modernity is de Man's own version of the post-structuralist deadlock of Law and Desire, in which the revolutionary impulse grows heady and delirious on its meagre prison rations.

De Man's resolute ontologizing and dehistoricizing of modernism, which is of a piece with the steady, silent anti-Marxist polemic running throughout his work, does at least give one pause to reflect upon what the term might actually mean. Perry Anderson, in his illuminating essay 'Modernity and Revolution' (*New Left Review* 144), concludes by rejecting the very designation 'modernism' as one 'completely lacking in positive content . . . whose only referent is the blank passage of time itself'. This impatient nominalism is to some degree understandable, given the elasticity of the concept; yet the very nebulousness of the word may be in some sense significant. 'Modernism' as a term at once expresses and mystifies a sense of one's particular historical conjuncture as being somehow peculiarly pregnant with crisis and change. It signifies a portentous, confused yet curiously heightened self-consciousness of one's own historical moment, at once self-doubting and self-congratulatory, anxious and triumphalistic together. It suggests at one and the same time an arresting and denial of history in the violent shock of the immediate present, from which vantage point all previous developments may be complacently consigned to the ashcan of 'tradition', and a disorientating sense of history moving with peculiar force and urgency within one's immediate experience, pressingly actual yet tantalizingly opaque. All historical epochs are modern to themselves, but not all live their experience in this ideological mode. If modernism lives its history as peculiarly, insistently *present*, it also experiences a sense that this present moment is somehow of the *future*, to which the present is nothing more than an orientation; so that the idea of the Now, of the present as full presence eclipsing the past, is itself intermittently eclipsed by an awareness of the present as deferment, as an empty excited openness to a future which is in one sense already here, in another sense yet to come. The 'modern', for most of us, is that which we have always to catch up with: the popular use of the term 'futuristic', to denote modernist experiment, is symptomatic of this fact. Modernism—and here Lyotard's case may be given some qualified credence—is not so much a punctual moment in time as a revaluation of time itself, the sense of an epochal shift in the very meaning and modality of temporality, a qualitative break in our ideological styles of living history. What seems to be moving in such moments is less 'history' than that which is unleashed by its rupture and suspension; and the typically modernist images of the vortex and the abyss, 'vertical' inruptions into temporality within which forces swirl rest-lessly in an eclipse of linear time, represent this ambivalent consciousness. So, indeed, does the Benjaminesque spatializing or 'constellating' of history, which at once brings it to a shocking standstill and shimmers with all the unquietness of crisis or catastrophe.

High modernism, as Fredric Jameson has argued elsewhere, was born at a stroke with mass commodity culture. This is a fact about its internal form, not simply about its external history. Modernism is among other things a strategy whereby the work of art resists commodification, holds out by the skin of its teeth against those social forces which would degrade it to an exchangeable object. To this extent, modernist works are in contradiction with their own material status, self-divided phenomena which deny in their discursive forms their own shabby economic reality. To fend off such reduction to commodity status, the modernist work brackets off the referent or real historical world, thickens its textures and deranges its forms to forestall instant consumability, and draws its own language protectively around it to become a mysteriously autotelic object, free of all contaminating truck with the real. Brooding self-reflexively on its own being, it distances itself through irony from the shame of being no more than a brute, self-identical thing. But the most devastating irony of all is that in doing this the modernist work escapes from one form of commodification only to fall prey to another. If it avoids the humiliation of becoming an abstract, serialized, instantly exchangeable thing, it does so only by virtue of reproducing that other side of the commodity which is its fetishism. The autonomous, self-regarding, impenetrable modernist artefact, in all its isolated splendour, is the commodity as fetish resisting the commodity as exchange, its solution to reification part of that very problem.

It is on the rock of such contradictions that the whole modernist project will finally founder. In bracketing off the real social world, establishing a critical, negating distance between itself and the ruling social order, modernism must simultaneously bracket off the political forces which seek to transform that order. There is indeed a political modernism—what else is Bertolt Brecht?—but it is hardly characteristic of the movement as a whole. Moreover, by removing itself from society into its own impermeable space, the modernist work paradoxically reproduces—indeed intensifies—the very illusion of aesthetic autonomy which marks the bourgeois humanist order it also protests against. Modernist works are after all 'works', discrete and bounded entities for all the free play within them, which is just what the bourgeois art institution understands. The revolutionary avant-garde, alive to this dilemma, were defeated at the hands of political history. Postmodernism, confronted with this situation, will then take the other way out. If the work of art really is a commodity then it might as well admit it, with all the *sang froid* it can muster. Rather than languish in some intolerable conflict between its material reality and its aesthetic structure, it can always collapse that conflict on one side, becoming aesthetically what it is economically. The modernist reification—the art work as isolated fetish—is therefore exchanged for the reification of everyday life in the capitalist marketplace. The commodity as mechanically reproducible exchange ousts the commodity as magical aura. In a sardonic commentary on the avant-garde work, postmodernist culture will dissolve its own boundaries and become coextensive with ordinary commodified life itself, whose ceaseless exchanges and mutations in any case recognize no formal frontiers which are not constantly transgressed. If all artefacts can be appropriated by the ruling order, then better impudently to pre-empt this fate than suffer it unwillingly; only that which is already a commodity can resist commodification. If the high modernist work has been institutionalized within the superstructure[i], postmodernist culture will react demotically to such élitism by installing itself within the base. Better, as Brecht remarked, to start from the 'bad new things', rather than from the 'good old ones'.

That, however, is also where postmodernism stops. Brecht's comment alludes to the Marxist habit of extracting the progressive moment from an otherwise unpalatable or ambivalent reality, a habit well exemplified by the early avant-garde's espousal of a technology able both to emancipate and enslave. At a later, less euphoric stage of technological capitalism, the postmodernism which celebrates kitsch and camp caricatures the Brechtian slogan by proclaiming not that the bad contains the good, but that the bad *is* good—or rather that both of these 'metaphysical' terms have now been decisively outmoded by a social order which is to be neither affirmed nor denounced but simply accepted. From where, in a fully reified world, would we derive the criteria by which acts of affirmation or denunciation would be possible? Certainly not from history, which postmodernism must at all costs efface, or spatialize to a range of possible styles, if it is to persuade us to forget that we have ever known or could know any alternative to itself. Such forgetting, as with the healthy amnesiac animal of Nietzsche and his contemporary acolytes, *is* value: value lies not in this or that discrimination within contemporary experience but in the very capacity to stop our ears to the Siren calls of history and confront the contemporary for what it is, in all its blank immediacy. Ethical or political discrimination would extinguish the contemporary simply by mediating it, sever its self-identity, put us prior or posterior to it; value is just that which *is*, the erasure and overcoming of history, and *discourses* of value, which cannot fail to be historical, are therefore by definition valueless. It is for this reason that postmodernist theory is hostile to the hermeneutic, and nowhere more virulently than in Gilles Deleuze and Félix Guattari's *Anti-Oedipus*.[6] In post-1968 Paris, an eyeball-to-eyeball encounter with the real still seemed on the cards, if only the obfuscatory mediations of Marx and Freud could be abandoned. For Deleuze and Guattari, that 'real' is desire, which in a full-blown metaphysical positivism 'can never be deceived', needs no interpretation and simply *is*. In this apodicticism of desire, of which the schizophrenic is hero, there

---

[i] Classical Marxism distinguished between the economic 'base' of a society and its 'superstructure' of cultural institutions such as religion, law, art, etc.

393

can be no place for political discourse proper, for such discourse is exactly the ceaseless labour of *interpretation* of desire, a labour of interpretation which does not leave its object untouched. For Deleuze and Guattari, any such move renders desire vulnerable to the metaphysical traps of meaning. But that interpretation of desire which is the political is necessary precisely because desire is not a single, supremely positive entity; and it is Deleuze and Guattari, for all their insistence upon desire's diffuse and perverse manifestations, who are the true metaphysicians in holding to such covert essentialism. Theory and practice are once more ontologically at odds, since the schizoid hero of the revolutionary drama is by definition unable to reflect upon his own condition, needing Parisian intellectuals to do it for him. The only 'revolution' conceivable, given such a protagonist, is disorder; and Deleuze and Guattari significantly use the two terms synonymously, in the most banal anarchist rhetoric.

In some postmodernist theory, the injunction to glimpse the good in the bad has been pursued with a vengeance. Capitalist technology can be viewed as an immense desiring machine, an enormous circuit of messages and exchanges in which pluralistic idioms proliferate and random objects, bodies, surfaces come to glow with libidinal intensity. 'The interesting thing', writes Lyotard in his *Economie libidinale*, 'would be to stay where we are—but to grab without noise all opportunities to function as bodies and good conductors of intensities. No need of declarations, manifestos, organizations; not even for exemplary actions. To let dissimulation play in favour of intensities.'[7] It is all rather closer to Walter Pater[j] than to Walter Benjamin. Of course capitalism is not uncritically endorsed by such theory, for its libidinal flows are subject to a tyrannical ethical, semiotic and juridical order; what is wrong with late capitalism is not this or that desire but the fact that desire does not circulate freely enough. But if only we could kick our metaphysical nostalgia for truth, meaning and history, of which Marxism is perhaps the prototype, we might come to recognise that desire is here and now, fragments and surfaces all we ever have, kitsch quite as good as the real thing because there is in fact no real thing. What is amiss with old-fashioned modernism, from this perspective, is just the fact that it obstinately refuses to abandon the struggle for meaning. It is still agonizedly caught up in metaphysical depth and wretchedness, still able to experience psychic fragmentation and social alienation as spiritually wounding, and so embarrassingly enmortgaged to the very bourgeois humanism it otherwise seeks to subvert. Postmodernism, confidently post-metaphysical, has outlived all that fantasy of interiority, that pathological itch to scratch surfaces for concealed depths; it embraces instead the mystical positivism of the early Wittgenstein, for which the world—would you believe it?—just is the way it is and not some other way. As with the early Wittgenstein, there cannot be a rational discourse of ethical or political value, for values are not the kind of thing which can be *in* the world in the first place, any more than the eye can be part of the field of vision. The dispersed, schizoid subject is nothing to be alarmed about after all: nothing could be more normative in late capitalist

---

[j] Walter Pater (1839–94), English critic who held aesthetic pleasure to be the highest good in life.

experience. Modernism appears in this light as a deviation still enthralled to a norm, parasitic on what it sets out to deconstruct. But if we are now posterior to such metaphysical humanism there is really nothing left to struggle against, other than those inherited illusions (law, ethics, class struggle, the Oedipus complex) which prevent us from seeing things as they are.

But the fact that modernism continues to struggle for meaning is exactly what makes it so interesting. For this struggle continually drives it towards classical styles of sense-making which are at once unacceptable and inescapable, traditional matrices of meaning which have become progressively empty, but which nevertheless continue to exert their implacable force. It is in just this way that Walter Benjamin reads Franz Kafka, whose fiction inherits the form of a traditional storytelling without its truth contents. A whole traditional ideology of representation is in crisis, yet this does not mean that the search for truth is abandoned. Postmodernism, by contrast, commits the apocalyptic error of believing that the discrediting of this particular representational epistemology is the death of truth itself, just as it sometimes mistakes the disintegration of certain traditional ideologies of the subject for the subject's final disappearance. In both cases, the obituary notices are greatly exaggerated. Postmodernism persuades us to relinquish our epistemological paranoia and embrace the brute objectivity of random subjectivity; modernism, more productively, is torn by the contradictions between a still ineluctable bourgeois humanism and the pressures of a quite different rationality, which, still newly emergent, is not even able to name itself. If modernism's underminings of a traditional humanism are at once anguished and exhilarated, it is in part because there are few more intractable problems in the modern epoch than that of distinguishing between those critiques of classical rationality which are potentially progressive, and those which are irrationalist in the worst sense. It is the choice, so to speak, between feminism and fascism; and in any particular conjuncture the question of what counts as a revolutionary rather than barbarous break with the dominant Western ideologies of reason and humanity is sometimes undecidable. There is a difference, for example, between the 'meaninglessness' fostered by some postmodernism, and the 'meaninglessness' deliberately injected by some trends of avant-garde culture into bourgeois normality.

The contradiction of modernism in this respect is that in order valuably to deconstruct the unified subject of bourgeois humanism, it draws upon key negative aspects of the actual experience of such subjects in late bourgeois society, which often enough does not at all correspond to the official ideological version. It thus pits what is increasingly felt to be the phenomenological reality of capitalism against its formal ideologies, and in doing so finds that it can fully embrace neither. The phenomenological reality of the subject throws formal humanist ideology into question, while the persistence of that ideology is precisely what enables the phenomenological reality to be characterized as negative. Modernism thus dramatises in its very internal structures a crucial contradiction in the ideology of the subject, the force of which we can appreciate if we ask ourselves in what sense the bourgeois humanist conception of the subject as free, active, autonomous and self-identical is a workable or appropriate ideology for late capitalist society. The answer would seen to be that in one sense such an ideology is highly appropriate to such social conditions, and in another sense hardly at all. This ambiguity is overlooked by those poststructuralist theorists who appear to stake all on the assumption that the 'unified subject' is indeed an integral part of contemporary bourgeois ideology, and is thus ripe for urgent deconstruction. Against such a view, it is surely arguable that late capitalism has deconstructed such a subject much more efficiently than meditations on *écriture*. As postmodernist culture attests, the contemporary subject may be less the strenuous monadic agent of an earlier phase of capitalist ideology than a dispersed, decentred network of libidinal attachments, emptied of ethical substance and psychical interiority, the ephemeral function of this or that act of consumption, media experience, sexual relationship, trend or fashion. The 'unified subject' looms up in this light as more and more of a shibboleth or straw target, a hangover from an older liberal epoch of capitalism, before technology and consumerism scattered our bodies to the winds as so many bits and pieces of reified technique, appetite, mechanical operation or reflex of desire.

If this were wholly true, of course, postmodernist culture would be triumphantly vindicated: the unthinkable or the utopian, depending upon one's perspective, would already have happened. But the bourgeois humanist subject is not in fact simply part of a clapped-out history we can all agreeably or reluctantly leave behind: if it is an increasingly inappropriate model at certain levels of subjecthood, it remains a potently relevant one at others. Consider, for example, the condition of being a father and a consumer simultaneously. The former role is governed by ideological imperatives of agency, duty, autonomy, authority, responsibility; the latter, while not wholly free of such strictures, puts them into significant question. The two roles are not of course merely disjunct; but though relations between them are practically negotiable, capitalism's current ideal consumer is strictly incompatible with its current ideal parent. The subject of late capitalism, in other words, is neither simply the self-regulating synthetic agent posited by classical humanist ideology, nor merely a decentred network of desire, but a contradictory amalgam of the two. The constitution of such a subject at the ethical, juridical and political levels is not wholly continuous with its constitution as a consuming or 'mass cultural' unit. 'Eclecticism', writes Lyotard, 'is the degree zero of contemporary general culture: one listens to reggae, watches a western, eats MacDonald's food for lunch and local cuisine for dinner, wears Paris perfume in Tokyo and "retro" clothes in Hong Kong; knowledge is a matter of TV games.'[8] It is not just that there are millions of other human subjects, less exotic than Lyotard's jet-setters, who educate their children, vote as responsible citizens, withdraw their labour and clock in for work; it is also that many subjects live more and more at the points of contradictory intersection between these two definitions.

This was also, in some sense, the site which modernism occupied, trusting as it still did to an experience of interiority which could, however, be less and less articulated in traditional ideological terms. It could expose the limits of such terms with styles of subjective experience they could not encompass; but it also remembered that language sufficiently to submit the definitively 'modern' condition to implicitly *critical* treatment. Whatever the blandishments of postmodernism, this is in my view the site of contradiction we still inhabit; and the most valuable forms of post-structuralism are therefore those which, as with much of Jacques Derrida's writing, refuse to credit the absurdity that we could ever simply have jettisoned the 'metaphysical' like a cast-off overcoat. The new post-metaphysical subject proposed by Bertolt Brecht and Walter Benjamin, the *Unmensch* [dehumanised man] emptied of all bourgeois interiority to become the faceless mobile functionary of revolutionary struggle, is at once a valuable metaphor for thinking ourselves beyond Proust, and too uncomfortably close to the faceless functionaries of advanced capitalism to be uncritically endorsed. In a similar way, the aesthetics of the revolutionary avant-garde break with the contemplative monad of bourgeois culture with their clarion call of 'production', only to rejoin in some respects the labouring or manufacturing subject of bourgeois utilitarianism. We are still, perhaps, poised as precariously as Benjamin's Baudelairian *flâneur*[k] between the rapidly fading aura of the old humanist subject, and the ambivalently energizing and repellent shapes of a city landscape.

Postmodernism takes something from both modernism and the avant-garde, and in a sense plays one off against the other. From modernism proper, postmodernism inherits the fragmentary or schizoid self, but eradicates all critical distance from it, countering this with a pokerfaced presentation of 'bizarre' experiences which resembles certain avant-garde gestures. From the avant-garde, postmodernism takes the dissolution of art into social life, the rejection of tradition, an opposition to 'high' culture as such, but crosses this with the unpolitical impulses of modernism. It thus unwittingly exposes the residual formalism of any radical art form which identifies the de-institutionalization of art, and its reintegration with other social practices, as an intrinsically revolutionary move. For the question, rather, is under what conditions and with what likely effects such a reintegration may be attempted. An authentically political art in our own time might similarly draw upon both modernism and the avant-garde, but in a different combination from postmodernism. The contradictions of the modernist work are, as I have tried to show, implicitly political in character; but since the 'political' seemed to much modernism to belong precisely to the traditional rationality it was trying to escape, this fact remained for the most part submerged beneath the mythological and metaphysical. Moreover, the typical self-reflexiveness of modernist culture was at once a form in which it could explore some of the key ideological issues I have outlined, and by the same stroke rendered its products opaque and unavailable to a wide public. An art today which, having learnt from the openly committed character of avant-garde culture, might cast the contradictions of modernism in a more explicitly political light could do so effectively only if it had also learnt its lesson from modernism too—learnt, that is to say, that the 'political' itself is a question of the emergence of a transformed rationality, and if it is not

[k] The allusion is to Benjamin's essay 'On Some Motifs in Baudelaire'. *Flâneur* is French for 'stroller, saunterer'.

397

presented as such will still seem part of the dead tradition from which the
adventurously modern is striving to free itself.

NOTES

1. Peter Bürger, *Theory of the Avant-Garde*, Minneapolis 1984.
2. Jean-François Lyotard, *The Postmodern Condition: A Report on Knowledge*, Manchester 1984, p. 45.
3. Paul de Man, 'Literary History and Literary Modernity', in *Blindness and Insight*, Minneapolis
   1983, p. 162.
4. For a vigorous critique of the political implications of de Man's arguments, see Frank Lentricchia,
   Criticism and Social Change, Chicago and London 1983, pp. 43–52.
5. See Fredric Jameson, 'Reification and Utopia in Mass Culture', *Social Text*, Winter 1979.
6. Gilles Deleuze and Félix Guattari, *Anti-Oedipus: Capitalism and Schizophrenia*, Minneapolis 1983.
7. Jean-François Lyotard, *Economie libidinale*, Paris 1974, p. 311.
8. Lyotard, *The Postmodern Condition*, p. 76.

24 Catherine Belsey

Catherine Belsey (b. 1940), who teaches in the English Department of University College, Cardiff, represents a distinctively British school of post-structuralist criticism which has emphasized the political and ideological rather than the epistemological and hermeneutic implications of European theory, and has taken its cue from Barthes and Foucault rather than from Derrida. In a loose sense Marxist, and certainly 'left wing', this school of criticism has sought to define the problem of meaning in literature as an aspect of the struggle for power in society at large, and has coupled the study of literature with commitment to political struggle in the areas of race, gender and class. Its characteristic strategy has been to expose and attack the assumptions and values of traditional literary education—manifested, for example, in the typical formulae of school and university examination papers—as protecting, in the name of humanism, the hegemony of a particular class.

Catherine Belsey's *Critical Practice* (1980), a vigorously written, iconoclastic primer, has been influential in disseminating an alternative programme for literary studies, based on such favourite post-structuralist ideas as the Death of the Author, the dissolution of the autonomous subject, the role of the reader in the production of meaning, the bad faith of classic realism, and the oppressiveness of the literary canon. She was a contributor to a symposium, *Re-Reading English*, ed. Peter Widdowson (1982) which stirred up a long-running controversy about these matters in *The London Review of Books*. (See Tom Paulin's review in *LRB* 4, 2, 1982, and subsequent correspondence.) In 'Literature, History, Politics' (reprinted from the journal *Literature and History*, 1983), Catherine Belsey seeks to retain classic literature as an object of study without surrendering commitment to 'a politics of change'.

CROSS-REFERENCE: 6. Derrida
                   9. Barthes
                  10. Foucault

Literature, history, politics[1]

To bring these three terms together is hardly to do anything new. *Literature and History* has been doing it since its inception; the Essex Conference volumes[a] do it; Raymond Williams has spent his life doing it; historians like E. P. Thompson and Christopher Hill, glancing sideways at literature, have frequently done it; a venerable tradition of Marxist criticism all over Europe does it. Less marginally, as far as the institution of literary criticism in Britain is concerned, T. S. Eliot, F. R. Leavis and E. M. W. Tillyard did it when they constructed between them a lost Elizabethan utopia where thought and feeling were one, where the native rhythms of speech expressed in poetry the intuitive consciousness of an organic community, and everyone recognised in the principle of order the necessity of submission to the proper authorities, social and divine.

And yet paradoxically to bring these three terms together *explicitly* is still to scandalise the institution of literary criticism, because it is to propose a relationship between the transcendent (literature), the contingent (history) and the merely strategic (politics). The institution is dedicated to the infinite repetition of the best that has been thought and said in the world, and this luminous heritage, however shaded by the Discarded Image of medieval ideas, or the Victorian Frame of Mind, stands ready to be released from history by the apparatus criticus which the academic profession supplies, and to reappear resplendent before every new generation of student-critics. The model for the institution's conception of history as a kind of perpetual present, and its conviction of the vulgarity of politics, is Arnold's essay, 'The Study of Poetry', where it is clear from the 'touchstones' Arnold invokes that great poetry from Homer to Milton, despite minor differences of language and setting, has always taught the same elegiac truth, that this world is inevitably a place of sorrow and that the only heroism is a solitary resignation of the spirit.

The sole inhabitant of the universe of literature is Eternal Man (and the masculine form is appropriate), whose brooding, feeling presence precedes, determines and transcends history as it precedes and determines the truths inscribed in the English syllabus, the truths examination candidates are required to reproduce. '"When we read Chaucer's early poems we feel the author's awareness of how complex and involved the events and circumstances of life are, of how they defy any single interpretation". Discuss.' (Oxford Honour School of English Language and Literature, 'Chaucer and Langland', 1980.) Miracu-

---

[a] The proceedings of the conference on the Sociology of Literature, held annually at the University of Essex. A selection of papers from these conferences has been published under the title *Literature, Politics and Theory*, edited by Francis Barker and others (1986).

lously, Chaucer's awareness of the complexity of it all precisely resembles mine, ours, everyone's. Every liberal's, that is, in the twentieth century: a modern 'recognition' is rendered eternal by literary criticism. Examination questions, the ultimate location of institutional power, identify the boundaries of the discipline, and define what it is permissible to 'discuss', as they so invitingly and misleadingly put it (Davies, 1982, p. 39). '"The sense of a peculiarly heightened personal dignity is at the centre of Donne's work." (Alvarez) *Either* discuss with reference to Donne *or* describe the sense of personal dignity in any other writer of the period.' (Oxford Honour School. . . . 'English Literature from 1600 to 1740', 1980.) Or any other writer of any other period, perhaps, because it is a reading from the present, from a position of liberal humanism, which finds the sense of personal dignity at issue wherever it looks.

Historians have been quite clear, at least since Eric Hobsbawm's seminal articles were published in *Past and Present* in 1954, that the seventeenth century was a period of general crisis. That general crisis has apparently no repercussions whatever for the literature of the period as it is defined in the broad run of examinations at O Level, at A Level and in the universities. Where the crisis is glimpsed, it is instantly depoliticised: '"Courtly poetry without a court." What do the Cavalier poets gain or lose by the decline and final absence of a Court? Discuss one or more poets.' (Cambridge English Tripos, Part II, 'Special Period, 1616–60', 1981.) Had the question asked what was gained or lost from the collapse of the Court by agricultural labourers, by an emerging feminism or by radical politics, the answer might have mattered. But that would be history. What matters in English is the implications of the Revolution of the 1640s for the Cavalier poets. Alternatively, the crisis is personalised as the idiosyncratic interest of an individual: '"Throughout *Paradise Lost* Milton's concern is to present and investigate a crisis of authority." Discuss.' (Oxford Honour School . . . 'Spenser and Milton', 1980.) What it is not possible to say in answer to that question is how a crisis of authority is at the heart of *Paradise Lost*, not as a matter for the author's investigation, but as a source of fragmentation within the poem and the writing of the poem. It is precisely the location of authority— in God and in the human will, in the subjectivity of the narrator and in a signification which is outside the narrator and appeals to all human cultures— or rather, it is these contradictory locations of authority which insist on the inadequacy of any reading of the poem that looks for 'Milton's concern' as a guide to its possible meanings. And among these possible meanings is the limits of what can be said about authority in a period when authority is in crisis.

When the institution of literary criticism in Britain invokes history, whether as world picture or as long-lost organic community, it is ultimately in order to suppress it, by showing that *in essence* things are as they have always been. The function of scholarship, as of conventional criticism, is finally to reinstate the continuity of felt life which the ignorance of a trivialising society obscures. No history: no politics. Because if there has never been change at a fundamental level, there are no rational grounds for commitment to change. No politics—or rather, no overt politics, since there is, of course, no political neutrality in the assertion of an unchanging essential human nature.

The radical theoretical work of the last twenty years has not always confronted the suppression of history and politics in literary criticism. Structuralism, widely regarded, when it began to appear in Britain in the sixties and early seventies, as the beginning of the end of civilization as we know it, quite failed to challenge the institution on this central issue. Saussure's *Course in General Linguistics* is a remarkably plural text. Insofar as its readers confined themselves to its discovery of an opposition which precisely replicated the classic liberal opposition between the individual and society, structuralism offered no threat to the equilibrium of the free West. Fired by the concept of the difference between *langue* and *parole*, which permitted utterance within the permutations already authorized by the language-system, the structuralists set off in quest of similar timeless enabling systems in other spheres, the form of all societies, the pattern of all narrative, the key to all mythologies. It was the signifying system itself which was held to lay down, long before the drama of history was inscribed in it, the elementary structures of culture and of subjectivity (Lacan, 1977, p. 148). Structuralism thus proclaimed Eternal Man and the suppression of history with a new and resounding authority. Ironically, Saussure's analysis of language as a system of differences was invoked to initiate the elimination of all difference.

But it was also Saussure's work, in conjunction with the Marxist analysis of ideology, which permited Roland Barthes on behalf of anarchism to identify Eternal Man as the product and pivot of bourgeois mythology (Barthes, 1972, p. 140), and subsequently to repudiate the structuralist equalization of all narrative 'under the scrutiny of an in-different science' (Barthes, 1975, p. 3). This was possible because one of the effects of the *Course in General Linguistics* was to relativise meaning by detaching it from the world outside language. Insofar as the value of a specific sign differs from one language to another, and insofar as language is the condition of meaning and thought, meaning and thought differ from one language to another, one culture to another. As linguistic habits alter, cultures are transformed. Difference, history, change reappear.

They disappear again, however, in American deconstructionism, which nails its colours to the free play of the eternal signifier. Here all writing and all speech is fiction in a timeless present without presence, and the subject celebrates its own non-being in an infinite space where there is no room for politics. Deconstructionism has nothing to say about the relationship between literature and history, or the political implications of either. Nothing explicit, that is.

What is at stake here is the elision of the signified. Saussure distinguished three terms or orders—the signifier (the sound or written image), the signified (the meaning) and the referent (the thing in the world). A certain elusiveness in Saussure's theory concerning the relationship between meaning and *intention* prompted Derrida's deconstruction of Saussure's phonocentrism, and in the interests of contesting the notion of a pure, conceptual intelligibility, a 'truth in the soul' which precedes the signifier (Derrida, 1976, p. 15), Derrida in that context treats as suspect, as he puts it, the difference between signifier and signified (p. 14). The other of the signified is subsumed under 'presence', which is understood indiscriminately as concept, intention or referent, so that meaning, being and truth are collapsed together. Elsewhere Derrida's notion of *différance* does not eliminate the possibility of signification. Meaning exists, neither as being nor as truth, but as linguistic difference, textually produced, contextually deferred (Derrida, 1973, pp. 129–60). But the opening pages of *Grammatology* invite vulgar deconstructionists to take it that there is no such thing as meaning, and in consequence, since meaningless language is literally unthinkable, that words mean whatever you want them to mean. This *Looking-Glass* reasoning leads at best to an anarchic scepticism, the celebration of undecidability as an end in itself, and at worst to the reinstatement of the mirror phase, where the critic-subject at play rejoices in its own linguistic plenitude. In the constant and repeated assertion of the evaporation of meaning there is no place to analyse the context for meaning, and therefore no politics, and there is no possibility of tracing changes of meaning, the sliding of the signified, in history.

It was at this point in the debate that political post-structuralism began to turn more insistently to the work of Foucault. (It was also, perhaps, at this point in the debate that Foucault's own work became more explicitly political.) Foucault goes beyond Derridean scepticism to the extent that he identifies the relationship between meaning (or discourse-as-knowledge) and power. Conceding that language does not map the world, but distinguishing signified from referent and intention, knowledge from what is true (because guaranteed by being or by things), Foucault reinstates politics in a post-structuralist world which, despite the heroic efforts of Althusser, could not support the concept of science. *I, Pierre Rivière* . . . documents Pierre Rivière's murder in 1835 of his mother, his sister and his brother. It is made clear that the meaning of Pierre's memoir exceeds any single reading of it, since reading always take place from a position and on behalf of a position. The question is not, 'what is the *truth* of Pierre Rivière's behaviour?', 'was he *really* mad?' but 'from what positions, inscribed in what knowledges, did the contest between the legal and the medical professions for control of Pierre Rivière take place?' And in addition, 'what possibilities of a reading of these documents are available now which were not available in the 1830s?' From the perspective of the present, the records of Pierre Rivière's act of unauthorized resistance can be read as a part of the history of the present, because they demonstrate the social and discursive construction of a deviant and at the same time permit him to speak. The 'humanitarian' practice which confines the criminally insane for life silences them even more effectively than execution, since whatever they say is rendered inaudible, 'mad'.

Foucault's work politicizes the polyphony of the signified. The plurality of meaning is not exclusively a matter of infinite play, as recent history demonstrates. Meanings produce practices and generate behaviour. It was explicitly in a contest for the meaning of 'aggression'—as colonialism, as theft, or as violence—that British and Argentinian soldiers killed and mutilated each other in the South Atlantic, both sides using might to establish that might is not right. In this as in all other just wars it was evident that the letter kills. While the American deconstructionists play, Reagan is preparing to reduce us all to radioactive rubble to preserve our freedom. The control of meanings—of freedom, democracy, the American way of life—the control of these meanings is political power, but it is a mistake to suppose that the abolition of the signified is the abolition of power.

On the contrary, deconstructionism collaborates with the operations of meaning-as-power precisely insofar as it protests that there is no such thing.

Foucault's work brings together two of my three terms, history and politics, in its analysis of the ways in which power produces new knowledges. It is a history of ideas in which ideas are understood as generating practices, a history of discourses in which discourses define and are reproduced in institutions. It offers a challenge to classical Marxist politics to the extent that it refuses to find a central and determining locus of power in the mode of production, and a challenge to empiricist history in its refusal to treat documents as transparent. In a sense we needed both challenges. Whatever the inadequacies of Althusserian Marxism, it was impossible for a post-structuralist politics subsequently to retreat from the decentring concept of overdetermination. To attribute a relative autonomy to ideology was to open up the possibility of a history of the forms in which people become conscious of their differences and begin to fight them out. These forms are precisely the classical superstructural forms of law, metaphysics, aesthetics, and so on, but with the addition of those areas where struggle has become increasingly pressing in the twentieth century—sexuality, the family, subjectivity. The theory of relative autonomy, however vulnerable in itself, permitted attention within Marxism to these areas as sites of struggle.

But if post-structuralist politics implied the dispersal of history into new areas, it also implied a historiography which was both more and less than the transcription of lost experience. To take a single example of the problem, Lawrence Stone's book, *The Family, Sex and Marriage in England, 1500–1800*, published in 1977, is extremely welcome insofar as it tackles precisely one of those areas which politics (specifically, in this instance, feminist politics) had brought to prominence. But Stone's vocabulary of 'evidence', 'sources', 'documents' and 'sampling' define the historian's quarry, however elusive, as something anterior to textuality, revealed through its expression in the mass of diaries, memoirs, autobiographies and letters cited. History is seen as the recovered presence of pure, extra-discursive, representative experience, 'how it (usually) felt'. What Stone produces in consequence is a smooth, homogeneous evolution, with over-lapping strata for enhanced verisimilitude, from the open lineage family of the late middle ages to the affective nuclear family in the seventeenth and eighteenth centuries. But the affective nuclear family begins to be glimpsed in discourse in the mid-sixteenth century, and there is evidence (if evidence is what is at stake) that this concept of a private realm, in which power is exercised invisibly for the public good, defines itself in this period in opposition to a control of marriage exercised directly but precariously by the sovereign as head of the church. What Stone's quest for the representative experience behind the documents eliminates is the *politics* of the history of the family, precisely the issue which put it on the feminist map, the contest for power, which is also a contest for meaning in its materiality, the struggle about the meaning and practice of family life.

Representative experience is understood to be whatever a lot of people said they felt, and it is held to be the origin of, and to issue in, representative behaviour. This notion of the 'fit' between documented feelings and recorded behaviour relegates to the margins of history any feelings or behaviour which were not dominant. Struggle thus becomes marginal, always the province, except in periods of general struggle, of the idiosyncratic few. But more important, modes of resistance to what was dominant are ignored if they could not be formulated in so many words, were not allowed a voice, were not experienced as resistance or can be defined as deviant. Stone makes no space, for instance, for a consideration of witchcraft as a practice offering women a form of power which was forbidden precisely by orthodox concepts of the family.

The point is worth dwelling on because Stone is by no means an isolated case. Even among those radical historians for whom struggle is heroic, if still idiosyncratic, the quest for experience and the belief that documents are ultimately transparent remain common. But documents do not merely transcribe experience: to the extent that they inevitably come from a context where power is at stake, they are worth analysis not as access to something beyond them, not as evidence of how it felt, but as themselves locations of power and resistance to power.

A post-structuralist history needs to re-examine Stone's mass of documents (and perhaps others), and to address to them a different series of questions. These include the following (borrowed, in modified form, from Foucault):

What are the modes and conditions of these texts?
Where do they come from; who controls them; on behalf of whom?
What possible subject positions are inscribed in them?
What meanings and what contests for meaning do they display?

(cf. Foucault, 1977, p. 138)

The answers to these questions give us a different history of the family, sex and marriage. This is the history not of an irrecoverable experience, but of meanings, of the signified in its plurality, not the referent in its singular but imaginary presence. It is, therefore, a history of struggle and, in consequence, a political history.

Such a history is not offered as objective, authoritative, neutral or true. It is not outside history itself, or outside the present. On the contrary, it is part of history, part of the present. It is irreducibly textual, offering no place outside discourse from which to interpret or judge. It is explicitly partial, from a position and on behalf of a position. It is not culturally relative in so far as relativism is determinist and therefore a-political: 'I think like this because my society thinks like this'. But its effect is to relativise the present, to locate the present in history and in process.

Foucault's work gives us a methodology for producing our own history and politics, a history which is simultaneously a politics, but it has little to say about my third term, literature. Literature is not a knowledge. Literary criticism is a knowledge, produced in and reproducing an institution. Some of the most important and radical work of the last decade has been devoted to analysis of the institution of literary criticism, challenging its assumptions, exposing its ideological implications and relativising its claims to universality and timelessness.[2] One of the central concerns of this work has been the interrogation of the idea of literature itself as 'the central co-ordinating concept of the discourse of literary criticism, supplying the point of reference to which relationships of difference and similarity within the field of writing are articulated' (Bennett, 1981, p. 139).

Tony Bennett's point here is an important one. 'Literature' signifies as an element in a system of differences. It is that which is *not* minor, popular, ephemeral or trivial, as well as that which is not medicine, economics, history or, of course, politics. 'Literature' designates a value and a category.

That conjunction—of value and category—issues in English departments as we know them, and generates, I have argued, the continuous production and reproduction of hierarchies of subjectivity (Belsey, 1982). We need, therefore, as Tony Bennett argues, to call into question both the category—the autonomy of literary studies—and the value—Literature as distinct from its residue, popular fiction. We need to replace the quest for value by an 'analysis of the social contestation of value' (Bennett, 1981, p. 143).

Work on the institution of literary criticism is centrally concerned with the reception of literary texts, with the text as site of the range of possible meanings that may be produced during the course of its history, and with the knowledges inscribed in both dominant and radical discourses. Its importance seems to me to be established beyond question. Here is a field of operations which brings together literature, history and politics in crucial ways, undermining the power of the institution and challenging the category of Literature.

The effect of this project, in other words, is to decentre literary criticism, to displace 'the text', the 'primary material', from its authoritative position at the heart of the syllabus, to dislodge the belief in the close reading of the text as the critic's essential and indispensable skill. Quite whether we can afford to dispose of the literary text altogether is not usually made clear, but it seems implicit in the project that we can do without it for most of the time. What is to be read closely is criticism, official reports on the teaching of English, examination papers, and all the other discursive displays of institutional power.

But before we throw out the Arden Shakespeares and the Penguin English Library (in order to make a space for the Critical Heritage and the Newbolt Report), I want to propose a way of recycling the texts, on the grounds that work on the institution is not the only way of bringing together literature, history and politics, of undermining literary studies as currently constituted, or of challenging the category of Literature. I want to argue in favour of at least one additional way of doing all those things (in the hope of forestalling one of those fierce bouts of either-orism which periodically dissipate the energies of the left).

Literature (or fiction: the fields defined by the two words are not necessarily co-extensive: what about Bacon's *Essays*, Donne's sermons, the 'Epistle to Dr Arbuthnot', *The Prelude*? But perhaps we read these texts as fiction now, so the term will perhaps serve to modify the ideological implications of Literature)— literature of fiction is not a knowledge, but it is not only a site where knowledge is produced. It is also the location of a range of knowledges. In this sense the text always exceeds the history of its reception. While on the one hand meaning is never single, eternally inscribed in the words on the page, on the other hand readings do not spring unilaterally out of the subjectivities (or the ideologies) of readers. The text is not an empty space, filled with meaning from outside itself, any more than it is the transcription of an authorial intention, filled with meaning from outside language. As a signifying practice, writing always offers raw material for the production of meanings, the signified in its plurality, on the under-standing, of course, that the signified is distinct from the intention of the author (pure concept) or the referent (a world already constituted and re-presented).

The intertextual relations of the text are never purely literary. Fiction draws not only on other fiction but on the knowledges of its period, discourses in circulation which are themselves sites of power and the contest for power. In the case of *Macbeth*, for instance, the Victorian fable of vaulting ambition and its attendant remorse and punishment is also a repository of Reformation Chris-tianity, morbid, demonic, apocalyptic; of the Jacobean law of sovereignty and succession; of Renaissance medicine; and of Stuart history. Equally, since narrative fiction depends on impediments (where there are no obstacles to be overcome there's no story), *Macbeth* depends on resistance to those knowledges, on what refuses or escapes them: on witchcraft seen as a knowledge which repudiates Christian knowledge, on regicide, madness, suicide, as evasions of a control which is thereby shown to be precarious. A political and historical reading of *Macbeth* might analyse these discourses, not in the manner of Tillyard, as a means to a deeper understanding of the text, and at the same time of a lost golden world where nature itself rose up to punish resistance to the existing order, but on the contrary, as a way of encountering the discourses themselves in their uncertainty, their instability, their relativity.

Narrative necessarily depends on the establishment within the story of fictional forms of control and resistance to control, norms and the repudiation of norms. And in the period to which English departments are centrally committed, from the Renaissance to the present, the criterion of verisimilitude, towards or against which fiction has consistently pressed, has necessitated that these concepts of control and normality be intelligible outside fiction itself. Thus, sovereignty, the family, subjectivity are defined and redefined in narrative fiction, problematised and reproblematised. *Macbeth* (again) offers, in the scene with Lady Macduff, an early instance of the emerging concept of the affective nuclear family—a private realm of domestic harmony shown as vulnerable to crisis in a public and political world which is beginning to be perceived as distinct from it. It presents, on the other hand, the fragmentation of the subject, Macbeth, under the pressure of a crisis in which the personal and the political are still perceived as continuous.

In *Critical Practice* I tried to distinguish between three kinds of texts, which I identified as declarative, imperative and interrogative. The declarative text imparts 'knowledge' (fictional or not) to the reader, the imperative text (propa-ganda) exhorts, instructs or orders the reader, and the interrogative text poses questions by enlisting the reader in contradiction (Belsey, 1980, pp 90 ff.). It now seems to me that this classification may have been excessively formalistic, implying that texts can unilaterally determine their reception by the reader. As we know, a reading practice which actively seeks out contradiction can *produce* as inter-rogative a text which has conventionally been read as declarative. Nonetheless, the categories may be useful if they enable us to attribute a certain kind of specificity to literary/fictional texts. The danger of formalism is to be set against the structuralist danger of collapsing all difference. That there is a formal indeterminacy does not mean that we can never speak of form, any more than the polyphony of 'freedom' prevents us from condemning police states. In the period of *Macbeth* many of the available written texts are imperative—sermons, tracts, pamphlets, marked as referring to a given external reality, and offering the reader a position of alignment with one set of values and practices and opposition to others (divorce, for instance, or patriarchal sovereignty). Fictional (declarative or interrogative) texts, by contrast, marked as alluding only indirectly to 'reality', informing without directly exhorting, offer a space for the problematisation of the knowledges they invoke in ways which imperative texts cannot risk.[3] Radically contradictory definitions of marriage in a divorce pamphlet inevitably reduce its propaganda-value; plays, on the contrary, can problematise marriage without affecting the coherence of the story.

To say this is not, I hope, to privilege literature (and certainly not Literature) but only to allow it a certain specificity which identifies its use-value in the construction of the history of the present. A vest is not a sock, but it is not in consequence obvious that one is better than the other. On the basis of this specificity which is neither privilege nor autonomy, I want to urge that lyric poetry, read as fiction, is also worth recycling. Sexuality and subjectivity are the twin themes of the lyric, and since any text longer than, say, an imagist poem, moves towards argument or narrative, and therefore towards crisis, similar definitions and problematisations of these areas of our history offer themselves for analysis here. Sexuality, gender, the subject are not fixed but slide in history, and this sliding is available to an analysis which repudiates both the quarry of an empiricist history (experience, the world) and the quarry of conventional criticism (consciousness, the author).

The quest is for, say, the subject in its meanings. The word, 'I', the fixed centre of liberal humanism, may always *designate* the speaker, but it *means* something new in the late sixteenth century, and something new again in the early nineteenth century. Equally, sexuality is not given but socially produced. We don't have access to the eighteenth-century experience of sexuality, but we can analyse the contest in that period for its meaning. It may be the case that the size of household in Britain has not changed much since the middle ages (Laslett, 1977), but the meaning of the family, institutionally and in practice, has changed fundamentally—and can therefore change again. This kind of analysis is a stake through the heart of Eternal Man, and the world of practice as well as theory is consequently laid open to effective radical political action.

The reading practice implied by this enterprise—the production of a political history from the raw material of literary texts—is a result of all that post-structuralism has urged about meaning: its often marginal location, its disunity and discontinuity, as well as its plurality. In this way the text reappears, but not as it 'really is', or 'really was'. On the contrary, this is the text as it never was, though it was never anything else—dispersed, fragmented, produced, politicized. The text is no longer the centre of a self-contained exercise called literary criticism. It is one of the places to begin to assemble the political history of the present.

I say 'to begin' because it is immediately apparent that such a history is not bounded by the boundaries of Literature or literature. Literary value becomes irrelevant: political assassination is problematised in Pickering's play, *Horestes* (1567) as well as in *Hamlet*. Equally, the subject is a legal and a psychoanalytic category just as much as a literary one; the family is defined by medical and religious discourses as well as by classic realist texts. And so the autonomy of literature begins to dissolve, its boundaries to waver as the enterprise unfolds. The text does not disappear though the canon does; and fiction is put to work for substantial political ends which replace the mysterious objectives of aesthetic satisfaction and moral enrichment.

Two projects, related but distinct, immediately present themselves. The first is the synchronic analysis of a historical moment, starting possibly but not inevitably from literary texts. This has perhaps been the project of the Essex conferences, focussed on a series of crises (1848, 1936, 1642, 1789), and subtitled, 'the Sociology of Literature'. The Essex volumes have made available some excellent work, but if the projected archaeology did not materialise in its entirety, there are reasons for this which have little to do with the value or the practicality of the project itself. I suspect that one of these reasons was that the project was not shared by all participants. (There is no reason why it should have been: it makes no exclusive claims.) Ideally the project is a collective one, but it's not easy to work collectively if you meet only once a year. It's also a long-term project involving deliberate and patient analysis, and it may be that the conference paper is not an ideal place for its presentation and discussion.

But if the Essex conferences have not achieved everything that was hoped for, they have produced work which in various ways suggests important directions for the future.[4] And in addition, there is a second and analogous project—what Foucault sporadically calls a genealogy because it traces change without invoking a single point of origin (Foucault, 1977, pp. 139–64, etc.). This is a diachronic analysis of specific discontinuities—in sovereignty, gender, the subject, for instance. And where else should we begin this analysis but by looking at fiction, poetry, autobiography? If we start with the texts on the syllabus—because they are available and for no other very specific reason—we shall not end with them, because the enquiry inevitably transgresses the boundaries of the existing discipline.

The proposal is to reverse the Leavisian enterprise of constructing (inventing) a lost organic world of unfallen orality, undissociated sensibility and uncontested order. In fact, in so far as it concerns the sixteenth and seventeenth centuries, the kind of archaeology I have in mind uncovers a world of violence, disorder and fragmentation. The history of the present is not a history of a fall from grace but of the transformations of power and resistances to power. The claim is not that such a history, or such a reading of literary texts, is more accurate, but only that it is more radical. No less partial, it produces the past not in order to present an ideal of hierarchy, but to relativise the present, to demonstrate that since change has occurred in those areas which seem most intimate and most inevitable, change in those areas is possible for us.

According to Foucault, who invents the verb 'to fiction' in order to undermine his own use of the word 'truth', 'one "fictions" a history starting from a political reality that renders it true, one "fictions" a politics that doesn't as yet exist starting from a historical truth' (Foucault, 1979, pp. 74–5). I want to add this: the literary institution has 'fictioned' a criticism which uncritically protests its own truth; we must instead 'fiction' a literature which renders up our true history in the interests of a politics of change.

NOTES

1. I am grateful for the comments of Francis Barker and Chris Weedon on an earlier draft of this essay.
2. See for example the work of Renée Balibar; Francis Mulhern, *The Moment of Scrutiny* (London: NLB, 1979); Tony Bennett, *Formalism and Marxism* (London: Methuen, 1979); Peter Widdowson ed., *Re-Reading English* (London: Methuen, 1982); the LTP (Literature Teaching Politics) conferences and journal.
3. I am indebted for this idea to Simon Barker.
4. See particularly in the *1642* volume (ed. Francis Barker *et al.*) essays by Francis Barker, Peter Hulme, Christine Berg and Philippa Berry.

BIBLIOGRAPHY

Barker, Francis *et al.*,	(1981)	*1642: Literature and Power in the Seventeenth Century*, University of Essex.
Barthes, Roland	(1972)	*Mythologies*, trs. Annette Lavers, London, Cape.
Barthes, Roland	(1975)	*S/Z*, trs. Richard Miller, London, Cape.
Belsey, Catherine	(1980)	*Critical Practice*, London, Methuen.
Belsey, Catherine	(1982)	'Re-Reading the Great Tradition'. *Re-Reading English*, ed. Peter Widdowson, London, Methuen, pp. 121–135.
Bennett, Tony	(1981)	'Marxism and Popular Fiction', *Literature and History*, VII, pp. 138–165.
Davies, Tony	(1982)	'Common Sense and Critical Practice: Teaching Literature', *Re-Reading English*, ed. Peter Widdowson, London, Methuen, pp. 32–43.
Derrida, Jacques	(1973)	*Speech and Phenomena*, trs. David B. Allison, Evanston, Ill. Northwestern U.P.
Derrida, Jacques	(1976)	*Of Grammatology*, trs. Gayatri Chakravorty Spivak, Baltimore and London, Johns Hopkins U.P.
Foucault, Michel	(1977)	*Language, Counter-Memory, Practice*, ed. Donald Bouchard, Oxford, Blackwell.
Foucault, Michel	ed.(1978)	*I, Pierre Rivière . . .*, Harmondsworth, Penguin.
Foucault, Michel	(1979)	*Power, Truth, Strategy*, ed. Meaghan Morris and Paul Patton, Sydney, Feral Publications.
Lacan, Jacques	(1977)	*Ecrits*, trs. Alan Sheridan, London, Tavistock.
Laslett, Peter	(1977)	*Family Life and Illicit Love in Earlier Generations*, Cambridge, CUP.
Stone, Lawrence	(1977)	*The Family, Sex and Marriage and England*, 1500–1800, London, Weidenfeld and Nicolson.

25 Geoffrey Hartman

Geoffrey Hartman (b. 1929) is Karl Young Professor of English and Comparative Literature at Yale, and a leading member of the deconstructionist school of criticism especially associated with that university (others include Paul de Man, J. Hillis Miller and Harold Bloom, all represented in this Reader). Hartman's restlessness under the constraints of the New Criticism was signalled by the title of his collection of essays, *Beyond Formalism* (1970). Like many other American critics of his generation, he responded eagerly to the stimulus of post-structuralist theory, especially the work of Jacques Derrida. Hartman's *Saving the Text* (1981) was a speculative commentary upon Derrida's *Glas* (a text that is itself an idiosyncratic commentary upon texts by Hegel and Jean Genet, reproduced on facing pages so that they 'mirror' each other). Other books by Hartman include *The Fate of Reading* (1975) and *Criticism in the Wilderness* (1980).

The essential instability of language postulated by Derrida and Lacan, the perpetual sliding of the signified under the signifier, or endless deferral of determinate meaning, in discourse, liberates the critic from the obligation to produce interpretive closure. Instead, he can explore the potential meaning of a text in a style of semantic freeplay not essentially different from poetic composition. In 'The Interpreter's Freud', Hartman suggests that Freud's analysis of dreams by means of 'free association' led him inexorably to the same conclusion—that human cognition is essentially polysemous—in spite of his faith in the possibility of a 'scientific' discourse about the mind. The paradox is deftly illustrated by an acute reading of that well-known poem by Wordsworth, 'A Slumber Did My Spirit Seal', which shows how the deconstructionist distrust of the superficial sense of a text can reveal new richness of meaning in it.

'The Interpreter's Freud' was originally delivered as the 1984 Freud Lecture at Yale, and is reprinted here from Hartman's *Easy Pieces* (1985).

CROSS-REFERENCES: 5. Lacan
                         16. Miller
                         21. De Man
COMMENTARY: Christopher Norris, *Deconstruction: Theory and Practice* (1982), Ch 6.

The interpreter's Freud

Freud alone proves Emerson's observation that a significant institution is the shadow of a great thinker. We cannot understand Freud without understanding the peculiar quality of his greatness: that quality which made him, which still makes him, a scandal, a shadow we negotiate with. He has imposed on us with the force of a religion. 'One must have a very strong and keen and persistent criticism,' Wittgenstein remarked about Freud, 'to see through the mythology that is offered or imposed on one. There is an inducement to say, "Yes, of course, it must be like that!" A powerful mythology.'

Freud, however, wished to found a science of mind and not a mythology. His first major book on *The Interpretation of Dreams* planted the banner of rational and methodical inquiry in the very swamp of unreason, where few had ventured and, of those, very few had come back, their sanity intact. Yet these rationalist aspirations of psychoanalysis by no means disprove its redemptive and communitarian nature. Though psychoanalysis is not a religion, it still exhibits many features of past religions, including reasoning about unreason, about the irrational forces we live with and cannot entirely control.

Where is language in this field of forces? Especially the language of the interpreter as it takes for its subject other language constructs, presenting themselves as textual, like literary artifacts, or presenting themselves as a mysterious code belonging also to another medium, like hysterical symptoms or dream images. It is not necessary to overemphasize what we have learned about language since Freud and again since Lacan. The discourse of the analyst remains within the affective sphere of the discourse it interprets; it is as much a supplement as a clarification; and instead of an asceptic and methodological purism, which isolates the interpreter's language from the so-called object-language, creating in effect two monologues, we have to risk a dialogue in which our own often unconscious assumptions are challenged. 'The analysand's discourse,' André Green has written, 'is a stream of words that . . . the analyst cannot shut up in a box. The analyst runs after the analysand's words.'

In psychoanalysis especially, because it involves transference and countertransference, because it puts the interpreter, not only the text or person interpreted, at risk, this exchange of words does not always lead to an urbane dialogue. The word *dialogue*, in fact, is deceptive, for there may be, in this situation, more imposition and resistance, more 'crisscross' or crazy connections than when Dostoyevsky or, for that matter, Hitchcock, gets strangers together on a train. The Romance of the Railroad penetrates the interpreter's discourse, which hurtles toward its uncertain destination along a branching track of words with exotic expectations, mysterious switches, and—hopefully—good brakes.

To understand Freud's power as an interpreter (whether or not we agree with his findings or their claim to be scientific) it is necessary to read him with an attention solicited by his own immense culture, in which a sensitivity to language stimulated by literature played its part. I begin, therefore, by taking a sample from *The Interpretation of Dreams* to give it a close, literary reading. It is equally important, however, to gauge the transferability of Freud's interpretative method. The second half of my essay, then, will take up a nonanalytic text, a poem of Wordsworth's, and do two things: see it in a Freudian context, but also see Freud in its context.

It is a striking truth that literary analysis, like Freud's dream analysis, does no more and no less than disclose a life in images or words that has its own momentum. Ambiguities, overdetermined meanings, and strange linkages are more obvious than the coherent design they seem to flee from. 'My thoughts crowd each other to death,' Coleridge wrote. He finds himself in the grip of what he named 'the streamy nature of association'; in his Notebooks, especially, not only the dreams he puts down but also his speculative etymologies and related word chains accelerate into a futile 'science of the grotesque' (a phrase I take from Kenneth Burke's fine essay on Freud, in *The Philosophy of Literary Form*). But many writers acknowledge explicitly an experience similar to that of 'racing thoughts.' 'I often felt the onset of madness,' Flaubert confesses. 'There was a whirl of ideas and images in my poor mind, and my consciousness, my ego, seemed to be foundering like a ship in a storm. . . . I played with fantasy and madness, as Mithridates did with his poisons.' Or Keats, in a lighthearted vein: 'I must be quaint and free of Tropes and figures—I must play my draughts as I please. . . . Have you not seen a Gull, an orc, a Sea Mew, or any thing to bring this Line to a proper length, and also fill up this clear part; that like the Gull I may *dip*—I hope, not out of sight—and also, like a Gull I hope to be lucky in a good sized fish—This crossing a letter is not without its associations—for chequer work leads us naturally to a Milkmaid, a Milkmaid to Hogarth Hogarth to Shakespeare Shakespeare to Hazlitt—Hazlitt to Shakespeare and thus by merely pulling an apron string we set a pretty peal of Chimes at work.'

'A pretty peal of Chimes. . . .' Keats' insouciance puts us at an equal distance from the purely formal character of rhyme, as it suggests a flirtatious harmony and the tongue-tying phenomenon of clang associations. When Freud encouraged 'free' association in himself and his patients, he simply took the burden of self-judgment away, so that this inner speech, to which Flaubert and Keats allude, might be fully disclosed. *The Interpretation of Dreams* remains a disconcerting work because of this: Freud's interpretive method is not as separate as one might expect from the dream which is its object. Both dream and dream analysis are streamy, associative structures. The only difference between reported dream and analytic commentary is that the dream is more elliptical in the way it passes from sentence to sentence or image to image. Freud's interpretation fills up these ellipses or 'absences' in the dream; as Keats too is aware of having to fill in spaces by moving figures across a chequer board without being checked.

Quite often too, like Keats, Freud introduces explanatory material that branches off with a digressive life of its own—especially when that material is a name. An example will be helpful here. In trying to understand a dream about three women, one of them making dumplings (*Knödel*), Freud recalls the ending of the first novel he had ever read, in which the hero goes mad and keeps calling out the names of the three women who had brought him the greatest happiness— and sorrow. One was called *Pélagie*; and by a path at least as eccentric as that of Keats, the three women become the three Fates; *Pélagie* becomes a bridge to the word 'plagiarize,' which then also throws light on *Knödel* as a name (the name of a person) rather than a common noun. Suddenly everything alliterates or 'chimes.' Here is a portion of Freud's analysis from the section on 'Infantile Material as a Source of Dreams' in chapter 5.

> In connection with the three women I thought of the Fates who spin the destiny of man, and I knew that one of the three women—the inn-hostess in the dream—was the mother who gives life, and furthermore (as in my own case) gives the living creature its first nourishment. Love and hunger, I reflected, meet at a woman's breast. . . . So they really were Fates that I found in the kitchen when I went into it—as I had so often done in my childhood when I was hungry, while my mother, standing by the fire, had admonished me that I must wait till dinner was ready.—And now for the dumplings—the *Knödel!* One at least of my teachers at the University—and precisely the one to whom I owe my historical knowledge . . . would infallibly be reminded by *Knödel* of a person against whom he had been obliged to take legal action for *plagiarizing* his writing. The idea of plagiarizing . . . clearly led me to the second part of the dream, in which I was treated as though I were the thief who had for some time carried on his business of stealing overcoats in the lecture-rooms. I had written down the word 'plagiarizing' without thinking about it, because it just occured to me; but now I noticed that it could form a bridge [*Brücke*] between different pieces of the dream's manifest content. A chain of associations (*Pélagie—plagiarizing—plagiostomes* or sharks . . .—a *fish's swimming-bladder*), connected the old novel with the case of *Knödel* and with the overcoats, which clearly referred to implements used in sexual technique.

This is not the end: a further train of thoughts immediately takes off from the 'honored name of Brücke,' leading ('as though the need to set up forced connections regarded *nothing* as sacred') to the memory of Fleischl (*Fleisch:* meat), a second respected teacher, linked to Freud's experiments with cocaine in what he calls the *Latin Kitchen* (the dispensary or pharmacy).

In literary studies we often ask what the genre of a work may be. It is a question raised when the reader confronts a new or puzzling form; and it certainly arises when we read *The Interpretation of Dreams*. It is hard to call the book a work of science, and leave it at that. Often the fugual connections and especially the word chains are not furnished by the manifest content of the dream: though they may belong to the dream thoughts they do so only by virtue of an analysis which is interpolative and like an elaborate joke. One is reminded of Freud's own aphorism: 'The realm of jokes knows no limits.' What, then, is the genre of this book?

My quotation from the Knödel dream suggests that Freud finds a strange and original way to write a *Confession*. I mean an autobiography that lays bare whatever it may be—certainly sexual wishes, guilt feelings, and social envy, as well as the infantile emotions that spur the quest for scientific fame. *The Double Helix*[a] is nothing compared to Freud in disclosing the *libido* of science. 'Freud's frankness,' Kenneth Burke wrote, 'is no less remarkable by reason of the fact that he had perfected a method for being frank. . . . what for him could fall within the benign category of observation could for [others] fall only within its malign counterpart, spying.'

It is the reversal of malign into benign *and vice versa*, which risked, as Burke saw, a 'drastic self-ostracizing act—the charting of the relations between ecclesia and cloaca.' Freud's *Confession*, entitled *The Interpretation of Dreams*, even transcends Augustine's and Rousseau's, because in addition to a very moving if oblique narrative of self-justification, it launches an extraordinary mode of reading, one that is both wilder and more daring in its very rage for order than either rabbinic exegesis or the figural and typological method of the Church Fathers. Freud's way of interpreting dreams becomes a powerful hermeneutics, rivaling that of the great Western religions. Though his dreambook is an unlikely candidate for a Scripture—being, I have suggested, more like a Confession—it fashions a secular key out of phenomena that this same civilization had repressed by calling them sacred, then irrational, then trivial. Freud not only redeems this excluded mass from insignificance, he also introduces strange new *texts* for our considerations: texts neither literary nor Scriptural but whose discovery throws doubt on the transcription of all previous inner experience. Freud reveals much more than a code for the decipherment of dreams: he invents a new textuality by transcribing dreams in his own way. It is not just the dream which is important, but also the dream text. After Freud we all have Freudian dreams; that is, we report them that way—except for those chosen few who are Jungians.[b]

Psychoanalysis, then, creates new texts as well as transforming our understanding of those already received. Yet because the religious systems of the past also disseminated methods of interpretation that were radically revisionary, it is important to emphasize two features that distinguish psychoanalytic interpretation from these influential modes.

The first difference concerns the transactive relation of text and commentary. The dream text is not an object with Scriptural fixity. Scripture itself, of course, or the many books (*biblia*) we now call the Bible, had to be edited and fixed by a succession of interpretive communities. But Freud allows us to see the commentary entering the text, incorporating itself with the dream: what he called his self-analysis, working on dreams he had, so invests and supplements an orig-

[a] The title of a book by J. D. Watson, published in 1968, describing how he and Francis Crick succeeded in being the first scientists to elucidate the molecular structure of DNA.

[b] Carl Jung (1875–1961) was a protégé of Freud, but broke away from his master's teaching to found a rival school of analytical psychology.

inal version that it becomes less of an object and more of a series of linguistic relays that could lead anywhere—depending on the system of rails and who is doing the switching. The dream is like a sentence that cannot find closure. Freud keeps coming up with fragments of something already recounted, as well as adding meaning to meaning. This extreme indeterminacy, even if it was there in what we now call Scripture, is no longer available to us, despite suggestive residues of freedom in the early rabbis whose midrashim[c] exposed every inconsistency or gap in the sacred text, or who elicited new interpretations by changing speculatively the received voweling, the *nekudoth*.

A second feature that distinguishes psychoanalytic interpretation is its *kakangelic* rather than *evangelic* nature. I admit to coining this discordant word. The New Testament claims to bring good news, and reinterprets the Old Testament— that is, the Hebrew Bible—in the light of its faith. If the Gospels emphasize mankind's guilt, they also counter it by the possibility of salvation. But Freud brings bad (*kaka*) news about the psyche, and offers no cure except through the very activity—analysis—which reveals this news. 'A single Screw of Flesh / Is all that pins the Soul' Emily Dickinson wrote; and her homely metaphor keeps the hope open that on the other side of the 'Vail' or 'Gauze' of the body, her soul could enter into its freedom and see God or the loved one in full presence. Yet in Freud the 'Screw of Flesh' or *la chose genitale* (Charcot) cannot be totally sublimated, not even through the noncarnal conversation which psychoanalysis institutes. For it is precisely through this conversation that the patient becomes more aware of the 'mailed [maled] Nerve' as something—pin, penis, pen—without which there is no soul, no signification, good or bad.

The dream analysis I have previously cited reflects this *kakangelic* vision, this 'inverse Freudian piety toward the sinister' (to quote Philip Rieff). Knödl, Fleischl, and Brücke do not appear as proper names in the dream, yet Freud's interpolative commentary dwells on the dream's misuse of such names. He calls it 'a kind of childish naughtiness' and an act of retribution for witticisms made about his own name. He also mentions a mock-heroic verse written by Herder about Goethe. 'Der du von Göttern abstammst, von Gothen oder vom Kote' ('Thou who art the descendant of Gods or Goths or dung'), and he answers it in the name of Goethe by quoting from the latter's *Iphigenia:* 'So you too, divine figures, have turned to dust!' That Freud takes it on himself to answer Herder's quibble with a line of such pathos (it alludes to the death of many heroes during the siege of Troy) indicates something more than a regressive sensitivity about one's name. The dialogue of those two verses makes a little drama whose subject is the ambivalence that surrounds great men who have become ego ideals; and the ease with which their names can be profaned, dragged in the dust, causes Freud to balance Herder's childish punning with a compensatory impersonation. In *Totem and Taboo* the avoidance of the name of the dead in primitive societies, though more elaborately explained, still hinges on the same kind of envy or ambivalence. Freud has realized, in short, the profaning power of dreams; yet

[c] Midrash was a Jewish method of Scriptural exegesis which could entail revising or amplifying an original text.

not of dreams only, but of language as it allows that chiming to mock and madden anything sacred. He has to decide whether *Goethe* or *Kot*, ecclesia or cloaca, evangelism or kakangelism is to be the dominant trend of his commentary. It happens that two members of that strange trinity, Knödl, Fleischl, and Brücke, are sacred to Freud; yet the dream degrades them from proper to ordinary nouns. As ordinary nouns, however, they can become quiet conduits for the dream work; though the plot thickens when we ask what the dream work is seeking to reveal.

For the teaching of two of these men nourished Freud's scientific ambitions: they were among his male Fates. We do not learn particulars of what they taught him, since the dream is after something more universal. If we suppose that the dream conspires with Freud's wish that dream analysis be recognized as a science, then a hieratic form of discourse must appear, analogous to the hieroglyphs the dream itself presents. Yet the dream's mode of expression remains distinctly vernacular rather than hieratic—that is, without terms from the *Latin Kitchen*. While the language of the dream, then, forged in the real kitchen of women and dumplings, reaches for a mysterious vernacular, or mother tongue, the chain of associations characterizing the language of the interpreter fails to transform the dream text into the 'purer' discourse or sacred instrument of the scientist: his white overcoat or sublime condom.

Freud is brought back to his childlike if ambivalent veneration for Brücke, Fleischl, etc. He also experiences a related anxiety, that he may be a plagiarist like Knödl and so must clear his name. The dream discloses what infantile jealousies still prop the scientific project; but part of that project—not analyzed by Freud—is the ideal of a flawless discourse, a Latin of the intellect, a dream-redeeming sacred commentary. *Not the dream is holy but the power of the interpretation as it methodizes and universalizes itself.*

'Behold, the dreamer cometh.' That is said mockingly of Joseph in the Pentateuch; yet Joseph gains fame not as a dreamer but as a dream interpreter.[d] We glimpse in Freud the dreamer rising to fame not through vainglorious dreams but through the art or science of dream interpretation, which he called 'the royal road.'

The name 'Sigmund Freud' is indeed a misnomer. For in wrestling with the angel of the unconscious, with the evasive dream thoughts, Freud strips away so many layers of idealization, so many euphemistic formulas, that only wounded names are left. But through his unconsciousness-raising we learn what we are up against: profanation, defamation, self-slander, equivocation, distortion, ambivalence, displacement, repression, censorship. Freud neither curses nor blesses that hardwon knowledge; and so his greatness, finally, may be his moral style, that he neither palliates nor inculpates human nature.

From Freud I turn to Wordsworth, respecting his own statement that 'The poets were there before me.' My text is from the Lucy poems, a group of short lyrics on the death of a young girl, which is a motif that goes back to the Greek

[d] The story is told in Genesis of how Joseph, the son of Jacob, sold into slavery in Egypt by his brothers, won favour with the Pharoah by correctly interpreting the latter's dreams.

Anthology and evokes three highly charged themes: incompleteness, mourning, and memory.

A slumber did my spirit seal;
I had no human fears
She seemed a thing that could not feel
The touch of earthly years.

No motion has she now, no force;
She neither hears nor sees;
Rolled round in earth's diurnal course,
With rocks, and stones, and trees.

'A slumber did my spirit seal.' After that line one would expect a dream vision. The formula is, I fell asleep, and behold! Yet there is no vision, or not in the expected sense. The boundary between slumber and vision is elided. That the poet had no human fears, that he experienced a curious anesthesia vis-à-vis the girl's mortality or his own, may be what he names a slumber. As out of Adam's first sleep an Eve arose, so out of this sealed but not unconscious spirit a womanly image arises with the same idolatrous charm. Wordsworth's image seems to come from within; it is a delusive daydream, yet still a revision of that original vision.

There is, however, no sense of an eruption from the unconscious: brevity and condensation do not lead, as they do in dreams, to remarkable puns, striking figures, or deviant forms of speech. Nor is it necessary to be psychoanalytic to recognize that the trance is linked to an overidealization of the loved person. The second stanza, which reports that she has died, should, in that case, express disillusionment. Yet remarkably this does not occur: the poet does not exclaim or cry out. Both transitions, the passage from slumber to dream, and the breaking of the dream, are described without surprise or shock.

Is there nothing which betrays how deeply disturbing the fantasy may have been? Perhaps, if the emotion was strong, it is natural enough that the words should seek to understate and to seal the impression. There is, however, an uncanny *displacement* on the structural level that is consonant with what Freud calls the omnipotence of thoughts and a general overestimation of psychical acts attributed by him to primitive cultures and, in contemporary civilization, to art.

This displacement is, rhetorically speaking, also a transference: in the initial stanza, the poet is sealed in slumber; in the second that slumber has passed over, as if intensified, to the girl. She falls asleep forever; and her death is specifically portrayed as a quasi-immortality not unlike what his imagination has prematurely projected onto her. 'Rolled round in earth's diurnal course,' she indeed cannot 'feel / The touch of earthly years.' This subtle transfer, this metaphor as extended structure rather than punctual figure of speech, is anticipated by at least one local condensation. 'Human' in 'I had no human fears' (line 2) is a transferred epithet. The line should read: 'I had no such fears as would have come to me had I considered her a human—that is, mortal—being.' We do not know which way the transfer goes: from the girl to the poet or vice versa. And yet we *do* know:

surely the illusion took rise in the poet and is an error of the imagination. Yet Wordsworth leaves that illusion its moment of truth as if it were natural, and not in any way out of the ordinary. He does not take pains to demystify it. Nature has its own supernatural gleam, however evanescent it is.

The supernatural illusion preserves the girl from a certain kind of touch, 'of earthly years' in the first stanza, but in the second she is totally distanced. Coleridge surmised that the lyric was an imaginary epitaph for Wordsworth's sister, and F. W. Bateson seized on this to claim that 'A slumber' (and the Lucy poems as a whole) arose from incestuous emotions and expressed a death wish by the brother against the sister. The poem removes an object of love by moving it beyond touch. In all but one important respect it confirms Freud's analysis about the way neurotics evade reality. Freud shows how the whole world is eventually embargoed, put beyond touch or contact by a widening fear of contagion. The only difference is that in Wordsworth the whole world enters in the second stanza as an image with resonances that are more positive than sinister.

Wordsworth's poem, moreover, practically offers itself for inclusion in a section of the dreambook that contains Freud's most famous literary interpretation. In 'Dreams of the Death of Persons of whom the Dreamer is fond' (chapter 5) he discusses the story of Oedipus. We readily respond to the death of Oedipus, says Freud, 'because it might have been ours—because the oracle laid the same curse upon us before our birth as upon him.' That curse is understood to be an unconsciously fulfilled wish, a pattern we also suspect is present in 'A slumber.' But the question for literary criticism, even as it engages with psychoanalysis, is why such a wish, at once idealizing and deadly, and as if fulfilled in the second stanza, does not disturb the poet's language more. Even if the death did not occur except in idea, one might expect the spirit to awake, and to wonder what kind of deception it had practiced on itself. Yet though the poem can be said to approach muteness—if we interpret the blank between the stanzas as another elision, a *lesion* in fact—Wordsworth keeps speech going without a trace of guilty knowledge. The eyes of the spirit may be open, but the diction remains unperturbed.

I want to suggest that Wordsworth's curious yet powerful complacency is related to euphemism: not of the artificial kind, the substitution of a good word for a bad one, or the strewing of flowers on a corpse, but an earthly euphemism, as it were, a balm deriving from common speech, from its unconscious obliquity and inbuilt commitment to avoid silence. To call it euphemism may be inadequate, but the quality I point to resists overconsciousness and demystification.

It is generally the task of the critic to uncover euphemism in any sphere: literary, psychological, political. When Freud tells a patient the meaning of one of her flowery dreams, 'she quite lost her liking for it.' A kakangelic unmasking may be necessary, although not many would go as far as Kenneth Burke, who praised Freud's method as 'an interpretive sculpting in excrement' and put praise in action by suggesting we read Keats' 'Beauty is Truth, Truth Beauty' as 'Body is Turd, Turd Body.' What makes Wordsworth's poetry so difficult to psychoanalyze is its underlying and resistant euphemism, coterminous with ordinary language, and distinguished from the courtly and affected diction of the time.

Consider the word 'slumber' as such a euphemism. Then consider the entire second stanza as a paraphrase for 'she is dead.' The negative aspect of these phrases can be heightened. The 'slumber' may remind us of bewitchment or fascination, even of hypnosis. It could be a hypnoid state in which one hears voices without knowing it, or performs actions on the basis of these voices. In another Lucy poem, 'Strange fits of passion,' such automatism is strongly suggested, and a voice does intrude at the end in the form of an incomplete sentence that expresses, in context, a premonition, but in itself is more ambiguous: 'If Lucy should be dead!'

That we may be in the domain of voices is made more probable by the word 'passion' in 'Strange fits of passion': it meant an outcry under the impact of strong emotions. Yet to pursue this analysis would mean to go from the issue of euphemism to how language is a synthesis not only of sounds but of speech acts, and especially—if we look to infancy—of threats, promises, admonitions, yesses and nos that come to the child as ideas of reference in vocal form, even if (or because) not every word is understood. Such an analysis would also oblige us to explore the text of poetry as an undoing of that synthesis, or a partial recovery of the elements behind the deceptive neutrality of language. Ordinary speech, from this perspective, is a form of sleep-walking, the replication of internalized phrases or commands without conscious effect; poetic speech is an exposure of that condition, a return to a sense of language as virtually alive—in any case with enough feeling to delay our passage from words to things. Speech re-enters an original zone of stress and inhibition and becomes precarious.

That precariousness is both acknowledged and limited by Wordsworth's euphemism. The second stanza of 'A slumber,' unlike the end of 'Strange fits,' does not cry out: as a periphrasis for 'she is dead' it amplifies and even embellishes that reluctant phrase. It is hard to think of the lyric as a stark epitaph skirting aphasia. And though the traumatic or mortifying event may occasion the euphemism, it cannot be its cause. We must find a 'feeding source' (to use one of the poet's own metaphors) elsewhere; and we can find it only in the other threat to speech: the near-ecstasy depicted in the previous stanza. A common source of inarticulate or mute behavior, such ecstacy, whatever its nature, carries over into the second stanza's euphemia.

Epitaphs, of course, are conventionally associated with consoling and pleasant words. Here, however, not all the words are consoling. They approach a negative that could foreclose the poem: 'No ... no ... Neither ... Nor. ...' Others even show Wordsworth's language penetrated by an inappropriate subliminal punning. So 'diurnal' (line 7) divides into 'die' and 'urn,' and 'course' may recall the older pronunciation of 'corpse.' Yet these condensations are troublesome rather than expressive; the power of the second stanza resides predominantly in the euphemistic displacement of the word *grave* by an image of *gravitation* ('Rolled round in earth's diurnal course'). And though there is no agreement on the tone of this stanza, it is clear that a subvocal word is uttered without being written out. It is a word that rhymes with 'fears' and 'years' and 'hears,' but which is closed off by the very last syllable of the poem: 'trees.' Read 'tears,' and the animating, cosmic metaphor comes alive, the poet's lament echoes through nature as in pastoral elegy. 'Tears,' however, must give way to what is written, to a dull yet definitive sound, the anagram 'trees.'

Pastoral elegy, in which rocks, woods, and streams are called upon to mourn the death of a person, or to echo the complaint of a lover, seems too extravagant a genre for this chastely fashioned inscription. Yet the muted presence of the form reminds us what it means to be a nature poet. From childhood on, as the autobiographical *Prelude* tells us, Wordsworth was aware of 'unknown modes of being' and of strange sympathies emanating from nature. He was haunted by an animistic universe that seemed to stimulate, share, and call upon his imagination. The Lucy poems evoked a nature spirit in human form, perhaps modeled after his sister, and the forerunner of Cathy Linton in *Wuthering Heights*. It makes no sense to suppose a death wish unless we link it to the ecstatic feelings in this poetry. Yet where do these feelings come from? Wordsworth does not actually say he projected his starry emotions upon the girl. It is, rather, *our* habit of giving priority to the psychological state of the writer, *our* inability to consider his euphoria as a contagious identification with the girl, that makes us assume it is a dream and a delusion. For to think otherwise would return us to the world of pastoral elegy or even to a magical universe, with currents of sympathy running along esoteric channels—the very world described as primitive in *Totem and Taboo*.

Reading Freud through Wordsworth now brings us closer to a critique of Freud. The discovery of the role played in mental illness by large-scale wishful thinking, by omnipotence of thought, is a proven achievement. Yet Freud's description of the thought process of primitives and their licensed contemporary relic, the artist, is for once not reflective or dialectical enough. Freud wants so badly to place psychotherapy on a firm, scientific foundation that he exempts himself from an overestimation of psychical acts. At the same time he has made it hard for *us* to value interpretations not based on the priority of a psychological factor. Animism is accepted as a functional belief only in fiction—in Jensen's[e] *Gradiva* or Wordsworth's poems or *Wuthering Heights*—but is considered dysfunctional in terms of mental health unless demystified by psychoanalysis. Perhaps the decisive matter here is not a compulsion to demystify (to be kakangelic) but a failure to draw a certain type of experience into that special dialogue established by psychoanalysis. For the problem with art as with nonclassical anthropological data is that interpretation cannot find enough associations for them. Psychoanalysis distrusts, with good reason, the appearance of autonomy in such artifacts, even while recognizing their force, which is then labeled 'primitive.'

Yet Freud could acknowledge, in passing, that his persistent, even obsessive, mode of interpretation might share the delusional character of superstitions it sought to analyze and dispel. He himself may have suffered from a fear of contagion that placed, as Jacques Lacan and others have claimed, too many

[e] Johannes Vilhelm Jensen (1873–1950), Danish novelist, essayist and poet.

protective barriers between his hermeneutics and religious hermeneutics. Those barriers are coming down, or do not seem as impenetrable as they once were. Indeed, in the first part of my talk, I suggested some analogies that made religion and psychoanalysis enemy brothers. But I can be somewhat more specific, in conclusion, about what Freud saw yet tried to close out.

He was always distrustful and demystifying towards eudemonic*f* feelings, the kind that Wordsworth expressed in 'A slumber.' He considered them a 'thalassal regression' (to use Ferenczi's phrase)*g*, an attempt to regain an inertial state; the nirvana of preoedipal or undifferentiated being. Wordsworth's attitude was very different. In all his most interesting work he describes a developmental impasse centering on eudemonic sensations experienced in early childhood and associated with nature. Whether beautiful or frightening, they sustain and nourish him as intimations of immortality; and though Wordsworth can be called the first ego psychologist, the first careful observer of the growth of a mind, he shows the strength and usurpation of those ecstatic memories as they threaten the maturing poet who must respect their drive. If there is a death wish in the Lucy poems, it is insinuated by nature itself and asks lover or growing child not to give up earlier yearnings—to die rather than become an ordinary mortal.

This developmental impasse is quite clear in the present poem. Divided into two parts, separated formally by a blank and existentially by a death, the epitaph does not record a disenchantment. The mythic girl dies, but that word seems to wrong her. Her star-like quality is maintained despite her death, for the poet's sense of her immutability deepens by reversal into an image of *participation mystique* with the planet earth. There is loss, but there is also a calculus of gain and loss which those two stanzas weigh like two sides of a balance. Their balancing point is the impasse I have mentioned: such a death could seem better than dying into the light of common day. Yet to think only *that* is to make immutability of such value that human life is eclipsed by it. Ideas of pre-existence or afterlife arise. My analysis has tried to capture a complex state of affairs that may resemble religious experiences or pathological states but which Wordsworth sees as an imaginative constant, ordinary and incurable. For those who need more closure in interpretation, who wish to know exactly what the poet felt, I can only suggest a phrase from his famous 'Ode: Intimations of Immortality from Recollections of Early Childhood.' The meanest flower, he writes, can give him 'thoughts that do often lie too deep for tears.' The girl has become such a thought.

Yet even here we meet a euphemism once more. Naming something 'a thought too deep for tears': is that not a remarkable periphrasis for the inability to grieve? This inability seems to be a strength rather than a weakness if we take the figure literally. 'Too deep for tears' suggests a place—a mental place—beyond fits of passion or feelings, as if Wordsworth desired that grave immunity. Yet to call the

---

f A eudemon is a benevolent spirit or demon.

g 'Thalassal' means: pertaining to the state of marine life. Sandor Ferenczi was an associate and protégé of Freud who eventually quarrelled with him. His phrase appears to refer to a reversal of the evolutionary process.

words euphemistic is to acknowledge at the same time that they are so affecting that mourning is not absent but continued in a different mode. The work of writing seems to have replaced the work of mourning. Is there a link, then, between writing and grieving, such that writing can be shown to assist those Herculean psychic labors Freud described for us, whose aim is to detach us from the lost object and reattach us to the world?

My main concern has been to understand yet delimit Freud's kakangelic mode of interpretation. Wordsworth enabled me to do this by showing that euphemism can be an ordinary rather than artificial aspect of language, especially when the work of mourning is taking place, which is pretty much all the time. I have argued that this euphemism cannot be demystified because it is not simply a figure of speech covering up naked truth. Looking closely at a poem by Wordsworth reveals a far more complicated situation. The strongest euphemisms in Wordsworth are also the most naturalized; they seem to belong to language rather than being imposed on it. They are not in the service of evading reality or putting the best face on things. They have an energy, a force of their own, one which counters a double threat to speech: expectedly, that which comes from loss; but unexpectedly, that which comes from ecstasy, even if it is a remembered ecstasy, and so touched by loss. I have sometimes talked of euphemia rather than euphemism, both because we are dealing with a feature basic to language, and not simply to one poet's use of language; and also because the aphasia it circumscribes remains perceptible. Wordsworth's euphemia, in short, is nourished by sources in language or the psyche we have not adequately understood. They bring us back to an awareness of how much sustaining power language has, even if our individual will to speak and write is assaulted daily by the most trivial as well as traumatic events.

This sustaining power of language is not easily placed, however, on the side of goodness or love (eros) rather than death. Writing has an impersonal, even impersonating quality which brings the poet close to the dead 'whose names are in our lips,' to quote Keats. *Personare* meant, originally, to 'speak through' another, usually by way of an ancestral mask, which made the speaker a medium or an actor in a drama in which the dead renewed their contact with the living.

It is not surprising, therefore, that there should be a hint of the involuntary or mechanical in stanza 2 of 'A slumber': a hint of the indifference to which the girl's difference is reduced, and which, however tragic it may be, obeys a law that supports the stability a survivor's speech requires. 'O blessed machine of language,' Coleridge once exclaimed; this very phrase is symptomatic of the euphemia without which speech would soon cease to be, or turn into its feared opposite, an eruptive cursing or sputtering as in Tourette's syndrome. Coleridge has to bless the machine *as* a machine; yet his blessing is doubly euphemistic, for he knew too well what the machine could do in its unblessed aspect, as an uncontrollable stream of associations which coursed through him by day and especially by night.

It is here we link up once more with Freud, who created a new hermeneutics by charting compulsive and forced connections which 'regarded *nothing* as sacred.' Someone said of a typical lecture by Emerson that 'it had no connection, save in God.' Freud's kakangelic method removes all vestiges of that final clause. The recovered dream thoughts have no connections save in the negative fact that their capacity for profanation is without limit. All other connections are the result of a secondary process extending from the dream work's disguises and displacements to more conscious revisions. At times, therefore, the manifest dream content may appear saner than an interpretation that reverses the dream's relatively euphemistic bearing or disintegrates its discursive structure. Instead of completing dreamtexts, or by extension literary texts (or, like Jung, encouraging their synthesis), Freud makes them less complete, less fulfilling. The more interpretation, it seems, the less closure.

But did Freud himself regard nothing as sacred? I have already suggested that if the dream is unholy, and is shown to be so by the interpretation, the power of that interpretation as it methodizes and universalizes itself is something very near to holy. One wonders how else Freud could have continued his work without falling mute, without being overcome by the bad news he brought. The dream peculiar to Freud, as interpreter and scientist, a dream which survives all self-analysis, is of a purified language that remains uncontaminated by its materials, that neither fulfills nor represses an all-too-human truth. I hope Freud's shade will understand this parting remark as a blessing on the only scientist I have ever been able to read.

26 *Juliet Mitchell*

Juliet Mitchell (b. 1940) was born in New Zealand but grew up in England and read English at Oxford University. She taught English at the universities of Leeds and Reading, but resigned in 1970 to become a freelance writer, occasionally attached to American and Australian universities. In the 1960s she was actively involved in politics, and, like many members of the British intellectual left at this period, was much influenced by Louis Althusser's reading of Marx, especially his redefinition of ideology as 'the way we live ourselves in the world' rather than as an epiphenomenon of the economic base of society. Her essay, 'Women: the Longest Revolution', contributed to *New Left Review* in 1966, heralded the emergence of a politically radical feminism; and when the Women's Liberation Movement gathered momentum a few years later Juliet Mitchell was one of its most powerful and controversial voices in the English-speaking world. While many of her sisters reviled Freud as a spokesman for patriarchy, Juliet Mitchell saw the usefulness of Freud's work, as re-read by Lacan and other post-structuralist theorists, in exploring 'the question of the subject' from a feminist standpoint. In 1974 she published *Psychoanalysis and Feminism*, and subsequently trained at the Institute of Psychoanalysis. She now works as a psychoanalyst in London.

'Femininity, Narrative and Psychoanalysis' is the transcript of a lecture delivered to a conference on Narrative held in Australia in 1972. Though brief, it has the advantage of bringing together within the limits of a single argument Juliet Mitchell's four primary interests: English Literature, politics, psychoanalysis and feminism. The appealing directness and lucidity of its expository style owes something to the occasion for which it was originally produced, but is also representative of Juliet Mitchell's work in general, and of the British (as compared to the European or American) tradition of critical and theoretical discourse. 'Feminism, Narrative and Psychoanalysis' is reprinted here from Juliet Mitchell's *Women: The Longest Revolution. Essays on Feminism, Literature and Psychoanalysis* (1984).

CROSS-REFERENCES: 5. Lacan
                               7. Bakhtin
                           17. Cixous
                           20. Showalter

Femininity, narrative and psychoanalysis

After some initial remarks on narrative in psychoanalytic practice I shall say a little about women in the early history of the novel, and turn from that to psychoanalytic theory; finally I shall illustrate some of my concerns with reference to *Wuthering Heights*.

As everybody knowns, psychoanalysis is a talking cure. Obviously the analyst is male or female, the patient is male or female. If, as we frequently hear, language itself is phallocentric,[a] what happens within the psychoanalytic practice? If language is phallocentric, what is a woman patient doing when she is speaking? What is a woman analyst doing when she is listening and speaking back? These stark questions are relevant to the type of work one can do on a literary text.

Psychoanalysts, at one level, are hearing and retelling histories. The patient comes with a story of his or her own life. The analyst listens; through an association something intrudes, disrupts, offers the 'anarchic carnival'[b] back into that history, the story won't quite do, and so the process starts again. You go back, and you make a new history. Simultaneously with that, the analyst, in analysing his or her own countertransference, performs the same process on himself or herself, listens to a history, asks, 'Why am I hearing it as that?': something from the analyst's own associations disrupts, erupts into that narrative—the analyst asks a question from a new perspective, and the history starts all over again.

I bring this up here because I think it relates to questions about the role of carnival, about the role of disruption. What can you do but disrupt a history and re-create it as another history? Of course, you have multiple histories, though you can only live within one at a time.

I want to look very briefly at one kind of history: that preeminent form of literary narrative, the novel. Roughly speaking, the novel starts with autobiographies written by women in the seventeenth century. There are several famous men novelists, but the vast majority of early novels were written by large numbers of women. These writers were trying to establish what critics today call the 'subject in process'. What they were trying to do was to create a history from a state of flux, a flux in which they were feeling themselves in the process of becoming women within a new bourgeois society. They wrote novels to describe that process—novels which said: 'Here we are: women. What are our lives to be about? Who are we? Domesticity, personal relations, personal intimacies, stories . . .' In the dominant social group, the bourgeoisie, that is essentially what a woman's life was to become under capitalism. The novel is that creation by the woman of the woman, or by the subject who is in the process of becoming woman, of woman under capitalism. Of course it's not a neat homogeneous construction: of course there are points of disruption within it; of course there are points of autocriticism within it. *Wuthering Heights*, for example, is a high point of auto-criticism of the novel from within the novel. I shall discuss it soon in that light.

As any society changes its social structure, changes its economic base, artefacts are re-created within it. Literary forms arise as one of the ways in which changing subjects create themselves as subjects within a new social context. The novel is the prime example of the way women start to create themselves as social subjects under bourgeois capitalism—create themselves as a category: women. The novel remains a bourgeois form. Certainly there are also working-class novels, but the dominant form is that represented by the woman within the bourgeoisie. This means that when contemporary Anglo-Saxon feminist critics turn to women writers, resurrect the forgotten texts of these women novelists, they are, in one sense, being completely conformist to a bourgeois tradition. There is nothing wrong with that, it is an important and impressive tradition. We have to know where women are, why women have to write the novel, the story of their own domesticity, the story of their own seclusion within the home and the possibilities and impossibilities provided by that.

This tradition has been attacked by critics such as Julia Kristeva[c] as 'the discourse of the hysteric'. I believe that it has to be the discourse of the hysteric. The woman novelist must be an hysteric. Hysteria is the woman's simultaneous acceptance and refusal of the organisation of sexuality under patriarchal capitalism. It is simultaneously what a woman can do both to be feminine and to refuse femininity, within patriarchal discourse. And I think that is exactly what the novel is; I do not believe there is such a thing as female writing, a 'woman's voice'. There is the hysteric's voice which is *the woman's masculine language* (one has to speak 'masculinely' in a phallocentric world) talking about feminine experience. It's both simultaneously the woman novelist's refusal of the woman's world—she is, after all, a novelist—and her construction from within a masculine world of that woman's world. It touches on both. It touches, therefore, on the importance of bisexuality.

I will say something very briefly about the psychoanalytical theories behind this position of the woman writer who must speak the discourse of the hysteric, who both refuses and is totally trapped within femininity. Then I'll lead on to some of the things that were said earlier about how to disrupt this.

There is much current interest in re-reading Freud in terms of the moment at which sexual division is produced within society: the moment of the castration complex, the moment when the heterogeneously sexual, polymorphously perverse, carnivalesque child has imposed on it the divisions of 'the law'; the one law, the law of patriarchy, the mark of the phallus. At that moment two sexes are psycho-

[c] See headnote on Julia Kristeva, p. 229 above.

logically created as the masculine and the not-masculine. At the point in which the phallus is found to be missing in the mother, masculinity is set up as the norm, and femininity is set up as what masculinity is not. What is not there in the mother is what is relevant here; that is what provides the context for language. The expression which fills the gap is, perforce, phallocentric.

In Lacanian thinking this is called the moment of the symbolic. The symbolic is the point of organisation, the point where sexuality is constructed as meaning, where what was heterogeneous, what was not symbolised, becomes organised, becomes created round these two poles, masculine and not-masculine: feminine.

What has gone before can be called the pre-Oedipal, the semiotic, the carnivalesque, the disruptive. Now one can take two positions in relation to that. Either the pre-divided child, the heterogenous child, the pre-Oedipal child, exists with its own organisation, an organisation of polyvalence, of polyphony. Or alternatively that very notion of heterogeneity, of bisexuality, of pre-Oedipality, of union in a dyadic possibility of child with mother, that image of oneness and heterogeneity as two sides of the same coin, is, in fact, provided by the law, by the symbolic law itself. The question to me has a political dimension to it. If you think that the heterogeneous pre-Oedipal polyvalent world is a separate structure in its own right, then the law is disruptable, the carnival can be held on the church steps. But if this is not the case, if the carnival and the church do not exist independently of each other, the pre-Oedipal and the Oedipal are not separate, discrete states—if, instead, the Oedipal with the castration complex is what defines the pre-Oedipal, then the only way you can challenge the church, challenge both the Oedipal and its pre-Oedipal, is from within an *alternative symbolic universe*. You cannot choose the imaginary, the semiotic, the carnival as an alternative to the symbolic, as an alternative to the law. It is set up by the law precisely as its own ludic space, its own area of imaginary alternative, but not as a symbolic alternative. So that politically speaking, it is only the symbolic, a new symbolism, a new law, that can challenge the dominant law.

Now this does have relevance for the two alternative types of feminist literary criticism which exist today. It was suggested in another paper at this conference that this area of the carnival can also be the area of the feminine. I don't think so. It is just what the patriarchal universe defines as the feminine, the intuitive, the religious, the mystical, the playful, all those things that have been assigned to women—the heterogeneous, the notion that women's sexuality is much more one of a whole body, not so genital, not so phallic. It is not that the carnival cannot be disruptive of the law; but it disrupts only within the terms of that law.

This suggests a criticism of the French school associated with Kristeva, and to me it explains why that school is essentially apolitical. One needs to ask why Kristeva and her colleagues, while producing very interesting ideas, choose exclusively masculine texts and quite often proto-fascist writings as well. Disruption itself can be radical from the right as easily as from the left. This type of disruption is contained within the patriarchal symbolic. To me this is the problem.

I shall just mention some things about *Wuthering Heights* here so that we can use it if we like as a text on which to hang some ideas. I do not want to offer a psychoanalytic reading of this novel; I want to use *Wuthering Heights* simply to illustrate some of the points that I have tried to make here.

Emily Brontë is not writing a carnivalesque query to the patriarchal order; she is clearly working within the terms of a language which has been defined as phallocentric. Yet she is, through a kind of irony, posing questions about patriarchal organisation, and I'll sketch in some of the questions that I think are asked by the novel. First, who tells the story? Emily Brontë's manuscript was stolen from her and presented to a publisher by her sister, Charlotte. It was eventually published under a male pseudonym: Ellis Bell. The author is a woman, writing a private novel; she is published as a man, and acquires some fame and notoriety. She uses two narrators—a man, Lockwood, and a woman, the nurse, Nelly Dean. The whole novel is structured through those two narrators. Lockwood is a parody of the romantic male lover. He is set up as a foppish gentleman from the town who thinks he loves all the things the romantic gentleman is supposed to love, such as solitude, or a heart of gold beneath a fierce exterior. These things are criticised from within the novel, particularly through the character of Isabella, who thinks that Heathcliff is a dark, romantic Gothic hero who will prove to be the true gentleman beneath all his cruelty.

The story of Catherine and Heathcliff is a story of bisexuality, the story of the hysteric. Catherine's father had promised he would bring her back a whip from his visit to Liverpool. Instead he picks up a gypsy child who is fatherless, who never has had and never will have a father's name, who is given just one name: Heathcliff, the name of a brother of Catherine's who had died in infancy. Catherine looks in her father's pocket, finds the whip broken; instead of this whip she gets a brother/lover: Heathcliff.

Heathcliff is what Cathy wants all the rest of her life. She, in fact, makes the conventional feminine choice and marries somebody with whom she cannot be fully united—Edgar Linton. Edgar provides only an illusion of complementarity. I do not mean that they do not have a sexual relation; they have a child whose birth in one sense—the most unimportant—causes Catherine's death. The person that Catherine wants to be 'one' with is Heathcliff. Breaking the incest taboo, she says, 'I *am* Heathcliff, he's more myself than I am.' And Heathcliff says the same of Catherine. Each is the bisexual possibility of the other one, evoking a notion of oneness which is the reverse side of the coin of diverse heterogeneity. This type of 'oneness' can only come with death. Catherine dies; she haunts Heathcliff for twenty years, which is the date when the novel opens: it opens with Lockwood, who is given Heathcliff's dream, thinking (because he is the parodic romantic figure) that he can also get oneness. Heathcliff himself waits the whole stretch of the novel to have his own dream, which is to get back to Catherine. He dies getting back to her. 'Oneness' is the symbolic notion of what happens before the symbolic; it is death and has to be death. The choices for the woman within the novel, within fiction, are either to survive by making the hysteric's ambiguous choice into a femininity which doesn't work (marrying Edgar) or to go for oneness and unity, by suffering death (walking the moors as a ghost with Heathcliff).

I want to end with my beginning, and with a question. I think the novel arose as the form in which women had to construct themselves as women within new social structures; the woman novelist is necessarily the hysteric wanting to repudiate the symbolic definition of sexual difference under patriarchal law, unable to do so because without madness we are all unable to do so. Writing from within that position can be conformist (Mills and Boon romantic novels) or it can be critical (*Wuthering Heights*). I think the novel starts at a point where society is in a state of flux, when the subject is in the process of becoming a woman (or man) as today we understand that identity. If we are today again talking about a type of literary criticism, about a type of text where the subject is not formed under a symbolic law, but within what is seen as a heterogeneous area of the subject-in-process, I would like to end with asking a question: *in the process of becoming what?* I do not think that we can live as human subjects without in some sense taking on a history; for us, it is mainly the history of being men or women under bourgeois capitalism. In deconstructing that history, we can only construct other histories. What are we in the process of becoming?

27 Colin MacCabe

Colin MacCabe (b. 1949) has taught at the Universities of Cambridge and Strathclyde, and at present divides his time between Pittsburgh, where he is a part-time Professor of English, and London, where he is Head of Production at the British Film Institute.

Colin MacCabe has a special place in the history of British responses to European structuralism and post-structuralism. As an undergraduate at Cambridge he collaborated with Stephen Heath and Christopher Prendergast on a little book called *Signs of the Times* (1971) which enthusiastically introduced to English readers the ideas of Roland Barthes, Jacques Derrida, Julia Kristeva and other Parisian luminaries. A few years later, he became a contributing editor of the BFI journal *Screen*, which, in its efforts to combine Althusserian Marxism with structuralist semiotics in the analysis of film, became perhaps the most important medium in Britain for the exploration and dissemination of Continental European theory in the 1970s. During this period MacCabe formulated an influential, if somewhat reductive, concept of the 'classic realist text', as that in which an authorial and authoritarian 'metalanguage' judges and controls all the other discourses in the text—a practice which the experimental modernist text subverts. The idea informs his approach to Joyce in *James Joyce and the Revolution of the Word*, published in 1980.

The denial of tenure to MacCabe by the Cambridge English Faculty, in the same year, became something of a *cause célèbre*, attracting the attention of the mass media, and polarizing attitudes to 'theory' far beyond the boundaries of Cambridge. MacCabe himself went to a Chair at Strathclyde University, where he instituted innovatory programmes in literary linguistics and media studies.

'Language, Linguistics and the Study of Literature' was first delivered as a paper in 1979, and is reprinted here from MacCabe's collection, *Theoretical Essays: film, linguistics, literature* (1985). The essay reflects a tempering of the somewhat dogmatic radicalism of his early work, and a move towards a *rapprochement* between post-structuralist theory and historical scholarship. But his insistence that literary discourse must be seen in relation to contemporary non-literary discourse, and that 'the description and specification of these discourses will never be purely linguistic but will necessitate an account of the institutional sites of language in use', suggests that his priorities are ultimately political, in a sense generally characteristic of contemporary British critical theory. MacCabe is also the author of a study of the French film director *Godard* (1981) and editor of *The Talking Cure: essays in psychoanalysis and language* (1981).

Language, linguistics and the study of literature

If one believes that genesis determines structure, a proposition which a linguist would be likely to dissent from although it is a common premise of literary criticism, then it should be obvious that the two disciplines cannot be considered separately. For if we look back to the first recognisable beginnings of linguistics, we find that they take place in the context of an attempt to establish and comment on literary texts. The scholars of Alexandria in the second century before Christ were motivated in their linguistic enquiry by the changes in the Greek language that had occurred since the literary masterpieces of fifth century Athens had been written. These changes in the language made it difficult to establish what Aeschylus or Sophocles had originally written and what had been interpolated later as an apparently obvious correction necessitated by linguistic change. It was in the context of this practical difficulty, rendered much more acute by the fact that the possibility of historical change in a language was not recognised, and within the theoretical framework provided by the controversy as to whether the basic principle of language was analogy or anomaly, that Dionysos Thrax produced his grammar of Greek. This grammar was predominantly a morphology that set up word-classes. Given that his work was intended as the basis for the establishment of uncorrupted texts, it is unsurprising that its concerns were heavily normative.

If Thrax's efforts were preceded by the linguistic enquiries of Plato, Aristotle and, more valuably, of the Stoics, it is, nevertheless, the case that the vocabulary of cases, tenses and word-classes[1] with which we are familiar is inherited from the Alexandrian scholars of the second century before Christ. Of course, linguistics is not simply grammar. Questions of etymology and phonetics are contemporaneous with the research into grammatical organisation. But it was not until the eighteenth century that etymology was to escape from its determination by concerns extraneous to the systematic organisation of language, an escape that phonetics had made a century earlier.[2]

It is Thrax's grammar which institutes the study of systematic differences in language which is the hallmark of linguistics, even if these systematic differences were given a justification in terms of meaning which weighed heavy on the investigation of the vernacular languages of Europe up until this century and, arguably, weigh heavy still. For example, the distinct inflections of the Latin and Greek verb enable one to refer to distinct tenses. However, these formal differences are interpreted in terms of a particular temporal order and it is this order which is then used to classify other languages even where there is no morphological basis for such an order. The most evident example of this is the classification of a future tense in English. There is no distinct inflection of the verb which expresses actions as taking place in the future and although it is evident that English offers a variety of ways to relate actions to the future, it is arguably preferable to class *will* and *shall* with other modal auxiliaries rather than understanding them in terms of the expression of a pure future.[3]

Indeed if one is impressed by arguments from origin, then it may be worth recalling the similar etymology of *literature* and *grammar*—one of which derives from the Roman word for letter (*littera*) and one from the Greek (*gramme*). But such arguments prove nothing—other than reminding us that our every activity has a history and a name. But it was to more substantial arguments that Roman Jakobson, the legendary Russian linguist, whose work has traversed nearly every important movement in twentieth-century linguistics and whose writing traverses five or six languages, made appeal when, some twenty years ago, he contributed a closing statement to a conference on the relations between literature and language. Jakobson ended his paper with the following remarks: 'All of us here, however, definitely realise that a linguist deaf to the poetic function of language and a literary scholar indifferent to linguistic problems and unconversant with linguistic method are equally flagrant anachronisms'.[4] Jakobson's optimism may seem historically misplaced when the majority of linguists persist in treating literature as a 'deviant' use of language and the majority of literary critics remain blissfully ignorant of current debates around the Extended Standard Theory and its revisions, or of the kinds of considerations of language produced in discussions between those who favour a truth-conditional analysis of meaning and those who would prefer an analysis in terms of speech acts. For twenty years literary critics have been urged to acquaint themselves with linguistic theory and, with rather more shrillness, literary critics have replied that linguists should first learn about language. This particular debate cuts across and confuses that even older debate which determined the institutional structure of literary criticism in the universities—that between the philologists and those who wished to make the study of literature more than a glossary of changes in the language.

What I wish to argue in the later part of this paper is that in so far as Jakobson postulates the two disciplines as distinct, and in so far as co-operation between the two is understood as co-operation between two definite bodies of knowledge, then this is mistaken. That linguistics ignores literature at its peril and that the study and practice of literature is deeply implicated in theories of language will be the argument of this paper. Such a statement does not, however, entail any belief that somehow linguistics and literary criticism should be united, although it may suggest that they should be jointly transformed.

Before, however, turning to the difficult problem of the linguist's theorisation of language and the relation of this to literature, it is necessary to emphasise at some length, and through a series of examples, the centrality of the results produced by linguistic study for any consideration of literature which is to be more than a vapid voluntarism. There is little doubt that our ability to read is dependent on a knowledge of changes in meaning, syntax and phonology and that our ability to analyse is dependent on the possibility of using grammatical and prosodic categories to articulate the literary effects that turn on them.[5] It is perhaps an indication of the parlous state of English as a university course that there are few students or teachers who would quarrel with this statement but there are fewer still who make any effort to understand the basic elements of the synchronic organisation or historical development of English.

Of the various fields of language study, it is undoubtedly the historical study of meaning change which is the most relevant to the student of literature and it is an index of the difficulty that meaning poses for contemporary linguistic theory that such a study is no longer an active part of linguistics. Throughout the nineteenth century such study was a fundamental byproduct of the ever increasing sophistication of philological techniques but in this century it has become a neglected, indeed for many linguists a non-existent, area. A recent survey of historical linguistics devoted only two pages to a consideration of meaning change[6] and, at least in England, it is literary critics like William Empson in *The Structure of Complex Words* or Raymond Williams in *Keywords* who have made recent contributions to accounts of historical change.

It is important, however, to recognise that the crucial importance of such studies is not in the restitution of meaning to words that have since fallen out of use but in the reconstitution of the play of possibilities articulated in one word.[7] When Hamlet complains that 'the toe of the peasant comes so near the heel of the courtier he galls his kibe', we are not likely to misread the final phrase even if we have to use a glossary to discover that *kibe* means *chilblains*. If, however, we consider the following speech of Falstaff's from *Henry IV Part 2* we find a more difficult set of problems:

> I have a whole school of tongues in this belly of mine, and not a tongue
> of them all speaks any other word but my name. And I had but a belly of
> any indifferency, I were simply the most active fellow in Europe: my
> womb, my womb, my womb undoes me. Here comes our general.
>
> (Act IV Scene 2: 18–23.)

If we are surprised by the masculine Falstaff claiming a womb, we may be unsurprised to find a gloss that informs us that *womb*, in this context, means *stomach*. The verb *to womb*, meaning to *enclose an empty space*, gave rise to a series of nominal derivations which included both the sexually unspecific *stomach* as well as the meaning of *uterus* that is current today. It is crucial to a reading of the role of Falstaff to recognise that both meanings were available at the end of the sixteenth century and we should not be surprised at Falstaff's consequent sexual ambiguity, particularly in the context of a claim about the disruption of the normal order of language, 'and not a tongue of them all speaks any other word but my name.'

It is usual to concentrate on the threat to political representation posed by

Falstaff but it must be recognised that this threat is more fundamental than any contemporary definitions of the political would suggest. It is not just political representation that Falstaff threatens but representation itself. He subverts linguistic representation by his refusal to treat language in terms of meanings but rather in terms of a constant battle for power between the speakers. Falstaff's rejection of the authority of language threatens the law far more fundamentally than do his express desires. And this threat to the level of representation is embodied in Falstaff's very theatrical presence, marked as he is not in terms of the chronicles that Shakespeare uses to authorise his other characters but as the visible successor to the figure of Vice in the Morality plays. He thus stands for an anachronistic theatrical order which threatens to undermine the more contemporary order that surrounds him. It is not surprising that such a figure should undermine even the possibility of representing sexual difference. Falstaff's body constitutes a polymorphously perverse threat to the possibility of representation. It even claims to undo the arbitrary and social nature of the sign and to speak its own name independently of any social order of language. It is this dislocation of language and the body, occasioned by the deposition of Richard II and the symbolic upheaval which that entails, to which Henry V is addressed as answer across the two parts of *Henry IV*. An essential part of the new order that Henry inaugurates is a reintegration of language and the body. The French princess whom Henry woos at the end of the play is not simply an index of a political union; she bears visible witness to the possibility of reordering the body in language, an ordering that is most evident in Act III Scene 4 as her maid Alice names the parts of the body in English and an arbitrary system of signs speak the body rather than the other way round. I am not suggesting that all this can be read out of one quotation but I am suggesting an importance for Falstaff's speech that we would be likely to miss without knowledge of the contemporary meanings of womb.

A knowledge of syntax is as necessary to an ability to grasp the processes of a text as, for example, in the following passage from the Aeolus section of *Ulysses*.

—He spoke on the law of evidence, J. J. O'Molloy said, of Roman justice
as contrasted with the earlier Mosaic code, the *lex talionis*. And he cited
the Moses of Michelangelo in the Vatican.
—Ha.
—A few wellchosen words, Lenehan prefaced. Silence!
Pause. J. J. O'Molloy took out his cigarette case.
False lull. Something quite ordinary.
Messenger took out his matchbox thoughtfully and lit his cigar.
    I have often thought since on looking back over that strange time that
it was that small act, trivial in itself, that striking of that match, that
determined the whole aftercourse of both our lives.

(*Ulysses*, Penguin edition, pp. 140–1)

It is in the newspaper headlines and the variety of rhetorics that compose the Aeolus section that the text of *Ulysses* loses any notion of a central meaning. The opening chapters of the book present Stephen or Bloom's thoughts as central but this is no longer the case in the newspaper office. A good example of this displacement can be read in those pages when J. J. O'Molloy is relating the speech made by Seymour Bushe in the Childs murder case. O'Molloy's repetition is punctuated by Stephen's thoughts and descriptions of other events taking place in the office. Many of these events are not linked to Stephen's consciousness and might seem to be recorded by an impersonal narrator, although such a description, which implies a centre for the text which can be located outside the text, is misleading. The lack of a centre becomes the explicit focus of the text as a messenger boy in the office takes out his matchbox and thoughtfully lights his cigar and it is the reflection that follows this action which plays on the syntax of the language to produce its effects. The monotonous repetition of 'that' confronts us with the impossibility of fixing a moment of presence outside language which would ground the text. This impossibility entails not only that the premises of naturalism and realism are incoherent but also that the division between author and text cannot be sustained. The sentence which comments on the striking of the match contains the word 'that' in three distinct grammatical guises. Four of its occurrences are as a demonstrative, but what they demonstrate, in their repetition, is that it is hopeless to link sign and referent outside a system of difference. Each 'that' invites a further 'that' as the world endlessly subdivides into a meaningless catalogue of demonstratives. This ruination of the referential powers of language, similar to processes at work in much modernist writing, is emphasised in the occurrence of 'that' as the restrictive relative specifying 'that striking of that match' as 'what determined the whole aftercourse of both our lives'. The function of a restrictive relative clause is to denote a limitation on the reference of the antecedent noun. But in this case the limitation, in its all-embracing nature, is no limitation at all. As the demonstrative increases the power of the microscope of language and the relative produces a telescopic view, the event escapes our control. The sentence provides a perfect example of a controlling metalanguage which promises a position of knowledge to the reader. However, its exaggerated form and its place in the text subvert this promise and delineate the sentence's own structure, the structure of a control that the text is in the process of dissolving. If naturalism assumed the ability to record events without any selection, this sentence demonstrates that events take their place within a selection already operated by language.

The other occurrence of 'that' is to subordinate the indirect statement to 'I have often thought'. The difficulty, however, is to locate the referent of the 'I'. Is this Stephen Dedalus as the future author he is to become looking back on the significance of a particular event? Such a belief would have to rest on the realist assumption that there are significant moments in a life. This position, unfortunately, is undermined by the facts of language that the text is forcing on our attention. If the description of an event can always by further differentiated then it becomes impossible to isolate a moment in the past to which significance can be attributed. To describe the past is not to map language against reality but to seek reality in the significant repetitions that bear witness to our constitution. Stephen Dedalus and James Joyce cannot be held apart: neither one is the cause of the other. As we read through *Ulysses* it becomes impossible to separate character and author.

As a final example of how both syntactic analysis and lexical knowledge are essential to even the most basic notions of reading a text, we can consider the famous passage in Book 1 of *Paradise Lost* which describes Satan moving towards the shore and then looking over his defeated army:

> He scarce had ceas't when the superior Fiend
> Was moving toward the shore; his ponderous shield
> Ethereal temper, massy, large and round,
> Behind him cast; the broad circumference
> Hung on his shoulders like the Moon, whose Orb
> Through Optic glass the *Tuscan* Artist views
> At Ev'ning from the top of *Fesole*,
> Or in *Valdarno*, to descry new Lands,
> Rivers, or Mountains in her spotty Globe.
> His Spear, to equal which the tallest Pine
> Hewn on *Norwegian* hills, to be the Mast
> Of some great Ammiral, were but a wand,
> He walk't with to support uneasy steps
> Over the burning Marl, not like those steps
> On Heaven's Azure, and the torrid Clime
> Smote on him sore besides, vaulted with Fire;
> Nathless he so endur'd, till on the Beach
> Of that inflamed Sea, he stood and call'd
> His Legions, Angel Forms, who lay intrans't
> Thick as Autumnal Leaves that strow the Brooks
> In *Vallombrosa*, where th' *Etrurian* shades
> High overarch't imbow'r; or scatter'd sedge
> Afloat, when with fierce Winds *Orion* arm'd
> Hath vext the Red-Sea Coast, whose waves o'erthrew
> *Busiris* and his *Memphian* Chivalry,
> While with perfidious hatred they persu'd
> The Sojourners of *Goshen*, who beheld
> From the safe shore thir floating Carcasses
> And broken Chariot Wheels; so thick bestrown
> Abject and lost lay these. . .

Paradise Lost, 1: 283–312

The entire sequence produces a continual changing of perspective, common to Milton's description of Hell in which metaphor and simile follow one another so quickly that there is no question of a basic description which the equivalences or comparisons elaborate. Instead the description simply becomes the passage through these comparisons and equivalences, a *transport*, to give metaphor its original force, of language. The comparisons that elaborate 'his Legions, Angel Forms' engage a constant change of perspective which turns on the seemingly infinite number of subordinate clauses and the heterogeneity of the literary references that Milton employs. The opening disjunction opposes the leaves that strew the brooks at Vallombrosa to the sedge which is scattered on the Red Sea. The interest of the disjunction is not simply one of scale, from a brook to a sea, but also of literary genre: the relative 'where th'Etrurian shades/High overarcht imbowr' and the adverbial 'when with fierce winds Orion armd/Hath vext the Red-Sea Coast' juxtapose the world of pastoral with that of classical epic while the relative which qualifies Red-Sea Coast introduces an Old Testament reference[8]. The complex pattern of subordination refuses any possibility of ordering the variety of references and it is not until after a further adverbial clause of time that a relative clause 'who beheld from the safe shore' provides the reader with a point of rest and vision. In this delay of a point of identification, in this rejection of a standard world of literary reference, Milton forces the reader to refuse any of the particular representations of the fallen angels in order that he may construct the truth of their situation. The necessary presupposition of Milton's poetic practice is an epistemology in which truth can actually reside in the processes of language and not simply in an external world which language is called to represent. Two such epistemologies were available in the Renaissance and although theoretically separate they were often combined.[9] The hermetic philosophers of the Renaissance evolved a theory in which language and the world were articulated together in a system of correspondences which allowed the possibility of finding relations between things inscribed in the language. Such theories often found their ultimate support in a conception of both the world and language as the product of God's wit. A more specifically religious theory of the truth to be found in language was provided by St Augustine. For Augustine, the redemption was also a redemption of language and if normal uses of language were arbitrary and excluded from any direct contact with truth, certain figurative uses of language did allow access to the realm of divine truth. Both theories were under political, ideological and religious attack at the time *Paradise Lost* was written; this attack finding institutional form in the Royal Society. One of the Society's most important functions was to promulgate a theory of language which destroyed the possibility of truth residing in language except in so far as language functioned as representation.

It is in the light of that contemporary ideological debate that one can consider the reference at the opening of the passage to Galileo, the 'Tuscan Artist'. If one looks at a standard gloss, it will simply carry the information that *artist* means *scientist*. While it is true that art and its derivatives still have that Renaissance meaning which covers every intellectual activity (and would, therefore, include what we now call science), it is important to recognise that elements of our current meaning which opposes art to science were developing at this time. Thus the first mention of such a meaning in the OED comes in 1678—just a decade after the first publication of *Paradise Lost*—when a manual on making sun dials records, 'Though we may justly account Dyalling originally a Science yet . . . it is now become to many of the ingenious no more difficult than an Art'. It would be dangerous to read this entry as using our current meaning of science, a development of the early nineteenth century, but it is significant that it opposes a realm of inquiry that can produce truth (science) to a mere practice which has no epistemological status (art).

At this point a linguist might quite reasonably interject that this is all very interesting and demonstrates how analyses of literature draw on studies in lexis and grammar but it has nothing to say to linguistics itself. For what is crucial to the establishment of linguistics is the specification within the heterogeneous material of language of a definite object which linguistics studies. Famously it was de Saussure who accomplished such a specification and, at the risk of pedantry, it is worth reviewing Saussure's argument both to understand the linguist's objection but also to indicate how the objection only has force within the realm of syntax and the object which he considers his own dissolves once one considers problems of meaning.

The major concept which Saussure develops is that of linguistic value. It is from this concept of value that all the other major Saussurean concepts (*langue/parole*, signifier/signified, diachrony/synchrony, syntagm/paradigm) follow one after another.[10] The problem that obsessed Saussure was simple; how could one say that two occurrences of the same word were the same word? And if one could not, how could linguistics claim to be a science when it could not identify its most basic objects? If I call a meeting to order by saying 'Gentlemen, Gentlemen', how can I claim that both words are the same when the pronunciation or intonation may be different? The problem can be dissolved once one recognises that what is at stake is a relational and not a material identity. This opposition can be grasped through Saussure's famous example of the 8.45 express from Geneva to Paris. What enables us to refer to this train is not a set of material identities—each day the train is made up of engines and coaches which are different—but the relational identity that it is given in the timetable—it is not the 8.30 for Lausanne or the 9.00 for Geneva.[11]

Certain consequences follow immediately from this notion of relational identity. Linguistics is not concerned with the positive characteristics of particular realisations of language but with the differential structure which allows those particular productions. It is this distinction that Saussure captures in his terms *langue* and *parole*. *Langue* refers to the specific set of systematic differences which allows the production of particular utterances of *parole*.

A linguist's reasons for professing lack of interest in the readings of Shakespeare, Milton and Joyce would turn on conceptions of *langue*—it might be argued that, whatever their incidental interest, they had nothing to say about linguistics' object of study. But whereas this is true in the case of syntax—the analyses do not reflect back on the syntactic distinctions they use—it is emphatically not the case at the level of meaning—where the examples produced do not just analyse specific uses of particular meanings but constitute those meanings in the analysis. Thus in Milton's use of the word *Artist*, it is not a question of specifying a meaning and then a use but rather of an account in which that meaning is in the process of changing as a word gets articulated in new, or in opposition to new, discourses. And the description and specification of these discourses will never be purely linguistic but will necessitate an account of the institutional sites of language use, an account which will draw on a wide variety

439

of facts and interpretations. The idea that there is an organisation of meaning which belongs to *langue*, and the analysis of which might be termed semantics, and separable uses of that organisation, which might be analysed under the various rubrics of pragmatics, socio-linguistics or stylistics, merely reproduces a distinction between logic and rhetoric, endemic to our thinking about language since the seventeenth century, which opposes an order of language determined by its relation to the order of things and another order, deemed inferior on this account, determined by its relation to the speaker. Such a distinction inevitably forces linguistics away from the study of language in its specificity and towards a mythical logic or psychology which will provide this universal ordering of meaning independently of specific uses of language.

It is at this point that the difficulty of simply proposing some institutional union of the disciplines of linguistics and literary criticism becomes apparent, for the difficulties of analysing meaning necessitate a recasting of both disciplines. Saussure's concept of value signalled, above all, a break with the primacy of meaning in specifying the object of linguistics. But Saussure himself allowed for the possibility of using the concept of linguistic value to analyse meaning. This decision indicates the extent to which Saussure himself underestimated his own theoretical achievement.[12] His belief in the possibility of analysing meaning linguistically is in contradiction with that impulse which led him to formulate the concept of linguistic value as a strategy for dislocating meaning from the field of linguistics. If it is perfectly legitimate to divorce the language from its situation in order to study phonology, morphology and syntax where differences of situation contribute only secondary characteristics—it is impossible to perform the same operation at the level of meaning where the relations of the meanings of a text to its socio-historical conditions (of both production and reception) are not secondary but constitutive. In short there is no such entity as *langue* at the level of meaning. And indeed; strictly speaking, there is no such thing as meaning in so far as the term assumes an entity independent of the different ideological, political or theoretical positions which inform language and the different institutional conditions of utterance. It is not that a word has different meanings for different speakers but that the same lexical item appears in different discourses.

If Saussure refused to allow meaning a position of centrality within linguistics, he retained a belief in its existence. That he failed to see the way in which at the level of meaning language is always discourse can be explained in terms of the two great lacunae of Saussure's theory: subjectivity and institutions. For Saussure there was no question but that the speaker's relation to his utterances was one of transparency. If the functioning of *langue* was unconscious and to be located in some notion of community, this functioning was simply at the service of the conscious intentions of the speaker. It was to this area of conscious intentionality that *parole* referred. The idea that we might produce meanings of which we were not conscious, that the workings of discourse and desire made our own speech as much material for interpretation as a foreign language is alien to the *Course in General Linguistics*. This belief in the transparency of the speaking subject is complemented by an inability to conceive of institutions as other than straightforward means for achieving ends that could be separately and naturally defined. This is made clear in another famous passage where he distinguishes *langue* from any other social institutions in the following terms:

> Other human institutions—customs, laws, etc.—are all based in varying degrees on the natural relations of things; all have of necessity adapted the means employed to the ends pursued. Even dress in fashion is not entirely arbitrary; we can deviate only slightly from the conditions dictated by the human body. Language is limited by nothing in the choice of means, for apparently nothing would prevent the association of any idea whatsoever with just any sequence of sounds.[13]

This rather naive view—that there is a determinate, evident and natural relationship between means and ends in institutions—complements the belief in a full subjectivity which simply uses the resources of *langue* in *parole*. Sixty years after Saussure's death, with both the variety of Marxist or sociological analyses which refuse such transparency to institutions and the discoveries of psychoanalysis which make clear the complexity of the subject's relation to language, it is impossible to understand language either as a transparent medium for individual expression or as a simple medium for communication within an institution whose functioning can be exhaustively described in the natural relationship of things.

In order to deal with the effects of meaning we must combine an analysis of the institutional sites of language together with an analysis of subjectivity in language to enable us to understand how specific practices of language both produce subject positions for individuals and articulate various practices within institutions. This statement may seem both blunt and unspecific but it is possible to give it some gloss (and one that will indicate the consequent transformation of linguistics and literary criticism) by considering and recasting one of the most influential characterisations of language in relation to literature—that provided by Jakobson in the paper already quoted from at the beginning of this article. Jakobson argued that any speech event could be analysed in terms of six linguistic functions:

> An outline of these functions demands a concise survey of the constitutive factors in any speech event, in any act of verbal communication, the ADDRESSER sends a MESSAGE to the ADDRESSEE. To be operative the message requires a CONTEXT referred to ('referent' in another, somewhat ambiguous, nomenclature), seizable by the addressee, and either verbal or capable of being verbalised; a CODE fully, or at least partially, common to the addresser and addressee (or in other words, to the encoder and decoder of the message); and, finally, a CONTACT, a physical and psychological connection between the addresser and the addressee, enabling both of them to enter and stay in communication.[14]

Each of these factors relates to a particular function of language: Addresser (*Emotive*), Addressee (*Conative*), Context (*Referential*), Code (*Metalingual*), Contact (*Phatic*) and, finally, Message (*Poetic*). The first five functions are perhaps evidently related to the relevant factors. They distinguish between the message's primary aims: to express the speaker's state of mind, to influence the addressee(s), to refer to some third element, to comment on the meaning of what is being said, or to establish that the message is being received. The sixth function is defined by Jakobson as a message which reflects on its own structure, the moment at which paradigmatic choices influence syntagmatic ones, or, to use his own words: 'The poetic function projects the principle of equivalence from the axis of selection into the axis of combination'.

Jakobson's whole analysis into factors and functions rests on an implicit appeal to a notion of *langue* functioning at the level of meaning as well as that of syntax and phonology (although it might be said that almost all the specific analyses in the paper concentrate on the phonological and the syntactic). If we refuse this assumption, which posits individual speakers in a common relation to a totality, then much of the analysis dissolves.

If we select the institutional sites of language as the starting point of our analysis rather than some notion of *langue* as a totality then, for example, addresser and addressee become functions of the variety of places allocated to the speaker in a discourse rather than basic elements given by syntax or pragmatics. Such a focus will also emphasise how it is impossible to split off some general referential function of language. Every particular discursive formation has its own methods of specifying and referring to the extra-discursive. It may be one of the continuing weaknesses of contemporary philosophies of language to imagine that these methods can be unified under some general principle. In each case there will be a complex of practices and discourses within which reference will take place and it is not possible to talk of some general relation between language and context while ignoring the specific practices with which the language is imbricated. The history of sciences is particularly rich in such examples: when Galileo referred to the evidence for his theory of the solar system, the reference was dependent, amongst other things, on the acceptance of the operations of the telescope. It is impossible to abstract language from conditions of verification in order to pose some general theory of reference.

It is only if we understand the complexity of the varieties of methods of referring (and one might hesitate to gather them under the general term of reference) that we can theorise the way in which the very positions of addresser and addressee may be transformed by a system of reference. Jakobson's model presupposes a simple and uncomplicated three person model of language in which syntactic and discursive distinctions coincide. The references that I make to a third person are theorised in such a way that they could have no effectivity on the fundamental and given positions of addresser and addressee. Much of the functioning of fictional forms, particularly the novel, can, however only be understood as the reworking of the position of addresser and addressee across a series of third person statements.

The point of these considerations is to suggest that there is no universal ordering of factors and functions of language that we can specify in advance. If there are certain general concerns which have been useful to date in analysing discourse, this does not mean that it is possible to exhaustively enumerate features of language in advance of particular investigations. As has been argued, it is not clear that the particular methods by which a variety of discursive formations produce and allow evidence can be brought together under the head of reference. And these considerations also affect the consideration of the notion of a metalingual function. If, at the level of meaning, there is no unified structure of language then there is even less a metalanguage which can specify those meanings. Once again, as in the case of reference, each discursive formation is very likely to have a specific set of rules for producing paraphrases and equivalences but it is precluding the investigation to decree in advance that these will provide an identical function. Even the phatic function cannot be simply universalised depending as it does on a complex series of institutional practices in, for example, law or science. One of the conclusions of these arguments is that there is no reason why every utterance or even the idealisation of certain forms of utterance will be investigable at this level. If we refuse to allow the existence of *langue* at the level of meaning then we must not shirk the consequences that only certain utterances will be amenable to analysis. Once again we will be faced with Saussure's problem of identifying the units for analysis and this will be a task which cannot be universalised across the whole language.

If we now finally turn to the poetic function it is clear that we must consider it not as a universal feature of language but rather in terms of the rules within and across certain discourses which allow paradigmatic choices to interrupt and reflect on syntagmatic organisation. It is possible to consider discourses that have very rigorous operations to prevent such operations and others which don't (not to forget that third possibility: discourses to which such a characterisation is simply not pertinent). Such a position might allow us to isolate literature as an institution whose changing material determinates do not affect a unity to be discerned in a peculiar privilege given to that aspect of language which Jakobson names the poetic.

So far it has been an implicit assumption that institutions and discourses have total autonomy and that one can postulate some homologous relation between them. This is, of course, not the case. Institutions overlap and conflict, discourses are not tied in some obviously physical way to their institutional sites. Indeed the very possibility of discursive transformation rests on these contradictory relations. It is here that there is another crucial change of emphasis from the simple listing of institutions and discourses and then their correlation; rather they will find their origin in some contemporary area of institutional and discursive change and contradiction and it is here that the determination of regularities in the corpus will be grounded. The argument that it is the situation of the investigator which is the final determinant of the forms and grounds of argument may sound alarmingly unscientific. Whatever its epistemological status, and this could be argued for, it should not alarm any analyst of literature because it has consistently been claimed that it is such forms of argument that distinguish English as a discipline. And it has been within the discipline of English that many of the most penetrating studies of language, in the form that I describe it, have taken place. Richards, Empson and, more recently, Raymond Williams have contributed a great deal to the study of language in this century. But it is a contribution that has often been ignored by linguistics. One of the major reasons for this has been a certain failure by this tradition, which could ironically be termed a Cambridge one, to consider rigorously the relation between their own work and the dominant schools of linguistics. It should now be clear that such a consideration would not be a prologomenon to some pious institutional union between linguistics and literary criticism but to an analysis of language which would recast the assumptions and disciplines of linguistics and literary criticism.

NOTES

1. The adjective is the only important word-class not identified by the Greeks. Its different status from the noun was only properly recognised with the detailed study of Romance languages.
2. Before these dates phonetics had been dogged by the belief that a straightforward correspondence between letters and sounds could be realised, and etymology by the failure to understand the principles of historical change in language.
3. For the details of this argument see Barbara Strang, *Modern English Structure* (1968: 162–170). For a statement of the more classical analysis of 'will' and 'shall' see Otto Jespersen. It should be noted that even in English it is not simply the future tense which is organised differently from the Latin. Sentences such as 'If I loved her, I'd send her flowers' suggest that what we traditionally call the past tense of the verb is an inflection which cannot be fully semantically analysed in terms of tense.
4. Roman Jakobson, 'Closing Statement: linguistics and poetics' in Thomas Sebeok (ed.) *Style in Language* (Harvard, 1960) p. 377.
5. Phonetics and phonology present so many special problems that I am not going to consider them in this paper. My personal view, however, is that there are fundamental universal questions about sound in language. Any work in this area would have to take as its starting point the work of I. Fönagy, *Die Metaphern in der Phonetik* (1963) and the second section of Julia Kristeva's *La Révolution du langage poétique* (1974), particularly the chapter entitled 'Rythmes phoniques et sémantiques' pp. 209–64. Independently of any theoretical questions, the fact that many students and teachers of literature have not the faintest idea how the poetry or prose they study would have sounded if read aloud at the time of its composition is a practically unparalleled example of scholastic blindness.
6. Theodora Bynon, *Historical Linguistics* (Cambridge, 1977).
7. Perhaps the best analysis of the play of possibilities available within a single word is Empson's analysis of Pope's use of 'wit' in the *Essay on Criticism* in *The Structure of Complex Words* (1977: 84–100).
8. If one considers the literary history of this simile, then Milton's use of it to heterogenise the range of literary references beyond the epic becomes even more evident. There is a useful account of its history in epic in C. M. Bowra *From Virgil to Milton* (1945: 240–1).
9. For a short summary of these two positions see Geoffrey Shepherd's introduction to his edition of Sidney's *An Apology for Poetry* (1973: 56–7).
10. For a brilliant account of the centrality of Saussure's concept of value see Oswald Ducrot, 'Le Structuralisme en linguistique' in *Qu'est ce que le structuralisme?* ed. F. Wahl (1968: 44–9).
11. Ferdinand de Saussure, *Course in General Linguistics* (London, 1974) pp. 108–9.
12. For a more detailed statement of this argument see Cl. Haroche, P. Henry, M. Pêcheux, 'Mise au point et perspectives de l'analyse automatique du discours', *Language* 37 (1971).
13. Saussure, *op. cit.*, pp. 75–6.
14. Jakobson, *op. cit.*, p. 358.

28 Umberto Eco

Umberto Eco (b. 1929) was born in Allesandra, Italy, and studied at the University of Turin. He has taught at universities in Turin, Milan, Florence and Bologna, and is a frequent academic visitor to the United States. In 1981, he achieved international fame with his novel, *The Name of the Rose*, which was both a bestseller and a literary success. Before that, he had established himself as an authority in the fields of semiotics, cultural studies and literary theory, with such publications as *A Theory of Semiotics* (1976) [first published in Italy 1975] and *The Role of the Reader: explorations in the semiotics of texts* (1981) [1979].

Semiotics is the general science of signs, of which linguistics, according to Saussure (see above, pp. 1–14) is a subdivision. One consequence of this way of looking at language has been to encourage comparative study of literary and visual media, especially in the area of narrative. Another has been to break down the traditional prejudice of the custodians of 'high culture' against the products of popular or mass culture. These tendencies are exhibited very clearly in Eco's work, which is notable for its broad range of illustration and eclectic methodology. He is as interested in the semiotics of blue jeans or the Superman story as in the dense polysemy of Joyce's *Finnegans Wake*, and this, combined with a lively, witty style, makes him one of the most accessible of critics in the structuralist tradition.

In 'Casablanca: Cult Movies and Intertextual Collage,' he turns his attention on one of the popular classics of Hollywood cinema, reading off its multiple meanings in a manner reminiscent of Roland Barthes (see above, pp. 172–95). In the famous Humphrey Bogart–Ingrid Bergman movie, Eco suggests, filmic archetypes (or clichés, as a more élitist critic might call them) are multiplied to the point where they begin to 'talk among themselves' and generate an intoxicating excess of signification. This process, by which *kitsch*, in its reception by a finely attuned audience, can allegedly achieve something approximating the sublimity of classic art, is a recurrent theme and subject of controversy in discussions of postmodernism.

'Casablanca', first published in this form in 1984, is reprinted here from a collection of Eco's occasional and journalistic essays, *Faith in Fakes* (1986) (published in the United States and (as a paperback) in Britain under the title, *Travels in Hyperreality*).

CROSS-REFERENCE: 9. Barthes
                               22. Jameson
                               23. Eagleton

Casablanca: Cult Movies and Intertextual Collage

Cult

'Was that artillery fire, or is it my heart pounding?'[a] Whenever *Casablanca*[b] is shown, at this point the audience reacts with an enthusiasm usually reserved for football. Sometimes a single word is enough: fans cry every time Bogey says 'kid.' Frequently the spectators quote the best lines before the actors say them.

According to traditional standards in aesthetics, *Casablanca* is not a work of art, if such an expression still has a meaning. In any case, if the films of Dreyer, Eisenstein, or Antonioni are works of art, *Casablanca* represents a very modest aesthetic achievement. It is a hodgepodge of sensational scenes strung together implausibly, its characters are psychologically incredible, its actors act in a mannered way. Nevertheless, it is a great example of cinematic discourse, a palimpsest for future students of twentieth-century religiosity, a paramount laboratory for semiotic research into textual strategies. Moreover, it has become a cult movie.

What are the requirements for transforming a book or a movie into a cult object? The work must be loved, obviously, but this is not enough. It must provide a completely furnished world so that its fans can quote characters and episodes as if they were aspects of the fan's private sectarian world, a world about which one can make up quizzes and play trivia games so that the adepts of the sect recognize through each other a shared expertise. Naturally all these elements (characters and episodes) must have some archetypical appeal, as we shall see. One can ask and answer questions about the various subway stations of New York or Paris only if these spots have become or have been assumed as mythical

---

[a] Like the more famous line, 'Play it again, Sam,' (actually 'Play it, Sam') this quotation is not quite accurate. Ingrid Bergman's words in the film are: 'Was that cannon fire, or is it my heart pounding?'

[b] The action of *Casablanca* (made in 1942, directed by Michael Curtiz) takes place early in the Second World War, when Morocco was controlled by the Vichy French government. The American Rick (Humphrey Bogart) runs a cafe–night club in Casablanca which is a place of passage for refugees trying to get exit visas to the United States, usually by bribing the Prefect of Police, Renault. A Czech Resistance leader, Victor Laszlo, turns up with his wife, Ilse (Ingrid Bergman), who had a love affair with Rick in Paris just before the German Occupation, when she believed her husband to be dead. On discovering that he was alive, she parted from Rick without explanation. Bitterly hurt by this experience, Rick is at first hostile to Ilse in Casablanca, but on learning the truth, and that she still loves him, chivalrously helps her and Laszlo to escape the clutches of the Gestapo chief Strasser, at considerable risk to himself. In the final sequence, Rick and the implausibly reformed Renault go off to join the Free French.

areas and such names as Canarsie Line or Vincennes-Neuilly stand not only for physical places but become the catalyzers of collective memories.

Curiously enough, a book can also inspire a cult even though it is a great work of art: both *The Three Musketeers* and *The Divine Comedy* rank among the cult books; and there are more trivia games among the fans of Dante than among the fans of Dumas. I suspect that a cult movie, on the contrary, must display some organic imperfections: It seems that the boastful *Rio Bravo* is a cult movie and the great *Stagecoach* is not.

I think that in order to transform a work into a cult object one must be able to break, dislocate, unhinge it so that one can remember only parts of it, irrespective of their original relationship with the whole. In the case of a book one can unhinge it, so to speak, physically, reducing it to a series of excerpts. A movie, on the contrary, must be already ramshackle, rickety, unhinged in itself. A perfect movie, since it cannot be reread every time we want, from the point we choose, as happens with a book, remains in our memory as a whole, in the form of a central idea or emotion; only an unhinged movie survives as a disconnected series of images, of peaks, of visual icebergs. It should display not one central idea but many. It should not reveal a coherent philosophy of composition. It must live on, and because of, its glorious ricketiness.

However, it must have some quality. Let me say that it can be ramshackle from the production point of view (in that nobody knew exactly what was going to be done next)—as happened evidently with the *Rocky Horror Picture Show*—but it must display certain textual features, in the sense that, outside the conscious control of its creators, it becomes a sort of textual syllabus, a living example of living textuality. Its addressee must suspect it is not true that works are created by their authors. Works are created by works, texts are created by texts, all together they speak to each other independently of the intention of their authors. A cult movie is the proof that, as literature comes from literature, cinema comes from cinema.

Which elements, in a movie, can be separated from the whole and adored for themselves? In order to go on with this analysis of *Casablanca* I should use some important semiotic categories, such as the ones (provided by the Russian Formalists)[c] of theme and motif. I confess I find it very difficult to ascertain what the various Russian Formalists meant by motif. If—as Veselovsky says—a motif is the simplest narrative unit, then one wonders why 'fire from heaven' should belong to the same category as 'the persecuted maid' (since the former can be represented by an image, while the latter requires a certain narrative development). It would be interesting to follow Tomashevsky and to look in *Casablanca* for free or tied and for dynamic or static motifs. We should distinguish between more or less universal narrative functions à la Propp[d], visual stereotypes like the Cynic Adventurer, and more complex archetypical situations like the Unhappy Love. I hope someone will do this job, but here I will assume, more prudently (and borrowing the concept from research into Artificial Intelligence) the more flexible notion of 'frame.'

[c] See headnote on Victor Shklovsky, p. 15, above.

[d] Vladimir Propp, *Morphology of the Folktale* (1928).

In *The Role of the Reader* I distinguished between common and intertextual frames. I meant by 'common frame' data-structures for representing stereotyped situations such as dining at a restaurant or going to the railway station; in other words, a sequence of actions more or less coded by our normal experience. And by 'intertextual frames' I meant stereotyped situations derived from preceding textual tradition and recorded by our encyclopedia, such as, for example, the standard duel between the sheriff and the bad guy or the narrative situation in which the hero fights the villain and wins, or more macroscopic textual situations, such as the story of the *vierge souillée* [dishonoured virgin] or the classic recognition scene (Bakhtin considered it a motif, in the sense of a chronotope)[e]. We could distinguish between stereotyped intertextual frames (for instance, the Drunkard Redeemed by Love) and stereotyped iconographical units (for instance, the Evil Nazi). But since even these iconographical units, when they appear in a movie, if they do not directly elicit an action, at least suggest its possible development, we can use the notion of intertextual frame to cover both.

Moreover, we are interested in finding those frames that not only are recognizable by the audience as belonging to a sort of ancestral intertextual tradition but that also display a particular fascination. 'A suspect who eludes a passport control and is shot by the police' is undoubtedly an intertextual frame but it does not have a 'magic' flavor. Let me address intuitively the idea of 'magic' frame. Let me define as 'magic' those frames that, when they appear in a movie and can be separated from the whole, transform this movie into a cult object. In *Casablanca* we find more intertextual frames than 'magic' intertextual frames. I will call the latter 'intertextual archetypes.'

The term 'archetype' does not claim to have any particular psychoanalytic or mythic connotation,[f] but serves only to indicate a preestablished and frequently reappearing narrative situation, cited or in some way recycled by innumerable other texts and provoking in the addressee a sort of intense emotion accompanied by the vague feeling of a déjà vu,[g] that everybody yearns to see again. I would not say that an intertextual archetype is necessarily 'universal.' It can belong to a rather recent textual tradition, as with certain topoi of slapstick comedy. It is sufficient to consider it as a topos or standard situation that manages to be particularly appealing to a given cultural area or a historical period.

The Making of Casablanca

'Can I tell you a story?' Ilse asks. Then she adds: 'I don't know the finish yet.'
Rick says: 'Well, go on, tell it. Maybe one will come to you as you go along.'
Rick's line is a sort of epitome of *Casablanca* itself. According to Ingrid

---

[e] Chronotope is a term coined by Mikhail Bakhtin (see pp. 124–56, above) to analyse the ways in which time and space are represented and related in narrative.

[f] As it does in the work of Carl Jung and critics influenced by him, such as Maud Bodkin and Northrop Frye. (See sections 14, 15 and 31 of *20th Century Literary Criticism*).

[g] Something already seen.

Bergman, the film was apparently being made up at the same time that it was being shot. Until the last moment not even Michael Curtiz knew whether Ilse would leave with Rick or with Victor, and Ingrid Bergman seems so fascinatingly mysterious because she did not know at which man she was to look with greater tenderness.

This explains why, in the story, she does not, in fact, choose her fate: she is chosen.

When you don't know how to deal with a story, you put stereotyped situations in it because you know that they, at least, have already worked elsewhere. Let us take a marginal but revealing example. Each time Laszlo orders something to drink (and it happens four times) he changes his choice: (1) Cointreau, (2) cocktail, (3) cognac, and (4) whisky (he once drinks champagne but he does not ask for it). Why such confusing and confused drinking habits for a man endowed with an ascetic temper? There is no psychological reason. My guess is that each time Curtiz was simply quoting, unconciously, similar situations in other movies and trying to provide a reasonably complete repetition of them.

Thus one is tempted to read *Casablanca* as T. S. Eliot read *Hamlet*, attributing its fascination not to the fact that it was a successful work (actually he considered it one of Shakespeare's less fortunate efforts) but to the imperfection of its composition. He viewed *Hamlet* as 'the result of an unsuccessful fusion of several earlier versions of the story, and so the puzzling ambiguity of the main character was due to the author's difficulty in putting together different topoi. So both public and critics find *Hamlet* beautiful because it is interesting, but believe it is interesting because it is beautiful.

On a smaller scale the same thing happened to *Casablanca*. Forced to improvise a plot, the authors mixed a little of everything, and everything they chose came from a repertoire that had stood the test of time. When only a few of these formulas are used, the result is simply kitsch. But when the repertoire of stock formulas is used wholesale, then the result is an architecture like Gaudi's Sagrada Familia[h]: the same vertigo, the same stroke of genius.

Stop by Stop

Every story involves one or more archetypes. To make a good story a single archetype is usually enough. But *Casablanca* is not satisfied with that. It uses them all.

It would be nice to identify our archetypes scene by scene and shot by shot, stopping the tape at every relevant step. Every time I have scanned *Casablanca* with very cooperative research groups, the review has taken many hours. Furthermore, when a team starts this kind of game, the instances of stopping the videotape increase proportionally with the size of the audience. Each member of the team sees something that the others have missed, and many of them start to find

[h] Antonio Gaudi (1852–1926), Spanish *art nouveau* architect best known for his (still uncompleted) Cathedral of the Holy Family in Barcelona.

in the movie even memories of movies made after *Casablanca*—evidently the normal situation for a cult movie, suggesting that perhaps the best deconstructive readings should be made of unhinged texts (or that deconstruction is simply a way of breaking up texts).

However, I think that the first twenty minutes of the film represent a sort of review of the principal archetypes. Once they have been assembled, without any synthetic concern, then the story starts to suggest a sort of savage syntax of the archetypical elements and organizes them in multileveled oppositions. *Casablanca* looks like a musical piece with an extraordinarily long overture, where every theme is exhibited according to a monodic line. Only later does the symphonic work take place. In a way the first twenty minutes could be analyzed by a Russian Formalist and the rest by a Greimasian[i].

Let me then try only a sample analysis of the first part. I think that a real text-analytical study of *Casablanca* is still to be made, and I offer only some hints to future teams of researchers, who will carry out, someday, a complete reconstruction of its deep textual structure.

1. First, African music, then the *Marseillaise*. Two different genres are evoked: adventure movie and patriotic movie.

2. Third genre. The globe: Newsreel. The voice even suggests the news report. Fourth genre: the odyssey of refugees. Fifth genre: Casablanca and Lisbon are, traditionally, *hauts lieux* [favourite places] for international intrigues. Thus in two minutes five genres are evoked.

3. Casablanca-Lisbon. Passage to the Promised Land (Lisbon-America). Casablanca is the Magic Door. We still do not know what the Magic Key is or by which Magic Horse one can reach the Promised Land.

4. 'Wait, wait, wait.' To make the passage one must submit to a Test. The Long Expectation. Purgatory situation.

5. 'Deutschland über Alles.' The German anthem introduces the theme of Barbarians.

6. The Casbah. Pépé le Moko. Confusion, robberies, violence, and repression.

7. Pétain (Vichy) vs. the Cross of Lorraine. See at the end the same opposition closing the story: Eau de Vichy vs. Choice of the Resistance. War Propaganda movie.

8. The Magic Key: the visa. It is around the winning of the Magic Key that passions are unleashed. Captain Renault mentioned: he is the Guardian of the Door, or the boatman of the Acheron to be conquered by a Magic Gift (money or sex).

9. The Magic Horse: the airplane. The airplane flies over Rick's Café Américain, thus recalling the Promised Land of which the Café is the reduced model.

10. Major Strasser shows up. Theme of the Barbarians, and their emasculated slaves. 'Je suis l'empire à la fin de la décadence/Qui regarde passer les grands

See note *d*, p. 365, above.

barbares blancs/En composant des acrostiques indolents. . . .'[j]

11. 'Everybody comes to Rick's.' By quoting the original play,[k] Renault introduces the audience to the Café. The interior: Foreign Legion (each character has a different nationality and a different story to tell, and also his own skeleton in the closet), Grand Hotel (people come and people go, and nothing ever happens), Mississippi River Boat, New Orleans Brothel (black piano player), the Gambling Inferno in Macao or Singapore (with Chinese women), the Smugglers' Paradise, the Last Outpost on the Edge of the Desert. Rick's place is a magic circle where everything can happen—love, death, pursuit, espionage, games of chance, seductions, music, patriotism. Limited resources and the unity of place, due to the theatrical origin of the story, suggested an admirable condensation of events in a single setting. One can identify the usual paraphernalia of at least ten exotic genres.

12. Rick slowly shows up, first by synecdoche (his hand), then by metonymy (the check).[l] The various aspects of the contradictory (plurifilmic) personality of Rick are introduced: the Fatal Adventurer, the Self-Made Businessman (money is money), the Tough Guy from a gangster movie, Our Man in Casablanca (international intrigue), the Cynic. Only later he will be characterized also as the Hemingwayan Hero (he helped the Ethiopians and the Spaniards against fascism). He does not drink. This undoubtedly represents a nice problem, for later Rick must play the role of the Redeemed Drunkard and he has to be made a drunkard (as a Disillusioned Lover) so that he can be redeemed. But Bogey's face sustains rather well this unbearable number of contradictory psychological features.

13. The Magic Key, in person: the transit letters. Rick receives them from Peter Lorre and from this moment everybody wants them: how to avoid thinking of Sam Spade and of *The Maltese Falcon?*[m]

14. Music Hall. Mr. Ferrari. Change of genre: comedy with brilliant dialogue. Rick is now the Disenchanted Lover, or the Cynical Seducer.

15. Rick vs. Renault. The Charming Scoundrels.

16. The theme of the Magic Horse and the Promised Land returns.

17. Roulette as the Game of Life and Death (Russian Roulette that devours fortunes and can destroy the happiness of the Bulgarian Couple, the Epiphany of Innocence). The Dirty Trick: cheating at cards. At this point the Trick is an Evil one but later it will be a Good one, providing a way to the Magic Key for the Bulgarian bride.

18. Arrest and tentative escape of Ugarte. Action movie.

19. Laszlo and Ilse. The Uncontaminated Hero and La Femme Fatale. Both in white—always; clever opposition with Germans, usually in black. In the meeting at Laszlo's table, Strasser is in white, in order to reduce the opposition.

---

[j] 'I am the empire at the end of its decline/Watching the great white barbarians pass/While composing idle acrostics.' (I do not know the source of this quotation.)

[k] *Casablanca* was based on an unproduced stage play entitled, *Everybody Comes to Rick's.*

[l] See note *a*, p. 57, above.

[m] Another Hollywood classic, made in 1934, also starring Humphrey Bogart and Peter Lorre.

However, Strasser and Ilse are Beauty and the Beast. The Norwegian agent: spy movie.

20. The Desperate Lover and Drink to Forget.

21. The Faithful Servant and his Beloved Master. Don Quixote and Sancho.

22. Play it (again, Sam). Anticipated quotation of Woody Allen.[n]

23. The long flashback begins. Flashback as a content and flashback as a form. Quotation of the flashback as a topical stylistic device. The Power of Memory. Last Day in Paris. Two Weeks in Another Town. Brief Encounter. French movie of the 1930's (the station as *quai des brumes*[o]).

24. At this point the review of the archetypes is more or less complete. There is still the moment when Rick plays the Diamond in the Rough (who allows the Bulgarian bride to win),[p] and two typical situations: the scene of the *Marseillaise* and the two lovers discovering that Love Is Forever. The gift to the Bulgarian bride (along with the enthusiasm of the waiters), the *Marseillaise*, and the Love Scene are three instances of the rhetorical figure of Climax, as the quintessence of Drama (each climax coming obviously with its own anticlimax).

Now the story can elaborate upon its elements.

The first symphonic elaboration comes with the second scene around the roulette table. We discover for the first time that the Magic Key (that everybody believed to be only purchasable with money) can in reality be given only as a Gift, a reward for Purity. The Donor will be Rick. He gives (free) the visa to Laszlo. In reality there is also a third Gift, the Gift Rick makes of his own desire, sacrificing himself. Note that there is no gift for Ilse, who, in some way, even though innocent, has betrayed two men. The Receiver of the Gift is the Uncontaminated Laszlo. By becoming the Donor, Rick meets Redemption. No one impure can reach the Promised Land. But Rick and Renault redeem themselves and can reach the other Promised Land, not America (which is Paradise) but the Resistance, the Holy War (which is a glorious Purgatory). Laszlo flies directly to Paradise because he has already suffered the ordeal of the underground. Rick, moreover, is not the only one who accepts sacrifice. The idea of sacrifice pervades the whole story, Ilse's sacrifice in Paris when she abandons the man she loves to return to the wounded hero, the Bulgarian bride's sacrifice when she is prepared to give herself to help her husband, Victor's sacrifice when he is prepared to see Ilse with Rick to guarantee her safety.

The second symphonic elaboration is upon the theme of the Unhappy Love. Unhappy for Rick, who loves Ilse and cannot have her. Unhappy for Ilse, who loves Rick and cannot leave with him. Unhappy for Victor, who understands that he has not really kept Ilse. The interplay of unhappy loves produces numerous

---

[n] *Play It Again, Sam* is the title of a film made by Woody Allen in 1972, about a neurotic film critic obsessed with Humphrey Bogart.

[o] Literally, 'quay (or railway platform) of fogs,' this was the title of a classic French film, directed by Marcel Carne in 1938.

[p] To be precise, Rick ensures that her husband wins at the roulette table, thus ensuring that the couple can buy their exit visas from Renault for cash, instead of the girl having to sleep with the police chief to obtain them.

twists and turns. In the beginning Rick is unhappy because he does not understand why Ilse leaves him. Then Victor is unhappy because he does not understand why Ilse is attracted to Rick. Finally Ilse is unhappy because she does not understand why Rick makes her leave with her husband.

These unhappy loves are arranged in a triangle. But in the normal adulterous triangle there is a Betrayed Husband and a Victorious Lover, while in this case both men are betrayed and suffer a loss.

In this defeat, however, an additional element plays a part, so subtly that it almost escapes the level of consciousness. Quite subliminally a hint of Platonic Love is established. Rick admires Victor, Victor is ambiguously attracted by the personality of Rick, and it seems that at a certain point each of the two is playing out the duel of sacrifice to please the other. In any case, as in Rousseau's *Confessions*, the woman is here an intermediary between the two men. She herself does not bear any positive value (except, obviously, Beauty): The whole story is a virile affair, a dance of seduction between Male Heroes.

From now on the film carries out the definitive construction of its intertwined triangles, to end with the solution of the Supreme Sacrifice and of the Redeemed Bad Guys. Note that, while the redemption of Rick has long been prepared, the redemption of Renault is absolutely unjustified and comes only because this was the final requirement the movie had to meet in order to be a perfect Epos of Frames.

The Archetypes Hold a Reunion

Casablanca is a cult movie precisely because all the archetypes are there, because each actor repeats a part played on other occasions, and because human beings live not 'real' life but life as stereotypically portrayed in previous films: *Casablanca* carries the sense of déjà vu to such a degree that the addressee is ready to see in it what happened after it as well. It is not until *To Have and Have Not* that Bogey plays the role of the Hemingway hero, but here he appears 'already' loaded with Hemingwayesque connotations simply because Rick fought in Spain. Peter Lorre trails reminiscences of Fritz Lang, Conrad Veidt's German officer emanates a faint whiff of *The Cabinet of Dr. Caligari*. He is not a ruthless, technological Nazi; he is a nocturnal and diabolical Caesar.

Casablanca became a cult movie because it is not *one* movie. It is 'movies.' And this is the reason it works, in defiance of any aesthetic theory.

For it stages the powers of Narrativity in its natural state, before art intervenes to tame it. This is why we accept the way that characters change mood, morality, and psychology from one moment to the next, that conspirators cough to interrupt the conversation when a spy is approaching, that bar girls cry at the sound of the *Marseillaise* . . .

When all the archetypes burst out shamelessly, we plumb Homeric profundity. Two clichés make us laugh but a hundred clichés move us because we sense dimly that the clichés are talking among themselves, celebrating a reunion.

Just as the extreme of pain meets sensual pleasure, and the extreme of perversion borders on mystical energy, so too the extreme of banality allows us to catch a glimpse of the Sublime.

Nobody would have been able to achieve such a cosmic result intentionally. Nature has spoken in place of men. This, alone, is a phenomenon worthy of veneration.

The Charged Cult

The structure of *Casablanca* helps us understand what happens in later movies *born in order to become cult objects*.

What *Casablanca* does unconsciously, other movies will do with extreme inter-textual awareness, assuming also that the addressee is equally aware of their purposes. These are 'postmodern' movies, where the quotation of the topos is recognized as the only way to cope with the burden of our filmic encyclopedic expertise.

Think for instance of *Bananas*,[q] with its explicit quotation of the Odessa steps from Eisenstein's *Potemkin*. In *Casablanca* one enjoys quotation even though one does not recognize it, and those who recognize it feel as if they all belonged to the same little clique. In *Bananas* those who do not catch the topos cannot enjoy the scene and those who do simply feel smart.

Another (and different) case is the quotation of the topical duel betwen the black Arab giant with his scimitar and the unprotected hero, in *Raiders of the Lost Ark*. If you remember, the topos suddenly turns into another one, and the unprotected hero becomes in a second *The Fastest Gun in the West*. Here the ingenuous viewer can miss the quotation though his enjoyment will then be rather slight; and real enjoyment is reserved for the people accustomed to cult movies, who know the whole repertoire of 'magic' archetypes. In a way, *Bananas* works for cultivated 'cinephiles' while *Raiders* works for *Casablanca*-addicts.

The third case is that of *E.T.*, when the alien is brought outside in a Halloween disguise and meets the dwarf coming from *The Empire Strikes Back*. You remember that E.T. starts and runs to cheer him (or it). Here nobody can enjoy the scene if he does not share, at least, the following elements of inter-textual competence:

(1) He must know where the second character comes from (Spielberg citing Lucas),[r]

(2) He must know something about the links between the two directors, and

(3) He must know that both monsters have been designed by Rambaldi and that, consequently, they are linked by some form of brotherhood.

The required expertise is not only intercinematic, it is intermedia, in the sense that the addressee must know not only other movies but all the mass media gossip about movies. This third example presupposes a '*Casablanca* universe' in which

---

[q] Film made by Woody Allen in 1971.

[r] *ET* was made by Stephen Spielberg; the *Empire Strikes Back* by George Lucas.

cult has become the normal way of enjoying movies. Thus in this case we witness an instance of metacult, or of cult about cult—a Cult Culture.

It would be semiotically uninteresting to look for quotations of archetypes in *Raiders* or in *Indiana Jones*: they were conceived within a metasemiotic culture, and what the semiotician can find in them is exactly what the directors put there. Spielberg and Lucas are semiotically nourished authors working for a culture of instinctive semioticians.

With *Casablanca* the situation is different. So *Casablanca* explains *Raiders*, but *Raiders* does not explain *Casablanca*. At most it can explain the new ways in which *Casablanca* will be received in the next years.

It will be a sad day when a too smart audience will read *Casablanca* as conceived by Michael Curtiz after having read Calvino[s] and Barthes. But that day will come. Perhaps we have been able to discover here, for the last time, the Truth.

Après nous, le déluge.[1]

[s] Italo Calvino (1923–1986), Italian experimental novelist.
[1] 'After us, the deluge'—Proverbial expression variously attributed to Madame la Pompadour and Louis XV of France.

INDEX

Note: the names of contributors to the Reader are printed in caps and small caps, and the page references to their contributions are italicised. Subject entries are printed in block capitals. The titles of novels, stories, plays and poems will be found under the appropriate author.

Abel, E., 344, 353
Abraham, Karl, 207
ABRAMS, M. H., xii, 108, *264–76*, 277–8, 284–5, 355, 357, 358 & *n.*
Abu-Lughod, Ibrahim, 308–9
Accius, Lucius, 136
Aczel, Richard, 385
Adams, M., 353
Adams, Sarah Flower, 44 & *n.*
Adorno, Theodor, 377–8, 380
Aeschylus, 135 & *n.*, 432
Afanasyev, A. N., 27
Akakia-Viala, M. A. E., 200*n.*
Allen, Woody, 452 & *n.*, 454 & *n.*
Allison, D. B., 195, 410
Alonso, Damaso, 358
Althusser, Louis, 359, 373, 384, 390, 403, 425, 431
Alvarez, A., 401
AMBIGUITY, 49–50, 313–18
Ammons, A. R., 245
Anderson, P., 391
Annensky, Innokenty, 17
Anstett, Jean-Jacques, 309
Antonioni, Michelangelo, 446
Apuleius, Lucius, 139, 142
Arbusow, L., 56
Archimedes, 258
Ardener, E., 346–8, 350, 353
Ardener, S., 346, 352
Ariosto, Ludovico
Orlando Furioso, 153, 284
Aristotle, xi, 27, 62, 72, 76, 200, 206, 259, 432
Arndt, Walter, 127
Arnold, Matthew, 259, 331, 400
Artaud, Antonin, 232 & *n.*, 238
Ashbery, J., 373
Athenaeus, 134 & *n.*, 137 & *n.*

Atwood, Margaret, 348, 352
Auden, W. H., 246
Auerbach, Erich, 258, 263, 265, 358
Auerbach, Nina, 332, 337, 351–2
August, M. A., 340
Augustine, St., 326
Confessions, 76, 78, 105, 415, 438
Austen, Jane, 213, 349, 353
Austerlitz, R., 56
Austin, J. L., 195, 371, 387, 388*n.*
AUTHOR, 167–72, 197–210
AUTOMATIZATION, 19–21, 27, 29, 236
Avenarius, Richard, 19
Ayer, A. J., 84*n.*

Babbitt, F. C., 134*n.*
Bachelard, Gaston, 73
Bachofen, J. J., 291, 293
Bacon, Francis, 201, 406
BAKHTIN, MIKHAIL, 2, *124–56*, 157, 229, 425, 426*n.*, 448 & *n.*
Balazs, B., 61
Bales, R. F., 61
Balfour, J. A., 297 & *n.*, 298, 305
Balibar, R., 410
Balley, C., 263
Baltaxe, C. A. M., 76
Balzac, Honoré de, 201
'Sarrasine', 166–8, 170
Baratynsky, E. A., 19
Barker, F., 294, 400*n.*, 410
Barker, S., 410
Barrès, Maurice, 300
Barth, Karl, 260
BARTHES, ROLAND, x, xii, 64, 76, 80, 107–8, 157, *166–95*, 196–7, 229, 253, 256–7, 260, 263, 359–61, 371, 399, 402, 410, 431, 445, 455